Cambridge
International AS and A Level

Business

Cambridge
International AS and A Level

Business

Malcolm Surridge
Andrew Gillespie

HODDER
EDUCATION
AN HACHETTE UK COMPANY

The questions, example answers, marks awarded and/or comments that appear in this book/CD
were written by the authors. In examination the way marks would be awarded to answers like
these may be different. Questions from the Cambridge AS and A Level Business papers are
reproduced by permission of Cambridge Assessment International Education.

Although every effort has been made to ensure that website addresses are correct at time of going
to press, Hodder Education cannot be held responsible for the content of any website mentioned
in this book. It is sometimes possible to find a relocated web page by typing in the address of the
home page for a website in the URL window of your browser.

Hachette UK's policy is to use papers that are natural, renewable and recyclable products and
made from wood grown in sustainable forests. The logging and manufacturing processes are
expected to conform to the environmental regulations of the country of origin.

Orders: please contact Bookpoint Ltd, 130 Milton Park, Abingdon, Oxon OX14 4SB. Telephone:
(44) 01235 827827. Fax: (44) 01235 400401. Lines are open 9.00–5.00, Monday to Saturday, with a
24-hour message answering service. Visit our website at www.hoddereducation.com

© Malcolm Surridge and Andrew Gillespie 2014
First published in 2014 by
Hodder Education,
An Hachette UK Company
Carmelite House
50 Victoria Embankment
London EC4Y 0DZ

Impression number   5
Year   2018

Cover photo © Kalafoto – Fotolia
Illustrations by Integra Software Services Pvt Ltd., Pondicherry, India.
Typeset in ITC Garamond Light 9/12 by Integra Software Services Pvt. Ltd., Pondicherry, India
Printed in India

A catalogue record for this title is available from the British Library
ISBN: 978 1444 181 395

Contents

Introduction xii

AS Level

Section 1: Business and its environment   01

Chapter 1 Enterprise 01
1.1 The nature of business activity 01
1.2 The role of an entrepreneur 07
1.3 Social enterprise 11

Chapter 2 Business structure 14
2.1 Economic sectors 14
2.2 Legal structures 15

Chapter 3 Business size 23
3.1 Measuring the size of a business 23
3.2 Small businesses 23

Chapter 4 Business objectives 27
4.1 Business objectives 27
4.2 The role of objectives in the stages of business decision-making 29

Chapter 5 Stakeholders in a business 33
5.1 Stakeholder groups 33
5.2 The importance and influence of stakeholders 34

Section 2: People in organisations   39

Chapter 6 Management and leadership 39
6.1 Leaders and managers 39
6.2 Management and managers 39
6.3 Leadership 43
6.4 Styles of leadership 45
6.5 Emotional intelligence 49

Chapter 7 Motivation 52
7.1 What is motivation? 52
7.2 Human needs 53
7.3 Motivation theorists 54
7.4 Motivation methods in practice: financial motivators 62
7.5 Motivation methods in practice: non-financial motivators 64

Contents

Chapter 8 Human resource management (HRM) 69

8.1 What is human resource management (HRM)? 69

8.2 Recruitment and selection 72

8.3 Employment documents 75

8.4 Disciplinary procedures, redundancy and dismissal 77

8.5 Training 80

8.6 Employee welfare and morale 81

Section 3: Marketing 87

Chapter 9 What is marketing? 87

9.1 The role of marketing and its relationship with other business activities 87

9.2 Supply and demand 89

9.3 Features of markets 92

9.4 Producer and consumer markets 94

9.5 Niche versus mass marketing 94

9.6 Segmentation methods 95

Chapter 10 Market research 99

10.1 What is market research? 99

10.2 Primary and secondary market research 100

10.3 Sampling 102

10.4 Quantitative and qualitative market research 103

10.5 Market research results 103

10.6 Cost effectiveness 103

Chapter 11 Marketing mix 105

11.1 The marketing mix 105

11.2 The role of the customer (the 4 Cs) 106

11.3 Product 107

11.4 Product life cycle 107

11.5 Pricing 112

11.6 Price elasticity of demand 116

11.7 Promotion methods 120

11.8 Channels of distribution (place) 124

11.9 Using the internet for the 4 Ps/4 Cs 127

11.10 An effective marketing mix? 128

Section 4: Operations and project management 131

Chapter 12 The nature of operations 131

12.1 Inputs, outputs and the transformation process 131

12.2 The benefits and limitations of capital and labour intensive processes 132

Contents

12.3 Effectiveness and efficiency 133
12.4 Creating value 135

Chapter 13 Operations planning 137
13.1 Influences on operations decisions 137
13.2 Flexibility and innovation 138
13.3 Operations methods 138
13.4 Location 140
13.5 Scale of production 144

Chapter 14 Inventory management 148
14.1 Inventory 148
14.2 Managing inventory 148

Section 5: Finance and accounting

Section 5: Finance and accounting 153

Chapter 15 Business finance 153
15.1 Why businesses need capital 153
15.2 Working capital 154
15.3 Revenue expenditure and capital expenditure 156
15.4 Sources of finance 157
15.5 Factors influencing the choice of sources of finance 162
15.6 Choosing an appropriate source of finance 164

Chapter 16 Forecasting and managing cash flow 167
16.1 Why businesses forecast cash flow 167
16.2 Cash-flow forecasts in practice 169
16.3 Methods of improving cash flow 172

Chapter 17 Costs and break-even 177
17.1 Revenue and cost information 177
17.2 Uses of cost information 182
17.3 Break-even analysis 185

Chapter 18 Accounting fundamentals 192
18.1 Income statements and statements of financial position 192
18.2 Using financial ratios 197
18.3 The main users of accounts 201
18.4 The limitations and uses of financial statements 202
18.5 Management and financial accountants 204
AS Level Cambridge International past paper exam questions 206

Contents

A Level

Section 1: Business and its environment   216

Chapter 19 Business structure and size 216
19.1 Local, national and multinational businesses 216
19.2 International trading links 218
19.3 Governments and businesses 220
19.4 Business growth 221

Chapter 20 The economic environment 227
20.1 The government's economic objectives 227
20.2 Economic growth and the business cycle 229
20.3 Inflation 234
20.4 Unemployment 236
20.5 Exchange rates 239
20.6 Redistributing income and wealth 242
20.7 The government's economic policies 244
20.8 Market failure 249
20.9 Conclusion 249

Chapter 21 Other external influences on business activity 252
21.1 Introduction 252
21.2 Political and legal factors 253
21.3 Consumer protection legislation 256
21.4 Technological change 258
21.5 Competitors and suppliers 261
21.6 Social factors 263

Section 2: People in organisations   272

Chapter 22 Further human resource management (HRM) 272
22.1 Different approaches to HRM: human resource strategies and flexible workforces 272
22.2 Measures of employee performance 277
22.3 Management by objectives 281
22.4 Labour legislation 282
22.5 Cooperation between management and the workforce 284
22.6 Workforce planning 286
22.7 The role of trade unions in HRM 288
22.8 Negotiation 290
22.9 No strike deals 293

Contents

Chapter 23 Organisational structure 295
23.1 Business objectives, organisational structure and people 295
23.2 Formal and informal organisational structures 298
23.3 Types of organisational structures 300
23.4 Key factors within organisational structures 303

Chapter 24 Business communication 310
24.1 The theory of communication 310
24.2 Why do businesses communicate? 311
24.3 How businesses communicate 312
24.4 Barriers to communication 316
24.5 Improving communication 317

Section 3: Marketing   320

Chapter 25 Marketing 320
25.1 Marketing planning 320
25.2 Elasticity of demand 320
25.3 Product development 322
25.4 The need to forecast marketing data 325
25.5 The need for and development of a coordinated marketing mix 333

Chapter 26 Globalisation and international marketing 338
26.1 Economic globalisation 338
26.2 International markets 339

Section 4: Operations and project management   344

Chapter 27 Operations and project management 344
27.1 Introduction 344
27.2 Enterprise resource planning (ERP) 344
27.3 Capacity and capacity utilisation 345

Chapter 28 Lean production and quality management 350
28.1 Lean production 350
28.2 Benchmarking 353
28.3 Kaizen 353
28.4 Just-in-time production 354
28.5 Quality 355
28.6 Total quality management (TQM) 357

Contents

Chapter 29 Project management 360
29.1 Projects 360
29.2 Critical path or network analysis 361

Section 5: Finance and accounting   367

Chapter 30 Costing methods 367
30.1 Issues in costing 367
30.2 Full costing 369
30.3 Contribution costing 371
30.4 Contribution costing and decision-making 372

Chapter 31 Budgets 377
31.1 Preparing and using budgets 377
31.2 Variance analysis 383

Chapter 32 Published accounts 388
32.1 Income statements 388
32.2 Statements of financial position 390
32.3 Further issues on statements of financial position 392

Chapter 33 Analysing published accounts 398
33.1 What is a financial ratio? 398
33.2 The return on capital employed ratio (ROCE) 400
33.3 Efficiency ratios 400
33.4 Gearing 402
33.5 Investors' ratios 403
33.6 The value and limitations of ratio analysis 406

Chapter 34 Investment appraisal 409
34.1 Introduction 409
34.2 Financial techniques for making investment decisions 411
34.3 Assessing the risks and uncertainties of investment decisions 416
34.4 Qualitative influences on investment appraisal 418

Section 6: Strategic management   421

Chapter 35: Strategic management 421
35.1 Corporate strategy, tactics and strategic management 421
35.2 Strategic analysis 423

Contents

Chapter 36: Strategic choice 430
36.1 The Ansoff Matrix 430
36.2 Low cost vs differentiation 432
36.3 Force Field Analysis 433
36.4 Decision trees 433

Chapter 37: Strategic implementation 437
37.1 Business plans 437
37.2 Corporate culture 437
37.3 Developing a change culture 442
37.4 Leading and managing change 443
37.5 Developing a strategy to manage change 444
37.6 Contingency planning 445

A Level Cambridge International past paper exam questions 449
Index 474
Acknowledgements 485

Student's CD contents

Key terms
Answers to short answer questions
Interactive tests
Examination structure, Planning your revision and Examination technique

Introduction

The textbook

This book introduces you to Business. It has been written to meet the requirements of the Cambridge International syllabi for AS and A Level. It provides coverage of the entire syllabus although we have divided some modules and combined others to make the subject more convenient for you to study.

The book will guide you through the Cambridge International AS and A Level Business programme of study, although you should supplement it with research into businesses in your own and other countries. You are fortunate that there is an immense amount of information available about businesses, their behaviour and the environments in which they operate. The internet is an enormous and valuable resource and you will find much relevant information in magazines, newspapers and on television programmes. However, business activity takes place around you all the time: when you are shopping, travelling to and from school or college or enjoying leisure activities such as visiting the cinema. There are many opportunities for you to see the operation of some of the theories and models that you will study.

This textbook includes the following features:

- guidance as to the material that is covered in each chapter
- definitions of key terms to assist you in mastering the language of Business
- maths moments to help you to develop relevant numerical skills
- study tips to help you to prepare for examinations in Business
- diverse case studies to illustrate how theories and concepts operate in the real world
- a range of questions and activities to help you to reinforce your learning and to develop the skills needed to succeed in examinations in Business
- a selection of past Cambridge examination questions.

A new feature of the syllabus is Key concepts. These are the essential ideas, theories, principles or mental tools that help learners to develop a deep understanding of their subject, and make links between different topics. An icon indicates where each Key concept is covered:

Change

Change is the only constant. Exciting new enterprises are often created in response to economic, cultural or technological changes. Existing businesses must adapt to change if they are to survive and grow.

Management

Management is relevant to every person in a business. Good leadership, strong motivation in workers, effective systems and clear communication are hallmarks of successful businesses.

Customer focus

Customer focus means a business will design and produce goods and services that people want to buy. Customers provide the revenue which sustains a business. Successful businesses really understand their customers and strive to provide products that their customers love.

Innovation

Innovation enables a business to re-invent itself and stay ahead of the competition. The business world is dynamic and companies must seek to innovate through product development, more efficient processes and finding better ways 'to do business'.

Creating value

Creating value is the core reason why any organisation exists. Effective organisations aim to maximise stakeholder value. For most businesses this will be about maximising shareholder value, but social enterprises will also have other, non-financial, aims. Stakeholders also need to measure the value that is created.

Strategy

Strategy is about knowing where you are, where you want to get to and how you are going to get there. Managers need to think about, decide on and put into action major long term plans – such as buying another business, entering a new market or developing a new technology.

The Student's CD-ROM

Accompanying this book is a Student's CD-ROM which we hope will help you further with your study of this subject. The CD-ROM contains the following features.

1 The answers to all the short answer questions included at the end of each chapter.
2 A selection of additional interactive tests designed to assess and strengthen your knowledge and understanding of Business. Answers are provided to these questions.
3 A glossary of key terms for AS and A Level Business.
4 Material to assist you in preparing thoroughly for your examinations in Business.

The structure of the Cambridge syllabus

AS Business

Students taking AS Business will take two examinations.

Paper 1 Short answer and essay

- This paper has two sections: Section A contains about four compulsory short questions; Section B comprises three essays based on the AS syllabus content from which you have to choose one.
- The examination lasts for one hour and fifteen minutes.
- This paper represents 40 per cent of your AS marks or 20 per cent of the A Level.
- The paper can be sat in October/November or in May/June each year.

Paper 2 Data response

- The paper is made up of two compulsory data response questions based on the AS syllabus content. Each of these contains some text and sometimes tables and graphs as well.
- Each question has about four elements which range from definitions to questions requiring discussion.
- The examination lasts for one and a half hours.
- This paper represents 60 per cent of your AS marks or 30 per cent of the A Level.
- The paper can be sat in October/November or in May/June each year.

A Level Business

Students taking A Level Business will take the two AS examinations described above plus Paper 3 below.

Paper 3 Case study

- This paper has two sections.
- Section A contains a case study and approximately five compulsory questions of varying mark allocations. All these questions are based on the case study.
- Section B comprises two essays, also based on the case study, from which you have to choose one.
- The questions on this paper are based on the Additional A Level syllabus content.
- The examination lasts for three hours.
- This paper represents 50 per cent of the A Level (the AS papers make up the other 50 per cent).
- Paper 3 can be sat in October/November or in May/June each year.

Succeeding in Business examinations

Examinations in Business require you to understand the relevant theories and concepts set out in the syllabus. This means that you have to learn the material set out in the appropriate sections of this textbook. However, this is not enough on its own. The examinations will also require you to organise ideas, construct arguments, make decisions, solve problems, conduct calculations and interpret data. You will need to complete as many practice and past questions as possible to develop these examination skills. Finally, it is important for you to apply many of your answers to the business scenarios set out in the data response materials or case studies that are a key part of the examination papers. For example, if a question is about retailers, you must relate your answer to retailers to achieve a high grade.

This textbook contains numerous questions throughout and at the end of each chapter, all of which have been designed to help you to develop these essential examination skills.

Business is a subject that will have relevance to your future life, whatever you choose to do. We hope that you enjoy studying it and wish you good fortune in your examinations.

Malcolm Surridge & Andrew Gillespie

1 Enterprise

Chapter overview

In this chapter we examine:
- the nature of business activity; for example we look at what businesses do and the purpose of business
- the role of the entrepreneur; for example we consider why entrepreneurs are important to the economy
- social enterprises; these are businesses that are not set up to make a profit but to benefit society.

1.1 The nature of business activity

The purpose of business activity

What will you do this weekend? Have you got a part time job to earn some money? Are you going to go out to the cinema or shopping in the town centre? Whatever you do you will come into contact with many different businesses either as a consumer buying and using their products or as an employee working to create them. Businesses are everywhere! Just think of the last time you went shopping – the outlet where you shop is a business, it has bought the products from a supplier, they were transported by a delivery business and the firm probably uses another business to help promote itself. In every transaction between a customer and a business, many other businesses will have been involved to bring about that exchange.

There are many different definitions of a business but what they tend to have in common is the idea of someone (or a group of people) working in an organised way to achieve a given target. Notice the key elements of this definition – firstly, the activities of those involved are organised in some way and secondly, the business is created with a specific purpose in mind: often the **business objective** is profit but as we shall see later there are many other reasons why people set up in business. Using a definition of organised activities and a given target, many organisations such as

hospitals and even schools could be classified as businesses. They may not have profit as a target but they do involve many different people working together, planning and organising what they do to achieve targets such as helping people get better more quickly or improving the quality of students' education.

> ### Key term
>
> **Business objectives** are measurable targets set by the business such as sales or profits that have to be achieved within a given time period.

The transformation process

All businesses are involved in the transformation process. They take inputs and transform them in some way to produce outputs that they hope consumers will want.

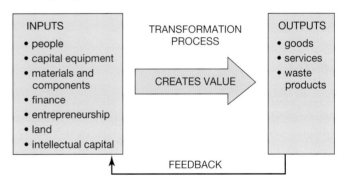

Figure 1.1 The transformation process

Inputs

The inputs into a business include:
- land
- labour
- capital
- intellectual capital.

Land

This involves choosing the location of the business. This is critically important for businesses such as shops and cafés. For other businesses such as farming, what will matter is the quality of the land in terms of the ability to grow different crops. The success of a farming business will be directly affected by changes to the quality of the land and the weather. The significance of land as an input will be particularly high in the **primary sector**.

Under the heading of land we also include premises. The amount of space available to a business can affect how much can be produced or how many customers can physically fit in the restaurant or store. The nature of the premises can also affect the working environment and people's motivation. For example, working in a modern office with a good canteen, parking spaces and a central location might be appealing to employees.

Labour

Organisations will need staff. The quality of employees in terms of their skills, their attitudes (e.g. to customers), their willingness to work and their natural abilities will have an influence on the success of any business. What makes a film a blockbuster? The quality of the writing, the acting and the production – people play a key role in the success of any film. Many films therefore promote themselves on the basis of who the actors are. Similarly, universities promote their professors. Music labels promote their bands. Publishers promote their author list. So people can be a crucial element of the transformation process.

Capital

The word 'capital' has many meanings. In this instance, we mean the equipment used by businesses. The coffee machines in the coffee shop, the ovens in the fast-food restaurants, and the scanning equipment in shops are all examples of capital equipment. The amount and quality of equipment in a business can affect the service it provides. For example, the online retailer Amazon is admired for the efficiency with which it processes an order and is able to make suggestions to customers of what else they might like to buy.

Intellectual capital

Intellectual capital involves the intelligence of the workforce. This includes the ability to develop new ideas, find new solutions to problems and spot business opportunities. Success does not just depend on what resources you use but how you use them, which is why intellectual capital is so important.

The choice of inputs and who supplies them can affect:
- the costs of a business
- the quality of the final product (and therefore sales).

In recent years, customers have become increasingly interested in what resources are used in a production process and where they

have come from. Firms may highlight the fact they use recycled materials or that their ingredients are 'natural' or 'organic'.

Firms will also face the choice of whether to buy in some materials or produce them themselves. Tyrrell's Potato Chips uses the fact that it grows its own potatoes when it promotes its products. Most other crisp manufacturers buy in their potatoes.

Outputs

The output of a business may be in the form of goods or services, or a combination of the two.
- A good (or a product) is a tangible item, such as a car or a laptop computer. A good is a physical item. Businesses can produce and stock them. This means that they can produce in advance of demand: for example, a store may stockpile new electrical goods before a busy selling period.
- A service is intangible. Services include education, creating music, hairdressing and physiotherapy. Most businesses in more developed economies are in the service sector. Services cannot be stored: they have to be produced for customers as they are needed. This can create problems because if there is a rush of customers there are no products stockpiled and so queues form or waiting lists have to be introduced.

In many cases, a business provides a combination of goods and services. For example, you may choose a restaurant because of the food you can eat there (the goods) but also because of the waiters, the environment and the way you are treated (the service).

Most outputs are intended for sale. A firm produces goods and services to sell to customers. However, there may also be by-products from the transformation process: for example, a firm's production may create waste and pollution. Many customers pay attention to these issues and, increasingly, firms are considering the effects of their production on other groups, such as the local community.

Case Study

Dabbawalla

Figure 1.2 A busy dabbawalla delivery in Mumbai

Every day in Mumbai, India, around 250000 people get their lunches delivered by 'dabbawallas'. A 'walla' means a 'doer of something' and a 'dabba' is a stainless steel lunchbox. The lunch is picked up from the person's home and taken to a sorting station. The lunch boxes are then divided up according to destination and delivered on bike, on foot or taken on the train to their destination. After lunch the box is collected and taken back to the person's home. This is an incredibly efficient but very labour intensive and low technology process with almost no boxes going missing or to the wrong address. The price is so low that it is easier to pay for the delivery than take your lunchbox with you on your journey to and from work.

Questions

1 Explain the transformation process of the dabbawallas in terms of input and outputs. [6]
2 Discuss how you would measure the success of this process. [10]

For most products there is a series of stages in the transformation process involved in taking the initial materials and ending up with the final product. The author J.K. Rowling took her imagination, a computer and paper and turned this into magical manuscripts for her Harry Potter books. The publishing company worked with the author, designers, a marketing team, a printing business, a distribution business and turned the manuscripts into a series of books. Book stores take a range of books and transform them into a retail experience for the customer. A series of transformations has gone on to get the idea from the author's mind into a book and into the hands of the reader.

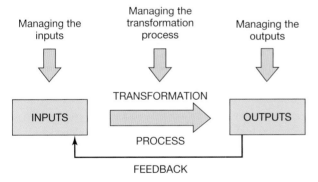

Figure 1.3 Chain of operations

Businesses need to identify exactly what they want to provide in terms of the range and quality of products they offer; do they want to specialise in a few types of items or provide a wide range of goods and services? Businesses also need to decide on the resources they will need to provide the product to the standard they want for their customers. There are a number of questions involved here: How many people are needed? What skills are needed? Will they be trained? What materials will be used? What equipment? And so on. Businesses need to find a way of generating a product that customers value so much that they will pay more for it than it cost to produce.

Case Study

Transformation processes

There are many different forms of transformation. These include:

● changing the characteristics of materials, information or customers. For example, manufacturers take components and build something new with them. Beauty salons and cosmetic surgeons take people and improve their appearance (we hope!). Doctors, dentists, physiotherapists, psychiatrists and teachers all help us to improve some aspect of ourselves. Accountants take our receipts and turn them into a set of accounts to show investors or government tax inspectors.

● changing the location of materials and information. Federal Express and Cathay Pacific simply move items or people around. Google helps you find something that is already there – it helps you to access information. An estate agent gives you information on houses that you might be interested in. This service saves time and money for the seller and helps the buyer sell the property more quickly.

● changing the ownership of materials. Wholesalers buy in bulk from a number of producers. Retailers then buy from wholesalers because it is easier to deal with them than with every single producer: it reduces the number of transactions and makes the process simpler.

Source: Adapted from Open University material at: http://openlearn.open.ac.uk

Questions

1 Explain the nature of the Federal Express transformation process. [6]
2 Discuss the possible reasons why a business might review and change its transformation process. [10]

When designing its transformation process a business person must consider questions such as:
● What level of output will be provided? Are you aiming to produce hundreds, thousands or millions of units? How many customers do you want to be able to have?
● What quality of service will be provided? How many people will you have serving in your shop? Will you deliver your products to people's homes? What will your policy be if people want to return items?
● How will you provide the service? Will you provide it online or via shops? Will you use high staffing levels or invest in more equipment?
● What aspects of the process will the business undertake for itself and what elements will be outsourced to or bought in from other providers? You may decide to manage the shop yourself but get cleaners in to tidy up, employ accountants to do the finances and use specialists to design the décor. You may produce a range of clothes but simply do the design work

yourself and get someone else to produce them like Benetton; alternatively, you may manufacture them yourself like Zara. All these decisions will have an impact on the costs, flexibility and the complexity of running your business.

The transformation process is ongoing and dynamic. If the output you produce is not acceptable or needs to be improved you will have to change the inputs and/or the way you produce. You will then monitor the results and, if necessary, change again. Change may also be due to external factors. For example, increasing concern about the environment has influenced what is produced and how it is produced.

Creating value

Value is created when outputs are produced that are worth more than the inputs brought in to provide them.

For example, artists such as Andy Warhol, Vincent van Gogh, David Hockney and Rembrandt took their imagination, paint and canvas and produced amazing works of art that sell for millions of dollars: far more than the cost of the items used up in their production. They created value via the transformation process.

Jamie Oliver, a famous cook, takes standard ingredients such as meat, herbs and vegetables, then puts them together in a unique way and comes up with a fantastic meal. He takes ingredients that many others may use but transforms them in a way that appeals to customers, packs out his restaurants, sells books and attracts viewers for his TV series. Clearly, he has created value by using his talent, creativity and personality.

Creating value can be done in ways that may seem odd. Here are some examples:

- Some companies buy new jeans and then stretch them, batter them and fray them to make them look distressed while, at the same time, more than doubling their price.
- A bottled water that was initially sold for $10 a bottle comes from King Island, near Tasmania. It is called 'Cloud Juice' and is claimed to be the purest in the world. It is rain water that has been collected from a plastic roof and then bottled. It is supposed to be so pure because it comes from rain clouds that travel 7000 miles from South America without passing over any land and therefore not encountering pollution.
- One of the most expensive coffees in the world is Luwak Coffee. This is made from coffee cherries that have been eaten and digested by common palm civets (a type of animal). The civets use their keen sense of smell to select the choicest and ripest beans. The beans are supposed to be much sweeter as a result of the digestion process and, having passed through the animal, they are hand-collected from the jungle floor.

To increase its created value, a business might aim to:
- reduce the costs of producing the product. This means cutting back on waste, ensuring the best price for the supplies and making sure that mistakes are not made. All activities that do not create value need to be examined to see if they are truly necessary.

- increase the perceived benefit of the product in the eyes of the customer. This could be through building the brand, developing a unique selling proposition (USP) or differentiating it through the service provided.

Study tip

When answering questions you may need to think about how different firms create value. What can businesses do to add more value? Should they focus on the benefits they are providing, or try to control costs more effectively?

Businesses and economic activity

Businesses make up an important part of any economy. They are important because they employ people, they pay employees' wages and salaries and they provide goods and services. Businesses provide the products we buy and give us the jobs and earnings we need to buy them. When businesses are doing well and expanding they employ more people and generate more income for the economy. Businesses innovate to win more customers: they create new goods and services and this can improve the quality of our lives by providing better food, better clothes and better electronic goods. Businesses therefore drive economies forward and this is why governments are eager to help new firms start up and compete, and why they often try to help businesses grow.

Choice and opportunity cost

In any economy there is a fixed amount of resources at any moment and therefore decisions have to be made about how these resources are used. Given the scarcity of resources, choices are inevitable in terms of what should be produced in the economy, how these products should be produced and who should receive them. Some of these decisions will be made by market forces: it will be the result of bargaining between consumers and businesses. If, for example, demand for a particular product increases, this will encourage businesses to use their resources to produce this instead of something else. Imagine you were a farmer and had limited land. You have to decide what to grow on it. This will depend in part on demand: if the demand for a particular crop increases you may switch to this and away from something less in demand.

Some decisions about what to produce and how to produce may be made by the government. For example, the government may provide some or all of the health services, the transport system or the education system in a country.

Governments tend to take control of goods and services they think are vital to their economy and where they want to ensure access for most people.

However, whenever decisions are made about what to produce – whether it be the free market or the government – it will involve an opportunity cost. Given that resources are limited, if they are used to produce more of one item, then this is at the expense of something else. Opportunity cost measures the sacrifice you make if you choose one course of action in terms of the next best alternative. For example, if a business decides to use its labour force to increase output of soft drinks then the opportunity cost is what could have been produced if the labour force had been used to produce something different. Whenever a business makes a decision it should consider the opportunity cost. A project that earns a profit of $100 000 may seem attractive but if the resources could have been used to earn $250 000 it is not so appealing. When judging the success of a business you should consider the opportunity cost. If Walmart, the huge US retailer, makes a profit of $10 million this may not be that impressive given the people, stores and equipment it has.

The business environment

Businesses do not operate in isolation. What they do is linked to what other businesses do, for example, their suppliers, the firms that distribute and promote their products, the banks that lend them money. They are also affected by many other external factors such as:

- **P**olitical and legal issues. For example, new laws by a government can prevent the way some products are promoted (such as cigarettes) and can affect the way employees must be treated and the way a business produces (perhaps to reduce its environmental impact).
- **E**conomic issues. For example, the amount of income in an economy can change over a period of time, affecting demand; the value of one currency in terms of another can alter, affecting the cost of importing supplies; and the cost of borrowing can go up, increasing costs.
- **S**ocial issues. For example, an increase in the size of the population or a change in the life expectancy of the population in a country can affect the level of demand and the types of products people buy.
- **T**echnological issues. For example, changes in the availability and speed of the internet can make it easier to find suppliers and sell across the world.

These external factors (known as PEST – political, economic, social and technological) will continually be changing and this will affect what businesses produce and the resources they use. If labour costs in one country become more expensive, for example, businesses might switch production to another country or start to use more machinery instead. If a government signs a treaty with another country to make trade easier its businesses might start to sell more to customers in the new partner country. Businesses therefore need to monitor their external business environment because it is dynamic (ever changing) and if necessary managers will need to change some of their decisions about inputs, the transformation process or the outputs they produce accordingly.

Case Study

Brazil

The Brazilian economy has been growing fast despite a slowdown in many other economies around the world. In 2012, the National Institute of Economic and Social Research (NIESR) said that Brazil had overtaken the UK in terms of the size of its economy. The Brazilian economy is now worth $2.5 trillion (£1.6 trillion) (compared to the UK's $2.48 trillion), making it the sixth biggest economy in the world.

Brazil is enjoying an economic boom because it is benefiting from revenue selling its food and oil at high prices.

Brazil is the largest Latin American economy and one of the so-called BRIC nations together with Russia, India and China. Its growth has been far faster than the US and western Europe in recent years.

With substantial oil and gas reserves being discovered off the coast of Brazil, the country is now the world's ninth largest producer of oil. Brazil has about 190 million people, in contrast to the UK's 60 million people.

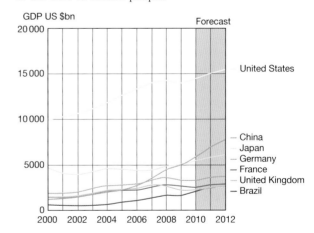

Figure 1.4

Source: IMF

Questions

1 Explain two possible reasons why the Brazilian economy might be growing so fast. [6]
2 Discuss the possible effects for Brazilian businesses of operating in such a fast growing economy. [10]

What does a business need to do to succeed?

To succeed a business needs to be more competitive than its rivals. This means it needs to provide better value for money. Its ability to achieve this depends on:

● The benefits it offers. For example, what does its product do relative to its competitors? Is it faster? Easier to use? Smaller? Bigger? Longer lasting?
● What price is being charged relative to the competition?

Different combinations of price and benefits are shown in Figure 1.5.

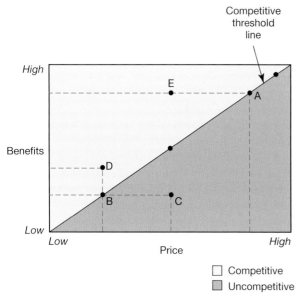

Figure 1.5 Competitive threshold diagram

Combinations A and B are on the competitive threshold; this means that they offer value for money relative to competitors. At B the benefits offered are relatively low – this is a basic product – but the price is low as well so consumers still think it is competitive. At A the price is high, but so are the benefits offered; this again means it can be competitive. Problems occur when the business is below the competitive threshold such as C; this means that given the price the benefits offered are relatively low (or to look at it another way, given the benefits the price is high).

What businesses will aim to do is move above the competitive threshold such as D, which means they are outperforming their rivals: they are offering the same benefits for less, or more benefits for the same price. The difficult part is deciding what it is that customers actually regard as a benefit, working out how to provide these and somehow doing this more cheaply than competitors or finding additional benefits without increasing the price. How businesses try to do this is examined in the rest of this book. Even if they do manage to become competitive they cannot afford to rest because competitors will soon follow their

lead; this means they need to keep improving and seeking ways of becoming more competitive. Many once famous businesses have now disappeared and those that are still successful can only keep that way by constantly improving.

Study tip

Remember that businesses often compete in different ways. Some may offer premium products and be able to justify high prices. Others may offer more basic products at low prices. An important thing to think about is how sustainable this approach is in the long term – will others be able to imitate the idea easily or can the business protect its success?

Why do businesses fail?

Businesses fail when they stop being competitive. This means that they stop providing good value for money relative to their competitors. This can be due to external reasons – perhaps they have a high level of borrowing and so their costs are hit badly when the cost of borrowing rises; or internal reasons such as poor training of staff leading to poor customer service. Businesses fail when they end up providing relatively low benefits given the price they charge. This can be because of their choice of inputs, their choice of outputs or the way they manage the transformation process. We hope that reading this book will help you avoid some of these problems if you decide to manage a business. Having said that, while many of the problems of business are avoidable, some – such as an earthquake – may be more difficult to plan for!

In fact many businesses fail early on in their life. This is because:

● The people managing them may not have had much experience of business. Often people who start up a business have an interest in a product but have not necessarily run a business before. They may be good at making things, for example, but not so good at dealing with customers or managing money. It may also be difficult to recruit experienced staff to join the business because they may want the security of a bigger business that has been around for longer and with a track record of success.
● New businesses do not have much market power, which can make it difficult to survive. For example, suppliers may be worried whether they will be paid and so demand payment in advance which can cause cashflow problems. Meanwhile, buyers may have a lot of power. Imagine being a new small supplier trying to sell to a big supermarket. The buyer may push the price down and be slow to pay, causing further financial problems for the new business. Given its lack of power it may have to pay more for supplies and advertising than more established businesses, making it difficult to compete on price.

Case Study

Small businesses in South Africa

Small business failure rates are as high as 63 per cent within the first two years of trading in South Africa. Reasons include inadequate access to finance and a lack of financial know-how. Other factors include poor management, infrastructure problems and a lack of government support required to run a business.

Entrepreneurs in South Africa who have failed often accuse banks, the government, their business partners and sometimes even their customers! However, the problem is often the entrepreneurs themselves and their business idea. Typical issues are that:

- there is not enough demand to make a profit
- sometimes they try to grow too fast and this leads to problems with cash flow
- their business operation is not good enough to be competitive.

Questions

1 Explain two reasons why businesses in South Africa fail. [6]
2 Discuss whether failure is inevitable for a business starting up in South Africa. [10]

Maths moment

Imagine 60 per cent of new businesses in a country fail in the first two years. Of those that survive another 40 per cent fail in the next three years.

Imagine 400 000 businesses start up in one year; how many would you expect to be left after five years?

1.2 The role of an entrepreneur

Entrepreneurs

An **entrepreneur** is someone who is willing to take a risk to start a new project or a new business. **Enterprise** refers to the skills needed to do this. An entrepreneur has an idea and then tries to make it work. Entrepreneurs see the resources that are available and the possibilities of combining them in a particular way to provide a product or service. Entrepreneurs create new businesses and in so doing provide new products and services. Some entrepreneurs, such as Richard Branson of Virgin and Stelios Haji-Ioannou of easyGroup, continually have ideas for new businesses and set up many different ones during their careers. Such people are called 'serial entrepreneurs'.

Key terms

Entrepreneurs are individuals who take the risk to create or start a new business or project.
Enterprise is the skill needed to make a new idea work.

Entrepreneurs create change and challenge the way things are done. They find and create new markets, generate income and employment and bring about innovation. They are extremely important to the growth of an economy and to improving the quality and range of goods and services on offer.

Enterprise (or entrepreneurship) involves discovering, evaluating and exploiting business opportunities.

Risk and reward

Entrepreneurs are prepared to take risks. They are investing time, money and effort into a new project that may or may not work. The danger is that it will not work and all their investment will be lost. Many new businesses fail. Look at the main shopping street in your nearest village or town. How long have the shops been there? Have some opened up recently? Have some closed down in the last year? The landscape of the centre of most villages and towns is changing all the time as some business ideas fail and others rise to take their place. The real risk to entrepreneurs is that they will lose much or even everything they have put into a project because the business idea eventually fails.

Some of the causes of risk are external. For example, there could be a change in the economy, meaning people have less money to spend than entrepreneurs had expected (and so demand for their products is lower than they hoped), or competitors may have changed their behaviour, making it more difficult for similar businesses to survive.

Alternatively, the causes of risk could be internal. It may be that an entrepreneur's understanding of the market is not as good as he had thought and he makes some bad pricing decisions. It may be that his judgement of people is poor and he hires the wrong people, with the result that the quality of service is not as good as he had hoped.

Entrepreneurs may sometimes undertake a project 'because it is there to be done'. They may be driven by a desire to do something new. This in itself may be a reward in terms of self satisfaction: they can hopefully look back on their careers and be proud of what they have achieved. However, they may also be interested in other rewards from setting up, such as the financial gain from owning their own business. These rewards can be high! For example, YouTube was set up in February 2005 by Chad Hurley, Steve Chen and Jawed Karim. The website includes music videos and movie and TV clips, as well as material posted by the general public. In 2006 the founders of YouTube sold their business to Google for $1.65 billion! Not a bad return in less than two years.

To go ahead with any venture, the expected rewards must justify the risk involved. In an ideal world a project would have a high reward and low risk, but typically new ventures are very risky because there are so many things that can go wrong. In fact, many ideas do not even get launched. Entrepreneurs hit so many setbacks or face so many difficulties that the project does not go ahead.

Table 1.1 Risks and rewards matrix: analysing projects

	Risk	
Reward	Low	High
Low	These are safe projects but do not generate high returns.	These projects are not of interest because of the high risk relative to the low rewards.
High	These projects are ideal: low risk but high rewards. However, it may not be easy to find projects like this!	These projects are of interest but risky. To go ahead, entrepreneurs must believe the rewards outweigh the risks.

Maths moment

If you estimate that a project has a 55 per cent probability of succeeding what is the probability of failure?

Case Study

Banyan Tree

The multimillionaire Ho Kwon Ping is the founder of Banyan Tree, a global chain of luxury holiday resorts in Asia.

After leaving school Ho Kwon Ping attended Stanford University in California, and later protested against the Vietnam War. He spent two months in jail in Singapore as a result of controversial articles he had written as a journalist for the *Far East Economic Review*.

After his release Mr Ho continued to work as a journalist and settled on one of Hong Kong's offshore islands with his wife. He joined the family business a few years after his father became ill. He decided the business needed to do something other than produce products for other companies. He realised that producing for others meant you had no brand presence and often your profits were squeezed by the bigger buyers.

He moved the company into the hotel business but struggled to get customers interested in the hotel they were going to build in Phuket, Thailand. So Mr Ho decided that the business should concentrate on creating a different type of hotel. It would be a luxury spa with villas rather than a hotel with rooms. This made the Banyan Tree stand out from the rest. He insisted on decisions others thought would not work because he was sure they would. For example, the staff at the spa did not wear shoes because being barefoot in Asia is a sign of respect, and they wore Asian clothes not the white uniforms staff in Europe tended to wear.

Banyan Tree now has hotels as far apart as Mexico and the Seychelles.

Questions

1 Explain two external factors that might have helped the success of Banyan Tree. [6]
2 Discuss the features you think make a successful entrepreneur. [10]

Study tip

Remember that any decision has a risk attached to it but the key question is whether this risk is worth it. Managers must try to assess the probability of any outcome and decide whether the business should pursue any course of action given the risk involved.

Why become an entrepreneur?

More than 3 million people, or 12 per cent of the UK population, have already set up business on their own. Research by Vodafone indicates that a further 6 per cent of UK adults are in the process of setting up their own business and nearly a third of all people are considering doing so. So what drives people to set up their own business?

There are many attractions to being an entrepreneur:

- You will experience a great feeling of satisfaction if your idea is successful. Imagine being able to look at a large business and know that you created it and helped it to grow.
- You will be your own boss. Fed up being told what to do? Dislike orders? Then being an entrepreneur may be the way forward. Setting up on your own means it is your business, to do with as you wish. This can be challenging and demanding but it does mean you are more in control of your own destiny. Some people prefer this to working for others: they like their independence.
- You keep the rewards. If you work in a business for someone else then the rewards belong to them. You may work very hard and very successfully and get a bonus, but the major rewards will usually go to the owners. If you are an entrepreneur, you are the owner and so any rewards belong to you. The downside is that if anything goes wrong the losses are yours as well.
- You have more control of what you do and when you do it compared to working for someone else. A survey by Yorkshire Bank found that almost three in five small-business owners first decided to become self employed because of a desire for more flexible working and an improved balance between work and their social lives. Two in five did so for greater financial control.

Awfully Chocolate

Figure 1.6 Lyn Lee

Living in Singapore – a very cosmopolitan city – Lyn Lee was amazed that she could not find a simple dark chocolate cake that she could eat whenever she wanted to! Most chocolate cakes in the market were either too sweet and creamy or not chocolatey enough. So she decided to set up a business to make the perfect everyday chocolate cake – soft, moist, very chocolatey but not overly sweet or creamy. With some friends, she tried different recipes and techniques every weekend for a year. As people not from the baking industry, they tried innovative methods to create a recipe they loved – and Awfully Chocolate was born.

The first Awfully Chocolate store opened in 1998 in Katong in Singapore. It was tucked away in an old side street with just one type of whole chocolate cake on offer. It was also unconventional in that the cake was not displayed, so the store did not look like a typical cake shop. This enhanced the quirky character of how Awfully Chocolate made its mark.

Friends and family thought the business would not last three months and even her supplier warned her about over-ordering boxes. But Awfully Chocolate gained a reputation for delicious handmade chocolate cakes and quirky design, and demand proved high. Cakes sold out every day and its reputation grew beyond Singapore.

But Lyn wanted Awfully Chocolate to grow on its own slowly so she only opened her second store in 2004, using the profits from her first shop. Awfully Chocolate's products now include more cakes, tarts, ice cream and truffles. It also owns brands

Everything with Fries, Sinpopo and Ninethirty by Awfully Chocolate. Apart from Singapore, Awfully Chocolate also has stores across Asia, including in China and Hong Kong.

Lyn says that every city has got its own character, personality and quirks, so you need to understand these to make it work.

According to Lyn, although people say the success is due to luck, it's actually due mainly to hard work!

Questions

1 Explain two reasons why demand for Awfully Chocolate's products may have been high. [6]
2 Discuss whether the success of a new business is likely to be mainly due to luck. [10]

What qualities is an entrepreneur likely to need for success?

There is no single set of qualities that has been identified that will definitely make someone a successful entrepreneur. Entrepreneurs can differ enormously in terms of their backgrounds, skills, interests and personalities.

However, it is likely that a successful entrepreneur is someone who:

- is prepared to work very hard, especially in the initial stages of setting up the business. This means you need determination and the ability to cope with stress and setbacks.
- a vision. Many entrepreneurs have stories about the various problems they encountered when they first started up. Problems with money, suppliers, equipment and so on are all fairly common. It is also quite usual for others around you to be more cautious and less certain that your project will work than you are. To be successful you need faith in your idea and a belief in your own vision, even when there are initial problems.
- is willing to take a risk. It takes a lot of nerve to give up your existing job and start out on your own and yet this is what many people do. You may have to give up the salary, the company car, the support from head office and the pension just to pursue your dream. You may also have to go through quite a long period of time with relatively low rewards before you make it a success (if you ever do!).

According to the Royal Bank of Scotland (RBS) a successful entrepreneur is usually:

- well-rounded: someone who can make the product, promote it, sell it and count the money
- able to bounce back: a person who can cope with mistakes and have the confidence to try again
- innovative: not an 'inventor' in the traditional sense but a person who is able to carve out a new niche in the market, often a niche that is invisible to others
- results-orientated: to make a business successful requires a drive that only comes from setting goals and targets and getting pleasure from achieving them

- a professional risk-taker: to succeed means taking measured risks. Often, successful entrepreneurs use a step-by-step approach to risk-taking, at each stage exposing themselves to only a measured amount of personal risk and moving from one stage to the next only as each decision is proved
- totally committed: hard work, energy and single-mindedness are essential elements in the entrepreneurial profile.

Study tip

There are many very different entrepreneurs so it is impossible to say exactly what qualities an entrepreneur must have. However, studies suggest that many entrepreneurs have some qualities in common such as being innovative and resilient.

Why do governments like entrepreneurs?

Governments like entrepreneurs because they set up new businesses in an economy. This means that entrepreneurs:
- create jobs and help keep unemployment low in the economy
- earn money and pay taxes
- create competition for the existing providers in markets and provide new products and services. This is good for customers, who get more choice, and this is likely to lead to better service.

Given the benefits of entrepreneurship, many governments are willing to help entrepreneurs to start up and grow their businesses.

The role of business enterprise in the development of a business and a country

Enterprise involves taking risks to develop new ideas. This is important to businesses and the country as a whole because a business enterprise finds solutions to problems, and new and better ways of doing things. This can help the business reduce costs and offer more benefits at a lower price than competitors.

For the country as a whole enterprise leads to innovation, which creates new products and economic growth. Enterprise challenges established ways of doing things and provides competition to existing providers. This can lead to more choice, better quality and lower prices for customers.

How can governments help entrepreneurs?

There are many ways in which governments can help entrepreneurs. They can provide:

- access to advice and useful information to help them get started. For example, a new entrepreneur may have little experience of financial matters and appreciate some advice in this area
- funding such as grants to help with the initial start-up costs
- legal protection for new ideas. For example, a patent provides legal protection for an invention. This means that inventors can make profits without their ideas being 'stolen' by others.

Maths moment

Imagine you need to raise $250 000 to start your business. The government will provide 3 per cent, and your savings equal 6 per cent. How much money do you still need to raise?

The entrepreneurial culture

If a country is said to have an entrepreneurial culture this means that entrepreneurs are highly valued and respected and that the business environment encourages and helps people to set up on their own. In America, for example, millions of people start their own business every year. It is generally accepted that some of these will fail, so if you have started a business and it has gone wrong, it is not seen as being particularly unusual. In other countries, if your business has failed the tendency is for people to be suspicious about your business skills and you can find it very difficult to start up again: for example, you may find it almost impossible to borrow money again. This type of culture would not encourage others to try to start up their own businesses because of the fear of failure.

The number of regulations in a country can also have a significant impact on the willingness and ability of people to start up in business. If there are many forms to fill in, and many restrictions on what can and cannot be done, it can make it difficult and expensive for entrepreneurs to set up. This can reduce the incentive to start up on your own.

Case Study

Government help in Singapore

There are a growing number of government organisations to support entrepreneurship in Singapore, which is helping the country maintain its important economic position in the region. The undoubted success of entrepreneurs is also due to the infrastructure available in Singapore, the business-friendly environment and efforts by the government to remove regulatory barriers.

In 2003, one of the recommendations of the government economic review committee was to make Singapore an 'entrepreneurial nation willing to take risks to create fresh businesses'.

Ease of doing business ranking
1 Singapore
2 Hong Kong SAR
3 New Zealand
4 United States
5 Denmark

6 Norway

7 United Kingdom

8 Korea, Republic

9 Iceland

10 Ireland

Source: World Bank 2012

Less than ten years later, Singapore ranks number one in the world for ease of doing business and number four for starting a business, according to the World Bank.

Singapore is considered a gateway to South East Asia. It is a relatively small market of 5 million people, which investors use as somewhere to save their money and then invest in much bigger markets such as Indonesia, Malaysia and the Philippines.

However, there are still some cultural barriers to entrepreneurship such as the fact that failure is not really acceptable in Asia. In the US failure is accepted as part of the process of being an entrepreneur; this is not so true in Asia.

Questions

1 Explain how culture may act as a barrier to entrepreneurship. [6]

2 Discuss the ways in which the government of Singapore might encourage entrepreneurship. [10]

Case Study
New York – the most competitive city in the world

A recent study commissioned by Citigroup found that New York was the most competitive city in the world. The city's then mayor, Michael Bloomberg, said that one of the reasons was that 'talent attracts capital far more effectively and consistently than capital attracts talent'.

In order to attract talented people New York City has tried to improve the quality of life, has invested in the services and facilities in the city and has tried to encourage innovation. It has also tried to make it easier than ever to start up, run and grow a business.

New York City's 200 000 small businesses employ more than half of the city's private sector workforce and are a critical component to the city's economic success. Services for small businesses include help raising finance, the provision of business courses and training, and support making sense of the various government regulations. The city has also worked hard at removing unnecessary and duplicate paperwork to make it simpler to run a business.

Questions

1 Explain two reasons why New York may be a good place to do business. [6]

2 Discuss whether your own city is a good place to do business. [10]

Case Study
Brazil's business labyrinth of bureaucracy

Despite its fast growth Brazil remains a country where it is difficult to set up in business. According to the World Bank's 2012 annual global report 'Doing Business', which evaluates the ease of starting a business, dealing with construction permits, registering property, and paying taxes, Brazil ranked 126th out of 183 countries. On average, it takes 13 procedures and 119 days of work to start a business in Brazil; and construction permits require an average 17 procedures and 469 days to finally get authorised.

The excess of laws, regulations, taxes, paperwork and time to fulfil the requirements when opening or running a business is one of the reasons why 40 per cent of Brazilian start-up businesses do not survive for more than two years after opening, according to recent data revealed by IBGE, Brazil's main government research institute.

Questions

1 Explain two reasons why starting a business in Brazil might be difficult. [6]

2 Discuss the possible consequences of making it difficult for businesses to open in a country. [10]

1.3 Social enterprise

Social enterprises

Not all enterprises are set up to make a profit. Local sports clubs, government organisations and charities, for example, do not have profit as the main objective. They are set up for some other purpose.

Case Study
Wikipedia

Wikipedia was created in 2001. It is a multilingual, web-based, free-content encyclopedia project and is now one of the largest online encyclopedias. It is written by volunteers all over the world. Its articles can be edited by anyone with internet access. Articles are continually updated and improved by online contributors. The website was created by the not-for-profit Wikipedia Foundation.

To find out more, visit www.wikipedia.com.

Questions

1 Explain the transformation process that Wikipedia provides. [6]
2 Discuss the ways in which the success of Wikipedia might be measured. [10]

Social enterprises are businesses that have social aims and which trade in order to benefit the community or society in general. Examples of social aims are job creation and training, providing community services and 'Fair Trade' with developing countries. Well-known social enterprises in the UK include Cafédirect, The Big Issue, The Co-operative Group, the Eden Project and Jamie Oliver's 'Fifteen', but there are many others (more than 55 000) operating in a wide range of industries from farmers' markets and recycling companies to transport providers and childcare. The number of social enterprises is increasing as people become more concerned about issues such as the environment and inequality.

Case Study
EnNatura

As interest in environmental issues grows, more and more industries are responding to an increasing demand for eco-friendly products. One company that has led the way here is EnNatura. This Delhi-based start-up produces a biodegradable ink. The company also claims its product has other benefits, such as making the process of cleaning printing machinery easier and more environmentally friendly.

The co-founders, Sidhartha Bhimania and Krishna Gopal Singh, were students at the Indian Institute of Technology (IIT). They intended to become academics but the excitement of creating a business proved too great.

They tried a number of ideas, considering options ranging from oil exploration to effluent treatment. Eventually they settled on a new form of printing inks, not least because it did not require a big lab space. The conventional printing process makes use of a lot of petroleum-based chemicals and solvents. These solvents are responsible for photochemical smog formation and ozone depletion as well as being hazardous to printers who are working in the industry. The challenge was to create an ink that would not only be eco-friendly but also have the vivid colours of conventional ink. The key was to develop their own resin from which the ink would be made. Krishna Gopal Singh and Sidhartha Bhimania set up EnNatura with a government grant, which provided them with a financial launch pad.

Questions

1 Explain why the government might have been willing to invest in EnNatura. [6]
2 Discuss whether businesses are good for society. [10]

Case Study
The Big Issue

The Big Issue is an international organisation that works with homeless people all over the world, from the United Kingdom to Africa, Asia and Australia. At the centre of its work is *The Big Issue* magazine, an award-winning entertainment and current affairs magazine which is produced by professional journalists and sold on the streets by homeless people. In the UK, the homeless buy the magazine for 70 pence and sell it on for £1.50, keeping 80 pence for themselves. Although financial exclusion is one of the key reasons why people remain homeless – and one of the core aims of The Big Issue is to give people a legitimate way of making a living – there are other benefits of becoming a vendor.

Not only does beginning to sell the magazine provide an opportunity to access the services of The Big Issue Foundation, but also the act of having to organise themselves and their money, as well as committing to a sales pitch, teaches new skills and self reliance, which in turn builds self confidence and can be the key to moving on. The Big Issue offers social as well as financial inclusion. Editorially, *The Big Issue* magazine is committed to giving homeless people a voice in the media and raising difficult issues that are overlooked in the mainstream press.

Source: www.bigissue.com

Questions

1 Explain how The Big Issue helps homeless people. [6]
2 Discuss the ways in which The Big Issue would measure its success. [10]

The Triple Bottom Line

For many businesses profit is an important measure of success. Profit is measured by the revenue or income a business earns from sales minus the costs of providing the good or service that it has sold. By making a profit a business has generated an excess in financial terms. This shows the business activity was worth undertaking and the amount of profit a business makes in relation to the scale of its operations is a common measure of success. The profits can be used to reward investors and to invest in the business so it can continue in operation and grow. Profit is therefore a financial (or economic) measure of success.

However, as we have seen with social enterprises, businesses may have other objectives. In fact businesses may have several objectives at any one moment. While profit does remain important to many organisations they may also be concerned about how this profit is made and the impact of the business on others. This means that businesses often have social and environmental objectives relating to how they treat suppliers, how they treat staff and the impact of their activities on the environment and other groups such as the local community. Businesses may be willing to accept lower profits if it significantly reduces pollution, if it ensures only recycled resources are used and if it helps the local community, for example. This increasing interest in social and environmental issues may be because there is more information about such things and so managers are making better informed decisions; it may also be a response to the fact that consumers, employees and investors are increasingly interested in such issues. Not only that, if competitors are demonstrating their environmental and social awareness then other businesses may have to follow to retain their competitiveness. Elkington suggested business performance should be measured by examining 3Ps: its Profits, its treatment of People and its impact on the Planet. This is known as the Triple Bottom Line (Profit, Planet, People).

Maths moment

You decide to give 1.5 per cent of your sales to charity. If your sales are $520 000 this year how much would you give to charity?

Test your learning

Short answer questions

1 State **two** resources used in a business. [2]

2 a Define what is meant by a business objective. [2]

   b Explain **one** reason a business might want to make a profit. [3]

3 a What is meant by scarcity and choice? [2]

   b Explain what is meant by opportunity cost with an example. [3]

4 a State **two** factors in the external business environment apart from the economy. [2]

   b Explain **one** way in which growth in the economy might affect a business. [3]

5 a State **two** reasons why businesses might fail. [2]

   b Explain **one** effect of business failure on an economy. [3]

6 a State **two** likely features of a successful entrepreneur. [2]

   b Explain **one** reason why entrepreneurs are important to an economy. [3]

7 a What is meant by social enterprise? [2]

   b Explain **one** way a social enterprise might measure its success. [3]

8 a What is meant by the Triple Bottom Line? [3]

   b Explain **one** reason why a business might set environmental targets. [3]

9 a What is meant by an entrepreneur? [2]

   b Explain **one** reason why people become an entrepreneur. [3]

10 a State **two** inputs that a business might use in its transformation process. [2]

   b Explain **one** reason why a business might use more machinery and less labour in its transformation process. [3]

Data response question

Caffe Habitu

In 2003, Jennifer Liu founded Caffe Habitu, a coffee chain, when Hong Kong's economy was suffering following the outbreak of Severe Acute Respiratory Syndrome (Sars) that killed nearly 300 people in the city.

As other businesses took fright and commercial rents plunged, Ms Liu leased a building in a new development in one of Hong Kong's busiest shopping districts.

The business benefited from some luck when one of her 20-strong chain of coffee shops featured in a romantic comedy called *Don't Go Breaking My Heart*, which was a box-office hit in China.

In the months after its release, Ms Liu had up to 200 enquiries a day from potential business partners in China.

She eventually selected a suitable partner and six branches are set to open in Shanghai, a move that could potentially allow Caffe Habitu to take on the likes of Starbucks in the world's biggest consumer market.

With its low taxes and light regulation, Hong Kong ranks second in the World Bank's 'ease of doing business' survey.

Questions

1 Explain why Jennifer Liu may have set up her own business. [6]

2 To what extent do you think the success of a new business is due to luck? [10]

Essay question

To what extent do you think business is important for society? [20]

2 Business structure

Chapter overview

In this chapter we examine:
- the different economic sectors in an economy, i.e. the difference between primary, secondary and tertiary sectors and the private and public sectors
- the advantages and disadvantages of different forms of legal structure, such as companies and sole traders.

2.1 Economic sectors

There are many types of businesses and it is useful to be able to categorise them to analyse their performance and the different issues they face. Typical ways of categorising business include by sector and by legal status.

Primary, secondary and tertiary sector businesses

The many businesses that exist in an economy operate in one of three sectors:

- Primary sector – this involves the first stage of production and includes extractive industries such as mining, farming, forestry and fishing. This sector is not very large in the UK economy but is bigger in some lesser developed economies. In Chile, for example, fishing is one of the biggest industries thanks to its 4000 km of coastline.
- Secondary sector – this represents manufacturing and construction industries.
- Tertiary sector – this represents the service sector (e.g. tourism, accountancy and music). This is often the biggest sector in developed economies in terms of both employment and the value of the output.

The public and private sectors

We can also distinguish between businesses that are owned by private individuals, which are in the private sector, and those that are government owned, which are in the public sector. Local supermarkets, clothes shops and hairdressers are likely to be in the private sector (although not always); the provision of electricity, water and health is often in the public sector – although again this will vary from country to country. Some products may be provided by both the public and the private sectors; for example, there may be government-run schools and private schools.

If a government takes control of a private sector business this is called **nationalisation**. If a government sells one of its organisations to the private sector this is called **privatisation**.

Typically the government is likely to run organisations:
- that have a strategic importance to the country, such as defence, in order to protect the country
- that provide essential services such as energy and water that the government wants to make sure everyone has access to regardless of income
- that individuals may not appreciate how beneficial they are if left to themselves, such as education and health. These are called **merit goods**.

Public sector organisations can have social objectives, not just profit objectives. This means they may provide non profit making services such as transport to remote areas; a private sector business would probably not be interested if there were not enough passengers but the government may provide this service for the welfare of its citizens.

Key terms

Nationalisation occurs when a government takes ownership of a business from the private sector into the public sector.

Privatisation occurs when a government transfers ownership of a business from the public sector to the private sector.

Merit goods are goods or services such as education and health that private individuals undervalue because they do not appreciate the full benefits of them and therefore do not consume enough unless the government intervenes.

The extent to which a government intervenes will vary from country to country and depends a great deal on political views about the role of the state. In countries such as North Korea there has been a belief that the government should mostly decide how resources are allocated and so there is a large public sector and small private sector. Countries such as the USA allow market forces to allocate resources to a greater extent so the public sector is smaller and the private sector is bigger. However, the role of government may change over time; for example in Cuba the government has been intervening less in recent years whereas in Venezuela it has been intervening more and taking control of many businesses.

Case Study

Cuba

Figure 2.1 A street scene in Havana, Cuba

Cuba is one of the world's most centrally planned economies, meaning that the government still runs most of the organisations that exist in the island. The government controls nearly 90 per cent of the economy and employs nearly 85 per cent of all workers. Although there have been some changes in recent years to encourage more private sector businesses, the number remains very small and the government still controls the majority of business activities. For most Cubans their jobs, their pay, where they live, their education, their transport, their health care and most of the products they buy are under the control of the government. At the moment the average Cuban has a relatively low living standard and many rely on state handouts. The country's dependence on imported food and oil leaves it vulnerable to world price fluctuations; it also relies on support from other countries such as Venezuela.

The main opportunities for the private sector are in tourism; licences are available for private sector restaurants and hotels, for example, to welcome visitors and bring in much wanted spending from abroad. Cuba has around

3 million visitors a year. Foreign investors are now allowed in some sectors that Cuba is eager to develop such as biotechnology and pharmaceuticals. There is growing pressure for more private sector opportunities and the government seems determined to make this happen although may want it to happen gradually.

Source: Adapted from www.ukti.gov.uk

Questions

1 Explain the potential benefits of a centrally planned economy. [6]
2 Discuss the possible reasons why Cuba has moved some way towards a market economy. [10]

2.2 Legal structures

When setting up in business, the founders must consider the most appropriate legal form for their enterprise. There are several different types of business organisation, each of which has its own legal structure. These include sole traders, partnerships, private limited companies and public limited companies, cooperatives, franchises and joint ventures.

Sole traders

Figure 2.2 Sole traders run their own businesses

When individuals run a business on their own they are known as 'sole traders'. Plumbers, decorators, window cleaners and hairdressers are often sole traders. The people running these businesses work for themselves. In some cases, sole traders hire other people to help them out, but they are the owners and remain responsible for the overall business and are actively involved in the running of it on a daily basis.

What does it take to be a successful sole trader?

As a sole trader you need to be someone who is willing to work on your own, who has the confidence to take your own decisions and who can turn your hand to almost any aspect of your business. As a sole trader, you may have to serve customers, decide what equipment to buy, deal with suppliers and keep accurate and up-to-date business records. This requires a wide range of skills and an enormous degree of flexibility.

Sole traders have to be used to working hard: running your own business is no easy task. You must also be good at managing stress. All the decisions of the business are yours alone, so if you get it wrong the responsibility is yours. On the other hand, if it is successful the sense of achievement and the rewards are yours, too!

Becoming a sole trader requires a high level of self-discipline because you are your own boss: there is no one to tell you what to do. This can be very exciting, because *you* decide what is going to happen. However, it also means that you have to motivate yourself to get things done. For example, you have to organise your day properly and use your time effectively.

The advantages of being a sole trader

One of the main advantages of being a sole trader is that it is so easy to start up in business. Unlike starting other types of organisation, you do not need to register with anyone or fill in any special forms: you can just start trading (provided you declare your profits to the government tax office at the end of each financial year!). If you suddenly decide you want to be a gardener, a web designer, an artist, an interior decorator or cleaner, you could start up in business tomorrow. It may be wise, however, to do some planning and get some training first!

Many people also enjoy not having to take orders from other people. They like the freedom to make their own decisions, to decide when and where to work, what to do and how to do it. You can also make decisions quickly as you don't have to check with anyone to get permission to do something. It can be incredibly motivating to be your own boss.

Another important advantage of being a sole trader is that you keep all the rewards of the business. You don't have to share the profits with anyone else.

Many entrepreneurs begin as sole traders for these reasons.

The challenges of being a sole trader

While being a sole trader can be very fulfilling, it also brings with it many challenges. Making all the decisions can be exciting, but you carry all the responsibility if anything goes wrong. If you work for someone else and there is a real problem, you have someone to work with to solve it. Being a sole trader can be quite lonely: some people find it difficult to cope with the pressure. The hours may be quite demanding, too. This is particularly likely to be an issue in the early years when you are trying hard to build up enough business. Also, you may not be able to take much time off for holidays because you may not be able to afford to close the business and risk losing customers.

Another difficulty is raising finance to set up and expand. You generally have to rely on your own money or money from friends and family (plus the money from the business itself, once it is up and running). Of course, it is possible to borrow from a bank or other financial institution but they often charge smaller businesses quite high interest rates because they are worried about the risk of failure and want to cover their losses.

Being a sole trader is also quite risky if anything goes wrong. This is because sole traders have **unlimited liability**. The sole trader keeps any rewards the business makes, but is also personally responsible for any losses. If their businesses have problems, sole traders can lose their personal possessions.

> ## Key term
>
> **Unlimited liability** occurs when an individual or groups of individuals are personally responsible for all the actions of their business. With sole traders, there is no distinction in law between the individuals and the business and so they could lose their personal assets if the business has financial problems.

In many ways, working for other people in a large organisation is much easier because you are likely to:
- have other people to share ideas with
- receive a more regular income
- be able to call on experts to help you solve problems.

On the other hand, there is not quite the same sense of achievement and satisfaction of having created something for yourself.

Table 2.1 Advantages and disadvantages of being a sole trader

Advantages	Disadvantages
Making your own decisions can be motivating.	Sources of finance are limited.
You can make decisions quickly and respond rapidly to changes in the market.	You rely heavily on your own ability to make decisions.
You have direct contact with the market.	You may work long hours and have limited holidays, leading to stress.
Setting up is easy.	You are subject to unlimited liability.

Partnerships

If you join with other people and set up a business together this is known as a partnership. This is common in professions such as accountancy, medicine and law. The benefits of forming a partnership over being a sole trader include:

- You have other people to share ideas with.
- There are more people to invest in the business and help finance it.
- You can benefit from each other's specialist skills: for example, if you have a legal practice you could have one partner specialising in tax law, another in marital law, another in company law and so on. This enables you to offer a wide service to customers.
- You can cover for each other if someone is ill or on holiday.

However, a partnership can present challenges:

- You need to consult with others and there may be disagreements between the partners over the policies and direction of the business.
- You are dependent on the actions of others. If, for example, one of the partners makes a mistake or brings the partnership into disrepute, it will have an impact on all the partners. You are liable for your partners' actions, which can be risky.
- In most partnerships the partners have unlimited liability, which means that there is no distinction between the individuals and the business. If the business is sued, for example, the individuals may lose their personal possessions. This is a risk that some people may not be prepared to take.

To reduce some of the possible problems of a partnership, the individuals involved are advised to write a Deed of Partnership. This document sets out the 'rules' of the partnership: for example, it sets out:

- how the partnership would be dissolved if someone wanted to leave. It would set out how the partnership would be valued and therefore what the person leaving would receive
- how to resolve disputes if the number voting for and against is equal
- how profits will be divided up: if this is not specified the profits are divided up equally.

Table 2.2 Advantages and disadvantages of setting up as a partnership

Advantages	Disadvantages
Share resources, ideas and the workload	Share profits
More sources of finance than sole trader	May disagree over decisions
Cover if someone is ill or on holiday	Unlimited liability

Maths moment

You have four other partners in your business. You have agreed to share profits. If your profits are $240 000 how much does each partner receive?

Companies

To avoid some of the problems of being a sole trader or a partnership, you may decide to establish a **company** instead. To set up a company, the owners have to complete various documents and register the business at Companies House. This process is known as incorporation.

A company is owned by **shareholders**. Each share in the business represents a part of the company. The more shares someone owns, the more of the company belongs to them.

A company has its own legal identity, separate from that of its owners. The company can own property, equipment and other goods in its own right and is responsible for its own debts. If the company fails, the shareholders can lose the money that they invested in the business when they bought shares, but they cannot lose more than this. This is because shareholders have **limited liability**.

Limited liability and its importance

Limited liability means that a company is responsible for the money it owes but that the personal possessions of its owners are safe. This is different from a sole trader, who has unlimited liability and could lose everything if the business had financial problems.

Having limited liability is essential for companies to be able to raise money by selling shares. Without it, investors would be far less likely to buy shares because of the risk to their personal possessions. If you invested in a business with unlimited liability it would mean giving money to others and risking everything. With limited liability, you know what the maximum amount is that you could lose.

Key terms

A **company** is a business organisation which has its own legal identity and which has limited liability.

A **shareholder** is an investor in and one of the owners of a company.

Limited liability means that investors can lose the money they have invested into the business but their personal possessions are safe. There is a limit to their risk.

Having company status means that:

- the business must pay to have its accounts checked annually by independent accountants (called auditors)
- the company accounts must be made public, so that outsiders can see the revenue and profits of the business, as well as what it owns. This means that there is less privacy of affairs than if you were a sole trader.

Why become a shareholder?

By investing in a company, shareholders become the owners of the business. This means that, if the business is successful, the value of their shares should increase. Shareholders should also receive some of the profits that the company makes each year. The part of the profits paid out to shareholders is called the **dividends**. The more profit a firm makes, the bigger the dividends are likely to be. Each year the shareholders will decide on the amount of dividends to be paid per share: the more shares a person has, the more dividends they receive in total.

Shareholders can also influence the policy of the business. Most types of shares grant their owners voting rights. Each share is worth one vote. So, by buying more shares, people can get more votes and have a greater influence over what the firm actually does. If someone owns more than 51 per cent of the shares, they control the business and, therefore, can decide company policy.

All companies must have an Annual General Meeting (AGM) to which the shareholders are invited and every shareholder must receive a copy of the company's Annual Report. The Annual Report reviews the performance of the business over the last year. At the AGM, the directors and managers give an overview of the company's position and respond to any questions that shareholders might have.

In the UK, financial institutions such as banks, pension funds and insurance companies own most company shares. These organisations buy shares to make a profit through the dividends they receive and by selling the shares at a higher price later on. They can then pass their profits on to their own investors.

Private limited companies

Private limited companies have 'ltd' after their names. They are owned by shareholders and the owners can place restrictions on who the shares are sold to in the future. For example, many (but not all) private limited companies are owned by families who limit the sale of shares to other members of the family: this makes sure that 'outsiders' do not become involved. Owners of shares in private limited companies cannot advertise their shares for sale: they have to sell them privately.

Public limited companies

Public limited companies have 'plc' after their names. Once again, they are owned by shareholders, but unlike private companies restrictions cannot be placed on the sale of these shares. Shareholders in public companies can sell their shares to whoever wants to buy them. This can cause problems if another firm starts to buy up shares in the business in an attempt to gain control of it. Some of the shareholders may want to resist this takeover, but they cannot stop fellow shareholders from selling their shares.

Another difference between plcs and ltd companies is that shares in plcs can be advertised in the media. This is why you can see the share prices of public companies listed in the newspapers, but not those of private companies. Most companies become public because they want to advertise their shares to the general public and raise relatively large sums of money. Most public companies are bigger than most private companies.

If the owners of a private company do not need to raise large sums via the sale of shares and want to maintain control over their company then they probably would not want to make it a public company.

Cooperatives

Another form of business is known as a cooperative. Cooperative businesses are owned and run by and for their members, whether they are customers, employees or residents. The members of a cooperative have equal voting rights and so it is a democracy. Members, such as farmers or freelancers, tenants or taxi drivers, can often do better by working together. Sharing the profit is a way to keep it fair and make it worthwhile.

Rather than rewarding outside investors, a cooperative shares its profits among the members. Around 100 million people around the world are employed by cooperatives, while nearly 1 billion are members.

There are different forms of cooperative, such as:

- **Employee cooperatives** These occur when the business is owned equally by all the employees who work there. Each employee has a vote in the business decisions and shares in the profits. The advantage of this is that employees may be more motivated to make the business a success because they are part owners. One of the problems, however, is that decision-making may be difficult if everyone has an equal vote but disagrees. Also, you cannot sell shares to those outside the business to raise finance, which might limit access to funds.
- **Community cooperatives** These are owned by members of a community to provide a local service such as a post office or pub.
- **Retail cooperatives** These occur when independent retailers join together. A group of independent stores may come together and operate under one brand name. This means they can get better deals from suppliers by buying in bulk and can share marketing costs.

Figure 2.4 Franchisor selling to franchisee

How do franchises work?

There are many different forms of franchise, but the basic elements of a franchise agreement are:
- The franchisor sells the right to the product in return for an initial fee and a percentage of the franchisee's turnover.
- The franchisee receives the right to the name and the systems used by the franchisor. This may include access to materials and training methods.

In the case of the McDonald's example, the company will want to keep close control over its brand name, products and reputation. Therefore if you buy a McDonald's franchise you have to follow very close rules in terms of what you sell, how you sell it, the pricing, the way the food is cooked, where it is bought, how you use the logo, and so on.

Figure 2.5 Some franchise logos

Franchises include:
- Ben and Jerry's ice cream
- Domino's Pizza
- McDonald's fast-food restaurant.

Buying a franchise

If you buy a franchise you are buying a product that has already been on sale and therefore has a track record. This means you can see whether or not it works. You can also learn from other franchisees who are already established, and benefit from their experience.

Cooperative facts and figures

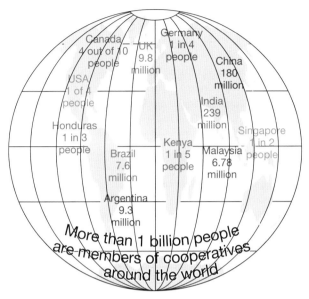

Figure 2.3 Number of people around the world who belong to cooperatives

Source: International Cooperative Alliance

Discussion question

Why do you think the cooperative approach is so popular around the world?

Franchises

If you do not have an idea for your own business or do not want to risk setting up completely on your own you might want to buy a **franchise**. A franchise occurs when one business (the franchisor) sells the right to use and sell its products and/or services to another business (the franchisee). Imagine you were interested in setting up a fast-food business. You could sit down and develop your own idea from scratch. However, it could prove to be difficult to come up with something that would capture demand and then decide on a brand image, a way of producing the food, a menu and décor for your stores. An alternative would be to buy the rights to sell, for example, McDonald's products in a given area. In this case, you would be buying a McDonald's franchise.

Key term

A **franchise** occurs when a franchisor sells the rights to use or sell his or her products to a franchisee.

The advantages of buying a franchise

Because you are joining other franchisees, then as a group you may have more bargaining power than you would have on your own. This may mean you get better deals with suppliers or when buying advertising space. Franchisees will often pool money to promote the brand on a national or regional scale. Any advert for the brand helps all the franchisees.

- You have the support of the franchisor and this can help you with decisions such as pricing, choosing suppliers and planning ahead. This should reduce the risk of something going wrong because there is more experience, joint power and support than if you were setting up alone.
- Buying a franchise may be less risky than setting up completely on your own. This is because there is past data for you to analyse before deciding whether or not to go ahead with the idea. At the same time it will be your own business and so there is still the incentive to make it successful, as you will benefit directly.

The problems of buying a franchise

The most obvious problem with buying a franchise is that it costs you money! This reduces the profits you make. However, you hope that by buying a franchise you will do better than you would have done on your own. Whether you are better off with a franchise therefore depends on its success and the terms and conditions of the contract.

Although one of the main benefits of buying a franchise is that you are linked to other franchisees, this can also be a problem. If, for example, the quality of service in other franchisees falls, it may damage the overall brand and hit your sales as well. You become dependent on others and vulnerable if there are problems elsewhere.

How much should you pay for a franchise?

Usually, there are several different types of payments involved in buying a franchise. For example, there may be an initial purchase fee plus a percentage of turnover each year. On top of this there may be money you have to invest each year to cover marketing and management expenses. The amount you pay will depend on:

- the likely turnover of the business
- the typical profits
- whether you have the exclusive rights to a particular geographical area and if so how big and attractive this area is
- the amount of training and support provided.

Maths moment

A franchisor asks for $12 000 fixed fee each year plus 2 per cent of profits after this fee and other costs are paid.

Your revenue this year is $650 000. Your costs (not including any costs associated with the franchise) are $420 000. What are profits this year?

Selling a franchise

One benefit of being a franchisor is that you benefit from the income generated from the franchisees. They will pay a fee to buy the franchise and a percentage of turnover. This generates earnings for the franchisor.

Franchising is also a way of growing fast. If you were trying to grow a business on your own, you would have to fund it all yourself. For example, you would have to find the funds to buy more premises and refurbish more shops. If you sell franchises, then the costs of opening a particular outlet falls to the franchisee. This may make fast growth much more feasible because individual franchisees are all funding their own enterprises. Domino's Pizza, for example, was founded in 1960 by Tom Monaghan. His ambition was to grow the business to three stores – that's why there are three dots on the company logo. However, through franchising the business has grown to become the world leader in pizza delivery. The company now has more than 8000 stores in over 50 international markets.

Another benefit of being a franchisor is that it may lead to more motivated managers because they are running their 'own' stores or businesses, rather than just being employees of a bigger business. This may help the business as a whole be more successful.

Case Study

Toni&Guy

Figure 2.6 A Toni&Guy hairdressers, UK

The Toni&Guy hairdressing business is a global brand with 435 salons all over the world including stores in Qatar, Kazakhstan, Japan and New Zealand. The business has grown via franchising.

Toni Mascolo, the founder of the company, grew up in Italy. When he was a boy, Toni would walk home from school past his father's hairdressing salon. 'I had a stool where I would sit and would wash hair, which made my father very proud. By the age of 12, 13, I was doing perms. It was a hobby. It's always been a hobby.'

He had originally thought of becoming a lawyer but that changed when his father moved the family to London. Mascolo, then 14, and known by his real name of Giuseppe, spoke no

English, so despite excelling at school back in Italy, he had little choice but to start working in his father's hairdressing business.

Toni&Guy started in 1963 when Toni and his brother Gaetano – who changed his name to Guy – decided to open their own salon in Clapham, south-west London. Other business interests apart from the salons themselves include:

- the production and distribution of products used and sold in the salons
- the Toni&Guy branded products, which have been developed with Alliance Boots
- another hairdressing chain called essensuals
- hairdressing training academies
- a business that supplies the salons with fixtures and fittings
- an IT business
- an in-house media agency.

Source: Adapted from *The Independent*, 15 October 2006

Discussion question

Do you think the business model adopted by Toni Mascolo would be easy for other hairdressers to adopt?

Study tip

When studying franchises you need to compare this way of starting up your own business with the alternatives. What are its advantages and disadvantages compared to other ways of starting up? What would determine whether an individual did this, rather than 'going it alone'?

Case Study

Franchise

Daily Bread is a leading bakery in India. It has recently started to franchise its operations across the country. Daily Bread has 20 stores in India and now wants growth in Bangalore, Hyderabad, Delhi and other cities in the country.

Why buy a Daily Bread franchise?

- The food and beverages industry is growing at a fast rate of 20 per cent a year. This makes it a good time to invest.
- The business is already established, which means you have minimal risks.
- Daily Bread treats you as a business partner so you can share your views and ideas with others in the business.
- You have a recognised brand.
- There is extensive hands-on training and support.

What is the profile of a Daily Bread franchisee?

- Prior experience in the hotel/food industry would be useful but is not essential.
- Individuals should have a drive to succeed and be highly motivated and committed.
- You will need the funds to invest between Rs 6 Lacs and Rs 15 Lacs. (1 Lac = 100 000 rupees, about $1700).
- You want to regard yourself as a partner not just an investor.

Options

Table 1.3

Options	Store size	Investment
Daily Bread Store	300 sq. ft to 400 sq. ft	Up to Rs.15 Lacs
Daily Bread Cafe	250 sq. ft to 300 sq. ft	Up to Rs.10 Lacs
Daily Bread Kiosk	120 sq. ft	Up to Rs.6 Lacs

Source: Adapted from www.dailybread.co.in

Questions

1 Explain why Daily Bread might franchise its business. [6]
2 Would you buy a franchise in Daily Bread? [10]

Joint ventures

A joint venture occurs when businesses collaborate on a project but do not formally join together all their activities. For example, in the car industry a number of manufacturers might share the research costs on developing an electric car but they would still compete with their other models. In the pharmaceutical industry two businesses may share their research skills for a new medicine. When entering a new market overseas a company may set up a venture with a local business to help make the contacts and develop the networks it needs to distribute its projects.

The benefits of a joint venture are that:
- businesses can share skills, resources and expertise and experience; this can benefit both parties
- businesses can collaborate on projects that are mutually beneficial without having to merge all their operations. This makes the process easier, less difficult to manage and less expensive than a full joining together (called a merger).

However, there may still be difficulties such as:
- agreeing on the division of the profits; there may be disagreements over the relative contribution of each business
- different views on how decisions should be made and what the priorities are
- different views on whether and how to end the venture.

Changing legal structure

It is relatively common for someone to set up in business as a sole trader and then to change the business into a private limited company (ltd) when they want to raise funds from selling shares or want the benefits of limited liability.

To operate as a ltd company a business must:

- have its accounts checked by an independent accountant (called an auditor) each year
- publish details of its accounts such as revenue and profits each year
- publish administrative details such the address of the company and names of its directors.

This means the business affairs of a private company are more open than those of a sole trader. If you want to keep your earnings private you would want to remain as a sole trader.

It may be that the owners of a private company want to make it public, as did Facebook in 2012. This gives the company access to more potential investors. To do this the business must make more information available to the public and there is greater regulation of the way it operates and the information it provides. Becoming a public company opens a business to even greater scrutiny and even bigger legal and accountancy bills! However, it does enable its shares to be sold more easily on the Stock Exchange and this makes the shares more attractive to more investors because they know they should be able to sell them if needs be to someone else (this means the shares of a plc are relatively liquid).

Test your learning

Short answer questions

1 Explain what is meant by the primary, secondary and tertiary sectors with an example of a business operating in each one. [6]

2 What is the difference between the private sector and public sector? [2]

3 a What is meant by a partnership? [2]
   b Explain **one** advantage of a partnership compared to a sole trader. [3]

4 What is meant by a company? [2]

5 Explain **one** advantage of creating a company rather than operating as a sole trader. [3]

6 a What is meant by limited liability? [2]
   b Explain how limited liability can benefit a company. [3]

7 a State what is meant by a franchise. [2]
   b Explain **one** reason for buying a franchise. [3]

8 a What is meant by a cooperative? [2]
   b Explain **one** benefit of being a part of a cooperative compared to a company. [3]

9 Explain **one** advantage of being a sole trader compared to a partnership. [3]

10 Explain **two** ways a company can raise finance. [2]

Data response question

Manchester United lowers stock float value

In 2012 Manchester United was forced to cut the value of its share flotation (which is when a company sells shares to the general public) in the US. It announced it would sell shares at $14 each, less than the $16 to $20 it announced a few weeks before. The club, which operates in the private sector, was selling shares that represented about 10 per cent of the business and hoping to raise $233 million (£150 million) to pay off some debt, well below the $333 million it had expected. The lowering of the initial share price suggests the club could not find buyers

at the higher prices. The shares will pay no dividend, and some analysts say that floating just 10 per cent of the club does not give institutional investors enough of a return opportunity.

In the documents issued to help sell the shares the 134-year-old club outlined its success on the pitch and the size of its fanbase, which generated a total global audience of 4 billion viewers in the 2010–11 season. Its commercial revenue grew from £66 million in 2009 to £103 million in 2011, as a result of sponsorship and merchandising deals. It made a profit of £13 million on continuing operations in 2011 and estimated it will have made profits of £23 million in 2012. The business said it intended to increase revenue and profits in coming years from sponsorship deals, sales of Manchester United branded products, broadcasting rights and improving its new media and mobile offerings.

It has also opened an office in Asia to try to attract new sponsors there, and is in the process of opening another one in North America. It already has retail shops in Singapore, Macao, India and Thailand.

Manchester United has been controlled since 2005 by the billionaire US sports investors the Glazer family, which paid £800 million for the club. They also own the Tampa Bay Buccaneers American football team. The Premier League giant came second last season and has won a record 19 titles.

Questions

1 Explain the terms
   a dividend [3]
   b private sector. [3]

2 Explain why Manchester United might want to sell shares. [6]

3 Discuss whether Manchester United should franchise stores to sell its branded products. [10]

Essay question

Discuss the advantages and disadvantages of forming a company compared to setting up as a sole trader. [20]

3 Business size

Chapter overview

In this chapter we examine:
- how the size of a business can be measured
- the significance of small and family businesses for the economy.

3.1 Measuring the size of a business

The size of a business can be measured by:
- the turnover (revenue) of the business
- the number of employees
- the market value of the business (e.g. the value of all of its shares)
- other indicators such as the number of stores or even the number of vehicles (e.g. for a bus company).

The best measure will depend on the sector you are considering. For example, in the public sector, that is businesses run by the government, organisations might not generate revenue (e.g. if the health service is provided free) so it may be more appropriate to measure the number of employees.

Note: Profit measures the success of the activities of a business. It is not in itself a measure of the size of a business.

Maths moment

Your company has 30 000 shares. The share price increases from $2.50 to $2.80. Calculate the old and new market value. Calculate the percentage change in the market value of the company.

3.2 Small businesses

The importance of small businesses and their role in the economy

In most economies the majority of businesses are quite small, often one-person businesses. For example, plumbers, hairdressers, restaurateurs, lawyers and photographers are often sole traders. Although these small businesses are the most significant in terms of number, the larger businesses tend to dominate in terms of the total number of people they employ and the value of the output they produce. There may only be one Sony or one Ford, for example, but they each employ a lot of people and have a very high turnover! Nevertheless, the small-business sector is very important to any economy.

This is because small businesses:
- create jobs, reducing unemployment
- provide competition for established businesses to ensure they remain competitive
- provide new sources of ideas. Small businesses are often very creative and many innovations start in smaller organisations
- can go on to grow in the future.

Advantages and disadvantages of being a small business

The advantages of small businesses are that:
- they are relatively easy to set up
- they are flexible because decisions can be made quickly (without having to consult lots of other people)
- they are often run by very motivated individuals because they probably set up and own the business and so want it to succeed because they personally gain the rewards

- they are often very creative because it is easy for those involved to communicate with each other and share ideas.

However, small businesses do have disadvantages:
- They lack power in the market – for example with suppliers and customers – and so can find it difficult to survive.
- They may lack much experience compared to more established firms.
- They may find it difficult to raise finance because of the high risk involved as so many small businesses fail.

This is why governments sometimes try to help small businesses by providing advice, lower taxes and less regulation to help them survive.

Small business finance

'Small- and medium-sized enterprises (SMEs) face challenges getting finance,' said the Vietnam Chamber of Commerce and Industry (VCCI) recently. It said that finance was expensive because the banks themselves are paying high interest of more than 13 per cent to get savers to provide them with funds. The banks also prefer to offer loans to large companies and state-run enterprises as they are a safer investment.

The Vietnamese government has ordered the banks to lend more to small- and medium-sized enterprises (SMEs).

Questions

1 Explain how high interest rates might make it difficult for small- and medium-sized enterprises to survive. [6]
2 Discuss why the Vietnamese government might be eager to lend more to SMEs. [10]

The role of small businesses as part of the industry structure in some industries

Small businesses are often very innovative. In industries such as pharmaceuticals and computers many of the breakthroughs are made by small businesses; bigger businesses then often take over or work with the smaller organisations to develop the ideas further.

Small businesses can also provide specialist services that bigger organisations might not be interested in providing for themselves; for example, while the larger firm concentrates on its core business the small firm might specialise in, say, digital marketing, specialist legal advice or provide expertise on a new market overseas. Small businesses can concentrate on small segments of the market (called **niches**) and sell their services to bigger organisations who buy in this expertise.

Key term

A **niche** is a small segment of a market.

Maths moment

The market as a whole is worth $960 000. Your niche is worth $60 000. What percentage of the market is this?

Family businesses

Figure 3.1 Family businesses are common in some countries, such as India

A number of businesses in an economy will be run by families. This is especially true in countries such as India where the culture tends to encourage families to work together.

Family businesses have some strengths:
- The family members may share values, leading to fewer disagreements.
- Those involved may work hard so that the family as a whole prospers; their ties to the business will be emotional as well as financial, which may make them more committed to the survival and success of the business. This may mean they will work harder and for longer than 'outsiders'.
- Individuals may be very supportive of each other because they are family members.
- Family members may be willing to plan long term because they will be looking for the benefits they can bring for future generations.
- A number of family members may be involved in providing finance and expertise.
- There may be decreased costs as family members may be willing to work for less than outside employees, at least in the short term.

However, there may also be weaknesses:
- Sometimes in a family business decisions may be made for emotional reasons rather than rational ones. It may be that the correct thing is to do 'A' but because we don't want to upset a family member we do 'B' instead.

- The family members may lack the right experience but there may be reluctance to bring in 'outsiders'. Sometimes the wrong people may be doing their jobs but family ties keep them in that role.
- It may be difficult to manage your relations easily.

Case Study

A family business

Nelson Assemany and his four brothers opened a shop together in Rio de Janeiro in 1967. Now employing their sons and nephews, today they have two shops, one selling fabrics, the other imported consumer goods.

While outsiders often think Brazilian business is dominated by big business such as the mining business Vale and oil group Petrobras, in reality 85 per cent of the country's companies are much smaller, family-run operations.

These businesses can easily adapt in a crisis compared to a company managed by a board of directors where you have to consult other people and get approval for everything.

Family businesses are also more likely to be focused on long-term growth, as the aim is to pass them onto the next generation.

Large companies are often too concerned with short-term results and shareholder profits.

The biggest difficulty for any family-run business is handing over power to the next generation when the current head of the family retires.

Questions

1 Explain what is meant by a company. [6]
2 Discuss the advantages and disadvantages of family businesses. [10]

Why and how a business might grow internally

The size of a business is not fixed – it can change over time. One way of doing this is to expand by buying up another business or joining with another business. This is called external growth and is discussed later in the book. Another way to grow is to expand your existing operations. This is called internal or organic growth.

To do this a business may:
- try to grow sales of its existing products in its existing markets
- develop new products for its customers
- find new markets where it can sell its existing products.

By growing:
- a business can get more power over suppliers and customers, which might help it to make more profits
- a business can reach more customers and there is the possibility of more profit through more sales
- the owners can eventually own something that is worth more
- the owners can have a sense of achievement because they can look back and be proud of having grown the business.

Test your learning

Short answer questions

1 Explain what is meant by the market value of a company. [3]

2 a State **two** ways of measuring the size of a business. [2]
  b Explain **one** possible advantage of being a big business compared to being a small business. [3]

3 Explain **one** problem of being a small business. [3]

4 Explain **one** reason why the government might want to support small businesses. [3]

5 What is meant by internal growth? [2]

6 a Explain **one** reason why a business might want to grow internally. [3]
  b Explain **one** problem of internal growth. [3]

7 State **two** ways in which a business might try to grow. [2]

8 Explain **one** advantage of being a family business. [3]

9 Explain **one** disadvantage of being a family business. [3]

10 a What is a niche market? [2]
  b Explain **one** benefit of operating in a niche market compared to a mass market. [3]

Data response question

Family businesses in Asia

From Samsung in South Korea and India's Reliance Industries to Hon Hai, the Taiwanese maker of the iPad, family businesses dominate Asia's, and increasingly the world's, business environment.

They make up half of Asia's publicly listed companies, a third of the region's stock market value and employ millions of people. However, many of these businesses are failing to plan for this transition, leading to uncertainty at best, and potentially ruinous family disputes. For example:

- Lee Kun-hee, the 70-year-old chairman of electronics giant Samsung, was sued by both his brother and sister over company shares left by their late father.

- India's richest man, Mukesh Ambani, was involved in a five-year dispute with his brother Anil over their father's vast Reliance empire.

- In Hong Kong a row emerged over the future of billionaire Stanley Ho's Macau casino business, which led to Mr Ho arguing against some of his own children.

Winston Wong, eldest son of the late Taiwanese tycoon Wang Yung-ching, sued to recover $4 billion worth of disputed assets that he claimed were taken by members of his father's third family. Wang founded Formosa Plastics, one of Taiwan's biggest companies.

Given that many of Asia's most successful business people are now in their eighties and nineties, the next decade will probably see a number of leadership successions.

Asia's biggest family businesses

- Samsung Electronics (South Korea)
- Reliance Industries (India)
- Hon Hai Precision Industries/Foxconn (Taiwan)
- Sun Hung Kai Properties (Hong Kong)
- Tata Consulting (India)
- Cheung Kong (Hong Kong)
- Hutchison Whampoa (Hong Kong)
- Wilmar International (Singapore)
- Bharti Airtel (India)
- Formosa Petrochemical (Taiwan)

Source: Credit Suisse

A recent study tracked the market performance of 250 family companies that underwent a succession. It found that, on average, these companies' market values declined by almost 60 per cent during the period starting five years before the succession, and up to three years afterwards. The success of a family firm is often down to the skills, charisma and connections of the founder, something that subsequent generations may find hard to replicate. This can be difficult to pass on.

Questions

1 Explain the following terms:
   a Publicly listed company   [3]
   b Stock market value   [3]
2 Explain why family businesses are so important to the economy.   [6]
3 Discuss whether family businesses are ultimately doomed to fail, it is just a question of time.   [10]

Essay question

Discuss the advantages and disadvantages of running a family business.   [20]

4 Business objectives

Chapter overview

In this chapter we examine:
- the nature and significance of business objectives in the private and public sectors
- decision-making and influences on business objectives.

4.1 Business objectives

An objective is a target. A good objective will state what is to be achieved (e.g. an increase in profit), how much the business wants it to be (e.g. $25 000) and when it wants this done by (e.g. in three years). This means a good objective should be:
- specific in terms of what the target is
- quantifiable (measurable)
- time specific in terms of when it should be completed.

A business will have an overall objective, such as a target of doubling its profits within five years. This will then give the business's managers the opportunity and information to set departmental targets.
 For example:
- The marketing department may have to increase sales by 40 per cent over an agreed period.
- The operations management department may need to reduce costs by 20 per cent over the next three years.
- The human resources department may have a target to increase labour productivity by 8 per cent over the same time period.

Within each department every individual should also have his or her own objective. For example, to reduce costs by 20 per cent, the person responsible for ordering supplies for the business may be set a target of finding a supplier that is 5 per cent cheaper. The manager in charge of sales for the South East of the country may be asked to increase sales in her area by 30 per cent to help overall sales rise by 40 per cent.

Those objectives which relate to the entire business, such as growth, are also termed corporate objectives.

The setting and pursuit of objectives of a business helps a business to coordinate its activities. It provides goals for employees at all levels within the organisation and helps managers to coordinate the activities of all employees. The Tesco case study below emphasises the importance of objectives within large and growing organisations.

Figure 4.1 Business objectives

Case Study

Tesco's growth objective takes it to Turkey

Tesco is a UK-based international retailer. It has stores in 14 countries in Europe and Asia. One of Tesco's objectives is to grow and this is clearly stated on its website. In order to achieve this corporate objective the company is seeking to expand its operations in several new markets. Another of Tesco's objectives is to be a 'successful international retailer'. The company's website states:

'In 1997, our international businesses generated 1.8% of the Group's profits. Today they represent 30% and we're now either number one or number two in eight of our 12 markets outside the UK. So we're already "successful" and are working to be an outstanding international retailer in stores and online.'

Source: www.tesco.com

Tesco entered the Turkish market in 2003 through the acquisition of five Kipa stores. Since then, it has expanded considerably and has 181 stores across 24 Turkish cities including Istanbul, Ankara and Izmir.

Questions

1 Explain how the Tesco employees responsible for its marketing might help the company to achieve its objective of growth in Turkey. [6]
2 Discuss the extent to which Tesco benefits from its clearly stated business objectives. [10]

Corporate social responsibility as a business objective

A business may have many objectives relating to different areas. For example, it may want to boost profits but at the same time may be aware of its impact on society as a whole and the environment in particular. Any business will have certain responsibilities to other groups by law. For example, there are laws in many countries determining the minimum an employee can be paid, the information businesses have to provide about their products and the procedures to be taken to make the working environment safe. All businesses should have an objective of acting legally. However, some may accept obligations to society over and above the legal minimum; this type of behaviour is known as corporate social responsibility (CSR). For example, a business may:

- believe it should ensure that work is interesting and that employees have a good career path within the organisation
- believe it has a responsibility to keep people in work as much as possible and therefore be reluctant to force anyone to leave the business
- believe that it is important to pay suppliers quickly rather than taking as long as possible and holding on to the money
- believe that it should invest in its local community to improve the area and quality of life of the community where it is based.

A business that acts responsibly believes it is a corporate citizen with obligations to society; this type of business will set targets to do more for society than it has to by law.

Case Study

Intel sets itself social objectives in Malaysia

Intel is one of the world's largest manufacturers of semiconductors, a component used in many electrical products including telephones and computers. It employs more than 82 000 people across the world. The company's mission statement is: 'This decade, we will create and extend computing technology to connect and enrich the lives of every person on earth.'

Figure 4.2 The Intel organisation believes in corporate social responsibility

In Malaysia Intel has set itself the objective of enhancing the quality of life in the communities in which they live and work as a means of achieving its mission. Some of its activities include the following:

- Intel Malaysia seeks to help local communities by involving its staff in volunteer programmes in the areas of education, environment and disaster aid relief. Intel Malaysia has committed 85 000 hours this year to community volunteer work.
- Its 'Back2School' programme, which aims to help economically-disadvantaged children in Kulim and Penang when they start school. Established in 1996, the programme provides children with Back2School kits each year. The kits include new school bags, uniforms, shoes and writing materials.
- Intel Involved volunteers have also participated in various disaster relief efforts around the region. To date, Intel Malaysia has donated MYR 285 000 (US$88 117) to various disaster relief funds and has sent 200 volunteers to help in tsunami relief efforts.

Source: Adapted from Intel's website at www.intel.com

Questions

1 Using examples, explain the difference between mission and objectives. [6]
2 Evaluate the extent to which Intel benefits from having a widely publicised mission statement. [10]

Mission statement, objectives, strategy and tactics

The mission of a business is the fundamental reason why it exists. A **mission statement** sets out the purpose of the business. For example, an airline may exist to be the 'best airline in the world'; a computer manufacturer may aim 'to help people work more effectively', and a cosmetics business may intend to 'bring beauty to everyone'. The mission will be determined by the owners of the business. The mission is a rather general statement and, unlike **objectives**, whether or not it has been achieved cannot easily be measured. What exactly does a business measure to decide if it is the best airline? It could be the number of planes it operates, or the number of passengers, or perhaps the level of customer satisfaction. This is why corporate objectives exist: to turn the mission into measurable, specific and time related targets.

Once these targets have been set the business has to decide how to achieve them most effectively. The long-term plan to achieve an objective is known as a **strategy**. For example, if a business wanted to increase profits by 30 per cent in three years the strategy might be to target overseas markets, as in the case of Tesco in the case study above. However, this strategy has to be put into action. For example, a decision has to be taken on which countries will be targeted. Tesco is clearly targeting China, India and Turkey to achieve its growth ambitions. However, other decisions have to be made too. In what order will the new countries be entered? What products will be offered in each? The shorter term action plans that combine to make up the strategy are known as **tactics**.

Figure 4.3 From mission to tactics

The importance of business objectives

Business objectives set out what the business wants to achieve. This provides a focus for all decisions. Employees know what they are supposed to achieve and can then make suitable decisions about the resources to use. Without objectives employees do not know the priorities and do not know how success will be measured. This can lead to a loss of focus and a wasteful use of resources.

Objectives can:
- motivate employees by providing a target
- provide a measure of control as progress can be reviewed against the target.

Key terms

A **mission statement** sets out the overall purpose of a business.
An **objective** is a target that is measurable and has a given timescale.
Strategy is the long-term plan to achieve the objective of a business.
Tactics are the short-term actions needed to implement the strategy.

4.2 The role of objectives in the stages of business decision-making

Managing a business involves many different decisions. For example, deciding on the objectives, deciding the best way of achieving these (which is set out in the company's strategy), and deciding how to bring the strategy about on time and at an acceptable cost through use of appropriate tactics.

Making the right decisions is therefore an important part of good management.

Decision-making involves:
- **Setting the objectives** This is essential because the success of a plan can only be judged against the objectives that were set. Making a profit of $100 000 may be disappointing if the objective was $300 000 but not if the target was $80 000! It is important to set realistic and achievable targets.
- **Gathering information** Before you decide what to do you need information on where you are at the moment, what else is happening and what your options are to analyse the situation.
- **Selecting a suitable strategy** Having analysed the information you can decide on the best strategy. For example, targeting the domestic or overseas markets.
- **Implementing the strategy** This is where the tactics come in to make sure the plan works well.
- **Reviewing** This is essential to see how you have got on and what, if anything, needs to be changed. After the review you can consider whether the objectives are still appropriate or not; you may need to set higher or different targets, for example.

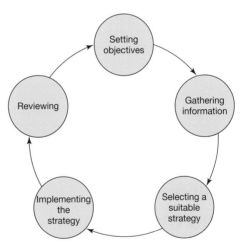

Figure 4.4 The process of decision-making

How objectives might change over time

Over time the objectives of a business may change. This can be for many reasons both internal (inside the business) and external (outside the business):
- **Internally** A business may have new owners or managers who want to achieve different things. Perhaps they want the business to grow faster, for example, or are more concerned about the environmental record of the business than the previous owners.

• **Externally** Perhaps the economy has gone into decline and so the organisation needs to reduce its growth target; perhaps competitors have entered the market, which means the profit target was too ambitious and needs to be amended downwards.

Decision-making is a continuous process in which decisions are being taken and reviewed and new objectives are set.

Turning objectives into targets and budgets

The overall objectives of a business need to be cascaded down into departmental and then individual targets for people. Using objectives throughout the organisation helps ensure everyone is working towards the same aim. With each objective there should be a strategy of how it is to be achieved and specific tactical targets showing the details of the activities that need to be undertaken. A plan will show:

• who is in charge of what
• what they have to do
• when it must be done
• how much they have to spend, that is, what **budget** has been agreed. A budget is a financial target that might set out expected revenues and also anticipated expenditure. This helps with financial planning. The size of the budget will depend on what the objective is and what has to be done to achieve it.

Key term

A **budget** is a financial plan.

The communication of objectives and their likely impact on the workforce

When setting objectives this should be done in discussion with the people who will be responsible for achieving them. This should help make sure the objectives are realistic and that the people involved are committed to achieving them. If a target is forced on an employee, they may not try very hard to achieve it because they may not think it is sensible or even possible to hit.

Having an objective can be very motivating because it provides a sense of direction so employees know what they are doing and why, and how this fits in with the overall strategy of the business. It can also motivate because it sets workers a target and so they have something to aim for and something that can be reviewed.

However, objectives may demotivate if the person who is set them does not believe in them and has no sense of

ownership. If an employee felt they were set a target that could not be reached or did not have the budget to make it possible they would probably feel demotivated. This means how an objective is set and what resources are allocated to it are very important.

Study tip

Remember that some of the businesses you will encounter in question papers may be large ones and that this can pose a challenge for the business to communicate corporate objectives clearly. This problem can be more serious if the business operates in different countries with different languages and time zones.

How ethics may influence business objectives and activities

Key term

Ethical behaviour is behaviour that is thought to be morally correct, and not necessarily the most profitable.

Business ethics refers to what is considered to be right or wrong in terms of business behaviour. For example, is it **ethical behaviour** to sell cigarettes if you know they can damage people's health? Is it ethical to produce a good or service if the process of producing it damages the environment? Is it ethical to show advertisements for children's toys between children's television programmes to get the children to pester their parents to buy them? Managers face ethical issues all the time in all areas of business. Sometimes the objectives of the business can encourage unethical behaviour. If employees are set extremely high sales targets they might decide to sell products to people who don't really need them, or to avoid telling people some of the problems that might occur with the product if they don't ask. The drive to boost sales can lead a business's employees to behave badly. In recent years there have been many sales scandals; for example insurance companies have sold people policies that were unlikely to ever pay out, or banks have not told people they could be earning higher returns if they changed to a different type of bank account. This behaviour is usually driven by a desire to hit high targets either to keep a job or to earn bonuses.

Ethics at Texas Instruments (TI)

Texas Instruments is based in Dallas, Texas, and makes a diverse range of electrical products including military equipment and calculators. It employs 34 500 people worldwide.

TI's board of directors established an ethics office in 1987 and appointed the company's first ethics director. Its ethics director and staff have three primary functions:

- to ensure that business policies and practices are continuously aligned with ethical principles
- to clearly communicate ethical expectations
- to provide multiple channels for feedback, through which stakeholders may ask questions, voice concerns and seek resolution of ethical issues.

The company's website makes its ethical position clear. 'Our challenge … is to provide the tools employees may need to make tough but appropriate decisions quickly. We work to ensure they have a clear understanding of the global rules and regulations that govern our operations, as well as our own values, principles and ethical expectations.'

Source: Adapted from the TI website at www.ti.com

Questions

1 Explain why Texas Instruments sets out its ethical objectives on its website. [6]
2 Discuss the case for and against Texas Instruments operating with ethical behaviour as a key objective at all levels in the business. [10]

Of course, unethical behaviour does not have to be the case but businesses must be clear on the behaviour they expect from employees in terms of how they reach their targets. This is why some businesses have a Code of Ethics or a Code of Conduct to make it clear to employees what is and what is not regarded as acceptable behaviour.

Test your learning

Short answer questions

1 a What is meant by a business objective? Give an example. [3]
  b State **two** features of a good objective. [2]

2 a Define the term mission statement. [2]
  b Explain **one** benefit to a multinational business of having a mission statement. [3]

3 a What is meant by the term corporate responsibility? [2]
  b Why is corporate responsibility important to an oil company such as BP? [3]

4 Using examples, distinguish between strategy and tactics. [5]

5 Explain **one** type of strategy a business that is entering new markets overseas might adopt. [5]

6 a What are the stages in the decision-making process? [3]
  b State **two** reasons why it is important to review decisions. [2]

7 a Define the term ethics. [2]
  b Explain **one** reason why businesses try to take ethical decisions. [3]

8 Explain **one** reason why a marketing manager might consider ethics when making a decision. [5]

9 a Define the term budget. [2]
  b Explain **one** advantage to a business of setting a budget. [3]

10 Explain **two** reasons why a growing business's objectives might change over time. [5]

Data response question

A different bank

New Zealand has five major banks which dominate its banking market. Two years ago, Provident Bank opened its first branches in Auckland and Wellington amid great publicity. The new bank's corporate objectives include achieving high rates of growth and establishing 20 branches through the country within its first three years of trading.

The bank has a mission statement which sets out its commitment to a high standard of customer service. This figures prominently on its website and is used in much of its publicity, including its recruitment materials.

Provident Bank has set out to differentiate itself from its rivals by adopting strongly ethical corporate objectives which influence its strategy and tactics. It does not invest in businesses whose actions damage the environment or those that supply armaments. It is a carbon neutral business. Its charges are higher than the large, established banks, but its marketing is distinctive and research suggests that it is appealing to wealthy New Zealanders.

Questions

1 Explain the terms:

   a corporate objectives [3]

   b tactics. [3]

2 Briefly analyse the reasons why Provident Bank considers its mission statement to be important. [6]

3 Discuss the case for and against Provident Bank adopting ethical corporate objectives. [10]

Essay question

Discuss whether the setting and monitoring of business objectives is only important for businesses that are growing. [20]

Past paper questions

1 Discuss how the objectives of a manufacturing business might be affected by ethical issues. [12]

Cambridge International AS and A Level Business Studies
9707 Paper 1 Q5b May/June 2008

2 Read the Rex Cinema case study on page 212 and then answer the following question.

Discuss the extent to which Rex's overall objective is being achieved. [10]

Cambridge International AS and A Level Business Studies
9707 Paper 22 Q2d October/November 2011

5 Stakeholders in a business

Chapter overview

In this chapter we examine:
- the different groups affected by business behaviour
- the relationship between a business and these groups.

5.1 Stakeholder groups

Key terms

Stakeholders are groups or individuals who have an interest in a business.

Shareholders are persons or organisations that own a part of a company.

All businesses involve and affect many other people and groups by their activities. These individuals and groups are called **stakeholders**. Stakeholders include:
- the owners of a business, such as the **shareholders** of a company
- the business's employees
- a business's managers, who take tactical and strategic decisions
- the suppliers of goods and services
- the banks and other organisations that provide loans
- customers, who buy the products
- the local community, which may be concerned about issues such as employment and pollution
- the government, which collects tax revenues and hopes for high employment levels.

Stakeholders may not have formal authority over a business, but it may be in the business's best interests to take their needs into account when making decisions. It has become more common for businesses to attempt to meet the needs of as many of their stakeholders as possible in order to generate a positive image.

Study tip

When responding to questions about stakeholders do not be too ambitious and write about too many stakeholders. This will make it difficult to develop arguments fully and to write analytically. Instead, you should select the two or three stakeholder groups that are most relevant in the circumstances and focus exclusively upon these.

Roles, rights and responsibilities of the stakeholders

Each of the stakeholder groups above will have their own objectives. For example, employees may want good rewards for the work done, job security, a safe working environment and some opportunities for promotion.

Shareholders will want financial rewards in return for the risk of their investment.

Suppliers may want to be paid on time and to be kept well informed of any changes in orders.

The government will want the business to act legally, for example, to pay its taxes on time.

Each stakeholder will have certain legal rights. As an example, employees may have a contract of employment that the business must adhere to, while the owners or shareholders are entitled to be kept informed of the business activities. These stakeholders may also have responsibilities to the business. In return for their wages employees are expected to complete their tasks competently; in return for payment for their products suppliers should supply goods and services of an appropriate quality and quantity. Businesses are therefore in a two-way relationship with their stakeholders.

Table 5.1 Summary of stakeholders' roles, rights and responsibilities

Stakeholders	Possible rights include	Possible responsibilities include
Employees	To be treated fairly, to be paid fairly, to be kept informed	To work effectively, to turn up for work on time
Suppliers	To be paid on time, to be informed of any potential changes in orders in the future	To provide good quality products meeting the set specifications at the time set
Owners/ shareholders	To receive a share of profits, to be kept informed by management	To treat management fairly
Customers	To be supplied the right quality products on time	To pay on time
Government	To be paid taxes, to have businesses obey the law	To protect businesses, customers, employees and the environment
Managers	To be rewarded appropriately for responsibilities, to have duties commensurate with seniority	To carry out duties to best of ability, to be discrete in handling sensitive business data
Lenders	To be repaid promptly and on time	Not to charge excessive interest rates or to withdraw loans without a reasonable period of notice
The local community	To live in an area that is free from excessive noise or other forms of pollution, to have a say in decisions which impact on the local community and to benefit from employment	To cooperate with the business in its daily activities

Case Study

Gold Fields Ghana engages stakeholders

Gold Fields Ghana is the country's largest producer of gold and the largest private sector employer with over 5 200 direct and 83 000 indirect employees. It has recently introduced a forum to discuss issues and listen to its stakeholders. The aim is to engage with and update key stakeholders on its operations and activities.

Those invited include government ministers, members of the community, financial institutions, investors and the media. The company is committed to sustainable development and has invested in socio-economic development projects in the community where it operates. Its investment focuses on education, health, water and sanitation and the development. A world-class water treatment plant has recently been constructed

at Tarkwa and this provides communities with access to clean water. The company has also tried to employ locals wherever it can – 97 per cent of the workforce are Ghanians.

Source: Adapted from Joy Online

Questions

1 Explain why employees and customers might be Gold Fields Ghana's major stakeholders. [6]
2 Discuss the extent to which Gold Fields Ghana may have benefited from holding its 'stakeholder forum'. [10]

5.2 The importance and influence of stakeholders

The interaction between a business's decisions or actions and its stakeholders

Any business decision can impact on stakeholders. Examples include the following:

- Employees may be affected by a decision to reduce the size of the business.
- Shareholders will be affected if the profits of the business are poor.
- Suppliers may be affected by an increase in orders and be able to grow their businesses.
- The community may benefit from the expansion of the business and greater income being earned and spent in the area.
- The government may be affected by the creation of more jobs and more taxes being paid.

The impact of business activity can be positive or negative. Sometimes one group may benefit and another may suffer. For example, a decision to cut wages would not be popular with staff but may enable higher rewards for the investors. A decision to shift production abroad would not benefit the government of the original country but may benefit the community where production now occurs.

If stakeholders do not welcome changes they can take various actions to avoid the effects of them. The following are examples of actions that may be taken by stakeholders.

- Shareholders can sell their shares and invest elsewhere.
- Banks can refuse to lend more or charge more for businesses to borrow.

- Employees can leave and work elsewhere or as a group they may take strike action, which means they withdraw their labour hoping to get the business to change its policy.
- Suppliers can refuse to supply the business or demand better payment terms such as payment on delivery.

Accountability to stakeholders

The shareholder concept

Businesses have certain legal responsibilities to their stakeholders. For example, there are laws controlling the ways in which businesses can promote their products and, for food manufacturers, the ingredients that can be used. Some businesses simply do what they have to by law and no more. They focus mainly on rewarding their owners. They will pay employees what they need to get the job done but do not think they have any more responsibilities other than this. They will try to get the lowest price for supplies perhaps by threatening to use different suppliers. They will pay governments the taxes they have to but will not think they have any obligation to invest more in their region or country. This is known as the shareholder concept and regards rewarding owners as the key business objective.

People in business

Milton Friedman (1912–2006)

Milton Friedman was born in Brooklyn, New York, in July 1912. He immediately drew attention as a brilliant student and received several state scholarships. He studied at a number of leading American universities.

In 1948 Friedman was appointed Professor of Economics at the University of Chicago, a post he held until his retirement in 1977 aged 65. Friedman soon began to attract attention for his criticisms of all forms of government intervention in the economy. This brought him into conflict with economists such as J.K. Galbraith, who supported the economic views developed by John Maynard Keynes.

Friedman was at the height of his powers and popularity in the 1960s and 1970s when he was the leader of the Chicago School of Economics. This group of liberal economists advocated the extension of free market economics and the reduction of the state in managing the economy. Many of his views attracted

much criticism. For example, he argued that government economic intervention in the form of imposing a minimum wage has an undesirable side effect, that of creating unemployment as businesses hire less of a more expensive resource.

Figure 5.1 Milton Friedman

Friedman also held strong views on the objectives that businesses should pursue. He argued that a business can best meet its **social responsibilities** by making the largest possible profit and then by using its resources as efficiently as possible, while operating within the law. He was a powerful advocate of the shareholder concept.

Friedman spent busy retirement years in California working at Stanford University, advising President Reagan on economic policy, writing best-selling books and appearing on television. He died in November 2006 at the age of 94.

The stakeholder concept

However, increasingly organisations are trying to work with their stakeholders and regard them much more as partners. This cooperative approach is known as the stakeholder concept. This view believes that it is better in the long term to treat stakeholders well.

For example, working closely with suppliers and paying them a fair reward for their work (even if this is more than the business would have to pay) will lead to better quality suppliers and much greater flexibility by suppliers to help out when needed. Focusing on employees' careers and showing concern about their welfare could lead to greater loyalty and commitment and as a result a better quality of work. Being interested in the environment could help save costs through initiatives such as recycling but also make the business more attractive to employees, customers and investors. The stakeholder concept fits in with corporate social responsibility in that it stresses the benefits of accepting obligations to stakeholders over and above what the law requires.

Hitachi

In 2011 Hitachi faced a number of natural disasters such as an earthquake in Japan, flooding in Thailand and earthquakes in Turkey. Hitachi City in north Tokyo, which is the headquarters of the company, was particularly badly affected by the Japanese disaster. These problems did disrupt the company's supply chain but the business continued to achieve good results. The managers believe its ability to survive such disasters was due to its stakeholders. The company has a good relationship with its different stakeholder groups such as customers, suppliers, national governments and various policy groups.

Hitachi believes it is important to be a good corporate citizen. For example, it says that environmental issues such as climate change are becoming a priority and there is increasing awareness of the relationship between businesses and human rights. The United Nations has asked companies to make broad contributions to society, mainly through corporate activities, with an eye on the environment but also alleviating poverty and protecting human rights. Hitachi is eager to do just this.

Source: Adapted from *Contributing to a Sustainable Society as a Good Corporate Citizen*, at www.hitachi.com

Questions

1 Explain two ways in which Hitachi could claim to be a good corporate citizen. [6]
2 Discuss whether or not working with stakeholders helps Hitachi. [10]

A business is made up of people with different opinions and sometimes very different views on what they want to achieve and how they think it should be achieved. Any major decision is likely to make some better off and others worse off; it is therefore likely to meet with opposition from some stakeholders.

Every decision will involve different stakeholders and will consider their objectives and their relative power. Do managers want to listen to them? Do managers need to listen to them? What will happen if managers ignore them? This means the managers of a business need to think about their relative power. A well-organised workforce that is unionised, for example, may be able to negotiate for more consultation and participation in decision-making than individual employees could on their own. Managers may want to pay more attention to an investor who owns 65 per cent of the company compared with one who has 1 per cent. A key supplier of a business's major component will have more influence than the supplier of a component that can

be bought in thousands of stores. So the more well organised a stakeholder group is, the more managers need a particular stakeholder, the more they like or agree with them and their objectives, the more they are likely to influence a manager's decision.

The role of different stakeholders can be shown using a stakeholder map:

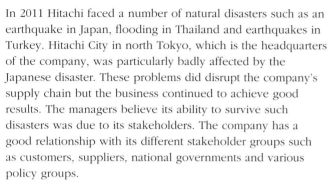

		Level of interest	
		Low	*High*
Power	*Low*	A Minimal effort	B Keep informed
	High	C Keep satisfied	D Key players

Figure 5.2 A stakeholder map and how a business may view different stakeholders

Groups in quadrant D are likely to influence decisions a lot. They are interested in what is going on in the business and are very powerful (e.g. major investors); managers will need to keep this group happy.

By comparison, stakeholders in quadrant A are not very interested and are not powerful (e.g. your milk delivery service or local newsagent); you do not need to worry much about this group.

How conflict might arise from stakeholders having different aims

One of the issues when dealing with stakeholders is that their aims might conflict; it might not be possible to please all of the groups all of the time. For example:

- Investors may push for lower costs to increase their profits and rewards and this may lead to fewer or lower pay increases for employees.
- In order to meet customer demands for cheaper products the business may relocate to cheaper production facilities overseas, so upsetting the local community.
- In order to meet government demands for more environmentally friendly operations processes the business may change its production system, leading to higher costs and higher prices for customers.

A business may have to juggle different demands and compromise on occasion.

Case Study

Foxconn changes its working practices

In recent years working conditions have improved enormously at factories owned and operated by Foxconn, a Taiwan-based electronics giant and Apple's biggest supplier. A report noted that Foxconn had introduced changes that it had earlier promised to implement. As a result working conditions have improved substantially at its two factories in Shenzhen and Chengdu, where it manufactures Apple's iPhones and iPads.

Foxconn has cut working hours to less than 60 hours per week, including overtime, and has improved health and safety measures. Foxconn has also improved the design of the machines used in its factories to avoid repetitive strain injuries, ensured all equipment is properly maintained and introduced regular breaks for all employees.

These changes have followed reports in the media of workers committing suicide, of dangerous working conditions and excessive overtime. Foxconn employees were reported to work an average of 56 hours a week while Chinese law only allows a maximum of 49 hours.

Foxconn has raised the workers' base wages on the mainland by between 16 and 25 per cent, giving a basic salary of about $283 (1800 Yuan). This was the third increase in two years, which has nearly doubled salaries.

Questions

1 Explain why some of Foxconn's stakeholders might not have approved of the changes that the company has implemented. [6]
2 Discuss whether Foxconn has taken the right decision by introducing these changes. [10]

How changing business objectives might affect stakeholders

As the objectives of a business change this may well affect the way it treats its stakeholders. For example, a greater emphasis on environmental issues may lead to more concern for society as a whole and future generations, and a focus on recycling, reusing and less waste and pollution. A demand for higher profits may lead to a drive to reduce costs and less investment in training, welfare and career development. A focus on better quality might lead to better treatment of suppliers. On the other hand, greater pressure for profits may mean managers start to cut back on training and career development and freeze wages; they might also bargain hard to push down prices to suppliers.

It is very difficult for managers to take decisions to satisfy all stakeholders simultaneously, especially at a time of change when major strategic decisions may be forced upon them. It may be that the best that is possible is to satisfy as many stakeholders as possible.

Test your learning

Short answer questions

1 a Define the term stakeholder. [2]
  b Explain why the UK government might be a stakeholder of a UK retailer. [3]

2 Explain how businesses and employees have responsibilities to one another. [5]

3 Distinguish between the responsibilities that a business manufacturing chemicals and the responsibilities it might have to its local community. [5]

4 a State **two** responsibilities that a business may have to its suppliers. [2]
  b Explain **one** likely reaction of a retailer's stakeholders to a decision to close 10 per cent of its shops to increase profitability. [3]

5 a State **two** possible responsibilities of the Indian government to its businesses. [2]
  b Explain how the adoption of an objective of growth might affect an airline's customers. [3]

6 a Define the term social responsibility. [2]
  b Explain **one** reason why a business might wish to be accountable to its bank. [3]

7 Explain why a large manufacturer might experience difficulty in meeting the objectives of its shareholders and its customers simultaneously. [5]

8 a State **two** reasons why a business might wish to be accountable to its employees. [2]
  b Explain **one** way in which a retailer could be accountable to its employees. [3]

9 Using examples, explain the difference between the stakeholder and the shareholder concepts. [5]

10 Explain the possible effect of a hotel's decision to increase its prices significantly on **two** of its stakeholder groups. [5]

Data response question

A change of approach

Multan Textiles Ltd has had a change of heart. Its new management team has decided to implement a range of policies intended to meet the needs of all of its stakeholders rather than solely its shareholders. The adoption of policies based on the stakeholder concept has significant implications for all of the company's stakeholders.

The company has agreed to raise its employees' wages over the next few years at a rate in excess of the current rate of inflation and to improve working conditions. It also has offered its suppliers more favourable credit terms to encourage a long-term relationship. It is also reviewing its manufacturing processes to minimise the impact of the chemicals on its employees and the local community.

The company has a long tradition of manufacturing textiles in the region and a good reputation. It is profitable although its shareholders have expressed some dissatisfaction at declining profit levels over the last few years.

Questions

1 Explain the terms:
   a shareholder [3]
   b stakeholder concept. [3]
2 Briefly analyse the benefits to Multan Textiles Ltd of implementing policies based on the stakeholder concept. [6]

3 Discuss the case for and against Multan Textiles Ltd retaining its original approach based on the shareholder concept. [10]

Essay question

Discuss whether it is possible for a large multinational oil company to satisfy all of its stakeholders fully. [20]

Past paper questions

1 Discuss how the objectives of stakeholder groups in a profitable business might be in conflict. [20]

Cambridge International AS and A Level Business Studies
9707 Paper 12 Q6 May/June 2010

2 Read the Joe's World case study on page 213 and then answer the following question.

   Evaluate how stakeholders in the farm, other than Joe, might react to the proposed contract with Wind4U. [10]

Cambridge International AS and A Level Business Studies
9707 Paper 2 Q2d October/November 2009

6 Management and leadership

Chapter overview

In this chapter we examine:
- the roles of leaders and managers within businesses and how these differ
- the functions of management
- the qualities of a good leader and the different leadership styles that exist
- the nature of emotional intelligence and Goleman's four competencies.

Table 6.1 The distinction between leaders and managers

Leaders	Managers
Look to the future	Focus on the present
Are willing to break the mould, innovate	Maintain the status quo
Have vision	Are implementers

The **management** writer Peter Drucker argues that a leader has the ability to generate a commitment and is capable of the 'lifting of people's vision to a higher sight, the raising of their performance to a higher standard, the building of their personality beyond its normal limitations'.

Key terms

Authority is the power or ability to carry through a task or action.

Leadership includes the functions of ruling, guiding and inspiring other people within an organisation in pursuit of agreed objectives.

Management is planning, organising, directing and controlling all or part of a business enterprise.

6.1 Leaders and managers

Many business writers draw a distinction between a leader and a manager. A manager is someone who gets things done. Managers tend to focus on the present and the short term and are responsible for implementing the decisions of others. They manage but they also follow. Their role in many ways is to maintain things the way they are.

Leaders, by comparison, are people who are followed, who have a vision of the future and a clear sense of where they are taking the business. A leader decides what needs to be done and is prepared to shake things up to get them done. According to a significant writer in this area, John Adair, '**Leadership** is the process of motivating others to act in particular ways.'

A leader should understand where he or she wants to take the business. They should be able to provide a clear direction for the business and motivate and inspire others. A leader is often brought in to make changes. The leader will know what needs to be done and is responsible for making it happen. Leaders may or may not always be liked but should be pushing (or pulling) the business forward.

6.2 Management and managers

Study tip

Do make sure that you distinguish between management and leadership in your answers and avoid using these two terms interchangeably. If the question is about management, make sure that is what you write about!

What is management?

Describing management is a complex task, and there have been a number of attempts by writers to classify what managers do within an organisation. For example:

- Henri Fayol, writing in the early twentieth century, set out the functions of management.
- In contrast, Henry Mintzberg identified ten roles carried out by managers.

We will consider both of these classifications in more detail in this chapter.

The functions of management

The management theorist Mary Parker Follett believed that management was 'the art of getting things done through other people'. From Fayol onwards, various writers over the years have argued that this involves different functions. However, those set out in Figure 6.1 would be considered the key functions that are carried out by most managers.

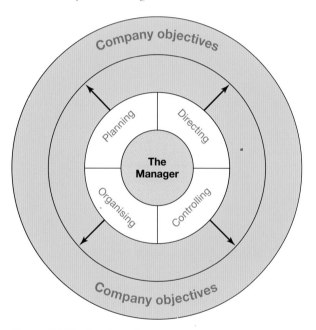

Figure 6.1 The functions of management

All businesses operate in different ways and may require managers to undertake varying tasks and duties. However, these various management duties and tasks can be categorised into four basic functions – the functions of management. The four principal functions of management are:

- planning
- organising
- directing
- controlling.

Case Study

Telenor and its Indian operations

Telenor is a Norwegian international communications company trading in a number of European countries as well as Asia. The company placed bids for licences to operate mobile phone services in several states in India. However, the company's managers were prepared to abandon the Indian market if the prices set at the auction to operate mobile phone services were too high.

In the event, the company announced that its bids were successful in Andhra Pradesh, Bihar, Uttar Pradesh East and West and in Assam. The company paid a total price of 8.447 billion rupees for the licences. The company's managers will face a heavy workload to ensure that the new services are available to Indian customers on time.

Telenor has 45 million customers in India and trades under a subsidiary brand name: Uninor. The company is the sixth largest mobile telephone company in India despite only entering the market just three years' ago.

Questions

1 Explain the difference between the roles of the leader of Telenor (the Chief Executive) and the company's managers. [6]
2 Evaluate which of the functions of management will be most important if Telenor's managers are to respond effectively to the opportunities resulting from its successful bids for the new licences. [10]

Planning

Planning is the first of the functions of management and involves looking to the future. It is the foundation upon which the other three functions of management should be based. Planning requires management to evaluate where the company is currently, and where it would like to be in the future. This allows managers to take decisions so that the company moves forward in an organised and coherent manner to give managers something against which to judge their decisions.

Planning may involve a variety of tasks, including the following:

- establishing objectives or targets for the business
- gathering together forecasts of key data such as costs and revenues
- drawing up plans for functional areas within the business such as finance, human resources or marketing – these plans should fit together to help the business achieve its objectives
- estimating the likely resource needs for any proposed plans.

The planning process is continual because external factors (such as successful bids for licences to operate in the Indian telecommunications market, for example) change all the time. These changes may cause a company to adjust its course of action to ensure that it achieves its objectives.

Planning helps managers to reduce the chance of projects failing in the future. A plan can highlight problems and encourage managers to develop solutions. It helps to make sure that managers have the resources they need. A plan can also be extended to help managers to overcome emergencies or crises – these are called contingency plans. Telenor might draw up a contingency plan to cover the consequence of many of its bids to operate mobile phone services being unsuccessful.

Organising

Management must assemble the resources that they need to carry out the actions set out in the plan. Through the process of getting organised, management will determine the internal organisational structure, establish and maintain relationships, as well as allocate necessary resources. Felda Global, the Malaysian palm oil producer, is entering the African market as part of its plans for 800 per cent growth by 2020. In order to organise this expansion, the company's managers will need a range of resources:
- land for its palm oil plantations and oil mills
- labour to plant the trees, build the mills and eventually harvest the fruit of the trees and to process it
- capital to finance the plan.

The company may also need to restructure its workforce in Malaysia to ensure that its planned operations in Africa run efficiently. A well managed business will use minimal resources to achieve its objectives.

Directing

The third function of management is directing. Through directing, management is able to influence and oversee the behaviour of the staff in achieving the company's goals, as well as assisting them by providing the necessary resources. Directing employees effectively entails motivation and communication.
- **Motivation** is the willingness to achieve a target or goal. Employees that are highly motivated generally perform better. This assists businesses in achieving objectives. For this reason, managers tend to put a lot of focus on motivating their employees. For example, they provide financial incentives programmes to encourage employees and also may grant them authority to take decisions to help improve motivation and performance.
- **Communication** is the exchange of information between one or more people. Effective communication can take a number of forms. It may simply be praise or clear guidance; alternatively, it could be detailed instructions. Whatever form it takes it can help to achieve high levels of productivity and encourages employees to use their initiative as well as to solve problems.

Controlling

Controlling involves setting standards using the company's objectives, and evaluating and reporting performance. Once management has done both of these things, it should compare the two to determine any necessary corrective or preventive action.

Managers can report on business performance in a number of ways.

- **Financial reports** Many companies publish details of their financial performance each year. This gives interested parties information on their sales, revenues and profits. In many countries there is a legal requirement for companies to report on profits or losses to assist governments in assessing whether the correct amount of tax has been paid.
- **Employee performance** Such reports may provide information on productivity (the quantity produced per employee per week, for example), levels of absenteeism or training costs. For many service businesses these can be vital measures of performance.
- **Social performance** Managers can measure a business's performance in terms of behaving ethically, minimising pollution and creating jobs.

Figure 6.2 A newly established palm oil plantation

Question

Discuss why it might be necessary for Felda Global to report on its social performance in Africa to ensure that its activities are controlled effectively. [10]

Felda Global may need information on each of the above areas to assess whether its planned expansion of palm oil production in Africa is progressing according to its plans. The control process is a constant task for managers. Through the process of control a manager is able to identify potential problems and take the necessary decisions to overcome them.

Analysing the functions of management gives some insight into what managers have to do to be effective and efficient. Some management writers have argued that when Fayol's writing on good management was accepted, productivity and living standards in America increased. However, this may have been the result of other factors too.

Mintzberg's roles of management

Henry Mintzberg is Professor of Management Studies at McGill University in Montreal and a renowned author on management.

One of his most famous pieces of writing in 1990 set out the ten roles performed by managers within businesses. He argued that management is not about functions but about what managers do.

Mintzberg argued that managers performed ten roles and that these fall into three categories as shown in Table 6.2.

Table 6.2 Henry Mintzberg's management roles and categories

Role	Category
1 Figurehead 2 Leader 3 Liaison	Interpersonal management
4 Monitor 5 Disseminator 6 Spokesperson	Informational management
7 Entrepreneur 8 Disturbance handler 9 Resource allocator 10 Negotiator	Decisional management This category of management role *uses* information to take decisions.

Interpersonal management

This category entails managing through other people.
- **Figureheads** represent their colleagues. They carry out social, ceremonial and legal responsibilities and are expected to be a source of inspiration. Figureheads are considered to have authority.
- **Leaders** create and maintain an effective working environment and motivate and develop more junior employees. In this role employees manage the performance and responsibilities of everyone in their team.
- **Liaison** In this role managers must communicate with internal and external contacts. They need to network effectively to gather information.

Informational management

The roles in this category involve processing information.
- **Monitor** In this role, managers search for internal and external information relevant to the business, looking for relevant changes in the environment. Monitors also look after their teams in terms of performance and welfare.
- **Disseminator** This is a central communication role. This type of manager passes on valuable information to others in the organisation.
- **Spokesperson** Managers represent and speak for their organisation. In this role they are responsible for transmitting information about their organisation and its goals to the people outside it.

Decisional management

This category of management role uses information to take decisions.

- **Entrepreneur** As a manager, the entrepreneur plans and initiates change within a business organisation.
- **Disturbance handler** In this role managers deal with the unexpected and also with crises. In such circumstances managers take control and attempt to solve disputes.
- **Resource allocators** take decisions on the most effective use of an organisation's resources including finance, staff and capital equipment.
- **Negotiator** In this role managers engage in important negotiations within and outside the business.

Case Study

Garuda Indonesia plans to double fleet

The Indonesian national airline Garuda Indonesia has announced plans to more than double its fleet of aircraft. The announcement comes ahead of the launch of Asean's open-sky policy, which comes into effect in 2015. This agreement will permit airlines from all ten member countries of the bloc to fly to any destination within the region.

Garuda Indonesia currently operates 92 aircraft, but this will be increased to 194 by 2015 under the company's plans. One of the company's planned purchases is five aircraft from Canada's Bombardier Aerospace, each with a seating capacity of 100, which will be employed on diverse routes once in use.

The airline will need to open new facilities in Makassar, Medan and East Kalimantan's Balikpapan to allow it to respond competitively to Asean's open-sky policy.

Questions

1 Explain why planning has been an important function for Garuda Indonesia's managers over recent years. [6]
2 This expansion represents a major challenge for Garuda Indonesia's managers. Evaluate which of Mintzberg's roles would be most important in the management of the company's growth. [10]

Mintzberg reached a number of conclusions from his studies.
- Senior managers are very busy and have heavy workloads! There is little free time and trying to get away from work is difficult.
- The work is fragmented; managers are moving from one task to another. They need to focus on what really matters and what really makes a difference (80 per cent of results usually come from 20 per cent of the effort, so they try to work out what that 20 per cent is).
- Managers focus on short-term immediate problems. They are often fire fighting, dealing with the problem in front of them; this pushes them away from long-term planning and thinking.

- Verbal contact is preferred to written as with the latter lots of information is received but it takes longer to get a response. Managers seldom get out and about; walking around is useful because it makes you visible and more aware of the issues within the business.

Managers actually control little of what they do day to day – things happen *to* them!

Mintzberg's work on management roles was based on observing senior managers and this is both a weakness and a strength of his theory. He did analyse what managers really do, but did not consider the working lives of middle or junior managers, so, in this respect, his analysis may be considered incomplete.

6.3 Leadership

The purpose of leadership

Leaders provide the vision that takes a business forward. They take the difficult decisions and bring about the difficult change. They can inspire or push through change. Leadership may not always be in the hands of one person – the leaders may be a team – but the direction needs to come from somewhere. Particularly in a crisis people look to a leader for guidance and to show them what to do; this is why, when an organisation is in trouble, a new leader is brought in.

The ability of great leaders in sport, in business, in politics and in all aspects of life to achieve great things is inspiring. Just think of someone like Nelson Mandela who helped bring about the end of the division between blacks and whites in South Africa and made this a peaceful process by leading through example.

It can be argued that leaders have a range of duties relating to all aspects of the business's operations. The tasks of leaders may include those listed below.

- Deciding objectives for the organisation. Leaders have to establish a sense of direction for the organisation and to establish objectives to move the organisation towards its overall aims. We saw in the case study above that Garuda Indonesia has set itself the objective of doubling its fleet of planes by 2015. Emirsyah Satar, the company's Chief Executive Officer (CEO), would have played a key role in this decision.
- Providing expertise and setting standards for the organisation. The leader is likely to be required to show enthusiasm in difficult times and to take a major role in solving problems as they arise.
- The leader will play a key role in determining the structure of the organisation – hierarchies and spans of control. He or she will determine lines of communication and control and will be instrumental in shaping the culture of the business.

- Leaders may become role models for individuals within the organisation and may choose to build alliances of senior individuals to protect their position.

The nature of leadership has changed over recent years for a number of reasons. Rapid advances in information technology have meant that leaders have far more information available to them to make decisions. This can help make better-informed decisions but it can also mean that they have too much data and experience difficulty in selecting the key elements of this.

Leaders may have been specifically recruited to change the way a business operates and may face resistance from employees who fear they will be worse off following the changes. Employees may try to block or disrupt the change. A leader's ability to implement change may depend upon the amount of support received from others within the organisation. It will also depend upon factors such as:

- the resources available to implement change; in some cases the leader may lack resources, making change difficult as, for example, funds are not available for training or recruitment
- the extent to which employees understand the need for change
- the support from other senior managers.

The challenge faced by leaders has been increased by developments such as the trend for many markets to become global. This has meant that many firms now operate in a larger and far more competitive environment. Decisions in such circumstances have become more complex and managers are now often required to attempt to organise production in a number of countries, facing a variety of languages, customs and cultures. Production difficulties are compounded by differing demands from customers across the globe.

Study tip

If asked to discuss the importance of leadership in a case study do look for evidence in the case study itself that you can use to support your arguments. For example, the business may trade in a very changeable market which a leader can do little about.

Leadership roles in business

An entrepreneur who is designing a structure for a new organisation, or amending an existing one, is likely to consider a number of roles for employees as part of the process.

Directors

Directors are found as part of the workforce of a company – either private or public. Directors are proposed by the Chief

Executive of a company and take up the role if they are subsequently elected by shareholders. The role of directors is largely strategic: they set and oversee the achievement of long-term goals for the business.

Directors can be executive, non-executive or independent. Executive directors are employed by the company in a senior capacity, possibly with responsibility for a part or function of the business such as marketing. Non-executive and independent directors perform similar roles, although the latter may not own shares in the company. These types of directors are not employed by the company and are usually appointed because they have a particular knowledge or skill. They also may protect the interests of the company's shareholders, employees, customers and other stakeholders if decisions are not taken with their interests in mind.

Directors exist within relatively small, privately-owned companies but are likely to fulfil broader roles than in larger companies because smaller companies employ fewer people.

Case Study

Trina Solar appoints non-executive director

Trina Solar Ltd is a manufacturer of solar photovoltaic (PV) products and one of the leaders in this particular market. The company has announced the appointment of Mr Henry Chow as a non-executive or independent director.

Mr Chow has held a number of posts as a director in the Asia Pacific region. He retired from IBM in 2009, having served as general manager and subsequently as chairman of the IBM Greater China Group. Mr Chow was also a member of IBM's Worldwide Management Council and IBM's Strategy Team. These groups advise IBM on its strategy and help it to respond to a changing world environment.

Mr Chow already holds a number of senior roles. He is a non-executive director on the board of AMD, an American company, and acts as an adviser to Bridgepoint, a British private equity company. Mr Chow is a graduate of the University of Hong Kong, holding a degree in electrical engineering.

Questions

1 Mr Chow has been a manager and a director at IBM. Explain the main differences between these two roles. [6]
2 Discuss the key benefits that you think Trina Solar Ltd will gain as a result of Mr Chow's appointment. [10]

Managers

Managers carry out a range of duties. These are often categorised as planning, organising, motivating and controlling. Managers

normally have authority over a number of junior employees and plan and monitor short- and medium-term strategies for the business.

In a small business, the owner may carry out the duties of manager and director, looking after all the planning for the business as well as organising and controlling day-to-day activities. This is one reason why many entrepreneurs are very busy people!

Supervisors

Supervisors represent a link between managers and the business's shop-floor workers. They are the first rung of management and are in regular contact with shop-floor workers. Supervisors are delegated some authority by managers to take decisions on day-to-day issues such as staffing or tactics to meet deadlines. Supervisors also act as a line of communication between managers and shop-floor workers.

Worker representatives

Employee representatives may be chosen by their fellow employees or appointed by management. Their roles can vary but most:
- receive information from and give information to management teams, for example about pay and conditions or major decisions to be taken by the company, such as an expansion
- pass on information to all employees within the workforce, often through meetings
- are consulted by management teams over certain workplace matters that are likely to have a significant impact on employees, such as the introduction of new technology into the business.

Worker representatives are frequently involved in issues concerning pay. They may take part in negotiations over future pay rates for the workforce of a business and recently, in some countries, have played a role in limiting the pay received by senior managers within businesses.

The qualities of a good leader

The business environment in which leaders operate has changed over recent years. Many subordinates will not just accept being given instructions; junior and middle managers are often well trained and expect to be able to contribute to decision-making. The modern leader has to take into account their views and to broaden ownership of decision-making. Indeed, given the complexity of many modern organisations, the leader relies upon support from others in the management team.

Furthermore, the increasing pace of change means that today's leaders have to be dynamic and flexible and able to respond effectively to changing environments. In particular, leaders of businesses providing technical products or services might experience and have to respond to rapid change.

What to look for in a top CEO

Four leading Ghanaian managers have offered advice on what makes a good leader and how to lead a successful business. Prince Kofi Amoabeng, Chief Executive Officer (CEO) of UT Bank, Jude Bucknor of Bucknor and Associates, Dr Kofi Amoah of Progeny Ventures and Michael Ikpoki, CEO of MTN, each spoke to an audience of Ghana's business leaders and received acclaim for their presentations.

The four speakers made up the panel at the fifth MTN Business World Executive Breakfast addressing the question 'Being an effective leader in Business'. The speakers emphasised the importance of having vision and being passionate about business matters.

Mr Bucknor said, 'It is essential for a good leader to have a vision that spells out clearly where you want to go and how you will get there.' He argued that innovation is also important and that leaders have to think creatively.

Michael Ikpoki, CEO of MTN, stressed the importance of a sense of responsibility and that generating high returns for shareholders was an essential element of success. He added that successful leaders make the most effective use of their workforces and develop talent in others.

Dr Kofi Amoah, CEO of Progeny Ventures, concluded that having a sense of humour and control over the workplace are central qualities in a successful leader in business.

Questions

1 Explain two key tasks of a leader of a large multinational company. [6]
2 Discuss the possible reasons why these experienced and successful CEOs have different views on the qualities needed for a successful leader. [10]

So, has the general view of a good leader changed over recent years?

Table 6.3 Traditional and modern views of good leaders

The traditional view of a 'good' leader	The modern view of a 'good' leader
• A strong decisive character. • An 'expert' in the relevant field of business. • An autocrat (to a significant degree). • Focus on profits and financial success. • Good communicator – but most comfortable with downward communication.	• Charismatic, with a flair for public relations. • Possessing principles, for example taking ethical decisions. • Excellent communicator – and a good listener. • Welcoming advice and support from specialists. • Flexible and able to flourish in a changing environment

Over the years many theories have been presented concerning leadership. Views have altered, and this has been reflected in the changing approaches to leadership adopted by businesses.

Trait theory

Many writers have argued that all leaders should have a number of traits or characteristics, though there is some disagreement as to the precise nature of these traits. However, the consensus is that certain personality traits differentiate a good leader from other people. Trait theories have developed from the concept of the charismatic leader – Nelson Mandela or Barack Obama, for example. Examples such as these have led to trait theory being termed 'great person theory'. Supporters of the idea of the charismatic leader contend that such individuals have identifiable characteristics that set them apart from ordinary mortals.

Some traits commonly mentioned by writers include:
- being informed and knowledgeable
- having the ability to think creatively and innovatively
- possessing inner motivation and the desire to achieve
- having the ability to act quickly and decisively
- projecting an air of authority.

One of the reasons for the decline in popularity of trait theories is that successful leaders have been found to exhibit different characteristics from each other.

Behavioural theories

These theories focus on how a leader behaves; trying to identify the right way of leading rather than what a leader is like as a person. There have been many studies looking at styles of leadership and considering which are successful.

One classification of styles is to consider the extent to which leaders 'tell' or 'listen to' their staff. Using this approach, leaders have been classified as being autocratic, democratic or laissez-faire (literally 'leave alone'). However, there are many more different styles of leadership that can be identified using this approach. The Tannenbaum and Schmidt continuum shown in Figure 6.3 on page 46 emphasises that there is a range of leadership behaviour depending upon the extent to which leaders take decisions or whether subordinates contribute significantly to decision-making.

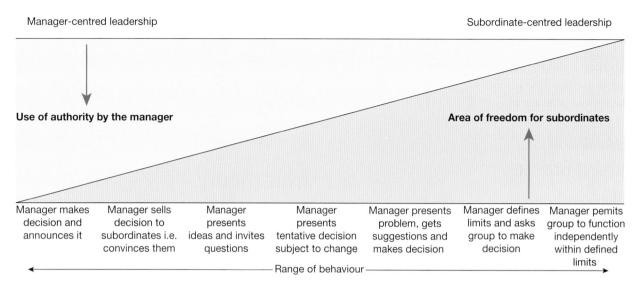

Manager-centred leadership   Subordinate-centred leadership

Use of authority by the manager   **Area of freedom for subordinates**

| Manager makes decision and announces it | Manager sells decision to subordinates i.e. convinces them | Manager presents ideas and invites questions | Manager presents tentative decision subject to change | Manager presents problem, gets suggestions and makes decision | Manager defines limits and asks group to make decision | Manager pemits group to function independently within defined limits |

⟵————————————— Range of behaviour —————————————⟶

Figure 6.3 The Tannenbaum and Schmidt continuum

A key factor in differentiating between leadership styles is communication. At the autocratic end of the spectrum communication is likely to be downward only as the leader or manager 'instructs' his or her subordinates as to their duties. Democratic leadership is more likely to result in two-way communication as consultation and 'selling' of the final idea take place. Laissez-faire leadership may result in relatively little communication as the problem or task may be outlined with subordinates having considerable freedom thereafter.

Autocratic leadership

This is also sometimes termed authoritarian leadership. It refers to a leadership or management style which assumes that information and decision-making are best kept at the top of the organisation. It is also characterised by:
- one-way communication (downward)
- minimal delegation or decentralisation
- close supervision of employees.

Martha Stewart, an American entrepreneur, built up a vast global business venture, including publishing, television broadcasting and online commerce, despite, or perhaps because of, her reputation as an autocratic leader. Under this style the leader determines objectives, allocates tasks and expects obedience from subordinates. In these circumstances employees become very dependent upon their leaders as they do not have the necessary information (or confidence) to act on their own initiative.

Organisations managed in an authoritarian style can face difficulties. People avoid making decisions so that matters to be decided are either passed up for the decisions to be made at a higher level, or decisions are made by committees as it is more difficult to dismiss all the members of a committee for jointly making a wrong decision. Senior management tends to be overworked and staff turnover tends to be high. This style of leadership becomes more difficult to operate successfully as an organisation grows.

As with all the behavioural leadership classifications the term autocratic manager covers a spectrum of actual styles. Extreme autocratic management will result in subordinates having no freedom of action. More benevolent autocratic leadership will allow for the possibility of some discussion or persuasion. This implies that limited two-way communication may occur.

Table 6.4 Autocratic management – circumstances in which it *may* be applicable

Appropriate	Inappropriate
• When a rapid decision is needed – perhaps in an emergency. • When it is important that the same message is given out by everyone in the organisation – maybe as part of crisis management. • When managers are responsible for a large number of (possibly unskilled) subordinates.	• When taking highly complex decisions requiring diverse knowledge and skills. • When leading a talented, self-motivated and creative group of employees. • In circumstances in which junior managers are expected to develop a full range of managerial skills.

Democratic leadership

Democratic leadership (sometimes called participative leadership) entails operating a business according to decisions agreed by the majority. Decisions may be agreed formally through a voting system, but are more likely to be the result of informal discussions. Typically democratic leadership encourages some or all of the following:
- the leader delegates a great deal and encourages decentralisation
- the leader and subordinates discuss issues and employee participation is actively encouraged
- the leader acts upon advice, and explains the reasons for decisions
- subordinates have greater control over their own working lives.

The successful operation of this style requires excellent communication skills on the part of the leader and the ability to generate effective two-way communications. A considerable amount of management time may be spent on communicating in one form or another. This approach helps to develop the skills of subordinates and generally results in a more satisfied workforce.

Case Study

Richard Branson assesses Apple's Steve Jobs

Figure 6.4 Flair: though their leadership styles differed wildly, Richard Branson of Virgin, top, was a great admirer of Apple's boss, Steve Jobs

Leadership doesn't have a secret formula; all true leaders go about things in their own way. It's this ability to think differently that sets them apart – and that enabled Steve Jobs to create perhaps the most respected brand in the world.

Steve Jobs's leadership style was autocratic; he had a meticulous eye for detail, and surrounded himself with like-minded people to follow his lead. While he was incredibly demanding of his people, he wasn't the best delegator – he wanted to involve himself in every detail, which is the opposite of my own approach. Personally, I have always believed in the art of **delegation** – finding the best possible people for Virgin and giving them the freedom and encouragement to flourish.

Steve Jobs was always at the centre of everything Apple did. Over his extraordinary career, he learnt that it is vital that you don't solely lead your company from a distance. Walk the floor, get to know your people. Even though I don't run Virgin's companies on a day-to-day basis any more, I still find it crucial to get out and about among our staff. No one has a monopoly on good ideas or good advice, so as a leader you should always be listening.

Of course, there will be times when strong and decisive leadership is necessary; to make sure the right moves are made. If you place the emphasis on getting the little things right, and address the everyday problems that come up, you can encourage a culture of attention to detail. Jobs may not always have been the best leader of people – which may, in part, have been due to his health problems – but he was innovative, determined and, above all, passionate. Finding gaps in the market, and creating products that make a real difference to people's lives, can only be accomplished if you have passion for what you are doing. If you make something you are proud of, that filters down to your staff, as well as your customers. Today, more than ever, you've got to do something radically different to make a mark.

Source: Adapted from the *Daily Telegraph*, 6 October 2011

Questions

1 Explain the key features of an autocratic leader, such as Steve Jobs. [6]
2 To what extent is being a good communicator, or being passionate about the business, more important than the leadership style adopted by a leader? [10]

Democratically led groups usually have low dependency on their leader, offer constructive ideas and suggestions and derive great satisfaction from their employment. As a consequence, such groups have high levels of self-motivation and may require relatively little supervision.

Key term

Delegation means passing authority down the organisational hierarchy. This is only genuine if the manager relinquishes some control to the subordinate.

There is evidence of a trend towards more democratic styles of leadership, though this depends on many factors including the size of a business and its culture. The trend towards democratic leadership has a number of possible causes.

- Management theory has developed and provided substantial evidence that people are more likely to be motivated (and productive) through the use of a democratic leadership style.
- Leadership has become more complex. Globalisation means that businesses are larger and more complicated organisations, the environment in which they operate is dynamic and subject to rapid change. Individuals are more likely to need the support that democratic leadership provides to succeed in these circumstances.

Study tip

Do learn the key terms in this chapter (and the other AS chapters) as it is likely that you will be asked to give one or more definitions in the Paper 1 questions.

Laissez-faire leadership

This approach is sometimes described as mild anarchy. Under this approach the leader has a minimal input into the operation of the business. Employees take the majority of the decisions with little reference to the leader. As a consequence the organisation can lack a sense of direction as well as coordination and planning.

The laissez-faire style of leadership may occur because of the shortcomings of the leader or the lack of the essential skills needed to carry out the role successfully. Alternatively, it may be a conscious and brave policy decision to give staff the maximum scope for showing their capabilities. It may be an appropriate style to adopt in certain circumstances. For example, the leader of a highly creative team may deliberately adopt this style in the expectation of bringing out the best in his or her subordinates.

Laissez-faire leadership may be successful in the following circumstances:

- The manager or leader is one among a number of equals in terms of experience and qualifications.
- The workforce is self-motivated and understands the role of managers.
- The workforce understands and agrees with the organisation's objectives.

Laissez-faire leadership tends to result in highly independent employees who are willing to voice their opinions. Staff may be satisfied or dissatisfied with this style of leadership, depending on their skills, the complexity of the tasks to be completed and their own personality.

Style versatility

Building on the contention that there is not a single perfect style of leadership, it is possible to argue that the best managers are those who adopt a style suitable to the circumstances. Thus, the most talented managers might be the most versatile, able to call on one or more of the styles we have discussed in order

to assess the demands of the situation. Therefore a versatile manager might adopt a democratic approach when reaching a decision on a proposed marketing campaign with a small group of writers and artists, but demonstrate a more autocratic style when dealing with a crisis.

Douglas McGregor's Theory X and Theory Y

Douglas McGregor was an American social psychologist who researched into management in large companies. His writing developed understanding of leadership by considering how the attitude of the leader might shape his behaviour. His book *The Human Side of Enterprise* was published in 1960. The book has received much acclaim and particularly his celebrated comparison of two types of leader as set out in Theory X and Theory Y. McGregor's theories were based on research he had conducted into the attitudes of managers towards their employees.

His research revealed that many leaders assumed their workers were motivated solely by money and had no real desire to work. McGregor referred to this type of manager as Theory X. He also discovered an alternative, and less common, type of manager, which he termed a Theory Y leader. Such leaders, according to McGregor, believed workers sought more than financial gain from employment. Thus, a poor performance by a group of workers may be the result of a work environment lacking stimulation and challenge for employees. The behaviour of employees, argued McGregor, is often the result of the way they are treated.

Key terms

Piece-rate pay is a system under which employees' wages are determined by the quantity of products they produce.

A **business culture** is the attitudes, values and beliefs that normally exist within an organisation.

McGregor did not believe in the views expressed by Theory X leaders. He set the theory only to disprove it as part of his support for the views expressed by Theory Y managers.

A Theory Y manager is more likely to be one who believes the following to be true.

- Workers seek satisfaction from employment and not just a pay cheque.
- Workers possess knowledge, creativity and imagination.
- Workers willingly commit themselves to organisational objectives.
- Poor performance by employees is due to repetitive and monotonous work or poor management.
- Employees wish to contribute to decision-making.

Theory X is derived from the work of F.W. Taylor and the Scientific School of Management who contended that workers were 'economic animals' motivated solely by money. Theory X leaders seek to get the best from their employees by use of techniques such as **piece-rate pay** and close supervision.

Alternatively, Theory Y stems clearly from Mayo's human relations approach and Maslow's work on human needs (see Chapter 7 on motivation). It focuses on meeting the social and psychological needs of individuals within the workplace. McGregor's work is, however, a theory of leadership and *not* one of motivation.

If leaders adopt a Theory Y style the implications can be significant for a business. These might include the following:

- greater delegation within the organisation, allowing those further down the hierarchy to have greater authority
- training for managers to encourage delegation and to improve two-way **communication**
- reviewing the business's culture to discourage managers from retaining what they might see as their 'authority'
- considering the organisation's structure and approaches such as delayering.

Businesses moving towards a Theory Y approach to leadership require planning, the support of managers and shop-floor workers and considerable training for all the employees involved.

6.5 Emotional intelligence

Daniel Goleman defined **emotional intelligence** as the 'capacity for recognizing our own feelings and those of others, for motivating ourselves, and for managing emotions well in ourselves and in our relationships'. Emotional intelligence (or EQ) is a relatively new managerial model, which received much attention following the publication of Goleman's book *Emotional Intelligence* in 1995. The EQ concept argues that IQ (intelligence quotient), a conventional measure of a person's intelligence, is too narrow as a measure of potential performance of employees, including managers and leaders.

The EQ model emphasises that there are areas of emotional intelligence that determine how well employees will perform. A high performing employee needs more than a high IQ (the normal measure of intelligence) because this ignores vital elements of a person's character and behavioural patterns. Some employees may be brilliant and have a very high IQ but lack personal skills and not get on well with other people. Research indicates that people with a high IQ are not automatically good performers in the workplace.

When researchers measured employee performance against IQ they discovered that:

- low IQ predicts low performance
- high IQ produces varying levels of performance from very low to very high.

The same results were found when the research included the professional skills that employees possessed. That means that an employee with a high IQ (and professional skills) can be a very high performer, but may equally be a very low one. Thus IQ and professional skills in themselves do not predict high performance. They are necessary for employees to perform well, but not enough on their own.

An important step in this area was to test for employee competencies and not just intelligence and professional skills. Research compared groups of high and average performers, to find the competencies that made the difference.

Key terms

Communication is the exchange of information or ideas between two or more parties.

Emotional intelligence is the capacity for recognising our own feelings and those of others, for motivating ourselves, and for managing emotions well in ourselves and in our relationships.

Goleman's 18 EI competencies

Goleman's work evolved to produce a model of 18 personal competencies grouped into four clusters as summarised in Table 6.5. His research tested these competencies against employee performance and this showed that possession of these competencies did coincide with high levels of employee performance in the workplace. Although there have been a number of studies of the importance and impact of emotional intelligence competencies, Goleman's work was carried out within businesses.

Table 6.5 Goleman's four competencies of emotional intelligence

Self-awareness	Social awareness
1 Emotional self-awareness	10 Empathy
2 Accurate self-assessment	11 Organisational awareness
3 Self-confidence	12 Service orientation
Self-management	**Relationship management (Social skills)**
4 Emotional self-control	13 Developing others
5 Transparency	14 Inspirational leadership
6 Adaptability	15 Being a catalyst for change
7 Achievement orientation	16 Having influence
8 Initiative	17 Conflict management
9 Optimism	18 Teamwork and collaboration

Source: Adapted from Transgrowth at www.transgrowth.com

Emotional intelligence and business

Emotional competencies have particular relevance for leaders and managers. Leaders have to be able to motivate and inspire others, establish good relationships and manage conflicts between subordinate employees. They also have to influence the ways other employees behave and be good communicators (including listening!). A leader's role is to motivate others to do their jobs effectively. Managers have to work within a team, be able to develop others (as part of delegation), be able to initiate change and also be able to manage conflict. To carry out these roles successfully, leaders and managers have to possess emotional competencies.

Research shows that exceptional leaders and managers possess a range of emotional competencies – both personal and social. Such competencies, it is argued, are the major factor determining the performance of leaders and managers. Emotional competencies can be learnt and may develop over time. Therefore training in this area can play an important part in developing all of an organisation's human resources.

Thus, emotional intelligence is increasingly relevant to the development of organisations and employees, because the EQ principles provide a new way to understand and assess people's behaviour, leadership styles, attitudes, interpersonal skills and, most importantly, their potential performance.

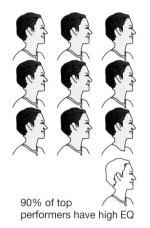

90% of top performers have high EQ

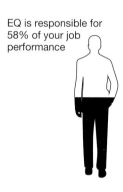

EQ is responsible for 58% of your job performance

$29 000
People with high EQ make $29 000 more annually than their low EQ counterparts

Figure 6.5 The importance and benefits of emotional intelligence

Source: Talent Smart

Test your learning

Short answer questions

1 **a** Distinguish between a leader and a manager. [3]

b State **two** functions of management. [2]

2 Explain how good communication might help a manager to carry out the functions involved in his or her job. [5]

3 **a** Why is organising an important function of management? [3]

b State **two** ways in which managers can report on business performance. [2]

4 **a** State **two** of Mintzberg's roles of management. [2]

b Explain why most managers normally focus on short-term problems. [3]

5 **a** Distinguish between autocratic and laissez-faire styles of leadership. [3]

b State **two** advantages of the use of democratic leadership. [2]

6 **a** Describe the leadership roles of managers and worker representatives. [3]

b State **two** qualities of a good leader. [2]

7 **a** Distinguish between McGregor's Theory X and Theory Y styles of leadership. [3]

b Explain how F.W. Taylor's theory of motivation might have influenced McGregor's Theory X style of leadership. [2]

8 **a** Define the concept of 'emotional intelligence'. [2]

b State **three** of Goleman's four competencies of emotional intelligence. [3]

Data response question

A growing business

Gadfly is a small private limited company that designs and manufactures bicycles. It competes with a number of large multinationals and its unusual designs have proved popular. The business is growing quickly (sales are rising by an average of 19 per cent each year) and it now has two factories, each with its own manager who is responsible for production at 'their' site. A major extension to one of the factories is expected next year. The number of employees is rising rapidly and last year reached 397, most of whom are relatively unskilled.

The business was established by Ali ten years ago and he hopes that it will continue to grow quickly. Ali is a natural autocrat and likes to take all of the decisions using little delegation. He is a good communicator and has 30 years' experience as an entrepreneur and also understands the bicycle manufacturing industry.

As the business grows it is changing. The company is having to produce a larger range of bicycles and needs more skilled employees to design new products and to sell the bicycles in new markets. For example, the company made its first sales in Australia and Argentina earlier this year. Ali is beginning to wonder whether his leadership style is suitable for his changing company.

Questions

1 Explain the terms:
  a delegation [3]
  b leadership. [3]
2 Briefly analyse why planning is an important part of the managers' role at Gadfly. [6]
3 Discuss whether Ali's use of an autocratic leadership style was suitable in these circumstances. [10]

Essay question

Discuss the importance of emotional intelligence in determining whether or not a person is likely to be a successful leader. [20]

Past paper questions

1 Discuss the qualities required by effective business leaders. [20]

Cambridge International AS and A Level Business Studies 9707 Paper 1 Q6 May/June 2008

2 Read the Newtown College case study on page 208 and then answer the following question.

Discuss the factors that NC needs to consider when recruiting and selecting an Office Manager. [10]

Cambridge International AS and A Level Business Studies 9707 Paper 21 Q2d October/November 2010

7 Motivation

Chapter overview

In this chapter we examine:
- the nature and importance of motivation as a management tool
- the needs of employees while at work
- some of the theories of motivation that can be applied in the workplace
- the practical methods of motivation used by businesses, both financial and non-financial.

7.1 What is motivation?

Key term

Motivation describes the factors that arouse, maintain and channel behaviour towards a goal.

There are two ways we can think about motivation at work and what causes it:
- **Motivation** can be the will to work due to enjoyment of the work itself. This implies that motivation comes from within an individual employee.
- An alternative view is that it is the will or desire to achieve a given target or goal that is the result of external factors, such as the promise of a reward, or to avoid the threat of punishment.

The first of these views assumes that motivation lies within the individual employee and the second that it is the result of some external factor. People in the workplace have differing views on the sources of motivation. A survey revealed that nearly 90 per cent of employers believe that money is the main motivator, while employees rank pay fourth, behind an interesting job, security and achievement.

This distinction is an important one and you should remember it when considering theories of motivation and how, in practice, leaders and managers can motivate other people.

Why is motivation important?

Whatever causes it, motivation is an important factor for all businesses. Having a well-motivated workforce is vital to assist businesses in achieving their objectives. This is arguably most relevant for organisations supplying services (such as airlines and restaurants) where employees are likely to have direct and regular contact with customers.

Key terms

Labour productivity measures the output per time period of an employee.

Labour turnover is the percentage of a workforce that leaves its employment with a business over some period of time, normally one year.

Absenteeism describes a situation in which an employee is absent from work without a good reason.

Organisations whose workforces possess high levels of motivation tend to show the following characteristics:
- a low level of **absenteeism** by employees at all levels within the business
- relatively few employees deciding to leave the organisation, giving a low level of **labour turnover**
- good relations between managers and other employees
- high levels of **labour productivity** from the workforce.

A business that enjoys the benefit of a highly motivated workforce is also likely to have a productive workforce. Low production costs offer firms two opportunities:
- to sell their products more cheaply
- to maintain price levels and enjoy greater profits.

Case Study

Al Rashed International Shipping Company

The Kuwait-based Al Rashed International Shipping Company trades in international markets and has benefited from high rates of sales growth since 2009 and plans further growth. The company depends on high quality staff to achieve its ambitious expansion plans.

Al Rashed International Shipping Company was established in 1952 in Kuwait, and was a new business enterprise for an existing business. The company is currently a major player in shipping markets in the Gulf. It supplies a range of services including ocean freight, international air freight and land transport both domestically and internationally.

General Manager Ravi Varrier, an employee of the company for more than 30 years, stresses that the company's success over the last half century has been based on the quality of its staff. The company aims to have an effective workforce and has carefully thought through systems of recruitment and selection as well as training. The company has strict policies to avoid any discrimination and encourages teamworking.

Training is organised by each department within the business. Training focuses heavily on communication and customer service. The company responds quickly and positively to any customer complaints.

The company's workforce in Kuwait and Iraq has increased from 180 to 350 since 2010. It has also invested approximately $5 million to develop its facilities in Iraq and Saudi Arabia. The company is investigating the possibility of entering the Libyan market following the political change in that country.

Questions

1 Explain why teamworking might improve motivational levels within the Al Rashed International Shipping Company. [6]
2 Discuss the benefits that you think this company might gain from having a well-motivated workforce. [10]

A high level of motivation within a workforce offers a business other benefits, too:

- Motivated employees are usually contented, making it easier for businesses to attract other employees – the firm will have a reputation as a 'good' employer. This helps to build the employer brand. For example, Google has a reputation as a good employer as illustrated in the case study below.
- Modern businesses protect their public image and spend vast sums of money to enhance it. The motivation (and thus the performance) of the workforce can be an important element of creating a positive corporate image.
- Over recent years, firms have become increasingly aware of the need to compete in terms of quality and customer service. If businesses are to compete in these ways, motivated employees are essential.

So, any leader or manager seeking to improve the performance of his or her workforce may be able to do so by taking steps to improve employee motivation. Understanding the various potential sources of motivation is an important part of taking such a step. A highly motivated and productive workforce is an important element in helping a business to achieve its objectives.

7.2 Human needs

> ## Key term
>
> **Human needs** can be defined as the elements required for survival and normal mental and physical health.

Artur Manfred Max-Neef is a Chilean economist who is perhaps best known for his work setting out the fundamental **human needs**. Human needs, as identified by Max-Neef are few, finite and interrelated. He believed that they are also the same for all countries and cultures and have not changed over time. He argued that what changes over time is how these fundamental human needs are satisfied. In Max-Neef's view, there is no hierarchy of needs (apart from the basic need for subsistence or survival) as some other writers have argued.

Max-Neef classifies the fundamental human needs as:
- subsistence, taking the forms of food, shelter and work
- protection, which may be provided through social security and health care systems as well as work
- affection, which can be satisfied through friendships and family ties
- understanding, which may be developed through education and literature
- participation in groups and communities, which gives rise to responsibilities and rights
- leisure, which may take the form of games or other non-work activities
- creation of objects and ideas
- identity, which can be expressed through language, religion or culture
- freedom in the form of equal rights for all.

How human needs may be satisfied at work

Employment does offer the possibility of satisfying some, but possibly not all, of these human needs. The following needs could be met through employment, but this may not always be the case.
- **Subsistence** Employment can provide an income sufficient to allow people to have shelter, food and clothes so that their lives are not threatened by the lack of these basic items.
- **Protection** Work can satisfy this need in a number of ways. A permanent contract of employment may provide the security of knowing that the income from employment will be received for the foreseeable future. Some forms of employment also provide health care and pensions to give employees an income in old age.
- **Participation** This can be achieved through working in teams, from teams of shop assistants through to membership of the board of directors of a large public company. Participation can also take the form of responsibilities within an organisation.

• **Creation** Many working environments offer opportunities for creativity and some may require this as an integral part of employment. Working in advertising or architecture requires creativity but this can also be an important part of manual work such as constructing houses. Creativity can take other forms including developing teams and building brands.

• **Freedom** Working in an organisation does offer surprising numbers of opportunities for freedom. In a democratically managed business, managers may empower employees. This gives them control over their working lives and a high degree of freedom not only to take decisions, but to decide which decisions to take.

Some other human needs may also be met through working. For example, many businesses provide leisure facilities for their employees and it is not unusual for people to engage in leisure activities with their colleagues from work.

Case Study
Working at Google

Though Google has grown a lot since it opened in 1998, we still maintain a small-company feel.

At lunchtime, almost everyone eats in the office café, sitting at whatever table has an opening and enjoying conversations with Googlers from different teams. Our commitment to innovation depends on everyone being comfortable with sharing ideas and opinions. Every employee is a hands-on contributor and everyone wears several hats. Because we believe that each Googler is an equally important part of our success, no one hesitates to pose questions directly to Larry or Sergey in our weekly all-hands ('TGIF') meetings – or throw a volleyball across the net at a corporate officer.

Our corporate headquarters, fondly nicknamed the Googleplex, are located in Mountain View, California, USA. While our offices are not identical, they tend to share some essential elements. Here are a few things that you might see in a Google workspace:

• Bicycles or scooters for efficient travel between meetings; dogs; lava lamps; massage chairs; large inflatable balls.
• Googlers sharing cubes, yurts and huddle rooms – and very few single offices.
• Laptops everywhere – standard issue for mobile coding, emails on the go and note-taking.
• Foosball, pool tables, volleyball courts, assorted video games, pianos, ping-pong tables and gyms that offer yoga and dance classes.
• Grassroots employee groups for all interests, such as meditation, film, wine tasting and salsa dancing.
• Healthy lunches and dinners for all staff at a variety of cafés.
• Staff rooms packed with a variety of snacks and drinks to keep Googlers going.

Source: Adapted from www.Google.co.uk

Questions

1 Explain how the human needs of participation and creation may be met by working at Google. [6]
2 Evaluate the extent to which human needs are met by working at Google. [10]

7.3 Motivation theorists

Many different views exist on motivation, and they differ because it is not clear why people work. Is it to gain money, to enjoy social interaction with other humans, or to fulfil personal needs such as achievement and recognition? Or is it a combination of some or all of these?

Motivation theories can be classified broadly into two different perspectives: content theories and process theories. Content theories consider 'what' motivates people and are concerned with individual needs and goals. Taylor, Mayo, Maslow and Herzberg studied motivation from a 'content' perspective. In contrast, process theories examine the 'process' of motivation and are concerned with 'how' motivation occurs. Vroom and McClelland studied motivation from a 'process' perspective.

Content theories of motivation

The content theories of motivation can be divided into three **schools of thought**. These are set out in Table 7.1.

Table 7.1 Schools of thought for content theories of motivation

School of thought	Key writers	Essential ideas
Scientific School	Frederick Winslow Taylor (1856–1917)	Motivation is an external factor achieved through money. Employees should be closely supervised and paid piece rate. Time and motion studies determine efficient means of production and workers are trained and told how to operate.
Human Relations School	Elton Mayo (1880–1949)	This brought sociological theory into management and accepted that employees could be motivated by meeting their social needs. More attention was given to the social dimension of work (e.g. communication, working as groups and consultation between managers and employees).
The Neo-Human Relations School of Management	Abraham Maslow (1908–70) and Frederick Herzberg (1923–2000)	This school highlighted the importance of fulfilling psychological needs to improve employee performance. Motivation, according to Maslow and Herzberg, depended upon designing jobs to fulfil psychological needs.

The School of Scientific Management

Motivating workers became an important issue as the size of businesses increased in the late nineteenth century. Managers developed the **division of labour** to its fullest extent in an attempt to increase efficiency and improve competitiveness. The introduction of mass production methods, along with the use of division of labour, increased the numbers of people working in factories. At the same time, their tasks became monotonous.

Against this background, managers began to investigate ways of increasing employee motivation to improve competitiveness and employee satisfaction. Frederick Winslow Taylor was the most notable of these early writers on motivation and became known as 'the father of scientific management'.

Taylor's theories were based on a simple interpretation of human behaviour, that people were motivated solely by money – his term was 'rational man'. He combined this principle with a simple interpretation of the role of the manager: to operate the business with maximum efficiency.

Key terms

Division of labour is the breaking down of production into a series of small tasks, carried out repetitively by relatively unskilled employees.

Schools of thought are individuals and groups who hold similar views on a particular matter – in this case on what motivates employees.

The key elements of Taylorism

- The starting point of Taylor's approach was work study. He measured and analysed the tasks necessary to complete the production process. He used a stopwatch to measure how long various activities took and sought the most efficient methods of completing tasks. He encouraged the use of the division of labour, breaking down production into small tasks.
- From this he identified the most efficient employees and the approaches they adopted. Using these as a basis, he then detailed 'normal' times in which duties should be completed and assessed individual performance against these norms.
- Employees were provided with the equipment necessary to carry out their tasks. This principle extended to giving stokers (men shovelling coal) a shovel of a size appropriate to their physique to maximise their efficiency. They were also given elementary training and clear instructions on their duties.
- Because, according to Taylor, employees were only motivated by money, the final stage of the system was to design and implement a piece-rate pay system. Under a piece-rate system, employees are paid according to the amount they produce.

Taylor, however, developed differential piece-rate systems to encourage efficiency among employees.
- Taylor also believed in close supervision of the workforce to ensure that they continued to make the maximum effort possible, motivated by pay.

Taylor's views were unpopular with shop-floor employees. His systems forced them to work hard and, by raising productivity levels, placed the jobs of the less efficient workers under threat. Taylor's approach raised efficiency and productivity, so businesses did not need as many employees. His ideas resulted in strikes and other forms of industrial action by dissatisfied workers.

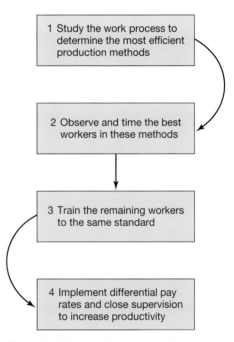

Figure 7.1 The essential features of Taylorism

Taylor's legacy

It is easy to dismiss Taylor and his ideas. His entire philosophy was based on the belief that employees were motivated only by money. He ignored any social dimension of employment and made employees work very hard for what was a meagre wage. His ideas resulted in workers endlessly completing monotonous tasks. There was considerable hostility towards his ideas and opposition from politicians and the business community.

However, Taylor made a significant and enduring contribution to the management of business organisations. He established management as a scientific subject worthy of research and study. His approach was adopted by many premier figures in the business community in the early decades of the twentieth century, including Henry Ford. His techniques encouraged the use of mass production and the conveyor belt system. Furthermore, his work provided a starting point for a later and more people-centred approach to management.

Case Study

Salary packages important for Indian employees

A recent survey carried out by TJinsite, research division of TimesJobs.com, revealed that 77 per cent of employees in India judge salaries to be more important than the location of the job. However, the respondents rated salary and job status to be of equal importance, although financial rewards are considered important by most people taking part in the survey.

The importance of pay varies between older and younger employees. Younger employees consider pay to be more important while older workers tend to rate job status more highly.

Employees in most industries in India rate salaries as important – there was minimal variation between different industries. Respondents said that factors such as job titles, location and status are significant, but an attractive salary is always a critical factor in persuading employees to apply for jobs.

Questions

1 Explain the possible reasons why salaries are an important element in choosing jobs for younger people.   [6]
2 Discuss other possible situations in which salary might be considered very important by employees.   [10]

Study tip

Avoid considering Taylor simply in negative terms. Certainly, many of his ideas would not be acceptable in modern businesses, but others (for example, simple piece-rate pay and work study) have endured. A balanced assessment of Taylor should take into account the lasting elements of his approach, as well as the shortcomings.

The Human Relations School

A fundamental weakness of the Scientific School was that its work ignored the social needs of employees. This, and the obvious unpopularity of the ideas of Taylor, led to the development of the Human Relations School. This school of thought concentrated on the sociological aspects of work. Its foremost member was an Australian-born psychologist, Elton Mayo (1880–1949). Initially, Mayo was one of Taylor's disciples, believing in the importance of scientific management to business efficiency.

Study tip

Don't just think of Mayo in terms of communicating with bosses, and his emphasis on social and sporting facilities. This is only part of his work. He advocated the benefits to employers and employees of working in teams: this aspect of his work is an important issue within many businesses today.

The Hawthorne effect

Mayo's views altered as a result of research he conducted at the Western Electric Company in Chicago. The research was to examine the effects of changes in lighting on the productivity of workers at the company's Hawthorne plant. Previous experiments on lighting and productivity had produced unexpected results. Researchers had anticipated that improving lighting would increase productivity because giving workers better working conditions would allow them to work harder and earn more money. They were astonished when productivity increased not only in the group who were given improved lighting, but also among a group whose lighting had not changed.

It became apparent that the employees were responding to the level of attention they were receiving as part of the investigations and because they were working together as a group. This became known as the 'Hawthorne effect'. As a result of this and similar experiments, Mayo stressed the importance of 'social man' within the workplace.

From these experiments, Mayo concluded that motivation was dependent upon:
- the type of job being carried out and the type of supervision given to the employee
- group relationships, group morale and the sense of worth experienced by individuals.

The implications of the 'Hawthorne effect'

Following the publication of Mayo's findings, managers gradually became more aware of the importance of meeting the social needs of individuals at work. Social environments at work and informal working groups were recognised as having positive influences upon productivity.

The acceptance of Mayo's views led to a number of developments in businesses during the 1940s and 1950s, many of which remain today:
- Personnel departments were established to ensure that employees' social needs were met at work wherever possible.
- Employees were provided with a range of sporting and social facilities to foster the development of informal groups among employees.

- Works outings and trips became a familiar part of an employee's year (for example, multinational retailer Marks and Spencer organises short-break weekends for its employees).
- Managers gave more attention to teams and **teamworking**.

Key term

Teamworking is the process of breaking down production into large units and using groups of employees to complete these tasks.

Mayo's recognition of the importance of teamworking is perhaps his most enduring testimony. Many firms have organised their workforce into teams, for example, the Japanese electronics manufacturer, Toshiba.

Mayo's work took management forward in general, and motivation in particular. He moved the focus onto the needs of employees, rather than just on the needs of the organisation.

The Neo-Human Relations School

This could also be called the new Human Relations School. Abraham Maslow and Frederick Herzberg are key members of this particular school and began to put forward their views in the 1950s. The Neo-Human Relations School considered the psychological aspects of employment and argued that motivation lies within each individual employee: managers merely need the key to unlock the motivational force.

By focusing on the psychological needs of employees, Maslow and Herzberg encouraged managers to treat their employees as individuals, with different needs and aspirations. Their work emphasised that, because people are different, the techniques required to motivate individuals will also differ.

Case Study

Motivating accountancy graduates

Respondents to an internet survey have judged training and development of skills to be more important than salary according to a survey by accountants Ernst and Young. Most of the 1051 respondents were accountancy graduates with additional experience in the industry. The key elements of the survey were:

- Approximately 44 per cent rated training as the most important factor attracting them to a job.
- A mere 18 per cent of respondents placed salary and benefits as the most important factor.
- The reputation of the business was judged most important by 12 per cent and 8 per cent identified the business's culture as the vital factor.

Questions

1 Explain why employees may be motivated by pay. [6]
2 To what extent do the results of this survey show that pay as a motivator is outdated and irrelevant for today's employees? [10]

Maslow's hierarchy of needs

In 1954, Maslow published his 'hierarchy of needs', setting out the various needs that, he argued, everyone attempted to meet through working. Maslow presented his hierarchy of needs as a triangle with basic needs shown at the bottom and his so-called higher needs towards the top (see Figure 7.2).

Key term

The **hierarchy of needs** is a theory that employees have successive requirements that can be fulfilled through work.

Maslow's argument was a relatively simple one. Employees, he argued, have a series of needs they seek to fulfil at work. These are in a hierarchy – once a lower level need is satisfied, individuals strive to satisfy needs further up the hierarchy. Abraham Maslow established five levels of human needs that can be satisfied through work.

The key point of Maslow's argument was that a business could motivate its employees by offering them the chance to fulfil a higher level of need once a lower one was satisfied (see Table 7.2). So once an employee's basic needs had been met, perhaps through a system of fair pay, he or she could be motivated further by the offer of secure and continuing employment. Similarly, a worker whose social needs were met through employment could next be motivated by the opportunity to satisfy self-esteem needs. This could be achieved by taking responsibility for a major project, offering the chance of achievement and recognition.

Maslow's theory was attractive to managers from the outset. It offered a more individualistic approach to motivating employees, recognising that not all people are the same. Managers had long realised that what motivated one person would not necessarily motivate another. Maslow's theory offered an explanation and an alternative approach for managers.

Frederick Herzberg's two-factor theory

Herzberg's two-factor theory was the result of a study designed to test the view that people face two major sets of influences at work. Herzberg's resulting theory was based on the results to questions asked of 200 accountants and engineers in the USA.

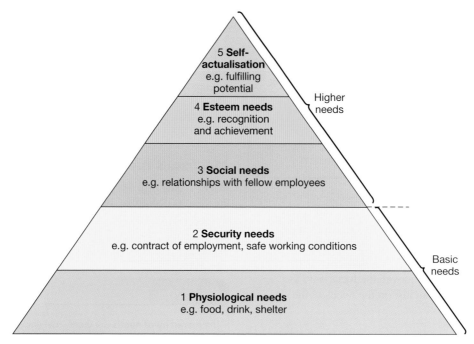

Figure 7.2 Maslow's hierarchy of needs

Table 7.2 An explanation of Maslow's hierarchy of needs

Maslow's level of need	Examples	Means of satisfying needs
1 Physiological needs	Food, water, shelter, clothing	Through pay and a warm and dry working environment.
2 Security needs	A safe and secure working environment for employees	Implementing a proper health and safety policy, providing employees with contracts of employment.
3 Social needs	Contact and friendships with other employees	Social and sporting facilities, opportunities to work in groups.
4 Esteem needs	Achievement, recognition and self-respect	Delegating authority to junior employees, offering promotion opportunities.
5 Self-actualisation	To fulfil one's potential completely	Providing opportunities to take new responsibilities and to develop new skills.

Herzberg's motivators – these **satisfiers** relate to the job itself and can create positive motivation

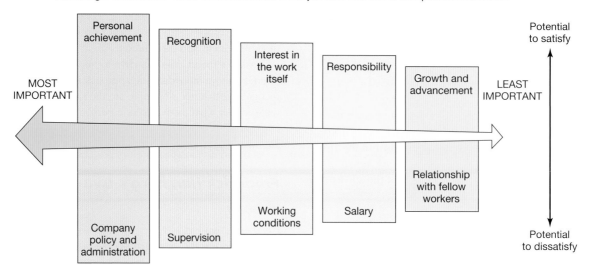

Herzberg's hygiene factors – these relate to the job environment and have the potential to dissatisfy

Figure 7.3 Herzberg's hygiene and motivational factors

The first part of Herzberg's motivation theory is related to the environment of the job. He identified a range of factors that shaped the environment in which people work and he called these influences **hygiene** or **maintenance factors**. These factors are all around the job, but are not a part of the job itself. Herzberg's research identified a number of hygiene factors, including the following:

- company policies and administration
- supervision of employees
- working conditions
- salary
- relationship with fellow workers (at the same level).

Key terms

Hygiene factors (also called maintenance factors) are a group of influences that may result in employee dissatisfaction at work.

Motivators are a series of factors, such as promotion, that may have positive influences on employees' performance at work.

Herzberg's crucial finding was that hygiene factors do not lead to motivation, but without them employees may become dissatisfied. So, according to Herzberg, an employee cannot be motivated by pay, but might be dissatisfied by inadequate financial rewards. Hygiene factors were so named because Herzberg believed attention to them would prevent hygiene problems. It is important to note that Herzberg's research classified pay as a hygiene factor and, therefore, as unable to motivate.

The second finding of Herzberg's research established those factors with the ability to motivate – the **motivators**. These factors relate to the job itself and can be used to positively motivate employees. He identified the following factors as motivators:

- personal achievement of goals and targets
- recognition for achievement
- interest in the work itself
- responsibility for greater and more complex duties
- personal growth and advancement.

Herzberg believed that these approaches (hygiene and motivation) must be used simultaneously. Employees should be managed so they have a minimum of dissatisfaction. They should get achievement, recognition for achievement, take interest in their work and be given responsibility to allow them to grow and develop within their work.

Assessing the work of the Neo-Human Relations School

The research and writing of Maslow and Herzberg has had a major impact on the way in which businesses have managed their employees. Although there are differences in their approaches, many similarities also exist. As illustrated in Table 7.3, Herzberg's motivators broadly correspond with Maslow's higher needs.

Case Study

Frederick Herzberg

Frederick Herzberg was born in Massachusetts in the USA in 1923. He attended City College, New York before enlisting in the army. During his military service he witnessed the survivors at Dachau concentration camp.

Figure 7.4 Frederick Herzberg

Herzberg gained a PhD in Psychology at the University of Pittsburg and began to turn his attention to business management. He became Professor of Management at Case Western Reserve University, where he established the Department of Mental Health. In 1972 he joined the University of Utah's College of Business.

Herzberg developed a reputation as one of the most influential thinkers on people at work and employee motivation. He combined his deep knowledge of employee psychology with a series of practical experiments in the workplace. His book *Work and the Nature of Man* (1966) was voted one of the ten most important books on management theory and practice in the twentieth century. He died in January 2000.

Questions

1 Using examples, distinguish between Herzberg's motivators and hygiene factors. [6]
2 Discuss the possible reasons why a book on employee motivation was voted one the twentieth century's most important management books. [10]

Table 7.3 Herzberg and Maslow compared

	Maslow	**Herzberg**
Motivation factors (higher needs)	• Self-actualisation needs • Esteem needs (higher needs)	• Achievement • Recognition • Responsibility • Interest in work • Personal growth
Maintenance factors (lower needs)	• Social needs • Security needs • Physiological needs (mainly lower needs)	• Company policy and administration • Supervision • Working conditions • Relationship with fellow workers

Both theories have the major advantage in that they were not simply theoretical writings – practical implications for management were within the theories. Both authors encouraged managers to utilise their employees' abilities by giving them challenging tasks.

Weaknesses do exist within these theories, of course. Herzberg's assertion that pay cannot be used to motivate might be true of many employees in wealthy, developed economies. However, this may not be the case with workers in poorer, developing countries. Equally, Maslow's theory is based upon a hierarchy and the assumption that individuals move from one level to the next. His work has been criticised on the grounds that people do not move through these needs in the same order. It also assumes that, once a need is fulfilled, it loses its power to motivate. This may not be the case, especially with the higher needs.

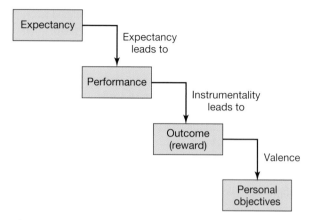

Figure 7.5 Victor Vroom's expectancy theory

> ### Study tip
>
> Many answers to questions on motivation receive low grades because students do not apply their knowledge to the scenario in the question. Ensure that you do not simply explain relevant theories: you must apply them to the scenario.

Process theories of motivation

Process theories of motivation look at what people are thinking about when they decide whether or not to put effort into a particular activity. Examples of such theories include expectancy and equity theories. They try to capture the process that employees go through when making choices with goals in mind. Unlike the other theories of motivation we have considered, they see the individual as an active decision-maker, rather than trying (in the case of the Neo-Human Relations School) to meet certain needs. Process theories emphasise the actual process (or method) of motivation.

Victor Vroom's expectancy theory

This theory, developed by Vroom in the early 1960s, argues that motivation depends on employees' expectations of the results of their efforts. If employees know what they want from an outcome and believe they can achieve the particular outcome, they will be motivated. In brief, Vroom's theory argues that the behaviour of individuals is such as to maximise pleasure and to minimise pain in whatever form it may occur.

Vroom's model consists of three major elements as illustrated in Figure 7.5.

Expectancy

This refers to the confidence that employees may have in their ability to complete a particular activity or task to an acceptable standard. Demotivation would result if an employee believes that he or she is not capable of completing the task in question satisfactorily.

Instrumentality

This is the belief of employees that the completion of a particular activity will lead to a desired outcome. In a situation of high instrumentality the employee has confidence that specific activities will result in the achievement of a valued reward. Instrumentality will be greater if employees recognise a clear link between actions and rewards and have confidence that they will receive the promised rewards for achieving their targets. The salesperson above may have high instrumentality if he or she is part of a clear bonus scheme and has received bonuses in similar circumstances previously.

Valence

This represents the strength of a person's desire to achieve a specific outcome. Valence is positive if a person prefers the outcome to not achieving it. If the person is indifferent to the outcome, then the valence will be zero. High values of valence mean that an outcome is highly attractive to employees and has great potential to motivate. In such circumstances managers can use the possibility of attaining this outcome as a means of motivation. For example, a salesperson may find the prospect of a monetary bonus for achieving an agreed sales target very desirable. The salesperson we have used as an example of this model must have confidence in his or her ability to achieve the number of sales necessary to receive the bonus.

David McClelland's theory of needs

The American writer David McClelland is perhaps best known for his work on achievement motivation. In his acquired needs theory, McClelland argued that an individual's motivation depends upon their needs and that these needs are determined by the individual's experience. David McClelland identified three types of motivational need:
- achievement motivation (n-Ach)
- authority/power motivation (n-Pow)
- affiliation motivation (n-Affil).

McClelland believed that these three needs exist, to differing extents, in all employees, irrespective of their role or status within the business. McClelland's work emphasised that the combination of these three needs determines:
- each employee's behaviour in terms of what motivates them
- how they manage and motivate other employees.

The need for achievement

People who have a high need for achievement (n-ach) aim for excellence. This means that they are likely to avoid low risk situations as they derive little satisfaction from meeting targets that are not challenging. Equally, they tend to avoid high risk situations as they fear not achieving. Therefore this type of person aims to attain realistic but challenging goals – ideally those in which they have a 50 per cent chance of success. This type of employee has a strong need for feedback on achievement and progress, and a need for a sense of accomplishment.

The need for authority and power

A person with a need for power (n-pow) can fall into one of two categories:
- a need for personal power and to direct or control other employees – this is a need which may be considered undesirable
- a need for institutional power – this is a need to organise other employees to attain the organisation's objectives.

Managers and leaders with a need for institutional power are likely to contribute more to a business enterprise than someone whose need for power is a personal one. The employee with a need for authority and power wants to have an effect on an organisation and to have some degree of control. He or she may also want to have more status within the organisation.

The need for affiliation

Employees who have a need for affiliation (n-aff) generally seek harmonious relationships with other people in the organisation. They need to feel accepted and are motivated to work with other people. This type of employee works well as a member of a team and enjoys social interaction. Employees who are motivated by the need for affiliation often work successfully and effectively in marketing, sales and customer service.

Case Study

Motivating generation Y employees

The CIMB Thai Group is a bank based in Thailand. It is relatively small with only 3700 employees. Despite this it experiences problems with its labour turnover rates, particularly among junior employees. In 2011 the Bank suffered an average labour turnover rate of 22.9 per cent while the figure for junior employees reached 34 per cent.

The Bank's executive vice-president for HR management, Dr Kongpob, commented: 'We're very serious about management of generation Y employees (those born after about 1983) since they are certainly going to be our future managers, so if you don't understand them, then work will be difficult.'

He continued to argue that generation Y employees dislike being forced or ordered to do something. In contrast employees born between 1946 and 1964 (called baby boomers) prefer to be in control and want others to follow them.

Dr Kongpob argued that generation Y employees perform most effectively if given challenging work, rewards related to performance and direct instructions. 'Give them challenging work, and if they achieve something, then recognise them for that achievement. It does not have to be a financial reward but something that will make them feel proud to be part of the team and organisation,' he concluded.

Questions

1 Explain the differences between McClelland's need for power and the need for achievement. [6]
2 To what extent do you think that David McClelland's explanation of the differing behaviour of the older and younger employees at the CIMB Thai Group is the only valid one? [10]

The implications of McClelland's work

McClelland's work has clear implications for leaders and managers. The principal one is that employees with different needs require different roles and tasks if they are to be motivated effectively.
- **An employee with a high need for achievement** Such employees should be given tasks which are demanding but ones which can reasonably be expected to be achieved. Such employees require regular feedback, especially of a positive nature.
- **An employee with a high need for authority and power** This type of employee is most likely to flourish and perform well when controlling others. For a junior employee this could be a supervisory role, while more senior employees may fulfil this need by managing large teams of employees.
- **An employee with a high need for affiliation** Working as part of a team, especially a cooperative one, is likely to allow employees to meet their needs for affiliation. Equally this type of employee is likely to perform best when interacting with other employees and should be provided with opportunities to do this whenever possible.

7.4 Motivation methods in practice: financial motivators

Managers and organisations use a variety of pay systems in an attempt to improve the performance of their workforce. Despite attention given to the views of Herzberg, which suggest that monetary methods of motivation are of limited value, pay remains a major incentive.

Table 7.4 Opinions on the motivational powers of pay

Writer	Opinions on the motivational power of pay
Frederick Taylor	Taylor saw pay as the primary motivating factor for all workers. He referred to workers as 'economic animals' and supported the use of piece rate.
Abraham Maslow	He saw pay as a reward permitting employees to meet the lower needs on their hierarchy.
Frederick Herzberg	Pay is a hygiene factor and a possible cause of dissatisfaction. In a few circumstances pay might be a motivator if, for example, it is used as a recognition for merit.

Time-based pay

Some employees receive payments based on the number of hours that they work each week or month. Their income is based on an hourly rate of pay. Thus an employee may be paid $11 an hour. If the employee works 36 hours in a particular week he or she will receive gross pay amounting to $396 ($11 x 36 hours).

This payment system has the advantages of being simple to understand and transparent. Many countries across the world have minimum wage laws based on specific hourly rates of pay which can be increased over time to compensate for inflation.

Time-based pay can result in employees becoming clock watchers and not being prepared to carry out any duties outside the hours for which they are paid.

Salaries and wages

Most employees receive their payment in the form of salaries or wages. Salaries are expressed in annual terms (e.g. a production manager might be paid a salary of $30 000 per year) and are normally paid monthly. Salaried employees are not normally required to work a set number of hours per week though their contract of employment may state a minimum number of hours.

On the other hand, wages are usually paid weekly and employees are required to be at work for a specified number of hours. Employees are normally paid a higher rate (known as overtime) for any additional hours worked.

Piece rate

Under this pay system, employees are paid according to the quantity they produce – a form of payment by results. Thus, an employee on a production line might receive an agreed amount for each unit of production they manufacture. **Piece rate** is common in a number of industries including textiles, electronics and agriculture.

Piece rate offers businesses a number of advantages and disadvantages. The introduction of a piece rate can increase the productivity levels achieved by many employees within a business. This can effectively reduce the business's labour costs for each unit of output that is produced. However, this rise in productivity may be at the expense of quality and consumer complaints may increase. A business using piece rate may lose customers as a consequence of its introduction, especially if quality is an important factor in consumers' buying decisions.

Bonuses and commission

Bonuses are additions to pay that are linked to individual or team performance measured against targets or objective criteria. Employers introduce bonus payments to reward individuals for doing well. By definition a 'bonus' payment is an extra and not part of basic pay.

Bonuses can be paid to employees in different industries and at different levels in an organisation.

- Profit related bonus, for example, to a manager in a retail organisation.
- Performance bonus payments to senior managers or directors or investment bankers.
- Bonus payments for reaching production targets in manufacturing.

Commission, like piece rate, is the payment for the quantity (or value) that is produced by an individual employee. In some industries, such as telesales, an employee's entire income may be made up of commission, although it may have to meet any conditions imposed by minimum pay laws. Employees can be paid a percentage of the value of any products they sell as commission. This form of payment has similar advantages and disadvantages to piece rate. However, in many countries it has become less common. One explanation for this may be that its disadvantages outweigh its advantages.

> ### Key terms
>
> **Performance-related pay** exists where some part of an employee's pay is linked to the achievement of targets at work. These targets might include sales figures or achieving certain grades in an annual appraisal.
>
> **Piece rate** is a system whereby employees are paid according to the quantity of a product they produce.

Profit sharing

Profit sharing is a reward system under which employees receive some part of the business's profits. This is a type of performance-related pay (see below), but not one which discriminates between the performances of individual employees. Such payments, which may vary according to the employee's seniority within the organisation, are separate from, and additional to, regular earnings.

Profits are paid to employees in the form of cash or company shares. Profit-sharing schemes can improve an employee's loyalty to the business by breaking down the 'us and them' attitude. Under profit-sharing schemes a greater level of profit is regarded as being of benefit to all employees, not just to senior managers. Employees may be more willing to accept changes designed to improve the business's profitability.

The danger with profit-sharing schemes is that they can provide rewards that are too small to represent a worthwhile payment for employees. On the other hand, if they are too generous, the business may lack sufficient funds for capital investment.

Performance-related pay (PRP)

Performance-related pay (or PRP) has become more widely used over recent years and has developed along with employee appraisal systems. PRP is only paid to those employees who meet or exceed some agreed targets. Under PRP, employees are paid for their contribution to the organisation, rather than their status within it.

Businesses of all sizes throughout the world have introduced PRP. It is widely used in Hong Kong and Japan with Nissan a prime example. Despite criticisms, PRP remains popular, and many employees support linking some element of pay to performance. However, there have been criticisms of the huge rewards paid to some senior managers and directors of moderately successful companies.

Criticisms of PRP

A number of criticisms of performance-related pay have been put forward:

- Many employees perceive PRP as fundamentally unfair. This is particularly true of those working in the services sector where individual employee performance is difficult to measure.
- Employees fear that they might be discriminated against because they do not get on with the manager who makes a decision on their performance. This can result in their performance worsening, not improving.
- A majority of businesses operating PRP systems do not put sufficient funds into the scheme. Typically, the operation of a PRP scheme adds 3–4 per cent to a business's wage bill. This only allows employees to enjoy relatively small performance awards, which may be inadequate to change employee performance.

Developments in PRP

Increasing numbers of businesses are implementing a system known as **variable pay**. Some managers argue that a business's performance often depends upon the achievements of the few.

Variable pay is really a development of PRP. It is similar in that it rewards employee performance, but there are differences. PRP operates according to a formula used throughout the company. Variable pay is far more flexible and the potential rewards for star employees are greater. If the business performs well employees benefit under variable pay, but can suffer financial penalties in a less successful period.

Some managers remain unconvinced of the value of PRP, no matter how sophisticated the scheme. The widespread use of PRP may, in part, be an attempt by managers to keep pay rates down for the majority of employees. PRP, or variable pay, treats employees as individuals, limiting the ability of trade unions to bargain collectively.

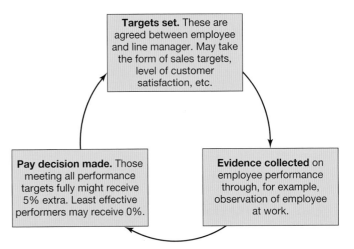

Figure 7.6 The operation of a typical performance-related pay system

Apple to introduce performance-related pay

Technology company Apple is about to increase the pay rates of its stores' workers. It is reported that the rises could amount to 25 per cent, but will be linked to the performance of the company's employees. At the same time the company is offering all of its employees the opportunity to buy its products at discounted prices.

Apple's employees in its retail outlets currently receive between $9 and $15 an hour, while those working at the Genius Bar within its shops are paid approximately $30 an hour. The *Wall Street Journal* has revealed that the company's employees are facing pay reviews and that Apple is expected to increase its pay rates, not just in the United States, but in other countries where the company operates as well.

A recent internal review by Apple uncovered that many of its employees were dissatisfied with the company's pay rates and this may be the reason why they are in the process of being improved.

Questions

1 Explain why Apple might expect its system of performance-related pay to improve the performance of its employees. [6]
2 Evaluate the possible problems Apple might face when introducing performance-related pay into its retail stores. [10]

7.5 Motivation methods in practice: non-financial motivators

Many non-monetary methods of motivation tend to focus upon the design of employees' jobs. Employees can be motivated by asking them to do a job that is challenging and interesting.

A good job should have at least a number of the features listed below.

- Employees carry out duties that result in a definite end product.
- Clear and challenging goals give employees something to aim at. Goals should be demanding, but not unattainable.
- Employees should be able to identify easily their contributions to the organisation.

- Jobs should be designed so that jobholders are involved in planning their own schedules of work, choosing their work methods, and coping with problems as they arise.

The main methods of non-monetary motivation attempt to incorporate some of these features into the working lives of employees.

Job re-design means changing the group of tasks or duties which make up a specific job.

Job enrichment occurs when employees' jobs are redesigned to provide them with more challenging and complex tasks. Also called vertical loading.

Job enlargement is giving employees more duties of a similar level of complexity. Also called horizontal loading.

Job rotation is the regular switching of employees between tasks of a similar degree of complexity.

Job re-design

Employers can change the design of employees' jobs to encompass more or different duties, or duties that are more challenging. **Job enrichment** occurs when employees' jobs are redesigned to provide them with more challenging and complex tasks. This process, also called 'vertical loading', is designed to use all employees' abilities. The intention is to enrich the employee's experience of work.

Frederick Herzberg was a strong supporter of job enrichment. He believed that enrichment provided employees with motivators that increase the satisfaction they might get from working.

Job enrichment normally involves a number of elements:

- redesigning jobs so as to increase not just the range of tasks, but the complexity of them
- giving employees greater responsibility for managing themselves
- offering employees the authority to identify and solve problems relating to their work
- providing employees with the training and skills essential to allow them to carry out their enriched jobs effectively.

Job enrichment involves a high degree of skill on the part of the managers overseeing it. They must ensure that they do not ask employees to carry out duties of which they are not capable.

Job enlargement does not increase the complexity of tasks carried out by an employee. Instead it increases the number of similar duties. It is also termed 'horizontal loading'.

A number of firms operating a policy of job enlargement simply require employees to carry out a number of similar tasks. Thus, a receptionist might be asked to carry out a number of duties in addition to dealing with telephone and personal enquiries from customers. The receptionist may also be asked to maintain records of petty cash and update customer records, for example.

Job enlargement offers benefits to the employee in that carrying out a range of duties, rather than a single one repeatedly, may stimulate their interest. The business gains an advantage from having an employee able to carry out a wider range of duties, possibly reducing their labour costs.

Job rotation is a particular type of job enlargement. Under this system employees switch regularly from one duty to another. Thus, a supermarket may require employees to spend a week on the checkout, a week stacking shelves and a week dealing with customer enquiries. Job rotation may reduce the level of monotony, but does not increase the challenge of the job.

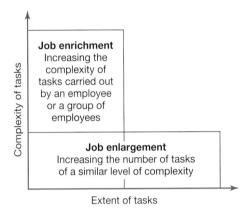

Figure 7.7 Job re-design: job enrichment and job enlargement

Employee empowerment

Empowerment involves redesigning employees' jobs to allow them greater control over their working lives. Empowerment gives employees the opportunity to decide how to carry out their duties and how to organise their work.

Empowerment can make work more interesting as it offers opportunities to meet a number of individual needs. Empowered workers can propose and implement new methods of working as they bring a new perspective to decision-making. They may spend a part of their working lives considering the problems they face and proposing solutions.

Key terms

Empowerment is a series of actions designed to give employees greater control over their working lives.

Job design is the process of grouping together individual tasks to form complete jobs.

Empowerment would receive the approval of Maslow and Herzberg. It provides motivators, as well as offering employees the opportunity to fulfil higher needs.

Employees require training if they are to be empowered. They are unlikely to have the skills necessary to schedule tasks, solve problems, recruit new employees and introduce new working practices. It takes time to implement empowerment and teething problems are common.

Teamworking

Teamworking exists when an organisation breaks down its production processes into large units instead of relying upon the use of the division of labour. Teams are then given responsibility for completing the large units of work. Team members carry out a variety of duties including planning, problem-solving and target-setting.

A number of different team types operate within businesses:

- **Production teams** Many production lines have been organised into distinct elements called 'cells'. Each of these cells is staffed by teams whose members are multi-skilled. They monitor product quality and ensure that production targets are met.
- **Quality circle teams** These are small teams designed to propose solutions to existing problems and to suggest improvements in production methods. The teams contain members drawn from all levels within the organisation.
- **Management teams** Increasingly, managers see themselves as complementary teams establishing the organisation's objectives and overseeing their achievement.

There has been a major trend in businesses towards teamworking over recent years. Teamworking is a major part of the so-called Japanese approach to production and its benefits have been extolled by major companies such as Honda.

Teamworking offers employees the opportunity to meet their social needs, as identified by Maslow; Herzberg identified relationships with fellow workers as a hygiene factor. However, much of the motivational force arising from teamworking comes with the change in job design that usually accompanies it. Teamworking requires jobs to be redesigned, offering employees the chance to fulfil some of the higher needs identified by Maslow, such as esteem needs. Similarly, teamworking offers some of the motivators, for example achievement.

Training

Some businesses invest heavily in training, often regarding it as a core element of managing their workforces successfully. Managers value training because they believe it improves employee motivation and performance. They believe that training helps to motivate employees because they feel valued by the business and this fulfils what Maslow would have called their esteem needs.

However, training has drawbacks as a technique of motivation. It can be very expensive, especially if it takes place away from the workplace and it may not be the most cost-effective method of motivating employees. A further danger is that employees may leave once they have acquired new skills and higher levels of motivation, attracted by higher pay elsewhere.

Employees may receive induction training when starting a new job. This type of training is intended to introduce a new employee to their job and working environment. Induction training can give employees confidence in their ability to do a job from the outset and this confidence may boost their motivation and performance in the workplace.

Employee participation

Employee participation is the involvement of employees in the process of decision-making within a business, possibly through the appointment of worker directors. Many businesses recognise the motivational and other benefits of involving employees in decision-making within an organisation. We consider employee participation more fully below.

> ### Key terms
>
> **Employee participation** is the involvement of employees in the process of decision-making within a business.
>
> **Perks** or **fringe benefits** are rewards received by employees in addition to their wage or salary. Common examples include company cars and private health care.

Perks

These are sometimes referred to as 'fringe benefits'. **Perks** are those extras an employee receives as part of their reward package.

Examples of perks include the following:

- a company car (or a mileage allowance for an employee's own car)
- private health insurance
- employers' contributions to pension schemes
- discounts for company products.

Firms tend to use fringe benefits to encourage employee loyalty and to reduce the number of employees leaving the firm. A danger of the widespread use of fringe benefits is that costs can increase quickly, reducing profitability.

Promotion and status

Promoting an employee to a more senior position within the business is likely to prove motivational. Herzberg recognised advancement as a motivator with the ability to create positive motivation and to improve employee performance.

Similarly, granting someone higher status within an organisation, perhaps through giving them their own office or parking space, may motivate them by fulfilling their need for self-esteem. However, some businesses have opted for a policy of single status in recent years. Single status means that businesses end discrimination between different grades of employees within the organisation by providing the same facilities and benefits for all.

Employee participation

As we have seen, employee participation is the involvement of employees in the process of decision-making within a business. Trade unions can be opposed to the use of employee participation because techniques such as quality circles can replace unions in the workplace.

Employee participation can take numerous forms, including those listed below.

- **Quality circles** These are groups of workers who meet regularly to identify methods of improving all aspects of the quality of their work. Quality circles normally involve four to ten employees drawn from all levels within the organisation and focus on supplying imaginative ideas.
- **Works councils** Managers and employees meet within works councils to discuss issues such as working conditions, pay and training. They are popular in many countries, especially Germany. Employee representatives on works councils are normally elected by the workforce and works council representatives may also be appointed to a company's board of directors.
- **Employee shareholders** Firms across the world operate schemes whereby their employees can buy shares in the company, often at discounted rates. Because employee shareholders have a financial interest in the business's performance it may be that their motivation levels and performance will improve as a consequence. If the business performs well, its share prices should increase, giving financial benefits to the employee.
- **Autonomous work groups** These are teams of employees who are given a high level of control over their working lives – in effect, another form of empowerment. Some such groups elect their own leaders and can appoint new staff as well as having considerable authority over what tasks to complete and in what sequence.

Case Study

Primark in Bangladesh

Primark is one of Europe's largest retailers of clothes. It operates more than 230 shops. The company has a well-publicised commitment to improve working conditions in its suppliers' factories in Bangladesh. It has established committees to allow employees to participate in decision-making in a number of its factories, allowing employees to make proposals to improve their working conditions. The programme covered factories in Dhaka, Savar Gazipur and Narayanganj. In preparation Primark provided training to 500 managers in the factories and more than 1000 employees to ensure they had the necessary skills to implement decisions to enhance working conditions in diverse environments.

Equipped with new skills, including those related to bargaining, the factory workers have reduced working hours and increased holiday entitlements while increasing hourly pay rates. The

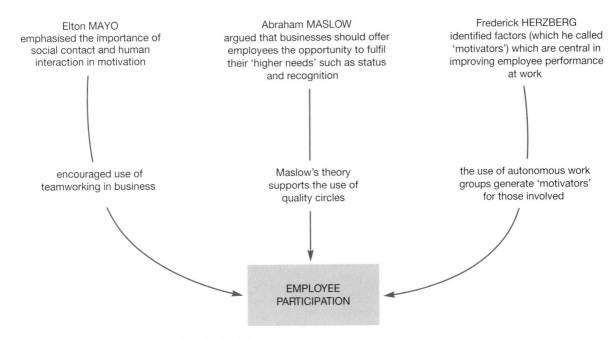

Figure 7.8 Employee participation and motivational theory

negotiations have also led to a number of administrative changes including transparent pay rates and accurate and detailed pay slips.

Primark plans to introduce this scheme into the remainder of its suppliers' factories in Bangladesh, and is prepared to pay for those resources required for its implementation. Primark has also supported the creation and publication of a range of posters setting out workers' rights. The whole scheme is designed to ensure that workers are empowered, educated, and effective communicators dedicated to improving working conditions in one of the world's poorer economies.

Questions

1 Explain the difficulties that Primark might face in establishing its worker participation committees. [6]

2 Evaluate whether Frederick Herzberg's theories of motivation offer the best explanation of the benefits that Primark might receive from setting up worker participation committees. [10]

Test your learning

Short answer questions

1 a Define the term motivation. [2]
  b State **three** characteristics of a highly motivated workforce. [3]

2 Explain how a business may benefit from having a highly motivated workforce. [5]

3 a Identify **two** human needs. [2]
  b Describe **two** key elements of F.W. Taylor's theory of motivation. [3]

4 a Distinguish between Herzberg's motivators and his hygiene factors. [3]
  b Name **two** of the levels of needs in Maslow's hierarchy of needs. [2]

5 a What is a process theory of motivation? [2]
  b Distinguish between the need for achievement and the need for power. [3]

6 a Distinguish between piece-rate pay and hourly pay. [3]
  b State **two** possible benefits to a business of profit sharing. [2]

7 Explain the features that an employer should include in the design of a job if it is to motivate employees. [5]

8 a Distinguish between Abraham Maslow's social needs and his esteem needs. [3]
  b Define the term empowerment. [2]

9 a Describe **two** different types of teams that may be used within a business. [3]
  b Identify **two** perks that a business may offer to its employees. [2]

10 a Define the term employee participation. [2]

b Describe **two** techniques that businesses may use to encourage employee participation. [3]

Data response question

A traditional business

Gibble is a long-established manufacturer of luxury pens. It is a traditional business with a tall organisational structure and many long-serving managers. Its products are recognised as being of the highest quality and it charges premium prices for its products. Its most expensive pen sells for £1250.

Despite the company's profits reaching record levels, its managers are seeking ways to improve the performance of its workforce. Some managers believe that pay is the best way to improve motivation and employee performance. Others would prefer the use of a flatter organisational structure and greater use of teams and techniques such as empowerment and job enrichment.

Questions

1 Explain the terms:

a empowerment [3]

b job enrichment [3]

2 Briefly analyse how the company might use monetary methods of motivation to improve the performance of its workforce. [6]

3 Discuss whether it is inevitable that the company will use non-financial methods to motivate its workforce. [10]

Essay question

Discuss the extent to which the careful design of employees' jobs is always the most important method of motivation. [20]

Past paper questions

1 a Explain how a business might use financial rewards to motivate workers. [8]

b Discuss why a business might use non-financial rewards to motivate its workers. [12]

Cambridge International AS and A Level Business Studies 9707 Paper 12 Q7 May/June 2010

2 Read the Loader Lorries case study on pages 209–10 and then answer the following question.

Discuss the extent to which the new employment contract has created the motivation problems at Loader Lorries. [10]

Cambridge International AS and A Level Business Studies 9707 Paper 21 Q1c May/June 2011

8 Human resource management (HRM)

Chapter overview

In this chapter we examine:

- the purpose and roles of human resource management (HRM)
- how businesses recruit and select employees
- key employment documents including job advertisements, job descriptions and employment contracts
- the ways in which businesses discipline employees, make them redundant and dismiss them
- the purpose, methods and importance of training employees
- issues affecting staff morale and welfare.

8.1 What is human resource management (HRM)?

Key terms

Human resource management (HRM) is the process of making the most efficient use of an organisation's employees.

Personnel management describes a range of discrete tasks necessary to administer the human dimension of business activities.

HRM comprises the acquisition, training, motivation and reward of human resources within the business. Although **human resource management** emerged in the 1940s, for many years businesses relied on the concept of **personnel management**.

There is a clear distinction between personnel management and human resource management. Personnel management considers the elements that comprise managing people (recruitment, selection and so forth) within organisations as separate elements. It does not take into account how these parts combine to assist in the achievement of organisational objectives. Personnel management within businesses carries out a series of unrelated tasks. Decisions relating to recruitment, training and pay systems are developed independently without considering the impact they have on each other and the achievement of corporate objectives.

Over recent years the influence of Japanese management techniques, and their evident success in managing people, has encouraged the adoption of human resource management by companies across the globe.

The purpose of HRM

HRM can help businesses to generate a significant competitive advantage over rivals and to achieve organisational objectives such as growth and increased profitability. Many companies have replaced traditional systems of personnel management with human resource management to enhance performance.

If implemented fully and operated properly human resource management recognises the individual rather than producing personnel policies for the whole workforce. All the elements of HRM (recruitment and selection, training and development, redundancy and dismissal) are geared to fulfilling the needs of the individual as well as those of the organisation. The key to HRM (or at least the 'softer' version of HRM) is that each employee should be nurtured and developed in pursuit of the organisation's objectives. All aspects of the HRM 'package' should be coordinated to ensure coherence and to assist the attainment of strategic targets.

If an organisation is successful in operating its HRM policy, the outcome should be motivated and creative employees who are committed to the firm and who do not seek to leave. Such employees should be aware of the goals of the organisation and understand how they can contribute towards the attainment of organisational targets.

Under this scenario a business should incur lower recruitment costs, enjoy higher levels of productivity and a reduction in faulty products. It may attract top class applicants to vacancies because of its reputation as a caring and enlightened employer. All of these factors should make the organisation more competitive and better able to cope with the rigours of operating in international markets.

However, in reality the case for human resource management is not so clear cut. Many businesses in the UK differ in their interpretation of HRM. Some see it as a confirmation of the value of employees who have to be developed to meet the needs of the organisation. Others take a 'harder' attitude, viewing employees as simply another resource to be used as effectively as possible. The latter approach has a much more short-term focus. The fact that different interpretations of the policy exist make it more difficult to assess its contribution to achieving objectives and overall competitiveness.

Two key arguments exist for the increasing use of HRM within businesses.

1 The nature of the workforce has changed over recent years. Greater use of part-time and peripheral workers, for example, has encouraged human resource managers to adopt a 'hard' style of HRM and view people as a resource to be deployed as effectively as possible. Simultaneously, the existence of a better educated workforce, along with the expectation that workers should carry out more complex tasks and duties, has led managers to view employees as valuable assets to be developed in the interests of the organisation. This approach to managing human resources is termed 'soft' HRM.

2 Changes in organisational structure have led to many managers taking on responsibility for managing people within the organisation. Techniques such as delayering and the development of empowered teams have been an integral part of the implementation of human resource management. Acquiring, developing, motivating and rewarding employees are, it is argued, best done by managers and colleagues close to the employee in question. Under HRM, managers can carry out many of the more routine tasks of traditional personnel management. Empowered teams can play a role in recruiting employees and identifying training needs. The 'soft' approach to HRM embodies a philosophy entirely in harmony with modern management techniques such as delayering and teamworking.

Case Study

The Central Bank of India

Central Bank of India has announced that it has introduced a human resource management package to improve the productivity of its 36 000 employees. This programme is intended to develop employees' skills and to ensure suitable candidates are available for future promotions.

The Bank has used technology to automate many of the functions of its HR department including paying employees, booking holidays and repayment of some expenses. Senior managers at the Bank estimate that this will save approximately 2000 employee days of work each month, resulting in a substantial cost reduction for the publicly owned Bank.

The automation of the HR function offers other benefits to senior managers. The new HR system gives managers instant access to all employees' qualifications, experience, performance appraisals and positions held. This will help the Bank's managers to manage the talent available more effectively and will ease the process of planning its future workforces.

Questions

1 Explain why HRM might be an important issue within the Central Bank of India. [6]
2 Discuss whether the advantages of the introduction of new technology into the Bank's HR department will outweigh the disadvantages. [10]

Planning the workforce

Key term

A **workforce** (or **human resource**) **plan** assesses the current workforce and actions necessary to meet the business's future labour needs.

Before a business recruits, selects or trains employees, it must establish future labour needs. This is not simply a matter of recruiting sufficient employees. Those recruited must have the right skills and experience to help the organisation achieve its corporate objectives. Managers will draw up a **human resource** or **workforce plan** to detail the number and type of workers the business needs to recruit, as well as the location where they will be employed.

Businesses require a range of information when developing human resource plans:

- They need to research to provide sales forecasts for the next year or two. This will help identify the quantity and type of labour required.
- Data will be needed to show the number of employees likely to be leaving the labour force in general (**labour turnover**). Information will also be required on potential entrants to the labour force.
- If wages are expected to rise, then businesses may reduce their demand for labour and seek to make greater use of technology.
- The plan will reflect any anticipated changes in the output of the workforce due to changes in productivity or the length of the working week.
- Technological developments will impact on planning the workforce. Developments in this field may reduce the need for unskilled employees while creating employment for those with technical skills.

Labour turnover

Labour turnover is the percentage of a business's workforce that leaves a business over a given period of time (usually one year).

$$\text{Turnover} = \frac{\text{number of staff leaving during the year}}{\text{average number of staff}} \times 100$$

This ratio measures the proportion of a workforce leaving their employment at a business over some period of time, usually one year. Low wages and inadequate training leading to poor morale among employees may cause high levels of labour turnover. Another cause is ineffective recruitment procedures resulting in the appointment of inappropriate staff. Other reasons include redundancy and retirement.

Maths moment

Last year 45 employees at Kenya Fuels Ltd left the company. The company had an average of 900 employees during the year. The company's HR manager had forecast that the company's labour turnover figure would be 4 per cent.

1 Calculate the labour turnover figure for this company.
2 How many employees would have left if the HR manager's forecast had been accurate?

Some level of labour turnover is inevitable. Managers seek labour turnover to bring new ideas into a business, but not so high as to impose excessive recruitment costs. A survey in the UK in 2012 by the Chartered Institute of Personnel and Development (CIPD) revealed that labour turnover in the UK was 12.7 per cent, compared with 12.5 per cent in 2011. Figure 8.1 shows the reasons why a selection of employees in the UK left employment in 2012. Labour turnover rates can vary considerably between industries and countries. In India labour turnover rates of 20–30 per cent are not uncommon and rates can reach 50 per cent in some Indian industries such as IT.

Managers attempt to manage labour turnover to achieve a balance between bringing new employees with enthusiasm and ideas into the business against the costs of recruitment. Surveys in the UK have shown that the impact of labour turnover of most businesses surveyed has a negative impact on performance and their ability to achieve organisational objectives. This suggests that most businesses face a higher labour turnover than desired or that they face unexpected recruitment costs.

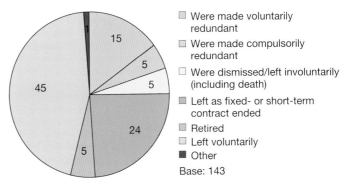

Were made voluntarily redundant
Were made compulsorily redundant
Were dismissed/left involuntarily (including death)
Left as fixed- or short-term contract ended
Retired
Left voluntarily
Other
Base: 143

Figure 8.1 Percentage of leavers by reason for leaving
Source: CIPD

Case Study

Labour turnover and hotels in Mumbai

Hotels and restaurants across the world face very high rates of labour turnover. Hotels in Australia have experienced rates in excess of 50 per cent, meaning that more than half the business's employees are leaving each year.

The hospitality industry in Mumbai, India, is no exception to this trend. There has been a high rate of growth in the industry as the city of Mumbai has prospered. A high rate of labour turnover has an immediate effect especially in the guest service areas and, therefore, a hotel suffers from the loss of efficient and skilled employees. In a market that is growing quickly new businesses may attract skilled employees from rival businesses by offering higher wages.

Hotel guests also develop a comfort level with an employee with whom they regularly interact and frequent changes reduce guest satisfaction levels. High rates of labour turnover affect regular operations which are vital to the smooth running of any hotel such as the restaurant and reception areas. Having skilled and experienced staff is vital in Mumbai's hotel industry where competitiveness is based heavily upon employee performance.

Questions

1 Explain why labour turnover rates 'in excess of 50 per cent' might cause problems for managers in hotels in Australia. [6]
2 Discuss the possible actions the managers of hotels in Mumbai might take to reduce rates of labour turnover. [10]

8.2 Recruitment and selection

Key term

Recruitment and selection is the process of filling an organisation's job vacancies by appointing new staff.

Recruitment

The process of workforce planning in which a business analyses its expected future labour needs and compares this to its current workforce may identify the need for recruiting new employees. Alternatively, the need for recruitment may arise because an existing employee opts to leave. The recruitment process is summarised in Figure 8.2.

Study tip

It is easy to get bogged down in the detail of recruitment and selection procedures. While such knowledge is fundamental it is vital to think about how successful different approaches to recruitment and selection might be in helping the business to achieve its organisational objectives.

In 2013 more than 60 per cent of businesses taking part in a UK survey said that they were experiencing recruitment difficulties. The key reasons cited were a lack of necessary specialist skills and insufficient experience (61 per cent). Recruiting is expensive: the average recruitment cost of filling a vacancy in the UK in 2013 was £6000 for senior managers and directors and £1800 for other employees. However, many managers would argue that these figures are less costly than appointing the wrong employee and perhaps having to repeat the process.

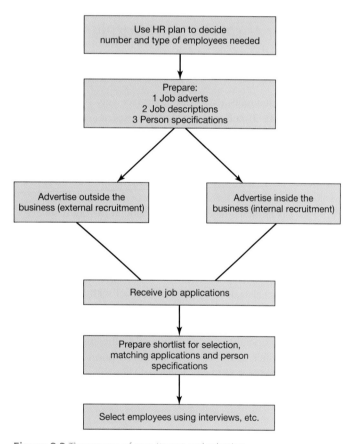

Figure 8.2 The process of recruitment and selection

Source: CIPD Resources and Talent Planning Survey, 2012

Recruitment is likely to be a more important activity in a business that is expanding or one which is developing new products or entering new markets. In such cases the business will require a substantial number of new employees and these may come from inside the business (existing employees) but are more likely to be recruited from outside it.

Internal and external recruitment

Firms may recruit internally through promotion or redeployment from within existing employees. Internal recruitment offers a number of benefits:

- Candidates will have experience of the business and its culture and will be familiar with the firm's procedures.
- Internal candidates may not require induction training.
- Internal recruitment provides employees with opportunities for promotion.
- It avoids the need for expensive external advertising.
- Selection may be easier as more is known about the candidates.

However, internal candidates are drawn from a limited pool of employees and the skills and experience of this group of people may be insufficient to meet the business's needs. This is more likely in the case of smaller businesses and with senior appointments or for rapidly growing businesses.

Managers may be keen to have a wider choice of candidates and may seek to recruit externally. This can result in applications from higher quality candidates, especially if recruitment is through national media or nationally based recruitment agencies. External recruits may bring fresh ideas and enthusiasm into the business. This can be a vital factor in an organisation with a low level of labour turnover.

External recruitment is likely to be very expensive. It also carries a greater risk as candidates are not known to the business. Firms can recruit externally by using a range of methods:

- Firms 'headhunt' employees who are currently working for other organisations in order to offer them employment. Those employees who are headhunted are usually either senior managers or people with specialist skills, perhaps in short supply. Specialist executive recruitment agencies exist which can target precisely the right type of candidates, but normally charge high fees.
- Websites operated by businesses and governments to bring together those seeking work and businesses intending to recruit. Examples include the privately owned Rozee website (www.rozee.pk) in Pakistan and the New Zealand government's jobs website (www.jobs.govt.nz).

- Employment agencies provide employers with details of suitable applicants for posts they may have vacant. Agencies usually charge considerable fees for bringing together employers and potential candidates.
- The government operates a number of training schemes to improve the skills and knowledge of the workforce. For example, in 2011 the Malaysian government introduced the '1Malaysia Training Scheme' to reduce youth unemployment by providing employable skills. In 2014 42 000 Malaysian graduates secured jobs after undergoing training on this scheme. Participating in schemes such as this offers firms a chance to consider the skills and aptitude of possible employees while they are on a training scheme. This is a relatively low-risk strategy and a cheap means of recruitment.

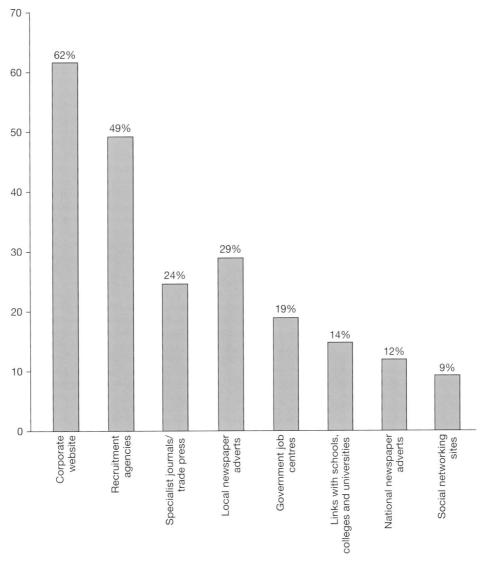

Figure 8.3 The most effective methods of attracting applicants from potential employees in the UK in 2013

Source: CIPD Resourcing and Talent Planning Survey, 2013

Selection

A number of selection techniques exist. Because of the high costs resulting from recruiting the wrong people, firms are investing more resources and time in the recruitment and selection process.

Table 8.1 Methods of selection used by a sample of UK businesses in 2009 and 2013

Method of selection	2013 Survey (%)	2009 Survey (%)
Competency-based interviews	82	69
Interview following contents of CV/application form	71	68
Online tests	22	38
Personality/attitude/psychometric tests	42	35
Assessment centres	43	35
Group exercises (e.g. role playing)	28	26

Source: Resourcing and Talent Planning, 2013 (CIPD)

Question

Does the data in Table 8.1 suggest that UK businesses are attempting to minimise costs of selection?

- Interviews remain a common form of selection technique. Interviews can involve one or two interviewers, or even a panel. They are relatively cheap and allow the two-way exchange of information, but are unreliable as a method of selection. Some people perform well at interview, but that does not necessarily mean they will perform well at work.
- Psychometric tests reveal the personality of a candidate. Questions are used to assess candidates' honesty, commitment or ability to fulfil a particular role.
- As managers become more aware of the high costs of poor selection decisions, they have made increasing use of assessment centres. In such centres, a number of candidates are subjected to a variety of selection techniques over a period of between two and four days. These might include some or all of the following:
  - simulations of circumstances that might occur within the job
  - a variety of interviews
  - role plays involving a number of the candidates and assessment centre staff
  - psychometric tests.

Evidence suggests that assessment centres are efficient at selecting employees for managerial positions. They are substantially more expensive than operating interviews, but their better performance compared with more traditional selection techniques might make them more cost effective in the long term. Businesses are also using online assessments as a low cost method of selection.

Recruitment is competitive in the Gulf States

Recent research has shown that employees seeking a new job have greater success if they apply directly through a business's website, rather than applying in person.

A study by Cazar, based on 3.9 million job applicants in the United Arab Emirates (UAE), the rest of the Middle East and Asia Pacific found that the highest proportion of candidates (24 per cent) were hired through company websites. Corporate talent pools, or databases of potential candidates set up by companies, emerged as the second highest source of new employees (22 per cent) while news, trade and social media websites came next, with 13 per cent.

With the increasing importance of the internet, the majority of recruiting activity today is done electronically. Many employers also use online tests to select employees. These are commonly used to reduce a long list of potential applicants to a smaller number of those who progress to further selection activities.

Some human resource specialists have warned businesses against relying too heavily on the use of corporate websites for recruiting and selecting new employees. Job applicants can post their CVs anywhere and also attend careers fairs. Companies can miss out on talented employees if their recruitment and selection methods are too narrow.

Source: Adapted from an article in *Gulf News*, 4 February 2014
http://gulfnews.com

Questions

1 Explain why some job applicants may not apply for jobs using company websites. [6]
2 Discuss the case for and against companies based in the UAE relying increasingly on their websites to recruit and select new employees. [10]

How recruitment and selection can improve a business's performance

Recruiting and selecting the right employees can improve the quality of a business's workforce. For example, appointing employees with the following types of skills can allow the business to meet the needs of its customers more effectively.

- **Innovative employees** Such employees can introduce new ideas into the business either in relation to the way that production is carried out or new ideas for products. They may bring knowledge and experience from other businesses.
- **Information technology skills** Most businesses use information technology in some way within the business – perhaps to monitor inventory or to collect information on customer preferences.
- **Customer service skills** Dealing effectively with customers and responding to their needs (and complaints) is an important element of successful business performance. Customers who are dissatisfied may move to other businesses and can also act as a source of adverse publicity for the business.

There are obviously many other skills that new employees can bring into a business. For many businesses, and especially those in the services sector, the quality of the workforce is a crucial element in its competitiveness. Some businesses base their advertising on the job-related skills that their employees possess. For example, IKEA, the Swedish furniture retailer, uses the quality of its workforce in its advertising.

However, recruitment can weaken a business's performance in the short term. Bringing in new employees who may be unfamiliar with the business's procedures and customers can result in errors and work being completed more slowly than normal. Recruitment and selection are not the only ways to improve a business's performance. Many businesses opt to give employees job-related skills through a programme of training; we will consider this aspect of HRM later in the chapter.

8.3 Employment documents

There are four key documents used in the process of recruitment and selection:

- job advertisements
- job descriptions
- person specifications
- contracts of employment.

Key terms

Job descriptions list the duties and responsibilities associated with a particular job.

Person specifications outline the skills, knowledge and experience necessary to fill a given position successfully. These are also termed job specifications.

A **contract of employment** is a legal agreement between an employer and an employee setting forth the terms and conditions of the employment arrangement.

Job advertisements

The start of recruitment is likely to be drawing up an advert for the job that is vacant. This advert could be placed in newspapers or magazines or on the internet. The advert needs to be targeted so as to attract suitable applicants while dissuading unsuitable candidates from applying. For example, if an international airline such as Pakistan International Airlines was recruiting a senior manager it may advertise the vacancy globally. In contrast, a retailer seeking to advertise a vacancy for a shop assistant would be more likely to advertise the job in a local newspaper. In part the choice of where to advertise a job will also be determined by cost; generally businesses are willing to spend more heavily on recruiting senior employees.

An effective job advertisement should contain sufficient information to attract and engage potential employees, but not too much so as to discourage them from applying. Figure 8.4 contains a checklist of possible information to include in a job advertisement.

✔ Job title

✔ Location of job

✔ Brief description of business, its products and markets

✔ Outline of job role

✔ Any special features of the job such as part-time or flexible hours

✔ Some indication of qualifications and experience required

✔ Salary or salary guide

✔ Other reward details such as a company car

✔ Explanation of how to apply and the recruitment process

✔ Contact details for the business

Figure 8.4 A checklist for writing job advertisements

United Nations Development Programme

The United Nations Development Programme (UNDP) and the Government of Singapore are establishing a Global Center for Public Service Excellence in Singapore. UNDP is recruiting a Director to head the Center, which is expected to be fully operational in the final quarter of 2012.

The Center will be (a) a hub for cutting-edge research, knowledge and dissemination on public services and (b) a convener of the best of experiences, case evidence and thought-leaders to exchange ideas, share experiences and articulate the same for a wider audience.

The Director should be a recognized expert in public services, covering areas of public sector management, institutional capacity development, public administration reform, and state–citizen interface platforms and processes. The individual should be an energetic leader capable of providing vision and operational dynamism as the overall manager of the Center, a convener of people; generator of ideas, and able to liaise on behalf of UNDP with peers and senior government officials around the world. The individual will be the public face of the Center, able to communicate effectively and build partnerships and alliances.

The Director will be based in Singapore, and will report to the Co-Chairs from UNDP and the Government of Singapore. S/he will maintain substantive and management relationships with UNDP's Bureau for Development Policy, UNDP's Regional Bureau for Asia and the Pacific, and the Special Unit for South–South Cooperation as the principal stakeholders of the Center from the United Nations System. The Director is expected to assume duties in Singapore by early January 2013.

More details about the job and terms of engagement are available at:
http://jobs.undp.org/cj_view_job.cfm?cur_job_id=32440
The closing date for applications is 30 September 2012

Figure 8.5 A job advertisement for the United Nations

Source: *The Economist*, 15 September 2012

Question

Do you consider Figure 8.5 to be an effective job advert?

Job descriptions

The next stage entails preparing **job descriptions**. These relate to the position rather than the person. Typically, job descriptions might contain the following information:

- the title of the post
- employment conditions
- some idea of tasks and duties
- the key aims and responsibilities of the job
- where the job fits into the organisation.

A job description is likely to form the basis of the contract of employment, which we consider below. It also offers other important information to employers and employees.

- It helps employers by allowing them to consider exactly what should make up the job and how this job relates to others within the organisation. It also can be used to judge performance of an employee at some point following their appointment. Employees can be set targets based on the information included in the job decription. During an interview, the job description might form the basis for the interviewer's questions.
- It provides potential employees with essential information to help them to decide whether or not to apply for a job. For example, the descriptions of tasks and duties will help them to decide whether they would enjoy the role.

Person specifications

Person or **job specifications** set out the qualifications and qualities required in an employee. They relate to the employee whereas job descriptions relate to the job. They include:

- educational and professional qualifications required
- character and personality needed
- skills and experience wanted.

Candidates' applications should be compared against the person specification and those applicants having the 'best fit' should be invited to interview or other selection procedure. This document, therefore, plays a vital role in helping an organisation decide which of the applicants for a post should be invitied to interview or other selection procedure.

Contracts of employment

A **contract of employment** is a legal agreement between an employer and an employee setting forth the terms and conditions of the employment arrangement. It is a legally binding agreement designed to protect the rights of employers and employees. In the UK the Employment Rights Act requires employers hiring workers for more than a month to issue a contract of employment. A contract does not have to be issued immediately an employee starts work, but its conditions are in force from the time an employee commences employment. Employees' contracts of employment may be verbal, implied (for example, through previous practice) or written, though the latter is more common and preferable in many ways.

The laws relating to contracts of employment vary between countries. Here we refer to those that apply within the UK.

A contract of employment in the UK should contain the following information.

1. The employee's and employer's names.
2. Date when employment began.
3. The scale (and rate) at which the employee will be paid and the frequency of payment.
4. The employee's usual hours of work.
5. The employee's entitlement to holidays – how many days and whether they can only be taken at certain times of the year.
6. Rules relating to absences due to sickness or injury, including sick pay conditions
7. The employee's right to a pension (if any) and employer's and employee's contributions.

8 The notice from either side to terminate the contract of employment. This states the period of time that must elapse between the employee stating their intention to leave the job and doing so. Similarly it may record the time period to be given to employees before making them redundant or dismissing them.

9 The job title and a summary of duties.

10 The location or locations of the work.

11 Details of any trade union agreements relating to the job.

12 Disciplinary procedures. This sets out the rules establishing standards of conduct at work and how the employer may respond to any breach of these rules.

13 Grievance procedures. This will state how an employee can make a complaint against other staff or their treatment at work.

A contract of employment may include implied terms which are not directly stated. Examples of implied terms include:

● employees not stealing from employers
● employers providing a safe and healthy working environment
● employers meeting legal requirements such as giving a minimum of 28 days' paid holidays
● employees should have essential qualities and qualifications to carry out the job, for example lorry drivers should have a relevant category of driving licence.

Case Study

Protests against 'precarious work'

Working for major employers while being employed by an agency has become common across the globe. Instead of employing people in permanent positions with clear and fair contracts of employment, many large corporations rely on agencies to supply workers. This approach to employment is used in many industries, from transport to the manufacture of consumer electronics. The use of agency workers minimises obligations on the large corporations to offer job security or decent working conditions.

A new global union coalition, the Geneva-based IndustriALL (www.industriall-union.org/home), has initiated a movement to combat this growing method of employment. The worldwide revenue earned by companies offering agency labour services to employers rose from $103 billion in 1996 to $203 billion in 2009. Businesses that use the services of these labour agencies benefit from a regular supply of employees (who can be dismissed at short notice) without the legal obligations that would result from providing a permanent contract of employment.

IndustriALL's report revealed some surprising statistics:

● In Spain more than 5 per cent of all jobs are provided through agencies.
● More than 55 per cent of the workers employed in Mexico's electronics industry are agency workers.
● Approximately 60 million Chinese workers are provided to businesses by agencies.

Questions

1 Explain the differences between agency labour and full-time employees. [6]

2 Evaluate the extent to which multinational businesses may be disadvantaged by employing agency labour in this way. [10]

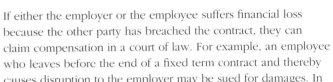

If either the employer or the employee suffers financial loss because the other party has breached the contract, they can claim compensation in a court of law. For example, an employee who leaves before the end of a fixed term contract and thereby causes disruption to the employer may be sued for damages. In many cases in the UK an employee may take an employer to an Employment Tribunal to settle a certain range of disputes relating to employment.

Employment tribunals

Employment tribunals in the UK hear claims about matters to do with employment. These may include unfair dismissal, redundancy payments and discrimination. Employment tribunals are similar to law courts, but are less formal. No one in an employment tribunal wears a wig or gown. Almost all hearings are open to the public, and evidence is given under oath or affirmation.

8.4 Disciplinary procedures, redundancy and dismissal

It is only possible for an employer to legally terminate the employment of a worker for specific reasons and having followed certain procedures. It may be that the employer takes disciplinary action against an employee; this may result in the employee leaving the business's employment. Similarly, employment may be ended as a result of redundancy or dismissal. We shall examine each of these situations in turn.

Key terms

Redundancies take place when an employee is dismissed because a job no longer exists.

A **dismissal** occurs when an employer terminates the employee's contract.

Disciplinary procedures state what behaviour is unacceptable in the workplace and what action will be taken if the rules are broken.

Disciplinary procedures

Most businesses in the UK have a set of **disciplinary procedures** to follow if they have concerns about the standard of an employee's work, their conduct or absences. Disciplinary procedures are a set way for an employer to deal with disciplinary issues. If an employer does not follow a suitable set of disciplinary procedures it may result in the employer having to pay higher levels of compensation to an employee who has been treated unfairly.

What should disciplinary procedures cover?

Matters to be covered by disciplinary rules will vary according to the type of business and the products it produces. However, the following issues may be included in the disciplinary rules of many businesses:

- timekeeping
- absence
- health and safety
- improper use of organisation facilities
- discrimination, bullying and harassment

- inappropriate personal appearance
- major acts of misconduct such as theft.

The law on unfair dismissal requires employers to act reasonably when dealing with disciplinary issues. What is classed as reasonable or unreasonable behaviour will depend on the circumstances of each case.

As shown in Figure 8.6, disciplinary procedures have to follow clear stages. The UK government advises employers to follow procedures such as those set out in the figure. Any employer failing to do so will be disadvantaged in any court case that arises from an incomplete or incorrect set of disciplinary procedures. Employers are advised to attempt to resolve disciplinary issues informally, without invoking the formal procedures whenever possible. If this fails, following the steps set out in Figure 8.6 is essential. Employers must ensure that employees understand why the disciplinary procedures have been invoked and what action is necessary on the employee's part to rectify the situation. Employers can help to avoid the use disciplinary procedures by:

- ensuring that employees have a clear understanding of what is required of them
- setting employee targets and reviewing employee performance on a regular basis.

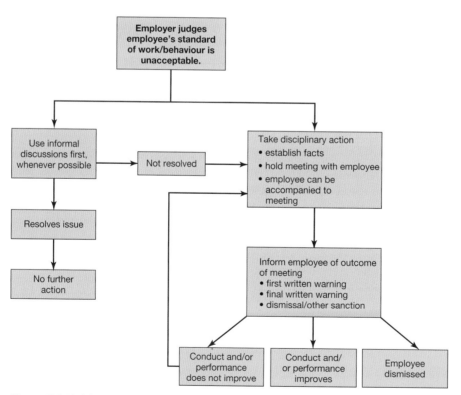

Figure 8.6 Disciplinary procedures
Source: ACAS 'Discipline and Grievances at Work'

Redundancy

What is redundancy?

Redundancy is a legal reason for an employer to dismiss an employee but it can only occur if a job no longer exists. Redundancies can take place for a variety of reasons, including:

- A business closes down and all its employees are made redundant.
- The jobs of some employees are replaced by new technology.
- A business moves some of its operations overseas and some jobs are lost as a consequence.

Case Study

Australian TV channel faces redundancies

It is estimated that the Australian television Network Ten will shed 116 jobs as a result of its poor financial performance during the last financial year. These jobs losses amount to about a third of its news staff in editorial and production.

Network Ten is one of five main free-to-air networks in Australia. Its stations can be found in cities across the country including Sydney, Brisbane and Perth. Network Ten will be seeking voluntary redundancies wherever possible although it has admitted that the jobs losses would take place across the country at each of its stations. The company hopes to replace local news staff with a centralised national news office. It is expected that this will cut the company's operating costs. This is essential after it recorded a loss of $12.9 (Australian) million in 2012.

It is believed 40 jobs will go in Sydney, 23 in Brisbane, 22 in Melbourne, 18 in Perth and 13 in Adelaide – a total of 116 positions. The jobs include journalists and producers as well as operations staff. Ten has already cut costs at the TV network by $42 million, or 6.6 per cent, over the past 12 months, more than the $30 million it forecast in April.

A trade union spokesperson, Christopher Warren, described the cuts as 'a savage blow that cuts to the heart of journalism in Australia's communities. Communities lose out when they lose their own local news. People want to know what's happening in their community,' he said.

Questions

1 Explain how trade unions may react to Network Ten's announcement of 116 redundancies. [6]
2 Evaluate the case for and against Network Ten arising from making 116 skilled employees redundant. [10]

Procedures for redundancy

If a business in the UK intends to make 20 or more employees redundant it is obliged to consult with any relevant trade union or other employee organisation at least 30 days before any redundancies occur. The employer must also consult with individual employees. If 100 or more employees are to be made redundant consultations must take place at least 90 days before the process of making people redundant can commence.

Part of this consultation may involve agreeing a procedure by which those employees who are to be made redundant are to be selected. It is likely to be beneficial to involve employees and their representatives in making such decisions. Businesses commonly seek to reduce the number of employees who have to be made redundant by:

- asking for volunteers for redundancy (these may be people who are close to retirement, for example)
- banning any overtime to maximise the number of jobs that are retained
- not replacing employees who are leaving for other reasons.

If, despite these measures, employees have to be made redundant there must be clear and agreed criteria for selecting them. The criteria for redundancy could be based upon employees' skills and experience (i.e. the business would retain the most skilled and experienced) or on absence and disciplinary performance (those with the best records keeping their jobs). Employees who are selected for redundancy must be given between one and twelve weeks' notice of their impending redundancy depending on how long they have been employed by the business.

Redundancy pay

Employees who have been continuously employed by the business for two years and who are made redundant due to the closure of the business or reduced need for employees are entitled to compensation in the form of redundancy payments. The calculation for statutory redundancy pay is:

- half a week's pay for each full year of service where the employee is aged under 22
- one week's pay for each full year of service where the employee is aged between 22 and 41
- one and a half week's pay for each full year of service where the employee is 41 or over.

The maximum number of years that can be taken into account in calculating redundancy pay is 20 years. Some employers may choose to pay higher levels of redundancy pay.

Many employers will have a set of redundancy guidelines with which they will comply to ensure that they do not break any employment laws relating to the process of redundancy.

Dismissal

Dismissal takes place when an employer terminates an employee's contract of employment. We saw above that redundancy is one reason for dismissal. Other reasons for dismissal include:

- when employees are unable to do their jobs properly, perhaps because they do not have the necessary skills or qualifications to be competent
- as a result of persistent or long-term illness (but not because of a person's disability)
- for 'gross misconduct' – theft or violence towards colleagues or customers may be considered gross misconduct
- a 'substantial reason' such as not agreeing to reasonable changes in employment terms or if an employee is given a prison sentence.

Employees should receive an explanation in writing of the reason for their dismissal within 14 days of it happening. Employees may also be entitled to receive up to 12 weeks' notice of dismissal depending upon how long they have been employed by the business.

Study tip

Do make sure that you distinguish between redundancy and dismissal. Redundancy is just one of the reasons why a business can dismiss employees fairly and legally. Dismissal is a more general term.

8.5 Training

Key term

Training is a process whereby an individual acquires job-related skills and knowledge.

Training can help employees to develop and improve their performance at work. Improvements in the performance of a business's labour force can assist the organisation in achieving its objectives. Training can result in higher levels of productivity or fewer faulty products. Both factors can help businesses to reduce their costs.

Almost all employees receive training at some point during their working lives. For example, they may receive training when commencing a new job. This is known as induction training and is intended to introduce an employee to the business.

Induction training may provide employees with information on the following:

- important policies such as health and safety, and disciplinary procedures
- the layout of the factory or office
- their new colleagues
- the basic duties of the job.

Induction training enables a new recruit to become more productive quickly. It can prevent costly errors resulting from employee ignorance and make a new employee feel welcome, thereby reducing labour turnover.

Case Study

Center Parcs

Figure 8.7 Center Parcs is a business that values its employees

Center Parcs opened its first UK village at Sherwood Forest in July 1987, offering short break holidays on a year round basis. Since then it has expanded its operations, opening three further holiday villages in the UK, with a fifth village opening in 2014.

Each UK holiday village is set in a forest environment, typically 400 acres (162 hectares) in size, and provides high quality accommodation in fully equipped villas, apartments and lodges, which are set among trees and streams. Each village offers an extensive range of sports and leisure activities plus numerous restaurants, bars and retail outlets and an Aqua Sana spa facility. Woodland, water and a natural healthy environment are the essential elements of a Center Parcs break.

The company values its staff and has the following statement on its UK website:

'We recognise that our staff are our most important asset and we continue to deliver initiatives to support and develop Center Parcs employees, whatever position they hold in the company.'

Source: www.centerparcs.co.uk

Questions

1 Explain the possible reasons why Center Parcs might have such a clear and highly prominent statement on its website. [6]
2 Evaluate the benefits of effective systems of training to Center Parcs which is expanding. [10]

Types of training

In addition to induction training, which we discussed earlier, training can be divided into two main categories.

Off-the-job training

This involves training outside the workplace, either at a college, university, or some other training agency. Off-the-job training can take the form of external courses such as lectures and seminars, self-study or open learning.

On-the-job training

This form of training does not require the employee to leave the workplace. He or she learns from experienced employees through observation and work shadowing. The trainee may work through instruction manuals or receive guidance from senior employees.

The case for and against training

Some businesses invest heavily in training, often regarding it as a core element of their human resource management. Some managers value it highly because they believe it improves employee attitude, motivation and performance. Others are less eager to spend money in this way, taking the view that 'if they cannot do the job already, why are we paying them?' Managers may be especially suspicious of off-the-job training, which can be very expensive.

In spite of being expensive, and sometimes disruptive, training does offer organisations a number of benefits. The costs and benefits of training are summarised in Table 8.2.

Table 8.2 The costs and benefits of training

Costs	Benefits
Training uses up valuable resources that could be utilised elsewhere in the organisation.	Training can improve employee performance and hence the competitive position of the business.
Training means that employees are unavailable to the organisation for a period of time.	Training should improve employee motivation and productivity.
Employees, once trained, often leave for better jobs.	Training is a core component of HRM and assists organisations in achieving strategic objectives.
Some managers avoid training their staff as it can lessen the degree of control they have over their subordinates.	A reputation for training will assist organisations in attracting and retaining high quality employees.

Factors influencing investment in training

It is more likely that firms will be willing to invest in training for employees if the market in which the firm operates is subject to intense competition. For example, firms may operate extensive training in an attempt to improve rates of productivity and gain a competitive advantage. Businesses manufacturing motor vehicles have tended to invest more heavily in training over recent years for these reasons. When products are similar, price is often the basis of competition and, in such circumstances, minimising costs is vital. A key part of this is making sure that labour is as productive as possible.

Investment in training is more likely if there are few employees in the labour market with the necessary skills and experience. This can result in a market where firms tend to 'headhunt' employees from rivals, rather than investing in training themselves. In a situation of scarcity, there is often no alternative to implementing training.

Managers who value techniques such as delegation and teamworking will be more likely to engage in large-scale training. Partly, this is a question of philosophy: democratic and communicative managers are more likely to value employees and therefore training. However, there are practical reasons why training will be needed in these circumstances. Businesses cannot expect to benefit from granting employees greater authority without preparing them for their change of role.

The financial position of a business may shape its attitude to training, certainly in the short term. There is some evidence that training is the first victim of the economy moving into a recession. If the firm is struggling to generate sufficient profits to satisfy its owners, it may reduce or eliminate training in an attempt to boost profitability.

It is easy to say that these are the benefits of training and these are the drawbacks. But the importance of these arguments to an individual firm will depend upon the circumstances of the firm. Training might be important in the long term, for example, but cutting costs to increase profits could be a more immediate goal. The objectives of the owners of the business could also be important. In relatively small firms it may be the case that owners wish to maximise short-term profits and not to seek growth. Such objectives may dampen the need to continuously improve employee performance and result in training being postponed or abandoned.

8.6 Employee welfare and morale

At its most basic, every employer is required by law to provide essential amenities such as toilets, sinks and clean drinking water for employees. Most employees also hope to find additional facilities such as a cloakroom and a clean and hygienic seating area for workers to use during meal breaks. There should be facilities nearby for heating food or water for hot drinks.

A 'good' employer who is concerned about **employee welfare** may also consider other issues besides the physical working environment. Such employers will seek to develop their employees as fully as possible to improve their performance at work. In part this may be achieved by a developmental **appraisal** system. Developmental appraisal measures an employee's performance with the aim of offering training to correct any shortcomings or to achieve further improvement. Businesses and employees can benefit from appraisal systems, especially those that develop employees' skills. Such appraisal systems can encourage employees to take actions intended to help the business achieve its objectives and can improve relationships between manager and subordinate alongside employee performance. Developmental appraisal systems can improve employee behaviour, enhancing productivity. Supporters of appraisal systems also argue that they can help in identifying staff training needs and ensuring that training undertaken is relevant to the needs of the individual and the organisation.

Key terms

Employee welfare is a broad term covering a wide range of facilities that are essential for the well-being of a business's employees.

Appraisal is the process of considering and evaluating the performance of an individual employee.

HRM, welfare and employee morale

Human resource management can play a central role in developing effective appraisal systems as well as improving the physical environment within which employees work. Recruiting people with the intention of developing their skills and improving their performance throughout a long-term relationship is at the heart of what is called 'soft' human resource management. Such an approach to HRM may well have a developmental appraisal system at its heart as well as a clear appreciation of the benefits to the business of providing good facilities for employees.

Case Study

Working at Google

Here's a taste of what we offer:

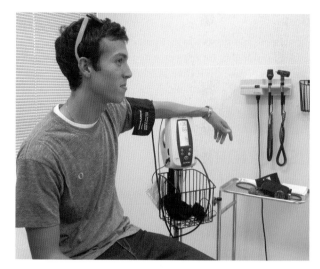

Figure 8.8 Stay healthy, save time

On-site physicians and nurses, convenient medical services, and comprehensive health care coverage help keep you healthy and happy. (Varies by location.)

Figure 8.9 Travel without worries

Googlers and their families are covered with travel insurance and emergency assistance, even on personal vacations.

Figure 8.10 More time with your baby

New parents get time off and some extra spending money to help them welcome their new bundle of joy.

Figure 8.11 Never stop learning

We'll reimburse you for classes or degree programs that help you with what you do.

Figure 8.12 Legal aid for less

Googlers get legal advice at no cost and, in the US, also get common legal services at a generous group discount.

Source: www.google.com

Questions

1 Explain how Google's employees might benefit from the company's commitment to continuous learning. [6]
2 Discuss the benefits Google might receive from treating its employees in this way. [10]

Work–life balance is a topic of increasing importance for employers as well as employees. The term work-life balance refers to the time an employee spends on work-related duties compared with time spent on non-work activities such as activities with his or her family.

Some governments have become concerned about the possible adverse implications for the health of employees and for rates of labour productivity of excessive working hours. The European Union has implemented a working time directive intended to limit working hours to a maximum of 48 per week, although exceptions can be made.

Case Study

International working hours

Despite concerns about the work–life balance of many employees, average working hours in many countries have

declined since 2000, as shown in Table 8.3 below. Many countries have laws to restrict the number of hours people may work, though these are not always enforced. For example, China has passed legislation to create a 44-hour maximum normal working week with overtime payments for hours beyond this. However, surveys suggest that this limit is ignored by many employers.

A survey released in December 2013 reported that Foxconn, a major manufacturer in China which supplies Apple among other businesses, had made progress towards improving its working conditions, but much room for improvement remained.

The group said Foxconn had constructed additional exits and restrooms at the three facilities, and had revised its policies to limit overtime hours to 36 per month and three per day.

But the report found that workers at one of the factories had worked more than 60 hours a week on numerous occasions between March and October of this year, and that all three had exceeded the monthly overtime limit.

Questions

1 Explain why many governments have passed laws to impose limits on the number of hours employees may work each week. [6]
2 Evaluate the case for and against Foxconn requiring its employees to work very long hours each week. [10]

Research has shown that long work hours can damage the health of employees, endanger their safety at work and increase levels of stress. The proportion of employees working more than 50 hours per week is not very large in the OECD's 34 member countries. Turkey has the highest percentage of people working very long hours (46 per cent), followed by Mexico with nearly 29 per cent. Overall, men spend more hours in paid employment and the percentage of male employees working very long hours across OECD countries is 12 per cent, compared with less than 5 per cent for women.

Table 8.3 Weekly working hours in a selection of OECD countries, 2000 and 2012 ·

Country	2000	2012
Australia	34.2	33.2
Chile	43.5	39.0
Mexico	44.4	42.8
Spain	33.3	32.4
Turkey	37.3	35.7
Average of OECD members	35.5	33.9

Source: Adapted from OECD, http://www.oecd-ilibrary.org

Many employers are concerned about long working hours and their impact on the work–life balance of the people who work for them. Long working hours can harm the performance of employees which may have a significant impact on the performance of the business itself.

Some major businesses have implemented policies designed to relieve the pressure on employees and to help them to achieve a sensible balance between work and non-work activities. The Colgate-Palmolive company is an American multinational manufacturer of consumer products such as soaps and detergents. It has acquired a reputation for employment practices that set realistic expectations for employees and it encourages the development of time management skills. Colgate-Palmolive also offers its employees the chance to work flexible hours and to telecommute. It provides nearby back-up childcare facilities to assist parents who work at home. As a result, Colgate-Palmolive has a high rate of employee retention, which offers it a range of benefits.

Policies for diversity and equality

Although the terms 'diversity' and 'equality' are frequently used together, and sometimes interchangeably, they have different meanings.

Diversity, in an employment context, refers to recognising the differences between individual employees and also the differences that may exist between different groups of employees. Businesses that operate diversity policies will treat people as individuals and will value the benefits that diverse individuals and groups in a workplace may offer to a business. Employee diversity could be based upon gender, race and ethnicity, disability, religion, sexuality, class and age.

In contrast, policies related to equality are intended to create a fairer society where all employees can contribute and fulfil their potential. One key aspect of this is to operate policies that allow all employees the opportunity to reach senior positions in a business, irrespective of their age, gender, ethnicity or sexual orientation. This is considered necessary as many groups such as women and ethnic minorities are under-represented in senior positions in businesses. This can mean that the skills and abilities of such employees are wasted.

A number of governments have enacted employment legislation to ensure that businesses design and implement policies for diversity and equality. For example, the UK government passed the Equalities Act in 2010. This offered protection to employees on the grounds of:

- direct and indirect discrimination
- harassment
- victimisation.

The Act identifies a number of 'protected characteristics'. These are:

- age
- disability
- gender reassignment
- marriage and civil partnership
- pregnancy and maternity
- race
- religion or belief
- gender
- sexual orientation.

The effect of legislation of this type is to encourage businesses to design and implement policies intended to encourage diversity and to promote equality. In the UK, businesses are offered advice on implementing policies for diversity and equality by ACAS (the Advisory, Conciliation and Arbitration Service). ACAS advises that a diversity and equality policy should include the following:

- a statement by the business's to encourage, value and manage diversity
- the business's commitment to providing equality for all
- the business's wish to attain a workforce that is representative of the communities from which it is drawn to secure the widest pool of talent possible.

Operating an effective policy for equality and diversity offers benefits to businesses. Drawing on all people within the local community when recruiting offers the best opportunity to employ the most talented employees, which will enhance the performance of the business. Similarly, promoting the most able employee, regardless of personal characteristics, secures the greatest level of talent for the business. Any other approach is likely to harm the business.

The elements of a policy designed to promote diversity can also bring benefit to the business. A diverse workforce may allow the business to understand the needs of a market which may be comprised of diverse consumers. This will assist the organisation in meeting the needs of its consumers more effectively. A business that acquires a reputation for operating an effective diversity and equality policy may become an attractive employer to potential employees. This process is called employer branding and can help businesses to attract highly talented and skilled employees, whatever their personal characteristics.

Case Study

Equality and diversity at the University of Cambridge

The University of Cambridge is one of the best known universities in the world. It was founded in 1209 and has over 9000 staff and 18000 students from countries throughout the world.

The University of Cambridge is committed in its pursuit of academic excellence to equality of opportunity and to a proactive and inclusive approach to equality, which supports and encourages all under-represented groups, promotes an inclusive culture, and values diversity.

The commitment applies to all protected groups and is underpinned by the University's Equal Opportunities Policy and Combined Equality Scheme (CES).

A new version of the University's E&D Essential online training module includes an introduction from the Vice-Chancellor and aims to help staff understand the main principles of equality and diversity, its impacts on the University and how members of staff and students can access support and other resources.

The module, which can be accessed on a variety of platforms, including tablets and laptops, is Cambridge-specific and takes about 30 minutes to complete.

Source: Adapted from the website of the University of Cambridge, www.cam.ac.uk

Questions

1 Explain how training might assist the University to implement its Equality and Diversity policy. [6]

2 To what extent do the benefits of the University of Cambridge's Equality and Diversity policy outweigh its costs? [10]

Firms take positive decisions on welfare and training because they have the potential to improve the morale and motivation of employees. We saw in Chapter 7 that there are different views on what motivates employees. Some writers on motivation argue that physical faculties are important or, as Herzberg believed, their absence has the power to demotivate employees. Many motivational theorists would argue that providing training and allowing employees to develop themselves and to fulfil their potential are powerful motivators. Maslow termed this 'self-actualisation' and argued that it was the highest form of motivation available to employers.

Test your learning

Short answer questions

1 a Define the term human resource management. [2]

   b State **three** activities that form part of human resource management. [3]

2 Explain the possible benefits to a business of an effective system of human resource management. [5]

3 a Define the term workforce plan. [2]

   b State **three** factors that might influence the workforce plan of an international retailer. [3]

4 a State **two** factors that might affect the level of labour turnover in a business. [2]

   b A business has 9500 employees. During the year 190 leave its employment. What is its rate of labour turnover? [3]

5 a Distinguish between recruitment and selection. [3]

   b State **two** methods of selection. [2]

6 a Distinguish between internal and external recruitment. [3]

   b Define the term job description. [2]

7 a State **three** items that might be included in a contract of employment. [3]

   b Define the term person specification. [2]

8 Explain the benefits a business might receive from preparing and using a person specification. [5]

9 a Distinguish between redundancy and dismissal. [3]

   b State **two** reasons why an employee may be made redundant. [2]

10 Explain why businesses invest in training despite its high cost. [5]

Data response question

The company behind the soaps and shampoos in hotel bathrooms

Cannell Ltd manufactures the soaps, shampoos and other complimentary toiletries that are available in hotel bathrooms. The company operates two factories with a combined workforce of 380, and labour costs are 47 per cent of its total costs. The company is relatively small and, selling throughout Europe, faces intense price competition from larger rivals. Recently the company has had to reduce its prices to retain some major customers. Profitability has declined in recent years – last year it fell by 14.5 per cent. The company has a highly skilled workforce although its labour turnover figure rose to 23.4 per cent last year from 14.9 per cent the previous year.

Cannell Ltd's managing director believes strongly in the importance of training, including induction training. He has proposed doubling the company's expenditure on training. Employees work in teams and the company updates its production line technology whenever it can afford to do so. The company has never had to use redundancy to manage its workforce.

Questions

1 Explain the terms:

   a induction training [3]

   b redundancy. [3]

2 Briefly analyse why Cannell Ltd should be concerned about its rate of labour turnover. [6]

3 Discuss whether or not the managing director is correct to argue that the company should double its spending on training. [10]

Essay question

Discuss the extent to which recruitment is always the most important element of human resource management. [20]

Past paper questions

1 a Outline the main factors which a manager of a large hotel might consider when carrying out manpower planning. [8]

b Discuss the extent to which the hotel manager might improve workers' motivation by re-designing their jobs. [12]

Cambridge International AS and A Level Business Studies
9707 Paper 1 Q5 May/June 2007

2 Read the Cheapo Air case study on page 211 and then answer the following question.

Discuss the human resource management (HRM) issues that would arise if Cheapo Air did switch from low cost flights to business flights. [10]

Cambridge International AS and A Level Business Studies
9707 Paper 21 Q2d May/June 2009

9 What is marketing?

Chapter overview

In this chapter we examine:
- the role of marketing and its relationship with other business activities
- the factors influencing supply and demand
- the features of different markets
- the difference between producer and consumer markets
- the difference between niche and mass markets
- different methods of segmenting markets.

Figure 9.1 Integrated business functions: for the business to succeed, the activities of the different business functions must be integrated effectively

> **Key term**
>
> **Marketing** is the process of identifying, anticipating and satisfying the needs of customers in a mutually beneficial exchange process.

9.1 The role of marketing and its relationship with other business activities

All organisations need customers. The purpose of all businesses is to understand and provide the goods and services that customers want. Indeed, according to Peter Drucker, a very influential management writer, there is only one valid purpose for a business, which is 'to create a customer'.

Marketing is the function of the business that is responsible for understanding customer needs and developing the right products, setting the right price and promoting and distributing products in the right way. Marketing provides the link between the customer and the production function of the business. Marketing ensures that what is being provided is actually wanted and needed, i.e. it is something of value, and communicates this and makes the product available to customers.

The importance of marketing

Effective **marketing** occurs when a firm fully understands the requirements of its customers and is able to meet these needs successfully. The marketing function helps the organisation to provide a product that the customer wants, is affordable, is perceived as good value and that leaves the customer and the organisation itself satisfied with the transaction.

Marketing is an ongoing process because:
- customers' needs change over time (e.g. the developing interest in health issues has increased demand for health clubs and reduced demand for high-fat foods)
- the business environment can change; for example, with new laws, changes in technology or the economic climate
- competitors enter the market with their own offerings and so businesses must respond to this
- a firm's own strengths change and develop.

Effective marketing will, therefore, change over time to ensure there remains a good match between customers' needs and the business's own strengths. Effective marketing will lead to high levels of customer satisfaction, which means that customers:
- are more likely to come back and buy more
- are more likely to tell their friends to come and try the products
- may be more willing to try new products launched by the business
- may become loyal to the product and less likely to switch to competitors.

Hugh Davidson

Hugh Davidson is a marketing writer who has advised many large companies around the world. One of his books is called *Offensive Marketing*. According to Davidson, 'Offensive marketing involves every employee in building superior customer value very efficiently for above average profits.' This is an interesting definition of marketing in that it highlights that:

- everyone is involved in marketing because everyone affects the quality of the service and the customer's impression of the product
- it is important to develop value for money that is better than your competitors', not just the same
- it is important to use resources efficiently (i.e. you must think about how much you spend on marketing and measure the returns from different types of spending)
- the aim is not just to do well but to achieve profits that are above average – the mark of a truly successful business.

Questions

1 Explain in your own words what is meant by 'offensive marketing'. [6]
2 Discuss the possible benefits of an offensive marketing approach. [10]

Defining marketing

A formal definition of marketing should include the following features:

- It is an exchange process – that is, it is two way. The business offers the customer a good or service and in return receives something, usually payment.
- It is mutually beneficial because both sides should gain from the exchange. Customers should be satisfied with the product and firms should make a profit (assuming that the firm is a profit-making organisation). Firms are unlikely to give away products for nothing.
- It aims to identify and anticipate customer needs. Entrepreneurs need to understand their customers to know what to offer them. However, it is not always enough just to identify customers' needs: in fact, sometimes the customers may not know themselves what their needs and wants are. In some markets, such as fashion and film, firms have to anticipate what customers will want in the future. They have to predict trends even before most customers know what these trends will be.
- It aims to delight customers. Nowadays satisfying customers may not be enough, as many other firms are also doing this. It's much better to delight the customer, so that they are more than satisfied and more likely to buy from you.

The purpose of marketing is to match the abilities and strengths of the business to the needs of the market. A business aims to supply goods and services that customers want and that will generate suitable rewards for the organisation.

Marketing involves a whole range of activities, including finding out what customers want, developing new products, packaging and promoting the products, and setting the price. All these activities are aimed at developing and providing goods and services which will satisfy the customer (so he or she will buy it), and make a profit for the firm.

The more effective the marketing, the better the value provided for customers and the greater the rewards the business should be able to make.

Marketing and other functions

The purpose of marketing is to ensure that the organisation meets the customers' needs in the present and in the future. Marketing is therefore a dynamic process. To be effective it must work with the other functions of the business to influence:

- what is produced, i.e. the precise nature of the firm's offerings; for example, in terms of design, features and quality
- how many are produced – marketing must estimate likely sales, which in turn will influence the quantity of goods and services the business must be able to provide
- the range of products offered (e.g. how extensive the menu or wine list should be in a restaurant; how many different models should be displayed in a store)
- the price at which products are sold; this therefore determines how much can be spent on materials and the transformation process if a profit is to be made.

Marketing will discuss and negotiate with:

- operations over how much can be produced, what benefits can be offered and what the costs will be
- finance over the amount that can be spent on developing, launching and promoting the product or service
- human resources over the number and skills of staff required.

There may be, for example, occasions when the business does not have the money, skills or capacity to develop a product.

Marketing objectives and corporate objectives

Marketing objectives are the targets set for the marketing function. Typically these include:

- **Sales targets** These might be set in terms of sales volumes or value. Specific targets may be set for the business as a whole and also for specific products or particular regions.
- **Market share** Increasing sales may not in themselves be particularly impressive if the market as a whole is growing fast and competitors' sales are increasing faster than yours. This is why a business may set targets in terms of the share of the market. Market share measures the sales of one product or business as a percentage of the total sales in the market.

A business may set a target such as its sales being 5 per cent of the market in the next year.

- **Brand awareness** A business may want to increase people's awareness of its brand relative to the competition.

The marketing objectives will be linked to the overall objectives of the business – the corporate objective. For example, if the business has a target of growth, the marketing department may have to increase sales. If the corporate target is to boost the profits of the business, the marketing team might focus on sales of the most profitable products and place less emphasis on others that sell but are not necessarily as profitable.

Key terms

A **marketing objective** is a marketing target for the business setting out what it wants to achieve and when.

A **marketing strategy** is a marketing plan to achieve the marketing objective.

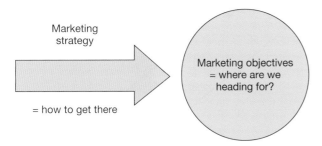

Figure 9.2 Marketing objectives and strategy

Case Study

BAT in Russia

BAT Russia facts

- Size of market: **349 billion cigarettes**
- BAT market share: **22%**
- Capital city: Moscow
- Population: **142 million**
- Language: Russian
- BAT employees: **3600**

British American Tobacco Russia is one of the leaders of the Russian tobacco market with a market share of over 20 per cent.

Our trade operations cover 673 cities around Russia. Our total sales volume in 2007 reached approximately 80 billion cigarettes.

BAT Russia's brand portfolio includes famous international and local brands such as DUNHILL, Kent, Vogue, Rothmans, Lucky Strike, Pall Mall, Viceroy, Yava Gold, Alliance, Yava.

Our company is one of the main contributors into the global business of British American Tobacco.

Most of our cigarette brands sold in the Russian market are produced in one of the three Russian factories, namely

BAT-Yava in Moscow, BAT-SPb in St Petersburg and BAT-STF in Saratov.

BAT Russia seeks to become the leader of the Russian tobacco market in every dimension. We do not limit the definition of leadership to the first place on the market in terms of sales volume and value, as it also refers to the company reputation and working conditions for employees.

Source: BAT

Questions

1 Explain why BAT may be targeting the Russian market. [6]
2 Discuss the possible reasons why BAT has several different brands in Russia. [10]

Study tip

Remember that marketing is not just about making customers happy: the business also needs to meet its objectives so think about issues such as the costs of any marketing action compared to its likely returns. Also, bear in mind what the business can actually deliver given its capacity, people and other resources.

9.2 Supply and demand

A market is made up of buyers and sellers. The sellers supply the product and the buyers demand it. If markets are allowed to work without government intervention and if they are competitive with many different sellers then the quantity produced and the price in the market will be determined by the forces of supply and demand. This can be shown graphically.

A supply curve shows how much producers are willing and able to supply at each and every price with all other factors constant. It is usually upward sloping because as the price increases producers are more willing and able to supply more; they are more willing because of the higher price and more able because the higher price means they can produce more even if their costs are slightly higher.

The supply of a product will depend on:

- the number of firms producing – with more firms supply may increase
- the time period – over time more firms can move into this market if it is attractive, which could increase supply
- technology – technological developments will increase the quantity supplied
- costs – if a business can reduce its costs; for example by using cheaper supplies or being more efficient in its operations, this means it can produce more at each price and supply can increase.

The demand curve shows how much customers are willing and able to buy at each and every price with all other factors unchanged. It is downward sloping because as the price falls customers can afford to buy more with the same income.

The demand for a product will depend on factors such as:
- the income of buyers as this will affect how much they can afford
- the price of rivals' products; if these are cheaper this is likely to reduce demand for your product
- the price of complementary products (for example if you buy a printer and print cartridges together these are complementary products); if a complement is cheaper you might buy more of it and more of your product
- marketing activities; effective marketing by a business should help increase demand for the product.

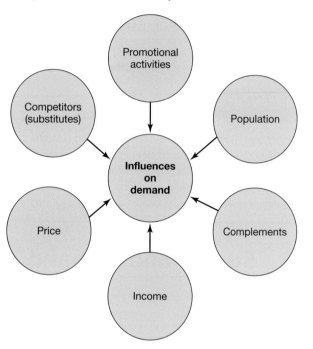

Figure 9.3 Influences on demand

Look at figure 9.4. If the price was originally at P_1 (figure 9.4a) then at this price the quantity supplied is greater than the quantity demanded – because the price is high producers want to sell more than customers want to buy. This leads to excess supply or a surplus. In a free market with no intervention the price will fall. As it does the quantity demanded increases, the quantity supplied falls until P_0 is reached. P_0q_0 is the equilibrium price and quantity; at this price the quantity demanded and supplied is equal and there is no incentive to change.

If the price was P_2 then at this low price the quantity demanded is greater than the quantity supplied and there is excess demand. This is known as a shortage. In a free market the price will increase; this increases the quantity supplied and reduces the quantity demanded until equilibrium at P_0q_0 is reached.

Of course, market conditions can change. With more income in an economy there will be more demanded of most products and so the demand curve moves to D_2 (figure 9.4b). The equilibrium is now P_3q_3; more demand leads to higher prices and output. If there is less supply in a market, perhaps because of poor crops, the supply curve would move to S_2 and equilibrium would be at P_4q_4 (figure 9.4c). Less supply in the market leads to higher prices and lower output.

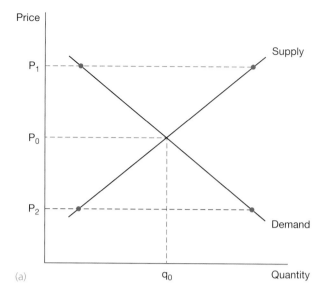

(a)

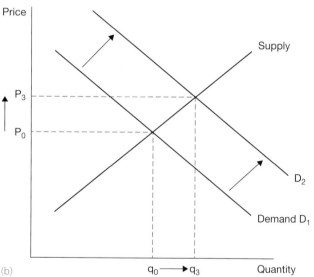

(b)

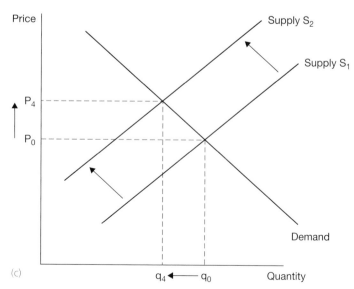

(c)

Figure 9.4 Supply and demand

Case Study

Luxury watches

Figure 9.5 Sales of Swiss watches are booming in the Middle East

Sales of luxury watches have continued to grow rapidly this year across the Emirates as Chinese tourists flock to the country's malls in search of internationally recognised brands.

Ahmed Seddiqi and Sons, one of the Middle East's largest watch companies, has seen double-digit growth in the first five months of this year over the same period last year and aims to expand across the country in response to demand.

The chief executive said that after the financial crisis people are going back to the reassuring brands and ones that are well known.

Ahmed Seddiqi has 50 stores across the United Arab Emirates, representing brands such as Rolex, Patek Philippe, AudemarsPiguet and Tag Heuer. About 152 000 visitors from China stayed in Dubai hotels last year. The Dubai Department of Tourism and Commerce Marketing said the figure for this year is expected to be at least 50 per cent greater.

According to a report released last week by the Federation of the Swiss Watch Industry, sales of Swiss watches in the UAE were 81 per cent higher in the first quarter than in the same period two years before.

The UAE and Saudi markets now account for about 6 per cent of total Swiss watch exports globally.

Questions

1 Explain two factors that might influence demand for luxury watches. [6]
2 Discuss how an increase in demand might affect retailers and producers of luxury watches. [10]

Case Study

Bordeaux

Sales of Bordeaux wine, which includes some of the most famous red wines in France, have been increasing recently but rather than French wine lovers, it is Chinese consumers who are behind this growth.

Indeed, China has become Bordeaux's largest export destination. This transformation is particularly remarkable given China's short history of mass wine consumption.

Over the past four years, some 30 French chateaux have been bought by Chinese investors, and around another 20 deals are currently in the pipeline.

This passion for French wine is part of a growing Chinese interest across Europe, seeking to satisfy domestic demand for what many Chinese consumers see as the finer things in life, such as French wines, luxury travel, foreign cars and fashionable clothes.

Bordeaux wine facts

- Vineyards total 117 500 hectares (290 000 acres)
- Annual harvest 730 million bottles (5.5 million hectolitres)
- There are 55 000 workers in the wine industry
- Grape varieties: Merlot, Cabernet Sauvignon, Cabernet Franc, Semillon, Sauvignon, Muscadelle

China, together with Hong Kong, now accounts for some 71 million bottles of Bordeaux a year.

Questions

1 Explain two factors that would influence the supply of wine from Bordeaux. [6]
2 Discuss the factors influencing the demand from China for French wine. [10]

Maths moment

Can you draw a diagram of supply and demand for wine for a given year if demand is increasing? Remember that in a given year there will only be a fixed quantity harvested whatever the weather.
Can you show what would happen if there was a good year and supply increased?

9.3 Features of markets

Markets will differ in nature. For example, they will differ in terms of:

- **Size** The size of a market can be measured in terms of the volume of sales or the value of sales. For example, there may be 20000 products sold (volume) or $100000 sold (value). If the volume of sales increases the value will also usually increase but this depends what is happening to the price. If the price falls it is possible that more units are sold but the value of sales declines.
- **The number of competitors** Some markets have many thousands of competitors – just think of how many hairdressers and cafés there are. In other markets there are relatively few providers – how many electricity companies or train companies are there, for example?
- **Growth** Some markets do not change in size very much; others grow fast; some shrink. The growth of a market is measured by the percentage change in its size over a given period. Generally businesses will prefer fast growing markets because they can all sell more. If the market is static then one firm can only sell more at the expense of another; this can lead to aggressive, competitive behaviour.

Key terms

The **market size** is the total number of items sold (this is measuring volume) or the total value of sales.

The **market share** of a business measures its sales as a percentage of the total market sales.

Maths moment

1 A business sells $20000 in a market worth $800000. What is its market share?
2 A business has a market share of 8 per cent in a market worth $400000. What are its sales?
3 A market was worth $300000 and increases in size to $360000. What is the market growth rate?
4 If a market was worth $500000 but grows by 2 per cent, what is it worth now?

☯ Consumer and producer markets

Consumer markets exist for products which are bought and consumed by the final user. For example, you buy a bar of chocolate and eat it. Consumer markets may have millions of potential buyers in them. In order to get the products to the customers, the producer may work with many intermediaries such as retailers. In producer markets the product is bought by another business. For example, its machinery is used to produce other goods. In producer markets your customers are other businesses who may have specialist buyers working for them. They will tend to be more rational in their purchasing and want to know how this product will make their own production more efficient or more effective. Think of buying a new car. When you go to the car showroom, this is the consumer market. However, to make that car the producer will have bought thousands of component parts in producer markets.

National, regional and international markets

Some products such as oil are sold on worldwide markets. There are international producers and the products are demanded all over the world. Other products tend to be more national; this means they are sold mainly or exclusively in the domestic country, such as a chain of clothes stores. Others may be traded only in the local area, such as a local taxi business or hairdressers. The markets in which a firm operates affect the likely sales, the nature of the competition and the complexity of the marketing challenge.

Customer (market) orientation vs product orientation

A customer-oriented (or market-led) business is one that bases its decisions on customers' needs. It continually monitors its environment to find out what customers want, what competitors are offering and what changes are occurring in the market. By being market-oriented, a firm should be able to ensure that the product or service it provides matches its customers' needs. If there is a high level of competition, then firms need to be market orientated to survive; if they are not, rivals will meet customer needs more effectively and reduce their sales. Any entrepreneur wanting to succeed should make sure there is demand for their product. This will usually be done via market research to try to identify the likely level of sales.

By comparison, a product-oriented (or product-led) business focuses more on what it can produce and hopes that this will fit with customer requirements. This is a very risky approach because the firm may produce something the customer does not want. If an entrepreneur assumes that because he or she likes the idea, everyone else will also like it, this is being product oriented. Not everyone thinks or behaves in the same way, so entrepreneurs must check that there is demand before starting out.

Although being product oriented is less likely to succeed than being market oriented, it can work if the customer has limited choice (for example, in some Eastern European countries, governments only allowed a few firms to produce particular products and so customers had to buy what was available). If it is lucky, the business may produce a product that people want, or in some cases people invent products that customers did not know they wanted until they arrived. However, over time, as customers find alternatives, product-oriented firms are likely to suffer.

Amazon

Table 9.1

Founded	Incorporated July 1994
Mission	To be Earth's most customer-centric company where people can find and discover anything they want to buy online.
Headquarters	Seattle, Washington, USA
Websites	We serve consumer customers through our retail websites, which include www.amazon.com, www.amazon.co.uk, www.amazon.de, www.amazon.co.jp, www.amazon.fr, www.amazon.ca, www.amazon.cn, www.amazon.it and www.amazon.es
Selection	Amazon and more than 2 million third-party sellers offer millions of unique, new, refurbished and used items in categories such as Books; Movies; Music; Video Games; Electronics & Computers; Home & Garden; Tools; Toys; Kids & Baby; Grocery; Health & Beauty; Clothing; Shoes & Jewelry; Health & Beauty; Sports & Outdoors; and Automotive & Industrial.

Questions

1 Explain what you think is meant by a customer-centric business. [6]

2 Visit the Amazon website (www.amazon.com). Discuss the ways in which Amazon might try to be the world's most customer-centric business. [10]

Problems associated with measuring market share and market growth

Measuring **market share** is not always easy. This is because the data you have on the sales in general may not be easy to collect: competitors, for example, may not want to share information. It will certainly take time and, at best, estimates of the market are likely to be a year or so out of date. While you will know your sales this month it may not be easy to compare this with other firms' sales accurately; market share data is therefore most likely to be accurate when looking backwards.

Similarly, data on **market growth** is difficult to estimate at any given moment because of the problems gathering data from all outlets and all producers. Again it is most likely to be accurate when looking backwards.

A further problem with calculating market share and market growth is actually defining the market in which a business operates. What is the market for your local bus company? Is it bus transport in your area – but how large do you define the area being considered? Or is it bus transport in the whole country? Or is it all forms of transport in your area? It is not always easy to define clearly the market a business operates within.

Market growth measures the percentage increase in growth in market sales over a given period

Implications of changes in market share and growth

A change in market share means that the sales of a business account for a greater proportion of the total sales in the market in the given period. If the market remains the same size or is growing then an increasing market share means higher sales. However, if the market is declining the market share could be increasing even if sales are falling.

When considering market share it is important to bear in mind the total market size. A small percentage of the global confectionery market is still a lot of sales!

The growth of a market shows the rate at which sales are increasing. In general, businesses might prefer faster growth to slower growth because it creates more sales opportunities. However, it is again important to bear in mind the size of the sales involved. A 1 per cent growth in the market for laptops is still a large amount of sales because the market is so big, whereas a 10 per cent growth of a very small local market might only mean additional sales of a few thousand. In well-established big markets growth may be slow but the numbers involved can still be huge.

The Chinese economy

After years of very fast growth in both sales and new products the Chinese economy is slowing down, which is worrying carmakers a little. But not too much because there is no way that the Chinese market is saturated yet: only about 3 per cent of the Chinese population owns a car currently, compared with 80 per cent in the United States. Many experts predict the Chinese market, which is already the world's largest, will require 30 million vehicles per year by 2020 – compared with 18.5 million sold last year.

But in the short term sales growth has slowed up: last year, sales grew just 2.5 per cent after growing by 35 per cent the year before. However, within the market, there are segments that are still expanding much more quickly, most notably luxury car sales that are aimed at the increasing numbers of China's super-rich people.

Competition in the mainstream Chinese market for cheaper, mass-produced cars is particularly tough as western producers such as General Motors, Ford and VW come up against domestic firms such as BYD, Geely and Chery. These Chinese carmakers are now preparing to export to, or even produce in, markets overseas.

Questions

1 Explain two ways in which car firms may compete against each other. [6]

2 Discuss the possible reasons why demand for cars in China has slowed down. [10]

9.4 Producer and consumer markets

There are different types of markets. In consumer markets the customer buys the product and it is consumed. For example, you buy food, music and clothes and then use (consume) these. However, these items will have had to be produced and that will have involved machinery, transport and technology. When you are selling products to be used in the production process such as a production line or raw materials, this is known as a producer (or an industrial) market. In this market the customer may be a professional buyer and therefore will be very interested in the technical specifications of what you are·offering, and a whole range of issues such as the payment terms, delivery times and your reliability as a supplier. Industrial buyers are professionals and may be more rational than we are when we go shopping; they are less interested in the packaging and more interested in the specifications of the products than we might be!

Table 9.2 Producer (industrial) markets and consumer markets

	Producer markets	Consumer markets
Number of buyers	Relatively small	Large
Nature of buyer	Professional	Individuals

Study tip

It is very important when answering marketing questions to think about the specific market the business operates in. It is no good simply repeating the textbook because you have to adapt your understanding for the particular market. Selling bars of chocolate may require heavy advertising; selling airplanes may require a very experienced sales team. Attractive packaging may help sell perfume but is less significant for selling tractors!

9.5 Niche versus mass marketing

Niche marketing occurs when a firm targets a specific segment of the market. For example, Aston Martin targets the luxury sports carmarket and Umbro targets the football market.

Key term

Niche marketing occurs when a business focuses on a particular (usually small) segment of the market.

By focusing on a niche, a firm can understand the specific requirements of the group and ensure its offering meets the group's needs precisely. It can tailor-make its marketing approach and avoid wasting time and money on activities that are not relevant.

Niche marketing is quite common for small businesses. This is because:

- it focuses on just one segment of the market and therefore the resources required may be relatively small; this makes it affordable and feasible for a start-up business
- by focusing on a small segment of the market this may not be perceived as a threat by larger, established firms. If a start-up is perceived as a real threat, the established firms may cut prices or try to influence stores to get them to stop distributing the product.

However, there are dangers associated with niche marketing:

- The total number of customers is likely to be quite low and therefore if anyone changes their mind and switches to something else, this can have a significant effect on the total demand.
- If the product does prove to be successful then larger firms may be attracted by this success and enter the market. Small firms may struggle to match the power and resources of larger firms and so may lose their share of the market.

By comparison a mass market approach targets the majority of the market. This usually involves high volumes of production and much higher capacity levels than niche marketing. This may make it unrealistic for a start-up business, especially given the high levels of promotion needed to generate the necessary demand to make mass production viable. However, over time a niche product may become more mainstream and therefore niche products may be moved into the mass market.

Study tip

When studying this topic you should be aware of the benefits and problems of a niche marketing approach. You should also appreciate the importance of understanding and monitoring customers' needs.

To make your business more effective you have to understand exactly what your customers want and provide them with excellent value for money.

9.6 Segmentation methods

Within any market, different segments may exist. A **market segment** is a group of similar needs and wants. For example, within the market for newspapers there are some readers who are most interested in sport, others who want financial news, and others who want celebrity gossip. Different newspapers have been developed to target these different groups.

Within the chocolate market the demand can be segmented into groups such as:
- snacking – you buy the chocolate and eat it there and then (e.g. a Mars bar)
- sharing – you buy the chocolate and take it home to share with others (e.g. Cadbury's Heroes)
- gift – you buy the chocolate to give to others (e.g. Thornton's chocolates).

There are various ways in which a market may be segmented, including:
- **Geographic segmentation** This focuses on the impact of factors such as the location of customers or the climate in different regions. Cars sold to Africa, for example, will have to withstand high levels of heat; cars sold to Scandinavia will need to cope with the cold. Cars targeted at people living in cities may be relatively small so it is easy to get around and park; people living in the countryside may want more rugged vehicles to cope with the terrain.
- **Demographic segmentation** This focuses on the impact of factors such as age, gender, income, occupation, marital status and stage in the family life-cycle. In the toys market, for example, the type of toys three-year-olds will play with is very different from those wanted by 13-year-olds. When you are single, you may be looking for a city centre, one-bedroom flat; when you are married with children you may want a three-bedroomed house with a garden, near a good school and out of the city.
- **Psychographic segmentation** This focuses on the impact of factors such as your personality, lifestyle, values, social class and attitudes. Are you someone who likes belonging to a group? Are you someone who is very ambitious? Do you want material things? Do you care how products have been made and their impact on the environment? These factors might all influence the way a product is promoted and the actual design of the product. Some holidays may be designed for adventurous, outgoing types. Others might target customers wanting a package hotel holiday in Spain. Your job and earnings are likely to influence a whole host of lifestyle factors:

the newspaper you read, where you shop, where you go on holiday, the interests you have and what you wear.
- **Behavioural segmentation** This focuses on the impact of factors such as whether you are a regular consumer, whether you are a heavy consumer, whether you are brand loyal and what makes you buy the product. Do you buy chewing gum to help you stop smoking? To have fresh breath? To help protect your teeth? Because you think it helps keep you calm? Promotional campaigns may be developed to focus on the specific motivations of different groups. Behavioural segmentation also includes when you buy and use the product. For example, do you tend to buy flowers to celebrate, or to apologise?

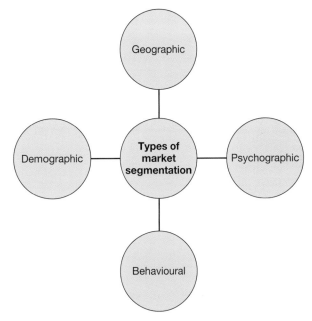

Figure 9.6 Types of market segmentation

For a market segment to appeal to a business it must be:
- measurable, so you can identify it exists and measure its size to decide on the likely earnings
- accessible, so you have the resources to offer what would be required and be able to get your products to the customers
- profitable, so you can meet customer needs and your own needs at the same time.

Benefits and limitations of market segmentation

By segmenting a market effectively, managers can identify which segments it wants to target. By understanding the requirements of a particular segment it can develop the marketing activities to meet these needs more closely. Hopefully, this should increase sales and boost brand loyalty. Effective segmentation should lead to effective marketing, with businesses providing exactly the right product in the right place at the right time and price. However, the more a market is segmented the more variations there are to the product and its marketing: imagine producing a different cleaner for the sink, oven, shower, toilet, floor, door handles, carpets, work surfaces, windows, walls and so on. Each one may meet a very specific need, but coordinating and providing such a range of products may be expensive. If possible, it would be easier and cheaper to produce an all-in-one cleaner to cover at least some of these functions. The firm may well get cheaper inputs if it buys in bulk and can spread one set of marketing costs over more units.

Businesses may therefore have to trade off the appeal of segmenting and meeting specific groups of needs more precisely with the benefits and cost advantages of producing a limited range of products on a larger scale.

Case Study

Bic for her

In 2012 Bic launched a pen aimed at women.

Figure 9.7 The Bic pen for women

Key benefits:

● Tinted barrel (pink, purple, blue, green or orange)
● Quality ink, quick drying and smooth writing
● Tungsten carbide ball, perfect sphere and very resistant
● Medium point: 1.0mm, line width 0.4mm
● Hexagonal barrel for comfortable handling
● Clear tinted barrel for visible ink supply

Source: Bic

Questions

1 Explain why Bic might want to launch a pen aimed specifically at women. [6]

2 Discuss the possible disadvantages of targeting many different segments in a market. [10]

Study tip

Although targeting specific segments may seem appealing from a marketing perspective it may make production more complex as it requires different models to be produced. Managers must balance the desire to meet the specific needs of customers with the costs and challenges this may generate.

Classification of products and how marketing might differ for different types of goods and services

There are many different types of products and these can be classified as:

● Consumer products, which are items bought by the final user. These can be subdivided into:
  ● Convenience items such as newspapers and milk – these are usually relatively cheap items and distribution is the key to marketing here. Customers will not spend much time searching for them in different stores; they pick up what is convenient in the nearest shop. This means producers have to get them distributed in many different places and displayed in a way that attracts attention; this is important because some convenience items are bought on impulse (e.g. chewing gum) when they are seen in the store.
  ● Shopping items – these are products such as clothes or electrical goods which are more expensive than convenience items. When you go to buy them you shop around comparing prices and features; you may go and look several times before actually buying. You may go to a retail area where you can quickly move from one store to another to compare. The producer has to clearly demonstrate value for money, for example, by stressing a unique selling point (USP) to show why its product is better than the competition's.
  ● Specialist products such as Rolex watches or Ferraris – these are products that customers have probably thought about for a long time and are willing to travel to find the right item. These may be distributed to relatively few locations but the nature of the outlet is very important to the overall brand image. These products are probably not very price sensitive because people want them for their status and their uniqueness.

Table 9.3 Classification of products

	Producer (industrial) products	Consumer products
Buyers	Professionals	Amateurs!
Number of buyers	Relatively few; selling to businesses	May be millions if mass market product
May focus on	Technical specifications and how it helps their business do better	Benefits in terms of consumption; may be more influenced e.g. by look or design or packaging
Promotion	Often uses sales force to approach customers	May be advertising for mass market product

- Industrial products, which are bought by businesses to use in their production process to produce the consumer goods. They include:
  - Installations – these are big items of expenditure such as production lines and new office space. Buyers will take a lot of care over the precise features of the item, especially any technical features, because it is a major item of spending.
  - Materials – these are materials used in the production process. There may be several possible suppliers so buyers will shop around. The quality, reliability and flexibility of supply will be very important when buying these products.
  - Supplies – these are basic items such as paper and light bulbs; there will be many suppliers and the buyer will look for a good prices.

Test your learning

Short answer questions

1 State **two** possible marketing objectives. [2]

2 a What is meant by a market segment? [1]
  b State **two** ways of segmenting a market. [2]

3 Explain **one** benefit of segmenting a market. [3]

4 a State **two** factors that influence supply in a market. [2]
  b Explain **one** factor that might increase supply in a market. [3]

5 a State **two** factors that influence demand in a market. [2]
  b Explain **one** factor that might increase demand for a product. [3]

6 a What is meant by market share? [2]
  b Explain **one** possible benefit of having a high market share. [3]

7 a What is meant by market growth? [2]
  b Explain **one** possible benefit of selling in a fast growth market. [3]

8 What is the difference between a producer and consumer market? [2]

9 a What is meant by a producer product? [2]
  b Explain **one** possible difference between marketing a producer product and marketing a consumer product. [3]

10 a What is meant by consumer orientation? [2]
   b Explain **one** possible benefit of being consumer orientated. [3]

Data response question

Poultry price rise

The price of poultry products has gone up in markets throughout the city by Rs 50 to Rs 60 per kilogramme (kg) following declining production and increasing demand of the commodity due to the ongoing winter season.

Demand for poultry products has increased from wholesalers and retailers as fast-food outlets and hotels place substantial orders and this has created shortages and pulled prices up.

Furthermore, big increases in prices of beef and mutton, which are currently priced at Rs 380 to Rs 400 per kg and Rs 550 to Rs 560 per kg respectively, have compelled consumers to turn to chicken meat.

However, the current sharp increase in chicken meat rates have largely disappointed such consumers resulting in a decline in its demand at the retail level.

The high prices have resulted in less domestic consumption of poultry meat as households could no longer afford it. The current price was likely to remain the same until next month when hatching and the production process would increase the supply.

Questions

1 Explain the meaning of the following terms
  a market [3]
  b shortage. [3]

2 Using a diagram show the effect of an increase in demand on the equilibrium price and output of chicken. [6]

3 Discuss the factors that might affect the supply and demand of poultry products. [10]

Essay question

Discuss the ways in which effective segmentation and targeting might benefit the marketing of a business. [20]

Past paper questions

1 a Outline the main determinants of demand for consumer goods in your country. [8]

b Discuss how a clothes retailer might segment the market for its goods. [12]

Cambridge International AS and A Level Business Studies
9707 Paper 1 Q7 May/June 2007

10 Market research

Chapter overview

In this chapter we examine:
- the meaning of market research
- the difference between primary and secondary market research
- methods of gathering information
- sources of information
- methods of sampling
- how to assess market research findings
- the importance of cost effectiveness in market research.

10.1 What is market research?

> ### Key term
>
> **Market research** is the process of gathering, analysing and producing data relevant to the marketing process.

Market research involves the gathering and analysis of data that is relevant to your marketing. For example, you might want to know:
- the size of the market – this can be measured in terms of the number of dollars spent in it (the value of the market) or the number of items purchased (the volume of the market)
- key market trends – for example, whether the market as a whole is growing, or whether particular types of products are growing in popularity
- what customers value about the product, how much they are prepared to pay for it, and what your product can do better than other products on the market
- key characteristics of customers (such as their age, lifestyle, attitudes and buying patterns). A customer profile is an outline of the customer base.

Market research can identify the fundamental reason for buying the product (for example, because you are thirsty or hungry) and customer wants (which shows which product you would like to buy). Having identified the need, the business will aim to make you want their products.

Market research provides a manager with information. This is important for effective decision-making. Imagine you are wandering around a house at midnight and none of the lights is working. You stumble, move slowly and make mistakes getting around: market research can provide the lighting in the room that enables you to move quickly, efficiently and effectively, to get to where you want.

By undertaking market research, managers should have a better idea of what people want and how they behave. This should mean that the firm can meet their needs more effectively and avoid wasteful marketing activities. Imagine that you are considering launching a new product. If you can find out who your target market is, what they like, what they read, where they shop, what they watch and listen to, then your marketing can be much more effective. For example, there is no point in spending money on a big Saturday evening television campaign if your target audience is at a nightclub.

Market research may be undertaken before the business is set up in order to decide whether or not it is viable. It can also be undertaken once the business is up and running to decide what to do next – for example, whether to change the price of a product or launch a new brand.

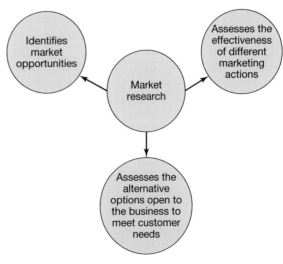

Figure 10.1 Research uses

Typically, market research is used to:
- identify market opportunities
- assess the alternative options open to the business to meet customer needs
- assess the effectiveness of different marketing actions.

10.2 Primary and secondary market research

Key terms

Primary market research gathers data for the first time for a specific purpose.
Secondary market research uses data that already exists.

Secondary (desk) market research

Given that the amount of money you have available to spend when starting up a business is likely to be limited, you will probably have to carry out most of your market research yourself rather than using specialist companies to do it for you. The cheapest and quickest way of doing this is to see what information about the market already exists. What data has been collected and published? A tremendous amount of information is available on the internet, in libraries and in newspapers, as well as from other sources.

Using data that already exists is called **secondary** or **desk market research**. It is particularly useful for general information on the economy, the market and on competitors.

While secondary data is usually quite quick to get hold of, it is not always in the right format for your needs, or up to date. The research may have been done in the previous year, when what you want is this year's figure. It may organise sales data according to the sales per country, when what you need is data focusing on a particular city. Nevertheless, secondary research is usually a good starting point. Once you have looked at secondary sources you can identify what else you need to know and what information needs to be gathered for the first time.

Primary or field market research

In some cases, you may have to gather new data for a specific purpose. This is called **primary** or **field market research**. For example, you may want to discover what people in your local area think of your specific idea, whether they are likely to use your particular service or what they think of your business name. This sort of information will not exist already, so you will need to undertake new research.

Primary research can be tailored precisely to your own needs but can be quite expensive and time consuming, compared with using information already collected. The danger is that because of cost constraints or because you are inexperienced you only ask a relatively small number of people, or a specific group that does not really represent the population as a whole. This means that your results may be biased and misleading. If you ask your friends, for example, they may tell you it is a great idea even if it isn't because they do not want to upset you!

If you are going to undertake primary research you need to make sure that you:
- don't lead people into giving you the answer you want (e.g. 'Why do you think my idea is so good?' is a leading question)
- ask a representative group of people (i.e. that you hope will represent your target group)
- ask enough people for the findings to be significant. One person's opinion may not necessarily reflect the views of the population as a whole.

Primary data can be gathered:
- by observation – for example, you may watch what is happening in the stores of your possible competitors or count how many people walk by a potential location for your shop on a typical day to calculate the 'footfall'. (In retailing, the footfall is an important indicator of the likely number of customers. The more people that walk past the more customers you may get.)
- through surveys – you may have been stopped in the street and asked your opinion about something. This is a face-to-face survey and is one way of finding out what people think. Firms also use telephone, mail or online surveys to find out the views of potential customers. Surveys may give you an idea of what people think of your idea and help you decide whether or not to go ahead.
- by asking a small group of people what they think (a focus group, see page 103)
- by test marketing. Sometimes a business may try a product in a test market such as a particular region for a while to see how it sells. If this goes well it might be rolled out to other areas, if sales are poor changes could be made to the product or the way it is promoted to see what happens then.

Table 10.1 The characteristics of primary and secondary market research

Primary (field)	Secondary (desk)
New data	Existing data
Specific to your needs	Gathered for another purpose
May take longer to gather	May be relatively cheap

Case Study

Marvel and DC Comics

The superheroes of American comics are now being aimed at Asian readers more used to manga comics.

With sales in decline at home, US comic-book giants Marvel and DC Comics are looking to foreign markets to grow their businesses.

Sales of comics in the US are down due to video games, social media and film.

Asia already has a rich culture of comics with a strong fan base. Japan's manga, which tends to portray ordinary people as opposed to superheroes, is immensely popular.

In a survey in ten cities in the region, manga had more than 50 per cent of the market in Taiwan and Hong Kong, while Western comics had less than 11 per cent, according to market research by Hakuhodo, a Japanese advertising firm. But sales are falling in Japan as well.

Meanwhile, the American comic-book companies have been reaching out to new audiences through movie franchises of characters such as Thor, Iron Man and the Fantastic Four.

And both DC Comics and Marvel are doing all they can to make sure they get it right this time, having failed to penetrate the market in the past. They are bringing in new artists, new writers and giving more creative control to these artists in Asia.

Table 10.2 Market share of comics in Asia (%)

Cities	Japanese	Western
Taipei, Taiwan	61	10.9
Hong Kong	48.3	5.5
Manila, Philippines	37	23.6
Bangkok, Thailand	27.6	9.9
Shanghai, China	25.4	7.5
Jakarta, Indonesia	18.9	6.2
Singapore	17.4	11
Ho Chi Minh, Vietnam	12.9	12.3
Kuala Lumpur, Malaysia	11.5	18.5
Mumbai, India	0.4	4.1
Average	27.4	10.2

Source: Market research by Hakuhodo

Questions

1 Explain why sales of comics in the US might be falling. [6]

2 Discuss the ways in which market research might help the US comic businesses. [10]

Case Study

Africa

Africa is one of the biggest emerging markets in the world. This rapidly expanding, competitive environment creates a growing need for market research. Consumers are the lifeblood of companies, but do companies actually possess sufficient knowledge about their consumers? Are their customers (perfectly) satisfied with their products/services? What are their opinions and wishes? How could their loyalty be improved? These are important questions for organisations and investors operating in Africa and also a stimulant not to fall into the common trap of seeing African consumers as 'poor and helpless people' but rather as real consumers.

The potential

Africa will be the fastest growing economy in the world in the next five years. For example, Uganda has an economic growth of 6.41 per cent per year, yet only 1 per cent of the total global market research budget is invested in Africa. The Basic Survivors (low income people living on or below one dollar a day) is a huge group in African countries (in Uganda, for example, this group is 65 per cent). Given the fact that Africa is the fastest-growing economy in the world, the Basic Survivors moves towards a regular middle class, with comparable incomes and western consumer behaviour. This means there is a huge potential for doing business but there is still an unused investment opportunity in African countries.

Companies that find new ways to overcome constraints and tap opportunities can gain insights, market share and customer or supplier loyalty, and will secure a strong position in this growing market.

Effective market research methods in developing countries

More than 500 million Africans use a mobile phone and the market is growing fast each year. Mobiles have penetrated to even those villages that have no electricity and no landlines. The rapid and accelerating penetration of mobile phones through all levels of society in developing countries means that it is possible to communicate with the Basic Survivors and emerging middle classes. This underlines the massive potential to use mobile phones in order to reach and interact with huge groups of people across the continent. The explosive growth of Africa's mobile communications industry offers a vast potential to interact with people on a personal level.

Figure 10.2 By 2016 there will be 1 billion mobile phones in Africa

Source: Research Africa

Market research is conducted by inviting people to participate in surveys and rewarding them with incentives such as mobile phone credits.

The mobile phone medium is particularly well suited to market research as it is cost effective, reliable and enables clients to obtain results virtually in real time. Furthermore, it allows consumers to participate in surveys when and where it suits them. These advantages have a positive impact on response rates, data quality and validity of results.

With a creative and innovative drive market research agencies are able to reach millions of low-income people who participate in incentive-based surveys and, as such, create new economic opportunities for people living in poverty. Among other benefits, this inclusive business model speeds up efforts to empower individuals through participation in countries affected by poverty and conflict.

Source: www.mckinsey.com

Questions

1 Explain the benefits of using the mobile phone to undertake market research. [6]
2 Discuss the potential benefits of using market research for businesses targeting Africa. [10]

Maths moment

Following market research, Nick estimates the market as a whole is worth $1 500 000. He believes his company can achieve a market share of 50 per cent. What would his sales be? Nick also thinks the market will grow by 5 per cent next year but he can retain the same market share. What would sales be then?

10.3 Sampling

If you decide to undertake a survey, the total number of people who you are interested in is known as your 'target population'. For example, if you have an idea for a website dedicated to your favourite football team, your target population would be all the fans of the club around the world. In most cases it will not be possible to interview all of the people in your target group. It may be too expensive or would simply take too long to talk to everyone. Imagine your website was aimed at the fans of a big club like Manchester United or Chelsea. There are hundreds of thousands of fans all over the world. Even if you managed to identify them somehow, all the cost and time involved in trying to talk to them would make it unrealistic, especially if you are a new business and therefore likely to have limited funds.

Instead of interviewing everyone in the target population, the firm might decide to take a **sample**. A sample is a group of people that is intended to represent the overall population. By interviewing, say, 500 fans you would hope to get an impression of what all the others think.

Obviously, the results will not be 100 per cent reliable, because you have not asked everyone in the population, you have only asked some of them. This means that you cannot be totally confident of the results. So it is important to choose a sample that is big enough to be representative of the whole market. The findings from a sample that is too small may not be very reliable.

Key term

A **sample** is a group of people or items selected to represent the population as a whole.

Sampling methods

There are three main ways of selecting a sample.

Random sample

With this type of sample, all the members of the target population have an equal chance of selection. If you wanted a random sample of 30 students at your school, you could take a list of names of all the students then pick 30 names at random. You would then have to find them to interview. This approach has the advantage that anyone could be asked. However, it can be quite time consuming because once the names have been selected you then have to go and find those people. If they were not in school on that day you would have to wait until they were, slowing up the whole process.

Stratified sample

This type of sample is based on particular proportions (such as 60 per cent males, 40 per cent females; or 20 per cent aged 16–35 and 80 per cent aged over 35). This type of sample is used when the target population has particular characteristics that you want reflected in your sample. You reproduce the characteristics of the target population and randomly sample within each category (for example, male, female).

Quota sample

With this type of sample the research sets proportions (e.g. male/female or different age groups) which may or may not reflect the target population. People who meet these characteristics are found as quickly and easily as possible, which means that a quota is not a random sample. For example, if you want to interview 12 students (5 male and 7 female) you simply approach people and see if they match these criteria and work with the first five male students and seven female students who agree to take part.

A quota sample is easier and quicker to complete than a random sample (as you do not need to know all the members of the population), but it is not random because members of the population do not have an equal chance of selection. To find 30 students, for example, you might simply find one class and ask them: this could lead to very biased results because they would all be a similar age and/or may all study the same subject. With a random sample you would expect a range of ages and interests, which might provide a better insight into the school as a whole.

Choosing a sampling method

The choice of sampling method will depend on factors such as:

- the time available. If time is limited a quota is likely to be used because it is relatively quick to do.
- your knowledge of the target population. To select people randomly you must have details of the target population. If you were selecting from a list of cardholders or club members this would be feasible. However, if you were interested in potential buyers of your product you would not necessarily know who they were and so could not select from this group randomly.
- the extent to which the target population has clearly differentiated groups of buyers. If the buyers can be differentiated clearly (e.g. 70 per cent male, 30 per cent female) then you would want to use a stratified sample.

Study tip

When deciding on the size and type of sample you need to think about issues such as the time available, the costs and how accurate the data has to be.

10.4 Quantitative and qualitative market research

Quantitative and qualitative market research are two different approaches to market research.

Qualitative research is based on the opinions of a small **focus group** or in-depth one-to-one interviews. This type of research aims to understand why customers behave in certain ways or to find out what they think of a product. It examines why customers do what they do. For example, a focus group might

be used to discuss consumers' views of a brand to understand their shopping habits. This often helps marketing managers understand what customers think of their product compared to another and can be a starting point in the research process. Focus groups may highlight particular issues or give a reaction to a business idea that can be examined in more detail. Given that qualitative research involves small groups, it means that the findings are not statistically reliable: this is why more extensive research is often used as a follow up.

Quantitative market research is based on relatively large samples and is therefore statistically valid. This sort of research is often used to show what has happened in a market and its findings can be expressed in numerical terms (for example, sales of Brand X have increased by 45 per cent; 12 million people watched *EastEnders* last week; the market for soft drinks is worth more than £4 billion). Quantitative market research is used to explain *what* has happened.

Key term

A **focus group** is a small number of people gathered together to talk about a particular issue in open discussion.

10.5 Market research results

When analysing the market research results a business needs to consider:

- Can the results be trusted to be relatively accurate – this means is the research valid?
- Would the research give the same results if it was repeated – is the research reliable?

The accuracy may depend on factors such as how the information was gathered, what the sample size was and how accurate you want the findings to be. Researchers often express their findings in terms of confidence levels based on a statistical analysis of the data. For example, they might say they were 95 per cent confident that sales would be between $20 million and $26 million in two years' time but only 68 per cent confident they would be between $23 and $25 million. The more precise you want the estimate to be the less confident the researchers are likely to be.

10.6 Cost effectiveness

The reliability and validity of market research depends on how it was conducted and may be linked to how much was spent on it. If the budget is limited this may mean only a small sample can be used, reducing the validity and reliability of the findings. By spending more on market research, better results may be acquired because the research may be more extensive. However, businesses will face competing demands in terms of the funds – for example, the production department may want to invest more into quality control, other marketing managers may want to spend more on promotion and the HR department may want to spend on training. This may limit the amount that can be spent on market research.

When deciding how much to spend on market research the business must consider the likely returns to decide whether or not it is worth it – how important are the findings? What are the likely consequences if the research is right or wrong? The bigger the likely returns the more a business may be willing to spend on market research.

However much is spent, managers will want to make sure the money is used well and therefore that the research is cost effective and money is not wasted. This will mean thinking carefully about how best to gather the data and planning the research effectively.

Test your learning

Short answer questions

1 **a** What is meant by market research? [2]

   b Explain **one** reason for undertaking market research. [2]

2 **a** What is meant by secondary market research? [2]

   b Explain **one** advantage of secondary research compared to primary research. [3]

3 **a** What is meant by primary market research? [2]

   b Explain **one** advantage of primary research compared to secondary research. [3]

4 **a** What is a sample? [2]

   b Explain **one** reason why a business may use sampling when undertaking market research. [3]

5 **a** What is the difference between a random sample and a quota sample? [2]

   b Explain **one** advantage of a random sample. [3]

6 State **two** features of effective market research. [2]

7 State **two** sources of information for market research. [2]

8 Explain **one** limitation of sampling. [3]

9 State **two** factors that might influence how much is spent on market research. [2]

10 Explain **one** reason why spending more on market research may not lead to higher sales. [3]

Data response question

Avon

The global beauty and cosmetics company Avon plans to launch more than 300 products in India this year as it aims to maintain its 40+ per cent growth rate. The company currently sells around 1500 products in India through direct selling agents. The new products would be launched across several categories, including jewellery and skincare.

The company, which currently sells its products in around 1200 towns and cities in the country, has set a target of reaching around 2000 towns. Avon currently sells its products through its representatives in 16 states covering around 70 per cent of the population. It aims to cover around 93 per cent of the population by 2015 and further increase its market share.

The company has a manufacturing unit at Dehradun, which produces 85 per cent of the products sold in India. The remaining 15 per cent of the products are imported from various locations.

Questions

1 Explain the meaning of the following terms:

   a company [3]

   b market share. [3]

2 Explain the ways in which Avon might research the market for its new products. [6]

3 To what extent do you think market research might help ensure the success of Avon's new products? [10]

Essay question

To what extent is secondary market research better than primary market research? [20]

11 Marketing mix

Chapter overview

In this chapter we examine:
- the elements of the marketing mix (the 4 Ps)
- the role of the customer (the 4 Cs)
- the importance of the product in the marketing mix
- the product life cycle
- types of pricing strategies
- the price elasticity of demand
- promotion methods
- channels of distribution
- using the internet in marketing
- an effective marketing mix.

A customer is influenced by many factors when deciding whether or not to purchase a product. The combination of these factors is known as the marketing mix. By developing an effective marketing mix, a business can meet the needs of its customers successfully. In this chapter we examine the different elements of the marketing mix.

11.1 The marketing mix

The **marketing mix** comprises all the elements associated with a product that affect whether or not the customer decides to buy it. A broad range of factors may affect customers' purchasing decisions.

Consider why a customer might choose to shop in one supermarket rather than another. The list below contains a number of factors affecting this decision.
- How far away is it?
- How easy is it to park?
- What is the range of products like?
- Are the prices competitive?
- What facilities are there (for example, a coffee shop)?
- Are the staff friendly and helpful?
- What services are provided (such as carrying shopping to customers' cars)?
- Does the supermarket offer a loyalty card?

There are clearly many factors that influence a consumer's decision to choose one business rather than another and these are all part of the marketing mix. An effective marketing mix offers the customer the right mix of benefits at the right price. Improving the mix will involve changing or enhancing the combination of elements affecting the customers' buying decision.

Figure 11.1 The marketing mix is commonly described as the 4 Ps

The marketing mix is often simplified and is commonly described as 'the 4 Ps'. This approach identifies four elements in the mix (all beginning with the letter P):
- **Price** How much are customers charged for the product and what are the terms of payment (e.g. can you put a deposit down and pay in instalments)? How does this price compare with that of rivals?

- **Product** This includes the many different aspects of a product, such as its design, its quality, its reliability, its features and its functions. For example, you may buy something principally because of its style (e.g. Bang & Olufsen, Apple), its reliability and durability (e.g. JCB, Caterpillar) or the brand values (e.g. DKNY, Gucci).
- **Place** This is the way the product is distributed. Is the product sold direct to the customer or through retail outlets? Can you buy online, or do you have to travel some distance to get to a shop where it is sold?
- **Promotion** This is the way the firm communicates information about the product to the customer. For example, it may use advertising or a sales force to highlight its strengths. The promotion of a product will affect the image that customers have of it and their awareness and understanding of the benefits of the product.

However the marketing mix can be extended to also feature a further 3 Ps:

- **People** A well-trained, well-informed, polite staff can influence people to buy from one shop rather than another. Customer service is an important marketing weapon.
- **Physical environment** This includes factors such as the layout, decor and parking and can be an important influence on which restaurant, pub or store a person chooses.
- **Process** The ease of ordering and paying can influence a purchase. Many supermarkets have introduced self-scanning to reduce queues and attract customers.

Key term

The **marketing mix** is the combination of elements that influence a customer's decision whether or not to buy a product.

Case Study

Doing business in Africa

With a solid understanding of the opportunity, companies seeking to do business in Africa must deliver a relevant, differentiated offering tailored to their target consumers.

African consumers have unique requirements that companies must take into account. For example, price remains the key consideration for the majority of African consumers, and all offerings should take this into consideration. In addition, community and family are strong elements of African culture, so companies need to ensure that branding and promotional efforts resonate with these values – for example, through corporate social responsibility and sustainable development programmes.

Consumer goods giants such as Unilever and Procter & Gamble have excelled in understanding and meeting the unique needs of African consumers. Unilever, which aims to serve all African consumers (including the Basic Survivors, those living on less than $1 each day), had to find a profitable way to make its

products available and affordable for the poorest of Africans. To achieve this goal, Unilever created the 'small unit packs/low unit price' concept: for example, selling small sachets of detergent or salt. This strategy has allowed Unilever to deliver the volumes required to support expansion while capturing the loyalty of lower income customers. This strategy has also prevented the margin-eroding resale of its bulk products in smaller portions.

Unilever collaborates closely with local wholesalers who not only assist Unilever to supply Africa's informal market but also provide the company with market insights and customer feedback. Unilever has embedded corporate social responsibility in its strategy to further boost the brand's relevance with Africans.

Source: www.accenture.com

Questions

1 Explain two features of the African market. [6]
2 Discuss how an understanding of the African market might influence marketing in this region. [10]

11.2 The role of the customer (the 4 Cs)

Another way of analysing the marketing mix is to consider it from the perspective of the customer. This is known as the 4 Cs approach:

- Cost – how much does the product cost the customer? (Price)
- Convenience to the customer – how easy it is to buy the product? (Place)
- Communication with the customer – what do we know about the product? (Promotion)
- Customer solution – what benefits does it offer? How does it meet a customer need to solve a customer problem? (Product)

Ways in which customer relations can be improved

Ensuring that you meet customer expectations is a key part of marketing. This means you need to:

- know what those expectations are through research
- manage those expectations through your communications – making sure you stress the positives but do not promise too much, for example
- know what your competitors are offering to ensure you continue to offer value for money
- follow up after sales to see what customers think and whether there are areas to improve
- look for ways to build a relationship with customers to understand their needs and see if there is anything else you can offer them that they would value. Amazon, for example, will start to recommend books you might like once you start buying from them.

Improving customer relations therefore involves investment in market research, training and ensuring a quality product that offers excellent value for money.

11.3 Product

Businesses will keep reviewing their products to ensure they are relevant and continue to meet customer needs. When doing this they will consider:

- **The core benefit that the product meets** For example, a soft drink satisfies thirst, a washing machine provides clean clothes and an aircraft moves people and cargo from A to B. Businesses have to be aware of new substitutes coming along – with more social networking and systems such as Skype and FaceTime people may not need to travel as much. With more emailing there may be less need for letter writing paper. The ways of satisfying a core benefit can change and businesses must be aware of this and prepare accordingly.
- **The nature of the product or service itself** In the case of a washing machine, for example, the business would consider what size, what features it had, what capacity, what types of wash were needed and what energy usage it had. These would vary from market to market – in some places people live in tower blocks and use industrial size washing machines in the basement areas. In other cities people have apartments with smaller washing machines in them. In some countries there tends to be a utility room with lots of space and the washing machine is a 'top loader' where people put the washing in from the top. In other regions the workspace on the top is needed and so washing machines are front loaders. Products must be developed according to how people are likely to use them.
- **The augmented features** This refers to aspects of the product such as a guarantee, after sales servicing or additional technical support which come with the purchase. Some people stick with their phone service or energy company because they trust them to fix things quickly if ever there is a problem. Some businesses buy their photocopiers or computers from companies that can maintain them effectively.

Product differentiation and unique selling point (USP)

One possible approach of marketing is to differentiate the products that the business sells relative to its competitors. Product differentiation occurs when the benefits of your product are perceived as clearly different from competitors. Your product may be perceived as easier, safer, better designed or trendier, for example. This differentiation can be achieved by having a unique selling point (USP); this is something about your product which is unique. For example, you might be selling the only water from Lake X or the best performing car according to a recent survey.

By promoting its USP, a business can differentiate its offering and may be able to charge more or offer better value for money.

11.4 Product life cycle

The **product life cycle** traces the sales of a product over its life. The typical path for a product can be divided into five stages.

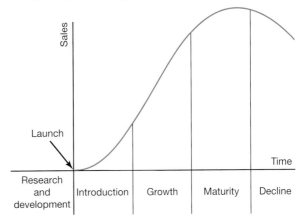

Figure 11.2 The product life cycle

The five stages of the product life cycle

1 The research and development stage

During this stage, the basic idea for the product is developed and tested. Mock-ups of a design may be made, models of a product may be produced or a new recipe may be taste tested. This stage can be expensive for a firm and no revenue is being generated during this period. This is a time of high risk because the product may never be developed successfully and the investment at this stage may not be recovered. For example, it took James Dyson 15 years and more than 5000 prototypes of the Dyson vacuum cleaner before he got it right, highlighting the time and money that can be used up in the development phase.

> **Key term**
>
> The **product life cycle** shows the sales of a product over its lifetime.

The length of the research and development process will vary from product to product. In the case of new pharmaceuticals, it can take 12 to 15 years to develop and test products before they can be launched, whereas developing a new design for a greetings card is likely to take months rather than years. Some products, such as newspapers, are modified on a daily basis (although significant changes, such as the size of the paper or whether to switch to colour, are far less frequent).

2 The introduction (launch) stage

This is the stage at which the product or service is launched and put on sale. Many product ideas will never actually reach this stage. They are abandoned after prototypes have been produced and tested. In the launch phase, promotion costs will be relatively high to make potential customers aware of the product, therefore a loss is still likely to be made. Producers may also struggle to get firms to stock their products or customers to try their service at this stage if the business is new, with no proven track record. Buyers may be reluctant to risk switching to or trialling a new product, particularly if there are heavy costs involved in doing so. For example, if there is a penalty payment for switching from one credit card, mortgage company, electricity company or gas company to another, customers are more likely to remain with their existing providers.

3 The growth stage

If the product becomes known and accepted by customers, sales should grow. At this stage, it should be slightly easier to get distributors to stock the products, as they will be more confident of sales and therefore willing to stock them. The firm should begin to make profits at this stage, as revenues begin to outweigh costs. (For example, sales of wine, teeth-whitening formulas, smoothies, men's cosmetics and laser eye-surgery are at their growth stage in several countries.) At this stage, you need to make sure you can meet the demand and manage the growth process. You may be taking on more staff, buying more equipment and expanding your premises: if this is happening rapidly it can be difficult to keep control. Making sure you can meet deadlines and maintaining quality can be major problems at this time.

Of course, some products never reach the growth stage: they are launched but are never successful and sales fail to take off.

4 The maturity and saturation stage

At this point in a product's life, the growth of sales slows down. The product may have been in the market for some time and competitors may have launched similar products. (Products such as washing machines and televisions are currently in their maturity stage.) The maturity stage can last for years in some cases. There is no rapid expansion and managers must consider what to do next with the product: for example, should funds be invested to try to boost sales or should the product be scrapped?

5 Decline

Eventually, the sales of any product are likely to fall. The business may find it more difficult to get the product distributed at this stage and may be forced to cut the price to maintain sales.

For example, you will have seen reduced-price CDs or books in the bargain areas of shops: the price has been reduced to try to increase sales. Products such as board games, road atlases and bow ties are in their decline stages in the UK.

Using the product life cycle

Managers may use the product life cycle model to identify which stage a product is in at any given moment and then adjust the marketing mix accordingly. For example, promotion may be used to announce the launch of a product in the introduction phase, but to stress the differences with competitors in the maturity phase. The price may be high initially if the product has some unique features, but may have to be reduced in later stages as competitors enter the market. Distribution may be difficult to get at first when a product is new, but easier over time when it has begun to prove itself. The business should be able to improve the firm's performance by recognising or anticipating where the product is in its life cycle and adapting the marketing mix accordingly.

Extending sales in the product life cycle

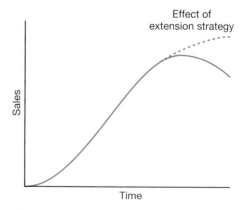

Figure 11.3 Extension strategies

A firm may try to prevent the sales of a product going into decline by using **extension strategies**. Methods to do this might include:
- Increasing the usage of the product on any given occasion – for example, shampoo products always advise you to wash once then rinse your hair and wash again, thereby doubling the usage rate.

An **extension strategy** occurs when marketing activities are changed to prevent sales falling.

- Encouraging the use of the product on more occasions – for example, Head & Shoulders shampoo was seen by consumers as a product to use when dandruff was already present. The company tried to change this perception to get people to use it all year round to prevent dandruff, as well as cure it.
- Reducing the price – as products approach the maturity stage, firms often cut the price to maintain sales. The success of this depends on the price elasticity of demand.
- Adapting the product – look around a supermarket and you will see endless examples of 'new, improved' products or products with added X, extra Y or less Z! These are all ways of trying to keep the consumer interested in the product.
- Introducing promotional offers – another technique often used by firms to try to prevent sales from falling is to have competitions or offers to boost their sales.
- Changing the image of the product – this has been done with a number of drinks, such as vodka and cider, which have had their image changed to appeal to a younger audience. New versions have been launched, such as vodka and mixers and cider with ice, and the branding and packaging have been changed to revitalise the image.

Table 11.1 Examples of how marketing decisions may change at different stages of the product life cycle

	Introduction	**Growth**	**Maturity**	**Decline**
Price	May be low to introduce	May be able to increase with demand	May hold	May cut to boost sales
Distribution	May be limited as stores unsure whether to stock	May increase to gain access to the market	May hold	May focus on best performing outlets
Promotion	May focus on awareness	May try to increase awareness	May highlight differences with competitors who may have entered	May try to reinforce existence and benefits of the product
The product	May be limited number of models/ varieties	May widen range with demand	May stop developing new models/ varieties	May focus on best performers

Case Study

Segway

Figure 11.4 Two Segways in use

The Segway was expected to revolutionise the way we travelled. It is a self-balancing electric scooter that was launched in 2001 by Dean Kamen, its American inventor. He imagined that this environmentally friendly form of transport would immediately catch on. The Segway can travel up to 12 miles an hour (19 km/h). However, when the Segway was launched in the UK the government declared it could not be used in any public place. It was too fast to be used on the pavement but not safe enough to be used on the road.

A recent study found that it took a few minutes to grasp the basic skills of Segway riding and three hours to become proficient. A rider simply leans forward to move forward and back to stop. On the original model, steering is controlled by twisting a handlebar grip. On a newer version, riders push the column left or right.

According to the company:

> 'We transform the way people work, play and live! Segway is based in New Hampshire and our products are "Made in the USA". We market a full line of zero-emissions Personal Transporters (PT) for indoor, sidewalk, cross-terrain and patrol use, which deliver impressive energy efficiency equivalent to 450 miles per gallon … We continue to focus our research and development efforts on creating green personal transportation solutions that challenge convention.
>
> Segway is passionately committed to innovation and the future of mobility to move you – easily, efficiently, intelligently, simply.'

Source: Adapted from www.segway.com

Questions

1 Explain two benefits of the Segway. [6]
2 Discuss the ways in which the marketing of the Segway might change as it moves from the introduction to the growth phase of the product life cycle. [10]

Extension: product life cycle and capacity utilisation

The **capacity** of a firm refers to the maximum amount it can produce at a particular moment in time. This will depend on the numbers and skills of its employees and the level and quality of its capital equipment and technology. **Capacity utilisation** refers to the amount that a firm is producing at any moment, compared with the amount it could produce. For example, a 50 per cent capacity utilisation means that a firm is producing half as much as it could be making; 25 per cent utilisation means it is producing a quarter of what it could produce. This is bad practice because resources are being wasted, and the firm is being inefficient because it could produce and sell more.

Key terms

Capacity measures the maximum possible output a business can produce with its given resources.

Capacity utilisation measures the existing output as a percentage of the maximum possible output.

When a firm first considers launching a product, it must predict the likely level of sales because this will determine the capacity it will need. In the early stages of the product life cycle, sales will usually be less than in the maturity phase, so if it enters the market with enough capacity for peak sales, the capacity utilisation will be low early on. This can be expensive because, although the firm has the resources to produce, say, 100 000 units, it may only be producing 20 000. This means that the cost per unit will be high – the cost of the equipment and staff have to be covered by relatively few sales. As the sales grow over time, these fixed costs can be spread over more units, thereby reducing the cost per item. On the other hand, if the firm sets up with a low capacity, it means that if demand does grow it may not be able to exploit this in the short term. In the long term a firm can, of course, increase capacity if sales are high enough. However, the decision to increase capacity may involve high levels of investment, so the firm must be confident that sales will continue to stay high to make sure that the new higher level of capacity is utilised.

Extension: product life cycle and cash flow

The cash flow of a business at the start of a product's life cycle is likely to be negative. This is because cash has to be spent researching and developing the product before any sales have occurred. Even when the product is launched, the firm is likely to be spending more money at first to promote it than is coming in as income. This means the business will need to monitor its cash flow effectively in the early stages to make sure it does not run out!

As sales enter the growth phase, the cash flow should become positive. This is because by this stage, there should be less need for extensive promotion as customers should be more aware of the product and also income should be higher.

In the maturity phase, there may be a need to spend money on re-promoting the product if sales are to be maintained. As a result, cash flow may begin to fall, but nevertheless it will usually remain positive due to the relatively high inflows. With falling sales in the decline phase, cash flow will drop.

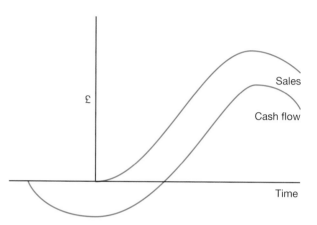

Figure 11.5 Sales and cash flow during the product life cycle

Maths moment

Over four years the sales of a product are as shown in Table 11.2.

Table 11.2 Sales of a product over four years

Year	Sales
1	$100 000
2	$150 000
3	$200 000
4	$220 000
5	$225 000

What stage of the product life cycle do you think sales are in? Explain your answer.

The value of the product life cycle model

The product life cycle model is valuable because it highlights the fact that marketing policies have to be adjusted at different stages in the development of a product.

However, it is important to remember the product life cycle is just a model and its shape will vary considerably between products. In the case of a new single release by a band, for example, the life span may be just a matter of weeks, whereas Marmite was launched in the early twentieth century and is still in its maturity phase. Toys often have short life cycles but some of them, such as Barbie dolls, have been around for many years. So marketing decisions in relation to the product life cycle are not clear cut; some products in decline have had to be taken off the market because they cannot be made viable; others, such as the drink Tango, have been rebranded and brought back to great success.

Often, it will only be clear in retrospect what stage a product was in; what appeared to be a slight dip may turn out to be the decline of a product, or what appears to be a decline may only be a slight dip: it only becomes clear later on. Unfortunately, businesses have to make decisions as they go. They do not have the luxury of waiting to see what would have happened if they had not acted.

Another limitation of the product life cycle model is that it traces the sales of one product over time. Most businesses have several products and therefore it is important to look at its overall position.

Product portfolio analysis (PPA)

Most firms have more than one product: some have hundreds. (For example, at the time of writing, Unilever owns a huge number of brands, including Bertolli, Birdseye, Findus, Hellman's, Knorr, Lipton, Slim-Fast, Comfort, Domestos, Dove, Lux, Pond's and Sunsilk, to name but a few.) The range of products and services a firm has is known as its **product portfolio**. As part of its planning process, a business will examine the position of these products in their markets. This is known as 'portfolio analysis'. One of the most famous models of portfolio analysis was developed by the management consultancy Boston Consulting Group and is known as the **Boston Matrix**. This model analyses the position of a firm's products in terms of their market share and the growth of the markets they operate in.

Types of product in the Boston Matrix

Each circle in the Boston Matrix represents one particular product or service. The size of the circle illustrates the turnover of the product; the bigger the circle the higher the turnover. The firm's products can be classified according to their market share and the growth of the market in which they operate.

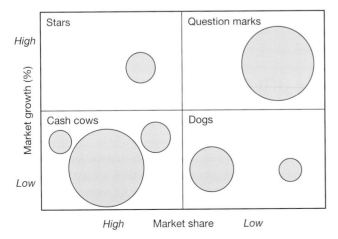

Figure 11.6 The Boston Matrix

Product portfolio analysis examines the market position of a firm's products.

The **Boston Matrix** is a method of product portfolio analysis that examines the products of a business in terms of their market share and the market growth.

- **Cash cows** are products that have a high market share but are selling in a slow-growing market. In some cases, this type of product will be the market leader in a mature market. Although the market may not be growing very fast, this may be because it has grown in the past leaving little room for further expansion. For example, the market for washing machines in the UK is quite big but is not actually growing very fast; given the size of the market a brand with a high market share will have sales worth millions of pounds. By comparison, the market for hybrid cars and organic food is still relatively small but has potential for very fast growth. A cash cow already has a large market share, so much of the promotional work will have been done already. The product is likely to have a good distribution system and people will be aware that the product exists. The firm is used to producing the product in relatively large volumes and so the cost per unit should be fairly low. As a result, this type of product is likely to bring in high levels of cash for the firm. This can be used to finance other products.
- **Question marks** (or 'problem children'). These are products that have a small market share of a fast-growing market. These products may go on to be very successful, but equally they may fail. They are quite vulnerable and their future is uncertain (hence the name). There is a high degree of risk associated with these products because you cannot be sure they will succeed. They need protecting by the firm and they require extensive marketing. Most new products are question marks because their future is so uncertain (although there are exceptions when a product takes off quickly).
- **Stars** These products enjoy a large share of a market that is growing rapidly. They are highly successful products for the business: however, they are usually expensive in terms of marketing. Money must be spent to ensure they retain their position in a growing market. For example, they may need to be promoted heavily to maintain customer awareness and to increase distribution in the market.
- **Dogs** These products have a low market share and are selling in a slow-growing market. A firm may want to get rid of these products unless it thinks it can improve its sales. However, dogs can sometimes be revived. Lucozade used to be seen as a drink to help sick people get better, until it was very successfully repositioned as a sports and energy drink.

The value of the Boston Matrix

The Boston Matrix provides a snapshot of the position of all of a firm's products at a particular moment in time (whereas the product life cycle focuses on just one product). This enables managers to see whether or not they have a balanced portfolio (i.e an appropriate mix of products). It can help a business to be more effective by providing an overview so the manager can take appropriate actions. For example:

- If a business has too many 'dogs', it may have insufficient new products to keep it going in the future. As a result, it may want to invest in new products.
- If, however, a business has lots of cash cows, it is generating relatively high levels of cash but, again, needs to think about the future: cash cows tend to be dominant products in markets that have already grown. A firm may want and need to be involved in newer markets as well and should therefore look to develop some star products.
- If a firm has too many question marks it may be quite vulnerable – question marks need protective marketing to maintain and grow their position in the market: this may drain a firm's resources.

With an appropriate mix of products, the cash cows can be used to finance the development of question marks and turn them into stars: this way the firm uses money from established markets to enter new markets and so protects its future.

Portfolio analysis, therefore, provides a good basis for effective marketing planning:

- Dog products may be sold off or production and sales halted.
- Star products may be invested in to maintain their position.
- Cash cows may be 'milked' to provide funds.
- Question marks may be protected.

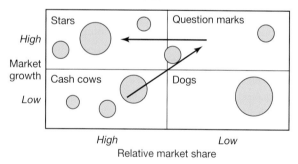

Figure 11.7 The Boston Matrix (2)

Crocs

Born in Boulder, Colorado, as a simple, comfortable boat shoe, today Crocs™ footwear can be found across the globe and in more than 120 styles for men, women and children. With distinct collections, Crocs offers colourful, lightweight comfort for any occasion and every season.

All Crocs shoes are uniquely designed and manufactured using the company's proprietary closed-cell resin, Croslite, a technology that gives each pair of shoes the soft, comfortable, lightweight, non-marking and odor-resistant qualities that Crocs wearers know and love. Crocs footwear is ideal for casual wear, as well as for professional use and recreational activities.

More than 100 million pairs of Crocs footwear have been sold to date.

The original Crocs products sold very well but then entered the maturity phase of the product life cycle. At this stage the managers used the original Crocs as cash cows to finance the development of new styles for different types of occasions.

Questions

1 Explain two features of Crocs that you would use when promoting the product. [6]
2 To what extent do you think the Crocs brand can last for another 30 years? Justify your answer. [10]

Study tip

You need to be able to discuss the value of the product life cycle model and product portfolio analysis. How can these models be used in marketing? What are their limitations? You also need to make sure you can apply them – can you tell from sales which stage of the life cycle a product is in? Can you identify a cash cow or dog product?

To make their businesses more effective, business managers need to monitor and develop suitable product portfolios. They must also adapt their marketing at different stages of the product life cycle. You need to be able to make recommendations such as how to extend the life cycle of a product or how to improve the portfolio of products of a business.

11.5 Pricing

The price of a product can have a major influence on its appeal and whether or not customers think it is good value for money. In this section we examine the factors influencing the price of a product and different pricing strategies. Getting the price right is an important element of effective marketing because it will determine whether customers believe they are receiving value for money.

How price affects purchasing decisions

The price of a product plays an important part in our decision about whether or not to buy it. If the price is too high, we simply cannot afford the product even if we want it! Even if we can afford it we may decide it is not value for money if the price seems too high compared to the benefits the product offers. The success of the low-costs airlines such as Southwest Airlines, Jetstar and Ryanair in gaining market share at the expense of firms such as British Airways shows how much the price can influence demand.

The price will, therefore, often play a significant role in the purchasing decision. However, the relative importance of price is likely to vary according to the product and the particular circumstances. For example, if two garages opposite each other are charging different prices for petrol, we are likely to choose the cheaper one. We are unlikely to be loyal to a particular brand of petrol. When buying a wedding ring, however, we do not always go for the cheapest! Similarly, when buying clothes and shoes we may be willing to pay more for an item if we think the brand justifies this.

Even if you wanted to choose the cheapest price it can be difficult to compare prices directly – look at how complicated the price structure is for mobile phones or electricity. The structure of special rates, different tariffs and different options is designed to make it difficult to know which is actually the best deal.

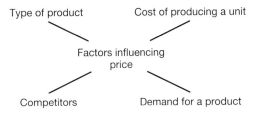

Figure 11.8 Factors influencing price

Fastjet

The Easyjet low-cost model adopted by Sir Stelios Haji-Ioannou and which proved so successful in Europe is now growing in Africa. Stelios recenty started up Fastjet, which will fly from Dar es Salaam in Tanzania for prices starting at 32000 Tanzanian shillings ($22) – plus the additional baggage charges and taxes.

Fastjet hopes to add Kenyan and Ugandan destinations alongside its regional service shortly and grow into a pan-African low-cost airline.

The business has merged with Fly540, an airline that will gradually disappear as Fastjet grows, but provides it with assets in Angola and Ghana as well as east Africa.

Africa is ripe for aviation investment, with huge distances between cities and poor road and rail infrastructure. However, a poor safety record has blighted African airlines, with many carriers prevented from flying in European airspace by safety regulators.

The Chief Executive of Fastjet said that getting around in Africa is incredibly difficult at the moment but if you put in a reliable service people will want it. The aim is to bring travel to people who don't even dream of flying.

Questions

1 Explain two factors that may have limited demand for air travel in Africa until now. [6]

2 Discuss the factors that may determine the success of Fastjet. [10]

Factors determining the price of a product

The price of a product will depend on the following range of factors.

The type of product

Demand for some products is more sensitive to price than others. When you are looking to buy a new microwave, for example, you are likely to look online or go to a shop that stocks several models. You may even go to a couple of different outlets to compare what they offer. This type of product is called a 'shopping good' because you shop around to find a good deal. These products are very sensitive to price differences so prices need to be competitive.

Other products are known as speciality items. These include high performance cars and luxury watches. Customers are likely to be willing to travel some distance to find these items and are heavily influenced by their design and branding factors. These products are less sensitive to price changes because they are so unique. This may lead to higher prices.

The cost of producing a unit

Although in the short term a firm may sell an item at a loss to get it established in a market, in the long term a product will nearly always have to generate a profit. This means the price has to be greater than the cost per unit. Some organisations (such as museums and hospitals) are non-profit making and so do not necessarily have to cover their costs. However, most firms in the private sector have to make a long-term profit to survive. The price therefore cannot fall below the unit cost for too long.

The ability of customers to pay

If the economy is doing well and customers have high income levels a firm may be able to increase prices. If, however, incomes are falling customers may be more sensitive to the price and look for a better deal (or wait before purchasing); this may delay any price increases by firms.

The demand for a product

The level of interest in and demand for a product will also affect the price that firms can charge. Holiday companies will often increase their prices in the school holidays when they know lots of families will want to go away. The holiday companies lower prices when demand is lower in term time.

The sensitivity of demand to price changes

The sensitivity of demand to price is measured by the price elasticity of demand (see page 116). Demand for some products is very sensitive to the price, as people shop around for the best deal. Other items may not be so sensitive, for example, if it is an exclusive item.

Competitors

The price that a business sets for its product must take account of competitors' prices. If competitors are offering a similar product or service and it is easy to switch from one to the other, firms are likely to set similar prices to each other.

This is why businesses will often stress the particular benefits of what they are offering, so they can justify a higher price. If customers believe a product provides better value for money, they may still buy it even if it is more expensive. Stella Artois beer, for example, ran a very successful 'reassuringly expensive' campaign in the UK, stressing that you pay more for high-quality lager.

There are now many websites offering price comparisons; this makes demand more sensitive to price as customers are looking around more. To see price comparison sites, visit www.kelkoo.co.uk and www.pricerunner.co.uk.

Pricing points

Some businesses aim to have a given range of products at particular pricing points in the market (e.g. the top or bottom end of the market) depending on the brand image and other elements of the marketing mix. Some businesses produce several different brands, priced at different levels. For example, a business may produce several different watches (often under different brand names): some in an exclusive range, some for the mass market and some discounted items.

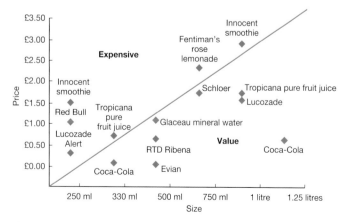

Figure 11.9 Competitors in the UK soft drinks market

Source: Mintel (2010)

Figure 11.9 shows competitors in the soft drinks market in the UK in terms of the size of the bottles sold and the price charged. This highlights which products appear to be good value and which appear to be expensive. The red line shows combinations of price and quantity. If a product is above the line this means that for the given quantity it is relatively expensive. If it is below the red line then for the given quantity it is regarded as relatively good value.

Question

1 Where would you choose to compete in this market? Justify your answer. [15]

The firm's objectives

The price charged by a firm will be influenced by its **objectives**. If a firm has a particular profit target, this will influence the price that is set per unit. If it wants to achieve $10 000 profit and expects to sell 20 000 units, it must make $0.50 profit per unit, if this is possible. If, however, it is aiming for a high market share (at least in the short term) it may be willing to sell at a lower price if this will help boost sales.

> **Key term**
>
> The **objective** of a business is the target it sets out to achieve.

The stage in the product life cycle

The price of a product is likely to be changed at different stages in the product life cycle. For example, when the product is in the maturity stage, the price may need to be reduced to avoid losing sales to competitors.

The rest of the marketing mix

The price a firm charges depends on the other elements of the marketing mix.

A heavily branded consumer product (such as Nike trainers or Coca-Cola) will be expensive compared to own-brand products, for example. An exclusive four-star restaurant will charge more than a fast-food store. A designer boutique will charge more than Primark.

Typically the price will be higher if the product:
- has a unique selling point
- is perceived as being exclusive
- is in high demand
- is sold through exclusive outlets.

There are therefore many factors that can influence the price of a product, and setting the price is a complex decision. If managers understand these influences, they can market their products more effectively by setting the right price for the market conditions. Managers can judge, for example, whether a price cut makes sense, given the market conditions.

Of course, a price is not fixed for ever and there are a number of times when a firm might reconsider the price it is charging for a product. In the following sections we consider different pricing strategies and approaches.

Vertu Ti

A luxury handmade mobile phone was launched in the UK in 2013 priced at more than £14 000 (about $24 000). The Vertu Ti is a titanium-cased, sapphire crystal-screened Android smartphone. Each one is handmade and signed by a single craftsman at the company's factory in Church Crookham, near Fleet in Hampshire.

It is the latest high-end phone by the British company, formerly part of Nokia, which was first in the news in 2002 when it offered a £15 000 Nokia phone available in 18-carat gold, white gold and top-of-the-range platinum cases. Its specifications put it alongside most other smartphones on the market, with an eight megapixel rear camera with flash, a 1.3MP front-facing camera and 64MB of internal memory. The company claims its 3.7-inch sapphire crystal screen is 'virtually scratch proof' and tested to be four times stronger than other smartphones against impacts. The company also claims its titanium case is around five times stronger than other smartphones.

Vertu has expanded on its concierge service that was available on previous handsets through a special button. It would allow wealthy users to call their own personal operator and ask for anything from local information to a table at the most exclusive restaurant in town. The 'Vertu key' on the new handset includes this but adds a 24/7 service including Vertu Certainty, which 'helps protect the device, its data and, where necessary, the customer'.

Source: www.vertu.com

Questions

1 Explain who you think is the target market for the new Vertu. [6]
2 Discuss the factors what would have influenced the price set for the new Vertu. [10]

Pricing strategies for new products

When a product is first launched into a market, a firm has to decide what price to charge. It has a number of options:

- **Penetration pricing** – this strategy uses a low price to enter the market and gain market share. This makes sense if there are cost advantages from producing on a large scale. For example,

in some markets a high level of investment is required to set up, such as when investing in premises and equipment. Once this investment has been carried out a firm may want to generate high levels of demand to spread the costs over many units. A low entry price might help do this.

Penetration pricing is also beneficial if the market is price sensitive (price elastic) in that a lower price will generate significantly higher sales and increase revenue (see page 116).

- **Price skimming** – this strategy uses a high price to enter a market. Even though the price is high, some people may still be eager to try a new product. Once sales from this group of people have been exhausted, the price can be dropped to attract a new group of customers. When this group is exhausted, the price can be cut again. A price skimming strategy is appropriate if the firm can protect its idea or invention so that competitors cannot enter with a cheaper version in the early stages. Price skimming makes sense if the market is not particularly price sensitive (i.e. it is price inelastic), so that a price cut would generate a relatively smaller increase in sales. This strategy is often used with new technology: the latest computer or computer accessory enters the market with a high price, which then falls quite rapidly a year or so later.

- **Competitive pricing** – some firms set their price at the same level as their competitors or deliberately undercut their rivals. The John Lewis Partnership claims it is 'never knowingly undersold'. Esso operates a 'Pricewatch' to monitor competitors' prices. Several retailers offer to refund the difference if you can find a similar product cheaper in another local store. Competitive pricing is common when consumers can easily make a direct comparison between different products. The rise in internet usage has made it easier for customers to compare prices between firms. This puts more pressure on firms to be competitive.

- **Price taking** – price takers are firms that accept the price which dominates in the market. A small independent electrical retailer, for example, may have to accept the price set by the major seller. Independent bookshops may have to follow the prices of major bookstores.

Figure 11.10 Pricing strategies

Penetration pricing is a pricing strategy aimed at gaining market share via a low entry price.

Price skimming occurs when a high initial price is set for a product and this is reduced over time.

By understanding these pricing strategies managers can decide on the best price to set when launching a new product.

11.6 Price elasticity of demand

Every business is interested in what affects demand for its products and services. What is it that makes its sales go up, or down? Will sales alter if it changes the price, or if incomes change? What is the strength of the relationship between, for example, price and sales? If the price is cut by 10 per cent, will sales go up by 5 per cent, or 50 per cent? Similarly, if average consumer income levels rise by 5 per cent, what impact will this have on demand for the firm's products?

The relationship between changes in demand and changes in factors such as price and income is measured by the elasticity of demand. There are several types of elasticity but one of the most important to businesses is the **price elasticity of demand**. This measures the sensitivity of demand to a change in price. A business can change its price, but before it does so, it will want to know the possible impact on the demand for its products.

Effective marketing involves an understanding of what influences demand and how sensitive demand is to different factors. This requires an understanding of the concept of elasticity.

Key term

The **price elasticity of demand** measures the sensitivity of demand to a change in price.

Why does the price elasticity of demand matter?

By calculating the price elasticity of demand, a firm can identify how changes in price may affect the quantity of its sales and, therefore, revenue. This is important for its marketing planning. If, for example, a firm is planning a price cut, it will want to estimate how much sales are likely to increase. This allows the business to ensure it has sufficient inventor or capacity to meet demand. It may also have implications in terms of employing people. For example, the firm may need to hire extra people or get staff to work overtime to meet orders. The business will also want to calculate whether the price cut is worthwhile financially. Will the price cut lead to higher profits, or not? An understanding of price elasticity should, therefore, lead to better pricing decisions.

Calculating the price elasticity of demand

The price elasticity of demand is measured by:

$$\frac{\text{Percentage change in quantity demanded}}{\text{Percentage change in price}}$$

Demand is said to be 'price elastic' if the value of the price elasticity of demand is greater than 1, i.e. every 1 per cent change in price brings about a more than 1 per cent change in quantity demanded.

For example, if demand rises by 20 per cent when the price is cut by 10 per cent, the price elasticity of demand will equal $+20/-10 = -2$.

The value of 2 shows that for every 1 per cent change in price, the quantity demanded changes by 2 per cent, i.e. by twice as much. The negative sign simply shows that the price and quantity demanded move in different directions. If price goes down, quantity demanded rises, and if price rises, quantity demanded falls.

Demand is said to be 'price inelastic' if the value of the price elasticity is less than 1, that is, if a 1 per cent change in price leads to a less than 1 per cent change in quantity demanded.

For example, a price cut of 10 per cent, leading to an increase in demand of only 5 per cent, will have a price elasticity of demand of $+5/-10 = -0.5$.

The negative sign shows that as price goes down, quantity demanded rises (i.e. they move in opposite directions). The 0.5 (which is less than 1) shows that every 1 per cent change in price leads to a 0.5 per cent change in quantity demanded.

This means that demand is not very sensitive to price changes (i.e. demand is price inelastic).

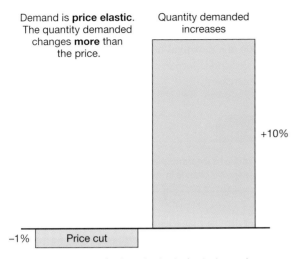

Figure 11.11 Price elastic and price inelastic demand

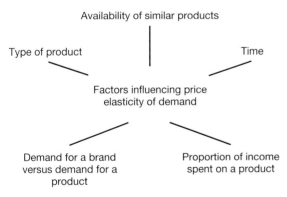

Maths moment

1 The price elasticity of demand is –0.8. What happens to sales if the price increases by 20 per cent?
2 The price elasticity of demand is –3. What happens to sales if the price increases by 20 per cent?

What determines the value of the price elasticity of demand?

Figure 11.12 Factors influencing the price elasticity of demand

The price elasticity of demand will be affected by a number of factors, such as:

● **The availability of similar products** If a consumer can switch easily from one product to another, its demand is likely to be quite sensitive to price changes (i.e. demand will be price elastic). When buying an energy-saving light bulb, for example, most customers do not care what brand they buy – faced with two types, they are likely to buy the cheaper one. Demand would therefore be price elastic. Many

businesses attempt to differentiate their products so that consumers do not switch to competitors' offerings (i.e. the firms try to make demand for their products price inelastic). Coca-Cola, for example, has worked hard to distinguish its products from other cola drinks. Coca-Cola hopes that relatively few consumers will switch brands even if its price is higher. Successful branding should, therefore, reduce the price elasticity of demand and make demand price inelastic.

● **Time** In the short term, customers are often loyal to their existing provider (for example, their credit card company, their bank or their insurance company). This may be because they can't be bothered to look for alternatives or because they think that changing isn't worth it in the short term as conditions might change again and so any advantage a competitor has may be temporary. However, over time, if customers feel they are getting a bad deal, this will act as an incentive to switch. They also have more time to explore their options. This means demand will become more price sensitive (i.e. more price elastic) over time.

● **The type of product** When buying convenience products, such as milk, purchasers tend to go to the nearest shop. Consumers do not spend much money on each item and are not too concerned about price. Demand for this type of product is likely to be price inelastic. In comparison, shopping goods such as clothes are likely to be much more sensitive to price (i.e. more price elastic): this is because customers spend time comparing their options.

● **The proportion of income spent on the product** If you spend only a small proportion of your income on a product you may not be very sensitive to price changes because they will have a limited impact on your spending. However, if you spend a high proportion of your income on something (such as housing) then a given percentage change will have a more noticeable effect and demand is likely to be more price sensitive.

● **Demand for the brand versus demand for the product** Demand for petrol is likely to be very price inelastic – most consumers would find it difficult or inconvenient to do without their cars. However, demand for one company's petrol is likely to be more price elastic than demand for petrol in general, as it is fairly easy to switch to another petrol company. Demand for a particular brand is therefore likely to be more price elastic than demand for the whole product category.

Price elasticity, total revenue and profits

A price cut and price elastic demand

If demand for a product is price elastic, a business can increase its revenue by lowering the price. Although it earns less for each item, its overall income increases because it is selling so many more products.

Imagine that a firm sells 10000 units at $5; its **total revenue** is 5 × 10000 = $50000. If the price is cut to $4 and sales jump to 15000 the new total revenue will be $4 × 15000 = $60000. A 20 per cent price cut increases sales by 50 per cent and revenue increases.

Whether this increase in revenue also means an increase in profit depends on what happens to the costs when the firm produces and sells more. If, for example, a firm has to increase capacity, it may incur significant additional expenses and so, although it is earning more, profits may fall. On the other hand, if revenue increases more than costs, profits will rise.

> **Key term**
>
> The **total revenue** is the income generated from sales. It is also called 'turnover' or 'sales'.

A price cut and price inelastic demand

If demand for a product is **price inelastic**, the revenue will fall when the price is cut. This is because the increase in sales is not big enough to compensate for the fact that each item is selling for less.

Imagine that a firm sells 10000 units at $5; its total revenue is 5 × 10000 = $50000. If the price is cut to $4 and sales increase to 11000 the new total revenue will be $4 × 11000 = $44000. A 20 per cent price cut increases sales by only 10 per cent and revenue falls.

In this situation, when demand is price inelastic the business could earn more by putting the price up. Although it would lose some customers, the fact that it is charging more per unit means its overall income will increase.

Imagine that a firm sells 10000 units at $5; its total revenue is 5 × 10000 = $50000. If the price is increased to $6 and sales fall to 9000, the new total revenue will be $6 × 9000 = $54000. A 20 per cent price increase cuts sales by only 10 per cent and revenue increases.

> **Key term**
>
> A **price inelastic demand** means that the impact of a change in price leads to a smaller change in the quantity demanded (in percentages).

Table 11.3 Summary table: price elasticity and revenue

	Price decrease	**Price increase**
Price elastic demand	Revenue increases	Revenue decreases
Price inelastic demand	Revenue decreases	Revenue increases

> **Case Study**
>
> ## Price elasticity of demand

Table 11.4 Price elasticity of demand

Goods	**Estimated price elasticity of demand**
Inelastic	
Salt	−0.10
Matches	−0.10
Toothpicks	−0.10
Coffee	−0.25
Tobacco products, short run	−0.45
Legal services, short run	−0.40
Taxi, short run	−0.60
Cars, long run	−0.20
Approximately unitary elastic	
Films	−0.90
Housing, owner-occupied, long run	−1.20
Private education	−1.10
Elastic	
Restaurant meals	−2.30
Foreign travel, long run	−4.00
Airline travel, long run	−2.40
Fresh green peas	−2.80
Cars, short run	−1.20 to −1.50

Sources: Bohi (1981); Cheng, and Capps Jr (1988); Gwartney, and Stroup (1997); Houthakker, and Taylor (1970); US Department of Agriculture

Questions

1 Explain what is meant by a price elastic and a price inelastic demand. [6]

2 Discuss the significance of the findings in Table 11.4 for marketing managers. [15]

Study tip

Students' understanding of elasticity is often imprecise and so when someone has actually grasped the concept accurately it stands out from the other scripts! It is worth learning elasticity carefully.

Think about your wording – a price inelastic demand means that the relative change in the quantity demanded is less than the change in price. It does not mean that there is no change at all. Remember that elasticity measures change in the quantity demanded relative to changes in other variables.

Case Study

Elasticity of air travel demand

The price elasticity of air travel demand varies according to the coverage and location of the market in which prices are changed and the importance of the air travel price within the overall cost of travel.

The estimate for the price elasticity of demand for a particular route was found to be −1.4 on average, whereas the price elasticity of demand for flights from any airport in one country to another were −0.8.

Air travel price elasticities on short-haul routes were higher than on long-haul routes. This largely reflects the greater opportunity for substitution on short-haul routes (e.g. travellers can switch to rail or car in response to air travel price increases).

Questions

1 Explain why demand for short-haul flights was more price elastic than demand for long-haul flights. [6]

2 Discuss the significance of the findings above for the pricing of fights on a particular route. [10]

Maths moment

The price elasticity of demand is −0.2.

The price is $200 and sales are 500 units. The price increases by 10 per cent.

1 What is the effect on sales?
2 What was the original total revenue?
3 What is the new total revenue?

The price elasticity of demand is −2.5.

The price is $200 and sales are 500 units. The price increases by 10 per cent.

4 What is the effect on sales?
5 What was the original total revenue?
6 What is the new total revenue?

Problems with the price elasticity of demand concept

It is important to remember that the value of price elasticity of demand at any moment is an estimate (you will never know exactly how sensitive demand is to price until you actually change the price and see what happens). Therefore, a specific value of price elasticity of demand needs to be treated with some caution. This is especially true because markets keep changing and this will affect the price elasticity of demand. New products, changes in consumer tastes, developments in distribution and competitors' marketing campaigns will all affect the demand for a product. This can make it difficult to know exactly what caused a change in sales following a price change. Was it the price change? Or was it government policies, or consumer confidence? While it may appear that a price cut of 1 per cent increased sales by 2 per cent, suggesting a price elasticity of −2, in reality the sales may have gone up for completely different reasons.

Having said this, with experience, by asking experts or by analysing the results from a test market, managers are likely to have some idea of approximately how sensitive demand is to price and may feel confident to base pricing decisions on this. Even if they do not know the exact value, an understanding of whether demand is price elastic or inelastic is useful when it comes to setting and changing prices.

Price discrimination

You will sometimes find that demand conditions for the same product can vary. For example, demand for pubic transport around 8a.m. is very heavy, as people want to get to work for

9a.m. Similarly, demand is busy between 5p.m. and 6p.m., as people want to get home. Demand is less heavy at other times of day. If a business can identify different demand conditions it may want to change the price in the different markets.

The demand for transport before 9a.m. and between 5p.m and 6p.m. is likely to be price inelastic: it is not sensitive to price because people have to get to and from work. At these times a transport business may increase price to increase revenue. At other times of day demand may be more price elastic (i.e. sensitive to price) because there is not the same pressure on people to travel; they can always delay their journey or not go at all. To raise revenue at these times the business may decrease price.

The result is that you pay different prices for the same journey at different times of day. This is known as 'price discrimination'.

Price discrimination may occur when firms charge different prices:

- at different times of day, for example, taxi fares may be higher after midnight
- to different age groups, for example, lower fares on the bus for children and pensioners
- to different customer groups, for example, discounts for members.

11.7 Promotion methods

A business has to communicate the benefits of its products to its customers. It has to let them know the product exists, what it does and why they should buy it. In this section we examine the importance of the promotional mix in marketing. Managing the way that a business communicates with its customers about its products is vital to its success.

What is promotion?

The promotion of a product involves communicating about it to existing or potential customers. These messages may be intended to:

- inform customers (e.g. tell them about modifications to the product, promotional offers or new releases)
- persuade them (e.g. highlighting your product's benefits compared with the competitors)
- reassure buyers they did the right thing by buying the product in the first place.

The promotional mix

The **promotional mix** refers to the combination of ways in which a business can communicate with its customers. The choice of promotional mix influences the effectiveness of the way in which the business is communicating: this in turn influences the effectiveness of the firm's marketing.

Key term

The **promotional mix** refers to the combination of ways in which the business communicates about its products.

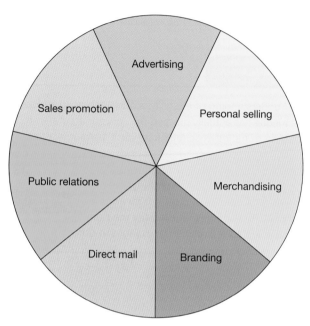

Figure 11.13 The promotional mix

The elements of the promotional mix include the following.

Advertising

Advertising is a paid for means of communication. Advertising is often used as a long-term strategy to build brand loyalty. There are, of course, many different media available in terms of advertising, such as newspapers, radio, television and billboards. Managers must determine the most appropriate media to use. This depends on the resources available, the target group and their lifestyles, the likely sales (which influences how much can be spent) and the nature of the product. Mass-market products such as cars may be able to justify television advertising, for example, whereas a local decorator may advertise in shop windows or the Yellow Pages. The difficulty with advertising is that many consumers are bombarded by different adverts and so getting a message through to your target group that they actually pay attention to can be difficult. With the growth of digital television and radio, as well as the internet, the volume of messages aimed at consumers is increasing all the time and this can reduce the effectiveness of some advertising. Advertisers therefore have to think carefully about what messages to deliver, what media to use and when to advertise.

Having said this, advertising can be very effective. For example, heavy investment in advertising built the Magner's cider brand so well that sales in 2006 rose by 225 per cent!

Effective advertising targets the customer cost effectively and communicates the key messages successfully.

Sales promotions

Sales promotions are attempts to boost sales using techniques such as promotional offers, competitions and price cuts. Offers can include 10 per cent extra free and 'buy one, get one free' (called 'BOGOF'). Sales promotions may be used as a means of boosting sales in the short term. When undertaking a promotional campaign a firm must consider:

- What will it cost?
- What will it do to the brand image?
- To what extent will the offer be effective (e.g. the type of offer you would give as a sportswear company is different from a wine or perfume business)?
- What is the likely impact on sales?

Personal selling

Personal selling is based on face-to-face contact with customers. This may be used by manufacturers to get distributors to take their products or in industrial markets and the service sector, where the producer often deals directly with the customer. Financial services, such as pensions, insurance and mortgages, are often sold in this way. Similarly, the sale of products, such as photocopiers, often takes place through a sales force. If a product is sold in low volumes, is technical and complex and needs to be explained to customers, then a sales force is likely to be an effective promotional method. The sales team can be absolutely essential in some markets. For example, manufacturers must work through the retailers; the manufacturers' companies' sales teams compete very aggressively to get their products displayed in the best way to get their promotions highlighted in the stores.

Public relations (PR)

Public relations activities involve contact with the media and the various groups that the firm deals with. It attempts to send out particular messages about the firm or its products. Whereas with advertising you pay for an advert to be run in the media, with public relations you are creating a story or event to attract attention that you do not have to pay for. Public relations might involve press releases to the media, handling customer complaints and organising events to promote particular messages.

Sponsorship is a common form of public relations activity. A business will sponsor an individual or event to raise its profile. You will often find major sports competitions are sponsored by businesses. In 2012, for example, Chelsea Football Club renewed its shirt sponsorship tie-up with Samsung, in a deal said to be worth about £18 million a season. Manchester United and US car giant General Motors have a deal worth $559 million (£349 million) that will last for seven years from 2014.

Case Study

Richard Branson and the Virgin brand

Figure 11.14 Richard Branson

Richard Branson was born in 1950 and educated at Stowe School. He went into business aged 16, publishing *Student* magazine. As a young entrepreneur it was clear he had a real flair for publicity. Having originally founded Virgin as a mail-order record company he later opened his first store in London's Oxford Street. The Virgin Records music label was formed in 1972. Mike Oldfield's *Tubular Bells*, recorded in Virgin's first recording studio – an Oxfordshire barn – and released in 1973, was a best-seller. When punk rock came along, Virgin signed the Sex Pistols, even though other record companies refused to touch them. This proved to be a marketing success. Many other stars were signed up including Genesis, Peter Gabriel, Simple Minds and The Rolling Stones, making Virgin Records a major player in the international music business. Since then, the Virgin brand has been expanded into air and rail travel, mobile phones, finance, weddings, wines, retail, drinks, hotels and gymnasiums. It now has around 200 companies in over 30 countries, employing more than 25 000 people.

One of Branson's strengths has been his ability to get free publicity for the business. He has had his picture taken in a wedding dress, as well as with Pamela Anderson, with Diana, Princess of Wales and Nelson Mandela. In 1985, Sir Richard set out from New York to beat the record for crossing the Atlantic by boat, but barely 100 miles (160 km) from home the boat hit some floating driftwood and sank. In 2004, he set the record for the fastest crossing of the English Channel by an amphibious vehicle to mark the twentieth anniversary of Virgin Atlantic. Branson's latest venture is space travel!

Source: Adapted from news.bbc.co.uk

Questions

1 Explain two key features of the Virgin brand. [6]
2 Discuss other products that you think the Virgin brand could extend to. Justify your choices. [10]

Direct mail

This type of promotion involves sending mailshots to customers. With increasingly sophisticated database information, these can be carefully targeted.

Branding

In some markets branding is very important. By building a **brand**, businesses hope to make customers more loyal. This may allow them to charge more for items, by making demand price inelastic. It may also make it easier to introduce new products under the same brand name as customers may feel reassured and be more willing to try them. If customers recognise a brand they can associate with all of its values and this in itself can provide a benefit – people may feel more secure driving a Volvo, more fashionable using an Apple Mac and smarter wearing Prada. Increasingly, some people want to identify with a brand and the lifestyle that is associated with it. Brand loyalty is very important because it is easier and cheaper for a business to sell more to an existing customer than it is to generate a new customer.

However, a brand has to be protected and managers have to be careful that it does not become associated with the wrong things. For example, in 2010 Toyota had to recall millions of cars due to a brake problem which damaged the company's reputation for quality.

Key term

A **brand** is a name, design, logo, symbol or indeed anything that makes a product recognisable and distinguishes it from the competition in the eyes of the customer.

Case Study

Best global brands

Table 11.5 Best global brands

2012	Name	Country	Estimated worth 2012 $m
1	Apple	USA	70605
2	Google	USA	47463
3	Microsoft	USA	45812
4	IBM	USA	39135
5	Walmart	USA	38320
6	Samsung	Korea	38197
7	GE	USA	33124
8	Coca-Cola	USA	31082
9	Vodafone	UK	30044
10	Amazon.com	USA	28665

Source: http://brandirectory.com

Questions

1 Choose one of the brands in Table 11.5 and explain what you think are the brand values (i.e. what does the brand stand for?). [6]
2 Discuss the benefits to a business of having a strong brand. [10]

Merchandising

This includes using the name of a product on a range of other items. Bands will sell CDs but also T-shirts, posters, mugs, toys and so on. The brand is being extended via merchandising. Merchandising also includes the various methods used to promote in-store sales, such as point-of-purchase displays (POPs).

Case Study

Swatch

The Swatch Group manufactures and sells finished watches, jewellery, watch movements and components. Its brands include: Tissot, Swatch, Flik Flak, Blamian, Brecquet, Omega, Rado and Calvin Klein. These brands target different groups and have different price points.

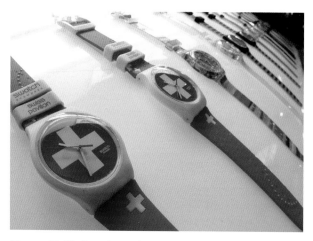

Figure 11.15 Swatch watches

Questions

1 Explain what is meant by segmentation. [6]
2 Discuss the possible reasons why a firm such as Swatch operates with different brand names. [10]

Each of the different methods of promotion has its own advantages and disadvantages, as shown in Table 11.6. For example, personal selling is obviously quite labour intensive and therefore expensive, but the firm gets immediate feedback from its customers.

Table 11.6 A comparison of promotional methods

Method of promotion	Advantages	Disadvantages
Advertising	• Wide coverage • Control of the message • Can be used to build brand loyalty	• Can be expensive, e.g. TV advertising
Public relations	• Can be relatively cheap	• Cannot control the way the story is covered by the media
Direct mail	• Relatively cheap	• May not get read
Sales promotions	• Can entertain and interest the consumer	• Often short-term effects • Can encourage brand switching
Personal selling	• Two-way communication • Can answer customer enquiries	• Can be expensive • Can only reach a limited number of customers
Branding	• Can enable higher pricing • Can launch other products building on brand loyalty	• Brands may get damaged (for example, through poor quality) and this affects any products sold under this name
Merchandising	• Can make the shopping experience better through the displays • May encourage purchase of items that were not originally intended (impulse buys)	• There will be a cost involved in providing displays in terms of both money and time

Case Study

Red Bull

Red Bull is an 'energy drink' that originated in Thailand and is sold to combat mental and physical fatigue. The marketing of the product has been highly successful and includes a number of unusual promotional methods. For example:

• Selected students (students are a key market) are given free cases of Red Bull if they throw a party; others are given a car with a model Red Bull on the top to drive around and be noticed by others. This is known as 'viral marketing'. It relies on a few key trendsetters spreading the word about a product and leading to others wanting to be associated with it.

• Sales teams identify key bars and clubs and promote heavily via merchandise such as branded coolers and POP displays.

• Heavy investment in brand building including promoting the slogan 'Red Bull gives you wings'.

• Red Bull sponsors many extreme sports events including cliff diving, BMX and skiing. Red Bull also sponsors the Red Bull Flugtag ('flight day' in German), a competition where entrants launch themselves off a 30-foot (9-metre) ramp in homemade 'flying machines' into a body of water.

• In recent years mainstream advertising such as television has also been used.

Questions

1 Explain the reasons why a business might choose to sponsor an event. [6]
2 Discuss other types of events you think it would make sense for Red Bull to sponsor. Explain your selection. [10]

Choosing the promotional mix

Businesses use a combination of promotional methods to communicate to potential customers about their products.

The composition of the promotional mix depends on numerous factors:

• **The nature of the product** Consumer durable products, such as televisions and washing machines, are likely to be advertised to the final customer. Firms usually use a sales team to deal with wholesalers and retailers but use advertising to get customers to demand the product in the stores. By raising awareness of the brand, customers will recognise it when they go to buy a product. Similarly, companies producing shampoos and household cleaners often advertise on television. By comparison, sales of heavy construction equipment are usually made direct to the customer and rely on the sales force. There are relatively few customers in this case, the product is expensive and sold in low volumes and there are many technical details that need to be explained. A sales force is likely to be much more effective than, say, an advert in a brochure.

• **The marketing expenditure budget** Inevitably, the budget acts as a constraint on all firms' promotional activities because it limits the amount of money available to spend in this area. Faced with a small marketing budget, for example, a firm cannot even consider television advertising and may have to rely on local newspaper advertising instead.

• **The available options** Technological developments are creating new possibilities, such as internet advertising and text advertising. Legal changes also influence what is possible, for example, what products can be advertised and how they can promote themselves. For example, there are strong restrictions on the promotional of alcohol and tobacco.

Improvements in the promotional mix may:
- reduce costs as cheaper ways of communicating are adopted
- boost sales as better ways of communicating are used to communicate more effectively and to more people.

> **Key term**
>
> The **marketing expenditure budget** is the amount of money a business allocates to spend on marketing activities such as promotion.

> **Study tip**
>
> You need to be able to understand the different messages a business might be trying to communicate to different groups such as investors and consumers.
>
> You also need to understand the different elements of the promotional mix and how these will be changed for different products and different situations. Think about whether some methods are more appropriate than others for specific products. Do not assume advertising is always the answer – there are many other ways of communicating that may be more effective for some products.
>
> To make its promotion more effective, a business might alter the total amount spent on it or review the promotional mix. As customers' habits change, the mix might need to be altered as well (e.g. switching to more internet advertising).

Above the line and below the line promotion

Above the line promotion refers to mainstream advertising such as television and posters. Below the line promotion refers to other promotional activities such as free gifts, discounts and special offers. Advertising is sometimes said to 'pull' customers into a shop or online store and below the line promotion activities are sometimes said to then 'push' you into buying. For example, you see an advert that makes you aware of a brand; then a special offer inside the shop makes you buy.

Types of packaging

Packaging can be an important element of the marketing mix, so much so that many people include it as a separate 'P' along with price, promotion and the others (see pages 105–06). Alternatively it can be included as part of the 'product'.

Packaging is important:
- to protect the product from damage in transport or in store
- to help promote the product, for example, if it is attractive in design
- to provide information to the customer.

11.8 Channels of distribution (place)

The distribution of a good or service refers to the way in which the ownership of it passes from the producer to the consumer. In some cases, the product goes directly to the end customer from the producer: for example, Dell Computers supplies some of its customers direct, without intermediaries, as does Avon cosmetics. Services such as insurance, health care and education tend to be provided directly to the end customers.

In other cases, producers use intermediaries: most producers of electrical goods, such as Sony and Phillips, have intermediaries between the producer and the final seller. These intermediaries include:
- retailers (such as Walmart), which are the final stage in the distribution chain. Many goods are sold through retailers rather than direct to the customer.
- wholesalers. These buy products in bulk from producers and sell these on to retailers, who then sell direct to the final consumer. Retailers use wholesalers because they offer a range of products and it is easier than dealing directly with them than with many different individual manufacturers.

> **Key terms**
>
> The **distribution channel** describes how the ownership of a product moves from the producer to the customer.
>
> The **distribution outlet** is where the product is actually sold, e.g. the shop.

The different **distribution channels** can be described in terms of the number of levels involved in the process:

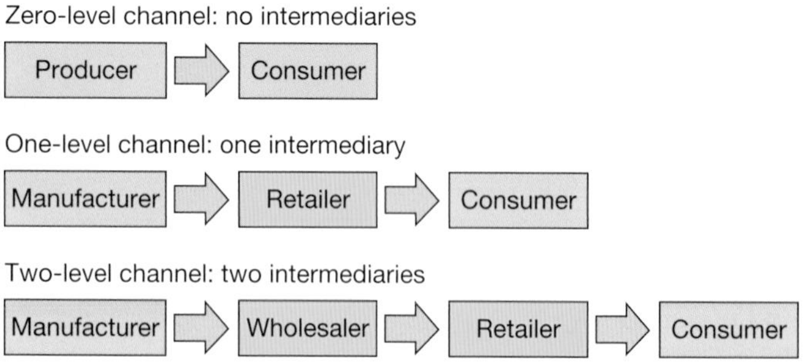

Zero-level channel: no intermediaries

Producer ⇨ Consumer

One-level channel: one intermediary

Manufacturer ⇨ Retailer ⇨ Consumer

Two-level channel: two intermediaries

Manufacturer ⇨ Wholesaler ⇨ Retailer ⇨ Consumer

Figure 11.16 Distribution channels

- In a zero-level channel, the good or service passes directly from producer to consumer without any intermediaries. For example, dentists, accountants and plumbers have zero-level channels.
- A one-level channel has one intermediary. For example, a retailer buys the product from the manufacturer and sells it to the consumer.

- A two-level channel has two intermediaries. For example, a wholesaler buys the product from the manufacturer and sells it on to retailers, who sell to the final customers.

The distribution strategy will vary considerably from product to product. In the case of milk, newspapers and chewing gum, for example, the aim is usually to generate as wide a distribution as possible. These types of goods are called convenience items because consumers are not willing to travel far to buy them – they need them to be easily accessible. In order to get to as broad a market as possible, several intermediaries may be used.

With products such as personal computers, vacuum cleaners, microwaves, and so on, consumers usually want to compare the features and prices of different brands. Manufacturers of these products need to get them distributed to certain stores where customers expect to go to find them. These shopping goods do not need to be distributed to as many outlets as convenience items, but the firm may have to fight hard to get intermediaries to stock them. Although with the growth of online shopping manufacturers do sell directly to customers, many sales are still through retailers.

More exclusive (or speciality) products, such as Rolex, Porsche, Bang & Olufsen and Bose have even fewer outlets, but the nature of these outlets is very important. They must reinforce the nature of the brand and so a great deal of time is spent ensuring they are well maintained and suitably exclusive. In some cases, the manufacturer owns the outlet to ensure it presents its products in a way that is appropriate to the brand.

Products that are sold to other businesses (i.e. business-to-business marketing) rather than the final consumer are called **producer** or **industrial goods** (rather than consumer goods). These tend to be distributed directly. This might include machinery, office equipment and specialised computer software.

> **Key term**
>
> **Producer** or **industrial goods** are sold from one business to another; they are used in the production of the final product.

Choosing a distribution channel

The choice of distribution channel will depend on factors such as:

- **Access to markets** If the target number of customers is relatively small (e.g. you are targeting a few large companies) then it may be possible to distribute directly. If, however, you have a mass-market consumer product, it is not realistic to try to distribute individually to all your customers – you will want to use intermediaries to help get your products to the market. Heinz could not distribute its baked beans to every individual household in the UK: it has to sell via wholesalers and retailers.
- **The desired degree of control** If a producer sells its products to other intermediaries then it hands over control of

the way they are marketed. The new owner can change the price, the way it is described relative to its competitors and where it is displayed in the market. Concern over the impact of such decisions on the brand may mean that a producer decides to sell directly or only via its own outlets.
- **Costs** It may be cheaper to sell a product direct to the customer. If the product goes through various intermediaries, all of whom add on their own profit margin, the final price will probably be higher than if the business sold direct to a customer.

Companies such as Amazon.com, Direct Line and lastminute.com have turned the distribution of their services into a major competitive weapon. By distributing directly to the customer, they have cut their own costs (enabling them to offer better value) and provide a more convenient service for customers. You can now order your weekly shopping, buy your books, check your bank account and book your holiday from home. The internet allows many firms (even very small firms) to deal directly with their customers on a global basis.

Choosing the right distribution channel is an important (and often underestimated) part of the marketing mix. It can have a big impact on the success of the business in terms of factors such as:

- market coverage
- costs
- control over the way the product is promoted and marketed in store.

Getting the right distribution outlet

Of course, the nature of the distribution outlet itself can have an impact on the buying experience. The layout of the stores, the decor, the availability of staff and changing rooms, the in-store displays all leave an impression and influence your view of a product. This is particularly important for speciality items such as luxury cars, jewellery or sophisticated technology. Visit a Mercedes dealership, a Gucci outlet or an Apple store and you immediately get a sense of the brand values.

If producers of such products are selling through stores (theirs or anyone else's) the store design and the way their products are displayed is very important. IKEA, the Swedish furniture retailer, is renowned for its highly effective store design. Its stores are very large and are placed out of town. This makes it cheaper for the company to offer a large number of parking spaces. The stores are relatively easy to get to for car drivers, which is important because the items bought are often big and bulky. Once customers get there, the stores are designed in such a way that they have to walk through all the displays to get to the tills – you cannot nip in and buy one thing. This tends to mean that customers buy more than they had planned.

Case Study

Dell Computers

Figure 11.17 Michael Dell

Michael Dell revolutionised the personal computer industry by missing out intermediaries and selling directly to the customer. He also innovated the way PCs were produced by developing a process to mass-produce individual made-to-order computers. Customers select from a variety of options what type of monitor, what memory, what base unit and so on they require. These are selected and then the computer you 'built' is produced for you. You can make these choices and order your computer online without having to speak to anyone.

Michael Dell was in born February 1965 and started his business in his University of Texas room in 1984 with just $1000 and an idea to provide affordable personal computers to college students. He went on to become Chairman and Chief Executive of a company with a net worth of more than $30 billion.

Michael Dell is the author of *Direct from Dell: Strategies That Revolutionized an Industry*. The book includes the story about his rise to the top and also his business philosophy.

Questions

1 Explain two benefits of selling online. [6]
2 Discuss the possible reasons why Dell changed its strategy in recent years and started to sell its products through retailers as well as online. [10]

In supermarkets, all kinds of techniques are used to make you buy more:
- The width of the aisles and the music being played affects the speed that you walk around the store.
- You will usually be greeted by the fresh fruit displays when you walk in; this creates an impression in your mind that all their products are fresh.
- The aroma in the store is likely to be fresh bread (many now have bakeries on site but even if they do not they can create the smell of fresh bread): this tends to create positive, warm feelings within us.
- You will usually enter on the left-hand side of a store because we tend to like to walk in and turn right.
- The basic items such as bread and milk will usually be at the back of the store so that you have to pass many other items to find them and hopefully buy other things along the way.
- Key items on promotion will be placed in display bins at the end of aisles so you see them when you turn, or by the tills: these are to prompt impulse items.
- Complementary items such as soft drinks and crisps will usually be placed near each other: buying one may prompt the buying of the other.

Store designers have become very aware of the effects that the decor and layout can have on customers and have therefore become much more sophisticated in their designs. The physical environment is an element of the marketing mix because it can have an important effect on where we choose to shop and how we behave as shoppers while we are there.

Case Study

Hotel Chocolat

Angus Thirlwell, managing director of the upmarket chocolate chain Hotel Chocolat, started an online chocolate business ten years ago but has found greater success with a conventional high-street presence.

He has put careful thought into the design of the stores, the first of which opened in Watford in the UK in October 2005, two years after the internet site launched.

'We chose dark walnut wood interiors and porcelain tiles. We've also used long counters like a hotel reception desk and made them spacious so that people can wander around, like in a hotel lobby,' he says. Whereas fast delivery was the sales pitch of the internet website, quality is the selling point of the stores.

The internet company out of which Hotel Chocolat grew was funded with £5000 each from Angus Thirlwell and his business partner, Peter Harris. It now turns over £40 million a year.

Questions

1 Explain two factors Hotel Chocolat might take into account when deciding where to open a new store.   [6]
2 Discuss the possible reasons why Hotel Chocolat was more successful when it opened stores than it was when it was just operating online.   [10]

Study tip

You need to think about the factors that influence a company's choice of distribution channel and its outlets and the effect this has on its costs and the quality of service it provides. A business may improve its effectiveness by reviewing its distribution, as this may influence its market coverage, the level of service provided and its costs.
Many people underestimate the importance of distribution but it is often vital to the success of a product. You will only sell chewing gum or newspapers if they are widely distributed and well displayed, for example.

11.9 Using the internet for the 4 Ps/4 Cs

The growth of the internet is an important external change which has, of course, had a big impact on marketing activities. For example:

- Businesses can now trade globally 24 hours a day seven days a week relatively easily.
- They can target marketing, for example, using Google Adwords so that your advert only shows when some key words are used.
- They can monitor consumer behaviour very accurately, for example, tracking how visitors to the website move around the site.
- They can enable different prices to be charged depending on where people are searching from and when they search. This is known as dynamic pricing and is used a lot by airlines and hotels. The price you are offered depends on when you enquire and what demand is at that stage; if there are still lots of vacancies the prices tend to be cheaper.
- It enables direct distribution from the producer to the consumer without the need for wholesalers and retailers. It also enables electronic distribution (e.g. of music and books) without a physical product being distributed, for example to e-readers and MP3 players.

The internet and the marketing mix

Table 11.7 Impacts of the internet on marketing

Element of the marketing mix	Impact of the internet
Price	The internet allows prices to be changed according to when people order (for example, how far in advance of an event), what time of day they order, whether they have visited the site before, whether they have bought from you before. The ability to adjust the price based on many factors so there is no 'one' price is known as 'dynamic pricing'. Businesses such as airlines and online retailers such as Amazon use dynamic pricing very effectively.
Promotion	Businesses can promote their products online and target who their adverts reach depending on, for example, where you are searching from and which terms you are using to search. Businesses can get others to help promote their products through viral marketing where their own campaign is forwarded via social media such as Twitter and Facebook by individuals to their friends. Methods of promotion such as blogs and Twitter are cheap ways of communicating.
Distribution	Businesses can now sell direct to the customer online rather than selling through intermediaries. By selling directly through e-commerce, a business may need fewer physical stores. This is known as 'clicks rather than bricks'.
Product	Some products can now be downloaded rather than having to be physically produced, for example music and e-books.
People	Interestingly, people are not necessarily removed from marketing due to the internet. In fact, many businesses now promote in their websites the ability to talk to a customer service representative at any time. The internet can interest you in an item and the sales representative can help you with enquiries or to make your choice.
Process	The internet can make the buying process more convenient in that you can search more widely than in a main shopping street.
Physical evidence	The design of a store may be less significant with the internet but the design of the website becomes the key. The appearance, the ease of finding information and navigating the site affect the customer experience.

Case Study

E-books

A recent report found that four times more US readers, or 15 per cent, are now reading e-books on a typical day compared with less than two years ago. In bed, however, the verdict is split. Around 45 per cent of those surveyed preferred e-books and 43 per cent prefer old-fashioned print.

These findings highlight the huge cultural and publishing changes as people do more of their book reading online.

The e-book industry has grown from $78 million in sales in 2008 to $1.7 billion in 2011, according to Albert Greco, a book industry expert at Fordham University. He has estimated e-book sales will be $3.55 billion in 2012.

Forrester, a consultancy, has forecast that nearly a quarter of Americans will own an e-book reader by 2016. Online retailer Amazon.com has about 65 per cent of the e-book market, according to Cowen & Co estimates.

Discussion question

Do you think there is anything publishers can do to increase sales of printed books?

11.10 An effective marketing mix?

The key thing to remember when discussing the marketing mix is that it must be part of an integrated approach for it to be effective. This means that all the different elements of the mix must work together and complement each other. There is little point trying to develop a high-priced, exclusive brand to target high-income earners if it is then distributed through bargain outlets.

In a well-managed mix, the elements fit well together and enhance the overall value provided to the customer. Think about when you last bought a mobile phone; you probably thought about the brand name, the features and design of a particular model, the various pricing plans that existed on networks, the length of the contract, the terms of insurance and any special offers available. Many different factors would have combined to influence you.

Having said this, the nature of the product and market conditions will mean that some elements of the mix are more important than others for particular products. For example:

- If you have a car insurance business you may invest heavily in advertising to generate enquiries and a sales team to take the enquiries: if you own a local bakery, you may not spend much on advertising at all and rely on word of mouth.
- If you are setting up a luxury hotel you may search for a long time to find the right place for your outlet: if you are a web-based business you may operate from home.
- If you are selling gift-type products then packaging may be very important to attract the customer and impress the consumer; if you sell computer equipment to businesses, packaging may be important only in terms of protecting the items during transportation.
- If you are selling exclusive handmade shirts, a high price may be used to reflect quality: if you are selling caravan holidays a low price may be important in order to compete.

What really matters for the mix to be effective is that the various elements combine and complement each other in such a way that the customer believes that the product provides better value for money than the competition. Improving the marketing mix may therefore involve:

- offering more benefits in relation to the price, perhaps by adding additional features
- promoting the benefits of the product more effectively so the customer identifies more closely with it or understands more clearly what it does
- making the product more accessible so that it is easier for customers to buy.

It is important to see the 4 Ps model as a rather basic model of what influences a decision to buy, or not buy, a product: the buying process is a very complicated one and involves many different factors. For example, we are influenced by factors such as the people who serve us, the way in which we can buy the product (e.g. can we order online or not?) and the ease with which the features of one product can be compared with others. The mix should be thought of as anything connected with a product or service that influences the buyers' decision.

Study tip

You need to remember that the right marketing mix depends on many factors, such as the type of the product and the competitive situation. You need to be able to analyse the marketing mix in the given context. Do not just list the 4 Ps whenever you get a question on the marketing mix; think about what is actually involved in marketing this particular type of product.
To make a business more effective, the entrepreneur needs to develop an outstanding marketing mix, with each element complementing the other.

Case Study

Barbie

Barbie, the best-selling fashion doll, was launched in 1959. The doll is produced by Mattel, Inc., and is a major source of revenue for the company. Ruth Handler, the creator of Barbie, watched her daughter Barbara at play with paper dolls, and noticed that she often enjoyed giving them adult roles. At the time, most children's toy dolls were representations of infants. Realising that there could be a gap in the market, Handler developed the idea of an adult-looking doll.

The first Barbie doll wore a black and white zebra striped swimsuit and ponytail, and was available as either a blonde or a brunette. Around 350 000 Barbie dolls were sold during the first year of production. Since then Barbie's appearance has been changed many times.

The promotion of Barbie was based extensively on television advertising: this approach has now been copied widely by other toys. It is estimated that more than a billion Barbie dolls have been sold worldwide in over 150 countries and Mattel claims that three Barbie dolls are sold every second.

Barbie products include not only the range of dolls with their clothes and accessories, but also a huge range of Barbie branded goods such as books, fashion items and video games. Barbie has also appeared in a series of animated films and makes an appearance in the film *Toy Story 2*.

Mattel estimates that there are more than 100 000 Barbie collectors. Ninety per cent are women, at an average age of 40, purchasing more than 20 Barbie dolls each year. Around 45 per cent of them spend upwards of $1000 a year.

Vintage Barbie dolls from the early years are the most valuable at auction, and while the original Barbie was sold for $3 in 1959, a mint-boxed Barbie from 1959 sold for $3552.50 on eBay in October 2004. In recent years, Mattel has sold a wide range of Barbie dolls aimed specifically at collectors, including porcelain versions and depictions of Barbie as a range of characters from television series such as *The Munsters* and *Star Trek*.

In June 2001, MGA Entertainment launched the Bratz range of dolls, a move that gave Barbie her first serious competition in the fashion doll market. In 2005, figures showed that sales of Barbie dolls had fallen by 30 per cent in the United States, and by 18 per cent worldwide, with much of the drop being attributed to the popularity of Bratz dolls.

In April 2005, MGA Entertainment filed a lawsuit against Mattel, claiming that the 'My Scene' range of Barbie dolls had copied the look of Bratz dolls.

Source: Adapted from http://en.wikipedia.org

Questions

1 Explain the ways in which Mattel might promote Barbie. [6]
2 Discuss whether the loss of market share to Bratz means that sales of Barbie are doomed. [10]

Market structures

A market where one firm dominates is called a 'monopoly'. A monopoly firm has power over the market and may well make high profits. As there is little choice for customers, the monopoly firm may be able to charge high prices. There may also be little incentive to innovate and therefore the quality of service may be reduced. Having said this, to remain a monopoly a firm may have to be innovative to stay ahead of the competition.

In many markets there are a few large firms that dominate the market rather than just one. This is called an 'oligopoly market'. For example, in the UK there are a few large banks, a few large supermarkets and a few large electricity providers. These are all oligopolistic markets. In this kind of market, the big firms will watch each others' movements and decisions very closely. There is a high degree of interdependence. This may lead to high degrees of competition as the dominant firms fight it out. This is often via promotional campaigns (just think of the numerous offers from banks and supermarkets to attract your business). However, it can also be via the way they do business. For example, does the bank have lots of branches? Can you do online banking? Does it offer insurance and investment advice? Is there a small-business adviser?

Oligopolies may also lead to collusion. This means that the firms combine to work together and act as a monopolist. This can lead to higher prices and less choice for consumers. A few years ago several UK private schools were accused of setting their fees in line with each other. Parents choosing private education were faced with high fees from a whole group of schools. Other markets are more competitive because they have far more firms of a similar size. This means that customers can choose between the alternatives and switch between them. In most towns there are several hairdressers, pubs, taxi firms and coffee shops. Customers can walk from one to the other if they do not like the service or price. This competitive pressure should lead to better value for money for customers. Firms may still try to differentiate what they do by building a brand, or by developing their offering, but the more choice the customer has the greater the pressure on firms to meet customers' needs in order to stay in business.

Summary

The decisions that managers make to ensure a business is competitive will be influenced by the market structure. The market structure depends on the number of firms in the market and the relative size of these firms. Other important factors in the competitive environment include the power of suppliers and buyers, the likelihood of new entrants into the market and the availability of substitutes.

Test your learning

Short answer questions

1 What is meant by the marketing mix? [2]
2 a What is meant by the price elasticity of demand? [2]
  b Explain the meaning of a value of the price elasticity of demand of −2. [3]
3 a State the stages of the product life cycle [2]
  b Explain **one** way in which the marketing mix might change at different stages of the product life cycle. [3]
4 a What is meant by an extension strategy? [2]
  b Explain **one** extension strategy with an example. [2]
5 What is the difference between above the line and below the line promotion? [2]
6 a What is meant by price penetration? [2]

b Explain **one** condition necessary for price penetration to be effective. [3]

7 a What is meant by price skimming? [2]

b Explain **one** condition in the market for price skimming to be effective. [3]

8 a What is meant by a distribution channel? [2]

b Explain **one** benefit of a short distribution channel. [3]

9 a What is meant by price discrimination? [2]

b Explain **one** benefit of price discrimination to the business. [3]

10 What is meant by a monopoly? [2]

Data response question

Harry Potter

Harry Potter features in a series of seven children's books by J.K. Rowling. The story is mostly set at Hogwarts School of Witchcraft and Wizardry, a school for young wizards and witches, and focuses on Harry Potter's fight against the evil wizard Lord Voldemort, who killed Harry's parents as part of his plan to take over the wizarding world.

The first novel, *Harry Potter and the Philosopher's Stone*, was published in 1997. Since its launch the books have gained immense popularity and commercial success worldwide, also leading to films, video games and various merchandise: from 'Quidditch' chess sets to 'HufflePuff' wall hangings, 'Goblet of Fire' candle holders to 'Hedwig' pillowcases.

Altogether, the books have sold well over 350 million copies, have been translated into more than 63 languages and reach readers via a variety of distribution channels. The success of the novels has made the author the highest-earning novelist in literary history.

Although the author did not have any age group in mind when she wrote the books, the publisher initially focused on the market segment of young children, aged nine to eleven. Rowling, whose first name is Joanne, was asked to use her initials rather than her first name because it was thought that young boys would not be interested reading a book written by a woman.

Word-of-mouth reviews, especially among young males, have been an important part of the books' success. Rowling's publishers were able to build on this buzz by the rapid, successive releases of the first four books, which maintained interest in the brand. The books also gained many adult fans, leading to two editions of each Harry Potter book being released in the UK, identical in text but with one edition's cover artwork aimed at children and the other aimed at adults.

The launch of a new Harry Potter book was a great event, with long queues forming outside the bookshops and some stores opening at midnight to sell the first copies.

Questions

1 Explain the meaning of the following terms:

a market segment [3]

b distribution channel. [3]

2 Explain two ways in which the marketing mix has been used to maintain sales of Harry Potter. [6]

3 If no more Harry Potter books are written, to what extent does this mean that sales of Harry Potter must inevitably decline? [10]

Essay question

To what extent is price the most important element of the marketing mix? [20]

Past paper questions

1 a Explain how the product life cycle might be used by the finance manager of a business. [8]

b Discuss how and why promotional activity might change at different stages of a product's lifecycle. [12]

Cambridge International AS and A Level Business Studies
9707 Paper 1 Q7 May/June 2008

2 Read the Cheapo Air case study on page 211 and then answer the following question.

Analyse the factors that CA would need to consider in setting a price for their business customers. [8]

Cambridge International AS and A Level Business Studies
9707 Paper 21 Q2c May/June 2009

3 a Other than price, outline **one** factor which could cause an increase in the demand for mobile phones. [2]

b A business sells a product whose demand is relatively price inelastic. Explain the effect on sales **and** revenue of a price increase. [3]

Cambridge International AS and A Level Business Studies
9707 Paper 1 Q2 October/November 2007

4 Read the Ganmor Cars case study on page 215 and then answer the following question.

Discuss the factors that would influence GC's choice of a marketing mix. [10]

Cambridge International AS and A Level Business Studies
9707 Paper 2 Q2d May/June 2008

12 The nature of operations

Chapter overview

In this chapter we examine:
- inputs, outputs and the transformation process
- the meaning of effectiveness, efficiency and productivity
- the meaning and significance of creating value
- capital intensive production versus labour intensive.

12.1 Inputs, outputs and the transformation process

Operations management, products and services

The process of transforming inputs into outputs is the responsibility of operations managers. They are there to make sure that the process occurs in the way that the business wants and that particular operations targets are met. For example, operations managers may be concerned with achieving a particular level of quality and ensuring that costs are not too high. The effectiveness of a business depends a great deal on the quality and cost of the operations process. If managers can improve the operations of the business, they can make it more efficient, increase the volume of output and improve quality. The marketing function identifies the opportunities within a market; the operations function then delivers this as effectively and efficiently as possible. Effective operations should lead to more sales and profits. Poor operations leads to mistakes being made, which can result in having to replace items, recall products or even paying damages.

Operations involves producing physical goods such as cars, but also providing services such as schools and hospitals which are intangible. These create particular issues: with physical products managers will consider how many inventories to hold, for example; with services it is not possible to hold inventories and so managers have to deal with queues if demand is high.

The precise nature of operations will, therefore, vary from business to business. If you are running a hotel, for example, operations management involves making sure the rooms are ready, the kitchens meet health and safety requirements, the televisions, kettles and trouser presses in the rooms work, the towels are washed and dried and there is enough food to feed the guests. If you are running a tyre and exhaust centre, operations management involves making sure you have enough spares in stock so that you can fix a customer's car quickly and safely, the equipment you have is suitable and working, and you can generate the bill accurately. If you are running a clothes shop it involves making sure you have the right number and mix of clothes on display, the store layout is appropriate, the queues are not too long and there is a security system to prevent theft.

Key term

Operations management oversees the planning, coordination and control of the transformation process turning resources into outputs.

Managing the operations process

The operations process involves all the different stages including:
- producing the initial idea (for example, in a research laboratory) to developing prototypes and testing these to check the product works and is safe to launch
- designing the best method of production to be efficient and hit volume and quality targets
- deciding on the levels of inventory to hold to keep production going and just in case anything goes wrong
- ensuring production goes according to plan
- delivering to the next stage in the process, such as a retailer
- if necessary, handling the recall of products if there are faults.

Study tip

Remember operations can affect the volume of production, the costs and the quality. Operational decisions will be linked to the other functions, e.g. they will be related to the sales, the overall finances of the business and the skills and number of employees required.

Using resources

Operations will involve the management of resources such as:

- **Land** This will include location decisions and finding the right base for a business, while considering issues such as the cost and ease of access to supplies; in some operations processes such as farming or wine making managing the land is a key part of the transformation process
- **Labour** This involves the number and skills of people you employ; in sectors such as sport, music and computer programming the skills of employees are absolutely critical
- **Capital** This refers to capital goods such as equipment and machinery; these are vitally important in sectors such as online businesses where the technology is at the centre of the business, or car production where production line technology determines output and quality and flexibility
- **Intellectual capital** This refers to the brains and minds of your staff; their ability to come up with new ideas, to find solutions to problems and be creative is very important in sectors such as advertising and consultancy.

Operations managers must decide on the right combination of resources for its transformation process given the desired targets and constraints such as budgets. This will depend on factors such as the nature of the process but also the cost and availability of different resources.

Case Study

The Zulfikarabad project

In 2012 the President of Pakistan announced that the Zulfikarabad project would reclaim land intruded by sea in the Thatta district. This would provide job opportunities to locals and bring in an era of development to improve the quality of life.

The project aims to transform the area into an economic hub. Roads are to be constructed and drinking water facilities provided in Thatta district under the Zulfikarabad project. Two small seaports will also be developed in the area. In total, 1.3 million acres (526 000 hectares) of land have been allocated for this project, of which 376 000 acres (152 000 ha) of land have been acquired, while 957 000 acres (387 ha) will be reclaimed from the sea.

At the moment the sea is eating away 18 acres (7.3 ha) of land every day and so the government will construct a 100-feet (30-m) high and 60-feet (18-m)wide dyke to protect this area from the sea.

Questions

1 Explain what resources would be used in this transformation process. [6]
2 Discuss the benefits of land reclamation to the region. [10]

12.2 The benefits and limitations of capital and labour intensive processes

A capital intensive process is one that involves a relatively high proportion of machinery and equipment; imagine a bottling process, for example. This type of process can produce high quantities of a standardised product at a relatively low unit cost (as the costs are spread over so many units).

However, a capital intensive process:

- can be expensive to set up
- can be relatively inflexible in terms of producing different versions of the product (although technology means this is now improving)
- is expensive per unit if only a few items are produced.

A labour intensive process uses a relatively high proportion of people; for example, a design business.

Using a high proportion of labour can enable the business to be very flexible and produce a wide range of personalised services. However, it may limit the volume of products that can be produced.

Table 12.1 Capital intensive vs labour intensive

Capital intensive	Labour intensive
Expensive to set up	Lower set-up costs
Can produce high volumes	May involve lower output levels
Can achieve lower average costs if volume is high	May be relatively expensive for high volumes as high amounts of labour are needed
May be relatively inflexible	Can be quite flexible

Study tip

Whether a process should be capital or labour intensive will depend on factors such as the importance of a personal service, the finance available for investment and the volume of output required.

12.3 Effectiveness and efficiency

The operations manager will want the process to be both effective and efficient. An operations process is effective if it achieves its set target; for example, it produces the target of 200 units a day. The process is efficient if it does not waste resources and minimises costs given the quantity and quality required.

A production process may be effective but inefficient if it is producing the target but at a high cost. Equally, it may be efficient at what it does but is producing the wrong thing or the wrong quantity, so is ineffective.

Study tip

Effectiveness focuses on what you do.
Efficiency focuses on how you do it.

Productivity: measuring efficiency

One measure of efficiency is **productivity**. This measures the **output** produced given the inputs used up. The more efficient a business is:

- the more output it produces from its inputs
- the less inputs it needs for a given level of output.

Productivity is very important to businesses because managers will want to get the most from the resources that they have.

Labour productivity specifically measures the output per worker. The equation to calculate this is:

$$\frac{\text{Output}}{\text{Number of employees}}$$

Labour productivity measures the output of the firm in relation to the number of employees. For example, if ten people produce 50 units in total each week, their productivity is 5 units each. The higher the labour productivity, the more is produced per person per time period.

Productivity is a crucial concept in operations management because it can have a significant effect on the costs of producing a unit. The higher the productivity, the more units each worker is making and, if wages are unchanged, the labour cost per unit will be cheaper. As a result, managers are constantly seeking ways of improving labour productivity because this means the firm can either make more profit per unit, can reduce the price to become more competitive or can produce more. Improving the effectiveness of the business may therefore be directly related to improving the productivity of its resources. Imagine a juice drinks business where employees are squeezing the fruit by hand; if they bought a juicer, productivity would increase so that more customers could be served or fewer staff may be required.

Maths moment

Complete Table 12.2. Assume that employees are paid $200 each per week.

Table 12.2 Calculating productivity

Number of employees	Weekly wage bill ($)	Output (number of units)	Productivity (output/ number of workers)	Labour cost per unit (weekly wage bill/ number of units)
100	$20 000	1000	10	$20
100	?	2000	?	?
50	?	1000	?	?
?	?	2000	40	?

Key terms

The **output** of a business is the total amount produced in a given time period.

Productivity measures the output per hour, per person or per machine.

How can productivity be increased?

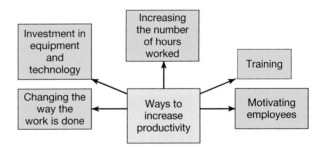

Figure 12.1 Ways to increase productivity

Productivity may be increased by using a variety of techniques:

- **Increasing the number of hours worked** If employees work more hours or more days each week, this could increase their output. However, this is not necessarily a long-term means of increasing employees' productivity because they are likely to get tired and stressed, and may therefore become less productive in the long term. Also, there is a limit to how many extra hours can be worked.
- **Training** This is a very important way of increasing productivity. Training can increase employees' output by helping them to gain more skills and to learn new and better ways of doing things.

- **Investment in equipment and technology** If employees have modern and more efficient machinery, they should be able to make more output than their colleagues who are using outdated equipment. As the UK's Department of Business and Skills says when commenting on the low productivity in the UK compared with many other countries: 'A worker can be 100 per cent efficient with a shovel but it won't count if his international counterpart is equipped with a JCB!'
- **Changing the way the work is done** If the way in which a product is made is changed, this can affect the speed and the effectiveness of the production process. Many firms have implemented teamworking in recent years, resulting in improved productivity levels. If activities in the process can be combined and undertaken simultaneously rather than in sequence, this speeds up production and enables higher productivity.
- **Motivating employees** If employees can be motivated (perhaps by offering more rewards or by giving people more responsibility – see Chapter 7) effort and productivity may increase.

At any moment managers will have to consider which of the above options are available given the firm's resources, and which will work best when it comes to boosting productivity. In one business the issue might be motivation; in another it might be a lack of modern equipment. If managers can boost productivity they will be improving the performance of the business.

> ### Case Study
> ## Finance Against Warehouse Receipts

Figure 12.2 Nyiombo Investments Ltd is now able to meet more than 60 per cent of Zambia's fertiliser demand

It is often very difficult for farmers in Africa to get loans that they need to buy essential materials such as seeds, fertilisers and pesticides. This is because they lack assets to act as collateral and so many banks are not willing to take the risk. Without these resources, farming is inefficient and so the returns the farmers gain are low. To help improve the situation the Standard Chartered bank has helped develop various financing schemes to enable farmers to get the finance they need. One of these is called Finance Against Warehouse Receipts. Under this scheme farmers use their crops as collateral; the corn, soya or wheat act as the security for the loan.

For example, through this scheme Standard Chartered has been able to finance farmers borrowing to buy fertilisers. The use of these fertilisers has boosted average crop yields to over a tonne per hectare – a significant increase in productivity. The programme has been so effective that it has helped the country move from importing maize to bumper harvests and becoming an exporter.

Source: Adapted from www.stanchartered.com

Questions

1 Explain how you would measure the productivity of a farm. [6]
2 Discuss the ways in which farmers might improve the productivity of their farms. [10]

> ### Case Study
> ## Assembly lines

Figure 12.3 One of the first assembly lines was for the Model T Ford

The Model T Ford was produced between 1908 and 1927. During that time Henry Ford introduced assembly line techniques which dramatically increased productivity. Each car moved along a line with parts being added to it; individuals specialised in a particular aspect of production. As a result, producing a car took just over an hour instead of 12 hours and this brought down unit costs so much that the price could fall from $890 to $240. The ability to produce a reliable car at a relatively low price made this a tremendous success; so much so that at its peak the Model T accounted for 50 per cent of all cars in the USA and 10 per cent of all the cars in the world.

Questions

1 Explain why unit costs usually decrease when productivity increases. [8]
2 Discuss the possible implications of introducing assembly line techniques. [16]

Extension: employee resistance to higher productivity

While managers might be eager to increase productivity, employees may resist such efforts, because:

- they do not want to work longer or harder
- they do not want to learn new skills
- they fear that higher productivity levels may lead to job losses
- they feel it is unfair that they are producing more unless they receive higher rewards.

Study tip

Remember that employees may not welcome efforts to increase productivity. Also, increasing productivity may lead to a fall in quality as production is rushed.

12.4 Creating value

Marketing, the operations process and operations decisions

Operations management involves all the stages of the transformation process and therefore is directly involved in the process of creating value. The more efficient the operations process, for example, the less resources are used up for the output produced and so more value can be added. Similarly, the better quality the product and the more effectively that it meets customer needs, the more likely sales are to be increasing the value created again.

Marketing is responsible for identifying the needs of customers; this department must work with operations to find the best way of fulfilling these needs while at the same time meeting the business objectives. For example, marketing will identify the key benefits customers want and the prices they are willing to pay; operations must then see if it can meet these targets at an appropriate cost.

Key term

The **created value** is the difference between the value of the final goods and services and the cost of the bought-in items.

Test your learning

Short answer questions

1 State **four** resources used in the operations process. [4]

2 Explain the difference between effectiveness and efficiency. [3]

3 a What is meant by labour productivity? [2]
  b Explain **one** way of increasing productivity. [3]

4 a If output is 300 units and the number of employees is 20 what is the labour productivity? [2]
  b Explain **one** reason why a business might want higher productivity. [3]

5 a What is meant by a labour intensive production process? [2]
  b Identity **two** processes that are labour intensive. [2]

6 a What is meant by a capital intensive process? [2]
  b Explain **one** possible disadvantage of a capital intensive process. [2]

7 a What is meant by creating value? [2]
  b Explain how a business may create more value. [3]

8 a What is meant by operations management? [2]
  b Explain **one** way in which effective operations management can increase the profits of a business. [3]

9 Explain **one** reason why a business may adopt a capital intensive rather than a labour intensive process. [3]

10 Explain **one** reason why employees may resist attempts to increase labour productivity. [3]

Data response question

The Singaporean economy

In the last ten years the economy of Singapore has grown by an average of 5 per cent a year. The country's productivity has also grown over the same period by about 1 per cent a year, which matches that of other developed economies. The majority of the population in Singapore benefited from a growth in earnings and a rise in their standard of living.

Even so, productivity gains have been slower than in the past due to more reliance on people for growth, for example in the service sector. The government of Singapore is eager to improve productivity and sees this as a key driver of economic growth. The government is focusing on ways of improving productivity through a number of programmes and schemes.

Source: Adapted from www.mom.gov.sg

Questions

1 Explain the meaning of the following terms:
   a productivity [3]
   b economic growth. [3]

2 Explain why an increase in productivity can help businesses and the economy to grow. [6]

3 Discuss ways in which productivity may be increased. [10]

Essay question

Discuss whether a capital intensive production process is better than a labour intensive one. Justify your answer. [20]

13 Operations planning

Chapter overview

In this chapter we examine:
- operations decisions
- the importance of flexibility and innovation in operations
- the advantages and disadvantages of different operations methods: job, batch, flow, mass customisation
- factors influencing location
- the significance of the scale of operations.

13.1 Influences on operations decisions

The influence of marketing

An operations manager like any manager must work with other functions within the business and will face constraints when making decisions. The starting point for new products will usually come from marketing. Marketing will have identified a market opportunity and then must liaise with operations to see what is possible:

- Can the business produce enough to meet the expected sales? Or will it need to increase its **capacity**?
- Can the business provide the right level of quality? What benefits can it provide effectively and efficiently?
- Can the business sell at the price recommended by marketing and still make a profit?

Many decisions will need to be reviewed to find the best solution. For example, is it better to find cheaper supplies so you can keep costs down or could you actually push the selling price up if the quality is better? Could you produce the item with fewer features without damaging demand significantly?

The constraints facing operations include:
- the technology it is working with and the existing capacity – for example, if the business is using **Computer Aided Design** (CAD) and **Computer Aided Manufacturing** (CAM) techniques it may be able to be more flexible and quicker to develop new products than competitors not using these

- the skills and numbers of its workforce – there will be some orders that the business will not want to accept because it lacks the expertise
- its suppliers – this may affect how easily it can increase output and the costs of production.

Computer Aided Design will enable a business:
- to develop models and prototypes on computer rather than having to build them.

This can:
- save time and money
- provide more flexibility and accuracy when it comes to adjusting the design. By saving and editing ideas it is easier to update them.

However, the ability to do this depends on the extent to which the CAD program can cope with complex design and replicate different testing conditions. The initial cost may also be high and staff will need training.

Computer Aided Manufacturing can:
- enable higher levels of accuracy and quality and therefore reduce costs
- speed up production.

However, there is:
- the initial cost, which may make it uneconomic for low levels of production
- the cost and time to train staff.

Its value will also depend on the sophistication of the CAM program.

Changes can be made in these factors – such as investment in new machinery – but this will cost money and take time and will have to be negotiated with the finance, marketing and human resources departments.

Key terms

Capacity measures the maximum output a business can produce with its existing resources.

Computer Aided Design (CAD) involves the use of computers to develop, explain and modify a design.

Computer Aided Manufacturing (CAM) is the use of computer software to control machines in the manufacturing process.

13.2 Flexibility and innovation

The importance of flexibility in operations

Targets in operations management include:

- the quantity that has to be produced and when the output is required given the expected sales pattern; operations will have to consider whether it can deliver the right quantity at the desired time
- the level of quality expected by customers, i.e. what benefits are they expecting?
- the expected costs to enable a profit to be made at the desired selling price.

The more flexible operations can be, the better. If, for example, a business can easily make a range of products at relatively low cost this will enable it to meet different customer needs. If a firm has all the capacity it requires and can deliver the quantities needed on time then marketing will be overjoyed. In reality there may be constraints limiting this flexibility:

- The business may be busy with another order and so cannot start a new one for some time.
- The business may not be able to offer all the desired features either because it lacks the necessary skills and technology or because it is too expensive.
- The business may not have the capacity to produce in the quantities required and therefore may need to look to others to produce some of it (called **subcontracting**).

Key term

Subcontracting occurs when a business uses other producers to produce on its behalf.

As ever, greater flexibility is likely to come at a cost: to be able to produce whatever is required whenever it is required is likely to be expensive!

Process innovation

Innovation involves developing new ideas. This may be developing new products, which is called product innovation, or developing new ways of doing things, which is called process innovation. For example, enabling people to order and pay online is a process innovation – it is making the old way of doing things seem slow and cumbersome.

Businesses will be looking for ways of being more efficient and this means looking to save costs. Process innovation can

enable a business to improve what it does and save money doing so; for example, using technology such as CAD and CAM to produce can enable better results, faster and at a lower cost. Just think how the internet has transformed the way we find information – think of the quantity and quality of information we now find quickly and the time saved going to the library and trying to find a book that someone else may already have borrowed! Think also of how much easier it is to check in for a flight these days thanks to online check-in; it makes it easier and more convenient for the consumer and can enable the business to reduce staffing levels and speed up the process at the airport.

Process innovation involves thinking about how you do something, whereas product innovation focuses on what you do.

Process innovation can occur:

- when businesses change the way they deliver a service – for example to enable ordering online
- when businesses change the way they produce or adopt new ways of producing. For example, they may automate a process by replacing people with machines. Several aspects of building cars are now undertaken by robots not people.

Study tip

Remember that innovation can lead to new products but also new ways of doing things – think of the way we listen to music, read books and book tickets these days.

13.3 Operations methods

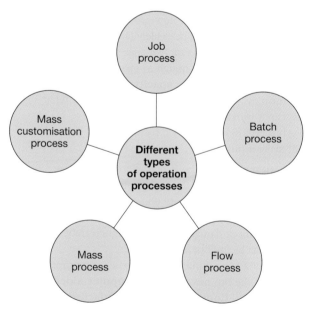

Figure 13.1 Different types of operation processes

There are different types of operation processes. Some of these are:

- **Job production** This involves one-off production. Imagine the work of a portrait artist, wedding photographer or architect. Each item is unique for each customer, which means that production is very flexible. It tends to require a wide range of skills because of the range of jobs that may be done. It also requires good project management skills because each order is unique and will have different planning requirements. As a result job production tends to be quite expensive.

- **Batch production** This occurs when items move together from one stage of a process to another. For example, when making wine or beer a 'batch' is fermented; similarly when producing bread you bake a batch at a time. This approach is cheaper per unit than job production because you are producing products in groups. At the same time you have some flexibility to switch the recipe or approach from one batch to another, meaning it has some flexibiliity.

- **Mass production** This involves large-scale production using production line technology. It is capable of huge volumes (e.g. of cans of beans or bottles of water) but produces relatively standardised products. Provided the volume is high then the unit costs will be relatively low but this means you need high levels of demand. Mass production suits mass markets. However, it is relatively expensive to set up to buy the production equipment and is not especially flexible in terms of producing a variety of products.

- **Flow production** This is similar to mass production except it means that the products literally do flow from one stage to another, for example, chemical production. It requires a heavy investment in equipment but if volumes are high the unit costs can be relatively low.

- **Mass customisation** This is a relatively new development made possible by technological advances. This type of process is on a large scale but whereas mass production usually lacks flexibility this technology enables a variety of models to be produced on the same production line. VW, for example, uses the same basic car platform for many of its cars. Mass customisation generally involves heavy investment in technology.

Table 13.1 Operations processes

Type of production	Features
Job	One-off, unique, tailor-made items
Batch	Items move as a group from one stage of the process to another
Mass	Large-scale production, e.g. using production line technology. Each item moves from one stage of the process to the next in large volumes
Flow	Items move continuously from one stage of the production process to another
Mass customisation	Large-scale production with the flexibility to produce a number of different models

Case Study

Hyundai

Hyundai Motor Co recently announced it was to become the first company to begin mass production of a hydrogen fuel cell-powered vehicle.

Figure 13.2 The Hyundai hydrogen fuel cell-powered car

The company plans to lease 15 of its ix35 vehicles to the Municipality of Copenhagen, Denmark, and aims to get 1000 of its vehicles on the road by 2015. These vehicles will be leased to private companies and governments. Hyundai hopes to start selling the car to consumers sometime in 2015.

The rollout is starting in Europe because it has a better hydrogen gas station infrastructure in place. With prices per vehicle in the 'upper $100 000s per car', the ix35 is too expensive for general consumers right now. However, the company hopes to bring the price of hydrogen cell cars down to about $50 000 by the time the company is ready to sell to consumers.

Fuel cell vehicles use hydrogen gas combined with oxygen from the environment to create electricity. The only waste product is water vapour. These vehicles have the potential to significantly reduce the dependence on foreign oil and lower harmful emissions that contribute to climate change.

Hyundai has been developing its hydrogen fuel cell technology since 1998, but until recently cars powered by the technology would have cost more than $1 million. Experts say the long-promised technology could one day replace internal combustion engines, but public concerns about safety and government indecision about which alternative fuel vehicle would be most appropriate for the US market have slowed things down.

Hyundai's vehicle can be refuelled in about the same amount of time as it takes to refuel a petrol car, has a top speed of 100 miles per hour (160 kp/h), goes from 0–60 mph (0–96 kp/h) in 12.5 seconds, and can travel 365 miles (587 km) on a single tank of petrol.

Questions

1 Explain two factors which might influence demand for Hyundai's new car. [6]

2 Discuss the factors Hyundai might consider before starting mass production of fuel cell vehicles. [10]

Problems of changing from one method of production to another

Changing from job to batch to mass production will depend on the nature of demand. Mass production requires high volumes and therefore is not appropriate for job production where each item is unique. Batch production enables relatively high outputs and some flexibility, for example, printing batches of different magazine titles, but is not appropriate if a customer wants something unique.

Moving from job to batch to mass production will require investment in capital equipment; it will enable higher volumes (assuming the demand is there) but there will be less flexibility in terms of tailor-making the product to customer needs.

13.4 Location

Factors that determine location and relocation

The location of a business can affect its costs, its demand, its image and its ability to attract employees to work for it. The location decision is therefore an important decision that can affect the ability of the business to compete. The decision of where to locate can also reflect the values of the business, for example if it wants to help employment in a particular area. So, location choices should not be taken lightly and will involve decisions at the most senior level.

A location decision can involve high levels of investment and have a major impact on competitiveness. The right location(s) may affect:

- the costs of production and of running the business
- the tax rates paid
- the availability of employees and the skills available
- demand for the products
- the ease of accessing markets.

Given the impact on costs and revenues a location decision will involve an assessment of the breakeven output and likely financial returns. Location decisions may involve several different elements: first which country, then which region and finally which specific plot of land.

Benefits of the optimal location

It may not always be possible to get the best (or optimal) location. You may find that a particular site is already taken or is too expensive. However, getting the best or nearly the best location can have several advantages:

- Lower costs may make the break-even output lower and reduce the risk of losses if sales are lower than expected. Lower costs may increase the return on investment and make a project worthwhile.
- Being closer to the customer (and therefore possibly getting more customers as a result) may boost sales and profits. Stores based in the city centre have a higher footfall than those a few streets away.
- Overcoming trade barriers (e.g. it is difficult to export to some countries because of barriers to trade) may increase sales. By basing itself inside a customs union such as the European Union, a firm may be able to sell in a particular country.
- It may add to the brand image. For example, having your flagship store on Fifth Avenue in New York or Covent Garden in London may be important for the status of your business.

Deciding where to locate

The decision on where to locate a business will be based on a combination of quantitative and qualitative factors. This means that it is a combination of factors that can be measured, such as the expected impact on costs and revenues (these are quantitative), as well as other factors that are less easy to quantify, such as the attraction of the surroundings and the quality of life in the area (these are qualitative).

Case Study

Bangladesh

An increasing amount of clothes are now being made in Bangladesh and exported to China thanks to the low labour costs. This helps businesses based there to continue to generate sales despite a slowdown in demand from Europe.

In Bangladesh the average monthly salary for garment workers is around $70 to $100, whereas China is experiencing increasing demands for higher wages from its employees. In some Chinese factories, for example, wages are now around $400 to $500 a month per worker. Chinese manufacturers say if they source clothes from Bangladesh, prices can come down by 10 to 15 per cent. Bangladeshi garment exporters say the other advantage they enjoy is that more than 90 per cent of their products, such as T-shirts, jeans, sweaters and casual trousers, enjoy duty free access to the Chinese market.

China's largest online clothing retailer has already shifted a portion of its shirts and casual trousers orders to Bangladeshi factories. Meanwhile, western fashion brands such as Ocean and H&M are also making clothes for Chinese customers in Bangladeshi factories.

However, Bangladesh's poor infrastructure and political instability have been a major concern for the clothing manufacturers. In addition, there have been violent labour protests in recent months with workers demanding better wages and conditions.

Questions

1 Explain two factors a business might consider when deciding whether to produce for itself or subcontract to other businesses.   [6]
2 Discuss the advantages and disadvantages of Bangladesh as a place to produce.   [10]

Case Study

Dov Charney and American Apparel

Figure 13.3 Dov Charney, founder of American Apparel

Dov Charney is the founder and chief executive of American Apparel, the largest T-shirt manufacturer in America. He is widely admired for almost single-handedly creating one of America's most successful fashion retailers, for devising his company's provocative approach to advertising, and for treating employees better than his rivals.

Mr Charney opened his first shop in 2003. He now has more than 140 stores in 11 countries selling casual clothes for men, women and children. Sales are more than $300 million and the company has an 80 per cent gross profit margin, which is well above the industry average of 60 per cent. Its unbranded, brightly coloured and moderately priced T-shirts, sweatshirts, underwear and jeans have become extremely popular among the young, cosmopolitan group that Mr Charney says represents the 'world-metropolitan culture'.

From the beginning Mr Charney has put great emphasis on making his employees happy. Pay is performance-related, and amounts to $12 an hour on average, far above California's minimum wage of $6.75. American Apparel staff can buy subsidised health insurance for $8 a week. They are entitled to free English lessons, subsidised meals and free parking. Their workspace is properly lit and ventilated. When the company goes public employees will receive an average of 500 shares, expected to be worth about $4500.

Anti-sweatshop activists praise Mr Charney as a pioneer of the fair treatment of garment workers. The benefits he provides are expensive: subsidising health insurance costs his firm $4–5 million a year; subsidising meals costs another $500 000. He considers his contented workers the reason for his success. Treating them well means they are less likely to leave, which saves money. 'American Apparel is not an altruistic company,' says Mr Charney. 'I believe in capitalism and self-interest. Self-interest can involve being generous with others.'

Whereas Gap, another American fashion chain, outsources 83 per cent of its production to factories in Asia, all of the 4000 or so workers involved in American Apparel's manufacturing process work in the same factory in downtown Los Angeles. But this is not because Mr Charney is opposed to outsourcing or globalisation. His motive, once again, is self-interest: it gives him control over every stage of production, and enables him to monitor the fashion market and respond quickly to new trends. In any case, he cannot outsource anything, he says, because he lacks the necessary infrastructure – and he has no plans to set it up.

Having become a public company, American Apparel now plans to open another 650 shops across the world. Retail analysts also doubt that American Apparel will be able to expand without resorting to outsourcing. Mr Charney insists that China is too far away for his T-shirt production, even though moving textiles by ship from Hong Kong to Los Angeles takes just 11 days.

Source: Adapted from www.americanapparel.net

Questions

1 Explain two potential benefits of outsourcing production.   [6]
2 Discuss whether American Apparel is right to base its production in the US.   [10]

Factors affecting a firm's location include:

- **Geographic** For example, the location of the market. In some cases, such as retailing, it will often be important to be close to the market. A central high street location is more likely to attract business than a site located some distance away from the main shopping areas. In other industries, such as telephone banking, it is not so important to be close to the customer.
- **The infrastructure of the region** The availability of energy sources and transport facilities will affect the ease, speed and cost of production. The importance of such factors will vary between industries, for example transport facilities are crucial to a wholesaler but less significant for an online insurance business.
- **Political factors** For example, political stability. The political climate can have an impact on the appeal of a certain area. For example, terrorist threats in countries post-11 September 2001 have created instability in certain regions, and the UK's

reluctance to commit to the single European currency has meant some overseas investors have been wary of locating in the UK because they have been worried about the possible impact of being outside the 'euro zone'.

- **The costs of a particular location relative to other options** For example, the cost of land itself will vary from area to area; so will the cost of labour and services such as electricity. Taxation rates can also vary significantly from country to country. The decision to locate can therefore have a significant impact on a firm's profits.
- **The availability of lower-cost locations abroad** has been a major factor for UK firms considering relocating to the Far East or Eastern Europe. Low-wage employees and a much lower cost of living often make it very financially attractive for UK firms to be based overseas.
- **The availability of government grants and incentives** If, for example, a government offers low rents or lower taxes to attract firms, this can obviously act as an incentive to locate there. In the last 20 years, for example, the development agencies in regions of the UK, such as Wales and Scotland, were very effective at attracting overseas investment not just because of financial aid but also because of the general level of local and national government cooperation in areas such as planning permission. Governments often use a combination of push and pull techniques to encourage firms to locate in particular regions. Incentives such as grants help to pull firms to an area; refusing permission to build in other areas helps to push firms to locate where the government wants them to be.
- **The nature of the business** itself – the extent to which a firm has freedom over the location decision depends in part on what it actually does. A self-employed website designer, for example, may be able to work from home. A fast-food restaurant, by comparison, must be located somewhere near its customers, while a mining company must base its production facilities where the actual minerals are.
- **Marketing** For example, market access. The location of a firm may affect its ability to trade in particular markets. Firms based outside the European Union, for example, must pay a tax (a tariff) to sell their goods within the EU. Firms located within the EU do not have to pay this tax. This is one reason why many Japanese firms have set up in the UK in the last 20 years – if they have UK production facilities using a proportion of UK components they can export to other EU states and not pay a tariff; this obviously makes their goods more competitive compared with exporting from Japan.
- **Exchange rates** If the pound is strong it is expensive for UK-based producers to export. On the other hand, it means UK firms have strong purchasing power overseas, which may lead some firms to relocate overseas when the pound is strong in value in terms of other currencies.
- **Demographic** For example, it may depend on the availability of labour with the right skills in the area.
- **Legal** For example, businesses may not be allowed to build in some areas where wildlife is protected, or if the process is dangerous (such as nuclear energy) a firm may not be allowed to set up near towns.
- **Resources** A firm may locate in a particular area because of the resources it offers. Microsoft located near Cambridge in the UK because it wanted easy access to top graduates and research facilities.
- **Image** A perfume company, for example, may benefit from being based in Paris or Milan but may not gain the same prestige from being located in Scunthorpe in the north of England.
- **Quality of life** For example, how attractive is the area in itself? What are the facilities like? What is the standard of living like?
- **Ethical issues** Some British firms have avoided locating in low-wage areas for fear of being criticised for 'exploiting' local staff or of taking jobs away from the UK. In many cases firms expand in areas where they already have established links (and therefore feel some responsibility to the community) rather than take jobs elsewhere. The Body Shop set up one of its manufacturing operations at Easterhouse in Scotland specifically to bring jobs to a deprived area.

Figure 13.4 Reasons for locating abroad

Disney

In the early 1980s the heads of Disney were looking for a location in Europe to open a new theme park. The first one outside the US was Japan and now Disney was looking for another base.

They initially came up with more than 1000 possible locations in Europe. By March 1985, the number of possible locations for the park had been reduced to four; two in France and two in Spain. Both of these countries saw the potential economic advantages of a Disney theme park and were offering financial deals to Disney. A strong possibility was a site near Toulon in southern France, not far from Marseille. The pleasing landscape of that region, as well as its climate, made the location a likely winner for the European Disney. However, thick layers of bedrock were discovered beneath the site, which meant construction would be too difficult. Finally, a site in the rural town of Marne La Vallée was chosen because it was close to Paris and its location was estimated to be no more than a four-hour drive for 68 million people and no more than a two-hour flight for a further 300 million. The agreement to build was signed in 1986.

Questions

1 Explain two operational issues involved in running a theme park. [6]

2 Discuss the factors that might influence where you locate a theme park. [10]

Qualitative factors affecting location

Although firms are likely to examine the potential impact on revenues and costs of selecting a particular site, the decision may also be affected by less measurable factors such as whether the location itself appeals to the managers, and the quality of life in the area. For example, many Japanese firms have been attracted to the UK because of the importance of the English language in business. It is also because English is learnt in Japanese schools – this makes it easier for these firms to set up in the UK than in France, for example. The culture of the country and the extent to which you think you understand its traditions, its ways of working and its customers are all very important. According to Rugman (2000), the probability of an American multinational opening its first operations outside the US in Canada or the UK is 70 per cent; these are similar countries and therefore appear familiar territories. The probability of an American multinational opening its second operation in Germany or Japan is 2 per cent; these seem less appealing as the cultures are more different.

Once a few firms have set up in a location this can also act as an incentive for others to locate there, as they may think this proves it is safe and that networking (i.e. using the expertise and experience of others) will be easier. The growth of Hollywood as a film centre and Silicon Valley as a centre for computing are in part because the success of some firms has drawn in others.

Other possible qualitative factors which could attract managers to particular areas include the fact that they like the region or because they have particular attachments to the place. William Morris, for example, set up a car factory based in Oxford simply because he lived there. Managers might also choose a location because the name of the place enhances the product's image; a fashion house in New York sounds more exclusive than a fashion house in Grimsby; an advertising agency in London may have more appeal than one in Dundee. The reasons a

particular location is chosen are, of course, varied: in the case of call centres, some firms have located in the north east or north west of the UK because callers like the accent of people from these areas more than the accents of people from the south east. Although this factor may well impact on a firm's profits it is difficult to place an absolute value on an accent and so this also counts as a qualitative factor. Interestingly, other firms have located to India to cut costs.

Types of location decision

There are in fact many types of location decision that managers may have to consider. There is the initial decision of where to set up the business. In many ways this is the easiest decision in that the managers have no commitments to existing facilities. On the other hand, it usually occurs at a time when money is tight and the firm will be heavily constrained by what it can afford. A key decision at this time is the desired capacity level – how big must the factory be? Or how much office space is needed? Managers may want to be optimistic about the possible growth of the business; at the same time they do not want to commit to large facilities and then find these are under-utilised.

Once a firm is established it may have to consider relocating at some point in its development. This occurs when a firm wants to move its facilities. This may be necessary because the initial reasons for choosing a place have now gone (e.g. government grants have been withdrawn or tax rates have been increased), or perhaps because the firm has outgrown its premises.

When relocating, a firm may have more experience of the type of facilities it needs than it did when it first chose its location; it may also have greater financial resources than when it started up. However, relocation brings with it all sorts of new problems, including:

- staff who do not want to move (or the firm does not want to pay to relocate) – these people may need compensation
- there could be a period of lost production time during the move
- the costs of notifying customers and suppliers, and administrative costs such as changing the firm's literature to include the new addresses.

A new location may also be part of an expansion process: a firm could be building new production facilities or opening up a new outlet, for example. The acquisition of new premises inevitably brings with it issues of management structure and control. A new facility will need to be controlled and the senior managers will need to decide on the best way of structuring the business, such as deciding what new jobs are created, what the reporting relationships will be and how to ensure effective communication.

Some location or relocation decisions may be within the local area; some may be within the local region; some may be overseas.

- The further afield you go the more complex and more difficult the decision becomes because you have more possible options.
- You may not know the region as well so it may take longer and you may need expert help.

143

- There may be more factors to consider; for example, when going international you need to consider different laws, cultures, political systems and exchange rate changes.

13.5 Scale of production

Factors influencing the scale of a business

When we talk about the scale of production, we are referring to a firm's output level; this will depend on its capacity. The capacity is the maximum output that an organisation can produce at any moment, given its resources.

The capacity of a firm at any moment will depend on:
- its capital, such as office space, store space, level of machinery and equipment
- the existing level of technology
- the number and skills of its employees.

If a business increases its capacity it is increasing the scale of its production. Deciding on the correct scale for an organisation is a critical decision for its managers. If the capacity is too low compared with demand, they will have to turn away orders, possibly losing customers. If the level is too high compared with demand, they will have idle resources such as equipment and machinery.

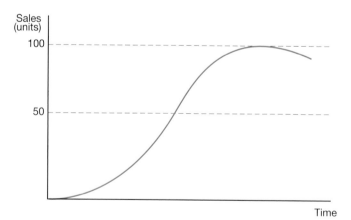

Figure 13.5 Product life cycle and scale decision

The 'right' scale for a business will depend on:
- **The expected levels of sales** The higher the level of demand, the greater the desired scale, assuming the demand can be sustained.
- **The costs involved in growing** Can the business afford to expand? Expansion often involves investing in the short term and may take months or even years to gain a return. The organisation may not be able to produce on the scale it wants because it does not have the money to buy all the resources it needs.

- **The resources available** For example, firms may not be able to recruit sufficient numbers of staff if the skills they want are in short supply.
  A firm can increase its scale by:
- investing in new capital, such as IT systems, equipment and technology
- investing in its labour, for example training the workforce to increase its productivity; hiring more employees to provide more 'people input'
- taking over another business or merging with another organisation (for more on mergers and takeovers see page 221).

As a business grows and changes its scale it tends to experience efficiency gains (called **economies of scale**) up to a certain scale and then inefficiencies (called **diseconomies of scale**) after that.

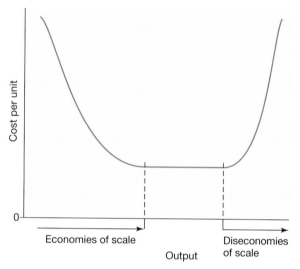

Figure 13.6 Economies and diseconomies of scale

Key terms

Economies of scale occur when the unit costs fall as the scale of production increases.

Diseconomies of scale occur when unit costs increase as the scale of production increases

Internal/external economies/diseconomies of scale

Internal economies of scale

Internal economies of scale occur when the cost of producing a unit (the unit cost) falls as the firm increases its scale of production (its capacity level). There are several types of economy of scale.

Technical economies of scale

As a firm expands, it may be able to adopt different production techniques to reduce the unit cost of production. For example, a business may be able to introduce a production line. This is expensive in itself, but if it can be used to produce on a large scale the costs can be spread over many units, reducing the unit cost. At Mars' Slough factory, 3 million Mars bars are produced each day.

Specialisation

As firms grow bigger, they are able to employ people to specialise in different areas of the organisation. Instead of having managers trying to do several jobs at once, or having to pay specialist companies to do the work, they can employ their own staff to concentrate on particular areas of the business. For example, they might employ their own accountants or market researchers. By using specialists rather than buying in these services from outside firms, the business can make better decisions and save money. For example, a specialist finance director may be able to find ways of reducing the tax burden or organising cheaper sources of finance. Specialisation also occurs when as a business grows it splits the process into a series of separate routine tasks. Each individual then completes their task and because they are focusing on a relatively small task and repeating it they become faster at it and more efficient.

Purchasing economies

As firms get bigger, they need to buy more resources. As a result, they should be able to negotiate better deals with suppliers and reduce the price of their components and raw materials. Large firms are also more likely to get discounts when buying advertising space or dealing with distributors. If a firm can become a big customer, the supplier will be eager to keep that deal and so is likely to offer better terms and conditions. The bargaining power of firms may mean lower unit costs and also better cash flow. This approach is what enables a business such as Walmart to compete so effectively.

Marketing economies

As the business expands the cost of a media campaign can be divided over more units of sales, making bigger campaigns more feasible.

Managerial economies

As businesses grow they can afford to employ managers in specialist areas such as human resources and a legal department; this is because the costs can be spread over more output. The use of specialists can lead to more effective and more efficient decision-making.

Businesses that grow also tend to benefit from 'learning by doing'. More experience of what to do, how to do it, what not to do and who to use to do it can make the whole process more efficient. This efficiency gain should not be underestimated. If you are trying to start a business, for example, there is a tremendous amount you simply do not know how to do; a more experienced business person will have made the errors in the past and will now be getting it right and operating more efficiently.

Economies of scale can be important because the cost of producing a unit can have a significant impact on a firm's competitiveness. If an organisation can reduce its unit costs, it can either keep its price the same and benefit from higher profit margins, or it can pass the cost saving on to the customer by cutting the price. If it chooses the first option, this may mean higher rewards for the owners or more funds for investment. If, on the other hand, it cuts the price, it may be able to offer better value for money than its competitors. The ability to lower price and still make a profit may be very important in a market with falling demand; this means such firms may be in a better position to survive a recession.

Firms with economies of scale may be able to price competitors out of the market if they wish; this can act as a threat to potential entrants who know they would be less efficient than the established business at first because they would be operating on a smaller scale and therefore may not want to take the risk of a price war. This means that economies of scale can act as a barrier to entry.

The extent to which economies of scale exist will vary between industries. In industries such as energy or telecommunications there is very heavy investment required to start operations and these costs can be spread over large outputs, meaning economies of scale are important. It is difficult for small businesses to survive in these industries because they are very inefficient relative to the bigger firms. In other industries such as hairdressing the costs are mainly labour and growth requires more people; this means economies of scale do not exist to the same extent and as a result many small businesses exist in this industry.

> ### Case Study
> ## The Thai auto industry
>
>
> The automotive industry is a vital sector for Thailand's economy and contributes greatly to exports and trade inflows. It is the country's second-largest export industry, after computer parts and components. It has had continuous support from the government and has a buoyant industry including suppliers. Continued growth has allowed the country's producers to benefit from economies of scale which, combined with a low-cost but experienced labour force, make them a strong competitive force.
>
> ### Questions
> 1 Explain two possible economies of scale the Thai automotive industry might experience. [8]
> 2 Discuss how important economies of scale are likely to be to the success of the Thai auto industry. [16]

Internal diseconomies of scale

Diseconomies of scale occur when a firm expands its capacity and the cost per unit increases. Diseconomies of scale are often linked to the problems of managing more businesses. As organisations grow they have more products, operate in more regions and have more staff, and simply keeping everyone focused and working together can be difficult.

Diseconomies of scale can therefore occur for several reasons.

Communication problems

With more people involved in the business, it can be difficult to ensure that messages get to the right people at the right time. Although developments in information such as emails and intranets have helped, it can still be quite difficult to make sure everyone in a large business knows exactly what they are supposed to know when they are supposed to know it. When businesses are in different parts of the world there can be differences in time zones; however, even if people are in the same buildings where there are hundreds of them it can be difficult meeting up. With increased numbers there is great reliance on email rather than face-to-face discussions and this reduces the quality of the communications. There may be more messages in your inbox but this does not mean communication is actually effective.

Coordination and control problems

Just as communicating properly gets more difficult in a large organisation, so does controlling all the different activities and making sure everyone is working towards the same overall goals. As the firm expands and sets up new parts of the business, it is easy for different people to be working in different ways and setting different objectives. It becomes increasingly difficult to monitor what is going on and to make sure everyone is working together. Culture differences are likely to emerge as differences in the values of different parts of the business become apparent. The UK division will do things differently from the French division, the operations team see themselves as different from the marketing team. These differences in approach, management styles and values can lead to difficulties in terms of how the different parts of the business work together, causing inefficiency. These differences can get worse and lead to resentment due to the communication problems outlined above.

Motivation

As a firm gets bigger, it can become much harder to make sure everyone feels a part of the organisation (again highlighting the importance of communication). Senior managers are less likely to be able to stay in day-to-day contact with all the employees and so some people may feel less involved. In a small business

there is often a good team environment; everyone tends to see everyone else every day and it is easier to feel they are working towards the same goal. Any problems can be sorted out quickly, face-to-face. As the organisation grows, its employees can feel isolated and have less sense of belonging. As a result, they can become demotivated. Think of Maslow's hierarchy of needs (see Section 7.3) and you can appreciate that social needs and ego needs may be neglected due to less personal contact.

Diseconomies of scale often occur when mergers and takeovers take place. Managers often anticipate economies of scale from sharing resources, synergy and the power of a large scale. In reality the difficulties of agreeing on standard policies, cultural clashes, different priorities and strategies can lead to significant diseconomies which lead to cost disadvantages overall. In practice, most takeovers and mergers lead to worse financial performance for the combined companies than they achieved individually.

To avoid diseconomies of scale, managers use practices such as:

- having a mission statement to unify the business and outline the central purpose
- managing by objectives – an approach in which all employees are set targets tying them to the overall corporate objective
- using appraisals to review individuals' progress and ensure that they feel involved and as if they are acting in line with the overall aims of the business
- communicating regularly in a variety of ways to ensure people feel informed. This could be via newsletters, corporate videos, emails or staff meetings.

> ### Study tip
>
> Remember to look at the case study to get an idea of how big the owners or managers want the business to be. Also:
> - check if the demand is actually there to justify expansion – there is no point producing more if you cannot sell it
> - check if it is possible to staff the expansion
> - check to see if the business has mechanisms in place (such as budgeting and appraisals) to try to ensure that diseconomies of scale do not occur if it grows.

Getting the 'right' size of firm is a crucial issue for managers. Firms want to be big enough to have market power and benefit from economies of scale, but not be so big that they suffer from diseconomies of scale. In industries such as brewing and pharmaceuticals, many firms have joined together to benefit from economies of scale. At the same time, other firms have split up into smaller units because of the problems of large size. There is, it seems, no ideal size. It depends on the particular nature of the business, its own culture and communication, and the nature of the industry.

External economies and diseconomies of scale

Internal economies and diseconomies of scale occur when a business expands the size of its operations. External economies and diseconomies occur when at each and every level of output the unit cost falls (for external economies) or rises (for external diseconomies). This happens due to factors outside of the business. For example, by locating close to similar producers a business may be able to benefit from economies of agglomeration, i.e. the benefits of being in an area with many suppliers and a well-trained labour force. This might make it cheaper than setting up elsewhere. It might also mean suppliers in that area could grow because of the number of firms to supply to, and so can gain internal economies of scale. This leads to lower unit costs for its customers creating external economies of scale for them. Alternatively, if suppliers have become too big and experienced diseconomies then businesses still buying from them might experience internal diseconomies of scale.

Test your learning

Short answer questions

1 What is meant by process innovation? [2]

2 a What is meant by job production? [2]
   b Explain **one** advantage of job production. [3]

3 a What is meant by batch production? [2]
   b Explain **one** benefit of batch production. [3]

4 a What is mass production? [2]
   b Explain **one** advantage of mass production. [2]

5 a What is flow production? [2]
   b Explain **one** disadvantage of flow production. [2]

6 State **two** factors that influence the location of a business. [2]

7 What is meant by an external economy of scale? Give an example. [2]

8 a What is meant by an internal economy of scale? [2]
   b Explain **one** internal economy of scale. [3]

9 What is meant by an internal diseconomy of scale? [2]

10 Explain **one** reason why internal economies of scale may help a business succeed. [2]

Data response question

Pantaloon Retail India Ltd

With more than 1000 stores and 16 million square feet (1.5 million square metres) of operational space, Pantaloon Retail India Ltd is now close to a point where it can gain the benefits of economies of scale, according to its founder and managing director Kishore Biyani.

In four years' time, the company aims to increase the size of the operational retail space to between 25 and 30 million square feet (2.3 and 2.8 million square metres), with annual revenues forecast to grow in the 30–35 per cent range between now and then.

Biyani recently said the company was very well placed in terms of its cost structures. 'We are eliminating all the excess costs that are there in the system and becoming very, very competitive.'

The retailing business throughout the world is known to be one with low profit margins, with profitability often determined by how efficiently a company manages its supply chain, and dependent on the scale of its operations.

Retailing in India

Large-scale retailing in India is still in its early stages of growth, with the population largely buying groceries and food items from the millions of small, independent stores.

Government restrictions on foreign direct investment have so far protected the local industry, and meant there has been a lack of investments required, noticeably in areas such as warehousing and cold-storage facilities.

In the past foreign retailers have been allowed to own up to 51 per cent in ventures that sell single-brand products, such as Nike sportswear. However, those who stock and sell multiple brands, such as Wal-Mart Stores, have been prevented from selling directly to consumers, although they can open cash-and-carry businesses that sell to wholesalers and other small businesses and shopkeepers.

Source: Adapted from http://articles.marketwatch.com

Questions

1 Explain the meaning of the following terms:
   a revenues [3]
   b supply chain. [3]

2 Explain two possible consequences of limiting the extent to which foreign retailers can compete in India. [6]

3 Discuss the importance of economies of scale in helping a retail business to compete. [10]

Essay question

Discuss the possible advantages and disadvantages to a business of expanding the scale of its production. [20]

Past paper question

Read the Bee's Meals case study on page 214 and then answer the following question.

Discuss the impact on BM and its workers of a change from batch to flow production. [10]

Cambridge International AS and A Level Business Studies
9707 Paper 2 Q2d May/June 2007

14 Inventory management

> ## Chapter overview
>
> In this chapter we examine:
> - the purpose, costs and benefits of holding inventory
> - how to manage inventory.

14.1 Inventory

Purpose of inventory

The term **inventory** refers to stocks held within a business. Types of inventory include:
- materials – these are items used in the production process
- semi-finished goods – these are items where some work has been done on them but they are not complete
- finished goods – these are products that are ready to be sent to the customer.

These inventories are held:
- to enable production to take place and so that orders can be met.
- just in case anything goes wrong. For example, you may want to hold excess materials in case there is a problem with deliveries from the supplier; you may want to hold inventories of semi-finished items in case there is a breakdown in part of the system; you may want to hold finished goods in case there is a rush order from a customer.

> ## Key term
>
> Inventory refers to the stocks held in a business such as materials and semi-finished goods.

Costs and benefits of holding inventory

The benefits of holding inventory are that you have products ready if you need them and if there are any delays or breakdowns in the process you can continue to operate.

However, holding inventory can lead to:
- costs of storage – for example, the costs of a warehouse facility
- opportunity cost – because the money invested in inventories could be used elsewhere to earn money; money in inventory is tied up and not generating more returns
- security costs – to protect the materials from damage or theft.
- the risk of the stock depreciating, i.e. becoming out of date – this may be because the stock goes off (e.g. in the case of food) or becomes unpopular (in the case of fashion items) and so is wasted.

14.2 Managing inventory

Buffer inventory, reorder level and lead time

Buffer inventory is the minimum amount of inventory a business wants to hold just in case of problems.

The lead time is how long it takes from ordering the supplies from a supplier to them arriving at the business.

The reorder level is the level of inventory left at which a business needs to place an order so that the new inventories arrive before the business goes below its buffer level.

The reorder quantity is the amount ordered each time.

Construction and interpretation of simple inventory (stock) control charts

In Figure 14.1, the business uses up 200 units a week at a constant rate. It wants to always hold 100 units as a buffer inventory just in case and the lead time is one week. This means the business needs to reorder at 300 units. As the supplies are being made and delivered (which takes one week) another 200 units will be used up, which means that when the order arrives the business is down to its buffer of 100. The reorder quantity in this case is 800 units a month (given the business expects to use up 200 units for each of the four weeks).

Figure 14.1 assumes that the usage rate of the inventory is constant each week.

In Figure 14.2 we show a situation where the inventory starts to be used up at a faster rate after week 8 and the business therefore runs out of inventory before new supplies arrive. This is known as an inventory out.

In Figure 14.3 the supplies do not arrive – perhaps due to a problem at the suppliers because stocks were not re-ordered – leading again to an inventory out.

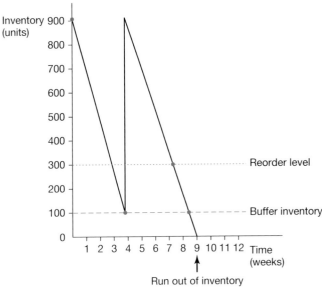

Figure 14.3 Effects of failing to reorder

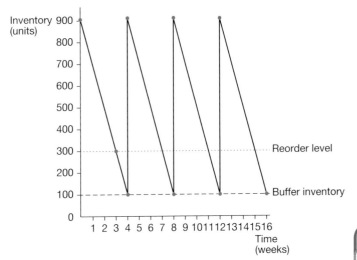

Figure 14.1 Inventory control chart

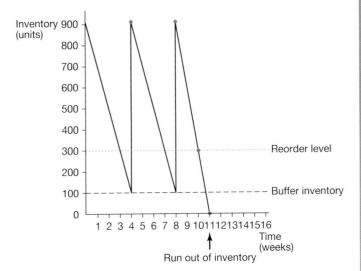

Figure 14.2 Example of a business running out of stock

Maths moment

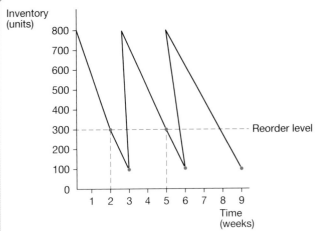

Figure 14.4 Inventory control chart

1 What is the reorder quantity in the inventory chart above?
2 What is the lead time?
3 How many units are used up each week?

Inventory (stock) control

The decision on how much inventory to hold is a trade-off between the costs of holding the stocks and the problems that might occur if stocks are not held.

The minimum amount of inventory that a firm wants to hold at any time is known as the buffer inventory (or the safety inventory). If the level of stocks falls below the buffer level, there may be a risk of running out; this could either halt production or mean that customers have to be turned away because no finished goods are available.

Several factors influence the level of buffer inventory a business holds:

- The rate at which stocks are generally used up – the faster stocks are used up, the more the firm will have to hold at any moment.
- The warehousing space available – the smaller the space the firm has for storage, the lower the level of inventory.
- The nature of the product – if the product is fragile or likely to depreciate, the firm will not want too much inventory in case it breaks or loses value rapidly.
- The reliability of suppliers – the more reliable suppliers are, the fewer buffer inventories the firm needs to hold because it knows it can get more as and when required.
- The suppliers' lead time – the lead time is the time it takes for products to arrive from when they are ordered. If the lead time is two days, for example, this means that it takes two days for supplies to arrive once you have ordered them. The shorter the lead time, the smaller the amount of inventories a firm needs to hold. If, however, the lead time is long, the firm will need to hold more inventory to last while it waits for a delivery.

Effective inventory management involves making sure that the business does not have too many or too few stocks.

Case Study

Car dealerships in China

Inventories at car dealerships in China were extremely high recently due to slower than expected sales. The inventory index (inventory divided by sales) was 1.98 this June. Typically the inventory index is between 0.8 and 1.2.

Dealers of Haima, a domestic brand based in South China's Hainan province, were the ones most seriously hit by excessive inventories. The average inventory index of Haima dealers reached 6.71 in June.

More than half of companies in the passenger car sector failed to meet their first-half sales targets. Chery, for example, sold 265 500 cars in the first half of the year, only 38 per cent of its full-year target of 700 000 units.

Therefore, carmakers have been pushing their inventories onto dealers in an attempt to boost sales. China's GDP growth slid to 7.6 per cent in the first half of this year from 9.2 per cent a year ago.

Some dealers have dropped their links with carmakers in the first half mainly due to excessive inventories.

According to a survey conducted by industry consultancy J D Power & Associates early this year, 63 per cent of auto dealers in China were profitable last year, down from 81 per cent the year before. Meanwhile, the proportion of dealers in financial difficulty increased to 20 per cent from 9 per cent.

The excessive level of inventory is likely to lead to price wars.

Source: www.chinadaily.com.cn

Questions

1 Explain why inventory levels are high in Chinese car dealerships. [6]
2 Discuss the actions dealerships could take if inventories are high. [10]

Just in time

One particular approach to inventory control is known as just-in-time (JIT) operations.

Just-in-time production occurs when firms produce products to order. Instead of producing as much as they can and building up inventories, firms only produce when they know they can actually sell the items. Similarly, components and supplies are only bought in by a firm as and when they are needed.

The aim of just-in-time production is to reduce a firm's inventory levels by as much as possible; in an ideal world there would be no inventories at all. Supplies would arrive and be used to produce items that are sold immediately to the final customer. A just-in-time approach should provide a firm with tremendous flexibility; firms produce what is required, when it is required. In the past, firms have tended to try to estimate what demand would be and produce this amount in advance of actual sales. This system works provided demand has been estimated correctly.

JIT production should also reduce costs. With no inventories, the firm does not have to pay for warehousing or security. The firm also avoids the opportunity cost of having money tied up in inventories.

Just-in-time production should help minimise wastage. If goods are produced and left to accumulate as inventories, they are likely to get damaged, to depreciate, to go out of fashion or be stolen. JIT avoids these issues. This means that JIT is part of a **lean approach** to business. Lean production seeks to minimise the waste of any resource, such as time and materials, to make a business more efficient.

Although the just-in-time process has many advantages, there are several potential problems or disadvantages as well.

First, the system relies on suppliers providing parts and components at exactly the time they are needed. If this type of flexible and reliable supplier cannot be found, the system breaks down. JIT can also cause problems if the suppliers fail to deliver on time. The manufacturer has no buffer inventory and so cannot produce. The system also means that the firm is vulnerable to action taken by employees. Any stoppage can be extremely expensive because production is halted completely.

The earthquake in Japan in 2011 was a disaster for those directly affected by it. It also caused enormous problems for businesses operating a just-in-time process and reliant on supplies from Japan. With a delay in supplies they struggled to produce.

Switching to JIT can also lead to an increase in costs because of the extra reordering. Because parts are ordered much more frequently, the firm may lose bulk discounts and will also have more administration costs.

Key term

Lean production is an approach that continally seeks to reduce any form of wastage in the production process.

Case Study

Toyota production halts

In April 2011 the Japanese carmaker Toyota had to temporarily halt production at its engine manufacturing plant on Deeside, Flintshire and five other of its factories across Europe.

The stoppage was due to a supply shortage from Japan, caused by the earthquake and tsunami.

The car industry in Europe relies on parts from Japan. Toyota uses a just-in-time system of supply which operates without a lot of slack in the system.

Questions

1 Explain what the potential benefits are to Toyota of a just-in-time approach. [6]

2 Discuss whether the halt in production at Toyota suggests that the company should stop using lean production techniques. Justify your answer. [10]

Study tip

Remember that the right level of inventory to hold will depend on how factors such as how well it can be stored, what it costs to store it, what the reorder time is, what the expected level of demand is and the operations strategy the business adopts.

Test your learning

Short answer questions

1 a What is meant by inventory? [2]
   b State three types of inventory. [3]

2 State two reasons why a business might hold inventory. [2]

3 State two costs of holding inventory. [2]

4 State two factors that influence the amount of buffer inventory held. [2]

5 a What is meant by lead time? [1]
   b Explain one factor that might influence the lead time of a supplier. [3]

6 What is meant by the reorder level? [1]

7 What is meant by just-in-time (JIT) production? [2]

8 Explain one reason why a business might use JIT. [2]

9 Explain one possible problem of JIT production. [2]

10 Explain one factor that influences the right level of inventory to hold. [3]

Data response question

Zara

The international retailer Zara is famous for its 'fast fashion'. It produces relatively small quantities of any one design and quickly changes the designs to ensure it stays up to date with fashion. Store managers monitor designs in other stores and sales patterns and send orders each week directly to the company's own factories. Unlike many other retailers, Zara has not subcontracted production and produces in Europe rather than Asia to ensure it keeps control of quality and can respond quickly. It has its own team of 200 designers able to imitate any new best selling designs that hit the fashion world. It designs more than 12 000 items a year. It can design and get an item in stores in weeks, whereas its competitors take months. Its approach is very much just in time; it produces in response to demand rather than ahead of it.

Questions

1 Explain the meaning of the following terms:
   a inventory [3]
   b subcontracting. [3]

2 Explain the possible advantages to Zara of holding relatively little inventory. [8]

3 Discuss the issues involved if a retailer wishes to adopt a fast fashion approach. [16]

Essay question

Discuss the possible advantages and disadvantages to a business of using just-in-time production. [20]

Past paper questions

1 Read the Loader Lorries case study on pages 209–10 and then answer the following question.

Using the information in Figures 1 and 2, analyse the differences between the two approaches to managing inventories (stocks). [8]

Cambridge International AS and A Level Business Studies
9707 Paper 21 Q1d May/June 2011

2 a Explain how JIT (Just in Time) could be used to manage stocks in a manufacturing business. [8]

b Discuss why businesses need an effective method of stock management. [12]

Cambridge International AS and A Level Business Studies
9707 Paper 1 Q7 May/June 2011

3 Read the Ganmor Cars case study on page 215 and then answer the following question.

Describe how lean production techniques might be used at GC. [6]

Cambridge International AS and A Level Business Studies
9707 Paper 2 Q2c May/June 2008

15 Business finance

Chapter overview

In this chapter we examine:
- why businesses need capital – to start up, to expand or to pay for day-to-day expenses (working capital)
- how the legal structure of a business affects its ability to raise finance
- the distinction between different sources of finance – short- and long-term, internal and external
- the factors that influence businesses' choices of sources of finance.

15.1 Why businesses need capital

Key terms

Capital is the money invested into a business either by its owners or by organisations such as banks.

Share capital is the money invested into a company by shareholders when they buy shares.

Loan capital is money invested by a business as a result of borrowing.

An **asset** is any item owned by a business that can generate an income for the enterprise.

Non-current assets are assets that a business expects to hold for one year or more. Examples include property and vehicles.

Capital is the money that is invested in a business, usually to purchase **assets**. There are two major circumstances in which a business needs to raise capital.

1 When it is first started

This is referred to as 'start up' capital for obvious reasons. The amount of capital raised by a business that is starting up is likely to be relatively small as an entrepreneur establishing a

new business is unlikely to have access to large amounts of finance and banks and investors may be unwilling to invest into an untried enterprise.

Start-up capital may be used to purchase the assets that a business needs to commence trading. In the case of a manufacturing business, this may be to buy a lease entitling the business to use a factory for an agreed period. It may also be required to buy machinery and vehicles. Start-up businesses supplying services may purchase slightly different **non-current assets** such as leases on shops or offices. Any start-up business is likely to require capital to finance its market research and also promotion to establish its brand and identity among potential customers. It can prove difficult for some start-up businesses to raise sufficient capital and this is an important reason why some business ideas never become reality.

Case Study

Creating a STORM of interest

The STORM Creative Events Agency was established in 2010 by Key is Ng. It is a fashion lifestyle events and public relations firm. Key is Ng has had a huge impact on the Singaporean and regional fashion scene.

The 24-year-old entrepreneur founded his company with a start-up capital of just $15 000. The company organises product launches, private parties, fashion shows and awards ceremonies to promote brands and business ideas. It is adept at gaining press coverage for its events and uses its contacts in the media throughout Asia to gain extensive coverage of its innovative events.

Questions

1 Explain how an entrepreneur starting a new business as a company might raise the capital needed to start the business. [6]
2 Discuss the reasons why Key is Ng was able to start the Storm Creative Events Agency with so little start-up capital. [10]

2 When it expands

Many businesses seek to grow; indeed for a number it is an important objective, as we saw in Chapter 4. This means a business will probably buy non-current assets. Business expansion can take a number of forms:

- A business may seek to increase sales of existing products, possibly by promoting them heavily.
- A business may seek to enter new markets, for example in October 2012 the Indian government announced that its supermarket sector would be opened up to foreign competition. As a consequence foreign multinational retailers such as Walmart, Carrefour and Tesco are likely to be developing expansion plans to enter this market.
- A business could develop new products to increase its market share or profitability. Apple announced the introduction of its new TV4 in 2014 and would expect to sell large quantities of this new product.
- A business may seek to take over (that is to buy control of) another business. In 2014 Microsoft completed its takeover of Finnish mobile phone manufacturer Nokia in a $7.2 billion deal.

Uses and sources of finance

Most expansion plans will require a business to raise finance and these may be very large sums of capital as in the case of Microsoft's takeover bid. A start-up business may require smaller sums of capital and has access to fewer possible sources of finance to find this capital. Table 15.1 sets out the different sources of finance that may be used by a business depending upon its circumstances.

Table 15.1 Sources of finance for start-ups and expansion

Start-up capital	Capital for expansion
Possible sources of finance include:	Possible sources of finance include:
• owner's finance, such as savings, redundancy pay, etc. • money borrowed from friends and family • bank loans • funds invested by outsiders, for example, venture capitalists • crowdfunding	• sale of shares (possibly using a Stock Exchange) • sale of non-current assets (e.g. property or vehicles) that are not used • loan capital – banks may be willing to lend for expansion • profits retained in the business from previous trading periods • crowdfunding

It is important to appreciate that businesses need capital for different reasons and that this means that they have different sources available to them.

- **Loan capital** This is raised from financial organisations such as banks. They may be willing to lend to an established business that is seeking to expand for two main reasons. Firstly, this type of business is likely to have a track record of successful trading and an established customer base.

Secondly, the business will most probably have assets that can be used as collateral for any loan. This means that the business might use its property as security for a loan. If it fails to make repayments, the bank can sell the property to regain its money and this reduces the risk of the loan.

- **Share capital** Although any company can sell shares to raise capital it is easier for large well-known public companies to do so. This is because they are able to use the facilities of the Stock Exchange to do so, enabling them to sell efficiently and cheaply to large numbers of shareholders.
- **Retained profits** This source of finance can only be used if a business is established and profitable. Thus, a firm considering expansion may be able to use this source if it has been financially successful in the recent past. It is not a source of finance that is available to start-up businesses.
- **Venture capital** Start-up businesses may be able to negotiate with venture capitalists who are wealthy individuals or organisations seeking higher risk investments. Venture capitalists normally offer a mix of loan and share capital and are unlikely to provide large sums of finance.

15.2 Working capital

Key terms

Working capital is the cash a business has for its day-to-day spending.

Current assets are items owned by a business that can be readily turned into cash. Examples include cash, money owed by customers (trade and other receivables) and inventories (stocks).

Current liabilities are short-term debts of a business, usually repaid within one year. An example is a business's overdraft.

Working capital measures the amount of money available to a business to pay its day-to-day expenses, such as bills for fuel and raw materials, wages and business rates. Much attention is given to the capital firms choose to invest in non-current assets, but of equal importance to the success of a business is the capital set aside to finance regular transactions.

Working capital is what remains of a business's liquid assets once it has settled all its immediate debts (see Figure 15.1).

Study tip

In some circumstances current liabilities might be greater than current assets. In this case, working capital will be negative (and may be called net current liabilities). As a negative figure it is often shown in brackets.

Working capital		Current assets		Current liabilities (Debts payable in the short term)
Essential, to pay for day-to-day expenses and keep the business operating	=	• Cash in the bank • Trade and other receivables due to settle their accounts soon • Inventories – raw materials and components	less	• Debts repayable to the bank, e.g. overdraft • Trade and other payables who expect to be paid in the near future • Tax due to authorities NB An overdraft only represents a current liability if the bank calls for it to be repaid

Figure 15.1 Working capital

It is possible to calculate the working capital of a business from its statement of financial position by using the following formula:

Working capital = current assets − current liabilities

A statement of financial position records a business's assets and liabilities. We look at statements of financial position (also known as balance sheets) in detail in Chapter 18.

Maths moment

Last year Darwin Hotels Limited had current assets amounting to the value of A$25.0 million and current liabilities totalling A$19.9 million.

1 Calculate its working capital for last year.
2 This year its current assets fell by 5 per cent while its current liabilities rose by A$1.1 million. Calculate its working capital for this year.

Working capital as a source of finance

Working capital is important to all businesses. It has been described as the 'lifeblood' of a successful enterprise. If any business is unable to pay its bills promptly, then it may be forced to close down as a consequence of insolvency.

However, working capital can also be a source of finance for a business. If a business manages its working capital effectively it may have a strong working capital position. To do this it may need to:

• make sure that its debtors (people or businesses that owe it money) pay on time
• ensure that it does not hold too high inventory (or stock) levels as this can tie up large amounts of cash for a business

• pay its own debts as late as possible so that as much cash as possible is held in the business at any given time.

If a business's **current assets** exceed its **current liabilities** on a regular basis this provides the business with a potential source of finance. However, this source of finance is only available on a short-term basis.

Case Study

MEO Australia raises A$9.3 million for working capital

MEO Australia has sold A$9.3 million of new shares to raise finance to ensure that it has sufficient working capital to fund its future plans. It sold 46.5 million shares to raise the capital it required and the directors said they were 'delighted' with the support of the shareholders in buying the shares.

MEO Australia operates in the oil and gas industry and is seeking to expand rapidly and provide energy to the rapidly growing Asian economies. This involves the discovery and extraction of oil and gas from different locations including the Timor Sea and the Gulf of Thailand.

In June 2012 the company announced losses of A$5.7 million for the financial year compared to profits of A$14.2 million for the previous financial year.

Question

1 Why might MEO Australia need large amounts of working capital? [6]

15.3 Revenue expenditure and capital expenditure

its trading activities. Spending on employees' wages is an example of revenue expenditure. Revenue expenditure is shown on a business's **income statement** as it is part of a business's trading costs or expenses. The differences between revenue expenditure and capital expenditure are summarised in Table 15.2.

We have seen that businesses need to raise capital to start up and to expand. Once a business has raised funds to finance its start-up costs, the business can start trading. In the case of expansion the business will require additional finance, in excess of that received from sales, to finance the purchase of additional non-current assets and other items.

If the start up or the expansion is successful the new or newly expanded business will earn revenue from its sales. This will be used to buy more labour services and raw materials to enable it to continue trading.

The expenditure carried out by a business can be divided into two categories: **revenue expenditure** and **capital expenditure**. Capital expenditure is on items that may be used many times, mainly non-current assets. A new computer system is an example of capital expenditure. Expenditure on items required to start up or to expand a business can be classified as capital expenditure. These will be shown on a business's **statement of financial position** as they include the purchase of non-current assets.

Revenue expenditure is on the goods and services needed by a business that will be used up in the short term as a normal part of

Case Study

Vardhman Textiles

Figure 15.2 A selection of textiles

Vardhman Textiles, one of India's largest textile manufacturers, plans to increase its capital expenditure by 142 per cent in 2012–13. The company expects to spend Rs. 7.5 billion compared to Rs. 3.5 billion in 2011–12.

The company manufactures fibre, yarn, sewing thread and fabrics, and forecasts significant rises in its revenue from sales and consequently its profits.

Vardhman's recently released Annual Report judged that yarn exports would be affected due to a slowdown in demand owing to global economic slowdown. However, it expects a revival in global demand and significant growth in yarn sales in 2013. The Report expects cotton prices to be relatively unchanged in 2012–13 following a 6.1 per cent fall in cotton prices in 2011–12. At the same time the prices paid by buyers of yarn have risen by 32 per cent to Rs. 210 per kilogram.

Table 15.2 Revenue and capital expenditure

	Revenue expenditure	Capital expenditure
Explanation	This is spending on assets that are used up in a relatively short period of time.	This is spending on non-current assets that will be used by the business for a prolonged period of time.
Examples	Spending on fuel, components and raw materials.	Expenditure to purchase property, vehicles and production equipment.
Effects on financial statements	This type of expenditure is recorded on the income statement under headings such as 'cost of sales' and 'administrative expenses'. It will only affect the accounts in the financial year in which the expenditure occurs.	The value of non-current assets purchased through capital expenditure is shown on the statement of financial position. The reduction in value of these assets over time is listed on the income statement. This type of expenditure affects the statement of financial position and income statements for a number of years.
Possible effects on profits	Revenue expenditure is essential to production but, if not controlled, can have an immediate and damaging effect on a business's profits.	This type of spending has no immediate effect on profits. However, capital expenditure is essential if a firm is to generate long-term profits.

Questions

1 Using examples, explain the difference between revenue and capital expenditure. [6]
2 Evaluate the view that this capital expenditure will increase the profits earned by Vardhman Textiles. [10]

15.4 Sources of finance

There are a number of sources available, but the one chosen will depend upon several factors:

- the amount of money required by the business
- the purpose for which the finance is required
- the period of time over which the loan is required
- the legal structure of the business
- the financial position of the business.

We shall look at a range of sources of finance in this section and consider how factors such as those listed above may influence a business's choice of sources of finance.

Short- and long-term sources of finance

Key terms

Short-term sources of finance are needed for a limited period of time, normally less than one year.

Long-term sources of finance are those that are needed over a longer period of time, usually over a year.

A business may need short-term finance to pay its bills and to keep its suppliers happy. This is an important part of cash-flow management. Managing cash flow can be difficult if a firm's customers are late in making payment for goods and services they have purchased or if sales are unexpectedly low. In either case the firm is likely to be short of funds to purchase raw materials and pay wages and salaries. Sudden increases in the costs of raw materials can also create a need for short-term finance. Short-term finance of this kind is usually repayable within a one-year period.

Besides the use of working capital there are two major sources of short-term finance.

Sometimes businesses need to purchase major capital assets such as land and buildings or they may decide to expand or to take over other businesses. To do this they will require long-term finance which will be repaid over a period of time in excess of one year and, on many occasions, much more than one year.

Table 15.3 on page 162 classifies a range of sources of finance according to whether they are short- or long-term.

Internal sources of finance

Key term

An internal source of finance is one that exists within the business.

An **internal source of finance** is one that exists within the business. The major internal sources of finance are retained profits, sale of assets, sale and leaseback, and working capital.

Retained profits

This remains a major source of finance, particularly for smaller businesses. Businesses can use profits from the current trading year or profits from previous trading years (technically these are called retained profits) as sources of finance. By using profits for reinvesting, a business avoids paying interest on a loan and this can avoid heavy interest charges if the loan required is a large one. Furthermore, using this source of finance may avoid the need for a company to sell further shares, enabling existing shareholders to retain control if they continue to hold a majority of the shares.

But using retained profits can have substantial opportunity costs – that is the business may lose out from not using these profits in another way. Reinvesting retained profits may not be popular with shareholders who are likely to receive a lower dividend as a result. Alternatively, the business may lose out on interest it may have received if it held the money in an interest-paying bank account.

This method of finance is only available to firms making a profit. Even then the profits may not be sufficient to purchase expensive capital assets.

Sale of unwanted assets

Firms can raise cash by selling assets that they no longer require – normally these are non-current assets. The sale of some assets can raise large amounts of finance for businesses. Thus a business might have land, buildings or other assets that are not required and they may decide to sell to raise capital. In 2014 India's GMR Infrastructure announced it was to sell two coal mines it owns in Indonesia for $600 to repay debts.

Raising finance in this way offers a key benefit in that the business is not committed to a stream of future interest payments, nor might its shareholders suffer dilution of control. However, the business would normally lose access to the assets it has sold.

Sale and leaseback

But what if the assets will continue to be required by the business? A popular technique of raising funds in recent years has been sale and leaseback. Under this arrangement firms sell valuable assets and lease them back again. This means that they have the capital from the sale of the assets as well as the continuing use of these assets, so that their business is not disrupted. The major drawback is that the business now has to pay for the use of assets which previously were freely available. This may have a negative impact on its long-term profits.

Case Study

The Thomas Cook Group

The Thomas Cook Group plc is a British registered company that sells holiday products to more than 19 million customers worldwide each year. The company's management team has announced its intention to reduce the amount of debt recorded on its statement of financial position and has been seeking the best source of finance to do this.

In 2012 the Thomas Cook Group agreed a number of sale and leaseback deals for some of its non-current assets.

- In October it raised £11.5 million ($19.4 million) by selling its offices in Ghent, Belgium, to Koramic Real Estate and leasing them back again.
- In May it signed a sale and leaseback deal with several other companies. This resulted in the sale and immediate leaseback of 19 aircraft, resulting in the company raising £182.9 million ($309.1 million).

Questions

1 Explain why the Thomas Cook Group might have wanted to reduce the amount of debt (or borrowing) that it had.   [6]
2 Evaluate whether sale and leaseback is the best choice as a source of finance for Thomas Cook Group plc in these circumstances.   [10]

Working capital

As we saw earlier in this chapter, working capital is the cash required by a business to pay for its day-to-day operations. Working capital is needed to pay for fuel, raw materials and wages. Reducing inventory levels, chasing up debtors (other organisations that owe the business money) more urgently and delaying payment to suppliers can raise cash generated from a firm's working capital.

Firms might seek to improve terms they are offered for trade credit. Many suppliers grant their customers an interest-free period of grace in which to pay for goods and services they have

received. From the customers' point of view this is a useful form of finance that helps fund working capital at the expense of the seller's cash flow. The typical credit period offered to customers is 30 days. If a business can extend this period to, say, 60 days, it is equivalent to a month's free loan. It may be, however, that suppliers are less willing to offer discounts on selling prices if they grant generous trade credit terms. Although the receipt of trade credit is a means of improving a company's working capital, it is technically an external source of finance.

External sources of finance

When individuals, other businesses or organisations such as banks or governments provide capital to a business, this is termed **external sources of finance**. Businesses are more likely to use external sources of finance when:

- a large sum of finance is required (as they will find it more difficult to raise such sums internally)
- the level of risk associated with the source of finance is low, encouraging outsiders to invest or lend money
- the company's profit levels are relatively low, reducing the possibility of the use of retained profits.

The first four external sources of finance we consider are all types of loan capital. The major difference between them is the timescale of the borrowing. An overdraft may be taken out for just a few weeks whereas a business mortgage could last for up to 50 years. Loan capital can be attractive to a business as a source of finance because it does not lead to any loss of control by the owners of the business.

Overdrafts

An **overdraft** is perhaps the best known method of short-term finance. It is a facility offered by banks allowing a business to borrow up to an agreed limit for as long as it wishes. Overdrafts are a very flexible form of finance as the amounts borrowed can vary as long as they are within an agreed figure. They are also simple to arrange – established business customers can often arrange, or increase the limit, without completing any forms.

However, overdrafts can be quite expensive with interest being charged at between 4 and 6 per cent over the bank's normal lending rate on a daily basis. This is not a problem unless a business seeks to borrow on overdraft over a long period of time. In these circumstances it might be better for a business to convert its overdraft to a longer-term method of finance. A further drawback of using overdrafts as a source of finance is that banks can demand immediate repayment, although this is rare.

Bank loans

Bank loans are relatively straightforward to arrange if the business that is seeking the credit is solvent and has a satisfactory financial history. The financial institution advances the business a set figure and the business makes repayments over an agreed period of time. If the bank lending the capital considers the loan in any way risky, then it is likely to charge a higher rate of interest. Small businesses, in particular, suffer from this effect. Normally banks charge about 2 per cent over their base rate of interest for loans such as these. Interest rates can be fixed or variable.

Banks will often require security for their loans and this will usually be in the form of property. Such security is often termed 'collateral'. If the business defaults on the loan the bank sells the property or other collateral and recoups the money that was lent. In this way the bank lowers the degree of risk it incurs in making loans to businesses.

Mortgages

Mortgages are simply long-term loans granted by financial institutions solely for the purchase of land and buildings. The land or building in question is used as security for the loan; they act as collateral. These loans can be for long periods of time – often up to 50 years. Mortgages can have fixed or variable rates of interest and are particularly suitable when a business wishes to raise large sums of money.

Some businesses may choose to re-mortgage their premises to raise capital. A re-mortgage either increases the existing mortgage or establishes a mortgage where one did not exist before. This source of finance is particularly popular with small businesses.

Debentures

Debentures are a special type of long-term loan to be repaid at some future date, normally within 15 years of the loan being agreed. The rate of interest paid on debentures is fixed. In some circumstances debentures may not have a repayment date, representing a permanent loan to the business; this is an irredeemable debenture. Debentures are normally secured by using the business's non-current assets as collateral. Debentures are another form loan capital and holders of debentures do not have voting rights in the business.

Case Study

Even banks need to raise capital

Bank CIMB Niaga, the fifth-largest bank in Indonesia, has announced plans to sell fixed interest bonds (similar to debentures) repayable after three or five years. Bonds to the value of 600 billion rupiah ($200 million) will be sold to raise capital that will be used by the Bank to provide loans to its customers. A bond is a certificate issued in return for the loan of an amount of money. It states an annual rate of interest and normally has a repayment date.

The Bank has issued a brief prospectus published in *Bisnis Indonesia*. It intends that the bonds will be able to be bought and sold on the Indonesian Stock Exchange. The bonds will offer a return of between 7.35 and 7.75% per cent. This issue of bonds is part of a larger issue that will take place by 2015.

Questions

1 Explain the advantages and disadvantages of borrowing a large sum of capital as Bank CIMB Niaga has done. [6]
2 Discuss the other sources of finance that might be available to a large bank such as CIMB to provide funds to lend to customers. [10]

Venture capital

Venture capital is an important source of finance for small- to medium-sized businesses which are considered to be risky and therefore in some danger of failing. It is normally a mix of loan and share capital. Financial institutions, for example, merchant banks, provide venture capital and wealthy individuals (who are known as business angels) are another source.

Organisations and individuals providing venture capital frequently wish to have some control over the organisation to which they are providing finance. The business's owners may need to sell some shares in their company (generally a minority stake) to the person or organisation providing the venture capital. Providers of venture capital may seek a non-executive director role in the business in which they are investing. Venture capital investors not only provide capital, but also experience, contacts and advice when required, which distinguishes venture capital from other sources of finance.

A significant drawback is that providers of venture capital will not advance huge amounts to businesses. It is unusual for venture capitalists to lend in excess of $850 000 in a single deal.

> ### Key terms
>
> **Venture capital** is funds, in the form of a mix of share and loan capital, advanced to businesses thought to be relatively high risk.

Share or equity capital

This is a very common form of finance for both start-up capital and also for additional capital in a later stage of the business's life. Firms raise capital by selling, quite literally, a share in their business to investors. A share is simply a certificate giving the holder ownership of part (or a share) of a company. The shareholders purchase shares and by selling large numbers of shares companies raise significant sums of capital. Issuing shares can be very expensive, which means it is only appropriate for raising very large sums of capital.

It is available to both private limited companies and public limited companies. However, in the UK, it is much easier for public limited companies to sell shares for two reasons:

1 They can sell shares on the Stock Exchange. This is an efficient international market which brings together buyers and sellers of shares and sets share prices.

2 Unlike private limited companies, public companies do not need the permission of other shareholders to sell shares.

Equally, existing shareholders can sell their shares freely. Both these factors make it easier to buy and sell shares in public limited companies and encourage shareholders to buy shares in the first place.

There are a number of benefits from selling of shares or equity as a source of finance. Although the companies will be expected to pay an annual return to shareholders (dividends) the level of this payment is not fixed and in an unprofitable year it may be possible for the company to avoid making any payment.

Case Study

Chinese mining company needs capital

The decision by the government of Myanmar to open its economy to foreign investment has created some attractive opportunities for Chinese companies, large and small. China Polymetallic Mining (CPM) is a small mining group based in Yunnan, close to the border between China and Myanmar. CPM's managers have stated that the company is in a good position to benefit from developing Myanmar's mineral resources and that global demand for them is rising. However, the company faces intense competition from larger competitors.

The company requires capital to undertake the expansion necessary to benefit from the mineral riches close by in Myanmar. It plans to double its production between 2012 and 2016. Crucially, the company has financial support from the Yunnan provincial government. The company may also raise further capital by issuing shares although this could prove to be a risky investment. The volatility of metal prices on world markets together with the possibility of natural disasters and changes in the regulations imposed by the Chinese government make predicting returns from mining in Myanmar difficult.

Questions

1 Explain the factors that China Polymetallic Mining (CPM) would take into account when deciding on the best source of finance to use for its planned expansion. [6]

2 To what extent is selling shares the best way for China Polymetallic Mining (CPM) to raise capital to fund its expansion? [10]

Microfinance

Key terms

Microfinance is the provision of financial services for poor and low-income clients.

Crowdfunding is a source of finance that entails collecting relatively small amounts of money from a large number of supporters – the 'crowd'.

Microfinance is a term that describes the provision of financial services for poor and low-income clients. Although much publicity has been given to the granting of small loans, microfinance includes other basic financial services such as savings, the transfer of money and insurance for those on low and very low incomes. An important element of microfinance is that it supports the transfer of remittances of income from people earning reasonable incomes to poorer relatives and friends in different countries. Without the services provided through microfinance this might not be possible.

Improving access to such services allows those on low incomes to fund activities which will create incomes, build assets and protect against risks. Microfinance is regarded by many as a solution to reducing poverty among low-income citizens across the globe.

Microfinance can entail a transfer of money from high income to lower income countries. The case study below illustrates its workings and benefits.

Case Study

Lendwithcare

Lendwithcare fights poverty and injustice in 87 countries around the world to help the world's poorest people find routes out of poverty. As part of its poverty-fighting work Lendwithcare provides microfinance services and is seeking to organise finance for María del Carmen Jimenez's business plan.

María is 28 and a single mother with one child and lives in Cariamanga in Ecuador. María is a primary school teacher. She has had the position for the last six years. Additionally, with her sister she runs a beauticians. Her sister works there full time while María joins her each day after finishing teaching at school.

María requested a loan in order to purchase new furniture and accessories for the salon. Hopefully, this will make their business more attractive and bring in more customers. María would also like to purchase extra inventories, specifically creams, soaps, and lotions as many of their customers are women and ask for facials and make-up.

María is seeking a loan of about $2000 and plans to repay it over one year. The loan would be granted by a number of Lendwithcare's supporters, each providing a small sum of money.

Figure 15.3 Maria del Carmen Jimenez

Source: Adapted from http://www.lendwithcare.org

Questions

1 Explain why banks in Ecuador might be unwilling to lend María $2000. [6]

2 Discuss the arguments for and against lending María a small sum of money. [10]

Crowdfunding

Crowdfunding is a source of finance that entails collecting relatively small amounts of money from a large number of supporters – the 'crowd'. It is common for businesses aiming to raise money through crowdfunding to use the interest to communicate with potential supporters. However, as the case study on page 162 shows, this is not always the case.

Crowdfunding has become popular in recent years, especially with small- and medium-sized businesses, because banks in many countries have been unwilling to lend following the financial crisis of 2009–10. Equally, savers with spare cash have received very low interest rates and these have often been lower than the rate of inflation, meaning that savings are losing value over time. Consequently, savers have sought other ways to generate income from their savings.

A number of entrepreneurs have set up internet-based businesses to meet the needs of savers and small- and medium-sized businesses. They have acted as a link between the two groups, providing information on businesses seeking finance and administering loans provided by the 'crowds' of savers. Each saver may lend a relatively small amount to any business; this limits the effect if the business fails to repay the loan.

Crowdfunding is attractive for businesses as it avoids the need to deal with local banks, which can be bureaucratic and slow to make decisions. Furthermore, even if the banks agree to grant a loan to a business they may charge higher interest rates than crowdfunders.

Government grants and loans

There is a wide range of grants and subsidised loans available to UK businesses. The Government offers grants and loans to support business expansion, to provide funding for researching and developing new products, to assist businesses in buying new premises or improving existing properties.

Government grants will usually only cover a proportion of the total costs of a start-up or an expansion. There is also likely to be a great deal of competition from other businesses for government grants and there is usually a fixed amount of money available under most grant schemes. However, the major advantage of government grants is that entrepreneurs and businesses do not have to repay them as long as they meet any conditions under which the grant was given.

There are various grants available to businesses for purposes such as start-ups and expansion from the European Union, the UK government and other agencies within the UK. An estimated 4500 grants and financial programmes are available to UK organisations amounting to a potential total value of £50 000 million.

Two major examples of grants available to UK businesses are described below.

1 **Selective Finance for Investment (SFI)** This is for capital expenditure including start-up costs and expansion. This is only given in circumstances in which jobs are created or protected and is normally for a maximum of 15 per cent of the total investment.

2 **Technology grants** These are to stimulate business growth through technological developments. This category of grant is available in a range of situations including researching and developing new products, marketing new technology-based products or for developing sources of renewable energy.

Maths moment

The UK government provided the maximum grant of 15 per cent of the start-up cost of a new business under its SFI scheme. The amount of the grant was £375 000.

How much was the start-up cost of the new business?

Taking on new partners

This is an option for small- and medium-sized enterprises. A partnership (whether it has limited liability or not) can take on a new partner who will invest into the enterprise in return for becoming a partner and owning a share of the business. Similarly, a private limited company can decide to sell more shares as long as the existing shareholders support the decision. In return for the ownership of a share of the business the new shareholder(s) will provide an injection of capital.

Crowdfunding: A different source of finance

Figure 15.4 The Brooklyn Warehouse in Halifax, Nova Scotia, is financed by crowdfunding

George Christakos owns and manages a restaurant in Nova Scotia, Canada, and, facing the normal difficulties in raising capital, decided to use his business's customers as a source of finance. He wanted to enlarge the restaurant in the town of Halifax that he co-owns with his father, Leo. George's first choice as a source of finance, the bank, decided not to lend him any money.

Not dismayed, George and his father decided to use crowdfunding to raise the finance they needed. This is a source of finance that invites small contributions from a large number of people.

Mr Christakos' crowdfunding effort was unique, but entirely suitable for his business, and comprised three options for his customers. For investing $50, a customer was rewarded with lunch for two and two T-shirts. The option of a four-course dinner for two for investing $100 proved to be the most popular. For customers with larger sums to invest, George offered two dinners a year for the rest of the restaurant's life.

Using crowdfunding as a source of revenue, the restaurant raised $23 000 from 115 contributors, 80 per cent of whom lived close to the restaurant. Crowdfunding campaigns can take many different forms. Some involve donations, while others, such as Mr Christakos' effort, involve the pre-purchase of goods or services. In any event the goal is to raise capital.

Questions

1 Explain why a loan from the bank might have been George Christakos' first source of finance. [6]

2 Discuss the major advantages and disadvantages of using crowdfunding as a source of finance. [10]

Table 15.3 Classifying sources of finance

	Internal sources of finance	External sources of finance
Short-term sources of finance	• Working capital • Retained profits	• Overdrafts
Long-term sources of finance	• Retained profits • Sale of assets • Sale and leaseback	• Bank loans • Venture capital • Mortgages • Debentures • Share capital • New partners • Government grants and loans • Crowdfunding • Microfinance

Table 15.3 classifies the sources of finance we have discussed according to whether they are short- or long-term, internal or external sources. You will note that retained profits can be classified as short- or long-term finance as a business can opt to use this type of finance over any timescale.

15.5 Factors influencing the choice of sources of finance

The business's legal structure

The legal structure of a business is a major influence on the sources of finance that are available to it. A major implication of a business's legal structure is that only companies are able to sell shares and only public companies in the UK can sell shares via the London Stock Exchange.

Start-up businesses, many of which may be sole traders or partnerships, normally have a more limited range of sources of finance to draw upon as they represent a greater risk to potential investors and have few, if any, internal sources of finance for use.

In contrast a public limited company has a greater range of sources of finance that it can use and, particularly in the UK, it benefits from being able to raise capital by selling shares on the London Stock Exchange.

Table 15.4 sets out the major sources of finance available to each of the major legal structures and offers some consideration of factors that decision-makers in each case may take into account.

Table 15.4 The legal structure of a business, possible sources of finance and key issues

Legal form of business	Possible sources of finance	Key issues for consideration
Sole trader or Proprietor	Owner's savings, banks, suppliers, government grants and loans	• Security for those lending funds • Loss of control by owner • Evidence that business has potential to develop • Financial history of business/owner
Partnership	Partners' savings, banks, suppliers, government grants and loans	• Problems of introducing new partner • Lack of collateral • Potential expense of raising large sums of money • Should they form a limited company?
Private Limited Company (Ltd)	Dependent upon the size of the private limited company: suppliers, banks, government grants and loans, venture capital institutions, private share issues	• Disagreement among existing shareholders • Difficulty finding suitable shareholders • Loss of control by existing shareholders • Lack of collateral and security for those lending funds • Element of risk in a loan
Public Limited Company (plc)	Suppliers, banks, government grants and loans, venture capital institutions, public share issues via the Stock Exchange	• State of economy and stock market • Ability to move to area receiving government aid • Recent financial performance • Reputation of company and senior managers

Cost of the source of finance

Key term

Opportunity cost is the next best alternative foregone.

For most businesses that are raising capital the cost of alternative sources might be an important criterion in making a decision as to the best source of finance. The costs incurred by firms raising capital can take a number of forms.

The rate of interest

The rate of interest charged by organisations granting loans can be a significant influence, especially if the loan is a large one. This will depend on the level of risk that the loan represents to the lender and the time period of the loan. A short-term loan to a high risk business might be charged at a high rate of interest.

Case Study

Pakistan's cement industry faces high borrowing costs

Paying interest on loans has become a major cost for Pakistan's cement industry despite three cuts in interest rates in 2012. Companies in the cement industry are paying interest rates over 12 per cent on long-term borrowing. Representatives of the cement industry have urged the government to provide some support so that the interest rates paid by the industry on its borrowing can be reduced.

The industry's financial position has been weakened further by stagnant demand in Pakistan for concrete products and by declining levels of exports.

Questions

1 Explain the benefits that Pakistani cement producers might receive from issuing shares as a means of raising capital. [6]
2 Discuss the reasons why high interest rates have been such a burden for businesses in the cement industry in Pakistan. [10]

The costs of selling shares

For a public limited company a share issue can be an attractive option. However, this can be an expensive method of raising capital as it entails considerable administration and promotion and, on occasions, a form of insurance if the sale is not successful. When shares are first sold by a company it has to use the services of other expert organisations to organise the sale. It is common for companies to use merchant banks for this purpose.

Public limited companies sometimes use rights issues to sell new shares. A rights issue entails selling additional shares to existing shareholders in proportion to the number of shares already owned. For example, existing shareholders may be offered the opportunity to buy one new share for each eight already held. Because of the relatively low cost of issuing shares in this way it is usual for them to be sold at a slight discount to encourage sales.

Study tip

Do not confuse the sale of new shares and second-hand ones. Firms sell newly issued shares directly to the shareholders. In contrast, second-hand shares are sold mainly through the Stock Exchange. When second-hand shares are sold on the Stock Exchange it is not a source of finance for the company whose shares are sold – it is merely a means of the shareholder recovering the investment by selling the shares to another person or organisation.

Opportunity cost

A decision to use a particular source of finance may have a cost in terms of what has to be given up as a consequence of the decision. For example, a decision to use sale and leaseback as a source of finance may appear a low-cost option. However, this source of finance will commit the company to paying each month or year for the asset that has been sold. Similarly, using retained profits for reinvestment into the company entails an **opportunity cost** which can be measured in terms of the reduction in the amount of profits that can be paid to shareholders (these are known as dividends). Finally, receiving trade credit from a supplier may be an attractive short-term source of finance, but it carries a possible opportunity cost in that the supplier may charge a higher selling price as it is, in effect, providing an interest-free short-term loan.

For many businesses, accessing sources of finance at the lowest possible cost is the most important factor.

Flexibility

Some sources of finance are highly flexible and can be adapted to meet a business's precise needs. The most obvious example is an overdraft. This source of finance allows a business to overspend its current account or not according to its needs (but subject to an overall limit). Thus, a business can use its overdraft only when it is necessary and can avoid any interest charges at times when its finances are stronger. This flexibility has a cost however: overdrafts are an expensive source of finance.

Although government grants are appealing to many businesses because they do not normally have to be repaid, they can be an inflexible form of finance. Many grants are only available with strict conditions attached. Many UK government and EU grants are only made if the business creates new jobs or at least maintains employment levels. This may be difficult to achieve in circumstances where labour is relatively expensive and the newly acquired finance could be used to introduce labour-saving technology.

Control

Some sources of finance may result in the original owners of the business losing some, or even complete control of it. Certain forms of finance are only available if the person or organisation investing gains a say in how the business is managed. This is perhaps most obvious in the sale of shares. If a private or public company makes a succession of share issues it may be that the number of new shares issued is greater than the number of 'original' shares. In this case the new shareholders may gain control of the company.

However, it may be possible for the company to issue shares that do not carry full voting rights. This can allow the original shareholders to retain control though, of course, it makes the issue of new shares much less attractive to potential shareholders.

Smaller businesses that do not trade as companies can also lose some degree of control if they opt to use certain sources of finance. For example, venture capitalists may only agree to provide finance to what may be a risky business if a part of their investment is in the form of shares and they have a say in the management of the business.

The purposes for which the finance is needed

Some sources of finance are suitable in certain situations. Thus, for example, a business that is seeking to raise finance to purchase property and has to rely on loan finance will probably consider taking out a mortgage. As we saw earlier, a mortgage is a long-term loan (and can be available at relatively low rates of interest) and the combination of these two factors makes it an ideal source of finance to purchase property, which can be very expensive.

If the finance is being raised to fund a risky start-up then an entrepreneur may experience difficulties in finding investors willing to put capital into the business. In this situation a venture capitalist may be the best choice as this source of finance specialises in investing in relatively high risk enterprises and may also provide support and guidance to novice entrepreneurs.

Finally, if the finance is needed to fund additional working capital, perhaps because a business is expanding, then an overdraft or perhaps trade credit may be selected as the funding will only be required for a short period of time until the business achieves a higher level of sales and an increased inflow of revenue. This additional revenue can repay the overdraft or settle the outstanding trade credit.

The level of existing debt

If a business has substantial amounts of existing loans, banks may be unwilling to agree to increasing the amount of debt. They may judge that further loans will represent a risk to them as the interest payments may be considerable, especially if interest rates rise.

In such circumstances a business may be forced to seek alternative sources of finance such as selling an asset (and possibly leasing it back) or selling shares if the business is a company. As a rule of thumb, if a business has borrowed more than half the total capital that it has raised, banks may judge further loans to be too risky.

15.6 Choosing an appropriate source of finance

Key term

Creditors are individuals or organisations to whom the business owes money.

The preceding section has highlighted that a business will base its choice of the best or most appropriate source of finance on a number of factors, including cost, flexibility and the need to retain control.

When making judgements on the most appropriate source, managers will have to take into account a range of factors relating to the business's internal position and the business environment in which it is trading.

- **The business's financial situation** Is it profitable? If so it may be able to use retained profits as a source of finance or at least be able to provide evidence to banks and other **creditors** that it can repay loans. Alternatively it may have assets that it can sell and lease back, or simply sell.
- **The business's reputation** A reputation as a reliable and popular business may also enable its managers to persuade suppliers to offer increased trade credit which can fund short-term needs for finance. Equally, such a reputation will assist a business in negotiating loans, possibly at favourable rates of interest, or in persuading shareholders to purchase the company's shares.
- **Its legal structure** This will play a role in making the decision on the appropriateness of sources of finance. Thus only companies will be able to elect to use share capital as a source to fund start-ups or expansions.
- **The business environment** The environment in which the business is trading will also shape the decision. If sales in a market are growing the business may be more able to finance the repayments on a loan as its revenues should increase in the future. On the other hand, if interest rates are high, making loan capital a relatively expensive source of finance, businesses may seek alternative sources.

Case Study

Venture capital scarce in the USA

Recent research has revealed that companies in the USA that rely on venture capital investment to expand their businesses and hire employees struggled to raise capital in 2012. Firms in the US arranged $6.9 billion in venture capital deals during the third quarter of 2012, a 32 per cent drop in value compared with the same period in 2011, according to a *Dow Jones VentureSource* report. It is likely that changes in the business environment in the USA are responsible for this change.

Venture capital investors in the US reduced lending and share purchase as a result of the recession and the slow recovery from it. The recession has made high risk companies even more risky and this has encouraged venture capitalists to be more cautious than in the past.

Although venture capital funds were relatively scarce in the United States in 2012, the position is slowly improving and funds are more available than in the 'dark days' of recession during 2009 and 2010.

Question

1 Explain the circumstances in which a company might choose to use venture capital as its primary source of finance. [6]
2 Discuss the other factors that may have led to the decline in the amount of money lent by venture capitalists in the third quarter of 2012. [10]

Study tip

If a question asks you to suggest and justify a source of finance for a given situation, do not always select a single source. It is very common for businesses to use several sources of finance to fund a project, especially if a large sum of capital has to be raised. It may also be easier to justify the use of a mix of sources as it reduces the impact of the disadvantages of any single source of finance.

As you can see, a business will take a range of factors into account when selecting the best source (or sources) of finance to use. There is no best source – it always depends on the circumstances.

Test your learning

Short answer questions

1 Explain **two** circumstances in which a business may need to raise capital. [5]

2 a Distinguish between loan capital and share capital. [3]
  b Define the term working capital. [2]

3 a Distinguish between revenue expenditure and capital expenditure. [3]
  b State **two** examples of capital expenditure. [2]

4 a List **three** external sources of finance available to a business. [3]
  b Describe a debenture. [2]

5 Explain, with examples, the difference between short-term and long-term sources of finance. [5]

6 a Describe what is meant by the term venture capital. [2]
  b Outline **one** advantage and **one** disadvantage to a business of using venture capital as a source of finance. [3]

7 a Define the term government grant. [2]

  b Explain why it is easier for a public limited company in the UK to raise capital by selling shares. [3]

8 a List **two** sources of finance that may be available to a partnership. [2]

  b Explain why a partnership may experience difficulties in raising large sums of finance. [3]

9 a Distinguish between an overdraft and a bank loan. [3]

  b Explain **one** disadvantage to a business of using an overdraft as a source of finance. [2]

10 Explain the advantages and disadvantages to companies of raising capital by selling shares. [5]

Data response question

Sunshine Tours looks to expand

Sunshine Tours plc is a London-based company that sells its shares on the London Stock Exchange. It sells holidays to European and American tourists. All of its holidays are based on the island of Mauritius. The company has suffered a decline in sales due to falling incomes in Europe and America, and its profits have steadily declined reaching just £48 million in 2012. However, sales are forecast to rise over the next three years at an accelerating rate.

The company's directors wish to expand the business. The company already has large long-term debts although it has repaid 30 per cent of these since 2010. Its business plan for 2015–17 sets out details of capital expenditure totalling £150 million, although the sources of finance to be used have yet to be decided.

The company's shares have been performing well despite its recent dip in profits and it has maintained impressive dividend payments to its shareholders. One of the directors believes that the company should raise all the capital it needs by selling shares. Another argues for the use of debentures as interest rates are low in the UK.

Questions

1 Explain the terms:
  a capital expenditure [3]
  b debenture. [3]

2 Briefly analyse the factors that the directors of Sunshine Tours plc may take into account when deciding which sources of finance to use to raise the £150 million it needs. [6]

3 Discuss whether or not Sunshine Holidays plc should sell shares as the only means of raising the capital it needs. [10]

Essay question

Discuss the extent to which it is always best for a business to use internal sources of finance. [20]

Past paper question

Discuss the suitability of the various sources of finance a large business might use when replacing old machinery. [20]

Cambridge International AS and A Level Business Studies
9707 Paper 1 Q6 May/June 2007

16 Forecasting and managing cash flow

Chapter overview

In this chapter we examine:
- the differences between cash flow and profit and the importance of cash flow to businesses
- the uses, construction, interpretation and amendment of cash-flow forecasts
- the causes of cash-flow problems
- the methods that businesses can use to improve their cash-flow positions; how to select the best method.

16.1 Why businesses forecast cash flow

What is cash flow?

A potentially profitable enterprise can fail because of poor management of **cash flow**. Equally, an unprofitable new business can enjoy a period in which it has plenty of cash – before the bills arrive!

Cash flow and profits are two very different concepts:
- A business makes a profit if, over a given period of time, its revenue is greater than its expenditure. A business can survive without making a profit for a short period of time, but it is essential that it earns profits in the long term.
- Cash flow relates to the timing of payments and receipts. Cash flow is important in the short term as a business must pay people and organisations to whom it owes money.

Unless a business manages the timing of its payments and receipts carefully, it may find itself in a position where it is operating profitably but is running out of cash regularly. This could be because it is forced to wait for several months before receiving payment from customers. In the meantime, it has to settle its own debts.

Businesses are especially vulnerable to cash-flow difficulties in their first months and years of trading and during periods of major expansion. It is for this reason that many financial institutions demand evidence that entrepreneurs and managers have planned the management of cash for a new or expanding enterprise before granting a loan.

The distinction between cash flow and profits

Profit is the surplus of sales revenue over total costs, if any exists. Just because a business is profitable, it does not mean that it will hold large sums of cash, or even have enough cash. There are a number of reasons why this situation might arise.
- Firstly, the business might sell large amounts of goods or services at profitable prices by offering customers 60 or 90 days' trade credit. This will mean that the business has to find cash to buy supplies and pay employees several months before the cash from the sale of the product flows into the business. This problem can be exacerbated if the business pays its suppliers promptly.
- Alternatively, a business such as a jeweller might hold large amounts of (expensive) inventory for customers to view before making a choice. This will entail large amounts of cash being tied up in the form of inventories and not available to the business for other purposes.
- A business may have paid for non-current assets and used large sums of cash to do so. These assets may support the business over many years, and will lead to future inflows of cash. However, the outflow of cash would be at the start and may place pressure on a firm's finances.

Thus a profitable business may find itself short of cash and possibly unable to settle its bills as they fall due. This could lead to the firm becoming insolvent and having to cease trading. A cash crisis is a major reason why many businesses fail.

In the long term, however, a business has to make a profit to satisfy its owners. They have invested funds into the business, quite possibly by purchasing shares, and expect to see a return on their investment. This is only possible if the business makes a profit in the longer term. A business may survive for some time without making profits if its owners are prepared to be patient, but cash has to be managed carefully in the short term to ensure that bills can be paid on time.

There are two main reasons why businesses might forecast their cash flows.

1 **To support applications for loans** Almost all new enterprises require loans to enable them to become established (and also during periods of expansion). Banks and other financial institutions are far more likely to lend money to a business that has evidence of financial planning. It is reassuring for the bank that the entrepreneur understands the importance of cash and has planned carefully to avoid cash-flow crises. Cash-flow planning gives the bank more confidence that the entrepreneur will be able to make the repayments of the loan as and when they are due.

Case Study

Saab runs out of cash

The Swedish car manufacturer Saab has become insolvent after failing to secure cash investment from potential Chinese companies. Saab had been in takeover talks with several Chinese companies, including Zhejiang Youngman Lotus Automobile.

The company stopped production of cars in its major factory in Trollhattan, Sweden, and the company does not have the cash to pay its suppliers. Saab's employees have also criticised the company for its failure to pay their wages.

Saab was established in 1945 when Swedish Aeroplane Limited, a Swedish aerospace and defence company, started a project to design a small car. The Saab 92, Saab's first production model, was launched in 1949. At the time of its insolvency the company employed 3200 people, produced more than 32 000 cars each year and generated an annual revenue of $1050 million.

Question

1 Explain why cash-flow forecasting would have been a very important activity for Saab. [6]
2 Discuss why a company that earns revenues of more than $1 billion dollars in a year might run out of cash. [10]

2 **To help avoid unexpected cash-flow crises** Twenty per cent of newly established businesses fail within two years of starting trading. A high proportion of these fail because of cash-flow difficulties. Similarly, many large and established businesses encounter cash-flow problems which can result in the closure of the business as in the case of Saab, the Swedish car manufacturer discussed in the case study. Planning can help avoid such difficulties. Cash-flow planning can help to ensure that businesses do not suffer from periods when they are short of cash and unable to pay their debts. By forecasting cash flows, a business can identify times at which it may not have enough cash available. This allows it to make the necessary arrangements to overcome this problem.

The importance of maintaining sufficient cash-flow balances

The case of Saab demonstrates the possible consequences of not holding sufficient cash. We saw in Chapter 15 that a business needs working capital to pay for its supplies of raw materials, components and energy as well as labour costs. Most businesses receive cash inflows from the sale of goods and services and have to ensure that they receive sufficient inflows to meet their obligations in time.

Some businesses need to hold larger cash reserves than others. Most supermarkets can trade securely and confidently despite holding relatively small cash balances. For example, Walmart, the world's largest retailer has annual sales of nearly $447 000 million, yet had only $6550 million of cash in January 2012. This is possible because supermarkets such as Walmart rely on customers paying at the time of purchase and frequently in cash. Thus it can rely on a regular cash inflow.

In contrast other companies, selling different products, need to hold larger cash reserves to trade safely and securely. House builders and ship manufacturers may hold greater cash reserves because they face a longer cash cycle. This means that there is a longer time period between the cash outflow associated with producing a product and the cash inflow from its sale.

Businesses that are judged to hold insufficient reserves of cash may experience difficulties when trying to raise capital to fund the purchase of new assets or the development of new products. Potential investors or shareholders may be concerned that the business will be unable to repay loans or to meet expected future financial commitments. In such circumstances potential investors may judge the business to be too great a risk and decide not to grant loans or to purchase shares.

Chinese companies short of cash

In 2012 a number of Chinese companies, both large and small, were reported to be short of cash. In part this was caused by the reluctance of many Chinese banks to grants loans to businesses. The shortages of cash were judged to be particularly severe in the construction, steel manufacture and machine building industries.

Chinese machinery manufacturers such as Zoomlion and Sany Heavy have been affected by cash shortages in the construction and property development sectors. Zoomlion, which is based in Hunnan, asked its shareholders for approval for new borrowing facilities.

At the same time there has been a significant rise in the level of inventories (stocks) held by businesses operating in these industries.

Questions

1 Explain why shareholders may be reluctant to invest in companies that are thought to suffer from cash-flow problems. [6]
2 Evaluate why the construction, steel manufacture and machine building industries might have been particularly hit by the cash problems. [10]

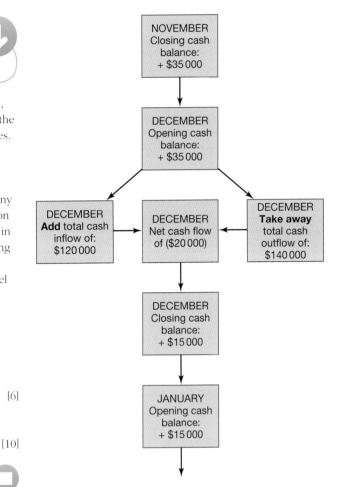

Figure 16.1 Opening and closing cash balances

16.2 Cash-flow forecasts in practice

Constructing cash-flow forecasts

A **cash-flow forecast** is a document that records a business's anticipated inflows and outflows of cash over some future period, frequently one year.

A simplified **cash-flow forecast** is illustrated in Figure 16.1. Although cash-flow forecasts differ from one another, they usually have three sections and are normally calculated monthly. An essential part of cash-flow forecasting is that inflows and outflows of cash should be included in the plan at the time they take place.

1 **Cash in** The first section forecasts the cash inflows into the business, usually on a monthly basis. This section includes receipts from cash sales and credit sales. Credit sales occur when the customer is given time to pay: normally 30, 60 or 90 days.
2 **Cash out** The cash out (or expenditure) section will state the expected expenditure on the goods and services. Thus, a typical section might include forecasts of expenditure on rent, rates, insurance, wages and salaries, fuel, and so on. At the end of this section the total expected outflow of cash over the time period in question would be stated.
3 **Net monthly cash flow** The net monthly cash flow is calculated by subtracting the total outflow of cash from the total inflow.
4 **Opening and closing balances** The final section of the forecast has the opening balance and the closing balance. The opening balance is the business's cash position at the start of each month. This will, of course, be the same figure as at the end of the previous month. The net monthly cash flow is added to the opening balance figure. The resulting figure is the closing cash balance for the month. It is also the opening balance for the following month.

A typical format for a cash-flow forecast is shown in Figure 16.2.

		January	February	March
1 Cash in	Cash sales			
	Credit sales			
	Total inflow			
2 Cash out	Raw materials			
	Wages			
	Other costs			
	Total outflow			
3 Net monthly cash flow	Net monthly cash flow			
4 Opening and closing balances	Opening balance			
	Closing balance			

Figure 16.2 A typical layout for a cash-flow forecast

Constructing cash-flow forecasts – a case study

Steve Marshall is planning to buy a bookshop. Steve knows that he needs to forecast his cash flow to help him to identify times when he might experience problems. Knowing when he is likely to be short of cash gives him the chance to arrange an overdraft or short-term loan. His bank is unlikely to advance him a loan unless he constructs a cash-flow forecast.

Study tip

Although you should understand how to construct a cash-flow forecast, it is unlikely that you will be asked to do this in a question paper because of time constraints. What you may be asked is to:
- fill in missing figures to show that you understand the structure and calculations
- identify problems that might occur – to demonstrate that you understand what the forecast tells you
- propose solutions to the cash-flow problems you have identified.

Steve has made the following forecasts about his business for the first four months of trading from June until September:
- Steve has raised $75000 from a bank loan and his savings to buy the lease on a property and to purchase books. He also intends that this money will be used to pay his start-up marketing costs.
- Steve expects his business to have an opening cash balance of $2000 at the start of June.
- Steve anticipates his cash sales to rise steadily for each of the four months (from $5750 to $9215) as his business becomes better known. However, he has already received an order to supply books to a local college. The order was for $10000. He expects payment in September, but will buy the books in June at the same time as he purchases his initial inventories.

- Each month Steve orders books from his suppliers to replace those he has sold.
- He has to pay his own wages and those of a part-time assistant. These normally amount to $1500 each month.
- Other costs, including his rent, rates, heating and lighting amount to $1500 each month in June and July, but are higher in August and September.

Steve's cash-flow forecast is shown in Table 16.1.

Table 16.1 Steve Marshall's cash-flow forecast

	June	July	August	September
Cash in				
Savings & borrowings	75000	0	0	
Cash sales	5750	7500	8475	9215
Credit sales	0	0	0	10000
Total cash inflow	**80750**	**7500**	**8475**	**19215**
Cash out				
Purchase of lease on shop	30000	0	0	0
Purchase of books	59000	4500	5000	6100
Wages	1500	1500	1500	1500
Marketing costs	2500	1500	975	400
Other costs, e.g. rent	1500	1500	1605	1630
Total cash outflow	**94500**	**9000**	**9080**	**9630**
Net monthly cash flow	**−13750**	**−1500**	**605**	**9585**
Opening balance	2000	−11750	−13250	−13855
Closing balance	−11750	−13250	−13855	−4270

Steve's cash-flow forecast illustrates many of the key principles. An important figure for each month is shown in the row entitled 'Net monthly cash flow'. This simply records the balance between the inflow and outflow for the month: June is a good example of how this operates. In June, Steve expected to receive $5750 from book sales. At the same time he planned to spend $94500 on his initial purchase of books as well as supplying the college's order, but also on marketing, wages and rent. Thus, in June he expected his net cash flow (cash inflows less cash outflows) to be − $13750 ($80750 − $94500). In cash-flow forecasts, negative figures can be shown in brackets or with a minus figure in front. Hence, the figure entered for net monthly cash flow in June could be ($13750).

This case study also highlights one of the key advantages of cash-flow forecasting. Steve's business will be short of cash during June, July, August and, to a lesser extent, September. The closing balances for these months indicate that he will require a maximum of $13855 of additional cash to enable him to pay his rent, wages, and so on. Knowing this in advance means that Steve can take steps to avoid a cash crisis, possibly by agreeing an overdraft with his bank.

Although the construction of cash-flow forecasts can help businesses to plan and manage their finances, the process does involve a degree of uncertainty. Managers cannot be certain about the accuracy of their forecasts of inflows, especially if they are engaging in a new venture such as launching a new product or entering a new market. Most businesses will base their forecasts of cash inflows on the results of market research. However, this may not be accurate if the managers carry out insufficient primary research or rely on out-of-date or inappropriate secondary research data. This is more of a risk for companies entering markets where current data is less available.

Forecasting cash outflows accurately can also be difficult. Unexpected changes in the price of resources can result in forecasts proving to be very inaccurate. For example, between January and February 2014 the price of a barrel of West Texas oil rose from $92 to over $104, an increase of 13.7 per cent. Forecasting cash outflows accurately can be challenging for businesses that use large quantities of products which have volatile prices, such as oil.

Amending cash-flow forecasts

Changes in the business environment can have a substantial effect on a business's cash-flow forecast and it may have to be amended as a consequence. It may be that a business's sales figures are lower or higher than forecast, resulting in the cash inflows being different from what was expected. For example, Steve Marshall's cash-flow forecast may have underestimated his cash sales in June. The actual figure may have been $6750. This would result in a number of changes to Steve Marshall's cash-flow forecast for June:

- the business's total cash inflow being $81750 in June
- the business's net monthly cash flow becoming –$12750
- the business's closing balance becoming –$10750.

It is also possible that a business's outflow may differ from its forecasts.

Maths moment

Use the information from Table 16.1 to answer the question below.

What would the closing balance have been in September if cash sales in September were $12715?

Causes of cash-flow problems

A major cause of cash-flow problems is a lack of planning. In our example above if Steve had not forecast the timing of his expenditure and income he may have been unaware of the impending crisis. Many businesses, once established, do not forecast in this way and frequently face unforeseen problems.

A number of other factors can contribute to cash-flow difficulties.

- **Overtrading** This occurs when a business expands quickly without organising funds to finance the expansion. Rapid growth normally involves paying for labour and raw materials several months before receiving payment for the final product. If this occurs over a prolonged period a business can face severe cash-flow problems.
- **Allowing too much credit** Businesses benefit in terms of cash flow by requiring customers to pay immediately for any products they purchase. However, most businesses offer customers trade credit – allowing them between 30 and 90 days to pay. This helps to win and keep customers. However, if a firm's trade credit policy is too generous it may lead to cash-flow difficulties.
- **Poor credit control** A firm's credit control department ensures that customers keep to agreed borrowing limits and pay on time. If this aspect of a business's operation becomes inefficient, cash inflows into the firm may be delayed. In some cases customers may not pay at all (this is known as bad debt). In these circumstances it is highly likely that a firm will encounter problems with its cash flow.
- **Other factors** A number of factors, normally beyond the control of a business, can lead to problems with cash flow. For example, a sudden slump in demand for its products may catch a firm unawares. In this situation a business might have a large quantity of unsold inventory for which it has paid and which it is unlikely to sell. Furthermore, the business may have to develop and market new products, placing a further strain on its cash flow.

Case Study

London taxi manufacturer bought by Chinese company

Manganese Bronze plc, the company that manufacturers the iconic London taxi cab, was taken over by a Chinese car manufacturer, Zhejiang Geely Holding Group, in 2013. Manganese Bronze had suffered a number of cash-flow difficulties, prior to the takeover being agreed. It was forced to recall 460 vehicles because of faults with the steering mechanism. The vehicle recalled, the TX4, is the only vehicle that the company manufactures. A spokesperson for the company admitted this had very serious implications for the company's cash-flow position.

The company has also been hit by falling demand for its taxis in the UK and was unable to fulfil an order for 1000 taxis from Azerbaijan. Zhejiang Geely invested $30m into the taxi manufacturer, following the takeover, to ensure it had sufficient cash to continue production.

Questions

1 Explain why a fall in demand for taxis may have contributed to Manganese Bronze's cash-flow difficulties. [6]
2 Evaluate whether a takeover was the best way to solve Manganese Bronze's cash-flow problems. [10]

Why cash-flow forecasts can be inaccurate

It would be foolish for businesses to imagine that their cash-flow forecasts will always prove to be accurate. A number of factors can lead to incorrect cash-flow forecasts.

- Inaccurate assumptions regarding the future levels of sales for the business or the prices it will receive for its products. A firm's forecasts of the cash it will earn can, of course, be too low as well as too high. A competitor suddenly increasing prices, for example, may lead to cash sales being higher than expected.
- Unexpected costs occurring. Prices of raw materials may increase without warning. The cost of labour may rise due, for example, to increases in the minimum wage. Similarly, machinery breakdowns can impose unanticipated pressures on a business's cash flow.
- Inexperience is often the cause of poor quality cash-flow forecasting. Many people set up firms with relatively little experience of managing a business. Forecasting sales and costs accurately in this situation is very difficult.

Researching the market carefully can reduce the risks of inaccurate cash-flow forecasting. Research can establish the prices customers are likely to pay and the probable level of demand for a firm's products. Further investigations with suppliers and organisations such as the local Job Centre can help to give accurate forecasts of the costs of raw materials and labour. Accuracy can also be improved by monitoring the operation of the forecast. Checking in this way can highlight possible problems early on and allow the appropriate action to be taken.

Most modern businesses use spreadsheets to construct and monitor their cash-flow forecasts. This technology makes analysing cash flows simpler and quicker.

16.3 Methods of improving cash flow

Key terms

Trade credit is a period of time offered by suppliers of goods and services before requiring payment to be made.

Debt factoring is the sale of customer accounts before they are due for payment for less than their face value.

Leasing is the hiring of assets used in production, such as machinery or vehicles for a specified period of time, usually more than two years.

Trying to prepare accurate cash-flow forecasts is only part of the solution. Businesses have to decide how they are going to improve their cash position – if they are able to do so. A number of techniques can be used to improve a cash flow.

- **Reducing costs** If a business is able to reduce its costs of production this will lead to a reduction in the amount of cash flowing out of the enterprise and will strengthen its cash-flow position. This reduction in costs can be achieved in a number of ways. A manufacturing business may seek lower-cost resources to reduce its cash outflows. For example, a furniture manufacturer may opt to use timber from non-sustainable sources because it is cheaper. A business supplying services may seek to reduce wages by cutting hourly rates or reducing the number of employees. Such actions may result in undesirable side effects even if the business's cash-flow position improves. Using lower quality resources may reduce the quality of a product and lead to a business having to reduce its prices, which may damage cash inflows. Moving away from the use of environmentally-friendly (and more expensive) resources or cutting wages and/or employment levels may attract adverse publicity. The outcome may be a fall in sales, which could reduce cash inflows. However, it is possible that a business may opt to use techniques such as recycling to reduce the costs of acquiring raw materials. This can have a positive effect on the business's image if it is perceived to be environmentally friendly and may result in rising sales.

- **Improving the management of trade receivables and trade payables** Most firms receive some trade credit from their suppliers; this is known as trade payables. This means they may be given 30 or 60 days to pay for supplies. If a business can persuade suppliers who have previously been reluctant to offer trade credit to do so, it will increase its trade payables figure and improve its cash-flow position. Remember, cash-flow management is a matter of timing: delaying payments always helps. Another important move might be to extend existing trade credit agreements from, say, 30 to 60 days. It may not, however, be possible for a small or newly-established business to negotiate favourable credit terms if it does not have a suitable financial history. Similarly, a business can help its cash-flow position by offering its customers less favourable terms for trade credit; this means it reduces its trade receivables. This may require all customers to pay for products within 30 days, whereas in the past trade credit was for 60 days. Good control of trade receivables and trade payables can mean earlier inflows of cash and fewer bad debts. If a business is not actively chasing up customers to ensure that they pay, and pay on time, cash-flow problems may be the result. Firms can improve their cash-flow position by managing these inflows and outflows more effectively.

Debt factoring

A firm can receive cash earlier by 'selling' its debts to a debt factor. A debt factor is another business, often a bank, that is able to provide short-term loans for a fee. Under such an arrangement the debt factor will pay up to 95 per cent of the value of the debts immediately. This can assist a firm's cash-flow position, but reduces its profits. This technique is also termed factoring.

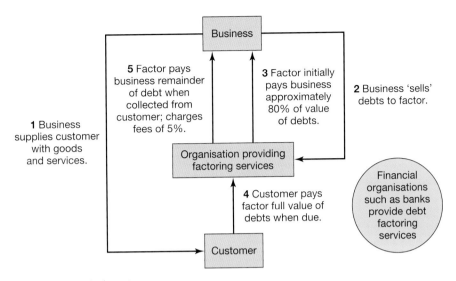

Figure 16.3 Debt factoring

Many small firms believe that to lose up to 5 per cent of their earnings means that factoring is uneconomic – it can eliminate much of their profit margin. However, factoring does offer a number of benefits:

- The immediate cash provided by the factor means that the firm is likely to have lower overdraft requirements and will pay less interest.
- Factoring means businesses receive the cash from their sales more quickly.

Debt factoring is generally used by small businesses. Businesses with a turnover above $1 million normally use an alternative technique (called invoice discounting) where the company retains the administration of the deal within the business. This way, its customers need not know that the company is using a debt factoring service. This can help a business to retain the confidence of its customers. Figure 16.3 illustrates the stages involved in debt factoring.

Maths moment

Melaka Industries has invoices to the value of $770 000 which it wishes to use for debt factoring. The factoring company has offered 80 per cent of the value of the invoices immediately and a further 15 per cent when they are paid by the customer in three months' time.

1 How much will Melaka Industries receive from the factoring company immediately?
2 How much will Melaka Industries receive from the factoring company in total?

Arrange short-term borrowing

The majority of businesses have agreed an overdraft with their bankers. An overdraft allows a business to borrow flexibly according to its needs up to an agreed limit. Overdrafts can be expensive but reasonably economical because a business only

borrows when it wants and as much as it wants. Alternatively, a business may arrange a short-term bank loan to provide an inflow of cash. This is less flexible as the business will have the full amount of the loan available (whether or not it is required) and will make monthly repayments including interest charges.

Sale and leaseback

This method of improving cash flow has been widely used by businesses over recent years. It entails a business selling a major asset – for example, a building – and then leasing it from the new owner. This provides a significant inflow of cash into the business, improving the cash position, but commits the firm to regular payments to lease the asset. Sale and leaseback has become an increasingly popular method of strengthening cash positions for larger businesses in most economies throughout the world.

Case Study

Nokia's sale and leaseback plans

Nokia, the Finnish manufacturer of mobile phones, has announced its intention to sell the office building that houses its headquarters to raise urgently needed cash. The company's headquarters is located in a stylish glass and steel building in Espo, close to the Finnish capital Helsinki. Nokia moved into the building in 1996 and enlarged it in 2001; it is currently the workplace for 1800 of the company's employees.

The company intends to sell and lease back the building as it is vital to its operations. Analysts estimate that it will raise $200 million to $300 million, which would provide a crucial cash inflow for the business.

Nokia has suffered from well-publicised cash-flow problems, particularly in recent months – its cash position weakened by $680 million over the last three months alone. A spokesperson for Nokia said: 'We have ample cash resources to do what we need. But to cut costs and conserve cash we are looking at all possible options with no stones being left unturned. One of those is the possibility of selling our headquarters.'

Questions

1 Explain two other ways in which Nokia may have raised $200–$300 million. [6]
2 Discuss whether the advantages of this sale and leaseback plan outweigh the disadvantages. [10]

Leasing

Leasing is a method of purchasing a range of assets that businesses need. Using leasing, a business simply leases (or rents) an asset rather than buying it, thereby conserving precious reserves of cash. Throughout the period of the lease, the finance company still owns the asset that has been purchased. Examples of non-current assets that may be leased by businesses include vehicles and also other equipment, for example, photocopiers and computers. The nature of some lease agreements means that the firm is able to purchase the asset for a relatively low price at the end of the lease period.

Businesses may lease assets rather than purchasing them outright, because this avoids the business spending a large amount of cash at one time. This is particularly valuable for a business that is short of cash, possibly because of expansion or difficult trading situations. On the other hand, the cost of leasing arrangements can be relatively high, which may have a negative effect on the business's longer-term cash position, although it does avoid major outflows of cash.

Hire purchase

Hire purchase is a means of obtaining credit for the purchase of a non-current asset. The business purchasing the asset pays a percentage of the purchase price as a deposit and the remainder in instalments (usually monthly) over an agreed period. The purchaser only becomes the owner of the asset once the final payment is made. The use of hire purchase to acquire non-current assets can improve a business's cash-flow position as it delays the outflow of the bulk of the payment for the asset until a series of dates in the future. The effect may be substantial as hire purchase may be used to finance the acquisition of relatively expensive assets such as vehicles and therefore have a considerable impact on the business's cash-flow position.

However, it is likely that the overall cost of the asset will be substantially higher using this method of purchase, with adverse consequences for profitability. Furthermore, if the business defaults on payment it does not own the asset in question.

Choosing the most effective method of improving cash flow

There is no single 'best' method of improving a business's cash flow. All the methods that we discussed earlier have their advantages and disadvantages, which are summarised in Table 16.2.

Table 16.2 The advantages and disadvantages of selected methods of improving a business's cash flow

Method	Advantages	Disadvantages
Improved management of trade receivables and payables	• Can be a 'free' method of improvement • Can be implemented relatively quickly • Available to most businesses	• Reducing trade credit offered may result in a loss of customers • May not be available to new businesses or those without a reputation as reliable payers
Debt factoring	• Can generate large and immediate inflows of cash • Available to businesses with little power to negotiate favourable trade credit terms	• Can reduce the amount of profit on each sale (by up to 5 per cent) • May not be viable for businesses making very small profits (such as start-ups)
Short-term borrowing	• Can be available to the business immediately • May be highly flexible (as in the case of an overdraft)	• Businesses with weak cash positions may be unable to negotiate short-term loans • Can be a relatively expensive option as interest rates may be high
Sale & leaseback	• Avoids the need for any interest payments • Retains the use of the asset for the business and can raise large sums of finance	• Only a business with saleable assets can engage in this method • This may reduce the business's long-term profits by increasing expenditure
Leasing	• Avoids the need for large cash purchases on assets that may decline in value • Can allow businesses to use the most up-to-date assets	• The business is committed to regular, smaller outflows • The company does not own the assets that are used
Reduction in costs	• Can boost the business's profitability as well as strengthening its cash-flow position • May improve the business's image if it involves techniques such as recycling	• May compromise quality of products if cheaper resources are used • Businesses may have to lower prices if quality is reduced
Hire purchase	• Can delay cash outflows by a considerable time period • May be used to finance the purchase of relatively expensive non-current assets, having a significant impact on a business's cash-flow position	• This is an expensive method of buying non-current assets and may reduce profitability • The business does not own the asset until the final payment is made

A number of factors will influence the methods a business might employ to improve its cash-flow position.

- **How established the business is** A new business may be unable to use some of the methods we have discussed to improve its cash-flow position. It may not be able to persuade suppliers to grant it trade credit if it does not have a record of prompt payment. It may also be unable to impose payment terms (such as paying within 30 days) at a time when it is seeking to win new customers to develop a customer base. Equally, it may not own assets that can be sold and leased back and banks may be unwilling to grant short-term loans when a business is new and poses a high risk. Thus, newly established businesses have a narrow and limited range of techniques to improve cash flow on which to draw.

- **The business's level of profitability** Businesses that generate low profit margins (profit margins are profits expressed as a percentage of sales revenue) may struggle to use certain techniques to improve their cash-flow position. For example, debt factoring can reduce profit margins by up to 5 per cent and this might push some marginally profitable businesses into a loss-making situation. Such businesses may also struggle to negotiate loans if banks or other financial institutions have any doubts about the ability of the business to repay debts because of low levels of profitability. It may be preferable for businesses in such a position to look at ways of improving their management of trade receivables

and trade payables which are likely to have little or no impact on profit margins.

Study tip

Do use numerical *and* written evidence when considering a business's cash-flow position and use this to guide you as to the 'best' method to improve the situation. The numbers in a cash-flow forecast may show a trend, which may be improving or getting worse. However, there may be evidence in a case study that will help you to judge the best method.

- **The type of business** It is increasingly common for businesses with valuable assets to engage in sale and leaseback deals to strengthen their cash positions. The earlier case study describes Nokia's proposed sale and leaseback of its headquarters and many high street retailers have opted for the same approach. It is usual for retailers to adopt this approach; Tesco, one of the world's largest retailers with stores in Asia and Eastern Europe as well as the UK, has conducted a series of sale and leaseback deals. Leasing is an attractive option for those businesses that require assets that need updating regularly. Firms that use large numbers of computers, such as banks or insurance companies, may opt for this method to improve cash flow as it avoids the need for regular major outflows of cash to ensure that the latest technology is available to employees.

Test your learning

Short answer questions

1 a Define the term cash flow. [2]
   b Explain **one** reason why a business might forecast its cash flow. [3]

2 Distinguish between cash flow and profit. [5]

3 a State **two** reasons why a profitable business might become short of cash. [2]
   b Explain why newly established businesses are vulnerable to cash-flow problems. [3]

4 Explain why some businesses need to hold larger reserves of cash than others. [5]

5 a Explain the term overtrading. [3]
   b State **two** other possible causes of cash-flow problems. [3]

6 a Define the term cash-flow forecast. [2]
   b Explain **one** reason why a business may prepare an inaccurate cash-flow forecast. [3]

7 a Define the term trade payables. [2]
   b State **three** methods a business might employ to improve its cash-flow position. [3]

8 Explain the advantages and disadvantages of the use of debt factoring as a method of improving a business's cash-flow position. [5]

9 a State **two** assets a business might lease rather than buy. [2]
   b Explain the disadvantages to a business of leasing assets. [3]

10 Explain why newly established businesses might face difficulties in using some methods to improve their cash-flow position. [5]

Data response question

Mugunga Mines Limited

The rising price of copper on world markets has resulted in some copper mines in Uganda being opened. In the past these might not have been considered profitable. However, the price of copper might fluctuate in the future. Mugunga Mines Limited is one company that has opened a large mine. It is a well-established company with a good record for being profitable. Opening the new mine has necessitated a large investment ($3.5 million) in mining equipment and preparatory work before mining can commence.

The company's customers want at least 60 days' trade credit before paying for the copper they purchase and the size of their orders is expected to rise quickly. The company may have to expand its operations within months and some directors fear cash-flow difficulties as a result of overtrading.

Questions

1 Explain the terms:
   a trade credit   [3]
   b overtrading.   [3]
2 Explain why Mugunga Mines Limited might be at risk of overtrading.   [6]
3 Discuss whether debt factoring is the best way for the company to deal with any future cash-flow difficulties. [10]

Essay question

Discuss the extent to which cash-flow forecasting can eliminate cash-flow problems for all businesses.   [20]

Past paper questions

1 a Explain why retail businesses should prepare cash flow forecasts.   [8]
   b Discuss ways in which a business might improve its cash flow.   [12]

Cambridge International AS and A Level Business Studies 9707 Paper 12 Q5 May/June 2010

2 Read the Newtown College case study on page 208 and then answer the following question.

   Calculate the value of X in the cash-flow forecast (Table 2). [3]

Cambridge International AS and A Level Business Studies 9707 Paper 21 Q2bi October/November 2010

17 Costs and break-even

Chapter overview

In this chapter we examine:
- why businesses need accurate information on costs and the types of costs they have to pay
- how cost information can be used to set prices and to monitor and improve business performance
- the calculation and illustration of break-even output
- the uses and limitations of break-even analysis.

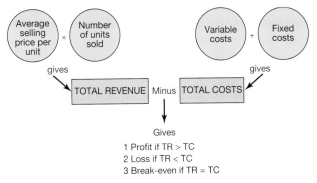

Figure 17.1 Costs, revenues and profits/losses

17.1 Revenue and cost information

Key terms

Costs are expenses that a business has to pay to engage in its trading activities.

Revenue is the income a business receives from selling its goods or services.

Break-even is the level of production or output at which a business's sales revenue is exactly equal to its total costs of production.

What is a **cost**? It is simply an expense paid by a business as part of its trading. Some of the expenses or costs firms have to pay include payments for raw materials, fuel and components as well as wages and salaries.

In contrast, revenues are simply a business's income or earnings over a period of time. Costs and revenues are vital data for most businesses. By comparing the total costs for a business over a period of time with the revenue that it earns, it is possible to calculate whether the business has made a profit or a loss. An important formula for many businesses is:

Profit (or loss) = total revenue − total costs

Business revenues

We saw earlier that **revenue** is the income received by a business from selling its products. You may also encounter the terms 'sales revenue' or 'turnover' which have the same meaning. Businesses calculate the revenue from the sale of a single product and from their entire product range. The latter is called total revenue. In either case the calculation is the same.

Revenue = quantity sold × average selling price

In most circumstances a firm can exercise some control over the quantity it sells and hence its revenue.

- If a business reduces its selling price, it can normally expect to sell more. Whether this increases its revenue depends on the number of additional sales it makes as a result of reducing its price. If competitors also reduce their prices, then few extra sales will result and revenue will be relatively unchanged.
- Similarly, a rise in price can be expected to reduce sales. The size of the fall in sales will depend on many factors including the loyalty of customers and the quality of the products. The amount by which sales fall will determine whether the firm receives more or less revenue following its price rise.

Some businesses attempt to maximise their revenues by setting a low price and selling as much as possible. This makes sense where consumers are judged to be looking for the lowest possible price and are not loyal to any particular products. For example, some supermarkets have adopted this approach to increase sales and revenues earned by the business.

On the other hand, some businesses sell products that are unique or regarded as highly desirable, perhaps because they are fashionable. Thus, some clothes producers, such as Allen Solly in India and Kuwaii in Australia, can charge high prices and accept lower sales than they might achieve with a lower price.

Maths moment

Rotorua Buses plans to cut the cost of its average fares for passengers from NZ$2.50 to NZ$2.00. It currently carries 5750 passengers weekly. It expects its price cut to increase the number of passengers by 22 per cent.

1 How much revenue does the company earn each week before it cuts its prices?
2 Will the price cut increase the company's weekly revenue?

Case Study

Palm oil prices

Analysts' forecasts for crude palm oil (CPO) prices for 2014 suggest they could reach RM3000 per tonne, and may increase further. The significant rises are expected as a consequence of a prolonged dry spell in Malaysia and the use of land for growing fuel for biodiesel production. Palm oil prices are also affected by increasing demand in developing economies such as India and China.

Godrej International Ltd director Dorab Mistry said weather would be the key for palm oil prices in 2014 and that a lack of rainfall would be crucial to revising price estimates going forward. Presenting his paper on the second day of the Palm and Lauric Oils Conference and Exhibition 2014, he announced that 'If the weather improves and rains come … it will not alter the price outlook to June 2014…With normal rainfall when the oil palm high cycle begun in July, prices could trade between RM2600 to RM2900 per tonne… However, without sufficient rainfall, crude palm oil prices may rise to RM3000 after June… Production is likely to be affected from late 2014 onwards and we may be looking at RM3500 per tonne.'

Source: Adapted from The Star Online (Malaysia)
http://www.thestar.com

Questions

1 Explain the likely effects of the increasing demand for palm oil in India and China on world prices. [6]
2 Discuss the possible effects of fluctuations in world prices for palm oil producers in countries such as Malaysia. [10]

Types of costs

Fixed costs

Fixed costs do not change when a business alters its level of output. For example, a business's rent will not vary if there is an increase or decrease in the level of production. Other examples of fixed costs include management salaries and interest payments made by the business.

Figure 17.2 relates to a business producing computers. You can see that whether the factory produces 10 000 or 60 000 computers each year, the fixed costs faced by the business will remain the same – $5 million.

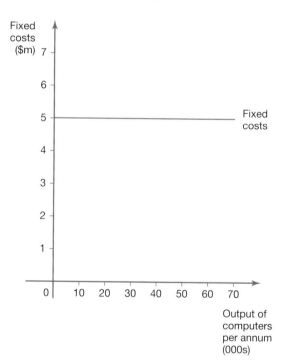

Figure 17.2 Fixed costs

The reason that these costs do not alter is that the business simply uses its existing facilities fully at times when it is receiving more orders. For example, in the run up to warm summer weather a manufacturer of sunglasses might increase its output thereby using its existing production facilities more fully. The firm's rent, rates and other fixed costs will be unchanged. Similarly, as winter approaches, sales and production of sunglasses are likely to fall, meaning some production facilities might be unused, but fixed costs will remain the same.

Variable costs

In contrast to fixed costs, variable costs alter *directly* with the level of a firm's output. This means that a firm increasing its output is likely to have to pay higher variable costs, whereas one reducing output could expect variable costs to fall. Expenditure on fuel, raw materials and components are all examples of variable costs.

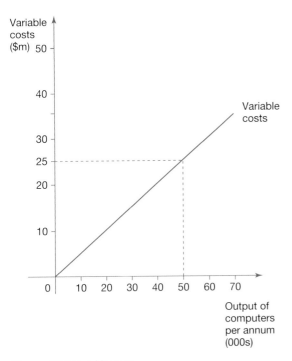

Figure 17.3 Variable costs

XYZ Computers Ltd in Figure 17.3 faces variable costs of $500 for each computer it manufactures; this is necessary to pay for the electronics, case and monitor. Thus to produce 20 000 computers means the company faces variable costs of $10 million (20 000 × $500); to manufacture 50 000 results in variable costs of $25 million (50 000 × $500).

It is usual to illustrate variable costs as a straight line as in Figure 17.3. This suggests that expenditure on items such as fuel, labour, raw materials and components rises steadily along with output. Variable costs are drawn this way for simplicity. In the real world the line may gradually flatten out as businesses frequently negotiate lower prices per unit when placing large orders. Thus XYZ Computers Ltd may be able to purchase components more cheaply, meaning that the variable costs associated with a production level of 50 000 computers might be $22.5 million. This means that the variable cost of each computer has fallen from $500 to $450.

Case Study

High fixed costs in Mauritius

Manufacturers of cement in Mauritius sell about 650 000 metric tonnes each year. Most of this (more than 80 per cent) is used in the construction of houses on the island with the remainder used in public buildings and roads.

Until 2011 the government of Mauritius controlled the price of cement as it was concerned that prices might be too high and prevent development. A major cause of this was a lack of competitiveness in the industry. High fixed costs of production meant that it was difficult for new businesses to raise enough capital to enter the industry and compete effectively with established producers. As a consequence the industry comprised two major suppliers. Since 2011 the government has taken action to make it easier for new businesses to enter this market.

Questions

1 Explain why a business entering an industry may want to keep its variable costs as low as possible. [6]
2 Discuss the reasons why high fixed costs may have led to the cement industry in Mauritius to have just two suppliers. [10]

Semi-variable costs

The distinction above suggests that it is easy to take each cost faced by a business and to decide whether it is fixed or variable. In reality this is not so easy. Some firms face costs that should be classified as semi-variable: they have fixed and variable elements.

Telephone costs are an example of a semi-variable cost. Most businesses pay a fixed quarterly charge for line and equipment rental. In addition, they face charges for each call made. The line and equipment rentals are fixed as they do not change as the firm increases or lowers its production levels. However, call charges are variable as they are likely to increase along with output as more calls are made to suppliers and customers, for example. Thus, taken together these elements mean telephone charges are semi-variable.

Total costs

The calculation of total costs assumes that all the costs faced by a business are either fixed or variable. This means total costs can be calculated simply using the following formula:

Total costs = fixed costs + variable costs

Total costs of production are an important piece of information for a business. Managers of a business can use this information in taking decisions on levels of output and prices to be charged. For example, firms that have very high levels of fixed costs, perhaps due to needing expensive equipment, will seek to produce large quantities of output. This reduces the effect of fixed costs on selling price by spreading them over a large quantity of sales.

Table 17.1 shows the cost information for XYZ Computers Ltd set out in the form of a table, rather than graphs as in Figures 17.2 and 17.3. One point to note is that a business's total costs when output is zero are only fixed costs as without any production there cannot be any variable costs.

Table 17.1 Fixed, variable and total costs of production

Level of production (thousand computers)	Fixed costs ($ million)	Variable costs ($ million)	Total costs ($ million)
0	5	0	5
10	5	5	10
20	5	10	15
30	5	15	20
40	5	20	25
50	5	25	30
60	5	30	35
70	5	35	40

At an output of 10 000 computers per year, XYZ Computers Ltd has total costs of $10 million. This means that, on average, it costs the business $1000 to manufacture each computer ($10 million divided by 10 000). What is the average cost of producing each computer when output is 50 000 per annum?

Other categories of costs

Key terms

Direct costs can be related to the production of a particular product and vary directly with the level of output.

Indirect costs are overheads that cannot be allocated to the production of a particular product and relate to the business as a whole.

Marginal cost is the extra cost resulting from producing one additional unit of output.

Marginal costs

This is the change in total costs when a business produces a single additional unit of output. **Marginal costs** do not really take into account fixed costs as they have to be paid whatever the level of production of the business. Thus, marginal costs are concerned with variable costs (the direct costs of materials and labour, for example). In most situations the marginal cost of an additional unit of a product is the variable cost of its production.

Direct and indirect costs

An alternative way of classifying the costs encountered by a business is to divide them into direct and indirect costs. **Direct costs** can be related to the production of a particular product and vary directly with the level of output. Examples include the costs of raw materials and fuel.

Indirect costs are overheads that cannot be allocated easily to the production of a particular product and relate to the business as a whole. Indirect costs include the costs of marketing and administration. Indirect costs are generally recognised as difficult to control. Unless managers are vigilant these costs can increase rapidly and reduce a business's profits.

The Honshu Motor Company
This manufacturer of motor cars may incur direct and indirect costs as set out below.

Direct costs	Indirect costs
• direct materials such as sheet steel and engine parts • direct labour, for example wages paid to employees on production line	• indirect labour costs, for example management salaries and wages paid to security staff • other indirect costs such as administration and distribution

direct costs + indirect costs = total costs of production

Figure 17.4 Direct and indirect costs of production

Indirect costs are also called overheads and are always fixed costs. Direct costs tend to vary with the level of production and are normally (but not always) variable costs.

Opportunity costs

The terms we have used above are 'accounting costs' – the terms that would be used by an accountant when discussing the financial aspects of a business's activities. However, there is another way of looking at costs, rather than giving a monetary value to the resources used by a business. Economists use a concept called 'opportunity cost' which values a product in terms of what has been given up to obtain it. Thus, an accountant might value a factory extension at $750 000, based on the resources needed to build it. An economist might say that the opportunity cost of the extension was a training programme for employees. This is because the management team of the business decided on an extension to the factory, rather than a training programme for employees.

Why is it important to calculate costs accurately?

Calculating costs accurately can help managers to make a number of important decisions. By combining cost information with expected revenues, managers can calculate whether or not a business (or an element within it) is likely to make a profit or a loss. From this information a range of other decisions may follow, including:

- whether or not to start up a new business
- whether to go ahead with a planned expansion
- whether to take on a particular order from a customer, which may be unusual in some way
- whether there is a need to reduce waste
- whether to engage in some activity, such as increasing security to prevent loss or wastage.

Without precise information on costs managers cannot make decisions that are likely to prove beneficial to a business. For example, a business may be considering a decision to enter a new market and its market research may indicate the likely returns from this expansion. A critical element of the decision, though, will be to calculate the costs of doing so, enabling the business's managers to forecast the likely profitability of this decision. Calculating the costs of this decision with a high degree of accuracy is not always easy, as we shall see in the next section.

Some businesses divide their operations into **costs centres**. This entails separating the business into elements for which the costs of production can be calculated. This process can assist managers in identifying how well specific areas of the business manage costs and to make comparisons to allow all areas of the business to adopt the best practice that exists within it.

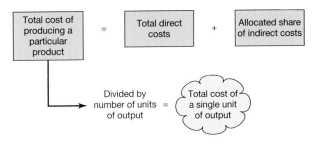

Figure 17.5 Key relationships for absorption (full) costing

Key term

A cost centre is an area, department or any other part of a business for which it is possible to calculate expenditure.

Difficulties in allocating costs

One problem faced by a business when attempting to calculate costs accurately is allocating or dividing up indirect costs between different elements of the business. This can be a particular problem for large businesses that produce a range of products.

One reason why it is difficult to calculate the total costs of producing a single unit of output is that indirect costs can be allocated in different ways and this can result in different cost figures. As a consequence, managers may take decisions that are incorrect.

When a business produces a number of products using a single office or factory it is difficult to calculate the total cost of producing a single unit of output of any of its products accurately. The problem it faces is how to allocate indirect costs such as marketing and administration.

One method of deciding upon costs is full costing, which is used by many businesses. This is also known as 'absorption costing'. This approach to costing involves charging all the costs of a particular enterprise to a unit of output. Thus all the costs associated with the production of a particular product are 'absorbed' by it. This approach may require managers to allocate indirect costs to all the business's cost centres.

Full costing can allocate (or divide up) indirect costs between different products produced by a business or its cost centres using a range of criteria such as the percentage of total direct costs used in the production of each product. This is a fairly arbitrary way of allocating indirect costs and may result in an inaccurate result.

However, it is possible to allocate costs in a more systematic manner and taking into account the type of indirect cost that has to be allocated. For example:

- The indirect costs of labour (such as security and administration) could be allocated according to the number of employees used directly in the production of each of the business's products.
- Costs such as rent and power may be allocated according to the proportion of the total space used by each of the products or cost centres within the business.

Case Study

Palm Foods allocates its indirect costs

Palm Foods manufactures a range of ready-to-eat meals aimed at high income consumers. The company's products can be divided into three divisions and each of these is a cost centre.

- Meat meals. These contain a range of foods based mainly on chicken and lamb.
- Fish meals. This is a smaller part of the company's production and is becoming less popular.
- Vegetarian meals. These are very popular as meals on their own or as accompaniments to some of the company's other products.

The company's managers want to know the cost of production for its three divisions to help with their decision-making. It uses the absorption approach to do this. The company's total indirect costs for 2013–14 were $6 million.

The company's accounts department has calculated some key statistics relating to the three divisions within the company.

Table 17.2

Accounting item	Meat meals	Fish meals	Vegetarian meals
Sales revenue (percentages)	50	20	30
Number of employees on each production line	30	25	25
Area of the factory floor used by each division (square metres)	2000	1300	1700
Total direct costs incurred in production (percentages)	40	30	30

Palm Food's accountants have decided to allocate the company's indirect costs for 2013–14 according to the area of the factory's floor space used by each of its three divisions.

As a consequence, the indirect costs were allocated as shown below:

Meat meals division: $2000/5000 \times \$6\,000\,000 = \$2\,400\,000$

Fish meals division: $1300/5000 \times \$6\,000\,000 = \$1\,560\,000$

181

Vegetarian meals division: 1700/5000 × $6 000 000 = $2 040 000

Questions

1 What allocation of indirect costs would have resulted if the company's accountants had used sales revenue as a guide? [6]
2 Discuss how the company should have allocated its indirect costs. [10]

In any event the allocation of indirect costs in this way is unlikely to be entirely accurate. This has significant implications because, by changing the way that indirect costs are allocated, the profitability of different areas of a business can be affected. For example, in the Palm Foods case study, if the company's accountants had decided to allocate indirect costs on the basis of the number of employees in each division, then the indirect costs allocated to the division producing meat meals would have been: 30/80 × $6 000 000 = $2 250 000. This is $150 000 below the method actually used and would have boosted the profits of this division by a similar amount assuming nothing else changes.

Maths moment

The accountants in the Palm Foods case study may have decided to use the number of employees working in each of the company's divisions as the basis for allocating its indirect costs.

Calculate how the total indirect costs would have been allocated between the fish and vegetarian meals divisions if this method had been used.

17.2 Uses of cost information

Calculating average, marginal and total costs

Key term

Average costs are the total cost of production divided by the number of units produced.

Managers can calculate a number of costs to assist with decision-making. Three vital ones are:
- average costs
- marginal costs
- total costs.

Average costs

Average costs are simply total costs at any level of output divided by that level of output. They are also called unit costs. In Table 17.1, it is possible to calculate average costs at each level of output. For example:
- At an output of 10 000 computers, the average cost is $10 000 000/10 000 = $1000 per computer.
- At an output of 40 000 computers, the average cost is $25 000 000/40 000 = $625 per computer.
- At an output of 70 000 computers, the average is $40 000 000/70 000 = $571 per computer.

Average costs tend to fall as a business increases its production levels because its fixed costs are spread over a larger output and so the amount allocated to each product is smaller as the level of production rises.

Marginal costs

Marginal costs are the extra cost resulting from producing one additional unit of output. In the example of our computer manufacturer XYZ Computers Ltd in Table 17.1, we know that to produce 50 000 computers would result in a total cost of production of $30 000 000. It may be that to produce another computer (making 50 001 in total) would result in total costs rising to $30 000 200. Thus the marginal cost of producing the additional computer is $200 in this case.

Total costs

These are simply fixed and variable (or direct and indirect) costs added together for some period of time. The right-hand column in Table 17.1 summarises this information.

Costs and pricing decisions

Key terms

Contribution is revenue from sales minus the variable costs of production.

Cost-plus pricing is the process of establishing the price of a product by calculating its cost of production and then adding an amount which is profit.

The costs of production can have a significant influence on a firm's pricing decisions.

Average costs and prices (cost-plus pricing)

Cost-plus pricing is the most commonly used method of setting prices. It entails deciding a price of a product by calculating its average cost of production by dividing total production costs by the number of units that are produced. To this value is added an amount which is called a mark up. The mark up is, in effect, profit.

For example, if a computer manufacturer is aware that a single product costs $500 to produce and decides to price the computer at $700, the pricing method is cost plus. In these circumstances the manufacturer can be certain the product will sell at a profit, but may be less sure about the level of sales. Cost-plus pricing does not take into account the state of the market or actions of competitors.

Scenario A	Scenario B
The company produces 1000 bicycles during the year. Total production costs are $100 000 + ($50 × 1000) = $150 000 **Average cost of producing one bicycle = $150**	The company produces 5000 bicycles during the year. Total production costs are $100 000 + ($50 × 5000) = $350 000 **Average cost of producing one bicycle = $70**

Figure 17.6 Average costs and prices

A firm can help to keep costs of production for each individual unit to a minimum by producing on the largest possible scale. Consider the two scenarios shown in Figure 17.6 for the Loddon Bicycle Company. This company has fixed costs of $100 000 and each bicycle has variable costs of $50 for materials and labour.

Manufacturing in the circumstances of Scenario B would allow the company to set lower prices for its bicycles or to enjoy higher profits – or both. For example, in Scenario B it could reduce its price from more than $150 per bicycle to, say, $100. This would allow it to make a profit of $30 per bicycle and it is likely that sales would rise significantly due to the price fall, boosting profits further.

Key term

Contribution pricing is based on the notion that any price set that is higher than the variable cost of producing a product is making a payment towards fixed costs.

Marginal costs and prices (contribution pricing)

By knowing how much it costs to produce an additional unit of output a business can be guided in setting prices or deciding whether to accept orders at specific prices. As we discussed earlier, marginal costs are based on the direct costs of production (and these are most likely to be variable costs). Indirect costs will not be affected by the decision to supply additional units and so it is the contribution from any sale that is critical.

Contribution can be calculated using the formula below:

Contribution = revenue − variable costs of production

The concept of contribution is useful when taking pricing decisions. If the manager or owner of a business sets a price in

excess of the variable cost of producing the product, then each sale will make a positive contribution to fixed or indirect costs. If sufficient sales are made, the enterprise will earn a profit. This approach to pricing is also called **contribution pricing**.

For example, the manager of a restaurant may calculate that the typical variable cost of serving a meal to a customer is $12. If the restaurant charges customers an average price of $25 for each meal, then it will make a profit as long as it attracts enough diners. It is certain that the revenue received from each customer will contribute $13 ($25 − $12) towards fixed costs.

Contribution pricing offers firms flexibility when deciding upon the amount to charge for their products. Businesses that have well-established products in high demand may be able to price significantly in excess of the variable cost of production. In these circumstances each sale makes a major contribution to fixed costs and profits. Fashion clothing is an example of a product where prices are set considerably above variable costs. Thus Allen Solly might charge the equivalent of $75 for a T-shirt that costs $10 to manufacture. The contribution of $65 from each sale is necessary because the business faces high fixed costs, spending heavily, for example, on marketing. Furthermore, products in the fashion industry have very short lives.

However, contribution pricing has its weaknesses. While setting a price that generates a positive contribution may result in the firm earning a profit, this depends upon the business in question achieving sufficient sales. This is far from certain as this approach to pricing places relatively little emphasis on the state of the market. Using contribution as a guide for pricing may result in low levels of sales because competitors' prices are lower or their responses may be unpredictable.

Study tip

Many students confuse contribution and profit, yet the distinction is vital and understanding it is important to gain top level grades. Profit is revenue less all costs, while contribution is revenue less just variable costs.

Extension: special order decisions

Businesses sometimes have to make decisions on whether to accept orders that are not on their normal terms. Thus a firm might receive a large order for its products at a price significantly lower than it usually receives. Alternatively, a business might receive an order that offers a price above the usual, but which requires special features or a very early delivery date meaning the supplier is likely to incur additional costs in fulfilling the order.

Firms faced with the dilemma of whether to accept this type of order are facing special order decisions. In these circumstances the concept of contribution can be applied to assist the business in reaching a decision on whether or not to accept the order. In general if the order will generate a positive contribution for the business it is probably worth accepting it, although there are a range of non-financial factors that may influence the decision. We look at special order decisions more fully in Chapter 30.

Costs and business performance

Managers of all businesses constantly monitor costs to ensure that:

- the costs incurred by separate areas of the business (divisions, branches or other cost centres) do not differ significantly without good reason
- they are not increasing unexpectedly and are similar to the forecasts set out in the company's **budgets**
- the business continues to hit profits targets.

We look at variance analysis in detail in Chapter 31.

Using costs to compare performance

A business that operates many similar branches or outlets may compare the costs of its branches and seek to reduce costs to those achieved by the most efficient performer. In this way, the company uses cost data as indicators of best practice and seeks to duplicate this approach in other areas of its business to improve performance and profits. It may be possible for senior managers to set cost targets for junior managers and to reward achievement of these targets. In this way large organisations are more able to control costs and enhance profitability.

Case Study

Starbucks enters Indian market

The American coffee retail chain Starbucks has opened its first coffee shop in India. The market of 1200 million people is very attractive to the company, but may require the company to change its approach in some ways. Starbucks, famous for its caramel macchiato and espresso, may find smaller and cheaper beverages the fastest way to win coffee drinkers in India.

The world's largest coffee chain will need options that are priced significantly lower than in the United States if it is to build a customer base in India. Starbucks' first coffee shop in India is in Mumbai – in a prosperous district that also has a Hermes store.

Starbucks' decision to enter the Indian market is the result of slow growth in sales in the United States and Europe as consumers cut spending on coffee products.

Questions

1 Explain why selling its products at lower prices in India might not necessarily reduce Starbucks' revenue. [6]
2 Discuss why the costs of operating a coffee shop in Mumbai might be different from those of operating in a city in the USA. [10]

However, for a large-scale global business such as Starbuck's in the case study, it may be difficult to compare performance in different countries in this way because of huge differences in costs. Thus monitoring and comparison of costs in this way is likely to be more effective if it takes place in a single country, or within countries with similar costs for resources such as labour.

Analysing why costs differ from forecasts

Most businesses draw up budgets to forecast their expected revenue, expenditure and profits over future trading periods. The business's managers monitor these budgets closely, looking for any differences between their forecasts and the actual figures. This process is known as **variance analysis**.

As the period covered by the budget unfolds, actual results can be compared with the budgeted figures and variances calculated and examined. Managers can then take the necessary decisions to improve the business's financial performance.

Monitoring profit targets

Budgets can be used to monitor how well costs are controlled, but also to calculate profits and to compare these with targets. This information can assist the business's managers in improving the business's performance. By using the cost and revenue information to calculate profits the managers can take decisions to improve the business's performance and especially its profitability. For example:

- If sales are rising its managers may be able to benefit from this popularity by charging higher prices and increasing profitability.
- It may be able to reduce its costs following such an analysis. If it is placing larger orders with other businesses for its supplies, it may be able to negotiate larger discounts for bulk orders. Alternatively, if it is not using all of its supplies it may reduce the size of its orders and its costs. This is vital if supplies are perishable.
- Labour is a major cost for many businesses, and especially those operating in the service sector. Monitoring labour costs is important to maximise profits. For example, if a business hires too much labour and it is not fully employed it is incurring costs that are not matched by revenue. Profitability will be damaged as a consequence.

17.3 Break-even analysis

What is break-even analysis and why is it used?

Break-even output is that level of output or production at which a business's sales generate just enough revenue to cover all its costs of production. At the break-even level of output a business makes neither a loss nor a profit. A business's managers may use break-even analysis for a number of reasons:

- to help decide whether the business idea will be profitable and whether it is viable
- to help decide the level of output and sales necessary to generate a profit
- the results of break-even analysis can be used to support an application by a business for a loan from a bank or other financial institution
- to assess the impact of changes in the level of production on the profitability of the business
- to assess the effects of different prices and levels of costs on the potential profitability of the business
- to judge whether launching a new product or entering a new market will be profitable given expected sales forecasts.

Contribution and break-even

Contribution is an important part of break-even analysis. Contribution can be defined as the difference between sales revenue and variable costs of production. This is illustrated in Figure 17.7.

Contribution is calculated through the use of the following formula:

$$\text{Contribution} = \text{revenue} - \text{variable costs}$$

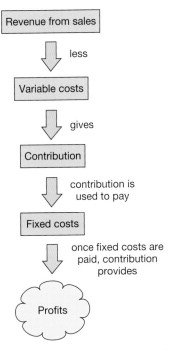

Figure 17.7 Contribution is the difference between sales revenue and variable costs of production

Contribution can be used to pay the fixed costs incurred by a firm. Once these have been met fully, contribution provides a business with its profits.

Contribution can be calculated for the sale of a single product. This is known as contribution per unit. It is calculated by using the formula:

$$\text{Contribution per unit} = \text{selling price of one unit of output} - \text{variable cost of producing that unit}$$

It is this method of calculating contribution that is useful when calculating break-even output.

Calculating break-even output

The manager of a business wishing to calculate the break-even point or level of output will require the following information:

- the selling price of the product
- the variable cost of producing a single unit of the product
- the fixed costs associated with the product: remember, fixed costs do not change as the level of production alters.

This information is used within the formula set out below:

$$\text{Break-even output} = \frac{\text{fixed costs}}{\text{selling price per unit} - \text{variable cost per unit}}$$

This formula can be rewritten given that contribution is the result of taking away variable cost from the selling price of a product.

$$\text{Break-even output} = \frac{\text{fixed costs}}{\text{contribution per unit}}$$

Case Study

Using break-even analysis

Sarah Feng is planning to expand her restaurant chain and to open a new restaurant in New York, specialising in Cantonese food. She has a lot of experience in the industry (already operating 12 restaurants in Sydney and Kuala Lumpur). Her new restaurant will maintain her reputation for serving high quality food in beautifully furnished buildings. Sarah plans to call her restaurant 'The River Palace'.

Sarah needs a loan to open The River Palace. She has already looked at a building which would seat up to 30 diners. She produced the figures set out in Table 17.3.

Table 17.3 Sarah's analysis for The River Palace

Type of cost or revenue	Amount
Average selling price per meal at The River Palace	$60
Variable costs per meal – ingredients, fuel, wages	$35
Monthly fixed costs of the new restaurant – lease for the property, rent and rates	$10 000

Using this information, Sarah was able to calculate how many meals she will need to sell (or how many diners she has to attract) in her restaurant if the project is to break even.

$$\text{Break-even output} = \frac{\text{fixed costs}}{\text{contribution per unit}}$$

Sarah knows her fixed costs will be $10 000 each month and this figure is entered into the top of the formula. To fill in the bottom Sarah has to take away the variable cost of producing a meal from the price the customer pays for a meal. The contribution earned from each meal in Sarah's new restaurant is $25 ($60 − $35). Thus:

$$\text{Monthly break-even output} = \frac{\$10\,000}{\$25} = 400 \text{ diners}$$

So, Sarah knows that, if her plan for The River Palace is to break even, she will need to attract at least 400 customers each month. If she attracts more than 400 customers, the project will make a profit. Sarah plans to open The River Palace on 25 evenings each month and would, therefore, break even if she had an average of 16 customers each night in the new restaurant.

Questions

1 If Sarah increased her prices to an average of $70 per meal, calcuate the level of her new break-even output. [6]

2 Discuss whether or not Sarah's planned price increase would be a good idea. [10]

While this calculation gives Sarah a quick guide to the number of customers her restaurant will need to break even, it tells her little more about the level of profit or loss The River Palace might make. A break-even chart is one way to work out the level of profits the business will generate if her forecast is proved to be correct.

Drawing break-even charts

The first stage in constructing a break-even chart is to mark scales on the two axes. Sarah knows that The River Palace can seat a maximum of 30 customers per night and that she normally opens for 25 evenings each month. Thus her maximum number of customers each month is 750 (30 customers × 25 nights). So her scale on the horizontal axis runs from zero to 750.

The vertical scale on a break-even chart records costs and revenues. Normally revenues are the highest figure. Thus Sarah has to calculate the highest possible revenue she could earn from her restaurant. At most she could attract 750 customers paying an average of $60 each. So the highest revenue she could possibly receive is ($60 × 750) = $45 000. Thus her vertical scale should have a maximum value of $45 000.

Having marked her scales, the first line to be drawn onto the chart is fixed costs. This is relatively simple as fixed costs do not change whatever the number of customers. Thus Sarah marks a horizontal line on the chart to show the monthly fixed costs she will have to pay – $10 000. This is illustrated in Figure 17.8.

The next stage is to include variable costs. As variable costs are expenditure on items such as components and raw materials, these costs will rise along with output. If Sarah has an increasing number of people dining at The River Palace she will need to buy more food and her wage bill will also rise.

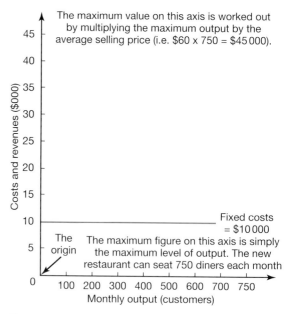

Figure 17.8 Fixed costs on a break-even chart

Variable costs always start at zero. The highest variable cost Sarah could encounter is to provide 750 meals, each having a variable cost of $35. Thus the highest variable cost would therefore be $26 250 ($35 × $750). This maximum figure is connected by a straight line to the origin as shown in Figure 17.9.

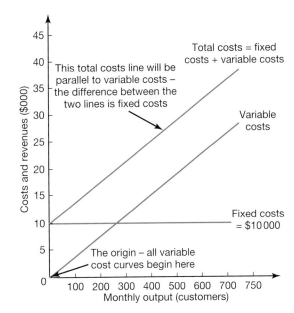

Figure 17.10 Including total costs on a break-even chart

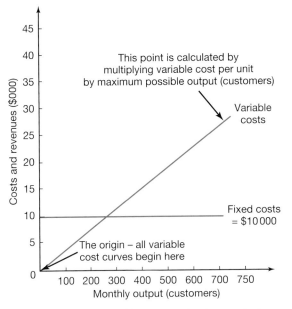

Figure 17.9 Adding variable costs to a break-even chart

Total costs are simply the sum of fixed and variable costs.
- If The River Palace has no customers in a month, it will not incur any variable costs. At zero output, total costs are the same as fixed costs. In Sarah's case, this will mean a total costs figure of $10 000 per month.
- At the other extreme, The River Palace might be full with 750 customers each month. Sarah will add together fixed costs (still $10 000, of course) and variable costs at full capacity (750 customers' meals each having variable costs of $35) equal to $26 250. Thus, total costs for the restaurant in these circumstances will be $36 250 ($10 000 + $26 250).

The line connecting these two points represents total costs. This line should be parallel to the variable costs curve and is shown in Figure 17.10.

Finally break-even shows the revenue The River Palace will earn. Sarah has already calculated that an average customer spends $60 on a meal in her restaurant. Once again there are two extreme situations.
- If The River Palace does not have any customers, it will not have any revenue. Thus the revenue line begins at the origin.
- If the restaurant is full, Sarah expects each of the 750 customers to pay $60 on average. If The River Palace attracts this level of custom, it will earn $45 000 ($60 × 750).

Figure 17.11 shows the break-even chart with the revenue line included. To make the chart easier to read, the variable costs line has been left out in this case.

The break-even chart tells Sarah that she needs 400 customers each month if The River Palace is to break even. This confirms the calculation we carried out earlier. However, a break-even chart provides much more information. Sarah can use it to read off the level of profit or loss her new restaurant will make according to the number of customers it attracts.

If the River Palace attracts fewer than 400 customers each month, it will record a loss. The amount of the loss is shown on the graph by the vertical distance between the total cost line and the revenue line at the relevant level of output. Similarly, if the restaurant attracts more than 400 customers in a month, it will generate a profit that month. Here the profit is shown by the vertical distance between the revenue line and the total cost line.

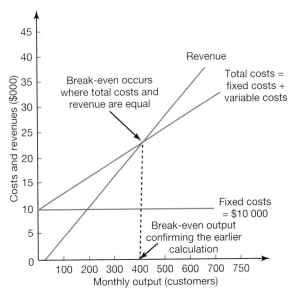

Figure 17.11 The complete break-even chart

187

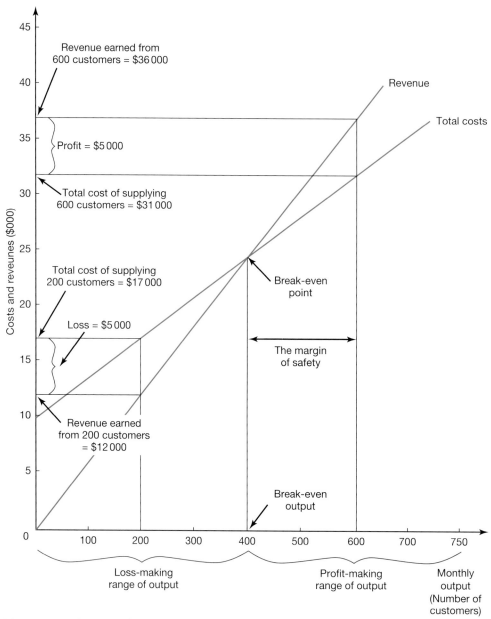

Figure 17.12 Showing profits and losses on a break-even chart

Figure 17.12 shows the level of loss and profit made by The River Palace if it attracts 200 customers and 600 customers per month.

Nigerian films fail to break even

The film industry in Nigeria is experiencing good times. Much of this is due to the efforts of Kunle Afolayan, a 38-year-old director. Kunle has produced a series of films since 2005 which have impressed knowledgeable film critics and recently received a highly favourable review in the *New York Times*.

Despite this international acclaim, it remains difficult to generate profits from making films in Nigeria. His latest film is a comedy called *Phone Swap*. To make the film, Kunle had to raise capital amounting to $500 000. About 40 per cent of this was raised from companies such as global mobile phone maker Blackberry. The film is still showing and earning revenues, but it is unlikely to break even. Most films produced by the Nigerian film industry (called Nollywood) fail to earn revenues of more than $200 000.

Questions

1 Explain two actions that Kunle Afolayan might take to help to make his film profitable. [6]
2 Discuss why a company such as Blackberry might choose to invest in a film which is not expected to make a profit. [10]

Mike plans to open a business providing people with help to learn how to use computers and the internet. Mike thinks his fixed costs will be $21 000 per year and the variable costs of each customer will be $100. His average price per customer will be $240. He expects to have 200 customers in his first year of trading.

1 If his figures are correct, will he break even in his first year of trading?
2 Calculate his expected profit or loss during his first year of trading.

The margin of safety

Key term

The margin of safety measures the quantity by which a firm's current level of sales exceeds the level of output necessary to break even.

A break-even chart can be used to show the **margin of safety**, although this can also be calculated. The margin of safety measures the quantity by which a firm's current level of sales exceeds the level of output necessary to break even.

If Sarah's new restaurant is successful and attracts 600 customers each month, the margin of safety will be 200 customers. This means that, in these circumstances, The River Palace could lose 200 customers each month before it began to make a loss. This is shown in figure 17.12 for an output of 600 customers per month.

The formula for the margin of safety = current level of sales − break-even output

This formula expresses the margin of safety as a number of units of output.

In our example of The River Palace restaurant at an output level of 600 diners each month, this calculation would give a margin of safety of 200 diners per month (600 diners − 400 diners). This means that the restaurant could lose 200 diners each month before it reached break-even output.

There is an alternative method of calculation which expresses the margin of safety as a percentage of current sales. The formula to use for this is:

$$\text{Margin of safety} = \frac{\text{current level of sales} - \text{break-even output} \times 100}{\text{current level of sales}}$$

Using this formula for our example we would get:

$$\frac{600 - 400 \times 100}{600} = 33.3\%$$

This tells us that the restaurant could lose just over 33 per cent of its sales before it found itself in a break-even position.

Changing variables and break-even analysis

Break-even analysis can assist managers in planning and operating their businesses. Break-even analysis can identify the number of sales a business needs in order to generate a profit at certain levels of costs and prices. However, break-even can deal with more complex circumstances including:

- analysing the impact of changing costs and/or prices on the profitability of the business
- deciding whether to accept an order for products and prices different from those normally charged.

In spite of its relative simplicity, break-even provides entrepreneurs with an effective and clear method of analysis and can assist in making decisions such as setting prices or accepting one-off orders.

Break-even analysis can show the consequences for a business in terms of changing profits (or losses) that may result from changes in fixed and variable costs or alterations in the firm's selling price. This is important for the planning of new businesses, for enterprises considering expansion and for those that operate in environments which alter frequently.

It is too simplistic for managers to assume that costs will remain constant or that prices in their markets will not alter over a period of time. Using break-even analysis for a number of 'what if' scenarios can increase the value of the technique in financial planning and decision making.

Table 17.4 illustrates the general effects of changing costs and prices on the break-even output of a business. To calculate the precise effect of changes at a particular level of production it is necessary to conduct calculations or to construct a break-even chart.

Sarah is conscious that rental values of properties in the Soho area of New York are rising rapidly. She realises that the rent of the historic building in which The River Palace is located is likely to rise and that this will increase her overall costs. If this happens this will reduce the profitability of the new enterprise. Sarah is concerned that a substantial rise in fixed costs (to say $12 500 each month) might make the business unattractive in financial terms. Break-even analysis could assist her in assessing the impact of this change as well as other changes in costs and revenues as illustrated by Table 17.4.

Table 17.4 Changing variables and break-even analysis

Change in business environment	Effect on break-even chart	Impact on break-even output	Other effects
Rise in variable costs	Total cost line **pivots** upwards	Greater output necessary to break even	Due to rise in costs greater revenue (and so more customers and sales) are necessary to break even
Fall in variable costs	Total cost line **pivots** downwards	Smaller output required to break even	Each sale incurs lower costs so that a smaller number of customers is needed to cover total costs
Rise in fixed costs	Fixed cost line and total cost line move upwards in a parallel shift	Greater output required to break even	Business incurs greater costs before earning any revenue, so more sales will be required to cover total costs and break even
Fall in fixed costs	Fixed cost and total cost lines make parallel shift downwards	Smaller output is necessary to break even	The business's total costs are lower and hence fewer sales will be required to break even
Rise in selling price	Revenue line **pivots** upwards	Break-even is achieved at a lower level of output	Each sale will provide the business with greater revenue whilst total costs are unaltered. Hence fewer sales will be necessary to break even
Fall in selling price	Revenue line **pivots** downwards	Break-even is reached at a higher level of output	Every sale will earn the business less revenue so, as total costs are unchanged, more sales will be required to earn sufficient revenue to break even

The uses and limitations of break-even analysis

Most financial techniques have uses and limitations, and break-even analysis is no exception. The uses of break-even analysis include the following:

- It is a simple technique allowing most entrepreneurs to use it without the need for expensive training. Because of this it is particularly suitable for newly established and small businesses.
- It is a technique that can be completed quickly, providing immediate results.
- It can be of value in supporting a business's application to a bank for a loan.
- By using break-even charts a business can forecast the effect of varying numbers of customers on its costs, revenues and profits.
- Break-even analysis can be used to analyse the implications of changing prices and costs on the enterprise's likely profitability.

However, break-even analysis has a number of limitations:

- It assumes that all products are sold. Thus Sarah might assume that she will attract 600 customers each month. She will

order the necessary food and hire sufficient staff. However, if only 500 turn up, she will not make the profit indicated for 600 customers on the break-even chart.

- It is a simplification of the real world. Businesses do not sell all their products at a single price and calculating an average is unlikely to provide accurate data. The technique is also difficult to use when a business sells a number of different products.
- Costs do not rise steadily as the technique suggests. As we have seen, variable costs can rise less quickly than output because of the benefits of buying in bulk.
- Any break-even analysis will only be as accurate as the data on which it is based. If costs or selling prices are incorrect, then the forecasts will be wrong.

Thus break-even analysis offers some support to businesses and especially to start-up enterprises or those seeking to expand by launching new products and/or entering new markets. However, it is only a guideline and its value should not be overstated. Perhaps, most importantly, entrepreneurs and managers should bear in mind that the value of the technique depends on the use of reliable data for costs, prices and expected sales.

Test your learning

Short answer questions

1 a Distinguish between costs and revenues. [3]

   b State the formula used to calculate a business's profits. [2]

2 a State **two** examples of fixed costs. [2]

   b Explain why if a business increases the selling price of its products, it may not receive a rise in revenue. [3]

3 a Distinguish between average costs and marginal costs. [3]

   b Why may average costs fall as a business increases its level of production? [2]

4 a Distinguish between direct and indirect costs. [3]

   b State **two** reasons why businesses need accurate data on costs of production. [2]

5 a State the formula needed to calculate contribution. [2]

   b Explain **one** reason why a business might accept an order for its products at a price that is lower than normal. [3]

6 a State **two** reasons why a business should monitor its costs closely. [2]

   b Explain why businesses should be cautious when minimising production costs. [3]

7 a Define the term break-even output. [2]

   b State **three** reasons why a business might use break-even to make decisions. [3]

8 a State the formula to calculate break-even output. [2]

   b If a business sells its products for an average price of $40, has fixed costs of $100 000 and contribution per unit of $15, what level of output is required to break even? [3]

9 a Define the term margin of safety. [2]

   b Calculate the margin of safety if a business has sales of 10 000 units per year and its break-even output is 6500 units. [3]

10 a State **two** reasons why a business might use the technique of break-even analysis. [2]

   b Explain why 'the assumption that all products are sold' is a major limitation of the break-even analysis as a management technique. [3]

Data response question

The new hotel

Santa Rosa Hotels has just opened its latest hotel in Huaraz, close to the Parque Nacional Huascaran in Peru. The area is a popular tourist destination and the numbers visiting are rising quickly. There are many other hotels in the area and the new hotel is not expected to be full at any time during its first year of operation.

The hotel's manager is keen to make the new business profitable and plans that every guest at the hotel will make a contribution to fixed costs. She is concerned about her pricing decisions as labour and other costs are expected to rise significantly over the next year or two.

Santa Rosa Hotels has not been a very profitable company since 2012 and its shareholders are keen to see an improvement in this area over the next year or two.

Questions

1 Explain the terms:

   a contribution [3]

   b fixed costs. [3]

2 Explain why it is important for the company to calculate its costs accurately. [6]

3 Discuss the case for and against the decision to use cost-plus pricing. [10]

Essay questions

1 Explain how having information about costs can help managers to improve the performance of a business. [8]

2 Discuss whether the limitations of break-even analysis mean that it is of little value to managers. [12]

Past paper questions

1 Discuss how, and to what extent, break-even analysis might be used as an aid to decision making in a large manufacturing business. [20]

Cambridge International AS and A Level Business Studies 9707 Paper 1 Q6 October/November 2008

2 Read the Cheapo Air case study on page 211 and then answer the following question.

   Analyse the factors that Cheapo Air would need to consider in setting a price for their business customers. [8]

Cambridge International AS and A Level Business Studies 9707 Paper 21 Q2c May/June 2009

18 Accounting fundamentals

Chapter overview

In this chapter we examine:

- the purpose and contents of income statements and statements of financial position
- the calculation and interpretation of liquidity and profitability ratios
- how businesses use ratio analysis to measure and improve performance
- the major users of published accounts
- the limitations on the usefulness of published accounts.

Income statements

Key terms

An **income statement** is an accounting statement showing a firm's sales revenue over a trading period and all the relevant costs generated to earn that revenue.

A **loss** is a situation where a business's expenditure exceeds its revenue over a specific trading period.

Profit can be defined in a number of ways, but is essentially the surplus of revenues over costs.

18.1 Income statements and statements of financial position

Since 2005 there have been significant changes to the way that public companies in the UK and the European Union present financial information. A European Union regulation required public companies to prepare financial statements complying with the International Financial Reporting Standards (IFRS) from 2005. This was to encourage a more global approach to the presentation of financial data, making comparisons and analysis more straightforward. Despite this there are some differences in the ways companies choose to present data in financial statements. This chapter will use the IFRS approach and terminology.

Businesses produce a range of financial statements recording their financial performance over a given trading period. For many companies around the world this is a legal requirement. We shall look at two financial statements in this chapter:

- income statements
- statements of financial position (previously called balance sheets).

What is profit?

At its simplest, **profit** is what remains from revenue once costs have been deducted. However, in the construction of the **income statement** two main types of profit are identified.

1 **Gross profit** This form of profit is calculated by deducting direct costs (such as materials and shop-floor labour) from a business's sales revenue. This gives a broad indication of the financial performance of the business without taking into account other costs such as overheads.

2 **Net profit** This is a further refinement of the concept of profit and is revenue less direct costs and indirect costs or overheads such as rent and rates, as well as interest payments and depreciation. This is a better indication of the performance of a business over a period of time as it takes into account all costs incurred by a firm over a trading period.

Net profit can take a number of forms.

- Trading or operating profit takes into account all earnings from regular trading activities and all the costs associated with those activities. However, this form of profit excludes any income received from, or costs incurred by, activities that are unlikely to be repeated in future financial years.
- Net profit before tax is a business's trading or operating profit plus any profits from one-off activities.
- Net profit after tax is the amount left to the business once corporation tax (or income tax in the case of a sole trader or partnership) has been deducted. This is an important form of profit. There are no more charges on this profit and the managers of the business can decide what to do with it.

The contents of an income statement

Figure 18.1 provides an initial guide to the contents of an income statement as presented by most companies. Negative figures are normally shown in brackets on financial statements.

The income statement comprises four main sections:

1 Firstly 'gross profit' is calculated. This is the difference between the revenue figure (this can be called sales revenue or turnover) and the cost of the goods that have been sold. The latter is normally expressed simply as 'cost of goods'. This element of the income statement is sometimes called the trading account.

2 Secondly, 'operating profit is calculated'. This is calculated by deducting the main types of expenses such as administration and selling costs.

3 Next, profit before taxation is calculated, which is arrived at by the inclusion of interest received by the business and interest paid by it. These are normally shown together as a net figure labelled 'financing costs'.

4 The final stage of the income statement is to calculate profit after taxation. This is arrived at by deducting the amount of tax payable for the year and shows the net amount that has been earned for the shareholders.

Public limited companies are required by law to publish their accounts. This means that they are available for scrutiny not only by the owners (shareholders), potential investors and bankers, but also by competitors.

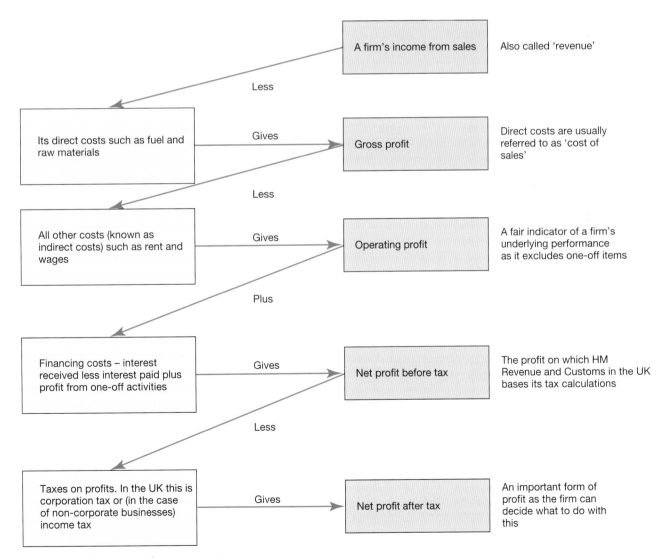

Figure 18.1 The contents of an income statement

When a company draws up its income statement for external publication it will include as little information as possible. Public limited companies usually supply no more detail than is required by law.

Case Study
Rolls-Royce

Rolls-Royce is one of the UK's best known companies. It manufactures engines for aircraft, ships and more general business use. It employs 40 000 people, and sells its products throughout the world for commercial and military use. Rolls-Royce operates joint ventures with companies and in Germany, India and Singapore.

Rolls-Royce Holdings plc's income statement is shown in a summarised form in Table 18.1.

Table 18.1 Rolls-Royce's summarised income statement

Summarised income statement for Rolls-Royce Holdings plc (years ended 31 December 2012 and 31 December 2013)		
	2013 £m	**2012 £m**
Revenue	15 513	12 161
Cost of sales	(12 197)	(9 432)
Gross profit	**3 316**	**2 729**
Administrative and other expenses	(1 781)	(1 351)
Operating profit	**1 535**	**1 378**
Profit from other sources	335	699
Finance income (interest received)	327	797
Finance costs (interest paid)	(438)	(108)
Profit before tax	**1 759**	**2 766**
Taxation	(380)	(431)
Profit for the year	**1 379**	**2 335**

Source: Rolls-Royce Holdings plc Annual Report, 2013
http://www.rolls-royce.com

Questions

1 Explain the possible reasons why Rolls-Royce's profit before tax may have fallen in 2013 despite its revenue increasing. [6]
2 Evaluate whether Rolls-Royce Holdings plc's financial performance was better in 2013 than in 2012. [10]

Maths moment

Suppose that Rolls-Royce plc had to pay tax on its profits (called corporation tax in the UK) at the rate of 36 per cent in 2013.

Calculate its revised 'Profit for the year' for 2013.

There is no single format for a limited company's income statement. In the UK the Companies Act of 2006 sets out the

minimum amount of information that must be included, though some modification can be made to ensure a 'true and fair view' of the business's performance.

The accounts of public limited companies also contain notes giving further details of the figures included in the income statement. This depth of information is important to allow shareholders and other interested parties to make an accurate assessment of the financial performance of the business.

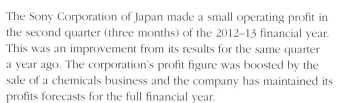

Case Study
Sony's profits fall

The Sony Corporation of Japan made a small operating profit in the second quarter (three months) of the 2012–13 financial year. This was an improvement from its results for the same quarter a year ago. The corporation's profit figure was boosted by the sale of a chemicals business and the company has maintained its profits forecasts for the full financial year.

Despite weak demand for its electronic products Sony reported an operating profit of ¥30.3 billion ($374 million) compared with a ¥1.64 billion yen loss in 2011. Sony's decision to sell its chemical business to the Development Bank of Japan for ¥58 billion had a significant impact on its profit figure. Business analysts anticipate further assets sales in the near future which should improve the look of its income statement at the end of the financial year.

Sony's financial performance is far from that achieved in the 1980s when it dominated global markets for consumer electronics with its Walkman portable music players. However, it has forecast a full-year operating profit of ¥130 billion.

Questions

1 Explain why a company's profit forecasts might prove to be incorrect. [6]
2 Discuss whether Sony is really a profitable business. [10]

How might a business use its profits?

One of the most important decisions taken by a business is how to use its profits, assuming that it makes any. The uses of profits can be divided into two categories.

- **Distributed profits** These profits are paid to the owners of the business and this will be in the form of dividends if the business is a company.
- **Retained profits** This portion of a business's profits is kept for investment in the business. Such profits may be used to purchase assets to help the business trade in the future. Examples include machinery, vehicles or properties.

A key issue in distributing profits is the balance between the short term and the long term. Distributing a high proportion of profits may keep the business's owners (most likely shareholders) happy in the short term, but might not be in the interests of those wanting a long-term investment. Some owners want to see the company grow over a number of years and to benefit from owning a share of a more valuable business.

As Rolls-Royce Holdings plc's profits for the year fell by nearly £100 million in 2013, the company's management team had to make a difficult decision about how much profit to retain. The team decided to increase the amount of profit distributed as dividends by 13.4 per cent despite the decline in profits.

Statements of financial position

Key terms

Assets are items owned by a business such as cash in the bank, vehicles and property.

Capital is the money invested into a business and is used to purchase a range of assets including machinery and inventories.

Creditors are people or organisations to which a business owes money.

Liabilities represent money owed by a business to individuals, suppliers, financial institutions and shareholders.

Inventories are the raw materials and other items necessary for production to take place. They also include finished products that have not yet been sold.

Liquidity measures the ability of a business to meet its short-term debts.

Reserves are a company's past retained profit.

What is a statement of financial position?

A statement of financial position is a financial statement recording the assets (possessions) and liabilities (debts) of a business on a particular day at the end of an accounting period. It was previously called a balance sheet and many companies, for example Rolls-Royce, still use this term. The statement of financial position only represents a picture of a business's assets and liabilities at a moment in time: it is commonly described as a 'snapshot' of the financial position of an organisation. Because of this, statements of financial position always carry a date on which the valuation of assets and assessment of liabilities took place. A consolidated statement of financial position is a statement of financial position for a business that includes information from all its divisions.

Key statement of financial position relationships

1 Assets = Liabilities

This is the fundamental relationship which helps to explain why the statement of financial position 'always balances'

2 Total assets = Current assets + Non-current assets

Businesses need to invest in a range of assets if they are to operate efficiently

3 Liabilities = Share capital + Borrowings + Reserves

Figure 18.2 Key statement of financial position relationships

By recording assets and liabilities the statement of financial position sets out the ways in which the business has raised its capital and the uses to which this capital has been put. The statement of financial position provides a great deal of information for those with an interest in a business and is the primary financial document published by businesses.

Statements of financial position are an essential source of information for a variety of business decisions and for a number of stakeholders. The precise information drawn from the statement of financial position will depend upon the stakeholder and the nature of their enquiry. We shall consider the users of financial information later in this chapter. However, it is important to appreciate that this particular financial statement contains a great deal of information.

Assets

An **asset** is simply something that a business owns. Thus assets are what a business purchases with its **capital**. There are two main categories of assets that appear on the statement of financial position. The distinction between the two categories is based upon the time the assets are held within the business.

1 **Non-current assets** These are assets owned by a business that it expects to retain for one year or more. Such assets are used regularly by a business and are not bought for the purpose of resale. Examples of non-current assets include land, property, production equipment and vehicles.

2 **Current assets** This category of asset is likely to be converted into cash before the next statement of financial position is drawn up. Therefore, cash and **inventories** (previously called stock) are examples of current assets as they are only retained by the business for a short period of time.

Liabilities

A **liability** is a debt owed by the business to organisations or individuals. Another way of thinking of a liability is that it shows the sources of capital the business has raised in order to purchase its assets. As with assets there are a number of categories of liabilities.

- **Current liabilities** In many senses these are the equivalent of current assets. They represent debts owed by the business due for payment within one year or less. Examples of such short-term debt are overdrafts and tax due for payment. Trade and other payables are organisations such as suppliers to whom the business owes money. These are normally classified as a current liability because payment is usually due within a short period of time.

- **Non-current liabilities** These are debts that a business does not expect to repay within the period of one year. Mortgages and bank loans repayable over several years are common examples of this type of liability.

- **Total equity** It may seem strange that the money invested into the business by its owners (shareholders in the case of a company) is a liability. However, if the company ceased trading, shareholders would hope for the repayment of their investment. Thus these funds (called total equity or total shareholders' equity) are liabilities. This element of the statement of financial position also includes reserves. These are the company's accumulated, retained profit.

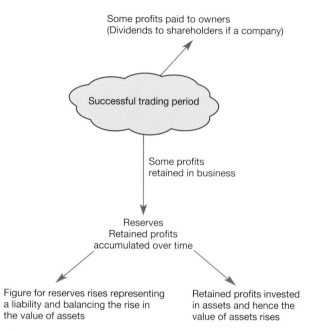

Figure 18.3 Assets, liabilities and reserves

Case Study

Burberry plc's statement of financial position

Burberry plc is one of the world's best known producers of luxury fashion products including clothing, perfumes, cosmetics and accessories. It published its accounts on 31 March, as it does each year. The net worth of the company, as measured by its net assets, had risen by 8.42 per cent from £1610.6 million ($2738 million) in 2012 to £1746.2 million ($2968.5 million) in 2013. Much of this increase was the result of rising values of the company's property and trademarks.

In both 2012 and 2013 the company's statement of financial position showed current assets to be considerably higher than current liabilities. In 2013 this gave Burberry a working capital figure of £403.0 million ($685.1 million); in 2012 its working capital was £419.7 million ($713.5 million), a very similar figure. Over the two years the company's non-current liabilities remained fairly constant at just under £130 million ($221 million).

Source: Adapted from Burberry plc's Annual report, 2013
http://www.burberryplc.com

Questions

1 Explain why a statement of financial position provides important information for Burberry plc's stakeholders. [6]

2 Evaluate the benefits received by Burberry plc's stakeholders as a result of the company having a healthy working capital figure. [10]

Reserves

An important feature of a statement of financial position is **reserves**. Reserves are simply profit accumulated during previous years' trading and not paid out to the owners of the

business. This accumulated profit is not held in the form of cash but is invested into a range of assets that are useful to the business and hopefully generate further profits.

If a business is successful, purchases more assets and grows, then its value will increase and so will the value of the assets. It may borrow money to achieve this growth; if it does, liabilities will grow at the same rate. However, if it funds its growth out of profits, then the matching liability will be recorded as reserves indicating that the owners' stake in the business has risen in value. Remember that the owners' funds in the business are a liability as this represents money lent to the organisation.

The format of a statement of financial position

Presenting statement of financial position data in a vertical format (as in Figure 18.4) is the most common format and all public companies in the UK are legally obliged to present their statement of financial position in this way.

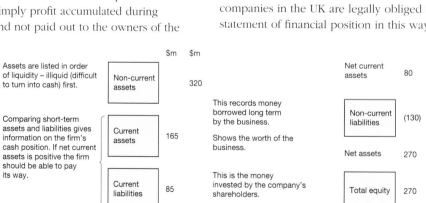

Figure 18.4 The format of a statement of financial position

Case Study

Rolls-Royce Holdings plc's statement of financial position

Table 18.2

Summarised consolidated statement of financial position for Rolls-Royce Holdings plc, 31 December 2012 and 31 December 2013	2013 £m	2012 £m
Intangible non-current assets	4987	2901
Tangible non-current assets	5258	5652
Inventories	3319	2726
Receivables and cash	9082	6704
Other current assets	417	163
Total assets	23063	18146
Current liabilities	(9780)	(7208)
Net current assets	3038	2385
Non-current liabilities	(6980)	(4942)
Total liabilities	(16760)	(12150)
Net assets	**6303**	**5996**
Share capital	456	374
Reserves and retained earnings	5847	5622
Total equity	**6303**	**5996**

Source: Rolls-Royce Holdings plc Annual Report, 2013
http://www.rolls-royce.com

Questions

1 Explain how this statement of financial position might help a supplier to decide whether or not to sell products to Rolls-Royce. [6]
2 Discuss the value of the information in this statement of financial position to a bank considering offering Rolls-Royce a loan of $790 million (£465 million). [10]

There are two key features on the statement of financial position that are worth examining in assessing the performance of a business.

1 **Working capital**

We looked at working capital in Chapter 15. A business requires working capital to pay its day-to-day bills as they arise. It is calculated by subtracting a business's current liabilities from its current assets. In Rolls-Royce Holdings plc's case, its working capital was positive in both cases: £3038 million ($5165 million) in 2013 and £2385 million ($4055 million) in 2012.

2 **The proportion of its capital that is borrowed long-term**

It can be risky for a business to borrow too heavily as it may not be able to continue to pay its interest charges if interest rates increase. In Rolls-Royce Holdings plc's case, in 2013 its long-term borrowing (which is recorded on its statement of

18.2 Using financial ratios

Key terms

Ratio analysis is a technique for analysing a business's financial performance by comparing one piece of accounting information with another.

A stakeholder is any group or individual having an interest in the activities of a business.

It is possible for **stakeholders** to use a series of relatively simple calculations to analyse a business's financial statements, including the income statement and the statement of financial position. The key feature of **ratio analysis** is that it compares two pieces of financial information. By comparing two pieces of data in this way it is possible to make more informed judgements about a business's performance.

A comparison of the financial performance of two companies during 2013 can illustrate the advantages of comparing two pieces of data to make more informed judgements. We saw earlier in this chapter that Rolls-Royce Holdings, one of the UK's best known companies, announced a profit before tax amounting to £1759 million ($2987.5 million) for the 2013 financial year. In comparison, Coca-Cola, another world-famous company, generated a profit before tax of $805 million in the same year. A simple judgement may be that Rolls-Royce had performed more successfully.

Table 18.3 shows that when we compare the profit before taxation to revenue earned, the performance of Rolls-Royce can definitely be judged superior. Rolls-Royce earned over 11 pence of profit from each £1 of sales. In contrast, Coca-Cola made less than 10 cents from each $1 of sales. Rolls-Royce had a higher percentage of revenue which was profit than Coca-Cola. Using this ratio, which is called the profit margin, it is possible to make a more accurate judgement than simply comparing the level of profit. We consider the profit margin in more detail later in this chapter.

Table 18.3 Comparing financial performance of two companies using a simple ratio

Company	Profit before taxation, 2013	Revenue, 2013	Profit as a percentage of revenue
Rolls-Royce Holdings plc	£1759 million	£15513 million	11.34%
Coca-Cola Enterprises	$805 million	$8212 million	9.80%

There are a large number of financial ratios that stakeholders can use. In this chapter we shall consider two groups of ratios only. These are:

- liquidity ratios
- profitability ratios.

Liquidity ratios

These ratios allow managers and other interested parties to monitor a business's cash position and can be calculated from data that is on the statement of financial position. Even profitable businesses can experience problems with liquidity and may be unable to pay their bills as they fall due. Liquidity ratios measure the liquid assets held by a firm (cash and other assets such as receivables that are easily convertible into cash). The value of these assets is then compared with the short-term debts or liabilities the business will have to pay. In this way stakeholders may evaluate whether the business's performance may be harmed as a result of liquidity problems. Creditors and suppliers are likely to be interested in a business's liquidity ratios, as well as managers, as they indicate its ability to pay money that is owed.

Current ratio

This ratio measures the ability of a business to meet its liabilities or debts over the next year or so. The formula to calculate this ratio is:

$$\text{Current ratio} = \frac{\text{current assets}}{\text{current liabilities}}$$

The current ratio is expressed in the form of a ratio, for example 2:1. This would mean that the firm in question possessed \$2 of current assets (cash, receivables and inventories) for each \$1 of current liability (payables, taxation and proposed dividends, for example). In these circumstances it is probable that the business would be able to meet its current liabilities without needing to sell non-current assets or raise long-term finance.

Using this ratio

- For many years holding current assets twice the value of current liabilities was recommended. This is no longer accepted, partly due to the use of computers in inventory control and the widespread use of just-in-time systems of production. A more typical figure might now be 1.6:1.
- In spite of this, the 'normal' figure for this ratio varies according to the type of business and the state of the market. Fast-food outlets such as McDonald's and banks typically operate with lower ratios, whereas some manufacturing firms may have higher ratios.
- Firms with high current ratio values (say, 3:1) are not necessarily managing their finances effectively. It may be that they are holding too much cash and not investing in non-current assets to generate income. Alternatively, they may have large holdings of inventories, some of which might be obsolete.

Firms can improve the current ratio by raising more cash through the sale of non-current assets or the negotiation of long-term loans. (NB: raising more cash through short-term borrowing will increase current liabilities, having little effect on the current ratio.)

Acid test (or quick) ratio

This ratio measures the very short-term liquidity of a business. The acid test ratio compares a business's current liabilities with its liquid assets (that is current assets minus inventories). This can provide a more accurate indicator of liquidity than the current ratio as inventories can take time to sell. The acid test ratio measures the ability of a firm to pay its bills over a period of two or three months without requiring the sale of inventory.

The formula is:

$$\text{Acid test ratio} = \frac{\text{liquid assets}}{\text{current liabilities}}$$

The acid test ratio is also expressed in the form of a ratio, for example 2:1.

Case Study

Chinese steel manufacturers face liquidity problems

Iron ore prices have dropped to a seven-month low amid concerns about waning demand from China, the world's top consumer of the steel-making ingredients. But after years of rapid growth in the Chinese steel industry, liquidity problems have appeared. Some manufacturers in Tangshan, home to about a quarter of China's steel industry, are empty and silent after owners ran out of cash to pay workers.

Xu Zhongbo, head of Beijing Metal Consulting, estimates that 40m–50m tonnes of steel capacity have been idled as production costs exceed prices by \$16.30 a tonne.

Another concern is the rise in iron ore stocks at Chinese ports to record levels. One interpretation is that the mountains of ore piling up at ports reflect the liquidity problems at the steel manufacturers, which are only buying raw materials when needed. As a consequence the steel manufacturers are holding minimal inventories of iron ore and coal.

Source: Adapted from BD Live, (Lucy Hornby), 27 February 2014
http://www.bdlive.co.za

Questions

1 Explain why manufacturers may be especially vulnerable to liquidity problems. [6]
2 Discuss the extent to which it is important whether or not a steel manufacturer holds a high level of inventory. [16]

Using this ratio

- Conventionally a 'normal' figure for the acid test ratio was thought to be 1:1, giving a balance of liquid assets and current liabilities. However, by 2008, a number of businesses were operating successfully with acid test figures nearer to 0.7:1.
- The value of the acid test ratio considered acceptable will vary according to the type of business. Retailers might operate with a figure of 0.4:1, because they trade mainly in cash, and have close relationships with suppliers. A manufacturing business might operate with a ratio nearer to the standard 1:1.
- Firms should not operate over long periods with high acid test ratios as holding assets in the form of cash is not profitable and does not represent an effective use of resources.

As with the current ratio the acid test ratio can be improved by selling non-current assets or agreeing long-term borrowing.

Liquidity ratios are based on figures drawn from the statement of financial position relating to a particular moment in time. Because of this some caution should be exercised when drawing conclusions from this type of ratio. The actual figures on the statement of financial position may be unrepresentative of the firm's normal position due to factors such as **window dressing** or a sudden and unexpected change in trading conditions.

> **Key term**
>
> **Window dressing** is the construction of financial documents in order to present a company's performance in the best possible light.

Interpreting the results of liquidity ratios

The results of the calculations in Table 18.4 show that Rolls-Royce Holdings plc is in a strong liquidity position. Its current ratio is 1.89:1, indicating that it has £1.89 of current assets for every £1 of current liabilities it has to pay. This should enable it to pay these short-term debts as they fall due and it has some current assets in reserve in case it encounters unexpected debts.

Its acid test ratio also looks very reassuring to stakeholders. It has £1.32 of liquid assets for every £1 of current liabilities. However, it is not unusual for manufacturers to hold relatively large amounts of assets which can be converted into cash reasonably quickly.

Apple is well known for its consumer electronics and especially the iPad. Its liquidity position is also very strong, which is perhaps not surprising for a highly successful multinational. One notable feature of its liquidity ratios is that the result of its acid test ratio is little different from that of its current ratio. These results show that Apple holds very low volumes of inventory. Partly, this is because it subcontracts its manufacturing operations to other companies such as Foxconn.

Finally, Carrefour is a French-owned retailer with stores in many countries. Its liquidity ratios may appear less comforting at first. However, it is not uncommon for retailers to operate with low liquidity ratios. Businesses such as Carrefour can rely on customers paying promptly and mainly in cash. Thus the company can be confident that it will receive a regular inflow of cash into the business.

Limitations of liquidity ratios

Thus, although it is common to see 'recommended' figures for liquidity ratios, the actual figure that is considered acceptable varies according to the type of business under consideration. This means that it is not always possible to make a judgement about a company's liquidity position from its liquidity ratios. A 'reasonable' figure for one business might not be so for another business operating in a different market. Our three examples in Table 18.4 highlight these differences.

It is also possible for a business to engage in window dressing its statement of financial position to improve its liquidity ratios. One simple way of doing this is to carry out a sale and leaseback deal. This entails selling an asset and leasing it back for continued use. We saw in Chapter 16 that Nokia, the Finnish manufacturer of mobile phones, is responding to a shortage of cash by selling and leasing back its headquarters near Helsinki. This is expected to raise $200–300 million for the company and this action would improve its liquidity ratios.

Table 18.4 The liquidity ratios for three multinational companies

Company	Rolls-Royce Holdings plc	Apple Inc	Carrefour SA
Type of business	Manufacturer of engines for military and civilian use	The company designs, develops and sells consumer electronics	A French supermarket chain with stores in 28 countries
Date of statement of financial position	31 December 2013	28 September 2013	30 June 2013
Current assets	£2 166.0 million	$73 286 million	€17 818 million
Inventories	£645.6 million	$1 764 million	€5 595 million
Current liabilities	(£1 148.8 million)	($43 658 million)	(€19 960 million)
Current ratio	1.89:1	1.68:1	0.89:1
Acid test ratio	1.32:1	1.64:1	0.61:1

Profitability ratios

These ratios compare the profits earned by a business with other key variables such as the level of sales achieved or the capital available to the managers of the business.

Gross profit margin

This ratio compares the gross profit achieved by a business with its revenue. Gross profit is earned before expenses such as administration and marketing costs are deducted. The ratio calculates the percentage of the selling price of a product that constitutes gross profit. The answer is expressed as a percentage.

$$\text{Gross profit margin} = \frac{\text{gross profit} \times 100}{\text{revenue}}$$

For example, in 2013 Rolls-Royce's gross profit was £3316 million. This was achieved from a revenue of £15513 million. Thus the company's gross profit margin = £3316m × 100/15513m = 21.4 per cent.

This gross profit margin may appear high, but a judgement should take into account that the company has not paid its expenses for selling the products and also its administrative costs. We will see later that the company's profit margin is considerably lower.

Using this ratio

- The figure for gross profit margin varies depending upon the type of industry. Firms that turn over their inventory rapidly and then can trade with relatively few assets may operate with low gross profit margins. Greengrocers and bakers may fall into this category. Firms with slower turnover of inventory and requiring substantial fixed assets may have a higher figure. House builders may fall into this category.
- The sales mix can have a major influence on this ratio. A farmer selling eggs at a 10 per cent gross profit margin and renting out holiday cottages at a 40 per cent margin could improve the business's overall profit margin (but reduce its turnover) by discontinuing egg production.

This ratio can be improved by increasing prices although this may result in lower turnover. Alternatively, reducing direct costs (raw material costs and wages, for example) will also improve the figure.

Profit margin

This ratio calculates the percentage of a product's selling price that is net profit after all costs have been deducted, but before tax is paid. Because this ratio includes all of a business's costs and expenses, it may be regarded as a better indication of performance than gross profit margin. Once again the answer to this ratio is written as a percentage.

$$\text{Profit margin} = \frac{\text{profit (profit before taxation)} \times 100}{\text{revenue}}$$

Continuing our example of Rolls-Royce Holdings plc, the company's profit before taxation for the trading year ending in March 2012 was £1759 million. The company's profit margin is shown as follows:

$$\text{Profit margin} = \frac{£1759\text{m} \times 100}{£15513} = 11.34\%$$

This confirms the result we calculated in Table 18.3.

Using this ratio

- Results of this ratio can vary according to the type of business, though a higher profit margin is preferable.
- A comparison of gross profit and profit margins can be informative. A business enjoying a stable gross profit margin and a declining profit margin may be failing to control expenses effectively. This may be due to the purchase of costly new premises, for example.

Maths moment

In 2012 Rolls-Royce's profit margin was 22.74 per cent and its profits before taxation were £2766 million.

Calculate the company's revenue in 2012.

Improvements in the profit margin may be achieved through higher selling prices or tighter control of costs, particularly expenses or indirect costs.

Interpreting the results of profitability ratios

The key issue here is the comparison between gross and net profit margins. A comparison of the two margins can inform stakeholders of a business's management of its costs.

A company's profit margins can be affected by the business in which it operates as well as its scale. Wal-Mart Stores Inc is the world's largest retailer and the second-largest private company in the world. It owns 11000 stores in 27 countries. Despite these formidable statistics the company only operates with a profit margin of 4.93 per cent. This is for two principal reasons. The grocery market in many countries in which Walmart trades is very price competitive with tough competition from other global retailers such as Tesco plc and Carrefour SA. Walmart promotes itself as a low-cost retailer and thus keeps its prices at a minimum to win market share. Secondly, as shown in Table 18.5, Walmart's scale means that it earns very high levels of revenue and thus a return of just under 5 per cent generates a profit before tax of $5697 million.

Table 18.5 The profitability ratios of three multinational companies

Company	Wal-Mart Stores Inc	Apple Inc	Panasonic Corporation
Type of business	The world's largest retailer	The company designs, develops and sells consumer electronics	A global producer of consumer electronics
Date of income statement	31 October 2013	28 June 2013	31 March 2013
Revenue	$115 456 million	$37 472 million	¥7 303 045 million
Gross profit	$28 840 million	$13 871 million	¥1 883 157 million
Profit/(loss) before taxation	$5 697 million	$10 143	(¥398 386 million)
Gross profit margin	24.98%	37.02%	25.79%
Profit margin	4.93%	27.07%	−5.46%

It may not be a surprise that Apple Inc, the American consumer electronics company, is highly profitable. The most noteworthy figure here is Apple's profit margin. This is over 27 per cent, meaning that 27 cents from each dollar of revenue received by the company represents profit. This is a measure of the company's global success but is also necessary if it is to continue to be a market leader in global consumer electronics. Continued success will require the company to invest consistently in developing new products and this high level of profit gives it the funds it needs.

Finally, Panasonic, the Japanese consumer electronics manufacturer, did not enjoy a very successful 2012–13 financial year. The company recorded a loss of nearly ¥4 billion for the year. Some business analysts believe that a significant reason for the company's relative failure is that the technology in its products has not always kept up-to-date with rivals such as Apple. The company's gross profit margin is respectable, suggesting that it may not be controlling costs such as administrative expenses effectively. In the 2012–13 financial year Panasonic would have had to raise its average selling prices by more than 5 per cent to cover its losses. However, in a highly competitive market this would have resulted in a substantial reduction in sales and possibly further losses.

Case Study

McDonald's net profit margin

The McDonald's Corporation is one of the world's largest restaurant chains with a menu based mainly on burgers. At the start of 2014 it had 35 000 restaurants in 118 countries, of which 28 000 were operated by franchisees and 7000 were operated by the company. The company has raised its dividends over a period of 36 consecutive years and has a globally recognised and valuable brand name as well as a clear focus on consumer needs.

The company's cash-flow position is strong: a surplus of $2.05 billion in its 2013 accounts. The company employs 1.8 million people, generates revenues of $27 567.00 million and profits of $8079 million, giving it a profit margin of 29.31 per cent.

Questions

1 Using examples from the case study, explain the difference between profits and cash flow. [6]
2 Evaluate the possible reasons why the McDonald's Corporation generates such a high profit margin. [10]

Limitations of profitability ratios

As with the gross profit margin, the profit margin figure can be massaged through window dressing. One method a business may use to achieve this is to bring forward sales from a future trading period into the current one. This can increase revenue without affecting costs and therefore gross profit and profit margins are improved. However, this is only a short-term policy as revenues and profit margins in the next trading period will be adversely affected.

18.3 The main users of accounts

A number of groups are likely to have an interest in a business's income statement and statement of financial position. These stakeholders are illustrated in Figure 18.5.

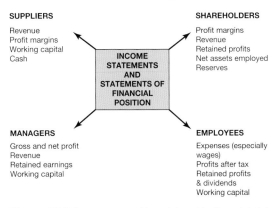

Figure 18.5 Some groups with an interest in financial statements

Shareholders

Shareholders are perhaps the most obvious group with an interest in the financial statements. Shareholders will be interested in a business's sales revenue and operating profit before taxation. This will provide some guidance as to the performance of the enterprise, especially when compared to previous years. They will also be likely to examine how profits have been utilised. Some shareholders may seek the maximum dividend possible. Others may be interested in a longer-term return and welcome substantial reinvestment in the expectation of future profits. The statement of financial position contains some vital information such as the value of the company (whether or not it is increasing) as measured by net assets employed. Reserves will also show the amount of profits that have been retained within the company over time and may provide some indication of expected future growth.

Managers

Managers use the income statement as an important source of information regarding the performance of the business. Managers are, of course, able to see the income statement in much more detail than that provided in the annual report and accounts. Published accounts contain the minimum amount of information required under law to avoid giving competitors any advantage. Managers will monitor sales performance through revenue figures and judge costs against sales revenue. If expenses and cost of sales rise by a greater amount than revenue, action may be necessary. Managers will also consider carefully the effects of one-off items on the financial statements.

On the statement of financial position working capital will provide a critical figure for managers and allow them to judge whether or not the business will face liquidity problems in the near future. Retained profits may also provide some indication of the capital available to invest within the business.

Employees

Employees may be interested in profits after tax if their pay is related to company performance through a profit-related pay scheme. They may also be interested in the level of dividends if they are shareholders. The level of profits after taxation may also be an indication of the company's ability to fund a pay increase or, alternatively, of the security of their employment.

The statement of financial position will advise them of the company's liquidity position which is a vital indicator of its future ability to pay its bills promptly and therefore to survive.

HM Revenue and Customs (HMRC)

HMRC is the organisation responsible for collecting corporation tax from companies on the UK government's behalf. HMRC will therefore scrutinise company accounts and use net profit before tax as the basis for its calculation of tax liability (the amount of

tax to be paid). It may also check that the income statement meets all necessary standards, e.g. the basis upon which non-current assets have been reduced in value – or depreciated. The statement of financial position provides further information about the value of non-current assets and how they have been depreciated. The rate at which a company depreciates its assets over time affects its profits and the amount of tax to be paid.

Suppliers

Suppliers will have a particular interest in a business's liquidity position and therefore its ability to settle invoices on time. If the statement of financial position records a healthy working capital position, suppliers may be more willing to grant trade credit to the business in question. Suppliers may also be interested in the business's income statement to analyse its trend in revenue (whether it is rising or falling) and its profit margins. This information will assist suppliers in making judgements about whether or not to increase prices charged for goods or services supplied.

18.4 The limitations and uses of financial statements

The information published in financial statements does provide a great deal of information as discussed throughout this chapter. It allows stakeholders to see and analyse trends in key figures such as revenue and profits. Similarly, interested parties can look at the company's ability to settle its debts as they fall due and make judgements about the risk involved in investing in the business based on the amount of capital that has been borrowed.

However, financial statements such as the statement of financial position and the income statement only include financial information. Inevitably they will not provide direct information on a range of important factors which are of significance to stakeholders.

Qualitative factors
Leadership

The quality of leadership of the business is not shown by financial data. Do senior managers have the necessary skills and experience to lead the business successfully and do they have the vision to inspire and direct the workforce?

The business's market standing

What is the position of the business in the market? It may have successful products that are selling well and generating acceptable levels of profit. However, the firm may be lagging behind in developing new products or in entering new markets and therefore likely to perform less well in the future. Financial analysis based on historical financial data is unlikely to reveal this.

The business's workforce

What about the motivation and performance of the workforce? Statements of financial position and income statements do not reveal productivity or levels of labour turnover, or even the rate of absenteeism which can indicate the level of morale within the business. For organisations supplying services, the quality of a business's workforce can be an important competitive weapon.

Historical financial information may not predict the future

All of the information that is included in financial statements is historical. The information on the statement of financial position relates to a single day at the end of the trading period, whereas the income statement contains data over the entire trading period. It is common for financial statements to include financial data from earlier trading periods. Many contain a five-year summary of the business's financial performance.

However, the assumption underpinning making decisions on the basis of analysing financial statements is that the future will be the same as the past. Clearly this is not always the case. Many of the world's economies suffered a major financial crisis in 2008–09 which led to a recession which has been prolonged in many cases. Analysing company accounts for 2007 would not have given an accurate forecast of likely future performance.

Other factors can lead to historical financial information proving to be an inaccurate indicator of financial performance. Competitors may launch new, innovative and highly competitive products, consumers' tastes and fashions may change or technology may change.

Case Study

Stoneage launches new campaign and store

Crescent Bahuman Ltd has announced that it has launched its latest 'Denim Forever' campaign along with a new flagship outlet in Lahore. The new product and store is based around the company's jeans brand Stoneage. The brand is famous in Pakistan for supplying western-style clothes for men and women.

The newly opened store will sell a broad range of denim clothes, including jeans, T-shirts and denim jackets. The company is one of Pakistan's leading exporters of denim products to a range of countries in and beyond Asia.

The company is optimistic that its new store and range will have a substantial impact upon the company's financial performance.

Questions

1 Explain why the Pakistan government and other clothes retailers might be interested in Crescent Bahuman Ltd's published accounts. [6]

2 Discuss the reasons why Crescent Bahuman Ltd's published accounts might not be a good indicator of its financial performance. [10]

Window dressing

In the section in this chapter on liquidity ratios, we encountered window dressing. This entails the construction of financial documents organised to present a company's performance in the best possible light.

Window dressing can be used to improve the look of a company's financial performance in a number of ways. We saw earlier that sale and leaseback deals can increase the amount of cash on a business's statement of financial position. Equally, bringing forward sales revenue from a later trading period can enhance a business's revenue and its profitability. Other methods of window dressing also exist.

- Businesses may maintain the value of intangible assets on the statement of financial position at what might be considered excessive levels to increase the overall value of the organisation. This tactic is only possible when the assets in question (for example, goodwill or brands) have been purchased.
- Capitalising expenditure. This means including as non-current assets items that might otherwise have simply been regarded as an expense and not included on the statement of financial position. Thus a firm might spend heavily on computer software and include this as a fixed asset on the basis that it will have a useful life of several years. This action will increase the value of the business.

The consequences of window dressing will most probably be improved figures for liquidity and profitability, making the business appear more attractive to diverse stakeholders such as suppliers and shareholders.

Not revealing the performance of individual parts of the business

Consolidated published accounts also bring together the financial data from all divisions or subsidiaries that make up a business. It would be unusual if the financial performance of all of the component divisions was similar; indeed some elements of a business may perform poorly, but this could be hidden by stronger financial performances from other elements of the business. This can be of enormous importance if the division that is performing poorly is one that the business is expecting to rely upon in the future.

Tesco struggles in some overseas markets

Tesco plc is one of the largest retailers in the world. It is the dominant retailer in the UK. In 2013 the company reported a fall in its annual profits for the first time in many years. Taking into account the cost of leaving the market in the United States, Tesco's profits after tax were £120 million, compared with nearly £2800 million in the previous year. The company has explained that its profits have fallen because it is investing heavily in improving its operational performance.

Tesco plc has also announced that it is selling its stores in the United States. The company operates 200 stores in Arizona, California and Nevada under the Fresh & Easy brand name. The withdrawal from the United States will cost the company an estimated £2.1 billion. Tesco is also abandoning its retail operations in Japan and reviewing how it operates in China.

Figure 18.6 A Fresh Easy store in America

Table 18.6

Division	Revenue £m	Operating profit £m	Stores	Employees
United Kingdom	43 600	2 272	3 146	313 885
Asia	11 500	661	2 131	125 797
Europe	9 300	329	1 507	94 712

Source: Tesco Annual Report, 2013

Questions

1 Explain why it is important for Tesco plc to make the maximum possible profit each year. [6]
2 Evaluate the impact that the poor performance of some of Tesco plc's overseas operations will have on the company as a whole. [10]

18.5 Management and financial accountants

Management accounting is a branch of accounting that analyses a business's financial performance and provides cost information to the internal management for the purposes of planning, controlling and decision-making.

CIMA (Chartered Institute of Management Accountants) in the UK defines management accounting as 'the process of identification, measurement, accumulation, analysis, preparation, interpretation, and communication of information that is used by management to plan, evaluate, and control within an entity and to assure appropriate use of an accountability for its resources'. Management accountants prepare information for senior managers to assist with planning and controlling operations within the organisation as well as decision-making. Some of the information provided by management accountants may be used to make strategic, long-term decisions. Management accountants provide information to other interested groups within the organisation.

On the other hand, financial accounting is concerned with the organising and reporting of financial information to stakeholders including shareholders, suppliers, creditors, and others who are outside an organisation. Financial accountants will prepare the business's published accounts such as its statement of financial position and income statement.

In summary managerial accounting provides and interprets vital information assisting the running of the enterprise. In contrast financial accountants prepare the statements on which a business's past performance can be judged.

Test your learning

Short answer questions

1 a Define the term profit. [2]

   b Distinguish between an income statement and a statement of financial position. [3]

2 a Explain the difference between gross profit and net profit. [3]

   b State **two** stakeholders that may have an interest in a manufacturer's income statement. [2]

3 a Distinguish between retained and distributed profits. [3]

   b State **two** reasons a retailer may retain some of its profits. [2]

4 a Give **two** examples of current assets. [2]

   b Distinguish between current and non-current assets. [3]

5 a Define the term liabilities. [2]

   b Distinguish between non-current liabilities and total equity. [3]

6 Explain what is meant by a company's reserves and why they may increase. [5]

7 a State the formula necessary to calculate a company's current ratio. [2]

   b A major retailer has an acid test ratio of 0.72:1 for its latest trading year. Why might the company not be concerned about this figure? [3]

8 a State the formula necessary to calculate a business's net profit margin. [2]

   b Explain how a business might improve its net profit margin. [3]

9 a State **two** qualitative factors that may influence a business's financial performance. [2]

   b Explain why shareholders may have an interest in a company's financial statements. [3]

10 a Define the term working capital. [2]

    b Distinguish briefly between management and financial accountants. [3]

Data response question

Plata Oils Inc

Plata Oils Inc is exploring for oil in the Atlantic Ocean close to Argentina. The company has discovered and operates large oilfields in other parts of the world although it has not opened a new oilfield for eight years. It is optimistic that it will find large oil deposits at a time when world oil prices are rising. It has invested heavily in oil exploration over the last five years.

Its recent financial performance has not been good as its profit margin has declined by 40 per cent, it has encountered liquidity problems and it has faced accusations of window dressing its accounts. The company has a well-established and consistent management team and many of its shareholders consider it to be a good long-term investment.

Questions

1 Explain the terms:

   a liquidity [3]

   b window dressing. [3]

2 Explain how the company might improve its profit margin. [6]

3 Evaluate the importance of Plata Oils Inc's accounts in judging the company's future financial performance. [10]

Essay questions

1 Explain how liquidity and profitability ratios may help managers to carry out their duties effectively. [8]

2 Discuss whether or not published accounts provide an accurate indication of a company's likely future financial performance. [12]

Past paper questions

1 a Explain the purpose of a company's statement of financial position and income statement. [8]

   b Discuss the usefulness of these accounts for managers and shareholders [12]

Adapted from Cambridge International AS and A Level Business Studies 9707 Paper 11 Q5 October/November 2009

2 Read the Loader Lorries case study on pages 209–10 and then answer following question.

   i Using the information in Table 1, calculate Loader Lorries' gross profit margin for 2010. [3]

   ii The gross profit margin for 2009 was 70%. Using Table 1, comment on the usefulness of the gross profit margin figures to the management of Loader Lorries. [3]

Cambridge International AS and A Level Business Studies 9707 Paper 21 Q1b May/June 2011

All the questions in this section are taken from Cambridge International's past papers in AS Business Studies. In each chapter we have recommended that you answer at least one part of these questions. However, you should attempt as many complete case studies as possible once you have studied the necessary chapters.

AS Level Paper 1

Section B (Essay)

Answer **one** question only.

5 a Outline the main factors which a manager of a large hotel might consider when carrying out manpower planning. [8]

   b Discuss the extent to which the hotel manager might improve workers' motivation by re-designing their jobs. [12]

6 Discuss the suitability of the various sources of finance a large business might use when replacing old machinery. [20]

7 a Outline the main determinants of demand for consumer goods in your country. [8]

   b Discuss how a clothes retailer might segment the market for its goods. [12]

Cambridge International AS and A Level Business Studies 9707 Paper 1 Q5, 6 & 7 May/June 2007

Section B (Essay)

Answer **one** question only.

5 a Explain why retail businesses should prepare cash flow forecasts. [8]

   b Discuss ways in which a business might improve its cash flow. [12]

6 Discuss how the objectives of stakeholder groups in a profitable business might be in conflict. [20]

7 a Explain how a business might use financial rewards to motivate workers. [8]

   b Discuss why a business might use non-financial rewards to motivate its workers. [12]

Cambridge International AS and A Level Business Studies 9707 Paper 12 Q5, 6 & 7 May/June 2010

Section B (Essay)

Answer **one** question only.

5 a Explain how a business might be affected by political and legal constraints. [8]

   b Discuss how the objectives of a manufacturing business might be affected by ethical issues. [12]

6 Discuss the qualities required by effective business leaders. [20]

7 a Explain how the product life cycle might be used by the finance manager of a business. [8]

   b Discuss how and why promotional activity might change at different stages of a product's life cycle. [12]

Cambridge International AS and A Level Business Studies 9707 Paper 1 Q5, 6 & 7 May/June 2008

Section B (Essay)

Answer **one** question only.

5 a Management has been described as getting things done through people. Given this
   description, explain the importance of management for a large business organisation. [8]

  b Discuss the view that a manager will be more effective by adopting a democratic rather
   than an autocratic leadership style. [12]

6 Discuss how, and to what extent, break-even analysis might be used as an aid to
  decision making in a large manufacturing business. [20]

7 a Information is collected by the Human Resources Department (Personnel). Explain how
   a business might use this information. [8]

  b Discuss the limitations of using purely numerical data when making business decisions. [12]

Cambridge International AS and A Level Business Studies 9707 Paper 1 Q5, 6 & 7 October/November 2008

Section B (Essay)

Answer **one** question only.

5 a With the aid of an appropriate diagram, explain the stages of a product life cycle. [8]

  b Discuss how a business might use a product life cycle to plan the marketing of a product. [12]

6 Discuss how the management of an airline might motivate its cabin crew*. You should make
  reference to relevant motivation theories you have studied. [20]

7 a Explain the usefulness to a new business of cash flow forecasts. [8]

  b Discuss the importance of published accounts to **three** stakeholder groups in assessing
   the performance of a company which is planning to expand. [12]

*cabin crew: in an aircraft, the people whose job it is to take care of the passengers.

Cambridge International AS and A Level Business Studies 9707 Paper 12 Q5, 6 & 7 May/June 2011

AS Level Paper 2

Newtown College

Newtown College (NC) is a successful college but is facing increasing costs and falling revenues. NC is in the private sector.

The college management is discussing a scheme to provide extra revenue by renting out facilities during the school holidays. Potential customers include:

- Local businesses (for training)

- Clubs (for sports events)

- Exam boards (for meetings).

Rooms will have to be improved to ensure high quality facilities and furnishings. There will need to be access to telephones, copiers and the Internet, as well as facilities for refreshments.

Following market research, the Principal of NC has prepared the following cash flow forecast for the next summer holidays if the scheme is implemented:

Table 2 ($000)

Week	1	2	3	4
Opening balance	0	−12	−16	−4
Cash inflow	0	10	20	30
Refurbishment costs	10	10	0	0
Operating costs	0	2	4	6
Staff costs	2	2	4	6
Closing balance	−12	−16	−4	X

The Principal would like to appoint an Office Manager to run the new scheme. The job would be part-time during term time and full-time during the college holidays. NC would not be able to afford a high salary. The Principal is keen on delegation. The Office Manager would be responsible for all aspects of managing the facilities including marketing.

a Explain the following terms:

   i   private sector (line 2)   [3]

   ii delegation (line 22).   [3]

b i Calculate the value of X in the cash flow forecast (Table 2).   [3]

   ii Using Table 2 and your answer to part **i**, briefly explain how this cash flow forecast might change if lower cash inflow is predicted.   [3]

c Analyse methods of market research that NC might have used to identify the likely demand for their facilities.   [8]

d Discuss the factors that NC needs to consider when recruiting and selecting an Office Manager.   [10]

Cambridge International AS and A Level Business Studies 9707 Paper 21 Q2 October/November 2010

Loader Lorries (LL)

LL is a public limited company which manufactures lorries (trucks) for use in road transport.

The lorry market has grown rapidly in recent years and LL has expanded. As a result LL has experienced diseconomies of scale.

However, the international lorry industry is now going through a difficult period. There is falling demand and excess production worldwide. As a result, LL's profits have fallen.

Table 1 Extract from accounts ($m)

	2009	2010
Sales	100	90
Cost of Sales (cost of goods sold)	30	35

In addition to falling profits, there are two problems which need urgent consideration: inventory (stock) control and workforce issues.

Inventory control

Recent data shows significant differences in the inventory levels of two key components: engines and gearboxes.

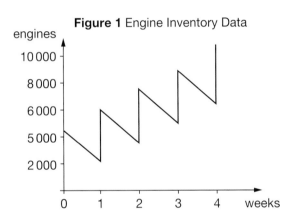

Figure 1 Engine Inventory Data

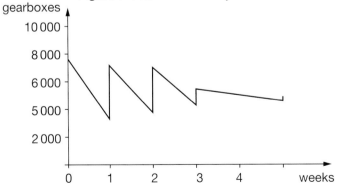

Figure 2 Gearbox Inventory Data

Bert, who orders engines, has argued that demand for lorries will soon recover. Fred, who orders gearboxes, is expecting a new, more efficient, gearbox to become available soon.

Workforce issues

There is evidence that the motivation of LL's workforce is declining, with increased absenteeism, poor quality production and increasing staff turnover. Industrial action over pay is possible.

In 2008 Voltaire, the Managing Director, negotiated a new employment contract with the production workers. The aim was to achieve a more flexible workforce and lower labour costs. The new contract included:

- Greater training opportunities

- Flexible but longer working hours

- Improved staff facilities including rest rooms

- Improved redundancy terms.

20

25

As a result LL's working conditions are better than for similar local businesses but LL's average wages are lower. The contract has produced improved efficiency, although many workers have been made redundant.

a Explain the following terms:

   i Diseconomies of scale (line 3)   [3]

   ii Cost of sales (cost of goods sold) (line 9).   [3]

b i Using the information in Table 1, calculate LL's gross profit margin for 2010.   [3]

   ii The gross profit margin for 2009 was 70%. Using Table 1, comment on the usefulness of the gross profit margin figures to the management of LL.   [3]

c Discuss the extent to which the new employment contract has created the motivation problems at LL.   [10]

d Using the information in Figures 1 and 2, analyse the differences between the two approaches to managing inventories (stocks).   [8]

Cambridge International AS and A Level Business Studies 9707 Paper 21 Q1 May/June 2011

Cheapo Air

Cheapo Air (CA) is a low cost airline operating only on popular routes. These routes are facing more and more competition from rival airlines. CA's profit margin is falling. CA is able to offer cheap flights by employing only the minimum number of staff. Customers get a flight and little more.

In order to restore profit margins, the Board of CA are considering changing from the low cost market to the market for business customers. CA would need to change the interiors of all their aircraft which would involve large capital expenditure. The change would mean a 33% reduction in the number of seats available on each flight. Business customers expect greater comfort and better service. This includes attentive cabin crew, meals and other refreshments, access to business services as well as more comfort and space. The business market is less competitive than the low cost market. The business market is relatively price inelastic.

CA has estimated the following financial information for the most popular route:

Table 1 Comparison Data

	Low Cost	Business
Available seats	300	200
Operating cost per seat	$100	$150
Price per seat	$150	$ not yet decided
Operating profit per flight	$15 000	$ not yet decided

CA's main competitor is charging $180 per seat for business customers but the service and comfort are not as good as what CA are planning.

a Explain the following terms:

  i   profit margin (line 2) [3]

  ii   price inelastic (line 10). [3]

b i   Calculate the price that CA would have to charge business customers to achieve the same operating profit per flight as for low cost flights. [3]

  ii   Briefly comment on your answer to **b i**. [3]

c Analyse the factors that CA would need to consider in setting a price for their business customers. [8]

d Discuss the human resource management (HRM) issues that would arise if CA did switch from low cost flights to business flights. [10]

Cambridge International AS and A Level Business Studies 9707 Paper 21 Q2 May/June 2009

Rex Cinema

Attendances at cinemas across the country have been declining for several years. For most cinemas, profits before tax (net profits) have been falling and some cinemas have closed recently. Ike and Tina, the owners of Rex, are worried that the business may make a loss next year unless something is done to increase revenues and reduce costs. Most of the costs involved in operating a cinema are fixed. Only the costs of hiring films and purchasing food and drinks for sale are variable or semi-variable costs.

Tina does not understand why attendances are falling. Rex's mission statement (their overall objective) is: 'we aim to be recognised as the best cinema in town'. Tina thinks that they have achieved this by providing comfortable seats at good prices. She wonders what else they can do.

Ike is interested in increasing revenue by putting on extra film shows, late at night. He believes that this will be profitable if more than 150 people attend each film show. He estimates the fixed costs to be $300 per show, with the variable costs at $0.50 per person. The cinema holds 175 people.

Tina does not know whether there is a market for these extra film shows. Friends have told her that they would attend once a week and she knows that another cinema in the same town has already started late night showings of particular types of films.

Some of Rex's customers think that Rex Cinema has:

- Uncomfortable seats

- High prices

- Boring films

- Expensive refreshments

- Poor facilities.

However, a recent review in the local newspapers praised Rex for providing 'imaginative and challenging entertainment in traditional surroundings'.

a Explain the following terms:

   i   profits before tax (net profits) (line 2)   [3]

   ii fixed costs (lines 12–13).   [3]

b i Calculate the price that Ike would need to charge in order to break even at 150 people per extra film show.   [3]

   ii If Rex charged $2 then the break-even would increase to 200 people. Comment briefly on the usefulness to Ike of the break-even information.   [3]

c Analyse the **methods** of primary research that Ike and Tina could use before making a decision about the extra film shows.   [8]

d Discuss the extent to which Rex's overall objective is being achieved.   [10]

Cambridge International AS and A Level Business Studies 9707 Paper 22 Q2 October/November 2011

Joe's World

Joe owns and manages a farm producing cereals for export. The farm has been in Joe's family for over 100 years. The export market is highly dependent on exchange rates. Joe's average net profit for the last three years was $30 000.

Joe has been approached by Wind4U, a business that installs and operates wind turbines for generating electricity. Wind4U say that the location of Joe's farm is ideal for a large wind farm (one hundred large wind turbines capable of supplying electricity for the nearby city). Joe would receive a rent from Wind4U. Joe would be unable to farm the land taken up by the turbines and he would also need to replace farm buildings and build access roads to enable him to continue farming. This would cost Joe $60 000 to set up.

Joe has made the following estimates ($000):

		Take contract with Wind4U	
Investment		60	
	Rent from Wind4U	Loss of Farm income	
Year 1	40	10	
Year 2	40	10	
Year 3	40	10	
Year 4	40	10	

Joe knows that in other countries wind farms have been very controversial. There are concerns about the impact on the local environment. However, without the development there will continue to be unreliable electricity supplies from sources that are less environmentally friendly.

The wind farm would be the first in Joe's country and he wondered whether building a Visitor's Centre, complete with café, would be a good enterprise.

a Explain the following terms:

  i export market (line 2) [3]

  ii net profit (line 2). [3]

b i Calculate the Average Rate of Return (ARR) for the contract with Wind4U. [2]

  ii Explain the usefulness to Joe of your answer to i. [2]

  iii Explain how exchange rates might influence Joe's decision whether to accept Wind4U's contract. [4]

c Briefly examine how Joe might research the market for the Visitor Centre. [6]

d Evaluate how stakeholders in the farm, other than Joe, might react to the proposed contract with Wind4U. [10]

Adapted From Cambridge International AS and A Level Business Studies 9707 Paper 21 Q2 October/November 2009

Bee's Meals

Mrs Bee runs Bee's Meals (BM) as a sole trader. She started her business 5 years ago providing cooked food to a local restaurant. The business now employs 5 of Mrs Bee's friends and her son, and she supplies 10 restaurants. Mrs Bee wants to continue expanding the business and she sees an opportunity to supply workers at an industrial site 10 km away with lunches (hot and cold). She would have to sell her current premises and move to new larger rented premises nearby. She would have to change the production system from batch to flow, which would involve buying new equipment.

She is concerned about how her employees might react to moving and to changes in the way that they work. She has the following information on the proposed change:

Table 1 Data for proposed new equipment

Cost	$100 000
Estimated payback period	2 years
Expected useful life	5 years
Residual value	$20 000

Mrs Bee is wondering about possible sources of finance for the expansion and she has the following financial information:

Table 2 Financial data and forecasts ($000)

	2006	2007 forecast
Retained Profit	25	50
Fixed Assets	50	50
Working Capital	10	20
Long term Loans	5	5
Owner's capital	25	25

Answer **all** the questions.

a Explain the following terms:

   i sole trader (line 1)   [3]

   ii payback. (line 12)   [3]

b **i** Calculate the annual depreciation on the new equipment using the straight-line method.   [3]

   ii Briefly explain how depreciation affects BM's accounts.   [3]

c With reference to Table 2 discuss possible internal sources of finance for BM's proposed expansion.   [8]

d Discuss the impact on BM and its workers of a change from batch to flow production.   [10]

Cambridge International AS and A Level Business Studies 9707 Paper 2 Q2 May/June 2007

Ganmor Cars

Ganmor Cars (GC) is a private limited company. It manufactures cars to customer specifications. GC is a small scale operation.

The following extracts highlight some of the issues of concern to the business.

Extract from Business News

Governments around the world are trying to tackle the problems arising from climate change. Many governments are considering taxes on 'gas guzzling' cars and increasing 'green' taxes on fuels such as diesel and petrol. 5

Extract from Car News

Large, multinational car manufacturers continue to face declining profits, particularly for their larger, more expensive cars. Car buyers around the world are expecting greater fuel efficiency and safety, as well as higher quality and greater reliability. These all add to production costs. Strong competition has meant lower prices for cars. 10

Extract from a Ganmor Cars press release

Ganmor Cars (GC), the manufacturer of specialist 'off road' cars, continues to see strong growth. Sales in our niche markets (farming, mining etc.) have been added to by sales to wealthy customers who buy our cars as fashion items, despite the high running costs. We are considering extending our product portfolio by adding a range of smaller family cars. This new range will be instantly recognisable as a GC car, but will be cheaper and more fuel efficient. We currently use job production to make each car to the customer's specification. We are planning to use lean production techniques including Total Quality Management for the new range of smaller family cars. This will enable us to achieve economies of scale, as well as maintaining our reputation for reliability and quality. 15 20

a Explain the terms:

  i multinational (line 9) [3]

  ii economies of scale (line 22). [3]

b Analyse how the Government might influence the activities of GC. [8]

c Describe how lean production techniques might be used at GC. [6]

d Discuss the factors that would influence GC's choice of a marketing mix. [10]

Cambridge International AS and A Level Business Studies 9707 Paper 2 Q2 May/June 2008

19 Business structure and size

Chapter overview

In this chapter we examine:
- local, national and multinational businesses
- international trading links
- governments and business – privatisation and nationalisation
- business growth – integration, joint ventures and strategic alliances.

19.1 Local, national and multinational businesses

Key term

Multinational businesses are those with production facilities in more than one country.

Local businesses

A local business will only sell its products within a relatively small geographical area. You are likely to be a customer of local businesses on a fairly regular basis. Such businesses will probably be relatively small in scale and may be sole traders. A business may decide to remain local because the owner(s) wish it to remain small or because the type of product or service is best supplied within a limited geographical area. For example, dentists tend to operate within local markets because it is not cost-effective for patients to travel long distances to receive dental treatment.

Table 19.1 A summary of local, national and multinational businesses

Type of business	Examples	Likely objectives	Possible legal structure
Local	Food retailers, hairdressers, state schools	Survival, satisficing, providing a service	Sole trader Private limited company
National	House builders, supermarkets, water supply	Maximising profits, providing a service, growth	Partnership Private company Public company
Multinational	Car manufacturers, airlines, computer manufacturers	Profit maximisation, growth, market domination	Public company

National businesses

A national business has all its production capacity within a single country, although it may sell its goods and services overseas. For example, the main intercity passenger train operator in Malaysia is Keretapi Tanah Melayu Berhad (KTMB), a business that is owned by the Malaysian government. It operates intercity passenger services on main lines and the Bukit Mertajam-Butterworth branch. The company is based entirely in Malaysia and it sells its services to foreign tourists and business travellers as well as Malaysians.

Businesses may remain national in scope because of practical limitations, as in the case of KTMB, or because its products are only in demand in one country – this may be the case for certain local food producers. Finally, a business may decide to operate at a national level because its owners do not wish to take the risk of operating in other countries.

Multinational businesses

A **multinational** corporation (MNC) is a business organisation which has its headquarters in one country but has operations in a range of different countries. There are numerous examples of such organisations, car manufacturers like Ford, Toyota, Honda and Volkswagen, oil companies like Shell, BP and Exxon Mobil, technology companies like Google, Microsoft and Amazon.

Multinational companies operate a global strategy making strategic decisions in terms of resources, facilities and markets available throughout the world. Many businesses trade as multinationals to exploit the cheap labour and other resources available in developing countries. Furthermore, by selling in global markets, multinationals can reap the advantage of economies of scale. The trend in many markets is towards fewer, larger producers. The global car manufacturing industry is an example of this with many mergers and takeovers in recent years. Business analysts forecast only three or four major producers will remain by 2015.

Multinational businesses, by their very nature, tend to be large or very large organisations. Research by the United Nations has revealed that approximately 35000 businesses in the world can be classified as multinationals. The largest one hundred of these companies account for about 40 per cent of international trade.

Their size means they often have considerable power and influence and as a result have come in for some criticism of their actions. Events such as the tax avoidance scandal in the UK and other European countries (covered in the case study below) have attracted much criticism and, sometimes, an assumption that MNCs are always a 'bad' thing.

Case Study

Multinationals under spotlight for tax avoidance

One of the UK government's most important committees has called for multinational companies that make substantial sales in the UK, but pay little tax there, to pay a fair and reasonable amount of tax on profits. This follows demands from politicians in other European and Asian countries for measures to tackle corporate tax avoidance. A number of multinational businesses, including Coca-Cola, Google, Amazon and Starbucks, have been strongly criticised for operating policies to reduce declared profits to avoid paying corporation taxes on these profits. Starbucks has received much adverse publicity for only recording a profit in one of its last 15 years' trading in the UK. Similarly Coca-Cola has been criticised by the authorities in Vietnam and has been investigated by tax authorities.

The UK government's Public Accounts Committee (PAC) said that the government should set down rules limiting activities that reduce companies' tax bills, as well as working with other countries to limit profit-shifting across borders.

'Global companies with huge operations in the UK generating significant amounts of income are getting away with paying little or no corporation tax here,' said Margaret Hodge, who chairs the PAC. 'This is outrageous, and an insult to British businesses and individuals who pay their fair share.'

Questions

1 Explain why multinational companies such as Coca-Cola are often able to make higher profit margins than those that operate in a single country. [8]

2 Evaluate the possible consequences for the UK or Vietnam if multinationals such as Google and Coca-Cola are forced to pay higher rates of taxation. [16]

Why do companies want to become multinationals?

For many companies, the following might be some or all of the reasons to expand into different countries:

- Reduce transport and distribution costs by producing nearer to markets. Thus some multinationals seek to expand to Asian countries as sales are growing for many products in that part of the world.
- To be able to sell in new markets by locating in them. This can help a business such as Lenovo or Walmart to develop a recognised brand.
- Secure supplies of raw materials or markets. There may be controls on exporting certain raw materials so, by locating in the country concerned, businesses can avoid such regulations.
- There may be cost advantages, most often in terms of low labour costs. Many countries have created production facilities in countries with low labour costs. For example, Coca-Cola established production facilities in Vietnam in 1993 to take advantage of low production costs.

The case for and against multinationals

The activities of multinational companies have attracted a lot of attention in the media over recent years and have provoked strong reactions among stakeholder groups.

The advantages of multinationals to host countries

- **Economic growth and employment** Multinationals bring foreign investment to countries that are not their home base. If they choose to expand by building production facilities they will be bringing investment into the country or cutting unemployment as well as helping the sales figures of local businesses which supply them with goods and services. The effects of the investment might be seen as essential for helping a country escape from poverty or vital in promoting economic development within the country.

- **Skills, production techniques and improvements in the quality of the workforce** It can be argued that multinationals bring with them new ideas and new techniques that can help to improve the quality of production and help boost the quality of human capital in the host country. Many will not only look to employ local labour but also provide them with training and new skills to help them improve productivity and efficiency.
- **Availability of quality goods and services in the host country** In some cases, a multinational's production in a particular country may be primarily aimed at the export market. However, in other cases, much of the multinational's production may be aimed at consumers in the country in which the products are produced. In the case of many Japanese car manufacturers, the investment made into UK production has enabled them to get a foothold in the European Union and to avoid tariff barriers. Consumers in the UK have had access to high quality vehicles at cheaper prices and the competition this has created has also led to improvements in working practices, prices and quality in other related industries.
- **Improvements in infrastructure** In addition to the investment in a country in production or distribution facilities, a company might also invest in additional infrastructure facilities like road, rail, port and communications networks. This can provide benefits for the whole country in that it creates employment as well as providing improved facilities for 'home' businesses.

The disadvantages of multinationals

If a country plays host to a multinational company it may pay one or more of the costs below.

- **The effect on employment may be minor** If the multinational uses skilled employees, many jobs might go to skilled workers from other countries rather than to domestic workers. Alternatively, a multinational company may operate capital intensive systems of production using little labour from the domestic country. Thus the effect on employment may be minimal and the wages paid to these workers may not stay in the host country.
- **Some MNCs may be 'footloose'** This means that they might locate in a country to gain advantages in terms of lower rates of taxation or lax regulations on environmental protection. However, the multinational may relocate elsewhere if regulations are tightened or tax rates increased. As a result there might not be a long-term benefit to the country.
- **Pollution and environmental damage** Some countries may have less rigorous regulatory authorities that fail to monitor the environmental impact of multinationals' activities effectively. This can cause long-term problems. In India, Coca-Cola has been accused of using up water supplies in its bottling plant in Kerala, Southern India, and also of dumping waste products onto land and claiming it was useful as fertiliser when it appeared to have no such beneficial properties.

- **Profits leaving the host country** Profits might go back to the headquarters of the multinational rather than being reinvested within the host country. This may lead to lower rates of employment and GDP in the host country than might have been expected.

19.2 International trading links

Deindustrialisation is the reduction in the relative contribution of the manufacturing sector to a nation's production.

The Asia-Pacific Economic Cooperation group is a loose grouping of 21 of the countries bordering the Pacific Ocean which have agreed to introduce policies to allow and encourage free trade.

The importance of international trade

International trade is important for businesses in economies throughout the world. It is important for a number of reasons.

- It provides supplies of raw materials and components for businesses at highly competitive prices. This enables importers to be price competitive in turn as costs are lowered below what they would have been without international trade.
- It opens up markets for the goods and services that they produce. This can assist businesses in increasing sales and profitability. The case study below shows how the Australian mining industry (and the Australian economy generally) have benefited from its export links with China. It also allows businesses to enter new markets benefiting from economies of scale.
- Engaging in international trade can increase and stabilise a business's sales over time. Trading overseas assists businesses to extend the life cycles of their products. For example, many London-based fashion houses are selling products in the southern hemisphere targeting Australia, New Zealand and South Africa in particular. Many items of fashion clothing have notoriously short life cycles and this is one way of extending a summer season for fashion clothes, boosting sales and profits. Equally, in a period of low economic growth such as that experienced by most European countries at the time of writing, overseas markets such as those in Asia can be highly lucrative and rescue flagging sales.
- Exposure to international competition can encourage domestic businesses to improve their efficiency to increase the chances of survival. It may also result in businesses adopting modern and more productive methods of production to enhance competitiveness.

International trade is forecast to grow steadily by 8 per cent per annum to 2030, outpacing GDP growth as barriers to trade are dismantled. This is shown in Figure 19.1. Between 2013 and 2030, the HSBC Bank forecasts that global GDP will grow by an average annual rate of just under 4 per cent.

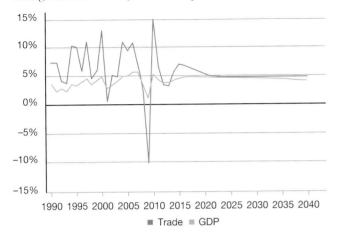

Figure 19.1 Growth in GDP and trade (% year growth)

Source: HSBC, October 2013 https://globalconnections.hsbc.com

Australia's mining boom

Figure 19.2 An open mine in Australia

The extraordinary economic growth rates achieved by China since the early 1990s have been a major influence on the Australian economy, and especially on its mining industry, much of which is located in Western Australia and the Northern Territory. As China's rate of economic growth has reached 10 per cent per year its demand for Australian resources soared to supply the roads, infrastructure and the products it exports throughout the world. Australian exports to China rose in value by ten times from $5 billion in 2002–03 to approximately $50 billion in 2010–11. There were a number of other significant changes resulting from increased exports of primary resources to China between 2002 and 2012.

- Weekly household incomes in Western Australia and the Northern Territory went up 66 per cent and 56 per cent respectively (compared to 30 per cent in the rest of Australia).
- In 2011–12, 250 000 people were employed in mining compared to 90 000 in 2002.
- Iron ore prices increased by 600 per cent, and coal prices rose by between 300 per cent and 500 per cent as China used more electricity in its homes and factories.
- Investment in mine projects or infrastructure in Australia increased from $12 billion in 2002–03 to more than $82 billion in 2011–12.

Since 2002 Australia's resources industry has benefited enormously from a prolonged surge of demand from China and other emerging economies. This has stimulated the national economy and kept export prices at historically high levels.

Questions

1 Explain the possible problems that businesses in China may face as a result of the high rates of economic growth in the country. [8]

2 Have all the stakeholders of Chinese manufacturing businesses benefited from the increasing levels of trade with Australia? Justify your opinion. [16]

Changes in the global economy and the pattern of international trade

There have been a number of changes in the global economy which have had significant consequences for the type of goods that are traded and the countries involved in international trade.

- **The emergence of regional trading blocs** In these blocs members freely trade with each other, but erect barriers to trade with non-members. The creation of these trading blocs, such as the European Union and the **Asia-Pacific Economic Cooperation group**, has led to more trade between members, while countries outside the bloc have suffered from a lack of access to certain markets.

- **A decline in trade in manufactured goods for some economies** Many developed economies such as the USA and the UK have experienced a decline in trade in manufactured goods relative to their trade in commercial and financial services. Many of these advanced economies have experienced **deindustrialisation**, with less national output generated by their manufacturing sectors.

Asia is forecast by analysts at the HSBC Bank to see the fastest growth in merchandise exports between now and 2030, with China, India and Vietnam averaging over 10 per cent annual growth, and South Korea not far behind.

Exports from the advanced European economies of the UK, Ireland, France and Germany are forecast to expand more slowly, at a little over 3.5 per cent a year, while Japan and the USA are both set for trade growth to average around 5.5 per cent a year.

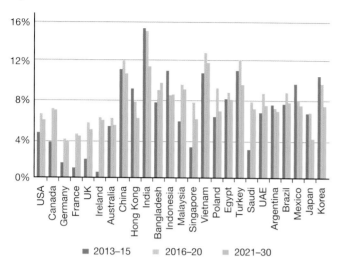

Figure 19.3 Growth in exports (% year growth)
Source: HSBC, October 2013 https://globalconnections.hsbc.com

Figure 19.3 shows the forecast rates of growth for exports for selected countries in three separate periods up to 2030. It is noticeable that some newer emerging economies such as Vietnam and Turkey are forecast to have high rates of growth in exports in the 2020s.

19.3 Governments and businesses

The extent to which a government owns and controls businesses within an economy varies across the world. It is also a matter of intense political debate. However, in many countries over recent years there has been a trend towards loosening the control that governments exercise over businesses. This trend is perhaps most noticeable in China since the early 1990s.

Nationalisation

Governments across the globe own and operate businesses or even entire industries. Such state-owned businesses are often referred to as nationalised businesses. There are a number of reasons why a government may opt to take control of a business through a process known as **nationalisation**.

- **Ensuring that the industry has objectives that assist the economy** If governments control a business or industry because it is nationalised it is possible to ensure that the enterprise operates in the best interests of the entire economy. In early 2013 the South African government announced that it would not nationalise its mining industry for fear that this would hit investment by foreign businesses. However, it did propose high taxes on the industry and the creation of a state-owned mining company to ensure that profits remained in South Africa and that domestic businesses could buy mined products at favourable prices.
- **Better industrial relations** In many cases trade unions and employees believe that they are treated more fairly by government-owned businesses rather than by privately owned businesses. It may be that some privately owned businesses focus squarely on short-term profits with adverse consequences for rates of pay and working conditions. As a consequence employee motivation and performance may be impaired.
- **High levels of investment are required** Some industries require long-term investment to improve facilities and services over time. This long-term investment may not be profitable in the short term, and this may discourage privately owned businesses from engaging in it. Thus certain industries such as railways may suffer from lack of investment without government intervention, possibly in the form of nationalisation. In such a circumstance consumers and other businesses may suffer.
- **Natural monopolies** Governments have nationalised certain industries because they are considered to be natural monopolies. An example of this could be the supply of water to homes and businesses. In such a situation it is most efficient to have a single business to avoid wasteful duplication of resources such as networks of pipes to supply water. Thus there is no benefit from competition. However, a privately owned natural monopoly could easily exploit its power and set higher prices to consumers. Thus nationalisation and government control of natural monopoly prevents this exploitation of monopoly power.
- **Avoidance of externalities** Some of the nationalised industries have the potential to create significant positive externalities (that is, benefits to those not involved in production or consumption of the product). For example, public transport plays a key role in reducing pollution and congestion by reducing the number of cars on the roads. A private business would ignore the positive externalities, but a government-run public transport system could invest in public transport to help improve the economic infrastructure and the well-being of all in society.

During the latter stages of the twentieth century criticisms of nationalised industries became more common. Much of the criticism centred on the potential for inefficiency because nationalised industries do not have the profit incentive. Thus inefficient operating practices existed, meaning that consumers were judged to be paying high prices for goods and services of questionable quality.

Furthermore, governments realised that by selling nationalised industries to private owners they could raise huge amounts of capital, allowing them to reduce rates of taxation without harming the government's financial position. As a consequence privatisation became increasingly common in many countries.

Privatisation

Privatisation is the process of transferring organisations from the state to the ownership and control of individuals and other businesses. In the 1980s and 1990s many major state enterprises were sold into the private sector and the policy has continued in recent years, although it has slowed as the state owns relatively few enterprises. In the UK since 2000 the London Underground system has been partly privatised, as has the port of Dover. In 1969 the Indian government nationalised the country's banks. In 2012 it passed an amendment to the country's banking laws which allows the private ownership of banks once again. The wheel has turned full circle.

The arguments in favour of privatisation are considerable.

- By removing potentially inefficient monopolies privatisation offers consumers the possibilities of lower prices and better-quality products. Businesses in competitive markets cannot afford to be inefficient. The policy is based on the unshakeable belief in the superiority of private enterprise.
- Private businesses are more likely to pursue long-term policies to increase the prosperity of the businesses, to the benefit of all in society. In contrast, the objectives of nationalised industries were unclear and inconsistent in the UK, often little more than breaking even.
- The process of privatisation can provide huge sums of revenue for the government. This can assist the government in improving the country's infrastructure or reducing rates of taxation on businesses. In addition, privatisation means that governments no longer have to subsidise inefficient industries. Pakistan has proposed privatising the Pakistan Steel Mills Corporation because it is incurring losses of 1.6 billion rupees per month.

However, the drawbacks of privatisation are apparent.

- Critics have argued that privatisation has not, in fact, resulted in more efficient industries. In the UK the establishment of watchdogs such as OFGAS and OFTEL have highlighted that, left to their own devices, the newly privatised companies might exploit consumers through excessive prices and poor quality products.
- Some economists have argued that having thousands of UK citizens as shareholders in privatised businesses has not encouraged long-term strategies to be implemented by the businesses. Shareholders, having limited understanding of business, have looked for a quick return. This has encouraged managers to maximise short-term profits – a policy not necessarily in the long-term interests of the company or the economy.

The perceived shortcomings of privatisation have led to a mild backlash against the policy. Countries such as New Zealand have created new nationalised industries, and even California has taken steps in this direction. Government proposals to privatise the UK's forests encountered much opposition and the plans were abandoned.

19.4 Business growth

Key term

External growth occurs when a business grows by merging with or taking over another business.

External growth occurs when one firm decides to expand by joining together with another. This may occur either by a takeover (also called an acquisition) or a merger. Mergers and acquisitions are both forms of integration.

If one company wants to take over another it must buy 51 per cent of the other business's shares so that it has control of the business. It may buy these shares either by using cash or by offering its own shares in return (this is known as a paper offer). The buying company will make an offer to the shareholders of the other company. The directors of the targeted company will decide whether or not they think the bid is fair and whether or not to recommend to their own shareholders that they should accept it; if they reject the offer the takeover becomes a 'hostile bid'.

If there are not enough shareholders willing to accept the offer, the buying company may decide to increase the amount it offers for each share. There is, however, a strict timetable that the buying company has to follow, so it cannot keep increasing its offer indefinitely.

In a merger the two (or more) firms agree to form a new enterprise; shares in each of the individual companies are exchanged for shares in the new business.

Table 19.2 Mergers and takeovers

Mergers	Takeovers
A **merger** is the combining of two or more firms into a single business following agreement by the firms' management teams and shareholders.	A **takeover** occurs when one company acquires complete control of another by purchasing more than 50 per cent of its share capital.
Mergers may be: - **Horizontal** (between firms at the same stage of production in the same market) offering economies of scale - **Vertical** (between firms operating at different levels in the same market) providing certainty of supply or retail outlets - **Conglomerate** mergers between firms in unrelated markets reducing risk and allowing the transference of good practice.	Takeovers may be horizontal, vertical or conglomerate. Takeovers can also be: - **Hostile** where a predator company's attentions are unwelcome and the target may try to reject the move. The predator has only a limited time to persuade the target company's shareholders to accept the bid - **Friendly**, in which case the company to be taken over welcomes the purchase of its business and is likely to recommend that shareholders accept the bid.

Types of integration

Integration is a general term describing businesses coming together, whether through mergers or takeovers. There are three types of integration: horizontal, vertical and conglomerate.

Horizontal integration

Horizontal integration occurs when one firm joins with another at the same stage of the production process in the same industry. For example, when the Bank of Rajasthan merged with ICICI Bank this was an example of horizontal integration because they are both providing banking services to business and private customers.

The possible reasons for this type of integration include:

- **greater market share** – by combining, the two firms will have a greater share of the market and, as a result, they are likely to have more power over other members of the supply chain, such as suppliers and distributors
- **economies of scale** – larger-scale production may bring a reduction in unit costs due to financial, production or purchasing economies. This offers the possibility of increased profit margins or of lowering prices in price elastic markets while maintaining profit margins.
- **the opportunity to enter a different segment of the market** and thereby spread risks to some extent as it is less likely that a number of markets or segments will suffer a slump in sales simultaneously.

Case Study

Exxon Mobil

Exxon Mobil Corporation is an American multinational oil and gas company based in Texas. It was formed on 30 November 1998 when Exxon and Mobil agreed to terms on a $75.3 billion horizontal merger. The announcement of the merger led some analysts to doubt whether it would survive, let alone prosper. The critics felt that the two companies had very different cultures and that the senior managers in each company may find it difficult to cede any degree of control.

The scale of the new company was, and is, enormous. It is the largest company in the world based on revenue generated and operates 37 oil refineries in 21 countries. It refines 6.3 million barrels of oil each day and is significantly larger than its rivals in the oil industry. The merger was expected to generate enormous cost savings for the new business and this has proved to be the case. The forecast cost savings were $730 million from cutting 9 000 jobs and closing offices; $1.15 billion from removing any duplication in the new business. Total savings were ultimately 14 000 jobs cut and $3.8 billion in reduced costs annually.

Since the merger the company's share price has risen much more quickly than the average of share prices in the United States. The company's shares have risen by 85 per cent compared with 21 per cent in a US's share index.

Figure 19.4 An Exxon Mobil oil platform in the North Sea

Question

1 Explain the reasons why two oil companies would choose to merge. [8]
2 Do you think that all of the company's stakeholders will have benefited from this merger? Justify your view. [16]

Vertical integration

Vertical integration occurs when one firm joins with another at a different stage of the production process in the same industry. Forward vertical integration occurs when one firm joins with another business at a later stage in the same production process. Backward vertical integration occurs when one firm joins with another business at an earlier stage in the same production process. An example of backward integration occurred in 2012 when an Anglo-Swiss commodity trading company Glencore merged with the multinational mining company Xstrata to create a business valued at $66 billion.

Firms may undertake vertical integration for various reasons.

- **In order to gain control over supplies** This may be important for a firm to ensure it can maintain its supplies (e.g. in times of shortage) or if it is essential to maintain the quality of its supplies. By gaining control of its inputs a firm may also be able to deny competitors the supplies they want.

- **In order to guarantee access to the market** By buying up retailers, for example, manufacturers may ensure that their products actually get to the market and are displayed and promoted in the way they want.

A conglomerate merger

A conglomerate merger occurs when firms in different markets join together, for example, if a chocolate manufacturer merges with or takes over a hotel company. An example of such a takeover took place when Siemens, the Europe-based electronics and electrical engineering business, purchased a railway company from Invensys, a UK company.

A firm may become a conglomerate in order to spread its risk. By operating in several markets or countries a firm is less vulnerable to changes in any one market. However, in some ways conglomerate mergers are much riskier than other forms of integration because managers may be entering markets in which they have relatively little experience.

Problems following a merger or takeover

Although, in theory, integration can offer many potential advantages such as economies of scale, many mergers and takeovers are relatively unsuccessful. One of the main problems following integration is coping with the different cultures of the organisations involved. Employees are likely to have different values regarding key areas such as customer service, quality, investment and training and this can cause conflict. Employees from one organisation may find that behaviour that was praised and rewarded in the past is now criticised. There will also be adjustment problems regarding pay and conditions, for example, employees in one of the organisations may have a significantly better remuneration scheme than in the other – either the firm increases the rewards for one (which is expensive) or tries to negotiate the rewards of the other downwards (which will be unpopular).

Many firms also find that they experience diseconomies of scale following integration. Despite improvements in information technology, communication can be a problem and there can be a lack of a common sense of purpose. The result is often demotivation and a lack of coordination.

Furthermore, many of the supposed benefits of integration do not appear – computer systems turn out to be incompatible, employees do not cooperate and share information and the business lacks focus or control. As a result, integrated companies can find that their costs increase and that the returns generated are lower than would have been expected if they had remained single. Studies show that more than 60 per cent of mergers and takeovers actually destroy shareholder value (i.e. the companies combined are

eventually worth less than they would have been if they had remained separate). It is surprising, therefore, how many large-scale deals continue to occur. Examples of this include mergers or takeovers between AOL/Netscape, Exxon/Mobil, British Petroleum/Amoco, NationsBank/BankAmerica and Deutsche Bank/Bankers Trust.

In many cases the big deals are driven by a demand for greater scale. However, in reality, diseconomies of scale often seem to be the result, particularly when the merger or acquisition involves significant cultural, political, psychological and geographical differences. Charles Handy, a leading thinker and writer on organisational behaviour and management, believed that: 'Businesses can grow more profitable by becoming better, or leaner, or deeper, or more concentrated, without growing bigger. Bigness, in both business and life, can lead to a lack of focus, too much complexity and in the end, too wide a spread to control. We have to know when big is big enough.'

De-mergers

Over recent years there have been a number of cases of companies splitting into two or more separate elements. Sometimes de-mergers follow a takeover that has not been successful, perhaps because the expected economies of scale have not materialised. In India in 2012 there were a number of de-mergers including Wipro and Pantaloon Retail. Companies may decide to sell off peripheral divisions to concentrate on their core activities.

Stakeholders and integration

Not all stakeholders benefit from the process of integration. Even those that may expect to benefit may, especially in the longer-term, be disadvantaged.

- **Employees** The employees of both companies may feel insecure following a merger or takeover. It may be that jobs are duplicated and a programme of rationalisation has been introduced to remove unnecessary staff and to cut costs. This may threaten jobs at all levels within the organisation. Remaining employees may find working conditions and pay rates change (not always for the better) or that they are redeployed to a new workplace.
- **Shareholders** This stakeholder group would expect to benefit from integration. The process may force up share prices and increase long-term profits. Benefits accruing from the existence of greater economies of scale could also be expected to benefit shareholders. However, as we saw earlier, many mergers and takeovers do not increase shareholder value.
- **Customers** It is possible for customers to benefit from lower prices due to economies of scale or through innovative products from enlarged businesses with greater resources for research and development. However, this may be balanced to some extent by a loss of choice, especially if the integration results in a reduction in brands available.

- **Governments** It is more difficult to assess the likely impact on this stakeholder group. It may suffer if the integration results in a business relocating overseas with a consequent loss of employment and tax revenue. On the other hand, it may be that the business's increased scale and range of activities increases profits and employment opportunities in a particular country.
- **Competitors** Mergers and takeovers are generally bad news for the newly enlarged business's rivals. The new business has greater resources to invest in new product development and promotion. Although it may face short-term difficulties it is likely to be a stronger competitor in the long term.

Joint ventures and strategic alliances

Key terms

Joint ventures take place when two or more companies start a project or establish a business division that they can operate between them.

Strategic alliances are agreements to cooperate by two or more businesses to achieve common objectives.

The distinction between joint ventures and strategic alliances is that, in the case of alliances, a new enterprise is not formed to carry out the common project. The cooperating businesses that make up a strategic alliance carry out their operations as separate firms.

Strategic alliances

Strategic alliances may be local, national or global. All are similar in approach and operation. A global strategic alliance is usually established when a company wishes to enter into a new business or new geographic market. Such alliances may be used where the government prohibits imports in order to protect domestic industry. Typically, alliances are formed between two or more corporations, each based in their home country, for a specified period of time. Their purpose is to maximise competitive advantages in their combined territories. Car manufacturers Renault and Nissan have operated a strategic alliance since 1999. The key features of this are as follows:

- The companies own shares in one another. Renault has a 44.4 per cent stake in Nissan, and Nissan owns 15 per cent of Renault.
- Combined vehicle sales for the two manufacturers increased from 4.9 million vehicles in 1999 to more than 8.03 million units in 2011.
- The alliance represented the world's third-largest automotive group in 2011.

- The alliance has a significant presence in many of the major world markets including the United States, Europe, Japan, China, India and Russia.

Joint ventures

Joint ventures involve the creation of a new jointly owned business. All parties to the venture own part of the new enterprise and normally contribute to its management. The companies concerned share revenues, expenses and assets. While joint ventures are generally small projects, major corporations also use this method to diversify into new products or markets. A joint venture can ensure the success of smaller projects for those that are just starting in the business world or for established corporations. Since the cost of starting new projects is generally high, a joint venture allows both parties to share the burden of the project, as well as the resulting profits.

The brewers SABMiller and the Molson Coors Brewing Company have operated a joint venture since 2007. This enterprise was established to sell well-known brands of beer such as Miller Lite and Molson Canadian. The aim of the venture is to combine the two companies' brewing facilities and other resources to help them to compete more effectively against large rivals.

Case Study

Sony Ericsson – a ten-year joint venture

Sony Ericsson was a joint venture created by the Japanese electronics company Sony Corporation and the Swedish telecommunications company Ericsson. The joint venture was formed to manufacture mobile phones. This venture offered the benefit of bringing together Sony's consumer electronics expertise and Ericsson's technological leadership in the communications sector. Both companies ceased manufacturing their own mobile phones.

However, in 2012 the joint venture was ended on Sony's initiative. The Japanese company invested more than $1.6 billion to take control of the handset manufacturing joint venture, Sony Ericsson.

The Japanese electronics corporation announced that the move was intended to create an integrated approach to its smartphones and enable it to use its content across its range of smartphones, PCs, TVs and tablets. These are all manufactured by Sony and the joint venture hindered this uniform approach.

A Sony spokesperson said that the purchase of Ericsson's 50 per cent stake in the former joint venture would enable it to be more innovative with its smartphones and allow consumers to connect with content 'wherever they are, whenever they want'. This would help to make the company's full range of products more attractive to consumers.

Smartphone sales are forecast to increase over future years and this move will assist Sony in selling consumers complete 'families' of products, increasing its sales and brand recognition.

Questions

1 Explain why these companies may have decided on a joint venture rather than a merger. [8]
2 To what extent do you think that Ericsson benefited from this joint venture? [16]

The benefits

- Businesses cooperating in these ways avoid the need for a complete merger and therefore at least some of the managerial, cultural and other problems that were discussed earlier.

- Joint ventures or strategic alliances can create synergy when well-matched organisations cooperate in the pursuit of agreed objectives.
- The cost of a joint venture or strategic alliance is usually shared equitably among the businesses involved, and is generally the least expensive way for all concerned to form a partnership.

The drawbacks

- There may be some loss of control over such important issues as product quality or operating costs which can affect profitability.
- Communication problems can still occur due to cultural differences or incompatible management information systems.
- If one business is a junior partner in the venture or alliance (say, having a 40 per cent stake) it loses effective management control of the new venture.

Test your learning

Short answer questions

1 a State **two** examples of local businesses. [2]
  b Explain why a business might decide to restrict its activities to its national market. [3]
2 a Define the term multinational business. [2]
  b Explain why a manufacturing business might want to become a multinational. [3]
3 a State **two** advantages to countries from hosting multinational companies. [2]
  b Explain why footloose multinational companies may bring limited benefits to host countries. [3]
4 a Define the term deindustrialisation. [2]
  b Explain **one** reason why international trade offers benefits to a business. [3]
5 a Explain **one** effect on businesses of the creation of trading blocs such as the European Union. [3]
  b State **two** examples of emerging economies. [2]
6 a Distinguish between horizontal and vertical integration. [3]
  b State **two** reasons why a business may integrate vertically with another business. [2]
7 a Distinguish between a merger and a takeover. [3]
  b What is meant by a hostile takeover? [2]
8 Explain the benefits to businesses arising from mergers. [5]
9 a What is a de-merger? [2]

b Explain **one** problem commonly encountered by businesses following mergers or takeovers. [3]
10 Explain the benefits that businesses may receive from engaging in strategic alliances. [5]

Data response question

The economy of Pakistan

Many diverse multinational companies are located in Pakistan. Examples include Berger Paints, Coca-Cola, DuPont (Chemicals), Philips (Electronics), Emirates Airlines and the conglomerate Unilever which is committed to an ethical business model. Such large businesses bring benefits to employees and customers in Pakistan as well as its government.

Since 1989 successive governments in Pakistan have carried through a controversial policy of privatisation. Industries subject to privatisation have included banking, oil and gas, and airlines. Over the same period Pakistan's economy has enjoyed good rates of economic growth, but unemployment has remained a problem and trade unions believe privatisation has increased it, quoting the privatisation of the Pakistan Telecommunications Company Ltd in 2005 as an example. Income differentials between rich and poor have widened. Pakistan's GDP rose by around 8 per cent per annum in the early years of the 21st century – some economists link this to privatisation.

Pakistan is a member of the World Trade Organisation (WTO), and has bilateral and multilateral trade agreements with many nations and international organisations. It is also a member of the South Asian Free Trade Area (SAFTA) agreement to reduce tariffs on imports. In recent years Pakistan has run a substantial deficit on its balance of payments – its latest figures amount to 2 per cent of its GDP. At the same time imports and exports have risen quickly.

Questions

1 Analyse the benefits that businesses in Pakistan receive from international trade. [10]

2 Consumers in Pakistan have been affected by its policy of privatisation. Discuss whether the advantages outweigh the disadvantages for consumers in the country. [14]

3 To what extent does Pakistan benefit from hosting multinational companies? Justify your view. [16]

Essay questions

1 To what extent is horizontal integration the best method of growth for a manufacturing business? [20]

2 Discuss whether shareholders are the only stakeholder group to benefit from mergers and takeovers. [20]

Past paper question

Read the Atlantic Steel Company case study on pages 449–51 and then answer the following question.

Discuss the impact of ASC's privatisation on the company's stakeholders, using data in Table 1 and other relevant information. [16]

Cambridge International AS and A Level Business Studies 9707 Paper 32 Q2b October/November 2011

20 The economic environment

Key terms

Economic growth is an increase in the value of goods and services produced by a nation's economy over a period of time.

Inflation is a sustained rise in the general price level and a corresponding fall in the value of money.

Unemployment is the number of people who are seeking a job but unable to find one.

The **balance of payments** is a record of a country's financial transactions with the rest of the world over a period of time.

Productivity is the relationship between inputs into the production process (such as labour and machinery) and the resultant outputs of goods and services.

The **level of economic activity** refers to the amount of spending and production in an economy. Governments aim to have smooth increases in the level of economic activity over time.

20.1 The government's economic objectives

Every business is affected to some degree by the national (or global) economy in which it operates. An economy is an immensely complex entity. It comprises millions of buyers (or consumers) and hundreds of thousands of businesses all making decisions to spend, hire labour, use certain machinery, produce more or less, lend money or borrow it to produce goods and services.

This scenario is then complicated further by the actions of governments that intervene in the working of the economy in order to achieve their social and economic objectives. Most governments aim to manage economies so as to maximise the standard of living of the country's inhabitants while pursuing other goals such as protecting the environment. The UK government aims to achieve economic stability in its management of the economy by avoiding, whenever possible, sudden and dramatic changes in the performance of the economy. It has a number of economic objectives as set out in Figure 20.1.

The key objectives for the UK are:
- **Sustainable economic growth** This means that the value of the economy's entire production of goods and services should increase over time. However, this should be at a rate which is

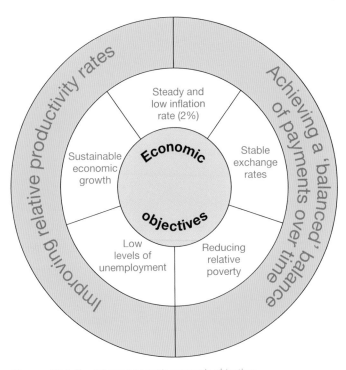

Figure 20.1 The UK government's economic objectives

sustainable – this means that it can be maintained over time while minimising the damage to the environment.

- **A steady and low rate of inflation** The UK government's inflation target at the time of writing is 2.0 per cent meaning that it aims to have prices rising in the UK at this rate annually. This is a major economic objective which the Bank of England pursues on behalf of the government.
- **Low levels of unemployment** It is not possible to eliminate all unemployment in an economy. The UK government (along with many others) wants to achieve full employment whereby those who are able and willing to work have a job.
- **Stable exchange rates** Significant fluctuations in exchange rates pose problems for many businesses and especially those which compete with foreign firms as relative prices can change quickly, affecting sales.
- **Redistributing income and wealth to reduce relative poverty** Many governments aim to reduce relative poverty among vulnerable groups in society such as children and the elderly. This may entail a range of policies including increasing pensions to ensure that the standard of living of these groups does not fall behind that of other groups in society.

Governments do pursue other economic targets such as achieving a balance between the outflows of money from its economy (caused, for example, by expenditure on imported goods and services and investment overseas) and inflows resulting from factors such as the sale of exports and the receipt of foreign investment. These flows, which are recorded in a country's **balance of payments**, should be equal over time. The UK government also aims to improve the level of productivity in the economy, hopefully by more than other economies. This means that by implementing policies such as improving the quality and extent of training or by encouraging investment in capital equipment, it attempts to increase the amount produced from the resources available within the economy.

The economic environment and business strategy

A business's strategy is simply the long-term plans through which it seeks to attain its corporate objectives – i.e. the objectives of the whole business. For example, a business may have growth

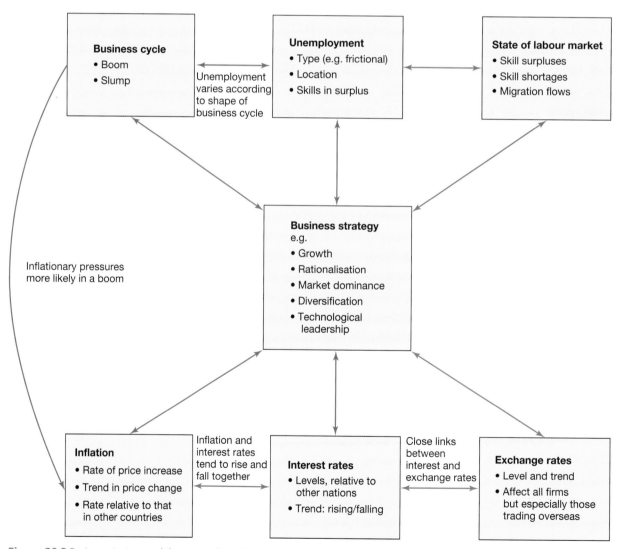

Figure 20.2 Business strategy and the economic environment

as a major corporate objective and will develop plans to achieve the desired rate of growth. These plans may include increasing innovation as part of the development of new products, entering new markets or pursuing a policy of takeovers and mergers. Figure 20.2 summarises some of the major economic variables that might impact upon businesses' strategic planning and decision-making. The diagram also emphasises the interrelationships that exist between the elements that make up the economic environment for businesses.

20.2 Economic growth and the business cycle

Key terms

A **recession** is characterised by falling levels of demand and declining levels of output and employment over at least a six-month period.

A **slump** takes place when production is at its lowest, unemployment is high and there are many business failures.

In this and the following sections we will look at each of the government's main economic objectives in more detail.

Economic growth

Economic growth is an increase in the value of goods and services produced by a nation's economy. Fluctuations in the rate of economic growth result in the business cycle, which we consider later in this section. If the rate of economic growth is negative (i.e. if the economy is getting smaller) for a successive six months, then it is said to be in **recession**.

Economic growth is normally measured by an increase in gross domestic product (GDP). In 2013 the GDP of the UK was £1 579 401 million. The population of the UK is approximately 63 million, giving a GDP per head, or per capita, equal to £24 755. Governments seek to increase this figure over time as it represents a rise in the country's standard of living.

Most countries' economies experience economic growth over a period of time though, in the short term, economies may stagnate or even decline in size. Figure 20.3 illustrates the economic growth rates for the UK from 2003 until 2013.

Governments aim to maintain steady and sustained economic growth over a period of time. However, this is a difficult target to achieve, as the operation of the business cycle tends to create the fluctuations apparent in Figure 20.3. Governments use counter-cyclical policies (including control via interest rates and taxation levels) to attempt to eliminate the more extreme fluctuations. High rates of economic growth are not desirable, as they tend to result in **slumps** whereby economic growth may become negative.

Governments can stimulate growth as a consequence of their economic policies. Short-term growth can be encouraged by cuts in interest rates and taxation which fuel borrowing and spending, prompting greater output and hence economic growth. The danger is, however, that firms and individuals purchase products from overseas, promoting growth in foreign economies. Supply-side policies may be implemented to achieve sustained economic growth. This type of policy entails increasing the productive capability of the economy by improving the skills of the workforce, encouraging more people into employment and promoting competition within markets to increase output and GDP.

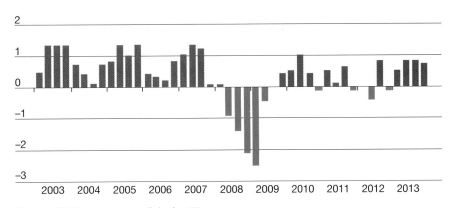

Figure 20.3 Economic growth in the UK

UK economy grew unexpectedly fast in 2013

The UK economy grew at the strongest rate in six years in 2013, having ended the year on a positive note as the recovery from economic recession became more apparent.

The UK's services and manufacturing sectors were the drivers of 0.7 per cent growth in the fourth quarter, taking the annual growth rate to 1.9 per cent, the strongest since 2007 before the financial crisis took hold. The economy grew in every quarter in 2013 according to the Office for National Statistics, providing a significant boost for George Osborne, the Chancellor of the Exchequer (Finance Minister), who has persistently argued that a strengthening recovery is proof that his economic plan is working.

Shortly after the figures were published Osborne said: '0.7 per cent growth in GDP is a boost for the economic security of hardworking people. Our long-term plan is delivering a brighter economic future.'

Average wages are growing at 0.9 per cent annually, which is half the rate of inflation, which was 2 per cent in December. The economy grew at a slightly slower pace in the final quarter of the year compared with the third, when gross domestic product increased by 0.8 per cent, but it was in line with economists' expectations.

Joe Grice, chief economic adviser at the ONS, said 'the economy does seem to be improving more consistently', but GDP is still well below pre-crisis levels. He added: 'Today's estimate suggests over four-fifths of the fall in GDP during the recession has been recovered, although it still remains 1.3 per cent below the pre-recession peak.'

Source: Adapted from *The Guardian*, 28 January 2014 (Angela Monaghan) http://www.theguardian.com

Questions

1 Explain why economic growth is an important macroeconomic objective for most governments. [8]
2 Evaluate the extent to which the economic data provided in the case study represents excellent news for all UK businesses. [16]

The case for economic growth is not clear-cut. Growth brings disadvantages as well as advantages. These arguments are summarised in Table 20.1.

The business cycle

All countries suffer fluctuations in the level of GDP and business activity within their economies. At times spending, output and employment all rise; during other periods the opposite is

Table 20.1 The benefits and drawbacks of economic growth for businesses

The benefits	The drawbacks
High rates of economic growth provide the government with increased tax revenues permitting greater expenditure on health, education and transport benefiting all businesses in the UK and encouraging further growth.	Not all regions within an economy benefit equally during periods of economic growth. Firms selling in the south of England are likely to enjoy increased sales while those in less prosperous regions such as Wales and the north of England may only see a marginal increase in revenues.
Growth provides opportunities for all in society. Individuals benefit from greater chances of promotion; high levels of consumer spending encourage enterprise. Businesses small and large may thrive in a growing environment.	Growth may result in shortages of labour and other materials. This may result in higher wages and prices fuelling inflation and creating uncertainty among the business community.
Businesses generally enjoy higher sales and increased profits. Expansion is likely for firms selling income elastic products such as cars and foreign holidays. Growth creates new markets for products.	Growth places individuals and businesses under pressure. Workloads increase and decisions may be rushed. In these circumstances it may prove impossible to maintain the quality of management and businesses may lose coordination and a clear sense of direction.

true. The value of a country's output over a period of time is measured by a nation's gross domestic product – this figure is dependent upon the level of economic activity. A rising level of economic activity will be reflected in a higher level of GDP.

The business cycle describes the regular fluctuations in economic activity (and GDP) occurring over time in economies. Figure 20.4 illustrates a typical business cycle.

Trade cycles generally have four stages:

- **Recovery or upswing** as the economy recovers from a **slump**, production and employment both begin to increase. Consumers will generally spend more in these circumstances as they are more confident in the security of their employment. Initially businesses may respond cautiously to signs of increasing consumer confidence. No major decisions are required to meet rising demand while spare capacity exists: firms simply begin to utilise idle factories, offices and other assets. As business confidence increases firms may take the decision to invest in further non-current assets (factories, machinery and vehicles, for example). Employees experience less difficulty in finding jobs and wages may begin to rise.
- A **boom** follows with high levels of production and expenditure by firms, consumers and the government. Booms are normally characterised by prosperity and confidence in the business community. Investment in non-current assets is likely to increase at such times. However, many sectors of the economy will experience pressure during booms. Skilled workers may become scarce and firms competing for workers may offer higher

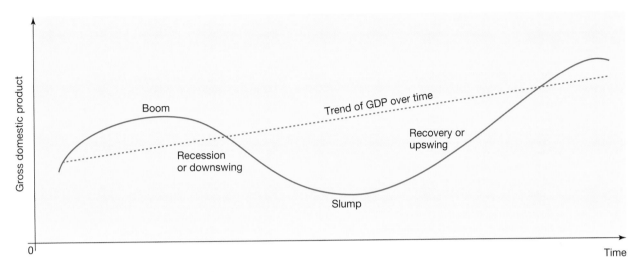

Figure 20.4 The stages of the business cycle

wages. Simultaneously, as the economy approaches maximum production, shortages and bottlenecks will occur as insufficient raw materials and components exist to meet demand. Inevitably this will result in their prices rising. The combination of rising wages and rising prices of raw materials and components will create inflation. It is the existence of inflation that usually leads to the end of a boom.

- A **recession** occurs when incomes and output start to fall. Technically a recession exists once GDP has fallen for two successive three-month periods – i.e. for six months. Falling sales will begin to eat into businesses' profits. In circumstances such as this the UK government has tended to lower interest rates in an attempt to stimulate demand and sales. Despite the falling interest rates, falling profits are likely to result in plans to invest in new factories and offices being delayed or abandoned. The level of production in the economy as a whole may stagnate or even fall. The amount of spare capacity within the economy will rise. Some businesses will fail and the level of bankruptcies is likely to rise.

- A **slump** often, but not always, follows a recession. In some circumstances an economy may enter the upswing stage of the business cycle without moving through a slump period. Governments may take action to encourage this by, for example, increasing their own spending or lowering interest rates. A slump sees production at its lowest, unemployment is high and increasing numbers of firms will suffer insolvency. (Note: In the UK limited companies become insolvent, while the term bankruptcy applies to individuals, sole traders and partnerships).

Figure 20.4 illustrates a smooth and regular trade cycle in operation. In reality the change in gross domestic product is likely to be irregular as economic cycles of different duration and intensity operate simultaneously. The business cycle is a major influence of the performance of businesses. As the economy moves from one stage of the cycle to another, businesses can expect to see substantial changes in their trading conditions.

The effects of the business cycle

Table 20.2 identifies some actions that different large businesses might take in response to the business cycle. However, not all businesses are equally affected by the changing trading conditions, as summarised in Table 20.3.

A number of businesses may find that demand for their products is relatively unaffected as the business cycle moves through its stages. Producers and retailers of basic foodstuffs, public transport and water services may notice little change in demand for their products. This is because these are essential items consumers continue to purchase even when their incomes are falling – demand for them is not sensitive to changes in income.

Demand for other categories of products is more sensitive to changes in income levels and therefore the stages of the business cycle. Examples include foreign holidays, electrical products such as televisions and laptops and construction materials such as bricks and windows.

Thus firms selling basic foodstuffs might have to take little or no action to survive a recession; in fact demand for their products might increase as consumers switch from more expensive alternatives. At the other extreme businesses supplying materials to the construction industry could be hard hit as firms delay or abandon plans to extend factories and build new offices. Their position might be made worse by a fall in demand for new houses as hard-up consumers abandon schemes to move home.

Government policy and the business cycle

Governments attempt to offset the most extreme effects of the business cycle. The UK government is no exception in this respect and it has taken a number of high profile actions in an attempt to lessen the effects of the recession that started in 2008 and was still affecting the UK and many economies around the world in 2014. The government implements **counter-cyclical policies**

Table 20.2 The trade cycle and business actions

Stage of business cycle	Key features	Likely reactions by business
Recovery or upswing	• Increasing consumer expenditure • Existing spare capacity used • Production rises • Business confidence strengthens • Investment increases	• Opportunity to charge higher prices • Rising numbers of business start-ups • Businesses take decisions to invest in non-current assets • Businesses operate nearer to (or at) full capacity
Boom	• Rate of inflation increases • Bottlenecks in supply of materials and components • Some firms unable to satisfy demand • Profits probably high – but hit by rising costs	• Firms face increasing pressure to increase prices • Businesses seek alternative methods to increase output • Wage rises offered to retain or attract skilled labour • Managers plan for falling levels of demand
Recession	• Government reduces interest rates • Firms reduce production as demand falls • Spare capacity rises • Business confidence declines and investment is cut • Profits fall	• Firms seek new markets for products – possibly overseas • Some products may be stockpiled • Workers laid off – or asked to work short-time • Financially insecure firms may become bankrupt or insolvent
Slump	• Increasing number of bankruptcies and insolvencies • Government lowers interest rates further • High levels of unemployment • Low levels of business confidence and consumer spending	• Firms offer basic products at low prices • Businesses may close factories to reduce capacity • Large-scale redundancies may occur • Marketing concentrates on low prices and easy payment deals

Table 20.3 Products affected and unaffected by the business cycle

Firms supplying these products may be significantly affected by the business cycle	Firms supplying these products are unlikely to be affected to a great extent by the business cycle – in fact demand may rise for some of these products in a recession/slump
• Leisure air travel • Sports and leisure goods • Jewellery • Household furniture • Cars	• Fuel including gas and electricity • Cigarettes and tobacco • Petrol • Water and sewage services • Unbranded basic foods

to limit the fluctuations in gross domestic product and hence the consequences of these fluctuations for businesses. These counter-cyclical policies have implications for businesses in the same way that the business cycle does.

In a slump the government seeks to lessen the impact of falling confidence among businesses and declining expenditure by individuals and businesses. By reducing interest rates and possibly cutting the level of taxes paid by individuals and businesses the level of economic activity may remain relatively stable. Recently many governments have favoured reducing interest rates in the expectation that they will encourage firms to undertake investment programmes as borrowing money becomes cheaper. Similarly, consumers may spend more if credit is less expensive.

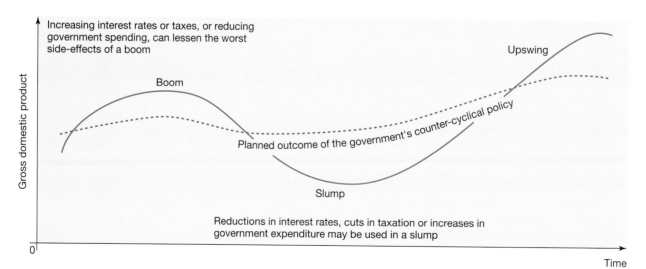

Figure 20.5 Counter-cyclical policies and the business cycle

At the time of writing the authorities in many countries are setting very low interest rates. In Malaysia the rate is 3 per cent, in Saudi Arabia it is 2 per cent and in the UK the Bank of England has set its base rate (which influences most other interest rates in the economy) at 0.5 per cent. This is its lowest rate ever.

At the other extreme a boom may result in governments raising interest rates in an attempt to lower the level of economic activity. Higher interest rates are likely to discourage investment by businesses and spending by consumers. Reducing expenditure in this way can assist in avoiding resources becoming too scarce as firms attempt to produce more than available resources will allow.

Businesses need to take into account the likely effects of counter-cyclical policies when considering their responses to changing trading conditions brought about by the business cycle. Such counter-cyclical policies can be beneficial as they avoid the need for firms to prepare for the worst excesses of boom and slump.

Case Study

Pakistan's central bank forecasts 4 per cent economic growth

Figure 20.6 The State Bank of Pakistan

Pakistan's central bank has estimated that the rate of economic growth in the country will increase to 4 per cent for the 2013–14 fiscal year, surpassing forecasts by international agencies.

The State Bank of Pakistan (SBP) announced its forecast in its belated annual report.

'SBP projects GDP growth in the range of 3 to 4 per cent … which is higher than the IMF's growth forecast of 2.5 to 3 per cent,' the bank said.

The International Monetary Fund (IMF) approved a $6.7 billion loan package for Pakistan in September last year, subject to strict economic reforms, particularly in its troubled energy sector and tax system.

The central bank forecast that the three-year deal should bring stability to the domestic foreign exchange market during the current fiscal year.

In the last fiscal year Pakistan's economy grew at 3.6 per cent, the bank said, and inflation fell to single digits. But it warned inflation could rise as high as 11 per cent in the current fiscal year, having reached 10 per cent last year. Economists say growth in Pakistan needs to be 7 per cent to absorb the country's booming population.

Source: Adapted from Dawn.com, 15 January 2014
http://www.dawn.com

Questions

1 Explain the benefits to businesses in Pakistan of the country's rapid growth in population. [8]
2 To what extent does the information in this article represent good news for businesses in Pakistan? [16]

Maths moment

Assume that Pakistan's average annual population growth is 1.75 per cent. Given that the country had 182 million inhabitants in 2012, what will be the revised forecast for 2025?

Business strategy and the business cycle

The business cycle is a permanent feature of the economic environment for firms, and one that is receiving a great deal of publicity at the time of writing. The effects of changes in the business cycle vary from industry to industry. Firms selling goods whose demand is sensitive to changes in income (known as income elastic goods) such as designer clothes and foreign holidays may find that sales rise in a boom and fall during recession. Conversely, businesses selling staple products such as foodstuffs where demand is not income elastic may be relatively unaffected by the business cycle.

It is possible to argue that the business cycle will only provoke short-term responses in many firms, because its effects are relatively short-lived. Booms and slumps do not last forever and businesses can take actions to see them through difficult trading periods. During boom periods managers may increase prices to restrict demand and increase profitability; they may subcontract work to other firms or seek supplies from overseas. Equally, in conditions of recession or slump, lay-offs may occur or short-time working may take place while overseas markets are targeted to increase sales. Well-managed firms will predict the onset of a boom or slump and take appropriate action in advance. Short-term responses may be all that are required if governments are successful in eradicating the more extreme effects of the business cycle.

20.3 Inflation

Inflation can be defined as a persistent rise in the price level and the associated fall in the value of money. For many businesses a low rate of inflation is not a problem. As long as wages are rising at about the same rate or higher, a low constant rate of price increase simply serves to help maintain demand. Inflation only becomes a major problem for businesses when it is high, rising rapidly or (worst of all) is doing both together.

Inflation in the UK, and in many industrialised nations throughout the world, has been at historically low rates over the last 15 years or so. Despite a rise in UK inflation rates to more than 5 per cent (as measured by the CPI) in late 2011, inflation in the UK is forecast to remain at 2 per cent or lower during 2014.

> **Key terms**
>
> **Counter-cyclical policy** is operated by the government with the intention of reducing the worst effects of booms and slumps.
>
> The **Consumer Price Index (CPI)** measures the rate of inflation based on the changes in prices of a basket of goods and services.

How is inflation measured?

The UK government measures the rate of inflation by use of the **Consumer Price Index (CPI)**. The CPI was introduced in December 2003 and measures the average monthly change in the prices of goods and services purchased by households in the UK and the government will use this to set targets for inflation in the future. The CPI is calculated using more than 650 separate goods and services for which price changes are measured throughout the country.

The causes of inflation

There are a number of factors that may cause inflation. Economists tend to classify the causes of inflation by **demand-**pull or **cost-push** factors. The cause of inflation can be an important factor for businesses as it provides some indication of likely future government policies to control inflation.

> **Key terms**
>
> **Cost-push inflation** happens when firms face increasing costs due to rising wages or increasing costs of raw materials and components.
>
> **Demand-pull inflation** occurs when the demand for the country's goods and services exceeds its ability to supply these products.

Demand-pull inflation

Demand-pull inflation occurs when the demand for the country's goods and services exceeds its ability to supply these products. Thus prices rise generally as a means of restricting demand to the available supply. The underlying cause of this might be the government allowing firms and businesses to have too much money to spend, perhaps as a consequence of cutting taxes or lowering interest rates.

Demand-pull inflation normally occurs at the boom stage of the trade cycle when the economy is at full stretch with most of its resources in use. At this high level of production shortages and bottlenecks occur in supply. Because resources and labour become relatively scarce, firms offer higher prices and wages and inflation is the result. Governments are alert for the first signs of demand-pull inflation and prepared to increase interest rates to prevent the economy overheating and prices rising.

Cost-push inflation

Cost-push inflation occurs when firms face increasing costs due to factors such as rising wages or increasing costs of raw materials and components. This type of inflation can arise from a number of sources.

- **Wage rises** If trade unions and employees are successful in negotiating pay increases significantly above the rate of inflation then further price rises might be the result. This becomes more likely if productivity is not increasing, allowing businesses to offset some of the increased wage costs against additional

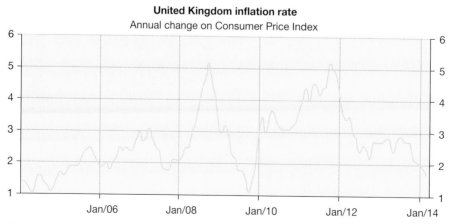

Figure 20.7 Inflation in the UK 2004–14

production. However, labour market conditions can influence the rate of wage increase and therefore inflation. For example, wages in Spain fell by about 20 per cent between July 2011 and January 2014 contributing to the country's very low inflation rate.

- **Imported inflation** One of the hidden causes of inflation is rises in import prices. The UK and Belgium are susceptible to this type of inflation as they are 'open' economies importing large quantities of raw materials, components and finished goods. Import prices rise when the exchange rate is falling and more of the domestic currency is required to purchase a given amount of a foreign currency. Although exporters might complain about rising exchange rates, they do help to control inflation.

The inflation rate was 2.5 per cent in China in May 2014. It had averaged 5.78 per cent annually from 1986 until 2014, reaching a high of 28.4 per cent in 1989 and a low of −2.2 per cent in April 1999. During 2013 Chinese exports prices fell, on average by 2.2 per cent while import prices rose by about 0.5 per cent over the same period.

Russia's inflation rate was 7.6 per cent in May 2014 and averaged 148.22 per cent annually from 1991 until 2014 with a high of 2330.3 per cent in 1992. Its lowest rate was 3.6 per cent in April 2012. The price of domestically produced products rose by 2 per cent between December 2013 and January 2014.

Case Study

Comparing the rate of inflation in China and Russia

Questions

1 Explain the likely effects of Russia's high rate of inflation on its businesses. [8]
2 Chinese businesses have operated in a better macroeconomic environment than those in Russia. Do you agree with this statement? Justify your view. [16]

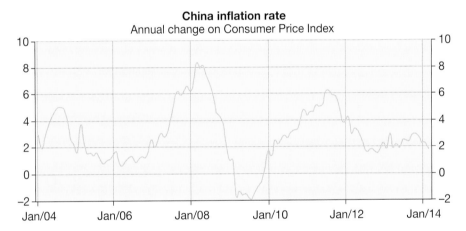

Figure 20.8 Inflation in China 2004–14

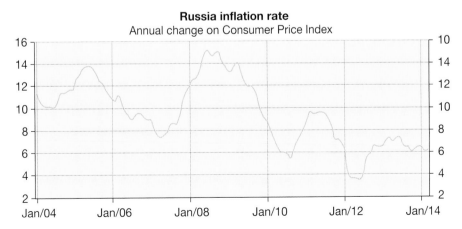

Figure 20.9 Inflation in Russia 2004–14

The impact of inflation on business

Inflation can have a number of effects on businesses.

- Many businesses may suffer falling sales in a period of inflation. Consumers might be expected to spend more during inflationary periods as they would not wish to hold an asset that is falling in value. However, research shows that people save more (perhaps due to uncertainty) and sales for many businesses fall.
- It can be difficult to maintain competitiveness (and especially international competitiveness) during bouts of inflation. Rising wages and raw material costs may force firms to raise prices or accept lower profit margins. Firms operating in countries with lower rates of inflation may gain the edge in terms of price competitiveness under such circumstances.

The impact of government anti-inflationary policies

We saw in an earlier case study that Russia is suffering from a relatively high rate of inflation. This places pressure on the government to control inflationary pressure. This can mean that businesses are frequently affected more by anti-inflationary policies than by inflation itself. Over recent years the Russian government has controlled the worst effects of inflation in a number of ways.

- Rises in **interest rates** have been the government's main weapon – the country's prime lending rate was 7.5 per cent in May 2014. Increasing the base or prime rate reduces the possibility of demand-pull inflation occurring. Consumers are discouraged from spending their money by higher rates on savings accounts and they are less likely to buy on credit as it is more expensive. Businesses reduce investment as borrowing becomes more expensive. Output and sales decline and the inflationary pressure is lowered.
- Over time the Russian government will seek to reduce the expectation of inflation. Recently the rate of inflation in India has begun to decline. This has helped businesses to be confident in setting prices and helped to dissuade employees from putting in excessive (and inflationary) pay claims. The falling rate of inflation enjoyed by Russia has helped in persuading foreign firms to invest in the country.

Other approaches can also help to control inflation. In the UK successive governments have introduced legislation designed to restrict the power of trade unions. Acts controlling picketing and making ballots compulsory before unions can take industrial action have served to reduce trade union power. This legislation has lessened the chance of cost-push inflation while reducing the number of days lost to strikes and other industrial action.

Inflation can offer some benefits to businesses, however. Some analysts suggest that low and stable rates of inflation may be beneficial. A steady rise in profits can create favourable expectations and encourage investment by businesses. Inflation can also encourage long-term borrowing and investment by businesses as the value of their repayments (in real terms) declines over time.

20.4 Unemployment

Unemployment remains an important issue in most countries. It is important because it represents a waste of resources if labour is unused – if all available workers were used the country concerned would be able to produce more and its citizens would enjoy a higher standard of living. The social effects of high and prolonged rates of unemployment can be devastating: poor health and crime are just two factors associated with unemployment and poverty.

Key terms

Interest rates are the price of borrowed money.

Cyclical unemployment is caused by the operation of the business cycle rising in slumps and falling in booms.

Frictional unemployment exists because people may be temporarily out of work between leaving one job and starting another.

Structural unemployment occurs due to fundamental changes in the economy whereby some industries reach the end of their lives.

Types of unemployment

People can be unemployed for a number of reasons. Governments find it useful to distinguish between the various types of unemployment, as each type requires a different remedy. Although many different types of unemployment exist, we shall focus on three main types.

Structural unemployment

Economies continually change: some industries die and others emerge to replace them. **Structural unemployment** occurs due to fundamental changes in the economy whereby some industries reach the end of their lives. Structural unemployment occurs for a number of reasons.

- The adoption of new methods of production.
- Significant and permanent changes in demand.
- Increasing competition from overseas.
- Rising income levels meaning demand for some products declines.

But structural change in the economy also offers opportunities to businesses. Rising incomes and technological developments have led to the development of the mobile phone industry. This industry employs a large number of people in manufacturing the product, supplying networks and in retail outlets.

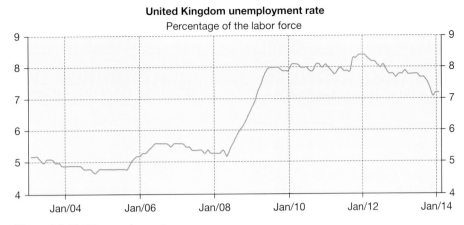

Figure 20.10 UK unemployment

Structural unemployment is a difficult problem for governments to solve. Because large numbers of employees may no longer have the skills that employers require, training is an important part of any solution. Other approaches include encouraging foreign producers to establish themselves in the country to provide employment for those with skills not needed by domestic businesses. The UK has been particularly successful in attracting motor vehicle producers from throughout the world.

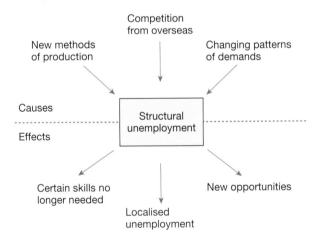

Figure 20.11 Causes and effects of structural unemployment

Cyclical unemployment

Cyclical unemployment arises from the operation of the business cycle – a topic we considered in detail earlier in this chapter. The boom stage of a business cycle will see this type of unemployment minimised as firms increase their production levels. At this stage of the business cycle those who have been unemployed for some time (and with relatively few skills) may find work.

At the other extreme much of the unemployment experienced during a slump will be cyclical. Figure 20.10 highlights the effect of cyclical unemployment as unemployment can be seen to increase substantially in the UK as the business cycle moved into a recession in 2008. Some businesses have moved to protect themselves against cyclical unemployment by the introduction of profit-related pay. Such schemes allow pay to fall during a recession along with profits, reducing the need to make workers redundant.

Frictional unemployment

People moving between jobs cause **frictional unemployment**. If a person leaves one job they may not be able to move into a new position immediately. While they are searching for new employment they are classified as frictionally unemployed. The government providing improved information on job vacancies available may reduce the level of frictional unemployment. A healthy economy will have some amount of frictional unemployment as people move between jobs.

Business and changing unemployment levels

Rises in unemployment can have serious implications for businesses, though the precise impact and likely responses of firms will depend upon their circumstances and the type of unemployment.

Study tip

It is important to relate the impact of unemployment – or changes in other economic factors – to the precise type of business under consideration. Some businesses rely heavily on labour as a key element of production – this is more likely to be true of businesses that supply services. Hence a change in the level of unemployment will have a greater impact on this type of business.

Cyclical unemployment might result in businesses suffering from falling sales. In the short term firms may be able to add any surplus production to inventories. Alternatively, businesses may seek new markets, perhaps by selling overseas. Not all businesses will be equally affected by changes in unemployment levels. Businesses selling essential products may be relatively unaffected by cyclical unemployment, while suppliers of luxury products could suffer substantial reductions in sales.

Structural unemployment can have a significant effect on businesses because it is frequently highly localised and often very persistent. Thus high levels of unemployment suffered by former coal mining communities would have considerable implications for most businesses in the locality. Unemployment brought about by the decline of an industry also has an impact upon associated industries. For example, falling production in the UK's shipbuilding industry contributed to the decline in the country's steel industry.

Case Study

Global migration

Migration is the movement of people between different countries. Over the last 20 years many European and North American countries have experienced significant inflows of migrants from parts of the Middle East, Africa and Asia. Although some people have left countries in Europe and America, the inflows have generally been larger creating a positive net inflow of migrants. Figure 20.12 shows the countries that have had net outflows and inflows of migrants.

The impact of migration depends upon a number of factors and not just the size of the net migration flow. If migrants possess suitable skills and are primarily of working age they offer substantial benefits to businesses in countries such as the UK and Australia. They can assist in overcoming skill shortages and reduce the expenditure that firms must make on training. In addition, the increased supply of people onto the labour market may help to prevent wages from rising. This is especially likely if migrants are willing to work for lower wage rates.

Questions

1 Explain the benefits that Australian businesses might receive from a net inflow of migrants. [8]
2 To what extent does a net inflow of migrants affect the competitiveness of businesses in the receiving nation? [16]

If there is a need to reduce output then rationalisation and redundancy might follow and factories and offices may be closed. Research and development plans may be abandoned or postponed as firms seek to reduce their costs to match their (reduced) revenues. A predicted fall in the level of demand may encourage the firm to diversify, possibly into foreign markets. Businesses may consider mergers with other firms to help reduce costs or to broaden product ranges.

Periods of low unemployment cause different problems for businesses and provoke different responses. Falling unemployment and accompanying skill shortages create problems that take time to solve. Businesses look to the government to assist through the provision of state training schemes and the development of relevant vocational courses in schools and colleges. Recent UK governments have attempted to support industry in these ways.

However, businesses can take action.

● Skill shortages encourage the development of capital-intensive methods of production in manufacturing and service industries.

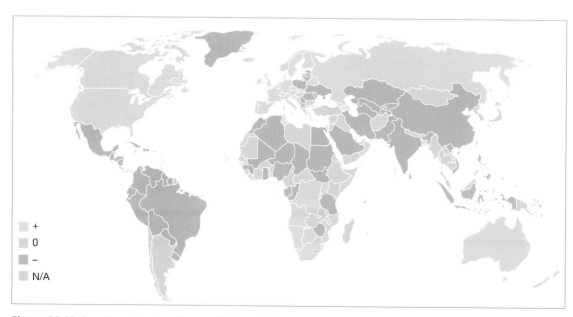

Figure 20.12 Countries with net outflows and inflows of migrants

Source: http://essay-eh.blogspot.co.uk

Using technology to replace labour can boost productivity thereby enhancing international competitiveness.

- Businesses may relocate to take advantage of more plentiful and cheaper sources of skilled labour. However, in the case of the UK, this may require location outside Europe as most of the EU is experiencing similar skill shortages.
- Businesses may invest in training schemes to develop the required skills in their employees.
- This may entail giving relatively junior or unskilled employees additional skills to enable them to carry out a wider range of activities. This can be a risky approach, however, as unscrupulous competitors may entice away skilled employees once training is completed.

The skills shortage creates difficulties for many businesses, but opportunities for others. Recruitment agencies and firms providing training for other businesses may enjoy increasing demands for their services during a period of skill shortages.

20.5 Exchange rates

An **exchange rate** is simply the price of one currency expressed in terms of another. Thus, at a particular time, the Chinese Yuan may be worth 400 Vietnamese Dong or 4.9 Thai Baht.

London is one of the premier international centres for buying and selling foreign currencies: each day transactions total billions of pounds. Exchange rates between most currencies vary regularly according to the balance of supply and demand for each individual currency.

Why do firms buy foreign currencies?

The main reason businesses purchase foreign currencies is to pay for goods and services bought from overseas. Firms purchasing products from abroad are normally expected to pay using the currency of the exporting country. For example, Sainsbury's (one of the UK's major supermarkets) purchases wine from Chile. Chilean wine producers would expect to be paid in their local currency – Chilean pesos (Ch$). Thus traders acting on behalf of Sainsbury's would sell pounds sterling in order to buy pesos on the foreign exchange market. This process is illustrated in Figure 20.13.

Demand for foreign currencies may also arise because individuals and businesses wish to invest in enterprises overseas. Thus a Hong Kong citizen wishing to invest in a business in Brunei Darussalam will require Brunei dollars to complete the transaction.

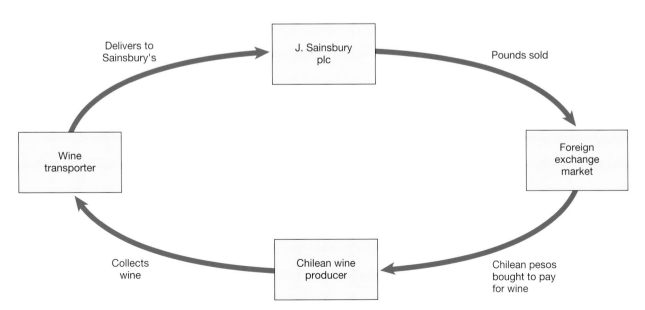

Figure 20.13 The operation of the foreign exchange market

The effects of exchange rate changes

Exchange rates can change significantly over time. A rise in the value of a currency is an **appreciation**; a decline in its value is termed **depreciation**.

In December 2012 the American dollar exchanged for 19.32 Uruguayan pesos ($U). By June 2014 the exchange rate was $1 = $U22.97. This meant that the value of the Uruguayan peso had depreciated by just under 19 per cent over the period. Alternatively, the value of the American dollar had increased (or appreciated) by the same amount.

Maths moment

In June 2014 an American company exported cars to Uruguay at an average price in dollars of $32 000 per car. Assuming no other changes, how much would an average car sell for in Uruguay?

Changes in the value of currencies affect the prices of exports and imports as shown in Table 20.4.

Table 20.4 The effects of changes in the value of the Uruguayan peso

The exchange rate of Uruguayan pesos	Prices of Uruguayan exports overseas (in foreign currencies)	Prices of imported goods in Uruguay (in pesos)
Appreciates (rises)	Increase	Fall
Depreciates (falls)	Fall	Increase

Using the information in Table 20.4 we can see that the fall in the value of the Uruguayan peso against the American dollar during 2013 and early 2014 would have had the following effects.

- Prices of Uruguayan exports to the United States of America (for example, wool from its Corriedale sheep) would have fallen by approximately 19 per cent. Sales would be likely to rise as a consequence, and Uruguayan exporters would receive the same amount in pesos per kilogram of wool.
- American products (for example, software for computers) imported by Uruguay would have been up to 19 per cent more expensive. However, the price the Americans received in dollars would not have changed. It is likely, however, that because prices were higher in Uruguay, American companies would sell smaller quantities of their products.

Small changes in the exchange rates of most countries occur all the time as demand for the currency and supplies of it alter. A series of slight rises and falls over a period of time is not necessarily a major problem for industry. Of more concern is

a sustained rise or fall in the exchange rate – or a sudden and substantial change in the exchange rate.

Exchange rate changes can create uncertainty for a number of reasons.

- If firms agree deals priced in foreign currencies, they may receive more or less revenue from a particular transaction than expected if the exchange rate alters in the intervening period. Thus, a deal to sell clothes to France may give Bangladeshi manufacturers less revenue than anticipated if the contract is agreed in terms of euros and the Bangladeshi taka then rises in value against the euro. In these circumstances, the amount of euros stated in the contract will convert into a smaller number of taka, causing a shortfall for the exporter.
- Changing exchange rates can affect prices and sales in overseas markets, even if the exporter avoids direct exchange risk by insisting on payment in domestic currency. For example, a London-based clothes designer may sell clothes overseas, but stipulate that they are paid in pounds sterling. A rise in the value of the pound may mean that foreign retailers are forced to increase the prices of the clothes to maintain profit margins. As a consequence sales may be lower than expected giving the London-based design company less revenue than forecast.
- Competitors may respond in unexpected ways to exchange rate changes. Foreign firms may reduce prices to offset the effects of an exchange rate change, putting rivals under pressure to do the same or lose market share.

Price elasticity can be an important part of a discussion on the possible effects of exchange rate changes. If overseas demand for a product is price inelastic, then an increase in the exchange rate may not be too harmful. It might be that Uruguayans will continue to buy American computer software when the price rises. In this case demand may alter little. If demand is price elastic exporters might be badly affected by a rise in the exchange rate, but benefit greatly from a fall.

Case Study

Argentina's currency falls against the dollar

For much of the latter part of 2013 the value of the Argentine peso fell steadily against the American dollar. The rate of the depreciation increased dramatically in the first two months of 2014. At the start of September 2013 approximately 5.75 Argentine pesos were required to buy one dollar. By January 2014 one American dollar was worth 6.5 Argentine pesos. By March 2014 one dollar exchanged for 7.87 pesos.

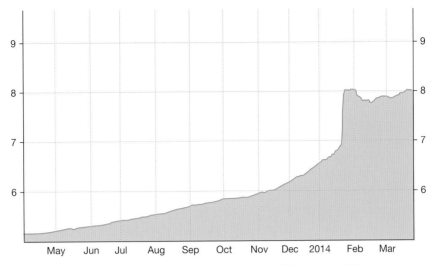

Figure 20.14 US dollar–argentine peso exchange rate, April 2013–March 2014

Source: www.bloomberg.com

Questions

1 Explain the effects of the significant fall in the value of the Argentine peso on the country's employees. [8]

2 Do you think that Argentine businesses benefited or suffered as a consequence of the changes in the value of the peso against the American dollar between September 2013 and March 2014? Justify your decision. [16]

Business strategy and exchange rates

Fluctuations in exchange rates create a great deal of uncertainty for businesses trading internationally. When exchange rates are volatile, businesses become uncertain about earnings from overseas trade. This adds to the risk businesses incur as part of their trading activities.

Firms like to operate in a relatively risk-free environment and to reduce uncertainty. The undesirable consequences of exchange rate changes can be reduced through the use of techniques such as forward foreign currency markets. This sets a guaranteed exchange rate at some future date (when transactions are completed) meaning that the amount received from overseas trading is more certain. However, fixing an exchange rate in this way does not guarantee a particular level of sales. Furthermore, the bank arranging this service may require a fee.

Exchange rate changes are more of a problem in markets where fierce price competition occurs. In these circumstances demand is more likely to be price elastic and businesses are under pressure to respond quickly to any change in exchange rates.

Businesses may respond to the pressures of exchange rate changes by seeking to create productive capacity in overseas markets to avoid the effects of changing currency values. A number of foreign motor manufacturers located in the UK have revealed that they are considering relocating in the euro zone in Europe to avoid the difficulties imposed by fluctuations in the value of the pound against the euro. In particular, Toyota has argued strongly for the UK to adopt the euro to eliminate exchange rate risk.

An alternative approach, currently used by Toyota, is to require suppliers to price their products in a different currency. The company, which sells cars throughout Europe, has announced that it intends to pay UK suppliers in euros. As a result, fluctuations in the exchange rate will have less impact on the company as it pays suppliers in the same currency that it receives from European customers.

Table 20.5 Changes in exchange rates

How might Zimbabwean firms respond to a rising value of the Zimbabwean dollar?	How might Zimbabwean firms respond to a falling value of the Zimbabwean dollar?
Exporters	**Exporters**
• Allow price to rise in foreign markets reducing probable sales. Remember exporters receive the same price in dollars for each overseas sale, but will sell less in this situation. • Leave prices unchanged in overseas markets. Sales should be unchanged but the exporter will receive fewer dollars from each sale. **Neither of these options is attractive to exporters – a rising exchange rate is bad news.**	• Exporters could allow prices to fall in overseas markets as a result of the exchange rate change. They will receive the same amount in dollars from each sale but should achieve higher sales. • Increase their prices to maintain price levels in terms of the foreign currency. Sales should remain constant (depending on competitors' actions) and revenue should rise in dollars as a result.
Domestic producers	**Domestic producers**
• Reduce prices to compete with cheaper imports. • Enjoy the benefits of cheaper imports of materials and components. • Emphasise other elements in the marketing mix, for example, the quality of the product.	• Enjoy increased sales as a result of rising prices of competitors' imported products, assuming foreign businesses do not hold prices down. • Increase prices (to some extent) to enjoy increased revenues from each sale. • Beware the increased cost of imported raw materials and components.

20.6 Redistributing income and wealth

Income and **wealth** are not equally distributed between the citizens of most countries in the world. This means that many societies include people who have large amounts of wealth and receive high incomes, while others are poor with little or no wealth and low incomes. It is the objective of governments across the world to use taxation and welfare benefits to redistribute income from richer members of society to poorer ones.

The scale of the problem of inequality

One way of measuring income inequality is through the use of the Gini coefficient. This measures the degree of equality of income distribution in a country using a scale of 0 to 1. A result of 1 indicates perfect equality while the closer the result is to 0, the greater the degree of inequality.

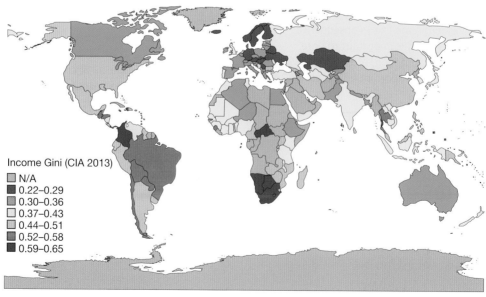

Income Gini (CIA 2013)
- N/A
- 0.22–0.29
- 0.30–0.36
- 0.37–0.43
- 0.44–0.51
- 0.52–0.58
- 0.59–0.65

Figure 20.15 The distribution of income in countries throughout the world

Source: CIA – The World Factbook, 2009

The distribution of wealth is generally more unequal than that of income. A few statistics will highlight this.

- In 2000, China had relatively equal distribution of wealth as there was little inherited wealth in the country. However, since then the distribution of wealth has become much more unequal. A survey in 2012 conducted by Professor Li Gan of the Southwestern University found that 10 per cent of households control 86.7 per cent of total wealth.
- In the United States of America the richest 20 per cent of the population own approximately 83 per cent of the country's wealth.
- The richest 20 per cent of Malaysians control 53.8 per cent of the nation's wealth, while the poorest 60 per cent of the population owns just 21.3 per cent of wealth.

The trend across many countries in the world is for the distribution of both income and wealth to become more unequal. A study in 2011 by the Organisation for Economic Cooperation and Development (OECD), looking at 34 countries in North and South America, Asia and Europe, reported that household incomes of the top 10 per cent grew faster than those of the poorest 10 per cent, leading to widening income inequality. Increases in household income inequality have been largely driven by changes in the distribution of wages and salaries, which account for 75 per cent of household incomes. With few exceptions (France, Japan and Spain), wages of the 10 per cent best-paid workers have risen relative to those of the 10 per cent least-paid workers.

The response of governments

Some analysts argue that a Gini coefficient figure higher than 0.4 can result in social problems resulting from gross inequalities in income distribution. Unequal distribution of income and wealth can result in large numbers of people suffering relatively poor living standards. It may also slow growth in an economy as the relatively poor may not have access to education and training and therefore have fewer job-related skills. Additionally, they may consume less, reducing demand for the products of a wide range of businesses.

This has led governments to implement policies designed to redistribute income and wealth from richer groups in society to poorer ones. Essentially these policies involve two elements.

- **Imposing taxes on income and wealth** Those sections of society that hold larger amounts of wealth or receive higher incomes may be subject to a range of taxes including income tax and inheritance taxes. These taxes may be graduated so that those with very high incomes or wealth pay a larger proportion of their income or wealth as tax.
- **Providing welfare benefits** This is the other part of a policy of redistributing income and wealth. Poorer households receive cash and non-cash benefits (also known as benefits in kind) from governments to supplement what may be meagre incomes. The benefits may be paid in the form of pensions to boost low income households or as compensation for loss of income due to unemployment. Non-cash benefits can be state provided healthcare or education.

Figure 20.16 illustrates the effects in the UK of the government's taxation and benefit policies on household incomes. The graph divides up the households into fifths – ranging from the poorest to the richest fifth of households in the UK. It is apparent that the redistribution of income policy does offset the inequality of income distribution to some extent.

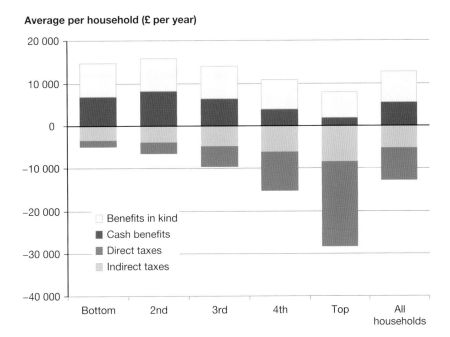

Figure 20.16 Taxes, benefits and the effects on UK household incomes in 2011

Source: ONS

20.7 The government's economic policies

Key terms

Fiscal policy is the use of taxation and public expenditure to manage the level of activity in an economy.

Direct taxes are taxes on income and wealth, for example income tax, corporation tax and inheritance tax.

Indirect taxes are taxes on spending, for instance value added tax (VAT).

Monetary policy is controlling the amount of money and/or interest rates within the economy in order to achieve the desired level of economic activity.

Supply-side policies are designed to improve the free operation of markets and therefore the total amount that is produced (or supplied) by the economy.

Governments operate a number of different policies with the aim of providing the best possible economic environment for businesses. This entails adjusting the level of activity in the economy to avoid the excesses of booms and slumps. The government's economic policies can be divided into three categories.

1 **Monetary policy** Using this policy the government (or the central bank such as the Bank of England acting on its behalf) manipulates the amount of money and/or interest rates within the economy in order to achieve the desired level of economic activity.

2 **Fiscal policy** This refers to the government's use of taxation and public expenditure to manage the economy. By adjusting the levels of taxation and government expenditure, the government can alter the level of activity within the economy.

3 **Supply-side policies** These are designed to improve the free operation of markets and therefore the total amount that is produced (or supplied) by the economy. Privatisation is one type of supply-side policy along with limiting trade union power and providing training for unemployed workers.

Monetary policy

This type of economic policy involves adjusting the amount of money in circulation and hence the level of spending and economic activity. **Monetary policy** can make use of one or more of the following:

- adjusting interest rates
- controlling the money supply
- manipulating the exchange rate.

Although at times all three techniques have been used, more recently governments have tended to rely upon altering interest rates to manage the economy. Since 1997 in the UK the Monetary Policy Committee of the Bank of England has had responsibility for setting interest rates. Giving this power to central banks is common in other countries, too. For example, the Reserve Bank of India performs a similar role. In the UK the Monetary Policy Committee sets interest rates monthly with the aim of achieving the government's target for inflation while attaining long-term growth in the economy. Table 20.6 highlights the aims that may lie behind the authorities altering interest rates and, importantly, the implications for individuals and businesses.

Broadly speaking, rises in interest rates depress the level of economic activity and reductions promote an expansion of economic activity.

Interest rates are the price of borrowed money. Although the Bank of England sets the base rate, many other interest rates operate in the UK. The precise rate of interest charged on a loan depends on several factors, including the time period of the loan and the degree of risk attached to it.

In the UK, expenditure is particularly sensitive to changes in interest rates. One prime reason for this is mortgage interest payments. Millions of UK consumers have mortgages, which are large loans taken out to purchase houses. A rise in interest rates increases the payments made on mortgages, leaving less money available for other types of expenditure. Similarly, a cut in rates reduces mortgage payments freeing money for other forms of expenditure.

Effects of changes in interest rates

The impact of rising interest rates will depend upon the size of the change as well as the initial rate. A small increase at a relatively high level of rates will have little impact, while a larger increase from a low base rate will have a significant impact.

Not all businesses are affected equally. We can identify several categories of businesses that are particularly susceptible to changes in interest rates.

- Small firms are often affected greatly by changes in interest rates as they have smaller financial reserves and a relatively greater need for borrowing. The Bank of England estimates that every 1 per cent rise in interest rates costs the UK's 1.5 million small firms an extra £200 million in interest rate payments. Significant rises in interest rates can lead to substantial increases in bankruptcies or insolvencies among small firms.

- Even larger firms with high levels of borrowing (and therefore high levels of gearing) can be affected by alterations in interest rates. For example, a rise in rates can lead to a hefty increase in interest payments forcing firms to reduce costs elsewhere or to pass on the extra expenses in the form of higher prices – if this is possible. Alternatively, a cut in interest rates offers

Table 20.6 Changes in interest rates – objectives and implications

Rising interest rates	Falling interest rates
The likely *objectives* of increasing interest rates include the following:	**Reductions in interest rates may be introduced with the following *objectives* in mind:**
Reducing the level of consumer spending	Reducing levels of unemployment
Limiting inflationary pressure in the economy	Stimulating the level of production in the economy
Slowing the level of economic growth (as measured by GDP)	Promoting exports sales by reducing the exchange value of the currency
Avoiding increasing imports creating a deficit on the balance of payments	Increasing rates of economic growth in the economy
(In general higher interest rates will assist in dampening down an economic boom.)	(Reducing interest rates can assist an economy in recovering from a slump.)
The likely *consequences* of increasing interest rates include the following:	**The *consequences* for businesses and individuals of falling interest rates include the following:**
Many businesses may experience falling sales as consumers increase savings	Demand and sales are likely to increase especially for products bought on credit
Demand for products purchased on credit may decline significantly	Production is likely to be stimulated, increasing employment
Businesses may cancel or defer investment plans	Export sales of price sensitive products may increase while imports become less competitive
Firms reduce borrowing by, for example, cutting levels of inventories	Businesses may undertake increased investment promoting growth in industries such as construction
Increased value of the currency increasing the prices of exports while reducing import prices	
(In general higher interest rates will assist in dampening down an economic boom.)	

a substantial reduction in expenses to such firms, improving their competitiveness.

- Firms trading overseas are affected by alterations in interest rates. Rising interest rates tend to lead to an increase in the exchange rates. This occurs because individuals and businesses overseas purchase, say, rupees to invest in Indian financial institutions to benefit from higher interest rates. A fall in interest rates would have the opposite effect.

Credit card worries in Singapore

The authorities in Singapore have released data that indicates consumers are facing difficulties in keeping up with payments. Data released by the Credit Bureau Singapore (CBS) shows that borrowers are falling behind on payments, and that the balances outstanding are increasing. In July 2013 62 830 credit card holders or other unsecured borrowers had not made a minimum payment in two months. This figure represented an increase of 12.7 per cent on the 2012 number.

Unsecured borrowing includes credit cards, overdrafts and personal loans that are not backed by collateral.

The total amount on unsecured cards, overdrafts and personal loans that are two months or more past due rose as well. It stood at $230.7 million in July, up from $212.5 million last year and $183.8 million in 2011.

'The steady rise in red ink is likely why the Monetary Authority of Singapore launched new rules on unsecured credit loans earlier this month,' said CIMB regional economist Song Seng Wun.

'After the binge, comes the belt tightening. When the bad loans are rising against the backdrop of an unexpected external shock or the risk of interest rates going up, the possibility of people on the margin and defaulting is there,' said Mr Song.

The new rules include barring financial institutions from giving out more loans to people whose unsecured debt totals more than 12 months of their income for 90 days or more.

Source: Adapted from The Real Singapore, 2 October 2013
http://therealsingapore.com

Questions

1 Explain the likely effects on businesses in Singapore of continued rises in unsecured borrowing if the authorities did not take steps to control it. [8]
2 Would the effects of a continued rise in unsecured borrowing be entirely bad for businesses in Singapore? Justify your view. [16]

Table 20.7 Interest rates and other economic variables

Other economic variables	Rising interest rates	Falling interest rates
Unemployment	Unemployment increases as levels of production decline	Unemployment decreases as the level of economic activity rises
Inflation	Falling demand and output reduces inflationary pressure	Increasing output and spending causes prices to rise, fuelling inflation
Economic growth	Will slow as businesses cut output and investment	Is stimulated by cheaper loans and rising business investment
Exchange rates	Exchange value of currency is likely to rise	Exchange value of currency generally falls
Balance of payments (current account)	Fewer imports purchased improving the current account balance	Increased spending will 'suck in' imports, worsening current account balance

However, it is not only the direct effects of altering interest rates that affect businesses. The use of interest rate policy by the authorities can have a profound impact upon the general economic environment in which businesses operate. The Reserve Bank of India changes interest rates to assist the Indian government in achieving its economic objectives. This means that altering rates affects the level of unemployment, inflation and growth existing in the economy. They also change business managers' expectations of these key economic variables, affecting their day-to-day and strategic decisions.

Table 20.7 illustrates the relationship that exists between the level of interest rates and key economic variables such as economic growth and unemployment.

Quantitative easing (QE)

Since March 2009 interest rates in the UK have been held at 0.5 per cent by the Bank of England, the lowest figure ever. This removed the possibility of lowering rates further to expand production and to help the economy achieve higher rates of economic growth and recover from the 2008–09 recession. But when interest rates can go no lower, a central bank's only monetary policy option is to pump money into the economy directly. That is quantitative easing (QE).

The way the central bank does this is by buying assets – usually financial assets such as government and corporate bonds – using money it has simply created. The institutions selling those assets (either commercial banks or other financial businesses such as insurance companies) will then have 'new' money in their accounts, which then boosts the money supply.

The hope is that this money is subsequently used to purchase goods and services and to boost output and growth. The UK government has injected more than £375 billion into the UK economy through QE since 2009. Quantitative easing has also been used by central banks in Japan, the USA and the European Union.

Fiscal policy

Fiscal policy is the use of government expenditure and taxation as a means of controlling the level of activity within the economy. In particular a government's fiscal policy is the relationship between the level of government expenditure and the amount raised in taxation in any given year. In the UK the fiscal year runs from 6 April to 5 April the following year; in many other countries it runs from 1 January to 31 December.

The balance between taxation and government expenditure in the UK is determined annually when the Chancellor of the Exchequer announces the annual budget. The government can operate two broad types of fiscal policy.

1 **Expansionary fiscal policy** This entails cutting taxation and/or increasing government expenditure on items such as health, education, social services, defence and transport. The effect will be to increase the amount the government borrows to fund its expenditure (known as the public sector net cash requirement or PSNCR) or to reduce the surplus held in the government's coffers at the end of the fiscal year.

2 **Contractionary fiscal policy** This is brought about by reducing government expenditure or increasing taxation or by both policies simultaneously. The effect is to cut the government's borrowing or to reduce the deficit on its budget for the fiscal year.

Figure 20.17 summarises the operation of fiscal policy. Fiscal policy can help to stabilise the economy (avoiding the worst effects of the business cycle) through the operation of the 'automatic stabilisers'. For example, lower unemployment when the level of economic activity is high means temporarily lower social security spending and higher income tax receipts. Higher company profits generate higher tax receipts, and higher spending by consumers yields higher receipts from indirect taxes. These factors together will have a contractionary effect, dampening an economic boom.

The effects of tax and expenditure policies

Tax and expenditure policies can have immediate effects on the level of economic activity, although the precise effects will depend upon the types of tax altered and the nature of government expenditure.

● **Direct taxes** These are taxes on income and profits and, in the UK, include income tax and corporation tax (levied on company profits). Direct taxes take a larger amount from individuals earning high salaries and companies

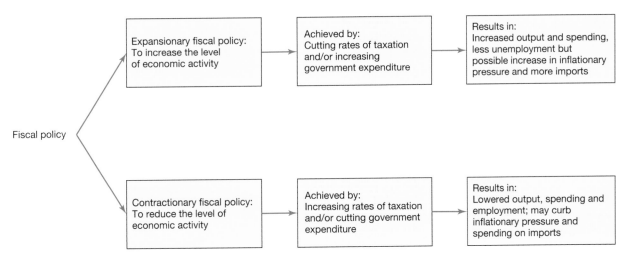

Figure 20.17 The operation of fiscal policy

announcing handsome profits. The government can forecast with some accuracy the effects arising from an increase (or reduction) in income tax. Although the overall effect may be predicted, the implications for individual businesses will vary according to the type of product supplied. Firms supplying luxury goods (long-haul foreign holidays, for example) might be significantly affected by a change in income tax rates, especially for those earning higher incomes, while those selling basic foodstuffs may be relatively unaffected.

● **Indirect taxes** VAT (value added tax) is the major tax on spending in the UK and other EU countries. It and other taxes on spending are classified as indirect. Changes in this type of taxation can have a rapid effect on the level of economic activity, although its effects are difficult to predict. An increase in VAT (as in the UK in January 2011, when it rose from 17.5 per cent to 20 per cent) lowered consumer spending, reducing demand for goods and services and eventually lowering the level of economic activity. However, the extent

of the fall in demand will depend upon the price elasticity of demand for the goods in question. Consumers will continue to purchase essentials such as fuel and food, although demand for products associated with home improvements, for example, may decline. An important side effect of increasing indirect taxes is that it is inflationary.

Government expenditure is the other half of fiscal policy. Governments may spend more in two broad categories.

1 **Transfer payments** This is expenditure on unemployment benefit, pensions and other social security payments. Changes in expenditure on these items will have a rapid impact as they are received by relatively poor members of society who will most likely spend the increase or cut back if necessary almost immediately. An increase in transfer payments often results in substantial increases in demand for basic goods such as food, public transport and gas.

2 **The infrastructure** Governments improve the infrastructure through their spending on housing, roads and flood protection. Investment in these areas can increase the level

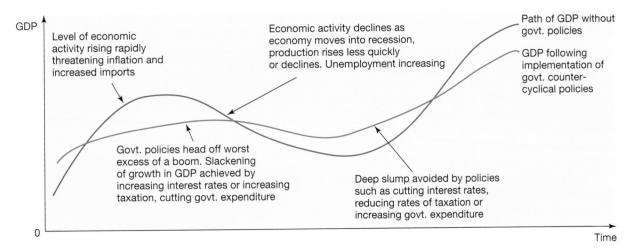

Figure 20.18 Government economic policies at work

of economic activity by boosting demand for the services of construction firms while reducing costs for other firms. A new road, for example, might cut a business's transport costs. This, however, is a much slower method of altering the level of economic activity. In 2013 the Chinese government announced that it was planning a number of new infrastructure projects including 15 expressways to prevent a loss of growth rates in the Chinese economy.

Supply-side policies

Supply-side policies are a range of measures intended to improve the operation of free markets and the amount that is produced by the economy. They can take a number of forms.

Labour market measures

In recent years many governments have implemented policies intended to allow labour markets to operate more effectively. The UK government has been a strong advocate of allowing labour markets to operate more freely and flexibly. For example, by reducing the power of trade unions businesses were enabled to implement policies to allow them to use labour more flexibly and efficiently. Employees were able to carry out a range of duties, rather than a limited role to avoid demarcation disputes. Disputes and confrontations became less common as a consequence of a series of laws.

Other policies have been implemented to encourage the effective operation of labour markets. The unemployed have been encouraged back into the labour force through the provision of training programmes designed to equip them with employable skills, by limiting the availability of unemployment benefit to those in genuine need and the cutting of income tax rates on low earners to encourage people into the labour force.

Privatisation

This is the process of transferring organisations from the state to the ownership and control of individuals and other businesses. In the 1980s and 1990s many major UK state enterprises were sold into the private sector and the policy has continued in recent years, although it has slowed as the state owns relatively few enterprises. Since 2000 the London Underground system has been partly privatised as has air traffic control and the port of Dover. In 2013 the Royal Mail was sold into the private sector.

However, many analysts argue that privatised industries do not operate more effectively. The perceived shortcomings of privatisation have led to a mild backlash against the policy. Countries such as New Zealand have created new nationalised industries, and even California has taken steps in this direction.

Other supply-side measures

Governments have tried to make other resources more freely available by removing controls on the operation of markets that provide capital and land. The negotiating of the free movement of capital throughout the EU has been a major factor in increasing the funds available to EU enterprises.

Case Study

Japan's economy shows signs of recovery

Japan's attempt to promote growth in its economy after years of falling prices is showing signs of success according to the country's central bank, the Bank of Japan. It said that economic conditions were starting to recover, signalling its confidence that the world's third-largest economy was about to make a long-awaited turnaround. The Bank of Japan's message was reinforced by a rise in Japanese exports, helped by a fall in the value of the yen, and some signs of a broader recovery in consumer confidence and consumer spending.

Reflecting its optimism, the central bank's policy-setting board left its monetary policy unchanged and stuck to its goal of hitting 2 per cent inflation within two years. To get money flowing again in the Japanese economy, the bank, led by its governor, Haruhiko Kuroda, has pledged to pump 60 trillion to 70 trillion yen, or about $600 billion to $700 billion, into the economy annually.

'Japan's economy is starting to recover moderately,' the bank announced. For proof, the bank pointed to a rise in business investment and profits, industrial production, and both business and consumer confidence.

Japan's economy is now growing faster than any of the world's leading economies, recording an annualised rate of 4.1 per cent in gross domestic product over the last three months.

Source: Adapted from the *New York Times*, 11 July 2013 (Hiroko Tabuchi) http://www.nytimes.com

Questions

1 Explain the likely effects of rising consumer confidence and spending on businesses in Japan. [8]
2 Discuss how the Japanese authorities might use economic policies to ensure that the economy continues to grow steadily over the next few years. [16]

20.8 Market failure

Governments can intervene in the economy for reasons other than adjusting the level of economic activity. One such reason for intervention is **market failure**.

When a market operates correctly it responds to the signals given by prices and increases or reduces the resources used by businesses in the market to supply more or less of the product. Over time global oil prices have risen from $19 per barrel in 1991 to more than $100 per barrel in 2014. The price has risen because consumers of oil (individuals and businesses) have demanded more of the product. In response to the signal of rising prices oil companies have sourced new supplies of oil and have increased production.

The failure of markets to work properly can come about for a number of reasons.

1 **Monopolies and cartels** The existence of monopolies and **cartels** might mean producers have too much power, resulting in insufficient output and high prices. As a consequence consumers may receive too little of certain products, resulting in a lower standard of living.

2 **Damage to the environment** Producers do not bear the full costs of production, and society as a result bears some costs such as those resulting from pollution. These are called external costs. These costs can result in severe damage to the environment with the potential of imposing high costs on future generations. This type of market failure creates oversupply of certain products as producers (and ultimately consumers) do not pay the full cost of production. Some of the costs of production are paid by others, for example, those who have to clean up the resulting pollution.

3 **Consumers and producers possess insufficient information about products** Consumers may underestimate their need for certain goods such as health and education, resulting in inadequate supply without government intervention in such markets. This form of market failure is likely to result in under supply as too few resources are allocated to producing goods and services in these markets. However, it can result in the over consumption of some products (drugs, for example) if consumers are unaware of the dangers they pose.

4 **Poaching of skilled labour** If a business invests heavily in training its workforce to provide job-related skills it can expect a consequent increase in productivity and a reward for devoting resources to training. However, one possible outcome is that highly skilled employees are attracted by rival businesses who are able to offer higher wages as they have not borne the training costs. Such poaching of labour can result in too few resources being allocated to training for fear of poaching. Thus the market fails.

Responses to market failure

1 **Monopolies and cartels** Many governments have enacted laws to encourage competition and to restrict a wide range of anti-competitive activities. Such laws prohibit the abuse of monopoly power (for example, by raising prices excessively to boost profit margins) and the operation of cartels. Such laws protect consumers from the adverse effects of monopoly power. Offending firms are normally fined, sometimes very heavily.

2 **Damage to the environment** Governments tend to control external costs in three main ways. They can impose indirect taxes with the aim of raising the costs of production to account for the external costs paid by other groups in society. This should lead to higher prices and lower profit margins, discouraging production and consumption of the products. Alternatively, governments can levy fines on businesses that damage the environment and thereby impose costs on others. Finally, a government may pass laws to ban processes and products that cause external costs.

3 **Lack of information** Governments frequently provide information about the benefits or drawbacks of products. For example, in many countries there have been health information programmes to advise smokers of the danger to health of consuming tobacco. Many such programmes have been successful and there has been a sharp decline in tobacco consumption in many countries.

4 **Poaching of skilled labour** This is difficult for any government. If it has sufficient funds available it may provide some training itself and can offer tax benefits to businesses that engage in staff training. However, such approaches can be very costly if they are to have any significant effect.

20.9 Conclusion

This chapter has shown that there are a variety of ways in which a government may intervene in an economy. The diverse forms of intervention can assist businesses as well as constraining their activities.

Table 20.8 summarises some of the methods of intervention and the expected effects on businesses and consumers and the general level of economic activity in the economy.

Governments have a range of fiscal, monetary and supply-side policies that they can use to pursue their economic objectives.

Most governments pursue the same economic objectives, although their relative importance may change over time. Thus, at the time of writing many economies have low rates of inflation and governments are focusing their economic policies on increasing the level of output or GDP and on reducing levels of unemployment at the same time.

Table 20.8 A summary of methods of government intervention

How governments' economic policies *help* businesses	
Method of intervention	**Expected effects**
Reductions in the rate of interest	Businesses may invest more in new production facilities as cost of borrowing is reduced and consumers may increase spending as loans are cheaper and saving is less worthwhile due to lower interest rates. The level of economic activity should rise.
Cuts in direct and indirect taxes	May encourage higher levels of production as it becomes more profitable and consumers may also increase spending as their net pay (after tax) rises or as the price of goods falls. Once again the level of economic activity should increase.
Increases in government spending (on infrastructure or welfare benefits, for example)	Lower income consumers in receipt of rising benefits are likely to increase spending on a range of basic products (as saving of such rises in benefits occurs rarely). Businesses in construction and engineering sectors may receive orders from government for infrastructure projects, directly increasing output. Government's expenditure on infrastructure also likely to increase pay of many associated workers, increasing spending and therefore production. These effects will increase the level of economic activity.
Helping unemployed back into work through policies such as training and improving information on job vacancies	These supply-side actions should increase the level of economic activity by increasing the number of people who are in employment and have the right skills to carry out a job efficiently. This can enable businesses to increase production and to do so in a cost-effective manner because they employ suitably skilled workers.
How governments' economic policies *constrain* business activity	
Method of intervention	**Expected effects**
Increases in the rate of interest	By making borrowing more expensive this is likely to dissuade businesses and consumers from borrowing for investment or to buy expensive products such as homes, cars and electrical products. It may also encourage saving, reducing consumption and investment further.
Increases in direct and indirect taxes	This reduces the take-home pay of employees and/or increases the prices of products. Either of these effects will reduce consumers' spending on goods and services and reduce the level of economic activity. Simultaneously, businesses may have reduced profits available to invest (and to encourage future investment).
Reductions in government expenditure	Reductions in transfer payments such as pensions directly affect the ability of less well-off consumers to purchase goods and services. At the same time the government may reduce orders placed with a range of domestic businesses. The effects of both types of cuts will be to reduce economic activity.
Implementing health advice policies, for example on the dangers of tobacco or alcohol	Economists call products such as tobacco and alcohol 'demerit' goods because they can be harmful and many consumers are unaware of this. As a consequence consumers are discouraged from consuming them through advertising and other policies. This can (and does) result in reduced sales, leading to lower levels of production and decreased levels of economic activity.

Test your learning

Short answer questions

1   a   State **two** possible economic objectives for a government.   [2]

    b   Explain **one** reason why businesses may benefit from a steady rate of economic growth.   [2]

2   a   Define the term recession.   [2]

    b   Explain **one** consequence of an economy moving into recession for a car manufacturer.   [3]

3   a   What is meant by the term inflation?   [2]

    b   Explain **one** effect of inflation on a major retailer.   [3]

4   Explain how a government's anti-inflationary policy may affect small businesses.   [5]

5   a   Distinguish between cyclical and structural unemployment.   [3]

    b   Define the term exchange rate.   [2]

6   a   Explain **one** reason why exchange rate changes can create uncertainty for businesses.   [3]

    b   What is meant by the term wealth?   [2]

7   a   State **two** ways in which governments may attempt to redistribute income and wealth within their economies.   [2]

    b   Explain **one** reason why an unequal distribution of income and wealth may pose a problem for businesses.   [3]

8   a   State **two** forms that monetary policy may take.   [2]

    b   Distinguish, using examples, between fiscal and supply-side policies.   [3]

9   Explain how a rise in interest rates might affect an India-based exporter.   [5]

10   a   Explain what is meant by the term market failure.   [2]

    b   State **three** examples of market failure that may affect businesses.   [3]

Data response question

The UK's economic performance

Since the global financial crisis of 2008–09, the performance of the UK's economy has been relatively weak, although there have been some encouraging signs. Some key data for the economy is shown in Table 1.

Table 1 Selected macroeconomic data for the UK, 2008–12

Year	2008	2009	2010	2011	2012	2013
GDP growth (%)	−1.0	−3.9	1.8	0.8	0.0	1.9
Inflation rate (%)	2.1	3.0	3.0	4.1	2.7	2.0
Unemployment rate (%)	7.9	8.4	8.2	8.1	7.7	7.2
Exchange rate (£/$)	1.47	1.61	1.57	1.58	1.62	1.64

The UK's working population in 2013 reached 32.5 million. The performance of the UK's economy over this period has varied between regions. London and the south-east of England have been less affected by slowing growth rates and increased unemployment. Some businesses have performed well despite the difficult economic conditions. For example, the Jaguar Land Rover Group has performed strongly, principally due to its buoyant export sales. In contrast, some of the UK's banks have struggled to restore their finances.

Questions

1   Analyse the possible consequences of the falling rate of unemployment for the UK's businesses.   [10]

2   a   Calculate the number of people who were unemployed in the UK in 2013.   [4]

    b   Evaluate the effects of the changes in the exchange rate over the period 2008–13 on UK exporting businesses.   [10]

3   Does the data in Table 1 suggest that UK businesses will be uncompetitive? Justify your view.   [16]

Essay questions

1   To what extent do government policies aimed at reducing inflation cause businesses more difficulties than inflation itself?   [20]

2   'All businesses in a country benefit from a sustained fall in a country's exchange rate.' Discuss the extent to which this statement is true for a country of your choice.   [20]

21 Other external influences on business activity

Chapter overview

In this chapter we examine:
- political factors affecting businesses
- legal factors affecting businesses – employment, consumer protection and health and safety legislation
- technological change and businesses
- competitors and suppliers
- social factors affecting businesses.

21.1 Introduction

In the previous chapter we saw how the economic environment can affect business behaviour. However, economic influences are not the only force shaping the external environment in which businesses trade. We can identify at least six other factors that contribute to the business environment.

1 **Political and legal factors** A range of political decisions can help to determine the business environment. For example, many countries operate minimum wages which can result in businesses paying increased costs for labour. Additionally, businesses face a variety of laws which constrain many of their activities including the emission of noxious gases and contributions to employees' pension schemes.

2 **Technology** Changes in technology are taking place at an increasing rate and can have an enormous impact on businesses. For example, the development of the internet and online retailing has forced many retailers to make significant alterations to their business models.

3 **Competitors and suppliers** The actions of competitors can act as a major constraint on business activities. For example, businesses can be under pressure to deliver new products or to sell at highly competitive prices. In contrast many businesses, and especially manufacturers, rely upon suppliers to deliver raw materials and components promptly and reliably.

4 **Social influences** Businesses are subject to pressures from groups in society and social change. Pressure groups in the UK are currently calling on a number of large businesses, mainly multinationals, to pay a 'fair' amount of tax on their profits. This may lead to businesses altering their practices to record more profits in the UK and therefore to pay a greater amount of corporation tax on profits. Simultaneously, social changes are occurring. One example is the increasing number of one-person households as more people opt to live alone. The number of one-person households worldwide reached 202.6 million in 2006, up from 153.5 million in 1996. This change has implications for house builders and suppliers of foodstuffs, both of whom may need to supply larger volumes of smaller-sized products.

5 **Demographic changes** This refers to changes in the population structure and size. Such changes can have profound implications for businesses. For example, the population of China is ageing quickly. By 2050 approximately 26 per cent of China's population will be aged over 65, compared with 8 per cent in 2011. This change will reduce the quantity of labour available to China's enormous manufacturing sector as well as creating a significant change in the types of products that are purchased. The movement of people, for example, from the countryside to cities is also a notable change in many countries.

6 **Environmental factors** Managing businesses to minimise the adverse impact on the environment attracts an enormous amount of attention from the media and the general public. At the same time consumers and businesses have become more aware of the impact of their activities on the environment. Businesses have responded to these concerns by changing the products they supply and the processes employed to do so.

Case Study

Advances in smartphone technology

Apple and Intel are working together to create a Bluetooth-equipped smartwatch, according to one Chinese technology news source. Technology site TGbus says the watch would connect to the iPhone, allowing the phone to be operated remotely from the user's wrist. This offers the possibility of sending out text messages, answering calls, or even updating Facebook status on the device while the user's iPhone is in a pocket or charging nearby.

An iPhone-compatible smartwatch is certainly in high demand. In 2012 a request for funding for a Pebble smartwatch raised more than $10 million in crowdfunding from 70 000 people who want one of the watches. Approximately $500 000 of that funding was raised during the company's first day of fundraising. This watch has been released onto the market, selling at a price of around $150. The watch is compatible with Android and IOS devices, it is enabled to read emails and SMS messages as well as to use apps. It also tells the time! By the end of 2013 the company had sold 300 000 of its smartwatches.

An article in the *Wall Street Journal* has revealed that Microsoft is expected to release a touch-enabled Windows watch. Apple and Google are expected to release their own products at a later date.

Questions

1 Explain, using examples, how changes in technology might affect businesses that are not in the technology sector. [8]

2 Discuss the possible benefits and drawbacks to businesses such as Apple and Intel of rapid changes in technology such as that illustrated in this case study. [16]

21.2 Political and legal factors

Key terms

Laissez-faire is a policy in which governments become less involved in the management of the economy by reducing taxes and controls on business activities.

Privatisation is the process of transferring organisations from state ownership to being owned and controlled by individuals and other businesses in the private sector.

In the previous chapter we studied the economic policies that are available to the government – fiscal, monetary and supply-side policies. We saw that the effects of their operation can have considerable implications for businesses. Governments can also influence the business environment through the implementation of other policies.

Government intervention in the economy

The issue of **privatisation** is at the forefront of the debate about the extent to which the government should intervene in the economy. Governments in diverse economies such as Argentina, Malaysia, New Zealand and the UK have implemented policies to reduce the state's role in the economy to allow markets and businesses to operate with the maximum degree of freedom. In part this was achieved through the policy of privatisation. In some countries privatisation has been accompanied by the reduction in government subsidies and grants to industry and by legislation limiting the state's role in business matters. For instance, in the UK wages councils (responsible for setting the wages of many low-paid workers) were abolished and regulations governing markets such as telecommunications and financial services were relaxed, allowing new suppliers and greater competition. This approach to managing the business environment is described as **laissez-faire** and puts faith in a greater degree of self-regulation by businesses.

There are, not surprisingly, advantages and disadvantages to businesses arising from trading under a government that takes a laissez-faire approach to economic management.

Businesses benefit through less interference in their activities. Government intervention tends to raise costs (insisting on the employment of safety officers, for example) reducing the competitiveness of national businesses. This can be a major handicap for firms operating in highly price-competitive markets where small cost differentials can lead to substantial loss of sales. The UK government is consulting on removing the requirement to pay national rates of pay; if this policy is introduced wages may fall in poorer regions such as the north of England and Wales, attracting new businesses and helping existing businesses become more competitive. Supporters of laissez-faire argue that this approach can be extremely successful in attracting overseas producers because of the lack of regulation of businesses. They contend that governments cannot prevent the operation of global market forces, and that it is a waste of money to try. Finally, the laissez-faire approach helps to promote an entrepreneurial society in which individuals take responsibility for their own economic welfare and are more creative and hard working as a result, to the benefit of all in society.

However, many individuals and groups oppose the laissez-faire style of economic management. They argue that it is vital that governments support struggling industries in poor regions to prevent heavy unemployment and poverty. The UK government is considering how best to intervene in the telecommunications market to ensure that all regions of the UK have access to fast broadband services. This is seen as essential in generating economic growth in more remote areas.

Governments should recognise that economic change is inevitable, and attempt to soften the blow of economic restructuring of this type. Allowing businesses to regulate their own activities with minimal interference from the authorities is likely to result in unscrupulous businesses exploiting workers (through low wages and poor conditions) and consumers (by charging excessive prices). Some controls, it is argued, are essential to prevent this happening, particularly where a business faces little competition and exploits its monopoly power.

Case Study

Vietnam announces minimum wage increase

The Vietnamese government has increased its minimum wage rates. A new minimum wage rate for workers, which will result in an increase in monthly pay of up to 300 000 dong (VND), equivalent to approximately US$14, was introduced in January 2014.

The country now has different minimum wage rates in four regions, determined by the level of economic development in each region. Zone 1 covers urban Hanoi and HCM City. Zone 2 covers rural Hanoi and HCM City as well as Can Tho, Da Nang and Hai Phong. Zone 3 includes provincial cities and the districts of Bac Ninh, Bac Giang, Hai Duong and Vinh Phuc. Zone 4 comprises the rest of the country.

Since January 2014 the monthly minimum wage has been VND2.7 million (US$128) for Zone 1, VND2.4 million (US$114) for Zone 2, VND2.1 million ($100) for Zone 3 and VND1.9 million ($90) for Zone 4. The minimum wage applies to employees in most businesses including cooperatives, farms and households.

Questions

1 Explain the likely effects of an increase in the Vietnamese minimum wage on the level of motivation among the country's workforce. [8]
2 Do you think that the existence of these minimum wage rates helps businesses in Vietnam to be more successful? Justify your decision. [16]

The legal environment

The law is a framework of rules governing the way in which societies operate. These rules apply to businesses as well as individuals. The legal framework affects businesses in a number of ways affecting almost all areas of business activity. Marketing, production, employment, relationships with customers and competitors and even the establishment of the business itself are examples of business operations influenced by the law.

Study tip

The questions in examinations will not ask you about specific laws, but you would benefit from some knowledge of the major laws in your country and the effects they have on local businesses. This chapter will refer mainly to laws in operation in the UK.

Employment legislation

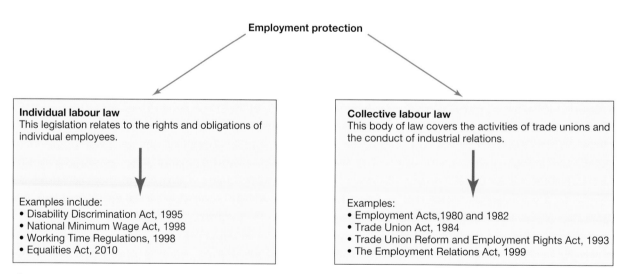

Figure 21.1 Employment legislation

Individual labour law

This aspect of employment legislation refers to the rights and obligations of individual employees. The amount and scope of individual labour law has increased in recent years, in part encouraged by the growing influence of the European Union on business matters in the UK.

A number of the most important Acts relating to individuals in employment are explained as follows.

- **Working Time Regulations 1998** This European Union legislation (hence the term regulation) set a limit of 48 hours on the number of hours that employees could be required to work each week. Employees can opt to work longer hours if they wish, but employers cannot insist that they do so without inserting an appropriate clause in their contract of employment. The regulations also gave employees an entitlement to four weeks' paid annual leave.
- **The National Minimum Wage Act 1998** This highly publicised Act came into force on 1 April 1999. The key features of this legislation are:
  - a general hourly minimum wage rate – £6.50 an hour from October 2014
  - a minimum level of £5.13 for 18–20-year-olds
  - all part-time and temporary workers must be paid the minimum wage.
- **Employment Equality (Age) Regulations 2006**
  - The main theme of this EU inspired law is that it will be unlawful to discriminate against workers under the age of 65 on the grounds of age.
  - Making someone redundant or barring workers from training or promotion because they are too old – or too young – will be illegal.
  - As they approach 65, workers will have to be given six months' notice that their employer wants them to give up their job and retire.
- **The Equalities Act 2010** This Act replaced a number of earlier anti-discrimination laws in the UK (such as the Disability Discrimination Act) to simplify legislation in this area. The Act relates to nine protected characteristics which cannot be used as a reason to treat people differently or unlawfully. Each person in the UK is protected by this Act, as everybody has one or more of these characteristics. The protected characteristics are:
  - age
  - disability
  - race
  - gender reassignment
  - marriage and civil partnership
  - religion or belief
  - pregnancy or maternity
  - sex
  - sexual orientation.

This Act makes unfair treatment unlawful in the workplace, in education and when supplying goods and services.

Collective labour law

> **Key terms**
>
> **Collective bargaining** is the process of negotiating the terms of employment between an employer and a group of workers.
>
> **Trade unions** are organisations of workers established to protect and improve the economic position and working conditions of their members.

This group of laws applies to the operation of industrial relations and collective bargaining as well as the activities of **trade unions**. Employers and employees are likely to negotiate on a variety of matters. These negotiations may include items such as working conditions and other workplace rules, basic rates of pay, overtime pay, hours of work, holidays, sick leave, retirement benefits and health care benefits.

For many years the law in the UK did not play a significant role in employer–employee relationships. However, this philosophy was changed when the Conservative governments of the 1980s and early 1990s passed a series of Acts intended to restrict the power of trade unions. Some examples of these laws, as well as a later one granting more powers to trade unions, are described below.

- **Employment Act 1980** Under this Act employers were no longer obliged to negotiate with unions – many unions were derecognised as a consequence. It also restricted picketing to employees' own place of work, thereby outlawing 'secondary picketing'. Closed shops were only permitted if supported by at least 80 per cent of the workforce in a secret ballot.
- **Trade Union Act 1984** This legislation made a secret ballot of employees a legal requirement before industrial action was lawful.
- **Trade Union Reform and Employment Rights Act 1993** Unions were required to give employers a minimum of seven days' notice before taking official industrial action. It also abolished wages councils and minimum pay rates.
- **Employment Relations Act 1999** Under this Act a trade union with a membership exceeding 50 per cent of the employees in any particular business can demand union recognition and the right to introduce **collective bargaining**.

Unfair dismissal

Many countries have a legal definition of unfair dismissal. Unfair dismissal is the termination of a worker's contract of employment without a legal reason. In the UK legislation relating to unfair dismissal only relates to workers once they have been in a particular job for one year or more. There are a limited number of reasons why an employee might be dismissed:

- where a job no longer exists – this is redundancy
- gross misconduct – examples of this reason include theft from the employer or behaving violently at work

- failing to carry out duties in 'a satisfactory manner'
- another substantial reason, e.g. the ending of a temporary contract.

All other reasons for dismissal are considered unfair. Employees who think they have been unfairly dismissed can claim compensation by taking their case to an industrial tribunal.

Health and safety legislation

Health and safety legislation has been enacted to discourage dangerous practices by businesses and to protect the workforce. The legislation in the UK is designed to *prevent* accidents in the workplace, and has developed steadily over the last 30 years.

The main Act in the UK is the Health and Safety Act of 1974. This is an example of delegated legislation whereby Parliament gives responsibility to government departments to update the scope of the legislation as necessary. This process avoids any particular aspect of legislation taking up too much of Parliament's time.

The Health and Safety at Work Act gives employers a legal obligation 'to ensure that they safeguard all their employees' health, safety and welfare at work'. The Act covers a range of business activities.

- The installation and maintenance of safety equipment and clothing.
- The maintenance of workplace temperatures.
- Giving employees sufficient breaks during the working day.
- Providing protection against dangerous substances.

Businesses are required to protect the health and safety of their employees 'as far as it is reasonably practicable'. This means that the business concerned must have provided protection appropriate to the risks. Thus, a chemical manufacturer would be expected to provide considerable protection for its employees.

The Act also requires employees to follow all health and safety procedures and to take care of their own and others' safety. The Health and Safety Executive (HSE) oversees the operation of the Act and carries out inspections of businesses' premises. The HSE also carries out investigations following any serious workplace accident.

Impact of employment and health and safety legislation on businesses

Employment legislation can help to motivate the workforce. Employees who work in a safe and secure physical environment will be more contented and probably more productive. Employers will also avoid the costs, delays and bad publicity caused by accidents at work or employee complaints about poor conditions. Furthermore, freedom from arbitrary dismissal may encourage a more cooperative and productive workforce, enhancing the performance of the business.

Employment legislation restricting the powers of trade unions has encouraged the development of more flexible workforces.

The ending of closed shops and the requirement for union recognition in many circumstances made it easier for businesses to implement changes in working practices, improving the productivity and competitiveness of UK businesses. Firms were able to adopt single union deals, making collective bargaining simpler and ending damaging and costly demarcation disputes (disputes between unions concerning the respective roles of their members in the organisation).

Following the legislation of the 1980s and 1990s, the UK has some of the most employer-friendly employment legislation in the western world. This has helped the country to attract the lion's share of foreign investment entering Europe. The UK is an attractive site for overseas businesses because its favourable employment legislation helps to minimise labour costs. The UK is the major recipient of inward investment into the European Union.

However, in spite of the employer-friendly approach in the UK, employment legislation does increase costs above the level that would exist if no legislation were in place. To take an example, the national minimum wage, introduced in 1999, raised the wages of an estimated 3 million employees. It is estimated to have added approximately 1 per cent to the nation's wage bill. Similarly, the requirement (under the Equalities Act) to make 'reasonable' alterations to the working environment to enable the employment of disabled employees adds to production costs.

Employment legislation also requires firms to employ greater numbers of non-productive workers such as human resource managers and safety officers. These employees add to the costs of production without making any direct contribution to the output of the business. Inevitably, costs increase as a consequence.

The effects of legislation may be greater on small firms that have fewer resources and are less able to keep up with changes in employment laws and may not be able to afford to respond in the appropriate manner. Larger firms have expert human resource specialists and are more likely to be geared up for change. They may also be able to afford specialist employment lawyers to advise them on avoiding some of the effects of a new piece of employment legislation.

21.3 Consumer protection legislation

The law covers the marketing activities of businesses. In the UK this is called consumer protection legislation. Consumer protection is a term used to describe a series of Acts designed to safeguard consumers against:

- businesses charging excessively high prices or rates of interest
- unfair trading practices, for example selling quantities less than those advertised
- unsafe products such as children's toys with sharp objects or toxic paint
- having insufficient information on which to take purchasing decisions.

Since 2014 the Competition and Markets Authority (CMA) has overseen consumer protection in the UK. It seeks to improve the position of consumers by giving consumers information to allow them to make better choices when purchasing goods and services. It also protects consumers by prosecuting offenders against consumer legislation and negotiating voluntary codes of practice with producers.

There is a considerable quantity of consumer protection legislation in the UK. The Acts listed below represent some of the highlights.

- **Sale of Goods Act 1979** The basic requirement of this Act is that the goods sold should be:
  - of merchantable quality – they must be undamaged and unbroken and must work properly
  - fit for the particular purpose
  - as described by the manufacturer.
- **The Consumer Credit Act 1974** This Act lays down that consumer credit can only be given by licensed organisations. It also sets out the terms under which credit may be given.
- **The Consumer Protection from Unfair Trading Regulations 2007** This bans a number of practices that have been deemed to be unfair to the consumer. An example of a practice that is banned is aggressive selling by businesses. The Regulations have also amalgamated a lot of previous consumer legislation, as well as keeping pace with new scams which are continuously being evolved and developed by scammers and rogue sellers.

Control of advertising

This is necessary to protect the public from improper use of the power of advertising. It involves a combination of legal controls and self-regulation.

- **The Trade Descriptions Act 1968** This Act makes misleading descriptions of goods and services an offence.
- **The Advertising Standards Authority** This body supervises the operation of this code of practice. It is an independent body; its members are not in the advertising industry. The ASA protects the public and deals with their complaints.

The impact of consumer protection legislation

Increases in the scope of consumer protection have had a number of implications for businesses. Meeting the requirements of consumer credit regulations, for example, entails additional processes and personnel, thereby increasing costs. Under this legislation, consumers expect firms to supply products that are safe and of consistently high quality. They expect the processes used in production to avoid any pollution and raw materials to be from sustainable sources. All of these expectations mean that production costs are greater, partly owing to additional costs of materials and employing extra workers to carry out the necessary checks.

Case Study

Queensland unveils new fast-food laws

The Queensland Government in Australia has announced plans to force fast-food outlets to display the energy content of meals and drinks on their menus. Heart Foundation figures show 4 million Australians buy meals at fast-food shops every day. The legislation, to be introduced next year, is designed to make it easier for customers to make healthy meal choices. New South Wales and the Australian Capital Territory (ACT) already have similar laws.

Queensland Health Minister Geoff Wilson says although some traders already provide nutrition information, he wants to see more. 'The new laws will mean that right across the state the major fast-food chains will be required to provide more information about the energy content of their standard food items,' he said. 'That'll mean that consumers get a win because they'll get more information.'

Mr Wilson says it is hoped the move will help reduce the rate of obesity. 'Obesity is reaching epidemic proportions in Queensland and Australia. One in three adults in Queensland is overweight at the moment and one in five is obese,' he said. 'By 2020 it'll be much worse and we want to make sure people are provided with as much information as possible to make the right choices to improve their health.'

Source: Adapted from ABC News

Questions

1 Explain how laws can constrain the marketing activities of fast-food businesses. [8]
2 Will such laws benefit the stakeholders of fast-food restaurants in Queensland? Justify your view. [16]

This has resulted in higher expectations on the part of consumers, in areas not necessarily covered by legislation. They require firms to provide advice and technical support and effective after-sales service and to behave in a socially responsible manner.

Study tip

It is easy to just think of laws as constraining business activity. Of course this is true, but legislation also offers opportunities to many businesses. For example, health and safety laws requiring firms to supply safety clothing and equipment provide sales for businesses supplying such equipment. Legislation requiring food products to have 'use by' dates created a small industry supplying specialised ink jet printers for use on production lines.

21.4 Technological change

In the twenty-first century the rate of technological progress is increasingly rapidly. The last few years have seen a number of technological advances that have significant implications for businesses. The internet has probably been the biggest single technological factor leading to change in business behaviour, but other sources of technological change such as biotechnology are also having and will continue to have substantial effects on business behaviour.

Technology and marketing opportunities

Technological advances have created new markets for new products and new ways to sell them.

Technology and new products

New technology can open up new markets for businesses. In 1990 mobile telephones were unheard of by most people. By May 2014 there were an estimated 6915 million in use across the world. Companies such as Nokia, Samsung and Apple have grown as a consequence of the developments in this field of communications technology. Analysts estimate that by the end of 2017 2.22 billion people across the world will own smartphones. Markets for MP3 players, satellite navigation systems and, more recently, tablet computers have been created as a consequence of technological advances. Today they are multi-billion dollar markets selling products to millions of consumers. Smaller, niche businesses have also developed, based on technological products, and we consider two very different examples below.

- **Electric motorbikes** Zero Motorcycles is a California-based company that designs and produces electric motorcycles that can be used on or off-road. Established by a former NASA engineer, Neal Saiki, the company describes its products as 'high performance electric motorcycles that are lightweight, efficient, fast off the line and fun to ride'.
- **Glasses to help correct the vision of the world's poorest people** Professor Josh Silver of Oxford University has used simple technology involving fluids, syringes and special hollow lenses to create glasses that wearers can adjust themselves to correct their own vision. This removes the need for specialist advice from an optometrist. More than 40 000 people in 20 countries are already using his glasses. However, Silver is ambitious for his project not to make money, but to help the needy. He hopes to supply 200 million pairs of spectacles to children in Africa who have eyesight problems. He is negotiating with the World Bank to make his vision a reality. In 2011 Silver was shortlisted for the European Patent Office's Inventor Award at a ceremony in Budapest.

Using technology in the products themselves, rather than in the production process, also offers great advantages to businesses. Firms possessing a technological lead over rival producers are frequently able to charge a high price for their products – at least until the competition catches up. This technique of price skimming is likely to boost profits. Possessing a technological edge may attract new customers to a business. Toyota's Prius hybrid car offered environmentally aware consumers the chance to buy a vehicle that switched off its petrol engine at low speeds and used a self-charging electric motor in its place. Toyota's hybrid car was first on the market and recognised to be of high quality. The company had a waiting list for this product despite its premium price.

Technology and promoting and selling products

One of the world's largest businesses – the Microsoft Corporation – has developed alongside the technological revolution in software and computing. Microsoft has benefited from technology in terms of being able to develop new products but also from using technology to promote and market its products. Technological advances have allowed the company to produce new products such as its software and gaming equipment, for example the Xbox, as well as providing a means to promote and sell its products online as consumers can download the company's software at any time.

It also has used technology as a basis for product development and to encourage consumer loyalty. Microsoft's Office product (Word, Excel, etc.) is designed to be used with its Windows operating system but is also highly compatible with the company's internet browser (Explorer). Thus technology has offered the company the opportunity to develop and sell a suite of products, rather than a single one.

Other businesses rely entirely on technology to distribute their products. Apple is famous for producing innovative technological products such as the iPad5, but the company also uses technology to distribute its products. Its iTunes store allows purchasers to download music, music videos, television shows, applications, iPod games, audio books, various podcasts, feature length films and movie rentals. It is also used to download applications for the iPhone and iPod touch.

Using technology in this way offers substantial cost advantages. Apple does not have to pay to distribute its products nor does it have to pay retailers commission on each sale. This increases the company's profit margin and increases its flexibility in pricing decisions. The company also receives marketing benefits in that it can easily collect large amounts of data about its customers and their preferences, enabling it to target its future marketing effectively.

Technology and production processes

Technology and communications

Technological advances also affect the ways in which businesses operate. Communications within businesses have been transformed by technology. Businesses can communicate simply, cheaply and (most importantly) quickly across the globe. Developments such as video conferencing have allowed employees in a business to see and talk with one another while at different locations.

This offers considerable benefits in terms of use of time and reduction of costs to multinational businesses, or even those operating more than a single site in the UK. Similarly, email allows employees and organisations to communicate immediately and messages can be sent to many recipients at the same time.

The development of extranets has created closer links between businesses, helping to improve efficiency. Companies like the giant American retailer Walmart share sales data through an extranet with suppliers such as Procter & Gamble, to enable production and deliveries to match demand in the stores. Walmart estimates that this improved its inventory control enormously when introduced and saves $2 billion in costs each year.

Technology and production

New technology offers a range of benefits to businesses and consumers. Perhaps the major advantage of technology to businesses is that it allows the development of new methods of production, resulting in lower costs. This permits the firm to enjoy higher profits on each sale. However, in an increasingly competitive global market firms seek to improve their market position by offering high quality and sophisticated products at low prices. Using ever-more sophisticated technology in planning and producing products is one way of achieving lower costs.

Figure 21.2 Computer Aided Manufacture (CAM) in Vauxhall's factory at Ellesmere Port, UK

Source: Carpages website

The process of manufacturing in many industries has been transformed by automation whereby machines do jobs previously carried out by people. The most dramatic aspect of this has been use of computer controlled technology on the production line. This is now an integral part of lean production. Its use allows businesses to control the production line to supply variants on a standard product to meet the precise demands of consumers. Thus Vauxhall's car factory at Ellesmere Port uses computer aided manufacturing systems to produce different colours and styles of cars in succession in response to customers' orders. This is part of the company's JIT (or 'pull') manufacturing system.

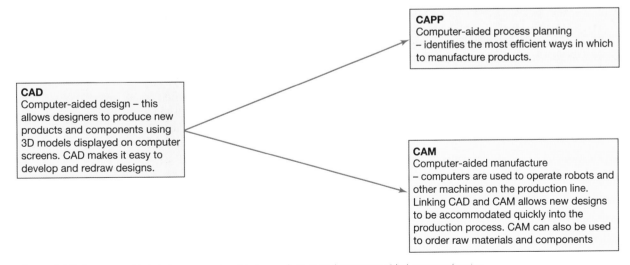

Figure 21.3 Computer aided design, computer aided manufacture and computer-aided process planning

Virtual design at Boeing

Before the first 787 Dreamliner entered service in 2011, designers at the American aeroplane manufacturer, Boeing, had created a virtual aeroplane to test and check their ideas before production of the aeroplane started.

Using a French software system, the American designers assembled an entire virtual Boeing 787 Dreamliner to check that the several hundred thousand parts that make up the airliner fitted together. Every component will have been modelled in 3D geometry, milled and shaped on digital machine tools, assembled several times in virtual factories, and maintained by people who had 'crawled' into digital equipment bays. Any parts that did not meet tough standards were redesigned to overcome problems.

The benefits of this approach were seen when the first Dreamliner was built: the model was assembled with few difficulties occurring. The costs of this process were also much cheaper than the traditional technique of actually constructing a prototype airliner to discover the potential problems.

Questions

1 Explain why the use of virtual design might increase Boeing's long-term profitability. [8]

2 Discuss the problems Boeing might have faced in introducing this type of technology. [16]

The use of CAD and CAM has assisted in improving productivity levels in many manufacturing industries, helping to keep costs down and enhance productivity. Because of this their use has spread to many industries including food processing and the manufacture of pottery.

Technology is not only used in production processes in the manufacturing sector. It is also widely used by businesses that supply services. For example, companies such as Aviva supply insurance policies using the internet. Policyholders enter their requirements onto the company's website and complete their personal details. Aviva's technology computes the price and deducts the appropriate sum from the customer's credit card before downloading the policy to the customer's computer. The whole production process is based on technology.

Technology and human relations

Humans within businesses are always affected by technological change. This is particularly true when new technology is introduced onto the production line. Such change may simply lead to some minor changes in the duties of employees. On the other hand technological developments can result in enormous changes for a business's workforce. For some it may be redundancy, replaced by technology as part of the process

of automation. Many high street banks have made workers redundant owing to advances in technology. Other employees may be required to undertake duties dramatically different from those with which they are familiar as a result of the increasing use of technology in the banking sector.

Employees' reactions to technological change can be equally diverse. For some employees it may represent an opportunity. They may have a chance to acquire new skills, to make their jobs more secure and enjoy higher wages or salaries. The new working practices may offer great benefits. Technology can allow employees greater control over their working lives, leading to increased responsibility and possibility of achievement. This can result in greater motivation.

Others may fear technological change as it increases job insecurity. This is likely to be true of those with few skills who carry out tasks that may be easily automated. Fear of unemployment may lead to industrial action as workers seek to protect their jobs. In such circumstances the introduction of new technology may be awkward and expensive. Redundancy payments may be expensive and corporate images may suffer.

New technology-based products create jobs and unemployment at the same time. For example, automated telephone switchboards have resulted in a loss of jobs for telephonists. Direct dial numbers and electronic answering systems have made telephonists obsolete in many firms. Simultaneously, employment has been created in industries manufacturing and maintaining the automatic telephone systems.

The reaction of employees to technological change may depend upon the culture of the business. Businesses operating traditional culture placing great emphasis on bureaucracy and convention may experience difficulties in adapting to technological change. The existence of a task culture may make the process less difficult. It may be most appropriate if the managers of businesses that are affected by technological change develop a culture that is responsive to change and where employees' attitudes are to embrace change rather than to resist it.

Google's culture

Though growing rapidly, Google still maintains a small company feel. At the Googleplex headquarters almost everyone eats in the Google café (known as 'Charlie's Place'), sitting at whatever table has an opening and enjoying conversations with Googlers from all different departments. Topics range from the trivial to the technical, and whether the discussion is about computer games or encryption or ad serving software, it's not surprising to hear someone say, 'That's a product I helped develop before I came to Google.'

Google's emphasis on innovation and commitment to cost containment means each employee is a hands-on contributor. There's little in the way of corporate hierarchy and everyone wears several hats. The international webmaster who creates Google's holiday logos spent a week translating the entire site into Korean. The chief operations engineer is also a licensed

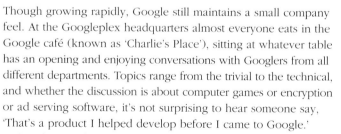

neurosurgeon. Because everyone realizes they are an equally important part of Google's success, no one hesitates to skate over a corporate officer during roller hockey.

Google's hiring policy is aggressively non-discriminatory and favours ability over experience. The result is a staff that reflects the global audience the search engine serves. Google has offices around the globe and Google engineering centres are recruiting local talent in locations from Zurich to Bangalore. Dozens of languages are spoken by Google staffers, from Turkish to Telugu. When not at work, Googlers pursue interests from cross-country cycling to wine tasting, from flying to frisbee. As Google expands its development team, it continues to look for those who share an obsessive commitment to creating search perfection and having a great time doing it.

Source: Google's corporate website

Questions

1 Explain why some employees in manufacturing businesses may fear technological change. [8]

2 Does Google's culture assist the business in embracing technological change? Justify your view. [16]

Threats and technological change

But technological change can be threatening as well as providing opportunities for businesses. The impact of technological change has been profound on one of the UK's most familiar organisations: the Royal Mail. From 2008–13 the company saw its volume of business fall by 6.3 per cent per annum as its average daily postbag declined by more than 8 million letters each day. The major reason for this change is increasing competition from email and digital delivery of information. Royal Mail expects the volume of terms it handles to continue to decline, but at slower rates, over the next few years. The company has estimated that the decline in its volume of business has reduced its operating profit by £500 million annually.

The threats of rapid changes from technology are considerable. Firms in high technology markets will face demands to research new products and to implement more efficient methods of production. Thus commercial pressures may exist to improve technology used in products and processes. New technology, in whatever form, can be a major drain on an organisation's financial resources. Installing new technology on the production line will involve a heavy capital outlay and disruption to production while the work is completed. Thus, a business may lose sales revenue at the time its expenditure rises significantly. Some firms may experience difficulty in raising the funds necessary to purchase new technology. Costs of research and development can be huge and many years may pass before any return is received on them.

Businesses operating in markets experiencing rapidly changing technology can be left behind – or find it too expensive to keep

up with other producers. Small firms can be particularly vulnerable even if they are well managed. This is one factor leading to mergers and takeovers in markets supplying high technology products. The series of mergers and takeovers in the world car manufacturing market has been brought about, in part, by the high costs of developing new products, especially environmentally friendly ones. Sir Alex Trotman, the former chief executive of Ford, has forecast that the global market for car manufacture will eventually comprise three large companies and the extent of investment in technology is one factor driving this change.

New production methods do not always work effectively from the start. Some sort of teething problems are inevitable following the introduction of state of the art technology onto production lines. Workers will take time to adapt to what is required of them and the technology may not behave as expected. This may result in lower levels of productivity and higher production costs.

21.5 Competitors and suppliers

Firms do not operate in isolation. There will be other firms offering similar goods and services and these are their competitors. If they operate in the same industry they are direct competitors, for example Coca-Cola and Pepsi-Cola both sell soft drinks. The degree of competition in a market and the overall structure of a market will affect the decisions a firm makes.

Market structure

When examining the structure of a market we should consider the number of firms in a market and their relative size.

The number of other direct competitors in a market varies considerably. Look online or in the local telephone directory and search for a plumber and you will find hundreds. In contrast, you may only find a company or two that produce sugar. Of course, when measuring the number of competitors you need to define the market carefully. The number of competitors in the Asian retail market is greater than the number in Singapore. There may only be a couple of cinemas in your town but there are far more in the whole county.

If there are relatively few competitors there may be less pressure on a business to maintain the quality of its service. It may become complacent because it is not competing so much to win and maintain customers. In a market with many more competitors customers have choice and the pressure is on to meet customers' needs more fully or lose their business to others.

The size of competitors is also important. There can be a big difference between a market with four equal-sized firms and a market with one large firm and three much smaller ones in terms of how those firms behave in relation to each other. If one firm dominates a market it is likely to have more power over suppliers and distributors and therefore may have lower costs (for example, it may bargain with suppliers and get a lower input price). This can mean that the smaller firms have to cooperate and collaborate with the larger firm because it could always undercut them if it wanted. For example, the smaller firms may be price takers and follow the price set by the larger firms.

Entry threat

The way a business behaves will not only be affected by the existing number of competitors in the market. It will also depend on how likely it is that other firms will enter the market in the future.

This in turn depends on the existence of barriers to entry. Barriers to entry are factors that make it difficult to enter a market. For example:

- **Entry costs** There may be heavy investment required to set up the business because of specialist equipment or facilities needed. You can imagine that setting up a hotel or leisure centre could require quite large sums of money. This will automatically make it difficult for some entrepreneurs to enter the market.
- **Brand loyalty** If the established firms have a high level of brand loyalty then it will be more difficult for others to enter the market because of the problems gaining sufficient market share to break even. For example, loyalty to Nike and Adidas sportswear and Wrigley's chewing gum make entry into these markets quite tough.
- **Legal restrictions** If the existing provider has a patent this means you cannot imitate the invention without permission (and usually paying a licensing fee).

Barriers to entry mean that the firms already in the market are relatively 'safe' from competition, at least for the moment. This means the competitive pressure is reduced and this may affect the quality of the service. On the other hand, if entering a market is very simple, the market is very competitive, forcing better service. For example, setting up a sandwich shop is not particularly expensive or difficult and so there is enormous pressure in terms of the prices charged and quality of food and service provided. There are always shops closing and opening and new forms of food emerging because of the very high level of competition. This is good for customers but not so good for the entrepreneurs who have to remain very responsive to market requirements to survive.

Buyer/supplier power

The competitive environment in a market also depends on the power of buyers and suppliers. If a business is reliant on a few key suppliers then they are likely to be able to charge more and the level of service they have to provide may not be that high because they are needed so much.

The power of a supplier depends on:

- the number of them – if it is easy for a business to switch suppliers then the supplier's power is less

- the size of the supplier and the extent to which it depends on other businesses – if the supplier is small and relies on a businesses then the business (buyer) has the power; if the business only represents a small percentage of the supplier's sales then the supplier has more power.

Similarly, buyer power affects what happens in a market. If the buyer has a lot of power he or she may be able to push the price down and insist that the product is amended to meet their requirements.

A buyer will have power if:

- there are relatively few of them so businesses rely on them heavily; for example, for suppliers of technical military equipment there are not that many military potential customers so the suppliers are dependent on them
- it has many alternative suppliers so it can switch away from one supplier relatively easily if it needs to. This puts the supplier in a weaker bargaining position.

Actions to change the competitive environment

Businesses will want to try to make the competitive environment more favourable. This means they would want:

- a high barrier to entry so that other businesses would not enter the market, which would remove a competitive threat
- few competitors and substitutes so that customers could not easily find alternatives
- low supplier power so that they have power over suppliers; this might mean they can demand a low price and do not have to pay quickly for the items (so they can hold on to the money and earn interest in the bank for longer)
- low buyer power so that they are dependent on your product. This should make demand more price inelastic and so you may be able to charge more for it.

People in business

Michael Porter

The analysis in this chapter is based on the work of business writer Michael Porter and his 'Five Forces' analysis.

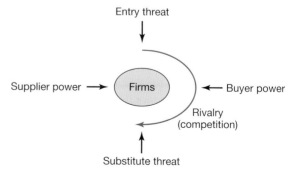

Figure 21.4 Porter's five forces

According to Porter, you can assess the likely profitability within an industry by examining the five forces. Businesses are likely to make more profit if:

- barriers to entry are high
- there are not many competitors
- there are not many substitutes
- suppliers are not powerful
- buyers are not powerful.

Businesses will want to change the five forces to make the industry more favourable. For example, they might:

- join together in an industry association to have more buying power over suppliers
- buy competitors' companies to reduce the degree of competition in the market
- develop USPs to reduce the ability of customers to find substitutes.

21.6 Social factors

Key terms

Social responsibilities are the duties a business has towards employees, customers, society and the environment.

Stakeholders are individuals or groups within society who have an interest in an organisation's operation and performance.

Corporate social reports (CSRs) are documents setting out a business's targets for meeting its social obligations and the extent to which previous social targets have been achieved.

A **pressure group** is a group of people with common interests who organise to influence public opinion and the decisions of businesses and governments.

Businesses are a part of society and are affected by social changes; equally, businesses' actions impact upon society. Social factors that affect businesses include migration and new patterns of demand created by changes such as ageing populations. At the same time the actions of businesses, such as their activities damaging the environment, also affect society.

Social responsibility

Stakeholders include shareholders, employees, customers, suppliers, creditors, **pressure groups** and the local community. The interest that stakeholders have in a business will vary according to the nature of the group.

Over recent years businesses have become much more aware of the expectations of stakeholder groups. In the past managers were expected to operate businesses largely in the interest of the shareholders. A growing awareness of business activities by consumers and other stakeholder groups has complicated the task of the management team. Businesses are also subject to the attentions of pressure groups pursuing a particular interest. For instance, Greenpeace campaigns to protect the environment and its activities have significant implications for businesses. For example, it is acting against uncontrolled deforestation in Indonesia and Malaysia to create palm oil plantations. Today's managers have to attempt to meet the conflicting demands of a number of stakeholder groups.

Social responsibility is a business philosophy that emphasises that firms should behave as good citizens. They should not merely operate within the law, but should consider the effects of their activities on society as a whole. Thus, a socially responsible business attempts to fulfil the duties that it has towards its employees, customers and other interested parties. Collectively these individuals and groups are termed a business's stakeholders.

Figure 21.5 Examples of a business's stakeholders

Meeting social responsibilities has many implications for businesses:

- taking into account the impact of their activities on the local community – protecting employment and avoiding noise pollution, for instance
- producing in a way that avoids pollution or the reckless use of finite resources
- treating employees fairly and not simply meeting the demands of employment legislation
- considering the likely sources of supplies (and whether they are sustainable) and the ways in which suppliers meet their social responsibilities.

Table 21.1 Stakeholders' interests

Stakeholder group	Possible nature of stakeholder's interest
Shareholders	Expectation of regular dividends Rising share prices Preferential treatment as customers, for example, lower prices
Employees	Steady and regular income Healthy and safe working conditions Job security Promotion and higher incomes
Customers	Certain and reliable supply of goods Stable prices Safe products After-sales service and technical support
Suppliers	Frequent and regular orders A sole supplier agreement Fair prices
Creditors	Repayment of money owed at agreed date High returns on investments Minimal risk of failure to repay money owed
The local community	Steady employment Minimal pollution and noise Provision of facilities (for example, scholarships, arts centres or reclaimed areas) for local community

Study tip

Figure 21.5 shows the primary stakeholders for businesses, although others exist. When writing about stakeholders it is important to develop answers fully. This is impossible if you attempt to cover too many stakeholder groups – just concentrate on the two or three that are most relevant.

Some businesses willingly accept these responsibilities partly because their managers want to do so, partly because they fear a negative public image. It can be argued that socially responsible behaviour can pay off for businesses in the long term, but may entail additional short-term expenditure.

Areas of social responsibility

The nature of a business's social responsibility will vary according to the nature of the business. A petrochemicals company is more likely to be concerned with polluting the environment than a bank. On the other hand, in an age of rapid developments in information technology, banks may see their social responsibility to be the maintenance of employment. We can identify a number of key elements of social responsibility beyond the responsibilities a business has to its shareholders.

- **Responsibilities to consumers** The consumer has become a force to be reckoned with over recent decades and this has been reflected in the development of consumerism.

Increasingly, consumers have been better informed about products and services and prepared to complain when businesses let them down. The rise of consumerism has meant that businesses have been required to behave more responsibly by looking after the interests of the consumer.

- **Responsibilities to employees** Businesses have a variety of responsibilities to their employees that are not a legal requirement. For example, firms should provide their employees with training to develop their skills as fully as possible and make sure that the rights of employees in developing countries (where employment legislation may not exist) are protected fully. This may mean paying higher wages and incurring additional employment costs.
- **Responsibilities to the local community** Firms can benefit from the goodwill of the local community. They can encourage this by meeting their responsibilities to this particular stakeholder group. This may entail providing secure employment, using local suppliers whenever possible and ensuring that the business's operation and possible expansion does not damage the local environment.
- **Responsibilities to customers** Customers are critical to businesses. Offering high-quality customer service, supplying high-quality products that are well designed and durable and at fair and reasonable prices should create satisfied customers and quite possibly generate repeat business.
- **Responsibilities to suppliers** Businesses can promote good relations with suppliers by paying promptly, placing regular orders and offering long-term contracts for supply. These are not legal requirements, and might result in higher prices for materials and components, but may also assist suppliers to meet their own responsibilities, for example in the maintenance of employment.

In what ways can businesses accept their social responsibilities?

Businesses can take a variety of decisions and actions, allowing them to meet their responsibilities to their stakeholders in general.

- For manufacturing businesses the impact of their sources of supply can be considerable. Using sustainable sources for resources means that future generations will have access to the same materials. Body Shop International's refusal to use any materials that are unsustainable or any components that have been tested on animals reflects a sense of responsibility to many relatively poor communities in developing countries and to animals.
- Many manufacturers have considerable potential to damage the environment. Altering production processes (sometimes at considerable cost) can reduce or eliminate many forms of pollution. Malaysia, the world's second largest producer of palm oil, has pledged to conserve a minimum of 50 per cent of its total land area as preserved forests. In 2010, 58 per cent of Malaysian land remained as forest.

Unilever says sustainability key to new business model

Consumer products manufacturer Unilever has unveiled a 'new business model' putting sustainability at the heart of its global operations. It pledged to halve the environmental impact of its products while doubling sales over the next ten years.

Chief executive Paul Polman said the new model was 'the only way to do business long term'.

The company said it would produce an annual report on its progress towards achieving these goals. Unilever, which makes a number of well-known and popular brands such as Persil, Dove, Flora, PG Tips and Ben & Jerry's, made three overarching commitments to achieve by 2020:

- cut by 50 per cent the environmental impact of its products in terms of water, waste and greenhouse gases
- source 100 per cent of its agricultural supplies from sustainable sources
- improve the health and well-being of one billion people across the world.

Polman continued: 'There is a compelling case for sustainable growth – retailers and consumers demand it and it saves us money.'

The company plans to deliver these commitments by doubling its use of renewable energy to 40 per cent of total energy use; reducing its water consumption by 65 per cent on 1995 levels; reducing waste sent for disposal by 70 per cent on 1995 levels and reducing levels of salt, fat and sugar in its food products.

The company admitted it would not be easy to achieve these goals, but said they could be achieved with the help of non-governmental organisations (NGOs), governments and suppliers.

Source: Adapted from BBC News (Richard Anderson), 15 November 2010

Questions

1 Explain how Unilever's sustainable approach might save the business money. [8]

2 Discuss how Unilever's shareholders might react to the launch of the company's 'new business model'. [16]

- Socially responsible firms put employees before profits. Maintaining employment, even when the level of sales is not sufficient to justify this, is an important means of fulfilling social responsibilities, as is the continuation of unprofitable factories to avoid creating high levels of localised unemployment. These types of policies are only really sustainable in the short term, unless the business in question is earning handsome profits elsewhere.

- Choosing suppliers is an increasingly important issue for firms which are keen to confirm that their raw materials and components come from socially responsible firms. Many firms operate a code of conduct for suppliers, including the American restaurant chain McDonald's. The fast-food company operates a code of conduct prohibiting suppliers from using child labour and insisting upon basic health and safety standards. The company has a contractual right to inspect suppliers' premises to ensure the code of conduct is implemented.

- Supporting the local community is an important way of fulfilling social responsibilities. It can provide the public with a clear perception of the 'caring' side of modern businesses. The Gulf Bank operates a 'Give Life' campaign to encourage more people to donate blood in Kuwait. The initiative, entitled 'Give Life', is designed to persuade the Kuwaiti community that blood donation is a worthwhile action. Recently, Gulf Bank announced that the campaign had reached a major milestone of saving more than one thousand lives due to the generosity of donors.

- More than 70 per cent of the UK's best-known companies (those making up the FTSE 100) are members of Business in the Community. This organisation exists to assist member companies in 'continually improving, measuring and reporting the impact that their business has on their environment, workplace, marketplace and community'. However, the state of the economy can influence the level of charitable donations given by businesses. Charitable donations in the UK have increased recently as the performance of the economy has improved.

Corporate social reports

Corporate social reports (CSRs) are documents setting out a business's targets for meeting its social obligations and the extent to which previous social targets have been achieved. These may also be called corporate responsibility reviews.

Analysts do not assess businesses solely in terms of profits, even during difficult financial times such as those the UK and other countries have experienced recently. It can be argued that businesses should also be judged in terms of their records on pollution, consideration of their employees and support for the community. A growing proportion of businesses are engaging in social responsibility reporting or **social accounting**. This form of reporting includes the costs to the business of acting in a socially responsible manner (charitable donations, for example) and the benefits received, which are usually difficult to quantify in monetary terms. A few businesses include their social reports within their annual reports. A 'successful' business might not be the most profitable, but the one of most value to all sections of the community in which it operates.

Social accounting (also known as corporate social reporting) is the process of communicating the social and environmental effects of a business's operations to its stakeholders.

Apple remains the world's most admired company in 2014

For the seventh straight year, Apple has been named the world's most admired company following voting by many global businesses. Despite a difficult year which saw Apple's share price fluctuate, the company remains the envy of the corporate world's eye.

The iconic tech company known for the iPhone and other stylish and user-friendly products continues in the top spot on this year's list, for the seventh year in a row. Apple, the most valuable brand on the planet according to Interbrand, brought in $171 billion in revenues and $37 billion in profits in 2013. The company is flush with cash, but the market is becoming impatient to see its next big innovative product. Many analysts forecast a smartwatch or Apple TV, but the company is also reportedly turning its attention to cars and medical devices.

Amazon and Google were No. 2 and No. 3, respectively, having switched places from their rankings in 2013. Among the other tech companies in Fortune's top-50 'all star' list: IBM at No. 16, Samsung at No. 21, Microsoft at No. 24, and Facebook at No. 38.

Source: Adapted from *Time*, 27 February 2014 (Matt Vella)
http://time.com

Questions

1 Explain how a company that charges very high prices for its products can earn profits of $37 billion in one year. [8]
2 To what extent is remaining the world's most admired company important for the management team at Apple? [16]

CSRs frequently have several elements. Firstly, firms are required to draw up and implement policies stating the ways in which they will conduct the aspects of their business which impact upon society generally. This may include issues such as:

- using sustainable sources of raw materials
- ensuring suppliers trade responsibly avoiding, for example, the use of child labour
- operating an extensive health and safety policy above the legal requirements, thereby protecting the well-being of employees
- engaging in a continuous process of environmental management and monitoring the effects of production on the environment
- trading ethically and taking account of the moral dimension in decision-making
- operating transparently to avoid corrupt practices such as paying customers a fee in return for the award of a large contract.

It is common for an independent body to monitor the effectiveness of these policies and the effects on society

generally. This helps to persuade stakeholders that the results published are genuine. Once the social report is complete firms review their social and environmental policies in the light of the information from the auditors.

CSRs can be a valuable exercise for firms to conduct. They may identify antisocial (or potentially antisocial) behaviour before problems arise. This helps to promote the corporate image of the business as a caring and responsible organisation. However, conducting an audit of this kind is not a guarantee that a firm is socially responsible. Managers must ensure that social policies are carried out effectively at all levels within the organisation and that employees are committed to them. Sufficient resources must be devoted to ensuring that the business remains socially responsible and problems identified in social audits should be resolved speedily. The danger of a less active approach is that social audits publicise weaknesses and firms are seen not to respond, with damaging consequences for their corporate image.

The trend to increase use of social and environmental reports continues with many large firms producing some form of report. However, the quality of the reports is improving, though some do not cover all the relevant issues. Many companies still do not have their corporate social reports independently audited to confirm their accuracy. A further criticism is that some firms do not analyse their supply chains. This means that suppliers could engage in practices such as employing children without it being revealed in the CSR. It is possible that the effects of slow rates of economic growth in many countries might reduce the numbers of businesses prepared to devote resources to producing a CSR, or to improving its quality and extent.

Global Reporting Initiative

Global Reporting Initiative (GRI) has pioneered and developed a comprehensive Sustainability Reporting Framework that is widely used around the world. The Framework enables all businesses to measure and report their economic, environmental, social and governance performance.

The Reporting Framework thus enables businesses to be more transparent about their economic, environmental, social and governance performance. This transparency and accountability builds stakeholders' trust in organisations, and can lead to many other benefits. Thousands of businesses of all sizes and in many different industries use GRI's Framework in order to understand and communicate their performances to stakeholders.

GRI has its headquarters in Amsterdam in the Netherlands. This acts as a hub, coordinating the activity of GRI's many network partners. GRI has regional offices in Australia, Brazil, China, India and the USA. Its global network includes more than 600 supporters as well as 30 000 people representing different businesses and industries.

Questions

1 Explain the difference between an oil company's economic and social performance. [8]

2 Discuss the benefits businesses might receive from using GRI's standard format to report their performance to stakeholders. [16]

Demographic changes

The UK's population has grown relatively quickly over recent years.

- **Changes in the composition of the UK population** The UK is subject to large migratory flows. There have been substantial inflows of migrants from parts of Asia and also Eastern Europe leading to the UK's population size passing 63 million in 2014 and the rate of increase is the highest since the 1960s. This has led to a demand for different types of products (as well as offering new sources of labour supply). In 2011, 579 000 Polish passport holders lived in the UK, compared with just 75 000 in 2003. This development has led to a new market niche and suppliers of Polish products such as foods and books have appeared. It is not just small businesses that have responded to the creation of this niche market. Tesco has launched a Polish language website to enable it to supply homesick Polish migrants in the UK with products from 'home'.

- **The UK's ageing population** The population of the UK is steadily ageing with larger numbers of people in the older age groups. In 2005, 34 per cent (20 million people) of the UK's population was over 50. In 2025 it will be 40 per cent, about 25.5 million people. In 2005 16 per cent of UK citizens were over 65 – that figure is expected to rise to 21 per cent in 2025, to as many as 13.5 million people. There are expected to be 4.5 million people in the UK aged over 85 in 2025. Figure 21.6 illustrates the main trends in the age structure of the UK's population until 2041. The older age groups represent substantial segments of markets for many products and businesses have responded to the increased spending power of older groups. Firms supplying products including holidays, clothes, insurance and housing have designed products for the older age group.

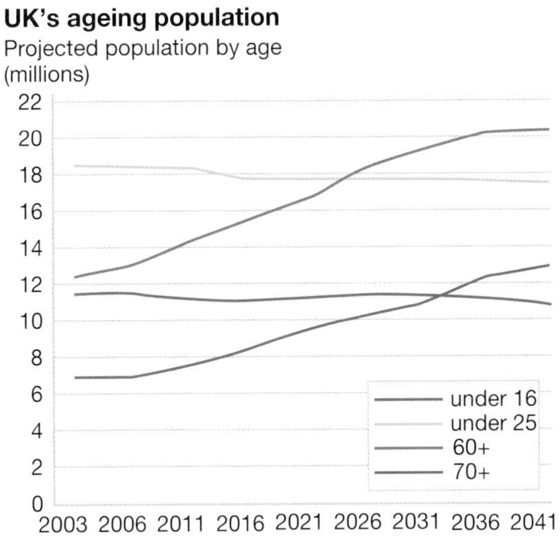

UK's ageing population
Projected population by age (millions)

Figure 21.6 The age structure of the UK's population 2003–41

Source: Government Actuary's Dept (2003 projections)

- **The rise in the number of single-person households** People in the UK are increasingly living alone, meaning that the country comprises more, smaller households. This has significant implications for businesses of all types. Table 21.2 illustrates how the number of single-person households in the UK is expected to rise until 2026. This trend has implications for businesses supplying houses, consumer durables and even food, where smaller packet sizes may be more commonly purchased.

Table 21.2 One-person households by age in the UK, 2003–26

	2003	2026	Average annual increase
Under 25	226 000	254 000	1 000
25–34	797 000	1 048 000	11 000
35–44	923 000	1 460 000	23 000
45–54	834 000	1 415 000	25 000
55–64	947 000	1 792 000	37 000
65–74	1 061 000	1 559 000	22 000
75 and over	1 659 000	2 359 000	30 000
Total	**6 447 000**	**9 886 000**	**150 000**

Source: News Distribution Service

Environmental threats and opportunities

The media take a great interest in business activities in relation to the environment. When firms are found to be guilty of some act of pollution, adverse publicity is likely to follow. Society expects higher standards of environmental performance than in the past.

There are many potential causes of damage to the environment. The major environmental concern identified by the government is global warming. This is caused by the release of a concoction of industrial gases (principally carbon dioxide) that has formed a layer around the Earth. This layer allows the sun's rays in but prevents heat escaping, causing the so-called 'greenhouse effect'. Other problems include the pollution of rivers and land and the dumping of waste, some of which is toxic and harmful to wildlife and humans alike.

Businesses contribute in many ways to the creation of environmental damage.

- The emission of gas through production processes.
- Pollution caused by transporting raw materials and products, particularly using road vehicles which emit noxious gases and create congestion and noise. A report by the EU suggested that pollution from vehicles in the UK could be responsible for up to 40 000 deaths among elderly people each year.
- The pollution of the sea by businesses using it as a 'free' dumping ground. The North Sea is one of the most polluted stretches of water in the world.
- Destruction of natural environments as a result of activities such as logging (cutting down trees for commercial purposes, as in the Indonesian forests) and the building of homes on greenfield sites.

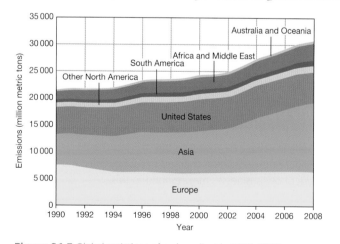

Figure 21.7 Global emissions of carbon dioxide 1990–2008

Source: The United States Environmental Protection Agency

Despite engaging in activities that damage the environment there is evidence that some businesses and some regions are improving some aspects of their environmental performance. Figure 21.7 illustrates that emissions of carbon dioxide by countries in Europe fell between 1990 and 2008. However, emissions in some regions with large numbers of developing economies, for example Asia, rose over the same period, as also shown in Figure 21.7.

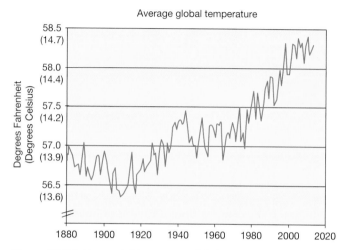

Figure 21.8 Evidence of rising average global temperatures 1880–2013

Source: Adapted from www.earth-policy.org/

There is a considerable body of evidence, as shown in figure 21.8, to show that world temperatures are rising. Although global warming is a controversial topic many scientists argue that a major contributor to this trend is businesses throughout the world. This development is linked to the rise in emissions of carbon dioxide shown in Figure 21.8.

Costs of polluting the environment

Businesses are acutely aware of their private costs (the costs of production they have to pay themselves) such as expenses for raw materials and wages. These are easy to calculate and form part of the assessment of profitability. However, environmental pressure groups and others have pressed for businesses to acknowledge the costs they create for other groups in society – the external costs of production.

Noise, congestion, air and water pollution all impose costs on other individuals and groups in society. A firm extracting gravel from a quarry may create a number of external costs. These could include congestion on local roads caused by its lorries. This would impose costs in terms of delay and noise pollution on local residents. The destruction of land caused by the quarrying could create an eyesore for people living nearby and may reduce the value of their properties. Dust may be discharged into the atmosphere. The quarrying firm will not automatically pay for these costs. It requires government action to ensure that it pays these external costs as well as its internal ones.

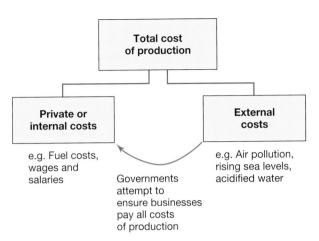

Figure 21.9 Internal and external costs of production

Thus, the total costs of production equal internal or private costs plus external costs borne by third parties. By ensuring that firms pay all the costs associated with the production of a product, governments can avoid what is termed market failure. As we saw in the previous chapter, market failure could occur as a result of pollution because suppliers may not be charged the full costs of production and oversupply might result, as profits are high.

The implications of environmental control for businesses

The need to alter business practice to take account of environmental protection has implications for most aspects of business activity.

- **Production** Firms face pressure to redesign products to use less materials and packaging and to make these materials biodegradable or recyclable. These requirements affect all types of businesses. For example, house builders are under great pressure to build on brownfield sites (land previously used for building, often in cities and towns) and to protect the countryside by minimising the use of greenfield sites. Strict controls on production techniques are intended to minimise pollution.
- **Purchasing** Businesses are encouraged to seek sources of supply that are sustainable and do not damage the environment, or to use recycled materials. For example, the paper industry makes a great deal of use of recycled materials and uses this as part of its promotion.
- **Marketing** Businesses use their 'green credentials' as an important component of their marketing strategy. Adverts will make reference to environmental protection and even projects to improve the environment. Packaging will confirm the company's concern to avoid pollution. This is particularly important to firms that are seen to have great potential to pollute (oil companies such as BP and China National United Oil Corporation (Chinaoil), for example) or for those who use this aspect of their operations as a USP – Body Shop International is an example of the latter. The case study on Unilever on page 265 shows the importance some managers place on an environmentally friendly business model.

- **Human resources** New processes and procedures in manufacturing make some jobs and skills obsolete, creating a need for redundancies or retraining. Environmental management has resulted in many businesses needing employees with new skills, requiring a retraining programme or recruitment. Environmental managers seek to minimise the effects of the business's activities on the environment and to ensure that the firm meets new legislative requirements as they emerge. Businesses may also seek to hire employees skilled in resource management and having the ability to influence corporate decisions to ensure the development of management strategies designed for the most efficient use of scarce natural resources.

The implications of environmental protection are profound especially for the so-called polluting sector (for example, chemicals and oil extraction and refining). They require a corporate response from senior managers within a business. But as with many external influences the environment provides opportunities for businesses as well as constraints.

New markets have been created for businesses supplying training in environmental management. Firms also offer to supply environmental control equipment to adapt production processes to minimise the possibility of environmental harm. Equally, a market exists for testing equipment to monitor emissions or the toxicity of waste products. Finally, businesses can use environmental policies as a means of obtaining a competitive advantage. The German car manufacturer BMW, for example, promotes itself as a manufacturer of cars that are almost entirely recyclable. This could prove attractive to environmentally aware consumers.

Case Study

New law for Philippines' mining industry

In July 2012, President Benigno Aquino III of the Philippines signed Executive Order 79 or the new Mining Law that intends to amend the Mining Act of 1995 and make the business of mineral exploitation more equal among the government, mining companies, communities hosting the mine, and indigenous people who hold rights to the land and its natural resources.

The new law, along with its implementing rules and regulations, signed by Environment and Natural Resources Secretary Ramon Paje, set a new policy tone for the industry. It also addresses the issues of environmental damage, climate change, protection of indigenous peoples, and equality in the distribution of wealth.

In the eyes of big mining companies, the new law spelled disaster. During the 2012 Mining Conference at the Sofitel Plaza in Pasay City, Mines Chamber president Benjamin Philip Romualdez protested about the losses the industry would suffer as a consequence of the ban on new mining projects until a new revenue-sharing measure is in place – one of the major problems the new law on mining is supposed to address. 'The $2 billion in mining investments we are expecting this year will not happen,' Romualdez said in his speech on the first day of the conference.

Questions

1 Explain who might benefit and who might suffer as a consequence of this law. [8]

2 Discuss the extent to which the benefits and drawbacks of this law may change over the longer term. [16]

Why should businesses accept social responsibilities?

It is easy to argue that by meeting their social responsibilities businesses are likely to reduce profitability. Providing workers with ongoing training, investing in facilities for the local community, trading with suppliers who do not use cheap child labour and only engaging in non-polluting production techniques will all increase costs, reducing a business's profitability and limiting its international competitiveness.

However, this is a relatively simple view and there are more subtle arguments in favour of businesses fulfilling their obligations to society.

- Some businesses have a high profile with regard to issues of social responsibility. Thus the public sees Shell and Exxon as having enormous potential to pollute. The directors of these companies have recognised this and regard socially responsible behaviour as an important competitive weapon. As an example, Shell supports education and produces much valuable material for use in schools and colleges. In particular, the company gives information on environmental matters. Clearly both Shell and Exxon hope that being seen to be socially responsible will improve their sales.

- Sometimes behaving in a socially responsible manner may reduce costs. Treating employees with respect and paying slightly above the going rate may improve motivation and performance and reduce labour turnover. For businesses where labour represents a high proportion of total costs (banking and insurance, for example) this could represent an important saving.

- In markets where little product differentiation occurs, adopting a socially responsible stance may improve sales and profits. In the UK the Co-operative Bank is alone in the banking sector in promoting its ethical and socially responsible views.

It may be that social responsibility might reduce profits in the short term, but over a longer timescale the marketing advantages may dominate and profits could increase.

Test your learning

Short answer questions

1 a State **two** external factors that might influence the external environment within which a business operates. [2]

  b Explain the implications of **one** social change for businesses. [3]

2 a What is meant by the term privatisation? [2]

  b Explain why many businesses oppose the intervention of the government in the economy. [3]

3 a Distinguish between CAD and CAM. [3]

  b Explain what is meant by the term unfair dismissal. [2]

4 Explain why the existence of employment protection legislation may be of benefit to businesses. [5]

5 a Give **two** examples of the marketing practices that consumer protection laws are designed to control. [2]

  b Explain **one** way in which a business's decisions may be influenced by the structure of the market in which it operates. [3]

6 a State **two** barriers to entry that an entrant to an industry may face. [2]

  b Distinguish between stakeholders and shareholders. [3]

7 a Explain the term social responsibility. [2]

  b Explain how a manufacturer might meet its responsibilities to the local community. [3]

8 Explain why a small retailer competing with much larger rivals might decide to meet its social responsibilities as fully as possible. [5]

9 a What is a corporate social report (CSR)? [2]

  b State **three** significant changes in the population of your country that might affect local businesses. [3]

10 a State **two** areas of business activity that might be affected by environmental control. [2]

  b Distinguish between internal and external costs of production. [3]

Data response question

Muirvale Housebuilders

The structure of the UK's population is changing quickly, especially migrationary flows and age patterns. Simultaneously, the number of single-person households is rising. By responding quickly and efficiently to such changes Muirvale Housebuilders, one of the UK's smaller house building companies, has increased its return on capital steadily, although its ROCE declined last year. It trades in a market that is dominated by large companies such as Taylor Wimpey. Muirvale's prices are 5 per cent higher than the market average.

Muirvale's corporate plan sets out:

- its intention to build a greater variety of properties than most of its competitors including large and small and retirement properties
- its commitment to meet its customers' needs as fully as possible, including after-sales service
- its aim to enhance its reputation for quality products.

Part of the company's strategy is its use of corporate social reporting (CSR) of which it was an early adopter. It uses sustainable materials and builds on more expensive brownfield (previously developed) sites whenever it can. It wishes to present itself as a socially aware business and, in particular, to be environmentally friendly as far as possible. It uses the results of its CSR extensively in its marketing.

Muirvale's market research has shown that, possibly owing to tougher economic conditions in the UK, demand for most types of housing in the UK has become more price inelastic. The research has also revealed a high level of awareness of Muirvale's socially responsible behaviour.

Questions

1 Analyse the demographic changes that may have influenced Muirvale Housebuilders' corporate plans. [10]

2 Discuss how the existence of larger competitors might influence Muirvale Housebuilders' decisions. [14]

3 Do you think that Muirvale Housebuilders should continue to produce its CSR? Justify your view. [16]

Essay questions

1 To what extent do laws on employee protection improve the performance of businesses? [20]

2 'Concern about possible damage to the environment is the most important social factor affecting the external environment for all businesses.' Discuss the extent to which this statement is true. [20]

Past paper question

Read the Eastern Motors (EM) case study on pages 468–70 and answer the following question.

Assume Eastern Motors has a factory in your country. Analyse the impact of any **two** legal controls on this factory's operations. [8]

Cambridge International AS and A Level Business Studies
9707 Paper 3 Q1 May/June 2009

22 Further human resource management (HRM)

Chapter overview

In this chapter we examine:
- different approaches to HRM
- the ways in which employee performance is measured
- the principles of need for employment legislation
- the benefits of employer–employee cooperation
- the reasons for and benefits of workforce planning
- the role of trade unions in HRM, negotiation, and collective bargaining and single union deals.

Key terms

Human resource management (HRM) is the process of making the most efficient use of an organisation's employees.

Labour productivity measures the relationship between the amount of labour used in production and the quantity of outputs of goods or services.

22.1 Different approaches to HRM: human resource strategies and flexible workforces

Hard and soft HR strategies

A human resource strategy is the medium- to long-term plan that is implemented to achieve the business's HR objectives. It is a central element of a business's approach to HRM. A number of factors have persuaded UK businesses to implement human resource strategies.

- A principal argument is that the Japanese have had apparent success in managing people using this approach. The Japanese have been seen to gain significant competitive advantage from managing a human resource that produces high-quality products at minimum cost. It is **human resource management** that is credited with achieving this match between employee behaviour and organisational objectives.

- Changes in organisational structure have led to many managers taking on responsibility for managing people within the organisation. Techniques such as delayering and the development of empowered teams have been an integral part of the implementation of human resource strategies. Acquiring, developing, motivating and rewarding employees are, it is argued, best done by managers and colleagues close to the employees in question. Under HRM, managers can carry out many of the more routine tasks of traditional personnel management.

- The increasing popularity of psychological approaches to motivation has encouraged the adoption of HR strategies. Human resource strategies demand styles of working that meet the social and psychological needs of employees. The adoption of flatter organisational structures and psychological techniques of motivation are essential elements of HR strategies – organisations that adopt these techniques and structures would naturally move towards adopting some type of HR strategy.

However, the adoption of HR strategies by businesses in many developed countries is not as sweeping and as clear-cut as some might suggest. Surveys have indicated that many companies have opted to select only the elements of the human resource management package that fit in with their philosophies, management style and corporate objectives. For example, a firm might choose to implement rigorous selection and appraisal methods but ignore other aspects, particularly developing employees through training.

This means that there is not a single HR strategy or approach to HRM. Different firms have interpreted HRM in different ways.

- **'Hard' HR strategies** Some firms operate 'hard' HR policies, treating employees as a resource to be used optimally. Such firms regard employees as yet another resource to be deployed as efficiently as possible in pursuit of strategic targets. Employees are obtained as cheaply as possible, controlled and disposed of when necessary.

Table 22.1 'Hard ' and 'soft' approaches to HRM

	'Hard' HRM	'Soft' HRM
Philosophy	Sees employees as a resource like any other available to the business	Sees employees as different from, and more important than, any other resource available to managers
Timescale	Sees HRM as a short-term policy: employees hired and fired as necessary	Takes a long-term view of using the workforce as efficiently as possible to achieve long-term corporate objectives
Key features	• Employees paid as little as possible • Employees only have limited control over working life • Communication mainly downward in direction • Leaders tend towards Theory X view of workforce • Employees recruited externally to fulfil human needs – giving short-term solution • Judgemental appraisal	• Managers consult with employees • Managers give control over working lives to employees through delayering and empowerment • Leaders tend towards Theory Y view of workforce • Emphasis on training and developing employees • Employees promoted from within, reflecting long-term desire to develop workforce • Developmental appraisal
Associated leadership style	Leaders operating this style of HRM are more likely to be at the autocratic end of the spectrum of leadership.	Leaders implementing 'soft' HRM are more likely to be democratic in nature.
Motivational techniques used	Probably mainly motivated by pay, with limited use of techniques such as delegation and teamwork.	Motivate through delegation and empowerment. Heavy use of techniques designed to give employees more authority.

• **'Soft' HR strategies** Other firms use an HR system that can be regarded as 'soft'. This approach is based on the notion that employees are perhaps the most valuable asset a business has and they should be developed to maximise their value to the organisation. This makes a long-term approach essential. Employees are seen as a resource to be valued and developed over time and in response to changing market conditions.

Appointing an HR manager

The following advert appeared in February 2014 on a global recruitment website.

HR Manager – International Automotive Company Shanghai

Date: 10 Feb 2014

Location: China, Shanghai

Salary: 80 000 – 130 000 per annum

An international manufacturer in the Automotive industry is looking for an HR generalist to become the HR Manager of their rapidly growing Chinese production operation.

Based in Shanghai you will be responsible for operational HR Management ensuring the HR function is able to facilitate and drive the wider development of the business. You will be responsible for ensuring that all HR deliverables are achieved according to both local and global HR objectives.

The person appointed will ensure a successful collaboration with all key stakeholders.

This is a broad HR generalist position and to be eligible you must have had a significant level of HR generalist experience in a production/manufacturing environment.

Desired Skills and Experience:

• Must have knowledge of Chinese employment law, policies and processes
• Strong tertiary educational background
• Experience in production/manufacturing or other relevant industrial sectors is highly preferred
• Ability to build strong working relationships with key senior stakeholders
• A broad HR generalist background with exposure to the full spectrum of hard and soft HR strategies
• Effective communication and negotiation skills

Source: Adapted from Sancus Associates website
http://www.sancusassociates.com

Questions

1 Explain the difference between hard and soft human resource strategies. [8]
2 Is it impossible to use hard and soft HR strategies within a single business with any success? Justify your view. [16]

Hard HR strategies

A hard HR strategy offers a number of advantages to a business.

- It makes it easier for businesses to adapt the size and composition of their workforces to match the needs of their customers. Thus, a business using this type of strategy will be prepared to hire and dismiss workers as necessary without the need to maintain the size of its workforce during a downturn in sales. This allows a business to cope more effectively when trading in markets that suffer from regular fluctuations in levels of demand.

- It can result in lower costs, especially in the short term. Adopting a 'hard' approach to employees may mean that a business only uses employees with minimal skill levels and relies on the use of technology and a small number of highly skilled core employees to meet the needs of its customers. This means that the business may be able to reduce expenditure on its workforce by paying low wage rates (perhaps minimum wage) and to avoid heavy and regular expenditure on employee training. Such a strategy, if successful, may boost profits to the satisfaction of shareholders.

- A 'hard' approach to HR allows managers to retain control over the workforce and to direct operations as they wish. Under such an approach employees will be told what their duties are, with relatively little opportunity for discussion on how to complete a job and limited input in terms of suggestions on how to improve the production process. This approach can assist a business in maintaining its focus on its corporate objectives.

However, the 'hard' approach to HR can also bring about a number of disadvantages.

- The level of **labour turnover** might be very high. This can impose a number of costs on the business. First, it has to recruit replacement employees. This can be costly in terms of advertising and using managers to select the new staff from the applicants. Secondly, even if the jobs are relatively unskilled some training is likely to be required, which may involve further expenditure. Finally, new employees are likely to be less productive during the initial period of their employment, which will detract from the overall levels of productivity achieved within the business.

- Employees may be demotivated by this approach to employment. The failure of managers to develop a long-term relationship with employees will mean that it is unlikely that what Herzberg identified as motivators will be present in the job to any great extent. For example, the chance to take responsibility for projects and opportunities for promotion will be limited. This approach relies heavily on pay as a motivator and ignores the potential of social and psychological factors to motivate employees and improve their performance at work.

Key term

Labour turnover is the percentage of a business's employees who leave the business over some period of time (normally a year).

Soft HR strategies

A soft HR strategy offers a number of advantages to a business, although in many cases these are the opposite of those discussed above.

- A soft HR strategy can help a business to build a reputation for being a 'good' employer. Good employers seek to offer their employees diverse and interesting jobs and the opportunity to develop their skills. The pay and conditions on offer are attractive and the employer ensures that employees receive regular training to improve their skills and enhance promotion prospects. Being regarded as a good employer allows businesses to attract higher-quality candidates, which in turn improves the quality of the workforce and the overall performance of the business. A recent survey showed that working for a respected employer was one of the most important factors to job seekers when applying for employment. This can make a soft HR strategy attractive to employers in Asia as the region is suffering from a severe shortage of employees with technical and professional skills. Attracting and retaining highly skilled employees is vital for the future of many businesses in the region.

- A soft HR strategy can improve knowledge management within a business. This means that the business is more likely to possess a workforce with the knowledge and skills essential for the business to continue trading effectively. This comes about because this approach usually results in a lower level of labour turnover and therefore employees develop long-term working relationships with businesses, allowing them to bring experience to bear in decision-making.

- A soft HR strategy may also develop a more creative workforce. Employees will be given more opportunities to contribute to decision-making and to provide suggestions and ideas on improving the operation of the business. This can motivate the employees (by meeting what Maslow identified as an individual's higher needs) and also provide an organisation with some excellent ideas without incurring the costs of hiring consultants. Because these ideas are generated from people with a different perspective on the organisation, they can be different and creative.

Of course, this type of human resource strategy does have its drawbacks.

- It can be very expensive, especially in the short term. The costs of training employees can be significant, particularly if they are given off-the-job training. These costs could be wasted to some degree if the employee leaves soon after completing the training, possibly as a consequence of being 'poached' by an unscrupulous rival – this is an example of market failure. Higher rates of pay and good working conditions can also add to an employer's costs.

- It can be difficult and expensive to alter the workforce in response to a change in market conditions. The soft HR strategy is likely to rely heavily on full-time and permanent employees and thus the business might have surplus capacity if demand falls, and little potential to increase output if demand rises.

The approach to HR strategy used will obviously depend upon the type of business. It may be that businesses employing less-skilled employees may opt to use a harder approach as the costs of losing employees may be less and the potential from increasing responsibility within the organisation is less obvious. On the other hand, a more skilled workforce might be more suited to a softer approach to make the most effective use of their talents and to minimise the risk of highly trained, skilled and productive employees leaving the organisation.

Study tip

It is essential, when dealing with questions on the advantages and disadvantages of the two types of HR strategy, to consider the nature of the business and its workforce. This may enable you to justify the use of a particular approach, either hard or soft.

Case Study

Outsourcing and HR

Outsourcing of HR functions is a reality for many companies, large and small, in the Asia-Pacific region today. The benefits can include cost savings, and access to highly skilled professionals and advanced technology, which can collectively result in a sustainable competitive advantage.

The broad adoption of HR outsourcing across Asia-Pacific has also emerged as a key finding of regional research conducted by Talent2, a leading HR and business process outsourcing provider. The Talent2 study found that in Australia, Hong Kong, China and Singapore, the majority of HR executives (80–90 per cent) are now considering HR outsourcing as a solution to key challenges including recruitment (64 per cent) and employee retention (50 per cent).

Commenting on these findings, John Rawlinson, CEO of the Talent2 Group, said: 'This research reinforces that ongoing skills shortages are hampering organisations across Asia from finding the people they need to drive top line business growth. What's interesting here is that HR executives are focusing on different ways to address these challenges – namely through outsourcing, and investment in learning and development.'

Source: Adapted from HRM Asia, 3 October 2013 (Shalini Shukla) http://www.hrmasia.com

Questions

1 Explain the problems a national business may face as a result of encountering significant skills shortages. [8]

2 Do you think that the skills shortages and move to outsourcing of some HR functions in the Asia-Pacific region will encourage companies to adopt 'soft' HR strategies? Justify your view. [16]

HR strategies and competitive advantage

Adopting and implementing the right HR strategy has the potential to provide businesses with a significant competitive advantage over rivals. Using the right strategy should make the organisation more competitive, and to some extent this is borne out by the performance of Japanese companies.

Soft human resource management recognises the individual rather than producing personnel policies for the whole workforce. Reward systems, training and development, appraisal and communication are all geared to fulfilling the needs of the individual as well as those of the organisation. The key principle of HRM (or at least 'soft' HRM) is that each employee should be nurtured and developed in pursuit of the organisation's objectives. All aspects of the HRM 'package' should be coordinated to ensure coherence and to assist in the attainment of strategic targets.

If an organisation is successful in operating its HR strategy, the outcome should be motivated and creative employees who are committed to the firm and who do not seek to leave. Such employees should be aware of the goals of the organisation and understand how they can contribute towards the attainment of organisational targets.

Under this scenario a business should incur lower recruitment costs, enjoy higher levels of productivity and a reduction in faulty products. It may attract top-class applicants to vacancies because of its reputation as a caring and enlightened employer. This process is termed employer branding. All of these factors should make the organisation more competitive and better able to cope with the rigours of operating in international markets.

However, in the real world there are differing views on the best HR strategy. Many businesses in the UK differ in their interpretation. Some take a 'hard' attitude, viewing employees as simply another resource to be used as effectively as possible. This approach has a much more short-term focus.

There are, however, theoretical arguments suggesting that whichever HR strategy is adopted, it may not enhance a business's competitiveness. Trade union recognition is a problem under the HR approach to managing employees. There is an obvious tension in an organisation that attempts to deal with its employees on an individual basis within a framework of collective bargaining. This tension may manifest itself in employee dissatisfaction or, in extreme cases, in industrial action. Both scenarios could prove extremely damaging to a business's competitive performance.

Further problems may exist if the culture of the organisation is not suited to a HR approach to managing people. Even a 'hard' HR strategy implies some degree of delegation and at least a limited commitment to training. This can involve a degree of expenditure and some managers may oppose the lessening of control that this entails. Furthermore, the adoption of any HR strategy may involve additional costs in the short term as managers and employees adjust to the new strategy and to revised roles within the organisation. The elevation of human resources to a strategic role may incite some opposition from those with responsibility for, say, marketing or finance. All of these factors can detract from the competitive performance of the organisation, especially in the short term.

Flexible workforces

Key terms

Flexible workforces exist when businesses place less reliance upon permanent full-time employees and make greater use of part-time and temporary workers.

Temporary workers have contracts of employment that only exist for a specific period of time – perhaps six months.

Annualised hours operate when an employer states the number of hours employees must work over a year. Weekly working hours can be varied to suit their circumstances.

In recent years a number of trends have emerged in workforces in many countries.

- **Rising numbers of temporary workers** The number (and proportion) of workers on temporary contracts (for a fixed time period) within the many OECD countries rose steadily from the early part of the twenty-first century until 2012, as shown in Table 22.2. The recession following the financial crisis in 2008 was one factor causing an increase in the proportion of **temporary workers** in the workforce in the UK and other countries. The average proportion of employees on temporary contracts across the 34 countries which are members of the Organisation for Economic Co-operation and Development (OECD) has increased by about 1.5 per cent. There have been significant rises in Mexico and the UK.
- **Part-time working** The percentage of employees who work part time has risen substantially across the OECD countries, with Chile, Mexico and Spain recording notable increases. Developing countries such as Pakistan exhibit the same trend. In 1999–2000 8.4 per cent of those employed in Pakistan worked fewer than 30 hours each week; by 2010–11 the equivalent figure was 10 per cent.
- **Contractors and consultants** Many businesses have replaced full-time employees with consultants or have contracted out duties to other organisations. For example, it is common for firms to employ contract staff to design and manage IT systems rather than use permanent full-time employees in these roles.
- **Full-time permanent employees** Firms across the world use fewer full-time employees than was the case in the early 2000s. Such employees are relatively expensive as the firm incurs all the costs of employment, such as making pension contributions and providing training. Using consultants and contractors avoids these costs and ensures employees are only hired when needed. Those full-time employees who are hired tend to be highly skilled and perform central roles within an organisation.

Businesses have opted for workforces containing increasing numbers of part-time and temporary employees. Labour forces with high proportions of these types of employees are called **flexible workforces**.

Table 22.2 Comparative data on percentages of employees working part-time and on temporary contracts in 2002 and 2012, selected countries

COUNTRY	Percentage of workforce on temporary contracts		Percentage of workforce working part-time	
	2002	**2012**	**2002**	**2012**
Australia	4.3***	6.1	54.6	56.4
Brazil	N/A	N/A	14.4	17.1
Canada	24.0	30.8	64.5	65.1
Chile	N/A	N/A	4.0	23.7
Germany	46.1	55.1	12.2	18.8
Korea (South)	35.7**	29.4*	N/A	N/A
Mexico	31.9	46.9	10.4	24.0
Poland	55.1	64.7	39.5	39.9
Russia	21.5	21.4	3.0	3.2
Spain	64.5	62.4	8.2	37.0
Turkey	19.8	20.8	1.8	7.8
UK	12.9	15.1	46.6	57.9
OECD average	24.5	26.0	34.8	40.5

* 2011 data; ** 2004 data; ***2001 data

Source: Organisation for Economic Co-operation and Development (OECD) http://stats.oecd.org

Core and peripheral workers

One way in which a flexible workforce can be organised is as part of a 'flexible firm'. This idea was developed by John Atkinson and The Institute of Manpower Studies. They explained that flexible workforces comprise a core workforce and a peripheral workforce, as illustrated in Figure 22.1 below.

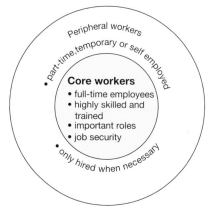

Figure 22.1 The organisation of a firm with a flexible workforce

The business's core workers would be highly qualified and trained and would be motivated and would be in permanent full-time employment with security of employment. In contrast, the peripheral workers would only be hired when necessary. They may be low skilled or have highly specialised skills that are not required at the time. An example of the latter category could be experts on environmental pollution. This would allow the business to respond to fluctuations in demand without incurring the ongoing costs of employing all its workers on a permanent basis. The peripheral workers could be employed part time or by using temporary contracts.

Other methods of flexible working

Businesses can also employ people flexibly using:

- **annualised hours contracts** – employees working in this way are be expected to work, say, an average of 38 hours each week, but can be employed to work longer hours during busy weeks, with an equivalent reduction in working hours during quieter periods
- **zero-hours contracts** – these are given to people who are employed by the business but only work and receive pay when both the business and employee agree to do so.

Case Study

McDonald's uses zero-hours contracts for 90 per cent of employees

McDonald's has emerged as potentially the biggest zero-hours employer in the private sector after admitting that it employs 90 per cent of its entire workforce in the UK, or 82 800 staff, on the controversial terms.

Zero-hours contracts have been criticised because they offer no guarantee of regular work and no stability of income. However, the Institute of Directors, which represents 38 000 directors including several bosses of FTSE 100 companies, attacked calls for a ban, claiming the UK could be in the same situation as Italy or Spain without a flexible labour market.

Andy Sawford, a Labour MP who has campaigned to abolish zero-hours contracts, said: 'McDonald's could lead on addressing this issue. There will be some employees working 20 to 30 hours a week, week in week out, and it is indefensible not to put those people on contracts. In the ordering of their food they know how to identify customer levels so they cook the right amount, so they could use that same information with staff levels and give employees more certainty.'

McDonald's employs 92 000 staff throughout the UK, running 1200 restaurants. A spokeswoman said prospective employees are asked during the application process to say which days they can work. She added: 'Many of our employees are parents or students who are looking to fit flexible, paid work around childcare, study and other commitments. Employee hours are scheduled in advance and we never ask people to be 'on call'.

'The zero-hours contracts which all our hourly-paid employees are on do not affect employee benefit entitlement and all of our employees are entitled to a range of benefits including life assurance, employee discounts and access to a range of training and qualifications.'

She said McDonald's has employed zero-hours contract workers since it entered the UK in 1974.

It has also emerged that a rival fast-food franchise, Subway, employs hundreds of staff on zero-hours contracts.

Source: Adapted from *The Guardian*, 5 August 2013 (Simon Neville) http://www.theguardian.com

Questions

1 Explain the possible implications of being on a zero-hours contract for an employee at McDonald's. [8]
2 Do you think that McDonald's should expand its use of zero-hours contracts to its restaurants in other countries? Justify your view. [16]

22.2 Measures of employee performance

Methods of measuring employee performance

Before managers decide on changes to the workforce as a result of recruitment or training it is important to assess the performance of the existing workforce. A number of measures are available to businesses to assess the performance of their employees. Armed with this knowledge managers are then in a better position to implement appropriate changes to improvement of the performance of the workforce and the business overall.

Labour productivity

$$\text{Labour productivity} = \frac{\text{output per period}}{\text{number of employees at work}}$$

This is perhaps the most fundamental indicator of the performance of a group of employees and has implications for a business's costs and hence the prices that it can charge. Productive workers produce larger quantities of output per worker per time period and this is a measure that is relatively easy to calculate.

Labour productivity depends upon factors such as the extent and quality of capital equipment available to the workforce as well as its skills and degree of motivation. Thus it is possible for managers to take a range of actions with the intention of improving labour productivity figures.

Research indicates that overall labour productivity in the UK increases by about 2 per cent per annum. This improvement in efficiency reduces the labour costs involved in producing a typical unit of output. Improvements in labour productivity allow businesses to enjoy increased profit margins or to reduce prices (while maintaining profit margins), hopefully leading to increased sales. Businesses can increase their competitiveness in terms of costs and prices if they can increase productivity at a higher rate than that of rival businesses.

Pakistan's poor productivity performance

Pakistan's labour productivity growth remains a matter of grave concern in all the country's economic sectors, ranging from 5.3 per cent in community, social and personal services to a negative 4.1 per cent in electricity, gas and water supply between 2000 and 2010.

According to the latest data of Asian Productivity Organization (APO), labour productivity growth in the country's agriculture sector stood at 0.1 per cent between 2000 and 2010. An almost negligible growth in the sector has put a huge dent in the country's overall labour productivity growth, which increased by 6.7 per cent in China, 2.5 per cent in India, 0.8 per cent in Bangladesh and 2.8 per cent in Sri Lanka during the period under review.

In the manufacturing sector, labour productivity grew by 2.3 per cent in Pakistan, 8 per cent in China, 3.4 per cent in India, 1.3 per cent in Bangladesh and 2.4 per cent in Sri Lanka.

Almost 60 per cent of Pakistan's exports are generated by the manufacturing sector, which, according to the APO, accounts for 13 per cent of the country's total employed workforce.

Questions

1 Explain the possible implications for a business if its workforce has negative labour productivity rates over a period of several years. [6]
2 To what extent is the use of more technology in the workplace the best way for Pakistani businesses to improve their labour productivity figures? [16]

Labour turnover

$$Turnover = \frac{number\ of\ staff\ leaving\ during\ the\ year \times 100}{average\ number\ of\ staff}$$

This ratio measures the proportion of a workforce leaving their employment at a business over some period of time, usually one year. Low wages and inadequate training leading to poor morale among employees may cause high levels of labour turnover. Another cause is ineffective recruitment procedures resulting in the appointment of inappropriate staff. Other reasons include redundancy and retirement.

Some level of **labour turnover** is inevitable. Managers seek some level of labour turnover to bring new ideas into a business, but not so high as to impose excessive recruitment costs. The 2013 Annual Survey by the Chartered Institute of Personnel and Development (CIPD) revealed that labour turnover in the UK was 11.9 per cent in 2012, compared with 15.7 per cent in 2008 and 18.3 per cent in 2005. In contrast, labour turnover rates in India are much higher. Rates of 20–30 per cent are normal and the IT industry has experienced figures approaching 50 per cent.

Key term

Labour turnover is the percentage of a business's employees who leave the business over some period of time, normally a year.

Job roles, labour turnover and reasons for leaving

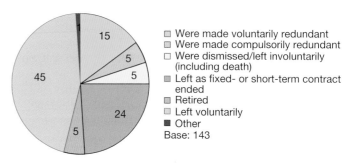

Figure 22.2 Reasons for leaving employment in a sample of jobs in the UK, 2012

Source: CIPD Annual Survey Report, 2012

Questions

1 Analyse the possible reasons why private services (for example, people employed in customer services or hairdressing) has a higher rate of labour turnover than senior managers and directors. [8]
2 Evaluate the extent to which a high rate of labour turnover poses a serious problem for small businesses. [16]

Managers attempt to manage labour turnover to achieve a balance between bringing new employees with enthusiasm and ideas into the business against the costs of recruitment. Research by the CIPD in the UK suggests that most businesses face a higher labour turnover than desired and that this results in unexpected recruitment costs.

Case Study

More feedback from CIPD

The costs associated with labour turnover can be high, not just in terms of replacing leavers but also the loss of skills and knowledge and consequent reduction in productivity. Just over a third of organisations wanted to reduce turnover in 2011, while just a quarter actually did so. In contrast, 25 per cent reported that they wanted to increase turnover during 2011, while 36 per cent reported that this happened.

Two-fifths of organisations report they want to reduce turnover in 2012. A smaller proportion (20 per cent) wants to increase turnover during 2012, perhaps due to a desire to reduce costs in tough economic conditions. Even among these organisations, however, there will still be key employees they wish to retain.

Source: CIPD Annual Survey Report, 2012

Questions

1 Analyse why a business might wish to increase its labour turnover. [8]
2 Discuss the reasons why a large and profitable retailer might experience difficulty in reducing its rate of labour turnover. [16]

Maths moment

Serendipity Ltd manufactures electrical components. Its managers recorded the following data over the most recent financial year.

- average number of employees: 750
- output of components (000s): 2250
- number of employees leaving the business: 50.

The company's managers also calculated that its productivity figure has fallen by 15 per cent since the year before.

1 Calculate Serendipity Ltd's productivity and labour turnover figures for the most recent financial year.
2 Calculate Serendipity Ltd's productivity figure for the 'year before'.

Absenteeism

$$\text{Absenteeism} = \frac{\text{number of staff absent (on one day)} \times 100}{\text{total number of staff}}$$

Absenteeism occurs for a variety of reasons, including industrial accidents and illness. The term is frequently used to describe a situation where an employee is absent from work frequently and without good reason. Thus, it is used as a measure of the morale and motivation of a workforce. High levels of absenteeism can dramatically increase a business's costs.

Study tip

Being able to interpret and comment on the results of measures of employee performance in relation to the business in question is important. For example, labour productivity may be important in some businesses operating in price competitive markets, while labour turnover could be critical where employees are highly skilled and expensive to train.

Key term

Absenteeism occurs when an employee is not present at his or her place of work.

Health and safety

$$\text{Health and safety} = \frac{\text{number of working days lost per annum for H\&S reasons} \times 100}{\text{total number of possible working days}}$$

This measures the safety of the working environment. A dangerous working environment not only lowers employee morale but may also damage the performance of the workforce. Absence due to accidents and injuries in the workplace increases the labour costs incurred by a firm and can lead to adverse publicity.

Managers need to measure employee performance to assess the efficiency (and competitiveness) of the workforce. In service firms (where labour costs are a high proportion of total costs) this can be a particularly important factor. Measures of employee performance also help to assess whether a workforce is fully motivated.

Methods of improving employee performance

There are a number of approaches a business can take to improve the performance of its employees. A logical approach to improving poor employee performance is to consider the causes and to implement policies intended to address this.

Training

One reason why employees may have relatively poor productivity levels is because they lack the skills necessary to perform their jobs efficiently. Businesses can invest in training to provide the job-related skills the employees require to carry out their work more effectively. Training can also improve a workforce's performance in terms of health and safety by alerting employees to dangers in the workplace and encouraging the use of safe working practices.

Figure 22.3 On-the-job training

However, training can be costly and there is always the risk that employees may leave the business for alternative higher paid employment once they possess these employable skills. Training to improve employee performance is more likely to be effective when employees are highly skilled or when improved employee performance can provide a distinct USP.

Motivation

A highly motivated workforce is likely to be highly productive with low levels of labour turnover and absenteeism. In Chapter 7 we considered a number of ways in which businesses may improve the motivation of their workforces. This may require businesses to redesign jobs to make them more attractive and fulfilling, perhaps by empowering employees and/or offering the opportunity to work in teams. Well-designed jobs can help to reduce labour turnover and absenteeism by allowing employees to fulfil Maslow's higher needs (such as self-esteem) at work. Herzberg argued that personal achievement, recognition and responsibility were key motivators. By creating jobs that allow employees to have responsibility, to achieve goals and to receive recognition, it is possible for businesses to satisfy larger numbers of employees and discourage them from leaving the business.

Study tip

Don't forget the materials that you studied at AS level. Your studies of motivation will help you to understand much of the material we cover in this chapter.

Pay systems

Businesses can use pay systems such as piece-rate or performance-related pay which reward employees according to the amount produced or for the attainment of specified targets. This approach can be effective in improving productivity, especially in manufacturing organisations.

A newer approach to pay, which is intended to improve the performance of teams within the organisation, is team pay. Team pay is a method of linking the pay of employees to the level of performance that they have achieved in a team. Team pay means that all members of a team receive some sort of financial incentive when a goal or target is reached. The goals might be financial, sales related or expressed in terms of quality. Team pay might be a supplement to basic pay or it might represent the entirety of an employee's pay.

Team pay is a very attractive technique as more businesses adopt flatter organisational structures and make more use of delegation. Modern businesses using these approaches to organising their employees require a workforce that can be flexible in its ability to deliver improvements in quality, profitability and customer service.

Team pay aims to reinforce behaviour that leads to effective teamwork. Being a part of a successful team can be very satisfying and may discourage absenteeism as individuals may be unofficially accountable to other team members and not want to let them down.

Table 22.3 Team pay versus individual pay

Team pay	Individual merit pay
Rewards teamwork and cooperation	Creates internal competition
Encourages group to improve work systems	Encourages withholding of information
Increases flexibility and ability to respond to changing needs	Individuals try to improve system – results in failure
Not incorporated in base pay	Decreases flexibility
Encourages information sharing and communication	Incorporated into base salary
Focus on wider organisation	No focus on wider organisation

Source: M Thompson, *Team-working and Pay* (1995) Institute of Employment Studies

Employer branding

Employer branding can be defined as creating a perception of the business as a really good place in which to work in the minds of current employees as well as other stakeholders such as customers and shareholders. A survey of 895 businesses in the UK by the CIPD revealed that 69 per cent of businesses consider that they have an employer brand and that this is particularly important to smaller businesses with fewer than 250 employees. Having a good employer brand helps to persuade employees to stay with a business and can be an important factor in retaining the services of skilled and potentially footloose employees.

22.3 Management by objectives

Peter Drucker spent many years researching major companies such as General Electric and DuPont in the United States. In 1954 he published *The Practice of Management*, one part of which was his theory of 'Management by Objectives' (MBO). This theory stated the central role of objectives in business management.

According to Drucker's theory of management by objectives, managers should:

- identify and agree targets for achievement with subordinates
- negotiate the support that will be required to achieve these targets
- evaluate over time the extent to which these objectives are met.

The objectives set at each level should be coordinated to ensure that the business achieves its corporate objectives. Each member of staff should make a contribution, no matter how small, towards the whole business achieving its overall objectives.

Thus, in our example in Figure 22.4 a business has a **mission statement** that sets the organisation the overall target of becoming the 'premier supplier of bottled beer in Europe'. The business's **corporate objectives** contribute to this mission – one might be to increase sales in Europe by a certain percentage each year. A business comprises functions such as marketing, finance and production. These functions should contribute to the achievement of corporate objectives by doing their bit. Thus, marketing should increase sales, raise production output, and so on ... Finally, the departments, teams and individuals at the bottom of the hierarchy should all make their coordinated contribution to the attainment of the objectives of the functional area of the business in which they work.

An important element of the operation of MBO is the review of the extent to which targets have been met and the development of new goals, targets and objectives in the light of this experience.

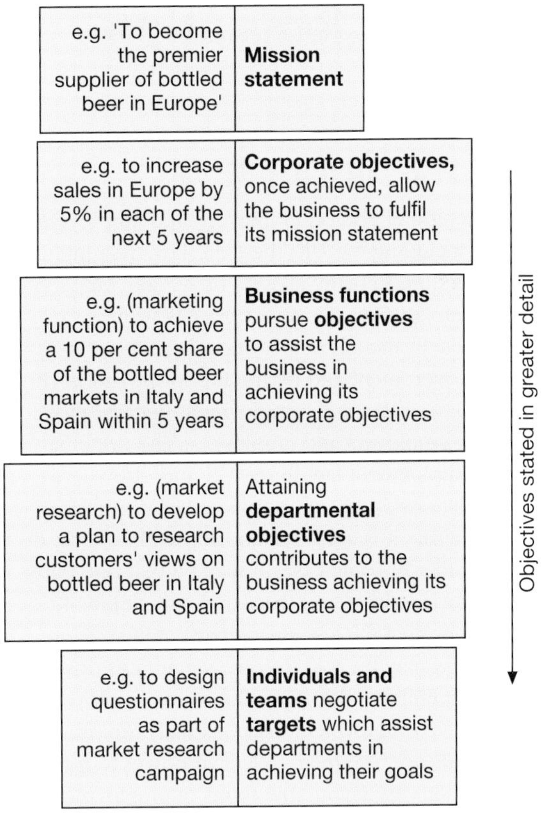

Key terms

Mission statements set out the overall purpose of a business.

Corporate objectives are the goals of the entire organisation, designed to assist in fulfilling the business's mission.

The advantages and disadvantages of management by objectives

MBO offers a number of advantages to businesses.

- MBO can improve communication within the organisation as the target-setting and evaluation process takes place. It can

Figure 22.4 Management by objectives

give managers a fuller appreciation of the duties and problems faced by their subordinates.

- Employees may be motivated by having a clear understanding of what they are trying to achieve, and how it helps the business achieve its overall goals. MBO has the potential to improve employee performance.
- MBO can highlight training needs for managers and subordinates, improving their performance and productivity.
- The attainments of goals can help all employees to fulfil some of the higher needs identified by Maslow.

Drucker recognised at the outset that MBO had a number of potential drawbacks.

- Some employees may find the setting of targets as threatening. Employees at different levels within the organisation have varying perceptions of issues, problems and their solutions. The manager might set targets that the subordinate considers unachievable.
- All employees within the organisation must be committed to the technique if it is to succeed and benefit the business.
- Setting targets for highly specialised employees can be difficult and tends to remove the focus from the mainstream corporate objectives.
- Modern businesses operate in a business environment that is changing rapidly, for example as a result of the globalisation of markets. Objectives can quickly become out of date if, for example, a technological development by a multinational competitor means that products are obsolete.

22.4 Labour legislation

The need for labour law

The law has far-reaching effects on employees and employers. In many countries, including the UK, there are laws relating to recruitment and selection, to many aspects of actually employing someone (for example, minimum rates of pay) as well as to dismissing employees. In the UK employment legislation is created by the UK government and by the European Union (EU). There is a need for laws relating to employment because two parties are involved: employers and employees. The principal objective of much employment law in the UK and elsewhere is to regulate the relationship between two parties of unequal power and to ensure that it is a fair relationship without abuses of power on either side. In some cases it may be that one party is much stronger than the other and that employment law is therefore needed to protect the less strong party. Thus a large and powerful business may be able to force wage rates down or to provide unacceptable working conditions for employees if little or no alternative employment exists. Equally, employees may form trade unions and use their collective power to force large wage rises and/or very favourable terms of employment on small businesses.

Study tip

You do not need to have specific knowledge of individual employment laws but rather a broad understanding of its purpose and the aspects of business activity that it affects.

As a consequence the government or other authority establishes and enforces certain rules or laws relating to employment to provide a fair and even framework within which employers and employees can operate.

Sources of employment legislation

There are three main sources of employment legislation in the UK.

- **Acts of Parliament** Each government passes a series of Acts to put into operation the ideas it set out in its election manifesto. Laws passed by Parliament are called 'statute law'. The House of Commons and the House of Lords pass these Acts before being signed by the Queen. Once all these stages are completed an Act becomes law. As an example, the Equality Act became effective in the UK with effect from April 2011, imposing additional responsibilities on employers to treat all employees fairly.

- **Common law** Much of the UK's business law is based upon decisions taken by judges. Common law often involves an interpretation of existing legislation, perhaps applying it to new circumstances. Higher courts, for example the Supreme Court, the Court of Appeal and the High Court, set common law. Common law is also called judicial precedent.
- **European Union law** The EU passes a great deal of legislation relating to UK businesses. The Working Time Directive is an example that has received a great deal of publicity. EU law is important to businesses covering topics such as free competition between firms, agricultural prices and working conditions. EU law overrules any UK national legislation that may conflict with it.

Additionally, UK businesses operate according to voluntary codes of practice frequently overseen by government agencies. Voluntary codes are normally an alternative to a new law or regulation. These codes are not law and are not enforceable in the courts. They are, however, in widespread use. For example, the UK Border Agency (which is responsible for managing migration into the UK) operates a series of codes of practice which govern the use of overseas workers by UK businesses.

Aspects of employment governed by employment laws

Most countries operate a range of employment laws designed to protect the rights of the individual employee who may be the weaker party in any employer-employee relationship. These cover a number of aspects of employment.

Discrimination

It is common in many countries for employment legislation to make discrimination in the workplace illegal. The types of discrimination that may be judged illegal could include discrimination of the grounds of:
- gender, marital status or sexual orientation
- colour, race, nationality or ethnic origin
- disability and age.

This legislation can benefit minorities but also businesses that may otherwise choose not to employ talented people who are from specific ethnic groups or perceived to be of the wrong gender. Discrimination laws can have a major impact on recruitment and selection policies operated by businesses.

Pay

Employment legislation may establish a minimum wage for employees working in a particular country. This is normally based on a wage rate per hour or day, although some countries such as Malaysia operate one based on monthly pay.

Minimum wage legislation is designed to protect employees with few employment skills and little bargaining power in labour markets and to provide them with an income which provides at least an acceptable standard of living. Some businesses have opposed the introduction of minimum wages, arguing that their implementation drives up costs of production and damages price competitiveness in global markets.

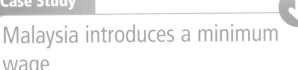

Malaysia introduces a minimum wage

Malaysia introduced its first minimum wage benefiting an estimated 3.2 million workers in July 2012. This brought the country's laws on low pay into line with neighbours Thailand and Vietnam. Prime Minister Najib Razak greeted the introduction of the legislation by saying that it would guarantee the lowest paid an income sufficient to lift them out of poverty.

From October 2012 employees on Peninsular Malaysia received a minimum monthly pay of 900 ringgit ($297). The legislation provides for different rates in rural areas: employees in the eastern Sabah and Sarawak states will receive 800 ringgit ($237) each month. From 1 January 2014 the Malaysian government sent officials from its Labour Department into businesses to enforce the new minimum wage rates.

The Malaysian government's decision comes at a time when a number of countries in Asia are either introducing or raising minimum wage rates amid fears about widening income gaps between rich and poor. Thailand increased its minimum wage to 300 baht ($9.75) a day throughout the country in January 2013, and by an average of 40 per cent in the rest of the country. In 2013 the Singapore Parliament discussed introducing a minimum wage for the first time.

Questions

1 Analyse the likely effects of a large pay rise for employees on the customers of the businesses. [8]
2 Discuss whether or not all businesses in Malaysia will benefit as a result of the government's decision which may increase wage costs by up to 40 per cent. [16]

Maths moment

Kulkar Industries employs 7500 people. Exactly 30 per cent of its employees receive annual pay of $3000 and a further 15 per cent are paid $2900 per annum. The government has introduced a minimum wage which is set at $3750.

Assuming no other changes to Kulkar Industries' wage rates, by how much will its annual wage costs increase following the implementation of the minimum wage?

Unfair dismissal

Unfair dismissal is the termination of a worker's contract of employment without a legal reason. Legislation relating to unfair dismissal only relates to workers once they have been in a particular job for one year or more. There are a limited number of reasons why an employee might be dismissed legally in the UK.

● Where a job no longer exists – this is redundancy.
● Gross misconduct – examples of this include theft from the employer or behaving violently at work.
● Failing to carry out duties in 'a satisfactory manner'.
● Another substantial reason, for example long-term illness, other laws which prevent continued employment or the ending of a temporary contract.

All other reasons for dismissal are considered unfair. Employees in the UK who think they have been unfairly dismissed can claim compensation by taking their case to an Industrial Tribunal.

Health and safety

Governments in most countries have put in place laws designed to make workplaces safe and healthy environments for all employees. Such laws normally require employers to identify potential risks and put in place policies and procedures for managing and minimising these. Such procedures might involve:

● changes in production methods
● education and/or training for employees
● the employment of specialist employees to manage the risk.

It is not unusual for businesses to be fined heavily if they fail to meet the necessary Health and Safety laws.

Workplace accidents in Zimbabwe

The National Social Security Authority (NSSA) has revealed that 38 people were killed in work-related incidences during the first half of 2013 while 2755 were injured.

According NSSA's occupational safety and health report the number of people dying in work-related accidents eased slightly to 38 compared to 43 fatalities during same period in 2012.

Most of the causalities occurred in Harare, which recorded 20 deaths from 1073 injuries.

NSSA's Director of Occupational Safety and Health, Rodgers Dhliwayo, said he blamed the fatalities and increased numbers of injuries on the failure by companies to invest in occupational safety.

'In short, they do not care much about the safety and health of their workers. The immediate causes of accidents ranged from ignorance, recalcitrance, stubbornness, short-cutting procedures and incompetence,' he said.

'Protecting employees from injury may require a certain amount of expenditure. When money is tight and economic conditions are difficult, it is tempting for business people to cut corners and avoid unnecessary expenditure.

'However, spending money on protecting the lives and health of staff is not unnecessary expenditure. It is essential expenditure for anyone who cares about the lives and welfare of those they employ. It is also, in the long run, in a business's own interests too.'

In 2012 there were 5141 serious occupational injuries which resulted in 103 deaths, the highest number of occupational injuries and deaths for several years. In 2011, there were 4158 serious work-related injuries recorded, 75 of which were fatal. In 2010 there were 4410 serious injuries, resulting in 90 deaths.

Source: Adapted from New Zimbabwe, 19 August 2013
http://www.newzimbabwe.com

Questions

1 Analyse the likely effects of safer workplaces on the motivation levels of employees in Zimbabwe. [8]

2 Do you think that spending money on protecting the lives and health of staff is always in a business's interests? [16]

Trade union activities

The degree of freedom to operate enjoyed by trade unions varies between countries. Many countries have enacted some laws to control the power of trade unions for fear that, if uncontrolled, their existence may upset the balance of power between employees and employers. The power of trade unions can be controlled by the law in a number of ways.

- Employers may not be legally obliged to recognise or negotiate with trade unions over workplace matters. In Pakistan trade unions' rights are not protected by laws at federal or provincial level and hence many employers do not recognise trade unions.
- Trade unions may have to operate secret ballots on key issues such as striking to ensure that decisions made by the trade unions' leaders fairly represent the views of the members of the union. In 2012 the government in New Zealand passed a law making secret ballots mandatory for trade unions.
- Some types of employees are not allowed to become members of a trade unions. Many countries, including Mauritius, make it illegal for police officers to join a trade union.

22.5 Cooperation between management and the workforce

> **Key term**
>
> **Industrial democracy** refers to ways in which employees can influence the decisions taken within a business.

Cooperation between the managers of a business and its workforce can take a number of forms.

Works councils

A works council is a forum within a business where workers and management meet to discuss issues such as working conditions, pay and training. This is a form of **industrial democracy**. Employee representatives on a works council are normally elected. It is common for works councils to be used in workplaces where no trade union representation exists. However, in businesses where works councils and trade unions co-exist, the former is normally excluded from discussing pay and working conditions. (We look at trade unions in more detail in a later section.)

Quality circles

Quality circles are groups of workers and managers who meet regularly to identify methods of improving all aspects of the quality of their products. Quality circles developed in Japan and consider working methods as well as the products themselves. They normally comprise three to ten employees from all levels within the organisation who assemble to discuss company problems and possible solutions. Quality circles meet for one or two hours two or three times a month, usually in working time, and can provide businesses with imaginative solutions to production problems. Quality circles have been used by numerous high profile businesses including Philips, Rolls Royce and Marks and Spencer.

Autonomous work groups

These are teams of employees who are given a high level of control over their working lives. Senior managers delegate considerable authority to those further down the hierarchy allowing them to decide what tasks to complete at what times and some control over the resources available to the group. In some cases autonomous working groups elect their own leader and appoint new staff. The intention behind the creation of such groups is improved motivation and productivity. Such an approach is unlikely to succeed without careful preparation and significant amounts of training.

A very common method of communication and cooperation between employers and employees is through the existence of trade unions in the workplace and collective bargaining. We will consider these topics later in the chapter.

The benefits of management–workforce cooperation

Benefits to employers

Managers can gain a number of advantages through cooperation with employees or groups representing employees.

- **Improved communication** It is less likely that employees will take industrial action in the form of strikes, bans on overtime working or adopting working practices to slow the rate of production if there is effective and regular communication between employers and employees. Misunderstandings are less likely to occur and disputes may be settled through negotiation. As a result of cooperation and enhanced internal communication a business may be more able to maintain its delivery of goods or services to customers and thereby benefit from a reputation as a reliable supplier.

- **Improved motivation of the workforce** Cooperation of this type can have positive effects on the motivation and performance of a business's workforce. Delegation of authority in the form of autonomous workgroups or involvement in decision-making can have real benefits in terms of generating factors that motivate. Improved motivation can result in higher levels of productivity and lower rates of absenteeism and labour turnover, which offer real financial advantages to businesses. Figure 22.5 illustrates how different methods of employee–employer cooperation relate to motivational factors identified by well-known writers on motivation.

- **Improved workforce performance** A business may find that increased cooperation with employees and their representatives can improve the performance of the workforce in other ways apart from increased motivation and productivity. Cooperation with employees (for example, through quality circles) may reveal improvements that may be made to operations systems and highlight dangerous aspects of production that could result in accidents.

- **Enhanced employer branding** We saw earlier in this chapter that employer branding is creating a perception of the business as a really good place in which to work in the minds of current employees as well as other stakeholders. Cooperation with the workforce and the creation of a harmonious and

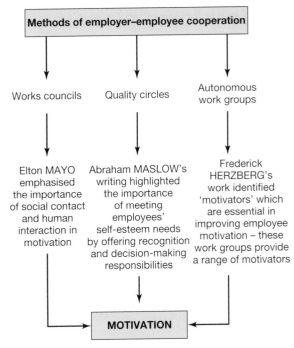

Figure 22.5 Methods of employer–employee cooperation and motivation

productive working environment is an important element of creating a positive employer brand. A positive employer brand offers two significant advantages to businesses:

- the possibility of recruiting higher quality employees attracted by the business's reputation as a 'good' employer
- reduced levels of labour turnover as more employees decide not to move to alternative employment.

Recruitment costs can be very high, especially for senior positions, so a positive employer brand can help to reduce costs as well as creating a positive corporate image for the business.

Benefits to employees

Effective cooperation between employers and employees can offer considerable financial advantages to employees. Firstly, by reducing the chance of industrial action taking place employees are more likely to be able to benefit from higher rates of pay from working overtime and the chance of periods without pay due to strikes is reduced. Increased productivity, which may result from such cooperation, may result in higher pay (if pay is linked directly to productivity) or in the employer becoming more profitable and having the ability to increase pay rates.

There may be non-financial benefits too. Cooperation in the form of works councils offers employees a chance to play a part in decision-making as part of a process of industrial democracy. Being part of a quality circle can allow employees to make proposals for changes in the way the business operates and have the satisfaction of seeing their ideas and decisions being implemented.

22.6 Workforce planning

A **workforce** (or **human resource**) **plan** assesses the current workforce and actions necessary to meet the business's future labour needs.

The components of workforce plans

Workforce planning is one of the core activities of human resource management. It entails a number of stages.

- The starting point of workforce planning is to consider the overall or corporate objectives of the business. The workforce plan must contribute to the achievement of the business's overall or corporate objectives.
- The next stage is to take a strategic view of employees, and to consider how human resources can be managed to assist in attaining the business's corporate objectives. This may entail considering factors such as the use of technology and how this might complement or replace some human input into the production process.

- At this stage those responsible for workforce planning will have to make a judgement about the size and type of workforce the organisation will require over future years.
- This desired future workforce is compared with that available to the business at the time of planning.
- Once this comparison is complete the firm can decide upon policies (e.g. recruitment, training, redeployment and redundancy) necessary to convert the existing workforce into the desired one.

This process is shown in Figure 22.6. The workforce plan will specify the business's desired workforce and how the business will implement its human resource policies. An important element of the plan is a skills audit to identify the abilities and qualities of the existing workforce. This may highlight skills and experience of which managers were unaware. For example, some employees could possess language skills which could prove invaluable to a business that trades overseas.

A business's workforce plan will contain at least the following information:

- **Information on the business's current workforce** This will set out:
  - the number of employees that this business currently has
  - the skills and qualifications possessed by its current employees
  - where its employees are currently employed (for multinational companies this could be in many different countries)
  - the age profile of its employees which will help to forecast likely future changes due to retirement, etc.

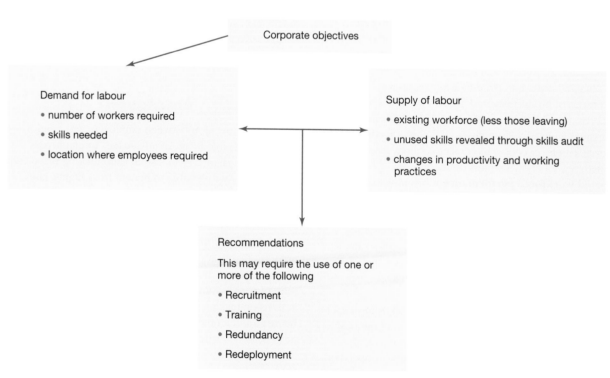

Figure 22.6 Workforce planning

• **An analysis of likely changes in the demand for the business's products** In turn this will affect the business's need for labour in the forthcoming period. Clearly, changes in demand will have a significant effect on the number of employees that are needed, especially if the business is heavily dependent upon employees as a central part of the production process. This is the case for many businesses providing services such as banks and hospitals.

Case Study

Working hours vary across the world

The Organisation for Economic Cooperation and Development (OECD) has researched the average annual hours worked per person in its 34 member countries. The OECD data includes full- and part-time salaried workers and the self-employed. It includes all the hours they work, including overtime. The survey shows South Koreans work the longest hours (2193 hours per year) with workers in Chile averaging 2068 hours annually.

European employees work fewer hours: British workers average 1647 hours and the Germans only 1408 – a little over 27 hours each week.

Figure 22.7 Employees in South Korea work the longest hours

The OECD was able to identify a number of trends from its research.

• Employees in Asian countries work the longest hours and have high proportions of workers who are employed for more than 48 hours per week.
• South Korea is unusual in that it is the only developed country to work very long hours. Most countries that are working long hours are developing economies such as Thailand, Malaysia and Bangladesh.

• Many countries whose employees work very long hours have low levels of productivity.

Questions

1 Analyse the benefits that a hotel chain may gain from employing a mixture of full-time, part-time and temporary workers. [8]
2 How useful might this information be to managers in large multinational businesses such as Nestlé? Justify your view. [16]

• **An analysis of the likely factors affecting the supply of labour** This could include a wide range of factors including forecast rates of labour turnover for the business, factors affecting the local labour markets such as the entry of a new business in the local area which may recruit heavily, or the arrival of large numbers of migrants from Eastern Europe into the local labour market.

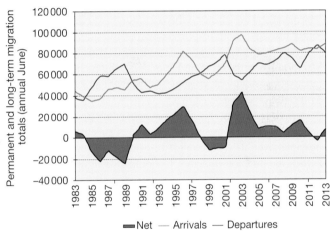

Figure 22.8 Net migration for New Zealand, 1983–2013

Figure 22.8 above shows that net migration to New Zealand (the balance between those leaving and entering the country) has been positive in most years since 2002. This may benefit employers as an increase in the available supply of labour can help to hold wages down.

Question

Comment on the implications of the data in Figure 22.8 for businesses in New Zealand's house construction industry. [10]

• **Recommendations on actions needed to acquire the desired workforce** These actions are likely to set out changes in recruitment, training, redeployment and redundancy. The workforce plan will set these out in detail and will also explain the impact on each element of the business and also the timescale over which the changes will be implemented.

A workforce plan assists a business in using its human resources effectively and at minimum cost in pursuit of its corporate objectives.

The reasons for using workforce plans

The process of planning can be highly beneficial to businesses. Workforce planning is no exception. It offers management the opportunity to coordinate and integrate the business's entire human resource management activities and to therefore avoid any inconsistencies or any waste of resources through duplication of activities.

Workforce planning offers businesses other benefits as well.

- The in-depth investigation of likely future events will encourage HR managers to think of the most effective (and cost efficient) ways of responding to these events. Managers have time to reflect on and discuss their responses and to consider the full implications of proposed actions. In this way all the data relating to any HR decisions can be collected and considered at length. This avoids crisis decision-making and reduces the likelihood of errors.
- HR managers are afforded the opportunity to consult with other managers with responsibility for other functions within the business such as marketing or finance. This allows HR decisions to be taken in an integrated fashion and to have the greatest possibility of assisting the business in achieving its corporate objectives.
- Workforce planning gives HR managers the opportunity to assess whether the business's human resource objectives are feasible given the constraints (for example, finance) under which the function operates. It should also allow the chance to change the HR objectives.

However, workforce planning can go wrong and be of limited value to a business. The value of workforce plans depends, to a great extent, on the accuracy of the company's forecasting of its future labour needs. In particular it will depend upon the company's ability to forecast the level of demand for its goods and services with some degree of accuracy. If the company underestimates demand it may have insufficient labour available and the result may be dissatisfied customers.

On the other hand, too many staff available means unnecessary costs and reduced profit margins. There are many reasons why forecasts of future sales (and therefore the required labour force) may be inaccurate. There may be a sudden and unexpected change in customer tastes. The economy may also perform differently to what was expected. In 2006 few economists were forecasting that many countries would go into recession in 2008. Finally, competitors may alter their behaviour by bringing out new products, or new competitors may emerge. So, forecasting labour demand can be a tricky business, especially if the forecast extends several years into the future.

The exact value of workforce planning will depend on the circumstances in which it is being conducted. The experience of the managers engaged in the process will play a part as will the volatility of demand for the products that the business sells. The time and resources devoted to the planning process will also affect the quality and accuracy of the outcomes and therefore its value. Finally, the timescale to which the plan relates is also important: the further into the future the plan extends, the less value it is likely to provide to the organisation.

22.7 The role of trade unions in HRM

> **Key terms**
>
> **Trade unions** are organisations of workers established to protect and improve the economic position and working conditions of their members
>
> **Union recognition** occurs under circumstances whereby the managers of a business accept the right of a particular trade union to negotiate on behalf of its members.

Most **trade unions** have similar objectives. These focus on improving the economic position of their members by fulfilling the following:

- **Maximising pay** Unions engage in collective bargaining to provide their members with the highest possible rates of pay.
- **Achieving safe and secure working conditions**
- **Attaining job security** Arguably, this is the most important objective of a modern trade union and one that is difficult to fulfil in the light of pressures resulting from globalisation and the increasing use of technology in the workplace.
- **Participating in and influencing decisions in the workplace** Trade unions may achieve this through collective bargaining or through having representatives on works councils and other employer–employee committees.

In addition many unions have social objectives such as lobbying for higher social security benefits, improved employment legislation and improved health care provision. Trade unions achieve their objectives by carrying out a range of functions to the benefit of their members.

- Their most important and time-consuming function is protecting members' interests over issues such as discrimination, unfair dismissal and health and safety matters.
- They negotiate pay and conditions for their members through collective bargaining.
- Trade unions provide their members with a range of personal services including legal advice, insurance, education, training and financial advice.

The value of trade unions

The case study below illustrates the benefits of trade unions to the UK economy and its businesses and employees. The report that features in the case study emphasises that employees benefit from the existence of trade unions in terms of more secure employment, better working conditions and higher pay.

Case Study

The value of trade unions to the UK

The Trades Union Congress (TUC) is an organisation that represents 54 individual trade unions in the UK that have 6.2 million members from many different occupations. The TUC has published a new report called *The Union Advantage* which looks at the advantages unions bring to the UK economy.

The Union Advantage says that trade union members get higher wages, better sickness and pension benefits, are much more likely to be able to take advantage of flexible working and are able to take more annual leave.

The report cites official statistics showing that workers in a union earn 12.5 per cent more an hour than employees in a non-unionised workplace in the UK, taking home average hourly earnings of £13.07 compared to £11.62.

The presence of a union is likely to push training up the workplace agenda, encouraging members to take up courses to improve their skills that their company can then benefit from in the form of improved productivity. More than 230 000 workers were helped into taking up some form of learning by their union last year, says the report.

The Union Advantage also says unions and their safety reps help make workplaces safer and reduce the chances of employees becoming ill because of stress, bullying and other workplace hazards. And as well as winning a better deal for their members, unions can also save the employers a lot of time, hassle and money, says the TUC.

The report cites official statistics suggesting that because unions give employees a voice and solve problems, people are much less likely to leave their jobs in a unionised workplace, saving employers between £72 million and £143 million in recruitment costs.

By cutting down on accidents at work, unions could be saving employers as much as £371 million a year says the report, and because they feel involved and listened to, unions help workforces become more productive, benefiting the UK economy to the tune of between £3.4 and £10.2 billion a year.

Source: Adapted from the Trades Union Congress website

Discussion Question

Do you think this report is biased? How might the view of managers differ?

The report also states the potential benefits that trade unions can bring to businesses. They can create a safer, healthier and more harmonious working environment leading to reduced labour turnover and higher productivity figures. Such a working environment can also benefit businesses because fewer accidents may occur, reducing costs and compensation businesses might have to pay as well as improving their corporate image.

The benefits to employees of a trade union membership

1 **Average rates of pay are higher** As a result of having greater bargaining power and skilled negotiators, trade union members receive higher rates of pay. In the UK it is estimated that the presence of trade unions increases wage rates by 8–12 per cent over non-union pay rates.

2 **Working conditions are improved** Trade union membership is likely to result in improved working conditions such as longer holidays and a safer working environment. Many trade unions train and provide health and safety stewards to minimise the risk of workplace injuries and they also ensure that employers meet their legal obligations.

3 **Trade unions can negotiate more and better training for members** Trade unions can provide courses to help employees learn new skills, improve existing ones and enhance their career prospects. Trade unions can negotiate agreements with employers to pay for courses and provide time off for employees to attend.

4 **Trade union membership reduces the possibility of discrimination** Trade unions in many countries campaign for tougher laws against discrimination on the basis of sex, race, age, disability or sexual orientation. Becoming a member gives trade unions more finance to carry out this work and larger numbers of members means greater credibility in negotiations with governments.

5 **Trade union membership can provide greater job security** Trade unions across the world fight to protect the jobs of their members, giving them a greater chance of a secure income. In the UK trade union members are only half as likely to be dismissed.

The benefits to employers of trade union involvement in the workplace

Businesses can benefit from working with trade unions for a number of reasons.

1 **Better communication** Trade union officials can act as an effective means of communication between the management team and the employees in a workplace. This can help to bring potential problems and causes of dissatisfaction to the attention of managers speedily and before they become the basis of a dispute. Trade union officials can also advise managers and perhaps dissuade them from taking decisions which might be highly unpopular with employees. They can also pass good ideas and suggestions to managers which may improve the performance of the workforce.

2 **Improvements in health and safety** Trade unions often appoint health and safety officers to ensure that employees are as fully protected in the workplace as is possible. This role can assist in preventing accidents and the damage to employee morale which often accompanies them. Improving health and safety performance can also avoid unnecessary expenditure by businesses on fines and compensation to injured employees as well as protecting the business's reputation as a good employer.

3 **Improved employer branding** Having trade unions within the workplace is likely to result in higher wages and improved working conditions for employees. Although this may increase a business's costs it can also enhance its reputation as a good employer and assist it in attracting high quality employees.

Welcoming trade unions may be part of a 'soft' HR strategy under which a business seeks to have long-term relationships with its employees. A combination of a soft HR strategy and a central role for trade unions in the workplace may result in a highly committed and productive workforce.

22.8 Negotiation

Negotiation is a method by which people and organisations settle differences.

Collective bargaining is negotiation between employers and the representatives of the workforce, usually trade union officials.

Individual bargaining takes place when a single employee negotiates his or her own pay and working conditions with management representatives.

Negotiation is a process by which compromise or agreement is reached while avoiding argument. In any disagreement, individuals aim to achieve the best possible outcome for their position (or an organisation that they represent). However, the principles of fairness, seeking mutual benefit and maintaining a relationship are the keys to a successful outcome.

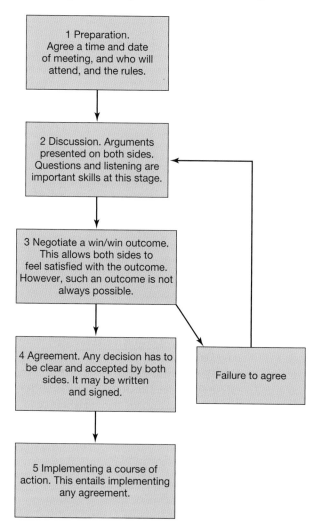

Figure 22.9 The process of negotiation

Stages of negotiation

It is common for negotiators to use a process involving stages such as those illustrated in Figure 22.9. The process of negotiation may involve the following stages:

- preparation
- opening discussions
- negotiation towards an outcome where both parties 'win'
- agreement
- implementation of a course of action.

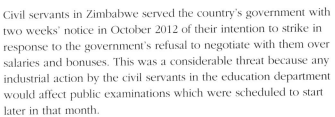

1 **Preparation** Prior to any negotiations the parties involved will have to agree the date and place of the meeting and precisely what is to be discussed and who will attend. This preparation meeting may also determine exactly what is to be negotiated and may set a timescale before a third party may be used to try to help to reach agreement. Thus this might establish whether negotiations between a trade union and an employer are just to be about wages or whether other issues such as working conditions will be discussed.

Preparation meetings can agree the 'rules' for discussions and can help to avoid further disputes and time wasting during negotiations, for example, about what is to be discussed.

2 **Opening discussions** Both parties will set out their positions at this stage and each should have the opportunity to do so fully. For example, a trade union might state its claim and its justification for such a claim. The employer may set out its offer and the reasons for it. All those involved should listen, ask questions and consider how they might reach agreement. Successful negotiators will try to identify the key areas on which disagreement exists and how to overcome these differences. A record should be taken of the discussions and parties may withdraw temporarily from the meeting to discuss separately how to proceed.

3 **Negotiate towards an outcome where both parties 'win'** This stage of the negotiation process targets an outcome where both parties can judge (with some justification) that they have achieved at least some of their objectives in the negations and therefore have 'won'. Such a position may not be possible if the opening positions are a long way apart or if there is one single area of disagreement and limited possibilities for trade-offs. If, for example, negotiation is simply about pay it may be impossible to balance any settlement with changes to working conditions. At this stage parties may put pressure on their opponents by threatening not to continue with negotiations unless they are prepared to change their position to some degree.

4 **Agreement** Agreement can be achieved once understanding of both sides' viewpoints and interests have been considered and a decision reached. This may take some considerable time. Any agreement needs to be made perfectly clear and recorded so that both parties know what has been agreed.

5 **Implementing the decision** From the agreement, a course of action has to be implemented, to carry through the decision.

Case Study

Zimbabwean government refuses to negotiate

Civil servants in Zimbabwe served the country's government with two weeks' notice in October 2012 of their intention to strike in response to the government's refusal to negotiate with them over salaries and bonuses. This was a considerable threat because any industrial action by the civil servants in the education department would affect public examinations which were scheduled to start later in that month.

The civil servants' representative David Dzatsunga stated that the civil servants intended to take advantage of the two weeks to mobilise their members if the government does not agree to take part in negotiations. The Zimbabwean government has continued to refuse to negotiate on the basic salaries received by civil servants and is opting to review only the allowances that are paid.

Questions

1 Analyse the ways in which low pay might affect the performance of Zimbabwe's civil servants. [8]
2 Evaluate the ways in which an agreement might be reached in these circumstances. [16]

Failure to reach agreement

If the negotiations break down and agreement cannot be reached a further meeting is normally scheduled and the process can return to stage two. It may be that other parties will become party to the negotiations to help to try and bring the sides together. This may involve conciliation or arbitration (see below).

Collective bargaining

Collective bargaining entails negotiations between management and employees' representatives, usually trade unions, over pay and other conditions of employment. Collective bargaining can only occur if the employer recognises the right of a trade union to act on behalf of the workforce. Under a collective agreement the terms negotiated by the employees' representatives are binding upon the entire workforce – this is the 'collective' aspect of this form of negotiation.

Some countries, such as the UK and New Zealand, have a tradition of collective bargaining, although even in these countries it has become less common as the proportion of firms recognising trade unions for the purposes of collective bargaining has declined. This trend has been reinforced by declining trade union memberships. However, in the UK the situation was reversed to some degree by the passing of the Employment Relations Act, which came into force in 2000. Under this Act a trade union with a membership exceeding 50 per cent of the employees in any particular business (of part of a business where negotiations take place) can demand union recognition and thereby the right to reintroduce collective bargaining.

Individual bargaining

The move away from collective bargaining has been driven by a change in philosophy within many modern businesses. The adoption of the principles of human resource management has resulted in many enterprises seeking to make the most effective use of each and every member of the workforce. This has had two main consequences.

1 Instead of paying a standard wage or salary to every worker carrying out a particular role (as would have been likely under collective bargaining) individual bargaining means that workers may be paid according to their contribution. This may reduce the labour costs of a business and has the potential to provide financial motivation for employees.

2 The other side to individual bargaining is that some businesses seek to develop their employees to encourage them to make the maximum possible contribution to the performance of the business.

Other firms have simply chosen not to recognise trade unions in the hope of being able to keep wage increases and costs to a minimum without the upward pressure of collective bargaining.

Arbitration and conciliation

Key terms

Arbitration is the attempt to settle an industrial dispute through the use of a neutral third party.

Conciliation is negotiations undertaken with the aim of reconciling differences between the parties to an industrial **dispute**.

Industrial dispute is a disagreement between an employer and employees (or their trade union representatives) over a range of matters, for example pay and working conditions.

It is normal for **industrial disputes** to be resolved without trade unions taking any form of industrial action. The decline in industrial disputes in countries including the UK over recent years has, in part, been a consequence of the effective use of measures outlined below.

Arbitration

Arbitration is a procedure for the settlement of disputes, under which the parties agree to be bound by the decision of an arbitrator whose decision is in some circumstances legally binding on both parties. The process of arbitration in the UK is governed by Arbitration Acts 1950–96. There are three main types of arbitration.

- **Non-binding arbitration** involves a neutral third party making an award to settle a dispute that the parties concerned can accept or not.
- **Binding arbitration** means that the parties to the dispute have to take the award of the arbitrator.

- **Pendulum arbitration** is a binding form of arbitration in which the arbitrator has to decide entirely for one side or the other. It is not an option to reach a compromise and select some middle ground. This system avoids excessive claims by unions or miserly offers by employers.

Arbitration is voluntary and both sides must agree to it. It can be used in settling an individual's dispute with an employer or as part of the process of collective bargaining. Arbitration may be a method of settling an issue that is fiercely disputed and where there may be some significant differences between the parties.

Conciliation

Conciliation is a method of resolving individual or collective disputes in which a neutral third party encourages the continuation of negotiations and the postponement (at least) of any form of industrial action. The conciliator's role does not involve making any judgement of the validity of the position of either party. The conciliator encourages the continued discussions in the hope that a compromise can be reached. This approach might be appropriate when a more informal approach is required to reach an agreement and could be more useful in settling individual disputes. This might be used to avoid a legal hearing before a court or a move to a more formal process such as arbitration.

Case Study

Indian pilots strike

Pilots at India's second-largest private airline, Jet Airways, walked out for five days in response to the sacking of two pilots. The two pilots were dismissed for establishing a trade union which was not recognised by the company. More than 400 pilots (out of a total of 760) at the company decided to take 'mass sick leave' which resulted in Jet Airways having to cancel hundreds of flights. This led to one of the largest disruptions of airline travel in India in recent years.

The company alleged that the 'strike' was illegal under Indian laws as the two parties had commenced conciliation talks before the industrial action was taken.

Jet Airways has recently announced an improvement in its financial performance following a period in which it recorded a loss. It is also engaged in talks with Etihad Airways over the sale of a 24 per cent stake in the company.

Questions

1 Analyse the reasons why pilots might take industrial action when conciliation talks have already commenced. [8]
2 Do you think that the 'strike' action was a good decision by the pilots in these circumstances? Justify your decision. [16]

22.9 No strike deals

In many countries the power and influence of trade unions within the workplace has been reduced. In consequence other types of arrangements have been agreed.

No strike deals

A no strike deal is an agreement between employers and unions whereby in return for a pay and conditions package a union agrees to refrain from strike action for an agreed period. Often such agreements are accompanied by a commitment by both parties to go to binding arbitration in the event of a dispute. This reassures the union that it is not making itself too vulnerable by agreeing not to take industrial action. A no strike agreement can benefit a trade union in a number of ways.

- By presenting itself as non-confrontational the union may attract a greater number of members from within the workforce, increasing its income and strength.
- A less confrontational stance might allow the union to appoint worker directors, increasing the union's influence and role in decision-making.
- Such agreements can improve the public perception of trade unions. This will assist the union in its activities in other businesses and industries and may persuade employers to recognise it.

A further advantage of no strike deals is that they may lead to a single union agreement strengthening the position of the union within the business.

Test your learning

Short answer questions

1 a Define the term labour productivity. [2]

   b Woodland Mines Ltd recruited 250 people last year and 200 employees left. Its average number of employees during the year was 6000. What was its rate of labour turnover? [3]

2 a Explain why absenteeism may be a problem for a business. [3]

   b State **two** methods a business might use to improve the performance of its employees. [2]

3 a Define the term management by objectives. [2]

   b Explain **one** advantage to a business of the use of management by objectives. [3]

4 a State **three** aspects of employment that are governed by employment laws. [3]

   b What is meant by unfair dismissal? [2]

5 Explain **one** benefit to an employer and **one** benefit to employees arising from their cooperation. [5]

6 a State **three** items of information that will normally be included in a workforce plan. [3]

   b Explain **one** reason why a business should use workforce planning. [2]

7 Define the terms trade union and collective bargaining. [5]

8 a Identify **two** reasons why an employee might join a trade union. [2]

   b Explain **one** benefit of trade unions to a business. [3]

9 Distinguish between arbitration and conciliation. [5]

10 a What is a zero-hours contract? [2]

   b Why might a large retailing business wish to use zero-hours contracts? [3]

Data response question

Punjab Sugar Mills Ltd

Punjab Sugar Mills has enjoyed a substantial rise in sales over the last four years, although its sales have fluctuated at times. It trades in a highly competitive market in which profit margins have declined steadily.

The company's workforce has grown rapidly too, although some HR managers support the introduction of more technology to replace people. The process of producing sugar is suited to the use of technology and this could help the company to achieve its overall aim of increasing its profitability. However, Punjab Sugar Mills Ltd has decided to invest heavily in training its employees at all levels during the last 18 months rather than buying technology, preferring to use labour-intensive production methods. The company's chief executive values his workforce and considers good employer–employee relations essential if the business is to succeed in the future. The company relies on the use of workforce plans.

The management team have been studying some key data for the company.

Table 1

Item	Last year	One year ago	Two years ago	Three years ago
Sales ($000s)	4785.6	4387.4	4401.9	4011.2
Sugar production (metric tonnes)	9570	8335	8282	8337
Profit margin (%)	9.22	10.43	9.14	7.95
Employee numbers	2512	2401	2456	2339
Labour turnover (%)	7.3	7.1	11.2	7.4

The price of sugar cane has fluctuated on world markets leading to significant fluctuations in the company's costs.

However, growing demand in Indian markets and in other Asian countries with rising incomes has boosted sales revenue.

Questions

1 Analyse the benefits that Punjab Sugar Mills Ltd receives from drawing up workforce plans. [10]

2 a Calculate the company's productivity figures for last year and two years ago. [4]

   b Assess the performance of Punjab Sugar Mill Ltd's workforce over the last four years. [10]

3 Do you think that the chief executive was correct to say that employer–employee cooperation was '… essential if the business is to succeed in the future'? Justify your view. [16]

Essay questions

1 Discuss the extent to which achieving high levels of cooperation between a business's management and its workforce is the most important task for human resource managers. [20]

2 To what extent is it true to say that labour productivity is always the most important measure of employee performance? [20]

Past paper questions

1 Read the Curry Cuisine case study on pages 471–73 and then answer the following questions.

   a Analyse **two** possible problems that might result from the approach to managing staff used within the Asian Experience kitchen. [6]

   b Evaluate the appropriateness of Ling's approach to managing staff with the Curry Cuisine restaurant. [14]

Cambridge International AS and A Level Business Studies 9707 Paper 3 Q2 October/November 2007

2 Read the Eastern Motors (EM) case study on pages 468–70 and then answer the following questions.

   a Using data from Appendix B, calculate for the Northcape factory in 2008.

      i The proportion of workers who left [2]

      ii Output of cars per worker [2]

   b 'If we can increase productivity and reduce wastage and absenteeism in the Northcape factory then this will make us more competitive.' (lines 46–47)

     Recommend an appropriate Human Resources strategy to achieve this objective. Support your recommendation. [16]

Cambridge International AS and A Level Business Studies 9707 Paper 3 Q2 May/June 2009

A Level
Section 2: People in organisations

23 Organisational structure

Chapter overview

In this chapter we examine:

- the types of organisational structure and their relationships with business objectives and people
- delegation and accountability
- control, authority and trust
- centralisation and decentralisation
- line and staff employees.

Key terms

An **organisational structure** is the way in which a business is arranged to carry out its activities.

Authority is the power to control situations or the decisions and actions of others.

Responsibility is the duty to complete a task and to be accountable for one's actions.

23.1 Business objectives, organisational structure and people

What is an organisational structure?

The **organisational structure**, which may be shown in an organisation chart, sets out:

- the routes by which communication passes through the business
- who has **authority** (and power) and **responsibility** within the organisation
- the roles and titles of individuals within the organisation
- the people to whom individual employees are accountable and those for whom they are responsible.

Figure 23.1 illustrates a simplified organisational chart for a large business.

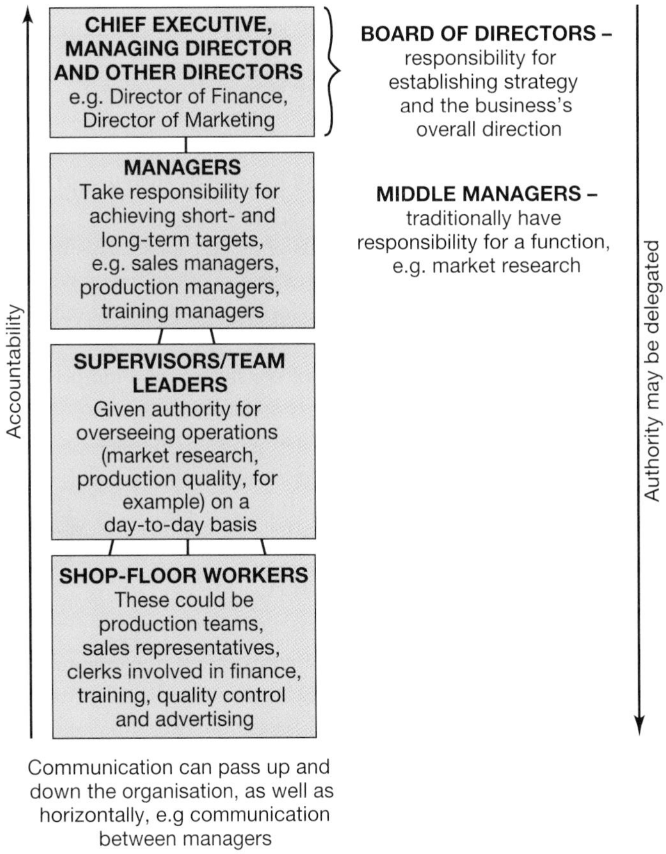

Figure 23.1 A simplified organisational chart

The organisation's structure plays a vital part in shaping the success of the business. This determines the ways in which its work activities are organised and how responsibility and authority are allocated. The structure of an organisation affects how employees (from the most junior to the very senior) carry out their responsibilities and use their authority, how they coordinate and work alongside others and the extent to which the business achieves its goals and objectives.

The case for flexible organisational structures

A flexible organisational structure is one in which workers can easily adapt to their customers' needs, efficiently complete their work and make decisions as and when necessary.

Management writer Peter Drucker was a strong advocate of flexible organisational structures. A common mistake by managers, Drucker argued, is that they tend to become obsessed by organising the business's structure just one way. At various times decentralisation has been the key element of a successful structure; later close control and command of employees was considered essential. 'There is no such thing as the one right organisation,' Drucker wrote. 'There are only organisations, each of which has distinct strengths, distinct limitations, and specific applications. It has become clear that organisation is not an absolute. It is a tool for making people productive in working together. As such, a given organisational structure fits certain tasks in certain conditions and at certain times.'

A flexible organisational structure is likely to possess a number of important characteristics.

● It will be continually changing and evolving to meet changing needs. Employees at all levels will be used to change and will be likely to respond positively to it.

● It will focus strongly on the needs of its customers. This may mean that, for example, employees may work in teams which can be disbanded, and new ones formed to meet customers' changing demands.

● The organisation may make use of consultants and temporary and part-time employees to supply specialist skills or to manage peaks and troughs in demand for its products.

Case Study

The structure of HSBC

The HSBC group operates in 85 countries across five regions: Europe, Hong Kong, the rest of Asia-Pacific including the Middle East and Africa, North America and South America. It has more than 254 000 employees.

The divisions that form the HSBC group provide a comprehensive range of financial services to personal, commercial and business banking clients. To more easily promote the group as a whole, HSBC was established as a uniform, international brand name in 1999 (see Figure 23.2). In 2002 HSBC launched a campaign to differentiate its brand from those of its competitors by describing the unique characteristics that distinguish HSBC, summarised by the words 'The world's local bank'.

HSBC's largest and best-known subsidiaries and their primary areas of operation are shown in Table 23.1:

Table 23.1

Subsidiary	Primary area of operation
The Hongkong and Shanghai Banking Corporation Limited	Hong Kong SAR, with an extensive network throughout Asia-Pacific
Hang Seng Bank Limited	Hong Kong SAR
HSBC Bank plc	United Kingdom
HSBC France	France
HSBC Bank USA N.A.	United States of America
HSBC Bank Brasil S.A.- Banco Múltiplo	Brazil
Grupo Financiero HSBC, S.A. de C.V.	Mexico

Source: HSBC website

Questions

1 Analyse the key issues in designing an effective organisational structure for a multinational business employing 254 000 people. [8]
2 Discuss whether the advantages to HSBC of organising itself in this way are greater than the disadvantages. [16]

Organisational structures should reflect businesses' needs

The organisational structure adopted by a business will depend upon the type and size of the business and will be designed to meet the needs of the business as fully as possible. A number of key factors will be taken into account by the business's managers when designing (or redesigning) the organisation's structure.

● **The business's size** As the business grows it is more difficult for managers to control growing numbers of employees. Thus, in order to manage their workloads efficiently, they will devise a structure that gives more authority to those lower in the organisational structure.

● **The type of product supplied by the business** A business that supplies a range of diverse products may organise itself traditionally into divisions. For example, Hard Rock Café operates in this way. It originally started as a restaurant business, established by Peter Morton and Isaac Tigrett, but later expanded into hotels and casinos. Key areas of the business such as casinos have some degree of independence, but operating within the overall structure of the organisation.

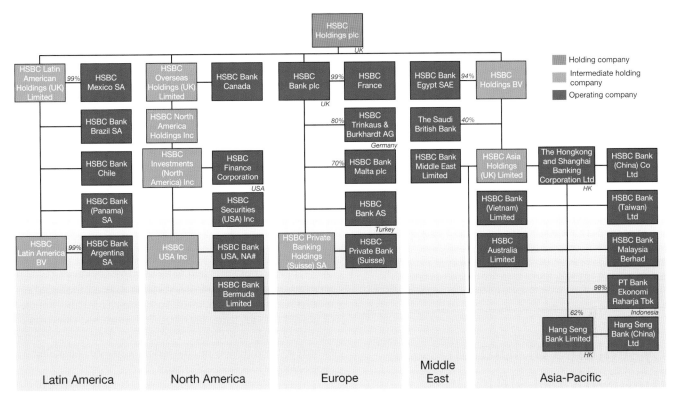

Figure 23.2 The simplified organisational structure for the HSBC

Source: HSBC website

● **The business's objectives** Businesses that are seeking growth may organise themselves so as to minimise costs and hence selling prices. This may encourage the use of organisational structures which pass considerable authority to relatively junior employees to minimise management costs. This may also motivate junior employees and improve productivity.

Organisational structures should facilitate growth and development

An organisational structure should allow and assist a business to increase its scale and to change in other ways to enable it to meet its corporate objectives. Thus an organisational structure should allow a busines to adapt to produce new products or to operate in different markets.

As a business grows, its chain of command from those at the top of the organisation to those at the bottom is likely to lengthen. This may require a structure that is flatter, with fewer layers of authority between senior and junior employees. This will make communication easier and more reliable, ensuring that decisions are more likely to be understood and acted upon and

that senior managers can readily gather information from below. If a structure has too many layers of authority, decisions may be slower and the organisation may become less competitive as it becomes slower to respond to changes in the market and other external changes.

Organisational structures are subject to factors requiring them to adapt if the business is to remain successful. Changes in technology, changes in competitors' behaviour, changes in government policies and changes in tastes and fashions can all act as a catalyst for a change in an organisation's structure. For example, a new competitor entering a market might result in an increase in price competitiveness, necessitating existing firms to cut costs. Reducing the size of the workforce and adapting its structure to contain fewer layers of authority may be one way to achieve this. However, if a structure is too rigid, this may not be possible.

Study tip

You should assess the strengths and weaknesses of any organisational structure by using all the information available to you and considering the extent to which the structure assists the business in achieving its organisational objectives.

23.2 Formal and informal organisational structures

Key features of formal organisational structures

Levels of hierarchy

A fundamental element of any organisational structure is the number of levels or layers of hierarchy. Organisations with a large number of layers (or levels) of hierarchy are referred to as 'tall'. That is, there is a substantial number of people between the person at the top of the organisation and those at the bottom. In contrast, 'flat' organisational structures have fewer layers of authority or **levels of hierarchy**. Figures 23.3 and 23.4 illustrate both tall and flat types of structure.

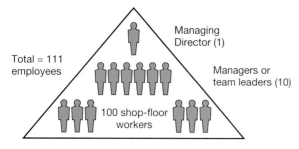

Figure 23.3 A 'flat' organisational structure

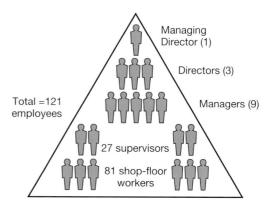

Figure 23.4 A 'tall' organisational structure

Traditionally, UK businesses have tended to use 'tall' organisational structures as they have grown. However, attracted by the prospect of faster and more effective communication, and influenced by the structures used by the some of the world's most efficient companies, many businesses have either adopted or moved towards flatter organisational structures. Drawbacks exist in making such a move. The process of flattening structures (which is called delayering) has led to businesses operating with significantly wider spans of control.

Chains of command

The organisational structure shows the business's **chain of command**. This is the way that authority is organised within the business and who has control over which other people in the enterprise. It also reveals how communication flows through the organisation and how many layers messages must pass through to move from the top to the bottom of the organisation – or vice versa.

Once businesses have adopted a tall organisational structure they have long chains of command from those at the top of the organisation to those at the bottom. Businesses with many layers of hierarchy frequently experience communication problems as messages moving up and down the organisation pass through many people and may be distorted or not passed on. Some business writers have estimated that each extra level of hierarchy in the structure reduces the effectiveness of communication within the organisation by approximately 25 per cent.

Spans of control

A **span of control** is the number of people who report directly to a manager. Spans of control and levels of hierarchy have a

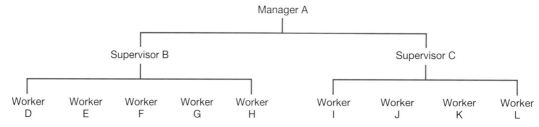

Figure 23.5 Spans of control

relationship. An organisation with a wide span of control will have relatively few levels of hierarchy – the 'flat' organisation in Figure 23.3. Conversely, 'tall' organisations have many layers of hierarchy, but narrow spans of control. Figure 23.5 illustrates a broad and a narrow span of control.

A narrow span of control allows team leaders, supervisors and managers to keep close control over the activities of the employees for whom they are responsible. As the span of control widens, the subordinate is likely to be able to operate with a greater degree of independence. This is because it is impossible for an individual to monitor closely the work of a large number of subordinates. A traditional view is that the span of control should not exceed six if close supervision is to be maintained. However, where subordinates are carrying out similar duties, a span of control of 10 or even 12 is not unusual. It is normal for a span of control to be narrower at the top of an organisation. This is because senior employees have more complex and diverse duties and are, therefore, more difficult to supervise.

Case Study

UBS

UBS is a Swiss financial services company which operates throughout the world. It provides a range of banking, investment and wealth management services for private individuals and businesses. In March 2014 it had over 60 000 employees with 37 per cent working in the Americas, 37 per cent in Switzerland, 16 per cent in the rest of Europe and 10 per cent in Asia and the Pacific. UBS has announced its intention to reduce its workforce to 54 000 by 2015 and to focus on its core services.

UBS chief executive Sergio Ermotti said: 'This decision has been a difficult one, particularly in a business such as ours that is all about its people. Some reductions will result from natural attrition and we will take whatever measures we can to mitigate the overall effect.'

UBS expects its reduced complexity and size will result in the removal of surplus layers of hierarchy but that spans of control will widen. By adjusting its organisational structure in these ways, UBS is expecting to reduce its operating costs by $1.44 billion a year.

Questions

1 Analyse the measures that UBS might take to reduce the effects of reducing its workforce by 6000 over a period of two years. [8]

2 Do you think that UBS is certain to be more efficient after these changes? Justify your decision. [16]

Delegation

Key term

Delegation is the passing down of authority through the organisation.

One key strategy entrepreneurs might adopt is to delegate authority as the organisation increases in scale. Giving people more authority is likely to lead to wider spans of control. Wider spans of control can operate effectively if junior employees have been delegated authority to take decisions. This reduces the workload on their manager or team leader as he or she does not have to monitor all subordinates so closely, freeing time for other duties.

The extent to which an organisation adopts **delegation** as a key element in its organisational structure depends upon the managers' views of control. Some managers like to retain as much control of decision-making as possible, and only delegate when the pressure of their workload makes this essential.

Centralisation and decentralisation

Centralisation and decentralisation are opposites. A centralised organisation is one where the majority of decisions are taken by senior managers at the top (or centre) of the business. Centralisation can provide rapid decision-making, as few people are likely to be consulted. It should also ensure that the business pursues the objectives set by senior managers.

Decentralisation gives greater authority to empower employees lower down the organisational structure. This may mean granting greater authority to employees in branches, departments or divisions of the business. Decentralisation may also entail relocating jobs and functions (such as managing budgets) to other parts of the organisation. Decentralisation may result in quicker and more effective decisions taken by employees with a good understanding of the customers' needs. It may also result in more motivated employees who relish greater authority. However, it does rely upon good communication and a clear focus on organisational objectives.

Informal structures

This type of structure exists where the organisation does not have an obvious structure. This is common in the case of professionals (doctors and lawyers, for example) where they operate as a team. The professionals normally receive administrative support from others within the organisation.

This form of organisational structure allows highly trained and motivated employees to organise their working lives and to take decisions with a high degree of independence. However, it is less appropriate for many businesses as it lacks coordination and control by senior managers.

23.3 Types of organisational structures

Businesses can adopt different organisational structures according to a number of factors including the size of the organisation, the environment in which it operates and the personal preferences of the owners and senior managers. We will discuss the factors influencing the choice of organisational structure in detail in the next section of this chapter.

Hierarchical structures

Hierarchical organisational structures share decision-making throughout the business and give all employees a clearly defined role as well as establishing their relationship with other employees in the business. It is common for this type of organisational structure to be based upon departments and because of the dependence upon agreed procedures it can be bureaucratic.

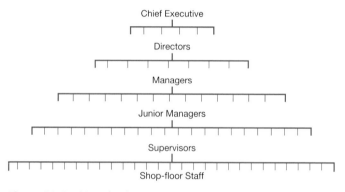

Figure 23.6 A hierarchical structure

If this type of structure is 'tall' it normally has a number of features.
- The organisation will be centralised with the most important decisions taken by senior managers.
- Hierarchy is important and senior managers expect to be treated with respect.
- Tradition is important and change is often implemented slowly.

Alternatively, as we saw earlier, it may be a 'flat' organisational structure which may result in a more decentralised organisation. A flat hierarchical structure may also make greater use of delegation as managers at all levels have to deal with wider spans of control. Close management may prove impossible if a manager has a large number of subordinates reporting to them and delegation can become a necessity.

Communication in formal organisations is principally downwards and uses established routes, moving down from senior to junior employees. Employees are aware of lines of command and communication and the position of their department or unit within the organisation. All employees appreciate the possibilities for promotion that exist in the

business. Furthermore, as the business becomes larger, decision-making can become slower as communication has to pass through many layers within the organisation. Simultaneously, coordinating the business's attempts to achieve its objectives becomes difficult. Senior managers become more remote and may take decisions that are not appropriate to local situations or to the needs of particular groups of customers.

Table 23.2 The advantages and disadvantages of traditional hierarchies

Advantages	Disadvantages
• Authority and responsibility are clearly established.	• Organisation can be slow to respond to customer needs.
• Promotion path is clearly signposted.	• Communication, and especially horizontal communication, may be poor.
• Flat structures may offer junior employees interesting jobs with delegated authority.	• Senior managers may become remote from junior employees and customers.
	• Managers can become overworked if the span of control is too wide.

Functional structures

Many hierarchical structures such as that shown in Figure 23.6 are based around functions within the business. Thus the hierarchy is based upon departments such as marketing, human resources and the other internal functions that are a part of most businesses. Figure 23.7 illustrates this.

This type of functional structure allows specialists to operate (for example, in marketing and finance) within their area of expertise. They can generate new and very innovative ideas, but other areas of the business may be unaware of such developments.

The disadvantages of this structure can become more apparent as the organisation grows in size. Departments may bid for resources in an attempt to increase their size and prestige within the business, rather than because this will benefit the organisation.

Organisational structures based on geography and products

This type of organisational structure can be seen operating in businesses throughout the world in slightly different ways. Some businesses organise their structures around geographical regions, possibly based on countries or even continents. Figure 23.2 on page 297 shows how the multinational bank HSBC structures its organisation based on geographical regions.

An alternative approach is to structure the organisation according to the products or brands that it produces. This allows the employees to focus on the needs of customers for a specific product rather than what might be a diverse range of products.

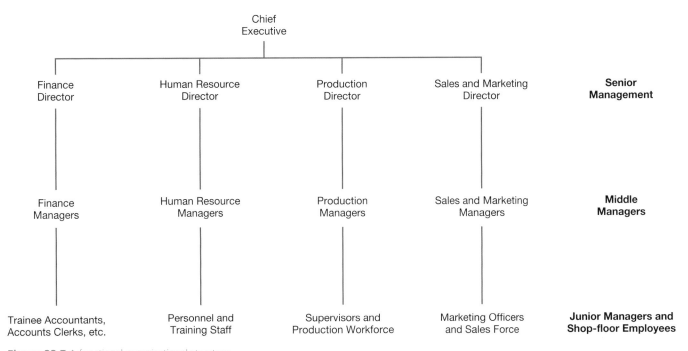

Figure 23.7 A functional organisational structure

The BBC

The British Broadcasting Corporation (BBC) is the largest television and radio broadcaster in the world. It is a public sector organisation owned by the state and operates under a Royal Charter. Its main task is to provide impartial television, radio and online services to the UK. It also operates an international broadcasting service, BBC World Service, which broadcasts in 28 languages and reaches many parts of the world. In 2011-2012 the BBC had approximately 23 000 employees.

The work of the BBC is overseen by a Trust which sets the corporation's objectives and makes sure that the BBC's senior managers meet high standards of performance. It also monitors the output of the BBC against the expectations of its audiences by holding a detailed review every five years.

The Executive is responsible for the operational management of the BBC and for fulfilling the objectives set by the Trust. The Executive comprises the Director-General of the BBC and other senior figures including those responsible for television, radio, news & current affairs and digital services.

Alongside the Executive, the BBC has the following operational areas:

● Television
● Radio

● News group
● Strategy and digital
● Finance & business
● BBC North
● BBC nations & regions.

In addition the BBC also operates BBC Worldwide Ltd. This is a wholly-owned subsidiary which sells BBC and other UK television programmes overseas.

The BBC's headquarters is at Broadcasting House in London. In 2011 it started the process of moving some of its operations to Salford in the north of England. BBC North is the division of the BBC that is based in Salford with a remit for production of programmes, technology development, digital media and training. The BBC expects to have up to 2 300 employees based in Salford eventually.

Questions

1 Analyse the problems the BBC may have faced in moving a significant proportion of its operations to Salford, more than 200 miles (320 km) away. [8]
2 The BBC Trust sets its objectives and the Executive is responsible for its operational management to achieve these objectives. Analyse the possible implications of this division of roles. [8]

Functional organisational structures have similar advantages and disadvantages to hierarchical structures. In addition they can generate high levels of motivation and loyalty to departments or divisions. However, this focus on departments or divisions can become harmful if decisions are taken without reference to other elements of the business or its overall objectives.

Some businesses such as HSBC opt to base their organisational structures on geographical regions because the products that consumers demand vary considerably in different countries. By organising itself in this way the Bank is able to meet the needs of its 60 million customers more fully. Indeed it promotes its services by emphasising that it operates in many different markets with customers who have different needs.

Other businesses produce highly differentiated products that require different production methods. As a consequence, they base their organisational structures around the supply of these products. This is the case with the BBC where its different divisions look after music, news and future media including its online services. Employees may need different skills to operate in these separate divisions to meet customers' needs effectively. Organising the business into smaller specialist divisions can improve the quality and speed of decision-making as well as the quality of the product itself.

Matrix structures

This type of organisational structure is task-orientated and based on the use of teams. It is intended to overcome many of the problems associated with the traditional or hierarchical structure. It is a combination of a vertical chain of command operated through departments or units and horizontal projects of product teams. A typical matrix structure is illustrated in Figure 23.9.

Businesses using matrix structures put together teams of individuals with the specialist skills necessary to complete a particular project. Each individual within the project team brings a particular skill and carries appropriate responsibilities. The aim is to allow all individuals to use their talents effectively, irrespective of their position within the organisation. So a project

manager looking to develop a new product may be able to call on IT and design skills from relatively junior employees elsewhere in the organisation.

Matrix structures focus on the task in hand – launching a new product, opening new retail outlets, closing down factories or entering overseas markets for the first time. Project groups often have strong senses of identity in spite of being drawn from various areas in the business. This is because they are pursuing a clearly defined objective providing team members with a sense of purpose and responsibility.

Matrix structures bring problems with them. Employees can find it difficult having two managers (project managers and departmental managers) because of divided loyalties. They can be uncertain about which parts of their work to prioritise and conflict can result. Matrix structures have a reputation for being expensive to operate: administrative and secretarial staff can be costly when used in support of a number of projects.

Table 23.3 The advantages and disadvantages of a matrix structure

Advantages	Disadvantages
● Focuses on tasks necessary for business success	● Employees can have divided responsibilities
● Encourages organisations to be flexible and responsive to customers' needs	● Conflict can occur between project and departmental managers, reducing performance of organisation
● Motivates and develops employees by providing varied and challenging tasks	● Heavy expenditure on support staff may be required

How and why organisational structures change with growth

In a very small organisation an entrepreneur or manager may be able to make all the necessary decisions and carry out many managerial tasks. He or she may not necessarily have the experience or knowledge to do this as effectively as possible, but lack of finance may preclude the employment of specialists.

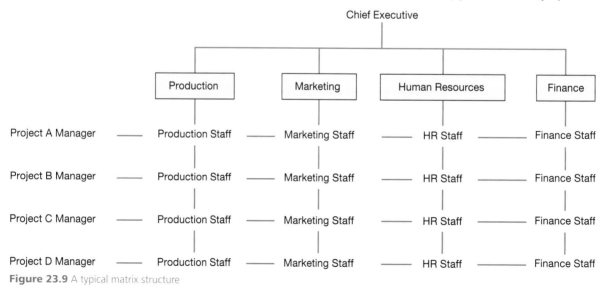

Figure 23.9 A typical matrix structure

However, as an organisation grows this may become more difficult – it becomes impossible for the entrepreneur to take all decisions. Because of this the structure adopted by the organisation might need to be adjusted as it develops.

Increasing levels of hierarchy

The most obvious change is that the organisation will introduce more levels of hierarchy to avoid managers having too heavy workloads. Thus a small business may initially be owned and managed by a single person, but growth may mean that the owner has to recruit two managers to take control of some of the business's functions. These managers may report to the owner, creating an additional level of hierarchy. Further growth and consequent recruitment of shop-floor employees may mean that the new managers' spans of control become too wide to be operated effectively. In turn this might require the appointment of more managers which may ultimately require the introduction of an additional level of hierarchy if the original owner's span of control and workload become unmanageable.

New divisions or departments

Another structural consequence of growth may be that as a business moves into new markets or starts to supply new products it establishes separate areas within the organisation to manage this. This can be necessary for two reasons.

1 The development means that the organisation is too large to manage as a single entity. Better quality decisions and a tighter focus on meeting customer needs may be achieved with a separate division.
2 The new development may require the provision of very distinct products requiring employees with different skills and distinctive operational procedures. This may be carried out most effectively within a separate part of the organisation.

Case Study

China's banks need to review organisational structures

The Chinese economy is entering a period of change. This has significant implications for the country's banks and leaves them facing three major challenges. Business analysts believe that China's banks should seek to increase their dealings with small- and medium-sized enterprises as well as with retailers. This is important as large enterprises use more non-bank finance.

Secondly, the banks must develop more new and innovative products to win new customers and to meet their changing demands.

Finally, the banks should adapt their organisational structures. Changes in types of customers and the need for new and innovative products will call for different organisational structures. The new organisational structures will require close cooperation and coordination among different divisions and groups of employees.

Questions

1 Analyse the issues that the Chinese banks may face if they implement a change in organisational structure. [8]
2 Evaluate the best type of organisational structure for the Chinese banks. Justify your view. [16]

Organisational structure and delayering

As an organisation reduces the number of levels of hierarchy through the process of delayering, it becomes a flatter organisational structure. This may be necessary because the business is becoming less responsive to its customers or because it needs to reduce the number of managers to lower costs and enhance its competitiveness.

A flatter organisational structure will entail fewer levels of hierarchy and wider spans of control. It does not necessarily mean that the organisation will adopt a different structure. Thus a business with a functional structure may not change its type of structure as it removes layers, it may simply operate with fewer levels.

23.4 Key factors within organisational structures

Delegation and accountability

We saw earlier in this chapter that delegation is the passing down of authority through the organisation. In contrast, accountability refers to the fact that responsibility remains with the manager or other person who has delegated authority. Thus a junior employee who is delegated responsibility to carry out specific tasks or to make certain decisions will be held accountable by the relevant manager if he or she performs poorly. This accountability can take several forms within a business.

● The poorly performing employee may not receive a bonus or other financial reward that is associated with the delegated task.
● If the employee is considered not to have the necessary skills to perform delegated tasks that are a central part of their employment, this may lead to a business offering further training.
● Alternatively if the employee is deemed to be incompetent in carrying out delegated tasks this may form the basis of a case for dismissal.

The key point here is that delegation passes down the organisational structure while accountability flows upwards from subordinates to managers.

Delegation is likely to be an effective element of the way an organisation structures itself and operates if a number of conditions are met.

- The process of delegation should commence with planning and preparation. Thus, both the junior and senior employees need to understand the objectives of delegating authority. In 2013 Starbucks continued its programme of opening coffee shops in India. The company will have delegated authority to its senior managers in the country and in turn the senior managers will have granted authority to branch managers to operate the branches successfully. This will have entailed careful preparation and the recruitment and selection of suitable employees.

- Both parties to delegation may require training to provide them with the necessary skills to be a successful part of an organisation that makes effective use of delegation. Managers may require training to help them to select the best people to delegate to, and on how to support employees through the process. Employees may require training to acquire the essential skills to carry out their new tasks. Trust must exist between manager and subordinate. The manager must trust the employee to carry out the delegated tasks effectively and be willing to give up control of the tasks that are delegated. On the other hand, the subordinate must trust that the manager will not interfere in the delegated tasks without good reason and that he or she will support the subordinate's decisions and actions.

- The manager may need to implement means to support subordinates carrying out delegated tasks. This is essential if the tasks are very complex or if the employee is new to having greater authority and a different role within the business. The support may be regular meetings or an ongoing programme of training.

Delegation and motivation

One key advantage of delegation not referred to in Table 23.4 is that it can have very positive effects on the motivation levels of junior employees. If subordinates are delegated authority to manage interesting and challenging duties it can enhance motivation.

- Maslow would argue that delegation allows employees to fulfil self-esteem needs by being involved in decision-making and having the trust of managers, which is a form of recognition.

- Similarly, Frederick Herzberg believed that delegation acts as a motivator. His research revealed that personal achievement, recognition and interest in the work itself are three of the most important means of motivation. If subordinates are delegated challenging and interesting tasks, Herzberg's theory suggests that this could have a highly positive effect on motivation.

Delegation and empowerment

Delegation frequently involves giving junior employees authority or power to make decisions on specified matters. For example, a shop manager may delegate the authority to recruit and select an agreed number of staff. In contrast **empowerment** is an extended form of delegation that allows managers more control over their work. Empowerment allows managers to decide which decisions are important and necessary and then to make them.

Control, authority and trust

Table 23.4 The advantages and disadvantages of delegation

Advantages	Disadvantages
• Delegation can speed up and improve the quality of decision-making. Decisions may be taken by employees who are close to customers and have a better understanding of their needs and they do not have to refer decisions to managers.	• The costs of training. Delegation may require a business to spend heavily upon training employees to ensure they have the necessary skills.
• Delegation can reduce the workloads of senior and middle managers, allowing them to focus on key tasks and to improve their performance.	• It may be inappropriate in some organisations where leadership styles are authoritarian and managers may be unwilling (or lack the skills) to pass control to junior employees.
• Delegation improves the skills of junior employees and prepares them for more senior roles in the organisation.	• Delegation is not a suitable strategy to adopt to manage a crisis. Such situations would require rapid decisions by experienced senior managers.

The relationship between spans of control and levels of hierarchy

Two fundamental features of an organisation's structure are span of control and levels of hierarchy. These two factors are interrelated: an organisation that reduces its levels of hierarchy is likely to widen the spans of control of many of its employees. Increasing the number of levels with approximately the same number of employees will narrow spans of control.

Earlier in this chapter we looked at the distinction between tall and flat organisational structures. Table 23.5 explores this relationship and its implications further.

Delayering has been a common feature of changes in organisational structures of many businesses in recent years. Delayering reduces the number of levels of hierarchy but widens spans of control. It is common for businesses to remove whole layers of management (and especially middle managers) as part of the process of delayering. The process of delayering offers a number of advantages to businesses.

- It can result in substantial reductions in wage costs which may be important for a business that operates in a price competitive market or one that aims to increase its profitability. Middle managers are frequently highly paid and so removing them results in a substantial saving on wage costs.
- By removing layers of hierarchy, delayering can shorten the chain of command, improving the flow of communication within the business and making it more responsive to the changing needs of its customers.
- Delayering (rather like delegation) results in junior employees having greater authority. This may enhance motivation as jobs will have to be redesigned and may become more diverse, challenging and interesting.

Despite these advantages the process of widening spans of control by removing layers of hierarchy can lead to disadvantages. Job losses are an integral part of delayering and this can threaten the security needs of all employees within the business, damaging motivation levels and employees' performance. Further issues are **knowledge management** and succession planning. A danger in delayering is the loss of knowledge that is essential to the organisation and the dismissal of the next generation of senior managers.

An organisation that is delayering needs to handle these issues openly and sensitively.

> **Key term**
>
> **Knowledge management** is the process of identifying, maintaining and effectively using an organisation's resources of knowledge.

> **Case Study**
>
> ## Google

Google has been reported to have nearly 60 staff for every manager, and it makes extensive use of small project teams. It also releases staff for about 20 per cent of their time for their own self-directed innovation projects. The company continues to produce innovative online services and functions including services which have revolutionised online commerce.

'We strive to maintain the open culture often associated with start-ups, in which everyone is a hands-on contributor and feels comfortable sharing ideas and opinions. In our weekly all-hands ('TGIF') meetings – not to mention over email or in the cafe – Googlers ask questions directly to Larry, Sergey and other execs about any number of company issues. Our offices and cafes are designed to encourage interactions between Googlers within and across teams, and to spark conversation about work as well as play.'

Google's approach to organising its employees is profitable: in 2013 the company generated revenues of $59.8 billion from which it made a profit of $12.2 billion.

Source: Google website

Questions

1 Analyse the problems that Google might encounter from allowing its employees to work unsupervised for 20 per cent of their time. [8]
2 Discuss the possible reasons why Google operates a flat organisational structure. [16]

Table 23.5 Spans of control, levels of hierarchy and tall and flat organisational structures

Balance between spans and levels	Associated leadership style	Other comments	Examples
Tall organisational structures with many levels of hierarchy and narrow spans of control	This is more likely to be authoritarian with managers having a Theory X view of employees.	• Managers can retain control of decision-making. • Employees may be relatively unskilled and less prepared to take decisions. • Motivation may depend upon financial incentives.	More likely to be used in relatively small businesses.
Flat organisational structures with few levels of hierarchy and wide spans of control	Leaders may use democratic methods based upon a Theory Y view of employees.	• Employees are more likely to be skilled, possibly multi-skilled. • Motivation will be linked to job design. • The business may engage in delayering and/or may make use of self-managed teams.	This structure may be used by large businesses and especially those operating multinationally.

Balancing control and trust

To be effective, delegation has to be based upon trust. The manager has to be willing to cede control to employees and to trust them to take the right decisions on the business's behalf. Giving trust has to be accompanied by a reduction in control. Delegation is ineffective if managers are continually looking over subordinates' shoulders. Such close supervision will not allow the junior employees to use their authority independently and is not an efficient use of the manager's time.

For some managers it can be difficult to give up control and to trust subordinates, especially if they have a 'Theory X' view of employees. Managers are more likely to be willing to trust employees if:

- the business's culture and leadership style encourage trust and delegation
- employees are skilled and prepared to exercise greater authority
- they have received training on effective delegation.

If these factors are present, trust is more likely. If managers are unable or unwilling to trust subordinates, they will retain control.

Authority and responsibility

Managers frequently delegate authority to more junior employees. This gives them power in relation to an agreed set of circumstances. For example, Pakistan International Airlines may delegate authority to one of its pilots to take decisions on a particular flight. However, despite this decision, overall responsibility for this flight remains with the senior managers at the Airline. Thus, if problems arise the senior managers are responsible for the well-being of the plane and all its passengers. Even if the pilot makes an error, responsibility will still lie with the senior managers, possibly because they gave authority to someone without all the necessary skills.

Thus it is possible to delegate authority but responsibility remains with the delegator (or senior employee).

People in business

Sergey Brin (born 1973)

Sergey Brin is one of the two entrepreneurs who established Google, one of the world's best known and most profitable companies. He and Larry Page founded the company and are reported to still own 16 per cent of its shares.

Brin was born in Russia and emigrated to the United States in 1979. He studied Mathematics and Computer Science at the University of Maryland and Stanford University. He met Larry Page at Stanford and together they established their business in a rented garage. Brin believes in the power and importance of knowledge and this is reflected in Google's mission statement: 'Organise the world's information and make it universally accessible and useful.'

Figure 23.10 Sergey Brin

Brin is a highly innovative person and encourages others to be the same. Google allows its employees to spend one day a week pursuing their own interests and this has resulted in the creation of many of the company's most famous products. He is committed to looking after the company's employees and to rewarding them well. Given the nature of Google's work and the skills of its employees, it is perhaps not surprising that he takes a democratic approach to leadership.

Centralisation versus decentralisation

We looked at centralisation and decentralisation on page 299. In recent years many businesses decentralised because it brings benefits to many stakeholders.

- Decentralisation provides junior employees with the opportunity to fulfil needs such as achievement and recognition through working. This should improve motivation and reduce the business's costs by, for example, reducing the rate of labour turnover.
- Decentralisation is doubly beneficial to managers. It reduces the workload on senior managers, allowing them to focus on strategic (rather than operational) issues. At the same time it offers junior managers an opportunity to develop their skills in preparation for a more senior position.
- Customers may benefit by having more decisions made locally which can encourage the business to meet their needs more fully. Many junior employees in the organisation may have better understanding of customers' needs and operational matters and delegation may allow them to use their skills and understanding to good effect.

However, some businesses remain centralised. This might be because the ssenior managers like to remain in control of the business and to take the major decisions. The decision to centralise may reflect the preferred style of management of the business's senior managers and their desire to retain authority. This may occur when employees are relatively low skilled and its managers are experienced decision-makers. In addition, if a business makes all its buying decisions centrally it is likely to benefit from purchasing economies of scale allowing the possibility of shareholders receiving increased benefits. In such circumstances an organisation is likely to perform more effectively if power remains at the centre of the organisation.

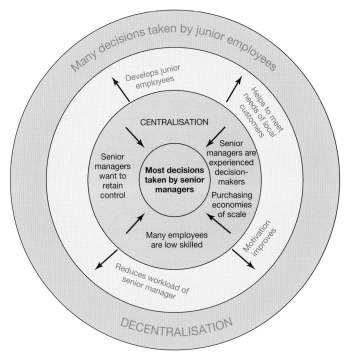

Figure 23.11 Centralisation and decentralisation

Opodo decentralises

Opodo is a European company owned by nine of Europe's leading airlines including British Airways, Iberia (now merged as IAG), Lufthansa and Air France. Opodo offers a 'competitively-priced' online global travel service with access to flights from over 500 airlines, over 65000 hotel properties and over 7000 car hire locations worldwide, as well as travel insurance. Opodo launched its first website in Germany in 2001 and currently operates in 14 countries.

In 2011 Opodo's parent company announced its sales had reached €3900 million. Ignacio Martos, chief executive of Opodo, said that one major reason the company was performing strongly was because the business had concentrated on its core business and had simplified its organisational structure through decentralisation. The company's decision to decentralise enabled it to concentrate on developing its operations and to invest heavily in IT for the next few years. Opodo states that it intends to maintain 'state of the art' technology and to develop

a comprehensive and reliable booking engine, giving customers first class customer service. Some business analysts believe that a democratic leadership style would be appropriate for the company once it has decentralised.

Sources: Adapted from Opodo and Eye for Travel websites

Questions

1 Analyse why Opodo might decide to operate a democratic leadership style. [8]
2 Evaluate the case for and against Opodo decentralising. [16]

> **Study tip**
>
> Do not assume that decentralisation is preferable. Whether a business should decentralise or not will always depend upon its circumstances.

Line and staff employees

> **Key term**
>
> **Line managers** have authority over specified people within the organisation.

- **Line managers** normally hold departmental responsibilities (including managing people and other resources) and derive their title from fulfilling a role in the line of command from the top to the bottom of the hierarchy. They have the power and authority to direct the actions of the subordinate who is accountable for carrying out certain duties. Line managers operate with the aim of assisting the business in meeting its corporate objectives.
- **Staff managers** are often appointed as the organisation grows in size and are used to relieve senior managers of some time-consuming duties. Examples of staff managers include IT and HR managers. Staff managers only indirectly contribute towards achieving corporate objectives. Instead, a staff manager is responsible for making sure all the supports are in place so the line staff are hired, trained, equipped and supported while they carry out the actual operations.

> **Key term**
>
> **Staff managers** have responsibility for support functions within the business such as information technology systems.

Causes of conflict between line and staff managers

The authority of staff managers is different from that of line managers. While the line manager focuses on generating revenue, the staff manager often has to engage in expenditure to support further operations. This can lead to tensions in the workplace, especially when there is no clear understanding of the difference in the authority of the positions.

Line managers do not always welcome the appointment of specialist staff managers. Line managers might feel that their positions and status are threatened and may believe staff managers only understand a part of the complexities of their jobs. When staff managers take decisions relating to their specialist areas, for example developing and implementing recruitment policies, line managers may not consider that they meet the needs of their particular division or department and may oppose their use.

Staff managers may sometimes feel that their opinions are not taken into account in corporate decisions. For example, when appointing a new member of staff the relevant line manager may have the final say, but a specialist HR staff manager may have a valuable contribution to make to the selection process and may be unhappy if he or she is not allowed to play a part in the decision.

Conflict is more likely in organisations where there is not a clear and well understood division between the authority of line managers with responsibility for operations and that of staff managers. If these authorities overlap it is the responsibility of senior managers within the business to make decisions to clarify and publicise responsibilities.

Is there a 'best' structure for organisations?

It is easy to criticise traditional hierarchical structures as being old fashioned, costly and having little relevance to modern businesses. This is not the case. We can list scenarios and circumstances in which such a structure would be appropriate and effective. Similar arguments can be put forward for matrix or functional structures.

We do, however, tend to think of an organisation as operating a single structure. It may be that large businesses in fact operate more than a single structure, reflecting the different needs of various areas of the organisation. Thus a large firm may organise itself as follows.

- Operate its research and development division on an informal basis to make the most effective use of talented and highly skilled scientists. This division would simply make sure that the scientific team received sufficient administrative support from clerical staff.
- Base its administration on a traditional structure in the expectation of achieving a continually high standard of work and benefiting from a consistent approach to this aspect of business.
- Its sales and marketing teams may be organised on a matrix structure and have clear targets and tasks to achieve. These could be in the form of developing existing markets, breaking into new markets or conducting market research.

It may be that these differing structures could be found within a single organisation. Dangers exist in this approach as the organisation could become difficult to coordinate and some divisions may begin to pursue objectives different from those of the overall business.

Test your learning

Short answer questions

1 a Define the term organisational structure. [2]

   b State **three** factors about a business that may be set out in its organisational chart. [3]

2 Explain **two** factors that might influence a business's managers when designing its organisational structure. [5]

3 a Define the term level of hierarchy. [2]

   b Explain why communication may be more difficult in a tall hierarchy. [3]

4 Explain **one** advantage and **one** disadvantage to a business of operating a functional organisational structure. [5]

5 a What is a matrix organisational structure? [2]

   b Explain **one** disadvantage to a business arising from operating a matrix organisational structure. [3]

6 a Distinguish between delegation and accountability. [3]

   b Explain **one** advantage to a large multinational business of engaging in delegation. [2]

7 a Define the term authority. [2]

   b Explain why authority can be delegated but responsibility may not. [3]

8 a Explain why trust is an important element of delegation. [2]

   b Why might a policy of delegation be difficult to implement within a business that operates with an authoritarian leadership style? [3]

9 a Give **two** reasons why a business may choose to operate a centralised organisational structure. [2]

   b Explain **one** benefit to a large multi-site business of implementing a policy of decentralisation. [3]

10 a Distinguish between line managers and staff managers. [3]

    b Explain **one** reason why conflict may occur between line and staff managers. [2]

Data response question

Nayudu Software Ltd

Janardan Nayudu's software company is growing quickly. It designs, installs and maintains software for a range of companies throughout India and in other Asian countries. All of its software solutions are individually designed to meet its customers' precise needs. It has excellent relationships with its customers (most of which are large businesses) due to the consistent quality of its work. It has a reputation for improving and developing on the work of some of its competitors and for having highly skilled employees.

Growth has led to a need to change the company's organisational structure: it increased its workforce by 24 per cent to 496 in 2013 compared with 2012. Many employees were attracted by pay rates 9 per cent above the industry average. Despite this, labour turnover remained at 12 per cent.

In 2013 the company employed 31 managers and these changes together led to a significant increase in its typical span of control. As a consequence authority has been delegated to all employees, including those newly appointed. Some managers are unhappy with this change.

Janardan Nayudu wishes the business to move to a matrix organisational structure. This will allow the employees to become more empowered. He is considering increasing the training budget (which was overspent in 2013), but considers maintaining profit margins a priority.

Questions

1 Analyse the possible implications for Nayudu Software Ltd of '… a significant increase in its typical span of control'. [10]

2 a Calculate the increase in the number of employees between 2012 and 2013. [2]

  b Calculate the company average span of control in 2013. [2]

  c Assess whether training is the most important factor for the company in preparing to empower its workforce. [10]

3 Should the company move to a matrix structure as Janardan Nayudu proposes? Justify your decision. [16]

Essay questions

1 Discuss the extent to which delayering will assist a business in achieving its corporate objectives. [20]

2 To what extent is it true to say that a matrix organisational structure is always likely to be more efficient than functional organisational structures? [20]

Past paper question

Read the Pyramid Televisions case study on pages 454–56 and then answer the following question.

Assess the advantages and disadvantages to the Research and Development department of changing the organisational structure of the business. [10]

Cambridge International AS and A Level Business Studies
9707 Paper 3 Q1b May/June 2008

24 Business communication

Chapter overview

In this chapter we examine:
- the purposes and methods of communication
- the channels of communication used by businesses
- barriers to communication
- the role of management in facilitating communication.

24.1 The theory of communication

What is communication?

Communication involves the transfer of information. This transfer can take place between people or between people and organisations or between different organisations. A transmission mechanism is simply the methods by which one person communicates with another. Letters and email are examples of methods of communication. Communication involves a number of elements as shown in Figure 24.1.

Study tip

Before reading this chapter, it is worthwhile revisiting the AS Business chapters on leadership, organisational structures and motivation. These will provide you with a good foundation for studying communications.

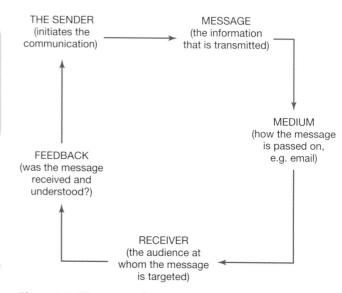

Figure 24.1 The process of communication

Case Study

Cathay Pacific

Figure 24.2 A Cathay Pacific aeroplane

Cathay Pacific is the international airline of Hong Kong. It operates scheduled passenger and cargo services to 151 destinations in 41 countries. It has seven wholly owned subsidiary airlines. Cathay Pacific is based at Hong Kong International Airport and operates 135 aircraft. The airline employs nearly 30 000 people and has a well-designed website. Along with its subsidiaries it carried 29 million passengers in 2013.

The company engages in communication for many different reasons, including marketing purposes. Over recent years it has made greater use of electronic communication both internally and externally.

Questions

1 Analyse the reasons why electronic communication may be important to Cathay Pacific. [8]

2 Do you agree that marketing is the most important reason for Cathay Pacific to engage in communication? Justify your view. [16]

Advertising provides an example of business communication.

- The sender is the company that commences the process of communication.
- The message is the information that the business wishes to send to its audience. In the case of Cathay Pacific, an advertisement may be transferring information about the quality of the airline's services.
- The medium is the way in which the message is communicated. Cathay Pacific might use newspapers and magazines to transmit its message.
- The audience. The target group at whom Cathay Pacific might aim its message would be fairly broad including any potential airline passengers on any of its routes.
- **Feedback** in Cathay Pacific's case, this could take the form of the company asking customers where they heard about the airline when making a booking. Cathay Pacific could also ask about the effectiveness of its advert to assess whether to use similar approaches in the future.

24.2 Why do businesses communicate?

Businesses communicate with their stakeholders in a variety of ways. It is not just a matter of communicating with customers through advertising.

Marketing purposes

Businesses need to communicate with potential and actual customers to research their needs through primary market research. In many industries this creates an ongoing need for two-way communication. Businesses also inform their customers of the products that they are selling through a variety of promotional activities and may use public relations events to present the business in a positive light to its stakeholders, including local residents and government. This category of communication will also include routine items such as arranging delivery of products to customers and negotiating prices.

Case Study

The Palm Court Hotel

The Palm Court Hotel in Bandar Seri Begawan, Brunei Darussalam, opened in February 2013. Bandar Seri Begawan is a popular destination for tourists from around the world who want to visit its beaches and experience the rainforest. The hotel has 34 bedrooms and a large restaurant to which it hopes to attract non-residents.

The hotel has 21 employees some of whom are part time and five have little experience of working in hotels. The hotel was established with the assistance of a bank loan and two private investors put up capital to fund the new business.

Shamsul Bahrin, the hotel's manager, has explained to his staff that effective communication is essential if the business is to succeed.

Questions

1 Analyse the communication problems that the employees of this hotel may face. [8]

2 Discuss the reasons why Shamsul Bahrin may believe that effective communication is essential to the hotel's success. [16]

Operational reasons

This forms a significant reason for communication within and outside the business. Internal communication will take place continually to ensure that operations are organised efficiently. For example, meetings may be held to discuss how to respond to a large order or complaints from customers. Alternatively, communication will be necessary with suppliers to order raw materials or components and to arrange delivery.

Managing the workforce

Effective communication is essential to create and maintain a productive workforce. This category of communication would include that essential to the process of recruitment and selection that we considered at length in Chapter 8. Negotiation with trade unions or other employee representatives over pay and working conditions as well as appraisal interviews are further examples of this category of communication.

Financial communication

Information on a business's financial information is vital to effective decision-making at all levels within the organisation. Junior managers will require budgets to enable them to control expenditure and to act as targets for revenue. More senior managers might look at data relating to cash flow and profitability produced by the business's finance department. This type of communication will also take place externally when businesses send invoices to customers or pay those sent by suppliers.

Legally required communication

Most businesses are obliged to communicate with external parties to provide key information. In the UK businesses have to engage in two-way communications with Her Majesty's Revenue and Customs (HMRC) to establish any liability to pay taxes and then to pay those taxes. Public companies have to publish an annual report and accounts containing specified information on financial and other aspects of the business's performance over the previous financial year.

This communication can be internal, that is with other individuals or groups within the business. Thus, an email sent from the director of human resources to team leaders concerning overtime rates would be an example of internal communication. External communication takes place between a business and other organisations or individuals. For example, a business providing details of job vacancies on its website as part of the process of external recruitment would be communicating externally.

Figure 24.3 summarises the key internal and external reasons for communication and emphasises that it is a two-way process.

24.3 How businesses communicate

Communication can take place in many different ways within a business. Some communication is interpersonal – just between two people. An example of this could be an appraisal interview. Individuals may also communicate with groups: a manager may brief a sales team prior to the launch of a new product, for example. Communication also takes place between groups within businesses, for example, between a management team and trade union representatives.

> **Key terms**
>
> A **communication channel** is the medium through which a message is transmitted to its intended audience such as a company newsletter or a mobile phone network.
>
> **Two-way communication** exists when information is passed up the organisational structure as well as down it, or outside the organisation and back in again.
>
> **Vertical communication** is the exchange of information between individuals or groups who are at different levels within the organisation, for example between managers and shop-floor employees.
>
> **Horizontal communication** involves individuals or groups at the same level of hierarchy within the business exchanging information, for example a meeting of a company's board of directors.

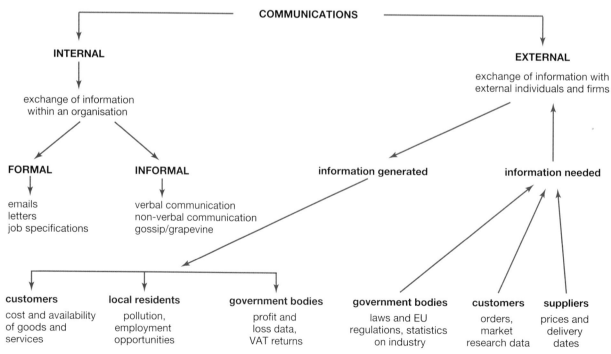

Figure 24.3 A summary of communication

Communication can be **two-way**, moving up and down the organisational structure perhaps as a part of discussion between managers and team leaders over the development of a new product. This entails those at higher and lower levels in the organisational structure initiating communication. In contrast **vertical communication** takes place either up *or* down the organisational structure. Figure 24.4 shows an example of a company's chief executive communicating with those lower down the organisational structure, for example over relocation plans. Finally, **horizontal communication** may occur between employees at the same level in the organisation, possibly a planning meeting between the company's managers.

Some communication takes place outside the official channels within a business. This is termed informal communication. Gossip between groups of employees during a break from work is an obvious example. Informal communication can be rapid but inaccurate and it is important for businesses to ensure that important matters are communicated promptly using official channels such as meetings to avoid wildly inaccurate information being transmitted. In contrast, formal communication uses official channels such as company meetings.

Spoken communication

- Telephone communication – this is widely used in business to transmit simple messages quickly and effectively. It allows contact with individuals and offers immediate feedback but does not offer a written record of discussions or allow callers to view each others' body language.
- Meetings – these occur in a variety of forms including board and shareholder meetings, meetings with customers and suppliers. Less formal meetings such as quality circles and social events are also forums in which information is exchanged. These can allow in-depth discussion and testing of ideas as well as providing a record of communication. However, they are time consuming and expensive, especially for multinational businesses.
- Presentations – these are frequently used in businesses, for example, internally to transmit information on new projects

and ideas and externally to attract new customers. Detailed information (especially relating to sales and products) can be exchanged using this method and the record of a presentation can be sent to any interested parties.
- Interviews – these are a formal method of communication that may be used to appoint new staff or to deal with disciplinary or grievance issues. This method encourages detailed discussions though they can only involve a relatively small number of people.

Written communication

This is more appropriate when detailed information needs to be exchanged. It can be slow, though modern technology (for example texts, email) can speed up the process.

- Reports are widely used to transmit information by businesses. They can relate to important issues such as an investigation into the establishment of a new nuclear power station or smaller topics such as reasons for low sales of a new product. They are also used to inform on the financial performance of companies.
- Business letters are a major external form of communication used, for example, to place orders with suppliers or to arrange other forms of communication such as meetings.
- Memoranda are extensively used internally to exchange information concisely and rapidly on a wide range of topics, though increasingly these are being replaced by emails.

Electronic communication

Developments in technology have transformed the way in which businesses communicate and bring benefits and drawbacks.

- Electronic mail (email) – this method of communication allows computers to speak to one another throughout the world for the cost of a local telephone call. Messages are stored on servers and can be accessed by the recipient through the use of a password. This is particularly useful for quick international communication across different time zones as messages can be stored until the recipient is available.

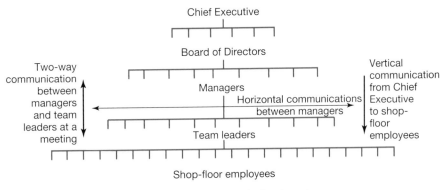

Figure 24.4 Communication flows through an organisational structure

- Websites – these play a central role in communication for most businesses, even relatively small ones. They offer a chance to communicate with stakeholder groups to publicise products, collect research data, achieve sales and to provide after-sales service. A rapidly increasing volume of business is conducted via the internet in most countries throughout the world. Many businesses operate Facebook pages to communicate with customers and other stakeholders, to respond to enquiries and to project a positive corporate image.
- Text messages – these are used by businesses to communicate with customers mainly for marketing purposes. Research shows that 99 per cent of texts are opened, making it an effective medium.

Case Study

Golden Screen Cinemas' Facebook page

Golden Screen Cinemas is Malaysia's largest cinema chain. The company operates 28 cinemas with 238 screens. Its largest cinema is in Mid Valley Megamall and has 18 screens and 2900 seats. Golden Screen faces tough competition from TGV Cinemas, which has 20 cinemas through Malaysia.

Golden Screen Cinemas makes effective use of its Facebook pages to communicate with its customers. This can be seen at https://www.facebook.com/GSCinemas. At the time of writing, the company has 925 000 likes and the pages have trailers for movies that it is showing or will show soon.

Questions

1 Analyse the possible reasons for Golden Screen Cinemas having a page on the Facebook website. [8]

2 To what extent do you think that Golden Screen Cinemas should rely solely on electronic communication for its marketing in the future? [16]

- Intranets – these are electronic computer-based communication networks, similar in nature to the internet, but used internally by individual businesses. They are ideally suited to large businesses, especially those with a number of locations. They provide an email service as well as access to information of interest to large numbers of employees.
- Video conferencing – this allows people to communicate face-to-face while in different locations, nationally or internationally. It saves time and avoids the need for employees to travel to meetings.

Visual communication

Visual communication uses images to transmit information to audiences. Methods of visual communication that are used by businesses include posters, displays, webpages and photographic communication. Some businesses use symbols to represent their products and image: Nike's tick is one example.

Visual communication can be an effective method of communicating a simple message or as a reminder of information previously communicated. It may be effective and is more likely to be used in certain industries, such as fashion clothing. Recent research suggests that people retain and recall information that is presented visually more fully than that which is presented verbally.

However, it does have a significant drawback in that it is often one-way and may not offer the opportunity for feedback.

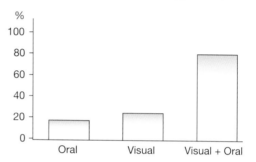

Figure 24.5 Oral and visual information: percentage retained

Source: Jerome Bruner, as cited by Paul Martin Lester in Syntactic Theory of Visual Communication

Selecting methods of communication

Owners and managers of businesses will select which method of communication to use on the basis of factors such as cost and speed of communication. Which factors are of prime importance will depend on the circumstances. A business that is experiencing cash-flow difficulties may consider costs closely, while for a news media organisation speed may be most important.

The costs of communication

Businesses will take into account the cost of any method of communication when deciding whether or not to use it. Most businesses attempt to control costs tightly to maximise profits and returns to owners such as shareholders. Costs of communication can include the purchase of relevant technology and associated training costs. Attendance at meetings involves opportunity costs for employees involved as they are not carrying out other duties.

Study tip

When weighing up the methods of communication do not just analyse costs incurred. Do consider the potential costs to businesses of poor or incomplete communication.

Speed of communication

In many situations businesses require communication to be rapid as well as accurate. Electronic communication has made this objective easier to achieve through use of telephones (landlines or mobiles), email, text messaging and video conferencing. Speed may be vital to meet the urgent needs of a customer, to advise of problems with a product or to communicate decisions to employees. Figure 24.6 assesses a selection of methods of communication in terms of speed and cost.

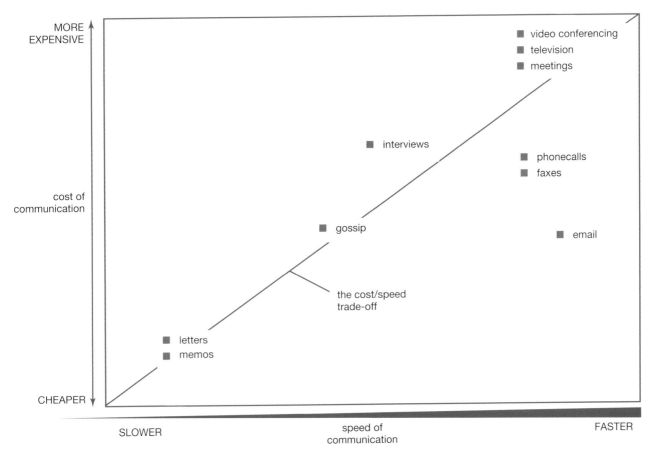

Figure 24.6 The speed and cost of a selection of methods of communication

The target audience

Some communication within businesses may simply involve an exchange of information between two people at the same location. In such circumstances a number of methods may be used including email, telephones or a face-to-face discussion. The problem of selecting the best method becomes more complex when larger numbers of people are used, especially if they are in different locations. Thus if the chief executive of a multinational business wishes to communicate with several thousand employees in many countries about the implications of the company's new strategy, email may be the chosen method to achieve a personal touch.

Case Study

Khosa Law Chambers

Khosa Law Chambers has operated in Lahore for more than 40 years. The law firm has represented clients in a wide variety of cases, some of which have attracted attention from national and international media.

A number of the company's cases have been important in legal terms with long-term implications. The legal practice is broad-ranging and handles cases in human rights, banking, immigration, corporate and real estate and crime.

The Chambers has represented some of the most important people in Pakistan including the former Prime Minister Benazir Bhutto and numerous other senior politicians and business leaders.

The company has a network of affiliates in major cities around the world, for example London and Toronto.

Questions

1 Analyse the reasons why effective communication is particularly important to Khosa Law Chambers. [8]
2 Evaluate the most important influences on the Khosa Law Chambers' choice of methods of communication. [16]

Keeping a record of the communication

Some types of communication require a record in written form for subsequent use. Thus a contract of employment is most likely to be written to avoid any disputes between employees and employers about what was agreed. Most agreements with legal implications will be in written form, and will therefore lead to the use of email, letters or memos.

The case for and against the use of technology in communication

Technology offers significant benefits and drawbacks to businesses in terms of communication.

- It provides a cheap and quick method to communicate and can transfer complex and highly technical information effectively. It is of particular value to companies that operate internationally or to those that sell to target groups which use electronic media as the major means of communication.
- It avoids the need for endless pieces of paper as businesses strive towards paperless administrative systems.
- It allows automatic generation of communications, for example re-ordering of inventories and invoicing of customers.
- Some employees may be resistant to the new technology and make ineffective use of it.
- New technology can be expensive to install and may require substantial training of employees, incurring further costs.
- High technology communication systems can generate enormous amounts of communication that may not improve the efficiency of the organisation. Technology does not necessarily encourage selective communication.

24.4 Barriers to communication

The use of jargon or technical terms

These are specialist terms used by people in particular industries which may be used when communicating with non-specialists. This is possible in a wide range of industries and not just technology companies.

Lack of understanding by managers

A principal cause of poor communication is that managers do not recognise that there is a problem. Symptoms of poor communication (such as poor industrial relations and low levels of motivation) may be thought to have other causes. Because senior managers have access to all the information they require and can communicate easily with all in the organisation they may be unaware that others in the business do not receive information essential to their jobs.

Inappropriate management and leadership styles

Some managers use leadership styles that discourage effective **two-way communication** within the business. Some individuals prefer to operate an autocratic leadership style and a traditional organisational structure. This only encourages downward communication, resulting in a lack of information at different levels in the organisational structure.

Equally, some managers may encourage working practices that keep managers and shop-floor employees apart (such as having separate facilities) and this may discourage effective communication, some of which may be informal.

> **Study tip**
>
> The importance of communication to a business cannot be underestimated. When dealing with case studies it is often an important argument to say that a business's performance can be improved in many ways through better communication.

Merger and takeover activity

Mergers and takeovers usually create larger and more complex business. This can create communication problems and the process itself can pose similar difficulties. The merger in 2012 between the Ghana Water Company Ltd and Ghana Urban Water Ltd was eased because of its relatively small scale. The chief executive of the newly merged business was able to lead meetings of employees discussing the implications of the change.

In contrast, in 2008 the Indian multinational company Tata took over the UK-based car manufacturers Jaguar and Land Rover. Tata paid $2.3 billion to buy these companies from another car manufacturer, Ford. Tata has business interests in over 100 countries spread across six continents and the purchase of Jaguar and Land Rover meant that the newly enlarged company had over 570 000 employees. Jaguar Land Rover has production facilities in India and Brazil as well as the UK. The global nature of both Tata and Jaguar Land Rover will make effective communications within and between these companies challenging.

Changes in business practices

The increasing need for information (and thus communication) has been further increased by developments such as delegation, empowerment, decentralisation and the widespread use of just-in-time techniques. Extending the roles and authority of employees creates a greater need for new channels of communication. In view of this it is perhaps not surprising that many businesses have been unable to keep up! The use of consultants and contract workers and the rise in teleworking have increased the diversity of communication required. Through the involvement of so many groups communication has become more difficult to carry out efficiently.

Many large businesses operate in several locations around the world. This means they have employees from different cultures using diverse languages and working in different time zones. All three of these factors can inhibit effective communication.

Too much reliance on IT systems

Some businesses have recognised the imperfections in their communications systems. However, many have relied upon IT to overcome these problems and have created further problems. If IT is to be effective it requires that employees be trained and that systems suit the precise needs. Simply throwing IT at the problem creates more, rather than better, communications.

24.5 Improving communication

The importance of effective communication

Effective communication is an essential element of business success. A survey by the Institute of Management and UMIST in the UK stressed the importance of good quality communications within businesses. The survey reported that good communication could assist employees of all types within a business.

- Good communication makes it easier to implement change – an important issue in a business environment subject to rapid and continual change.

- It encourages and develops commitment to the business from employees at all levels within the organisation.
- Effective communication helps to ensure that the business is coordinated and that all employees pursue the same corporate objectives.

The role of a manager in a modern organisation is to communicate with everyone – shareholders, the media, customers and suppliers. The measure of today's manager is how well they communicate, and good quality communication by managers with the business's stakeholders offers many benefits.

Successful decision-making requires that managers have access to as much relevant information as possible. The key management roles of planning, prioritising, coordinating and controlling depend upon access to information. This indicates the importance of good communication to businesses.

For example, modern techniques such as just-in-time production place great emphasis on effective communication systems. If supplies of components or raw materials are not available when required, businesses are likely to incur substantial – and unnecessary – costs as well as being unable to provide high quality customer service. Similarly, techniques such as Kaizen (continuous improvement) rely heavily upon effective two-way internal communication.

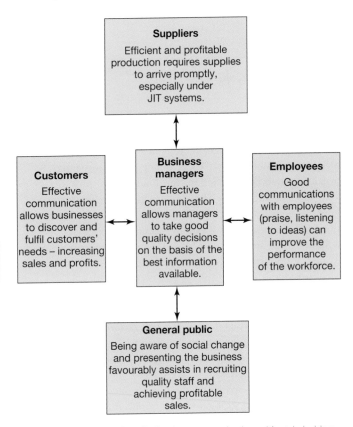

Figure 24.7 The benefits of effective communication with stakeholders

Good communication can have a positive impact upon employee motivation and performance. Praise and recognition are widely seen as motivators, but rely upon communication.

Communication can also give employees important feedback about their performance and help to improve it in the future. In this respect appraisal systems (and especially developmental appraisal systems) have been of considerable value.

> ### Study tip
>
> When answering questions on the importance of effective communication avoid the temptation to try to develop too many arguments. Select the best two or three and develop these as fully as possible.

Communication is the cornerstone of coordination. In large businesses it is easy for different departments or parts of the organisation to pursue differing objectives. Regular and effective communication can help to ensure that all employees remain closely focused on agreed corporate objectives.

Effective communication with customers is essential for businesses. The pursuit of quality means that businesses have to satisfy customers' needs. A key element here is to establish exactly what the customer requires, possibly through market research. It is also important to make sure that these needs are being satisfied on an ongoing basis.

> ### Case Study
>
> ## APN News & Media
>
> APN News & Media Limited is a media company operating in New Zealand and Australia. The company is partly owned by an Irish media group. APN has interests in several different markets including publishing newspapers, online publishing, radio broadcasting and advertising in New Zealand and Australia.
>
> In New Zealand, it has three of the top five national radio networks with NewsTalk ZB, Classic Hits and Coast as well as four additional major networks. In Australia, APN's major metro radio networks are Mix and Classic Hits, connecting audiences in Sydney, Melbourne, Brisbane and Adelaide. It also operates The Edge in Sydney.
>
> APN publishes 20 daily and more than 100 non-daily newspapers across Australia and New Zealand. It is the leading publisher in New Zealand, with *The New Zealand Herald* spearheading public opinion in the country. In Australia, it focuses on providing relevant and engaging publications in some of Australia's fastest growing regions.
>
> The company has market-leading online sites such as NZ Herald Online and a strong audience connection with its radio and news-branded web and mobile sites. APN is committed to expanding its digital businesses.
>
> Source: Adapted from APN News & Media Ltd's website

Questions

1 Analyse the possible barriers to communication that APN News & Media Ltd might encounter. [8]
2 Discuss the most important reasons why effective communication is essential to APN News & Media Ltd. [16]

Methods to improve communication

Good quality communication is essential for successful management. Globalisation is resulting in businesses becoming larger and more diverse, meaning that to operate successfully good communications are even more important than ever. To adapt to the changing demands of the global marketplace a business can take a number of actions to improve its communications.

- **Train employees in communication skills** Modern business communication is a complicated activity often requiring competence in a range of activities: listening, speaking, writing and reading skills, to say nothing of technological skills. To carry out all these activities satisfactorily employees will require training at regular intervals – it is not a one-off action. In spite of this, training in communications skills is a priority with a relatively small number of businesses and is often cut during less prosperous periods.

- **Avoid the danger of generating too much information** Modern technology has substantially increased the risk of this occurring and many firms simply invest in technology when facing communications problems. By evaluating communications needs before taking any action a business increases the probability of implementing an effective solution. A survey in the UK revealed that nearly 50 per cent of voicemail systems were switched off within a year of installation, indicating that many managers do not spend time evaluating the position before taking decisions.

- **Recognise that cultural and linguistic differences exist** These are common within a large multinational and can inhibit effective communication. Honeywell, the computer manufacturer, operates in 11 countries, employs 132 000 people and encourages its employees to be sensitive to cultural differences when communicating. The company stresses that it is important to respect and value cultural differences, to be aware of prejudice, and to ensure that employees have the full picture when communicating before making judgements. Multicultural communication is set to become a common feature in the lives of more employees as business becomes increasingly global.

Test your learning

Short answer questions

1 a Define the term communication. [2]

   b Distinguish between the message and the medium in the process of communication. [3]

2 a State **two** reasons why businesses communicate. [2]

   b Explain why feedback is an important element of successful communication. [3]

3 a Define the term communication channel. [2]

   b Using examples, explain the difference between vertical and horizontal communication. [3]

4 a Distinguish between formal and informal communication. [3]

   b State **two** examples of electronic communication. [2]

5 Explain **one** advantage and **one** disadvantage of using written communication within a large multinational company. [5]

6 Explain **two** factors that the owner of a newly established business might consider when deciding on the best way to communicate with actual and potential customers. [5]

7 a State **two** methods of technological communication that a retailer may use. [2]

   b Explain why a small business may decide not to make extensive use of technological methods of communication. [3]

8 a Explain why agreeing to a merger may result in communication difficulties for both the businesses involved. [3]

   b State **two** other barriers to communication. [2]

9 a Why is it important for businesses to communicate effectively with suppliers? [2]

   b Explain why good communication can help to improve the motivation of a business's workforce. [3]

10 a Define the term effective communication. [2]

    b Explain **one** action that the managers of a business with six restaurants may use to improve communication. [3]

Data response question

Vina Casa Rosa

Chile has a long history of producing wine. In recent years the industry has grown rapidly and much of its output is exported to countries throughout the world. Vina Casa Rosa, a medium-sized vinery, has an 80 hectare site in Atacama, a popular wine producing region.

The vinery's owner uses an autocratic leadership style, insisting that all 24 current employees assemble for an unpopular 30-minute briefing each morning where the instructions for the day are issued. The large numbers of temporary and seasonal employees attend too. Little use is made of electronic methods of communication such as computers or mobile phones; the company has not made a decision on whether to create a website. The wider management team has developed a good personal relationship with the buyers of their wines, but sales and profits have fallen slowly in recent years. Competitors are promoting themselves and selling directly overseas, responding to a changing market and increased overseas sales.

The vinery's workforce is dissatisfied with the leadership style and the use of spoken instructions. This year its productivity declined by 5 per cent to 8550 litres per employee. At the same time the rate of labour turnover of full-time employees rose to 25 per cent. Most employees believe internal and external communication is poor.

Questions

1 Analyse the strengths and weaknesses of Vina Casa Rosa's reliance on spoken communication. [10]

2 a Calculate the labour productivity for Vina Casa Rosa's employees for *last* year. [4]

   b Recommend whether or not Vina Casa Rosa should invest in technology to improve its communication. Justify your decision. [10]

3 Discuss the extent to which the autocratic leadership style is the major factor determining the quality of communication at Vina Casa Rosa. [16]

Essay questions

1 Discuss the extent to which technology can help large businesses to improve their communication. [20]

2 To what extent is it true to say that the most important barrier to communication for all businesses today is the trend towards globalisation? [20]

Past paper question

Read the Chan Beauty Company case study on pages 452–54 and then answer the following questions.

a Analyse **two** possible reasons for the communication problems in the factory. [8]

b Evaluate **two** ways in which communication might be improved in the factory. [10]

Cambridge International AS and A Level Business Studies
9707 Paper 32 Q1 October/November 2009

25 Marketing

Chapter overview

In this chapter we examine:
- the importance of market planning
- different forms of elasticity such as income, cross-price and promotional
- the importance of product development
- the value of research and development
- the value of protecting ideas
- the significance of forecasting
- the value of market analysis
- the importance of a coordinated marketing mix
- factors influencing a marketing strategy.

25.1 Marketing planning

A **marketing plan** sets out what a business intends to do in relation to its marketing activities.

It includes:
- the marketing objectives such as increasing market share, increasing sales of particular products in particular regions, smoothing out sales across the year or improving brand awareness
- the marketing strategy, i.e. how the objectives will be achieved; for example, by new product development or targeting new segments
- the marketing budget, i.e. how much can be spent on marketing activities
- details of marketing activities showing what will be done, by when, who is responsible and how much will be spent on each activity.

The benefits of marketing planning

By producing a plan the marketing department is forced to think carefully about what it has to do. It has to make choices between what to spend its money on. It has to debate when

is the best time to undertake different activities and how long they are likely to be. This is an important process that can highlight potential problems and possibly highlight new ways of doing things.

The marketing plan is vital because:
- It shows how much needs to be available to sell and at what times; this is crucial for the operations department.
- It will influence the human resource planning in terms of numbers and skills of staff needed at particular times.
- It will influence the financial forecasts showing expected profits and cash flow.

Having a plan:
- helps to coordinate action between departments
- can motivate by setting clear targets for different people
- can enable a proper review to see whether the targets have been achieved and if not, why not.

Key term

The **marketing plan** sets out the marketing objectives, strategy, budget and the activities necessary to achieve objectives.

Maths moment

1 If your sales are $200 000 and your market share is 3 per cent what is the size of the market overall?
2 If you set a target of a market share of 5 per cent what level of sales would you need?

25.2 Elasticity of demand

At AS we looked at the significance of the price elasticity of demand and how it helps businesses make pricing decisions. However, firms are not just interested in how price influences demand; they also want to analyse the relationship between other variables and demand. Another common measure of elasticity is the income elasticity of demand: this is analysed below.

Income elasticity of demand

The amount that demand changes in relation to changes in income can be measured by the income elasticity of demand.

$$\text{Income elasticity of demand} = \frac{\text{percentage change in quantity demanded}}{\text{percentage change in income}}$$

For example, if demand increases by 20 per cent when income rises by 10 per cent, then:

$$\text{Income elasticity} = \frac{+20}{+10} = +2$$

This product is income elastic because the demand has changed by more than the percentage change in income. These are 'luxury' products such as health clubs.

Alternatively, if demand increases by 5 per cent when income rises by 10 per cent then:

$$\text{Income elasticity} = \frac{+5}{+10} = +0.5$$

This product is income inelastic, because the demand has changed by less than the percentage change in income.

In both the above cases demand increased when income increased. These are called 'normal products' and have a positive income elasticity of demand.

If demand *falls* as income rises, the product is known as an 'inferior' product. This leads to a negative income elasticity of demand.

For example, if the quantity demanded falls by 2 per cent when income rises by 6 per cent, then:

$$\text{Income elasticity of demand} = \frac{-2\%}{+6\%} = -0.33$$

Products such as basic own label items may be perceived as inferior products; with higher levels of income customers switch to other items that are perceived as better.

Maths moment

1 If demand rises by 5 per cent when income rises by 20 per cent what is the income elasticity of demand?
2 If demand rises by 15 per cent when income rises by 5 per cent what is the income elasticity of demand?
3 If demand falls by 4 per cent when income rises by 8 per cent what is the income elasticity of demand?
4 If the income elasticity of demand is +1.8 what is the impact on demand of an increase in income from $20 000 to $22 000?
5 If the income elasticity of demand is −0.2 and sales are 5000 units, what is the effect of a 4 per cent increase in income?

Other types of elasticity that it would be possible to calculate include:

- **Cross-price elasticity of demand** This shows how much demand for one product (A) changes when the price of another product (B) changes:

$$\frac{\text{Percentage change in quantity demanded of A}}{\text{Percentage change in the price of B}}$$

This can show the nature of the relationship between the two products. With substitutes, customers will buy more of A when the price of B increases, and the cross-price elasticity will be positive. With complements, customers will buy less of A when the price of B increases (e.g. high-priced computer consoles reduces sales of consoles and of computer games, so the games and consoles are complements), so the cross-price elasticity is negative. The size of the cross-price elasticity of demand will show the strength of the relationship between the products (e.g. the extent to which they are close substitutes).

Maths moment

1 If the cross-price elasticity of demand is +0.2 what is the effect on demand for B of a 5 per cent increase in the price of A?
2 If the cross-price elasticity of demand is −2.5 what is the effect on demand for A of an 8 per cent fall in the price of B?
3 If the quantity demanded in A falls from 12 units to 10 units when the price of B rises from $20 to $24, then what is the cross-price elasticity of demand?

- **Promotional elasticity of demand** This will show the sensitivity of demand in relation to changes in promotional expenditure:

$$\frac{\text{Percentage change in the quantity demanded}}{\text{Percentage change in promotional expenditure}}$$

A positive result would show a positive correlation between the spending on promotional expenditure and the quantity demanded. The bigger the figure, the stronger the relationship. For example, a result of +0.1 means a 1 per cent increase in promotional spending increases sales by 0.1 per cent; a value of +3 means a 1 per cent increase in promotional spending increases quantity demanded by 3 per cent.

- **Weather elasticity of demand** This shows the sensitivity of demand in relation to changes in factors such as the temperature or rainfall:

$$\frac{\text{Percentage change in quantity demanded}}{\text{Percentage change in rainfall}}$$

When using these different elasticity of demands, care must be taken. The concept measures the change in quantity demanded in relation to a change in one other variable such as income or promotional expenditure with all other things unchanged. In fact, many things are changing in the marketing environment at the same time. It might appear as if a change in promotional spending has boosted sales significantly leading to a high positive result for the promotional elasticity, but in fact it may have been due to an increase in the income of customers. It can be difficult therefore to isolate the effect of a change in one variable.

Also, the value of an elasticity can only really be calculated by looking backwards and seeing what happened when income changed, the price of a substitute changed or promotion changed. This value may be of limited use now because the environment may have changed so much. In the time since a business last changed promotion it may have more competitors, a recession and fewer potential buyers in which case an 'old' value for elasticity will not help much.

Study tip

Remember to be precise when using the concept of elasticity of demand in your answers. Is it the price elasticity or the income elasticity you are referring to, for example? Remember that when demand is income inelastic, this does not mean that demand never changes at all; it simply means that the change in demand is smaller than the change in income.

25.3 Product development

A common strategy in marketing is to focus on new product development. This can be seen in the Ansoff Matrix (see Figure 25.1). Developing new products involves investment in research and development to produce new products and spending on testing and launching new products. The failure rate of new products is relatively high and therefore new product development involves a high degree of risk.

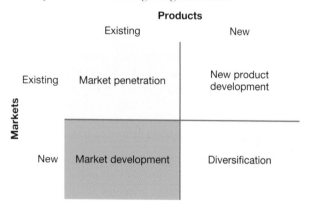

Figure 25.1 The Ansoff Matrix

Ideas for new products

Firms may generate the ideas for new products internally or externally. Internally, ideas may simply come through discussion, employees' suggestion schemes, brainstorming activities or the firm's own research department, if it has one. However, to generate good ideas for new products regularly requires a culture in which innovation is valued. This means people will be encouraged to question, to challenge and to improve the existing way of doing things (rather than adopting an attitude of, 'it's always been done like that'). This means the business will want to build an innovative culture.

Externally, many new ideas are registered at the Intellectual Property Office; firms may search the patent office records and if they find a product or process they would like to use they can pay a fee to the owner of the patent for the right to use their technology. Alternatively, a firm might buy a **franchise** to produce under another firm's name; in return for this right a firm pays a fee and/or a percentage of its turnover.

A firm's customers can also be a valuable external source of new ideas. You will notice that many companies have a customer phone line or a comments book to gain feedback from their consumers on their service and to discover more about what customers really want. Innocent drinks, for example, has a 'banana phone' which customers can ring with their ideas.

Key term

A **franchise** occurs when one business (a franchisor) sells the right to use its name and processes to another (a franchisee).

The importance of research and development

Research and development (R&D) is part of the innovation process. It refers to the generation and application of scientific knowledge to create a product or develop a new production process. For example, it may involve a team of employees at a confectionery company researching into a new flavour or a new variety of sweet or candy and then trying out different versions until they have one they (and the customers) are happy with. Or it may involve another team in the business focusing on new ways of producing the confectionery.

Case Study

The leading investors in R&D in Europe

In some sectors, such as the car industry, pharmaceuticals and energy, research and development can take many years and be very expensive. Glaxo calculates that on average a new pharmaceutical takes 10 to 15 years and costs around £500 million

Table 25.1 The leading investors in R&D in Europe

Rank	Company	Sector	R&D/net sales ratio 2010 %	Operating profit 2010 % of net sales
1	Volkswagen	Automobiles and parts	4.9	7.1
2	Nokia	Telecommunications equipment	11.6	4.5
3	Daimler	Automobiles and parts	5.0	7.1
4	Sanofi-Aventis	Pharmaceuticals	13.6	23.0
5	GlaxoSmithKline	Pharmaceuticals	13.2	13.5

($852 million) to develop. However, research and development is often very risky. This is because you may never have an idea that is actually viable. Even if you do manage to launch a product, you may find that you do not have very long to recover the costs of development. In the software industry, for example, new products are being developed very rapidly indeed; a successful film may only be showing for a few weeks. In Formula One, innovation is so fast that the car that is the fastest at the start of the race season would be last by the end if it failed to develop its technology.

Source: http://ec.europa.eu

Questions

1 Analyse how research and development (R&D) can benefit a business. [8]
2 Discuss the possible factors that determine the amount that a company invests in R&D. [16]

Figure 25.2 An original Sony transistor radio

Case Study

Akio Morita

Akio Morita was the founder of Sony. After serving in the Japanese navy he set up a small electronics company, Tokyo Telecommunications Engineering, with his friend Masaru Ibuka. Ibuka was an engineering genius who created many of the technical advances behind the brand Morita created.

The company became very successful in the 1950s when it produced a small transistor radio. The transistor was invented in America, but Morita bought a licence from Bell Laboratories to produce it in Japan. By the end of the decade Morita was exporting from Japan to the US and Europe. In 1958 he changed the company's name. After weeks of searching he found the name Sonus, which is Latin for 'sound'. He changed this to Sony because 'sony boys' is Japanese for 'whizz kids'. In 1961 Sony became the first Japanese company to be listed on the New York stock exchange.

After further successes with televisions and videotape recorders Morita developed the Sony Walkman. This product (which changed the way we listened to music) was launched with almost no market research and against the views of many within the business.

'The public does not know what is possible. We do,' said Morita. Interestingly, Apple's Steve Jobs had the same message many years later. 'The visionaries have the ability to look beyond where we are now to develop what customers want, whether or not they know it.'

In 1998 the Sony Walkman was declared the number one consumer brand in America. Morita's famous view of globalisation was 'think globally, act locally'. In America Sony was seen as American; in Japan it was seen as Japanese.

Source: Adapted from Economist.com, 7 November 2008

Questions

1 Analyse how market research can help with research and development. [8]
2 Discuss whether you think it is right to develop products without market research. Justify your answer. [16]

Protecting ideas for new products

If a firm manages to develop new products and new processes successfully it will naturally want to protect these from being copied or imitated by competitors. If an innovation is genuinely new, a firm may protect it by taking out a **patent**. In the UK, under the 1988 Copyright, Designs and Patents Act the holder of a patent has the right to be the sole user of a process or manufacturer of a product for 20 years after it is registered.

The owner of a patent may sell the right to produce the product or use a process to others. This can be a valuable source of income to some organisations. If one firm suspects another of illegally producing a patented product or using its patented technology, it can sue the offender. However, this can be costly and time consuming. To protect a product or process worldwide a firm must register the patent in different countries; this can also be an expensive and slow process.

By comparison, the work of artists, writers and musicians is automatically protected by copyright; copyrights do not have to be registered, although once again it is up to the copyright holder to sue offenders. Designs and logos can be protected by registering a trademark.

Case Study

L'Oréal Group

Figure 25.3 A selection of L'Oréal products

For more than a century L'Oréal has been pushing back the boundaries of science to invent beauty and meet the aspirations of millions of women and men. Its vocation is universal: to offer everyone, all over the world, the best of cosmetics in terms of quality, efficacy and safety, to give everyone access to beauty by offering products in harmony with their needs, culture and expectations.

With the opening up of the emerging markets, L'Oréal's mission is broadening in response to the vast diversity of populations. The whole company is focused on this new horizon: teams enriched by their cultural diversity, a portfolio of international brands present in the different distribution channels, and research that is capable of grasping the world's complexity. The exploration of new scientific and technological territories is being enriched by this global dimension. Knowledge of different cultures and rituals worldwide enables the laboratories to anticipate and invent the products of the future.

- 23 global brands
- operating in 130 countries
- more than 66 000 employees
- more than 600 patents filed in 2010 alone.

Questions

1 Analyse why L'Oréal might want to target emerging markets. [8]
2 Discuss whether innovation is crucial to the success of L'Oréal. Justify your answer. [16]

Case Study

R&D spending

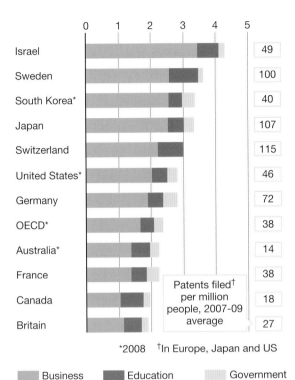

*2008   †In Europe, Japan and US

Business   Education and non-profit   Government

Questions

1 Explain the benefits of having a patent to a business.   [6]
2 Discuss the possible reasons why the number of patents filed per million people varies so much from country to country.   [10]

25.4 The need to forecast marketing data

Before setting a marketing objective and before deciding how best to achieve this, managers will want some understanding of market conditions. This means they will want to analyse the market to find out more about it and decide what to do next.

Market analysis occurs when a firm undertakes a detailed examination of the characteristics of a market. This is an essential part of marketing planning. Only by knowing the features of a market will a firm be able to plan effectively what to do next. A good understanding of markets should help the business to target the right segments and to market its products effectively in

a targeted way. A lack of analysis may mean the wrong markets are selected and/or the marketing is wasteful because it is not targeted.

Analysing a market involves gaining an understanding of the following.

- **The market size** This may be measured in terms of the volume or value of sales. For example, in the soft drinks market a firm may measure the number of cans or bottles sold (**volume**) or the monetary value of the total sales (**value**). A firm must ensure that the market is big enough to generate sufficient returns to make it worth competing in. If a market is only worth $2 million a year in revenue but would cost, say, $10 million to enter then it is unlikely to be worthwhile. A business will be interested in the whole market but also segments within it; for example, within the cereals market cold cereals sell more than hot cereals.

Key terms

The **value of sales** measures the amount of money spent on products in a market.
The **volume of sales** measures the number of units sold in a market.

- **The market share of firms within the market** This measures the sales of a firm relative to the total market size. In some markets, such as banking, airlines, petrol stations, sugar refining and pharmaceuticals, a few firms dominate. These are called oligopoly markets. In other markets there are no dominant firms – there are many smaller firms competing; for example, the hairdressing, advertising and taxi markets tend to have a large number of relatively small firms.
- **The likely costs and difficulties involved in entering the market** What is the typical spending on marketing in the industry, for example? What are the main channels to market and how easy is it likely to be to access these? How brand loyal are customers?
- **The trends within the market** For example, is the overall trend of sales upwards? At what rate is the market growing? For example, the growth of demand for takeaway foods has been rapid in recent years, whereas the growth in demand for high-fat foods has been slower. A firm will be reluctant to enter a declining market. When measuring the change in the size of the market, the firm will want to examine what is happening to the value of sales as well as the volume. If it finds the volume of sales has been going up but the value has been falling, for example, this means the average price has been falling. Will it be able to make a profit if this continues?
- **Patterns of sales** Managers will also look for patterns within the overall trends. Are sales seasonal, for example? This could have implications for cash flow and production. Think of sun cream, fireworks, school clothes, textbooks, garden furniture and holidays. Are some segments growing faster than others (e.g. the demand for mints has grown faster than the demand for chocolate within the overall confectionery market)? This could have implications for new product development.

- **Substitute products** Managers will be interested not just in this market but in substitute markets as well and how likely customers are to switch. If customers decide not to buy cereal, for example, then what else are they buying? Fruit? Toast? Yoghurt? Developments in these markets such as new forms of yoghurt may damage sales of cereal.

When analysing markets, a business will want to analyse the position at a given moment in time and to monitor the trends over time.

Maths moment

1 If a market is growing by 8 per cent by volume and 3 per cent by value what does this show?
2 If a market is growing by 5 per cent by volume and 7 per cent by value what does this show?

Why analyse markets?

It may be possible to set a marketing objective and develop a plan to achieve this target without gathering or analysing any data. You could simply rely on a hunch or your 'gut feeling'. Akio Morita, for example, is said to have launched the hugely successful Sony Walkman with very little reference to market research. Steve Jobs at Apple said that market research was of little value because customers did not know what they wanted.

However, while this can obviously work it is likely to be a high-risk decision equivalent to trying to find your way around a house in the dark – you may get lucky but the chances are you will cause some damage. Gather valuable data and interpret it correctly and this is the equivalent of having the lights turned on – navigating your way around should be that much easier. You know where you are, you can see where you want to go and how to get there. The marketing spending by businesses can run into millions of dollars in some cases. Analysing markets should help to reduce risks and ensure marketing is focused and relevant and does not involve wasteful activities.

Case Study

Africa

Africa is a diverse continent, with an estimated 1500 languages grouped into six linguistic families.

- In 2010, Sub-Saharan Africa (SSA) was populated by more than 856 million consumers. The region will have more than 1.3 billion consumers by 2030.
- The most populous country in SSA is Nigeria, with a population of 151 million, while the smallest, Seychelles, has just 100 000 people.

- While the global economy is predicted to grow by 2 per cent to 3 per cent between 2011 and 2020, SSA is poised to grow by 5 per cent to 6 per cent, making it one of the world's fastest-growing regions.
- African countries received $72 billion in foreign direct investment in 2008, which is five times the amount received in 2000. While lower than China's investments ($92.4 billion), this amount exceeds that received by other emerging markets such as Brazil ($45.1 billion).
- Consumer expenditure in SSA equalled nearly $600 billion in 2010, accounting for almost 8 per cent of all emerging market spending, and is expected to reach nearly $1 trillion by 2020.
- Consumer spending in South Africa and Nigeria accounts for 51 per cent of SSA's total expenditure.
- Poverty in SSA is decreasing rapidly – from 40 per cent in 1980 to less than 30 per cent in 2008 – and is expected to fall to 20 per cent by 2020.
- By 2050, almost 60 per cent of people in SSA will live in cities, compared with 40 per cent in 2010. This means 800 million more people will live in urban environments.
- By 2012, over 50 per cent of all Africans – or more than 500 million people – will own a mobile phone. In 2014, this portion was expected to increase to 56 per cent (more than 600 million people), giving Africa one of the world's highest mobile usage rates.

For companies looking for growth via emerging markets, Sub-Saharan Africa looms large. The continent's sheer size merits attention: since 2000, Sub-Saharan Africa has experienced rapid growth in consumer spending of 4 per cent reaching nearly $600 billion in 2010. Consumer spending is expected to rise to nearly $1 trillion by 2020. Accompanying the growth are rapid improvements in income levels, infrastructure and the business environment which promise continued growth as a consumer market.

Companies will have to adjust their strategies and expectations when entering Africa. Logistics can be unreliable and infrastructure lags behind much of the developed world. Furthermore, understanding the diverse nature of opportunities in Africa can be challenging. As a result, many executives planning on entering Africa want to know why Africa's consumers are an attractive proposition, which segments they should focus on, and how they can capture the market's potential most effectively.

Segments within the market exist, as shown in Figure 25.5.

Questions

1 Analyse the benefits to business of segmenting the market. [8]
2 Discuss whether Africa provides a good opportunity to business in the future. [16]

1
Basic Survivors

Basic Survivors are the largest consumer group in Africa and are characteristically low income consumers. They tend to live in urban slum areas or rural areas and make day-to-day decisions based on basic needs.

2
Working Families

Working Families are the second largest consumer group. They focus their spending on their children's needs and they value stability and routine in their lives.

3
Rising Strivers

Rising Strivers are emerging from the first two segments, having built their purchasing power through access to credit or other resources. They value upward mobility and buy based on convenience, quality, or even more 'expressive' factors.

4
Cosmopolitan Professionals

Cosmopolitan Professionals are typically located in urban areas. They are busy with work but often have active social lives. As a result, these consumers value pragmatic products but are also brand conscious and influenced by the media.

5
The Affluent

The Affluent of Africa have disproportionately high purchasing power, and are considered wealthy regardless of where they travel across the globe. This group is extremely small and very fickle.

Figure 25.4 Five key sub-Saharan African consumer segments
Source: Accenture Analysis

It is useful to analyse the markets you are in or want to be in before you set an objective or develop a plan. Only when you know where you are and what is going on around you can you really set a target to say where you hope to end up in the future. Analysis is also important to determine where you are and what you might do next (i.e. it helps you to assess the alternatives), and it helps you to assess the effectiveness of any action you take. If you are going to put resources into a particular marketing activity (advertising or promotion, for example) you need to know whether this will be a good use of funds.

By undertaking a market analysis a firm should be able to identify existing market conditions. However, analysis will also be used to predict where the market is going in the future. Analysis should help identify possible opportunities and threats for the future. An opportunity is a future possible event that could benefit a business. A threat is a future possible event that could harm the business. Opportunities may include particular segments that are likely to grow fast; threats may be markets that are about to decline.

Methods of analysing trends

Managers are naturally interested in how markets will develop in the future as well as their present situation. It is important, therefore, for firms to look ahead when undertaking marketing. Marketing managers will be eager to forecast what sales in the market are going to be in the future. From this they can estimate the likely sales of their own products and produce their sales forecasts.

A firm's sales forecast sets out targets for overall sales and for particular products and services. It is a key element of a marketing plan and influences decisions throughout the organisation.

Study tip

There are many sources of information that may help with a market analysis, such as internal, external, primary and secondary. Although the temptation may be to gather as much data as possible this can lead to too much data and actually delay action. A challenge to all businesses is getting good-quality information – the right amount at the right time, telling you the right things. Also, look at how the data is gathered – the value of market analysis depends on the quality of the information used. If information was gathered using a small sample or leading questions were asked then it may be very misleading.

To understand market trends managers might use one or more of the following methods of analysing trends.

Calculating moving averages

If you look at the sales data in Figure 25.5 and plot the figures on a chart, you will see that the sales are quite erratic during the year. In June, for example, sales are relatively high, whereas in July they are lower.

	Sales $000		Three-month moving average $000
January	9		
February	12	(9 + 12 + 15)/3	12
March	15	(12 + 15 + 15)/3	14
April	15	(15 + 15 + 18)/3	16
May	18	(15 + 18 + 21)/3	18
June	21	(18 + 21 + 9)/3	16
July	9	(21 + 9 + 18)/3	16
August	18	(9 + 18 + 21)/3	16
September	21	(18 + 21 + 24)/3	21
October	24	(21 + 24 + 12)/3	19
November	12	(24 + 12 + 24)/3	20
December	24		

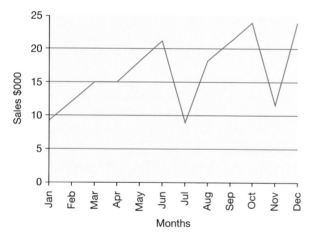

Figure 25.5 Monthly sales

However, although the sales clearly change from month to month, the overall trend is clearly upwards.

One way of plotting the underlying trend is to calculate the moving average. This looks at several periods at a time and averages out the data; by doing this, the effect of particularly high or low figures is reduced because an average has been taken.

For example, for a three-month moving average we average out the figures for January, February and March. Then we average out February, March and April; then March, April and May, and so on.

The three-month moving average highlights the underlying trend of the sales figures, as shown in Figure 25.6.

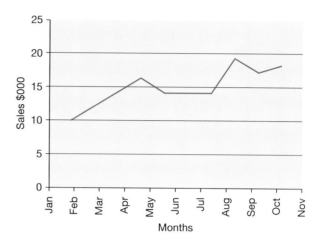

Figure 25.6 Three-month moving average

Extrapolation

To estimate the future sales in a market, managers may look back to identify trends that have occurred (using, for example, moving averages) and then, based on these, predict forwards. This is known as **extrapolation**. A holiday company experiencing a fall in the number of enquiries in a particular month compared with past years may change its sales forecast downwards. This technique is useful, provided the trends identified in the past continue into the future. If, in fact, there has been a major shift in buying patterns (e.g. the timing of buying has changed or the economy has unexpectedly entered a recession) extrapolation could be misleading.

> ## Key terms
>
> **Extrapolation** involves identifying the underlying trend in past data and projecting this trend forwards. In Figure 25.7, for example, the underlying trend in sales figures is clearly upwards. If we assume this trend will continue we can project it forward and estimate future sales.
>
> **Correlation** occurs when there are apparent links between variables (e.g. promotional spending and sales).

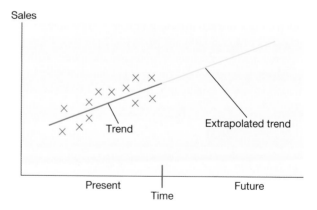

Figure 25.7 An extrapolated trend

Extrapolation is thus only likely to be effective if market conditions continue to develop in the future as they have in the past, i.e. extrapolation only works if past trends actually continue. The problem is that many markets are very dynamic and change rapidly. The market for cameras, for example, has seen rapid change in the last 20 years with the arrival of digital cameras; in this situation extrapolation may be very misleading – examining the past may provide little indication of what is going to happen in the future. Sales can drop suddenly regardless of what has happened in the past, perhaps due to a recession, competitors launching a new product or a problem with production. In the 1990s UK farmers could hardly have predicted the collapse in the sales of beef due to the BSE crisis. Similarly, Coca-Cola could not have predicted the short-term drop in sales in 2000 when it had to take some of its products off the shelves temporarily due to a health scare, or Toyota when its cars experienced quality problems in 2011.

Extrapolated figures must therefore be treated with caution – their reliability depends entirely on the extent to which the future will imitate the past. Obviously firms can learn from past trends – retail sales are likely to increase in the run-up to Christmas, holidays in Spain are more likely to be popular in the summer, central heating is likely to be used more when the weather is colder and so on – but they must also look out for future changes in the market conditions. Rapid developments in technology, for example, can lead to major changes in terms of what we produce and how business is conducted, and this may make extrapolation more risky. Sales of netbook computers looked to be soaring upwards until tablets such as the iPad were launched.

Correlation

Rather than using extrapolation, future market sales may be estimated using **correlation**. This process attempts to identify whether there is any correlation between different variables and the level of sales. Correlation occurs when there appears to be a link between two factors. For example, a firm might discover a correlation between its sales and the level of income in an economy – with higher income consumer sales might increase.

Correlation analysis examines data to see if any relationship appears to exist between different variables. This is important for marketing managers because, if they can identify the key factors that determine demand for their goods, and they can estimate what is happening to these factors (e.g. estimate income growth), they can estimate total market sales and then their likely sales.

Examples of different types of correlation are shown in Figures 25.8 and 25.9:

● 'Positive correlation' means that there is a direct link between the variables. An increase in advertising, for example, might lead to an increase in sales and vice versa. The sales of a product might be positively correlated with income levels and the number of customers in the market.

● A 'negative correlation' means that the two factors are inversely related; an increase in price, for example, is likely to lead to a fall in sales, so price and demand have a negative correlation.

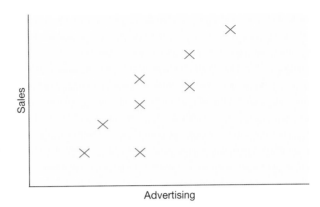

Figure 25.8 Positive correlation between advertising and sales

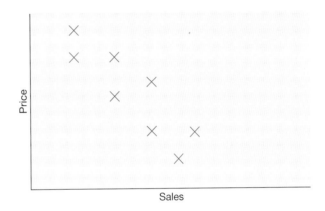

Figure 25.9 Negative correlation between price and sales

It is important to note that correlation analysis simply identifies an apparent link between the two factors; it does not show cause and effect. For example, there is often a strong link between coffee drinkers and smokers; people who smoke often drink a lot of coffee as well. There is a link between the two but this does not mean that drinking coffee actually makes you smoke or vice versa. It is important, therefore, to treat correlation figures with some caution. Just because sales figures and the amount of money spent on advertising expenditure are both increasing does not necessarily mean that the advertising is boosting sales. In many cases firms feel that the high sales mean they can spend more on advertising, i.e. sales may determine advertising spending rather than vice versa. Alternatively, the increase in sales could be coincidental – it could be caused by factors other than advertising.

However, the more times the correlation appears to exist (e.g. if the firm has regularly advertised and at the same time sales have regularly increased), the more likely it is that managers will believe that a link does occur.

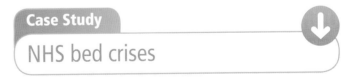

NHS bed crises

Health service managers in the UK try to avoid bed crises by using weather reports to forecast when people will fall ill. The

Meteorological Office has set up a unit using new technology to give doctors up to two weeks' notice of how many patients are likely to develop bronchitis, heart attacks and strokes. The service, which claimed to be the world's first, allows hospitals and surgeries to prepare for increases in demand using warnings generated by a supercomputer.

In the past the National Health Service has been caught out by sudden changes in the number of patients suffering respiratory and cardiovascular diseases. Meteorological Office experts say the timing was due almost entirely to changes in temperature and climatic conditions. According to a spokesperson, 'there is a very close link between weather conditions and illness. We can predict almost the day when large numbers of patients will seek treatment.'

More patients die in Britain from weather-related illnesses than almost any other country in western Europe. For every one degree fall in temperature, 1.37 per cent more people die; this is much higher than in other countries because the British are less well prepared; they do not dress warmly against the cold, their houses are less well heated or insulated and they take less exercise.

Questions

1 Analyse why the National Health Service in the UK analyses weather patterns. [8]
2 Discuss other factors that are likely to influence demand for healthcare services. [18]

Study tip

In many of the cases you are likely to face, a business will be making a major decision. In this type of situation large sums of money may be at stake and the future of the business may be at risk. It is possible but very unlikely that in this situation a decision will be made without some market analysis. You may question the way the analysis has been undertaken, but some information is likely to be better than none.

Other ways of estimating future sales

Using market research

Market research can be used to try to identify likely future trends rather than assuming they will be similar to the past. The value of this research depends on whether it is primary or secondary and the quality of the information. If a small sample is used, for example, the forecast is less likely to be accurate than if

a larger sample had been used. Types of research might include test marketing (trying out the product in a given area) or surveys. A test market is a representative selection of consumers which the firm uses to try out a new product. Having seen the results in the test market the firm can estimate how the product might sell elsewhere and produce a sales forecast. By using a test market the firm can see customers' reactions before committing to a full-scale launch. If necessary, changes can still be made before the product is widely available. Many film companies, for example, show their films to a test audience before they go on general release, to assess the public's reaction.

Key terms

Market research is the process of gathering, analysing and presenting data relevant to the marketing process.
Primary market research uses data gathered for the first time.
Secondary market research uses data that has been gathered previously (it uses the data for the second time).

The disadvantage of using test marketing is that competitors have an opportunity to see what you are planning to launch. This gives them time to develop a similar product and race you to launch first on a wide scale.

A test market may also give misleading results. This might be because the test market chosen is not representative or because competitors' actions lead to misleading results. For example, rivals might increase their promotional activities in the test market to reduce a firm's sales and lead it to believe that the new product will not do well.

Using your best guess

Managers could use their own experience or hire industry experts for their opinion of what is most likely to happen. This approach to forecasting is common if the rate of change in the market is great or if the firm is facing a new scenario and does not have past data to build on. In the Delphi technique, managers assemble a group of experts who are all asked individually for their views. These views are analysed and key areas extracted. These findings are circulated again to the experts for feedback.

Case Study

The flawed market research of new Coke

In 1985 the chairman of Coca-Cola announced, 'the best has been made even better'. After 99 years the Coca-Cola company decided to abandon its original formula and replace

Figure 25.10 A poster from the 1985 Coca-Cola relaunch

it with a sweeter version named 'New Coke'. Just three months later the company admitted it had made a mistake and brought back the old version under the name 'Coca-Cola Classic'!

Despite $4 million of research the company had clearly made a huge mistake. The background to Coca-Cola's decision to launch a new product was much slower growth in its sales in the 1970s, especially compared with Pepsi. Pepsi was also outperforming Coca-Cola in taste tests. The relatively poor performance was even more disappointing given that Coca-Cola was spending an estimated $100 million more than Pepsi on advertising. The taste testing of the new recipe for Coca-Cola involved 191 000 people in more than 13 cities. In all, 55 per cent of people favoured New Coke over the old formula.

However, once the launch was announced the company was amazed by the negative response; at one point calls were coming in at a rate of 5000 a day. People were most annoyed by the fact that Coca-Cola dared to change the formula of one of the USA's greatest assets.

What went wrong? Possibly one problem was that when undertaking the testing, customers did not know that choosing one cola would mean the other was removed, i.e. that if they chose a new flavour the old one would be withdrawn. Also, the symbolic value of Coca-Cola may have been overlooked.

Questions

1 Analyse the ways in which Coca-Cola may have researched the market. [8]

2 Coca-Cola did extensive (and expensive) market research and yet still made a mistake. Discuss whether this means that market research is a waste of time. [16]

The method of forecasting used by a firm will depend on the nature of the product and the market situation. When the National Lottery was launched in the UK, for example, Camelot (the organiser of the lottery) could have forecasted sales by looking at existing national lottery systems in other countries and tried to adjust this data to take account of the differences in culture and the precise nature of the system in the UK.

Camelot might also have used **secondary research** to identify gambling trends within the UK and **primary research** to identify customers' likely reaction to the lottery scheme. However, although the company probably used very sophisticated research techniques it is likely there was also an element of hunch in there too. After all, it was a completely new product within the UK and so there were no past data within the country to build on. Obviously once the lottery had been up and running for a few months the organisers were able to make better predictions of expected weekly sales because they were accumulating back data and gaining a better insight into the market.

The benefits of sales forecasting

Inevitably a firm's external and internal conditions are likely to change and this can make it extremely difficult to estimate future sales. It depends in part how much good-quality data you have gathered and the rate of change in the environment. However, the fact that there are difficulties in forecasting does not necessarily make this a useless management tool. The simple process of forecasting makes managers think ahead and plan for different scenarios. This may help to ensure they are much better prepared for change than if they did not forecast at all.

Also, even though a forecast may not be exactly accurate it may give an indication of the direction in which sales are moving and some sense of the magnitude of future sales, which can help a firm's planning. Ultimately it may not matter much whether sales are 2 000 002 units or 2 000 020 units, but it makes a big difference whether they are 2 million or 4 million in terms of staffing, finance and production levels, i.e. provided the forecast is approximately right it can still be very useful even if it is not exactly correct.

It is also important to remember that sales forecasts can be updated. A firm does not have to make a forecast and leave it there. As conditions change and new information feeds in, the managers can update the forecast and adjust accordingly.

Gathering data

Many organisations are likely to have a great deal of data available to them. They may, for example, have details of customers' locations, their orders and the frequency of purchase. Part of developing a management information system is considering exactly what information needs to be gathered, how to collect it, how to analyse it and how to make the findings available to those who need it.

Gathering and analysing data has become a lot easier, faster and cheaper with developments in information technology. Store cards, such as Tesco Clubcard, enable the business to collect huge quantities of data on shoppers and their habits and to link this to the address of the card holder. Tesco can then build up a map of the UK and see how customers respond to different incentives and external changes, such as more rain. This provides a detailed insight into UK shoppers which is invaluable to Tesco's marketing decisions.

Managers can also use secondary sources of data, such as industry surveys produced by the media, for example the *Financial Times* and *The Economist*. Secondary research is also available (for a fee!) from businesses such as Mintel (Market Intelligence – a market research company).

This does not mean that every business has all the information it needs at any moment, but there is a lot of data available at any time and managers need to be careful not to just gather more instead of thinking carefully about what they need. Think of applying to university – rushing to visit every university and get every prospectus is quite an inefficient and time-consuming way of going about things; much better to plan what you need and target key information.

> ### Study tip
> Remember how important a sales forecast is. If you do not have any sense of the scale of the possible sales, how can you plan how much to spend, how much to produce, how many people to employ?

The reliability of forecasts

Forecasts are most likely to be correct when:
- a trend has been extrapolated and the market conditions have continued as before
- a test market is used and is truly representative of the target population
- the forecast is made by experts (such as your own sales forces) and they have good insight into the market and future trends
- the firm is forecasting for the near future – it is usually easier to estimate what sales will be next week rather than estimating sales in five years' time.

> ### Key term
> A **sales forecast** is an estimate of the volume or value of a firm's sales in the future.

Why might forecasts be wrong?

Forecasts can only be predictions of the future. A variety of factors may make them wrong.
- **Customer buying behaviour changes suddenly** For example, customers may suddenly decide that a product is unsafe or unfashionable following a problem, such as a fault emerging with the product or ethical issues emerging regarding the way the product was produced. Changes in the weather might also change sales levels, along with other external factors such as economic change. **Sales forecasts** may therefore be wrong because of internal factors (e.g. poor quality control) or external factors (e.g. new entrants into the market).
- **The original market research was poor** This may be because the sample was too small or was unrepresentative. Alternatively, it may be because the results were wrongly interpreted; this could be because the firm was in a rush to launch the product. In some cases the research may actually have been ignored – managers may have been certain that they knew best and gone ahead with the decision regardless of the findings of market research.
- **The experts were wrong** Even the best-informed people can misread a situation and make mistakes – just look at the predictions of so-called experts before any horse race or football match, or the many different and often conflicting forecasts of growth in the economy that are often published in the media.
- **You are looking too far ahead** It may be possible to estimate sales with some degree of accuracy in the short term but the further ahead you look the less likely it is to get it right. The numbers for a sales forecast are really very tentative when you are looking, say, seven years ahead.
- **The value of any sales forecast will depend on the information gathered and the time, cost and nature of the method used** A sales forecast will be presented with a degree of confidence based on the way it is produced and the range given. For example, if you are asked to predict exactly what sales will be in three years' time you cannot be very confident of getting it right. If you can predict sales will be between $3 million and $8 million the range is so wide that you can be more confident of getting it right.

> ### Key term
> A **confidence level** shows how certain the market researcher is of the results given.

> ### Case Study
> # Best Buy
>

In 2012 the struggling US electronics chain Best Buy reported a major fall in its profits.

Net profits fell to just $12 million on revenues of $10.6 billion in the second quarter of the year. Profits were $150 million in the same period a year earlier. Best Buy said uncertainty over its future sales meant it could not provide any guidance on its full-year profits. The company owns 50 per cent of UK-mobile phone chain Carphone Warehouse.

Best Buy's shares, which have lost almost 70 per cent since their peak of $56.66 in May 2006, fell another 4 per cent after the latest financial results. The firm is struggling to compete with online rivals such as Amazon which are able to sell goods cheaper. In March, Best Buy announced a major restructuring that included closing 50 stores, cutting 400 corporate jobs and trimming $800 million in costs.

Best Buy has been trying to cut costs to improve its profit margins. One of its priorities is to stop its large stores simply becoming a showroom, where shoppers look at electronic products, but then buy them cheaper online. Best Buy has seen annual declines in revenue at stores open at least a year for two of the last three years.

Questions

1 Analyse two problems facing Best Buy. [8]
2 Discuss the problems Best Buy might have trying to forecast its sales. [16]

25.5 The need for and development of a coordinated marketing mix

The **marketing mix** is the combination of features such as the price, product, communications and distribution that influence a customer's decision to purchase an item. The elements of the mix must complement each other to be effective. A new cutting edge consumer electronics product would need to be promoted as top end and you would expect a high price – in fact you might be suspicious of a lower price! A premium, exclusive watch should be distributed in specialist retail outlets; if it was sold at petrol stations it would damage the brand. Marketing managers must build an integrated mix where the elements complement each other and take account of the nature of the product and the buying process. A convenience item such as milk is likely to be relatively cheap and distributed widely. A new television will need a promotional campaign to stress it benefits and will need to be priced competitively because customers will take time to compare it with alternatives.

Getting the mix right is therefore a great skill.

Development of marketing strategies that are focused towards achieving specific marketing objectives

The **marketing strategy** is the long-term marketing plan aimed at achieving the **marketing objectives**. Imagine we want to increase sales by 50 per cent over the next five years. How can we do this?

1 We may decide to boost sales of our existing products. If we do this we could try to:
- increase the amount existing customers buy when they purchase it (e.g. spend more every time they visit our shops)
- increase the number of customers (e.g. encourage people to switch to our shop)
- increase the number of times they buy (e.g. more visits to the shop)
- increase the amount they spend (e.g. get them to trade up to premium items).

2 Or we may decide to develop new products.

There are therefore different ways of achieving an objective. Each strategy selected will have different implications in terms of the precise marketing activities being carried out.

Case Study

Barbie

Barbie has been experiencing real competition from Bratz dolls in recent years. To boost sales of Barbie, managers could target different segments:

- those who buy Barbie already and try to get them to buy more
- those who used to buy Barbies but are older now, to try and get them to return to the dolls (e.g. adult collectors)

- those who do not buy Barbies but buy Bratz dolls; they could try to win over these customers
- those who do not buy dolls at all.

Each of these would be a different strategy to achieve the same objective of increasing sales.

Questions

1 Analyse the value to Barbie of identifying different segments in the market. [8]
2 Discuss which of the above strategies you would recommend. Justify your answer. [16]

Deciding on a marketing strategy

When deciding on a marketing strategy there are many issues to consider, such as:

- The marketing objective – does the business want to focus on existing or new products? Does it want to target local or international buyers? Does it want to be seen as a low price or premium provider?
- Where should the business compete and which segments should it target? For example, should the firm compete in a niche market or try to compete head-on with the major players in a mass market? Should it compete in particular regions, in the country as a whole, or globally?
- What should it offer? For example, what product lines should it offer? How many different types of products should it offer? How similar should these be?
- How should it compete and position itself against competitors? For example, should the firm try to match competitors' offerings but sell them more cheaply (a low-cost strategy), or should it aim to differentiate itself and charge more (a differentiation strategy)?

Managers will make different decisions in answer to these questions.

- Lobbs, for example, is an exclusive shoemaker producing expensive made-to-measure shoes – this is a niche, differentiation strategy. Clarks competes much more in the mass market.
- Primark aims at the mass market via low prices; Karen Millen aims more for the expensive fashion market.
- The Ford Ka is for the younger driver (perhaps their first car); the Aston Martin DB7 is for the highly successful executive.

A firm's marketing strategy should aim to exploit its market opportunities and defend it against threats. It should naturally build on the firm's strengths and avoid entering market segments or offering products where its weaknesses will be exposed.

Figure 25.11 Forming a marketing strategy

When assessing a marketing strategy, make sure you are clear about:

- the characteristics of the target market
- the positioning of the business relative to competitors
- the nature of the strategy (is it aiming to justify a premium price or is it offering a low price?)
- the link between the marketing strategy and the other functions
- the marketing objectives (how will success be judged?)
- the risk involved in any strategy relative to the likely returns
- whether it fits with the business strengths – could Primark suddenly move into the premium market, for example? What about Gucci chewing gum? Ryanair luxury hotels? Virgin old people's homes?

Study tip

Remember how important the marketing strategy is. The price and the promotional mix are only likely to work if you are actually competing in the right market in the first place and in the right way. If your strategy is clear, for example you decide you want to be a low price competitor then much of the marketing mix becomes straightforward – you are likely to offer basic products at a low price with a message of value for money.

Case Study

Unilever

Unilever is a large multinational business. Its mission is 'to add vitality to life. We meet everyday needs for nutrition, hygiene, and personal care with brands that help people feel good, look good and get more out of life.'

Its marketing strategy is now focused on what it calls 'power brands', i.e. key brands such as Dove and OMO that it wants to develop globally. These brand names will be extended to a wider range of products, but lesser-known brands have been or are being sold off. To achieve growth in the future Unilever is targeting emerging markets.

In these markets it has two strategies:

- to buy products for the first time
- to get customers to trade up.

Source: www.unilever.com

Figure 25.12 Some of Unilever's power brands

Questions

1 Analyse the possible benefits of a strong brand. [8]
2 Discuss the possible reasons why Unilever has decided to focus on power brands. [16]

Using SWOT analysis

When considering a marketing strategy a firm's managers should consider the following:

- What is the firm trying to achieve, i.e. what are its marketing objectives? There is no point in cutting prices, for example, if the firm is trying to build an exclusive brand image. Similarly, there is little point diversifying if the firm's objective is to focus on its core products.
- What are the market opportunities? What market segments appear to be growing? Businesses will be unlikely to target declining markets or segments that are small relative to the investment needed to enter them and compete in them.
- What are the firm's strengths and key capabilities? What is it good at? What are its competencies, i.e. the areas where it has expertise? Does it have any unique selling points (USPs)? Some businesses are good at innovating (e.g. W. L. Gore); others are good at extending the brand onto other products (e.g. Virgin); others are excellent at changing the price to match demand

conditions (e.g. easyJet) – these key capabilities should influence the chosen strategy if a firm is to play to its strengths.

- What resources does the firm have? For example, what is its financial position? Will it be able to finance any plans for expansion, for example? Some firms have a good liquidity position and can finance growth internally. Others may be heavily in debt (this is known as highly geared) and therefore cannot easily borrow more, which might limit the marketing strategy.

The marketing strategy should therefore be firmly based on an effective SWOT analysis, which examines the **s**trengths, **w**eaknesses, **o**pportunities and **t**hreats facing a firm.

Figure 25.13 SWOT analysis to develop a strategy

Why change a marketing strategy?

It may be necessary for a firm to change its marketing strategy for a number of reasons, such as:

- It may have changed its marketing objectives – rather than wanting more sales from a given product range managers may now seek to diversify (e.g. to spread risk) or there may be more pressure from investors to boost profits.
- Market conditions may have changed – the slowing down of the rate of growth in the PC market has led firms like Microsoft to look for new markets to enter, such as computer games. The decline of the traditional film camera market led the UK-based camera shop Jessops to reconsider what it offers. Concerns over diet have made McDonald's think about how to make its offerings seem healthier.
- Competitors' actions – a head-on attack from other firms may force an organisation to move into a new segment or to focus on particular areas of its business where it has a competitive advantage. In the UK, the threat of supermarkets such as Walmart attacking its core business led to Boots, which sold mainly healthcare and beauty products, moving more into segments such as photography, optical and dental care.

- The firm's own strengths – as a firm develops its staff, technology and product range it may find that its strengths create new opportunities and this brings about a change in strategy.
- Poor performance – if your strategy is working well you are likely to keep on with it. If your strategy is failing you need to rethink. In 2008 Woolworth's went into administration in the UK. It had no clear position in the market. Was it a confectionery store? A music business? A children's clothes shop? It was not clear to a buyer why you would go there, and in each of its areas it faced attacks. In this situation (or hopefully before it happened) a business would reconsider its corporate and marketing strategy.
- A change in marketing strategy may be prompted by the possibility of exploiting an opportunity and/or to protect a business against threats or poor performance.

Changing your marketing strategy can be a difficult process. For example:

- If you keep the same brand name and try to move upmarket it can be difficult to win customers over. For many years Skoda was trying to reposition itself as a relatively low priced but reliable, well-designed brand; for older buyers who remember quality problems in the past and its very basic design this was quite a shift in its positioning and buyers took time to be convinced. Equally, changes to the strategy can damage the brand and hurt the long-term success of the business. At one point Burberry was growing so fast and using its brand on so many products that it started to devalue the image and the company had to be more selective to maintain a premium image.
- It will involve changes in the other functions. For example, the operations process may need to change perhaps to achieve higher volumes or fewer defects or faster service; equally, responsibilities and duties of staff will change which can be disruptive and resisted.
- More funds may be needed to enable the strategic change. This may be to research the options, develop new products or launch them in the market. This can be difficult if, for example, the reason for the change was that the business had financial difficulties.

Test your learning

Short answer questions

1 a What is meant by marketing planning? [2]
   b Analyse **one** benefit of marketing planning. [3]
2 a What is meant by the income elasticity of demand? [2]
   b Analyse what is meant by an income elasticity of +2. [3]
3 a Analyse what is meant if the promotional expenditure elasticity is +0.5. [2]
   b If the promotional elasticity is +0.8 what is the effect on demand of an increase in promotional spending from $4 million to $5 million? [3]
4 a What is meant by the cross-price elasticity of demand? [2]
   b Analyse what is meant if the cross-price elasticity of good A in relation to the price of B is –3. [2]
5 State **one** problem of the concept of elasticity when making decisions. [2]
6 What is meant by a moving average? [2]
7 a State **two** ways of forecasting sales. [2]
   b Analyse **one** reason why it is important to forecast marketing data. [3]
8 State **two** sources of ideas for new products. [2]
9 a What is meant by a patent? [2]
   b Analyse **one** way in which a patent helps a business. [3]
10 What is meant by extrapolation? [2]

Data response question

Kellogg's

Kellogg's, the US breakfast cereal and snack maker, has said it will not change its marketing strategy to children despite concerns about obesity. Its managers said that the obesity issue was about calorie intake and exercise, not 'bad food'. Kellogg's plans to launch its Kashi brand of wholegrain cereals in the UK and will soon introduce a new version of All Bran to Japan.

The development illustrates how US food companies are responding to increased concern about the contribution of some processed foods to obesity, and marketing to children by highlighting efforts to develop healthier products.

The company's chief financial officer said: 'The whole issue with obesity is really calories in, calories out. There aren't any bad foods, it's all about balance.'

Concern about the role of food companies in contributing to obesity increased with a landmark lawsuit against McDonald's by New York teenagers who claimed the fast-food company played down the health effects of eating Chicken McNuggets. Kraft Foods has focused attention on the issue by voluntarily pledging to stop marketing in schools, advertising to children under six and shifting food promotions to the 6–11-year-old towards healthier items.

Asked whether Kellogg's would be changing its promotional strategy in the wake of Kraft's move, the company's chief executive said: 'We don't move based on what the competition does.'

Both Kellogg's and its main rival in the breakfast cereals, General Mills, have in the past year stepped up the introduction of cereals containing whole grains, including those aimed at children.

The chief executive said: 'Kids have been eating our products for decades. Offering options for what kids may want and what their mothers may want them to eat is certainly a thing we're interested in doing.' The vice-president in charge of marketing said: 'We think advertising cereal to kids is a very good thing to do and we'd like to do it more. Twenty-five per cent of kids walk out of the door in the morning having eaten nothing. We think that those kinds of problems are really much more significant and if we can put a dent in that, that would be very positive.'

Questions

1 Analyse the factors that might influence the ways in which Kellogg's promoted a new cereal. [10]

2 Discuss the ways in which an understanding of elasticity might benefit Kellogg's. [14]

3 Discuss whether Kellogg's should stop all advertising to children. [16]

Essay questions

1 To what extent is the concept of elasticity useful in marketing planning? [20]

2 Discuss the possible benefits of market analysis to a business. [20]

Past paper questions

1 Read the Chan Beauty Company (CBC) case study on pages 452–54 and then answer the following question.

Assume Option 1, the market development option, is chosen. Discuss the important features of a marketing plan for a successful launch in your country of the ethical beauty products. [16]

Cambridge International AS and A Level Business Studies 9707 Paper 32 Q5 October/November 2009

2 Read the Pyramid Televisions case study on pages 454–56 and then answer the following questions.

a Using the data in Appendix A calculate, for both PT and its major competitor, the:

i Income elasticity of demand

ii Promotion elasticity of demand. [8]

b Discuss possible changes to PT's future marketing strategy based on these results and other information in the case. [14]

Cambridge International AS and A Level Business Studies 9707 Paper 3 Q4 May/June 2008

3 Read the Curry Cuisine case study on pages 471–73 and then answer the following question.

Assume that Chas and Ling decide to go ahead with the "ready made meals" proposal. Evaluate the arguments for and against developing a marketing plan for this project. [20]

Cambridge International AS and A Level Business Studies 9707 Paper 3 Q7 October/November 2007

26 Globalisation and international marketing

26.1 Economic globalisation

In recent years the amount of international trade involving businesses buying and selling across borders has increased. This is because:

- Political agreements have opened up markets by removing or reducing protectionist measures such as tariffs (taxes on foreign imports), quotas (limits on the numbers of imported goods) and administrative restrictions, making it difficult for foreign businesses to sell or operate in your country. These still exist – for example, it is difficult for the big Western retailers to get permission to open in India – but they have been falling in recent years due to the work of governments and organisations such as the **World Trade Organisation**. Governments realise that trade enables their businesses and citizens to access new markets and thus stimulates economic growth.
- Better transport and communications technology has made it easier and cheaper to find markets, to move products around the world and to manage businesses in other countries.

Look at the labels on your clothes to see where they were made, find out where the different components of your laptop or mobile phone were made and look at the source of items on the shelves at your local shop and you will appreciate how global the world has become. Many businesses buy in products and services from abroad and sell their products abroad.

Not only that, money also flows around the world, being invested in overseas banks and used to buy foreign companies. Many famous 'British' brands, for example, are now owned by overseas companies: Jaguar and Tetley Tea are owned by Tata from India and Manchester United FC is owned by the Glazers from the USA.

Key term

The **World Trade Organisation** is an organisation of countries aimed at reducing protectionism across the world.

The implications for marketing of increased globalisation

Globalisation from a marketing perspective opens up enormous opportunities and threats. It creates the possibility of new markets and literally billions of new customers if you can successfully target them. For example, there are enormous numbers of people moving out of poverty and eager to buy consumer products in the emerging BRIC economies of Brazil, Russia, India and China. Other economies to watch because of their potential for fast growth have been identified as CIVETS by some commentators (Cambodia, Indonesia, Vietnam, Egypt, Turkey and South Africa) or the MINT economies by others (Malaysia, Indonesia, Nigeria and Turkey). However, it also creates the possibility of new competitors from abroad entering your markets. This means you have to be even better at what you do in your own market.

Case Study

The NFL

The National Football League (NFL) has experienced numerous problems in its marketing efforts to globalise American football. Its attempts began in the 1970s with some exhibition games played worldwide. In the 1980s the NFL created a European League but this closed down in 2006 as fans were disappointed by the quality of the European game compared to the US ones. The NFL then focused on playing more games around the world in countries such as Mexico and Canada where they felt there would be a market. These countries are a reasonable size, have a strong interest in sports and media interested in sports content.

Figure 26.1 American football has struggled to become popular internationally

However, while local events and partnerships had some impact the biggest change has been due to technology. Social media and online opportunities have created new ways for the NFL to distribute its products to a growing market worldwide. Technology has enabled localised messaging and communication.

Source: *Looking beyond the obvious*, Ernst & Young, 2013

Questions

1 Analyse the problem the NFL might have in bringing its sport to new markets around the globe. [8]
2 Discuss whether technology has made it easier for all businesses to succeed globally. [16]

26.2 International markets

Overseas expansion may be appealing for several reasons.

● **The domestic market is saturated** Many markets in the UK for example, are mature (e.g. the demand for microwaves, fridges and televisions). Companies can only generate replacement sales rather than many first-time buyers. In emerging economies such as Brazil, Russia, India and China the economies are growing much faster, creating opportunities for a rapid growth in sales. If investors are pushing for fast growth it may be that this is more likely to come from abroad.

● **The domestic market is subject to increasing competition or regulation** Tesco, for example, cannot expand much more in the UK for fear of being blocked by the Competition Commission for having too big a market share. It has expanded overseas in countries such as South Korea, Thailand, the USA and India to enable faster growth.

● **The benefits of particular market opportunities overseas** For example, China has a population of more than 1 billion that could be targeted.

Entering a foreign market does, of course, bring various problems. Perhaps most importantly the firm is unlikely to know

the market as well as its domestic market. It will need to ensure it fully understands market conditions, including consumer buying behaviour, legal and economic factors and the possible response of the competition. Given that the market is not known as well, entering an overseas market can be seen as risky. This is why many firms entering overseas markets find a local partner to help them understand the market.

Study tip

International marketing offers many opportunities in terms of new sales – for example, in China alone there are more than 1 billion potential customers. However, understanding the needs of customers, the competition and the nature of the market can be very complex when going overseas.

Case Study

Tesco withdraws from Japanese market

Tesco, the UK retailer, recently put its poorly performing Japanese firm up for sale having failed to gain enough scale in a country that is highly competitive and difficult for foreign retailers to compete in successfully.

The UK retailer had 129 stores in Japan, mainly in the greater Tokyo area. It entered Japan in 2003 when it acquired the C Two-Network, a discount supermarket chain.

The withdrawal showed that Tesco's chief executive was willing to take difficult decisions to improve the performance of the firm. Initially, Tesco seemed to believe that the C Two-Network's smaller supermarkets met a need among Japanese consumers for local stores that stocked essential items they would buy daily. It also invested in its own private brand products for Japan as well as food processing centres to allow it to deliver fresh processed foods to its stores. However, it struggled to compete against Aeon and Ito Yokado, the two largest supermarkets in Japan which enjoyed large economies of scale. Carrefour, the French supermarket, withdrew from Japan in 2005 after just five years. Walmart has also been struggling to achieve appropriate profitability. Tesco has found it difficult to get consumers to switch from their existing stores, especially when economic conditions are weak and competitors have large scale.

In other Asian markets Tesco is doing well. Tesco's biggest operations outside the UK are in South Korea. Analysts say Tesco owes much of its success in Korea to its appointment of Lee Seung-han of the Samsung Group as the local chief executive. They say he quickly moulded Tesco to a Korean retail model while Walmart and Carrefour, which pursued international models, had to quit Korea. In Korea Tesco has strength in its size with 129 hypermarkets and 255 smaller express outlets.

In Thailand, Tesco Lotus is the country's largest retail grocer. Its sales are more than 12 per cent of the market and includes more than 700 stores.

Source: Adapted from www.ft.com

Questions

1 Analyse two reasons why Tesco is expanding outside of the UK. [8]
2 Discuss the possible reasons for the failure of Tesco in Japan. [16]

Case Study
Food and drink in Asia

Figure 26.2 Minute Maid Pulpy

Coca-Cola recently launched the Minute Maid Pulpy in Malaysia. The drink, which debuted in China, is accompanied by a marketing campaign that focuses on the content of orange pulp within the beverage. Coca-Cola claim people of the region enjoy chewing on the orange pulp as they consume the drink, and so developed the Minute Maid Pulpy to meet local tastes. Coca-Cola plans to expand the product in other markets in the coming months.

According to Coca-Cola, Minute Maid Pulpy is already the best-selling drink in China, Taiwan and Hong Kong. However, rival beverage company Pepsico recently announced plans to invest $2.5 billion in the Chinese market over the coming three years. Pepsico currently markets several products in the Asian region including Tropicana Guo Bin Fen juices and Cao Ben Le drinks, which are inspired by Chinese medicine.

Western food and beverage franchises hoping to dominate the Chinese and Asian markets have a history of making significant changes to their products in an effort to appeal to regional tastes and sensibilities. McDonald's, Starbucks and KFC all offer products in Asia which are specific to the area, McDonald's menus include Corn Cups, and Starbucks sells green tea Frappuccinos in their Chinese franchises.

The Chinese mainland fast-food and beverage market was estimated to be worth $200 billion in 2008 and has grown at a rate of 16 per cent per year since.

Questions

1 Analyse the benefits to Coca-Cola of having many different brands around the world. [8]
2 Discuss the advantages and disadvantages of changing the recipes of products for different regions. [16]

As with entering any market, the marketing department needs to carefully analyse marketing opportunities when thinking of expanding overseas. This means looking at factors such as the market size and the potential for growth. The analysis will use techniques such as correlation and extrapolation but the firm may need to use local expertise to try to understand the market better.

The market analysis should help identify possible markets for the firm's products, looking at the market conditions and the strengths of the brand and the products themselves.

Once options have been identified the firm must choose which ones to target and then develop an entry plan, thinking about when and how it will enter the markets; for example, will it simply sell to the market or set up and produce locally as well.

Understanding overseas markets can be difficult because of differences in language, climate, culture and buying patterns. There is therefore potentially a high amount of risk involved so managers must consider the likely rewards and how much time and effort to spend on market research.

The method of entry into international markets

Typically, firms will begin to export abroad. This means they will continue to focus on the domestic market but accept orders from abroad. This is a low-risk strategy – it simply involves a firm sending its products to other countries. It may at this stage do some marketing abroad, for example advertising its products or attending promotional events. If sales from abroad continue to grow the firm might look for an agent or representative overseas. This means it has someone based abroad who knows its firm well and understands local conditions. They will try and generate business for the firm and may be paid on commission. Again, the risk of this approach is relatively low.

A bigger commitment would be made when the firm finds a partner and forms a joint venture or alliance. For example, it might collaborate on projects and share the profits. At this stage it is not just someone representing the firm, but someone who the firm is working with locally to generate more sales. For example, a drinks company might have an alliance with a local drinks company to share distribution costs or to gain access to some outlets. It might also franchise if that was appropriate. This would mean it was working with local partners who would understand the political, legal, economic, social and technological issues better.

If the market overseas looks as if it will prosper long term, a firm might take over a foreign partner or invest itself to set up its own operations there. These show real commitment and are major strategic decisions; this involves a high degree of risk and expenditure. Several UK businesses have found it difficult to succeed abroad because of the real differences in approach between regions.

Globalisation or localisation?

Once the decision has been made to enter an overseas market a business must consider the extent to which it will adapt its offerings to local conditions. Is it possible to market the product in almost the same way in every country (as Gillette does with its razors), which is known as a **global strategy**, or will the marketing have to be adjusted for each market? If a business pursues a global strategy this means it is adopting essentially the same marketing mix wherever it competes. A pan-global marketing strategy has been adopted by businesses in several markets, such as jeans, soft drinks, cigarettes and luxury goods. A Rolex watch, for example, is positioned and marketed in a very similar way across the world.

One advantage of a global approach is that it offers marketing economies of scale, for example, the business can develop one advertising campaign and one approach to packaging worldwide. However, this type of strategy does not respond to the requirements of different national markets and so the business may lose sales to competitors who focus more on local needs. In markets such as food and drink and the media, a business may need to adapt significantly to local requirements. On the other hand, a more local approach may meet customer needs more precisely but may be more expensive and more complex to manage.

In reality, most companies will choose a balance between the global and local approach. Unilever, for example, has built several superbrands such as Dove. These are global brands that sell in many different markets. They have the same name and logo everywhere. However, some adjustments are made in the way the product is promoted to reflect local conditions. Unilever calls itself a 'multi-local multinational'. This is reflected in its structure – it has brand managers who look after a brand globally and local country managers who look after all related issues in their areas. This approach is also called a 'think global, act local' strategy. Companies try to find economies of scale where they can by doing things the same but, where necessary, adjusting to the local market. McDonald's has the same basic brand image and approach everywhere but sells wine in France, does not sell pork in Muslim countries and adjusts the menu in different areas. Coca-Cola sells its main brands globally but has more than 200 local brands that only sell in limited areas.

Factors to consider when entering overseas markets

When considering entering an overseas market, marketing managers think about:

- the likely costs to establish the product in the market and continue promoting
- the likely risk – given that they may not be familiar with factors such as the culture, the legal system or competitive environment, the risk could be relatively high
- the likely competition
- the understanding of the market
- the time frame
- the link with the business's strengths and experience
- how to enter
- the likely returns – these could be huge in some markets but must be balanced against the risk.

Case Study

LEGO

The Danish company LEGO has recently become the world's second-biggest toymaker by sales.

The maker of billions of coloured toy bricks every year has almost tripled its sales since 2007 despite the financial crisis and the popularity of digital games. Lego's sales overtook those of Hasbro (which makes Transformers, My Little Pony and Play-Doh), which was previously number two behind Mattel.

LEGO's new range of Friends building sets – designed to appeal to girls – sold well alongside ranges such as City, Star Wars and Ninjago.

Figure 26.3 A LEGO model of the Star Wars Death Star

CEO Jorgen Vig Knudstorp credited LEGO's high-selling video games and website with helping the company to engage with children in the digital age, but added that physical play was still important.

The 80-year-old company used to be under-represented in big toy markets such as North America and the UK, but it has pushed to increase sales in the US, which is now its biggest market. It is also looking to expand into Russia, Latin America and Asia as the middle classes swell in emerging markets.

LEGO is 75 per cent owned by an investment vehicle belonging to the founder's family and 25 per cent by the LEGO Foundation. Mr Knudstorp said LEGO only kept cash needed for operating purposes but otherwise gave it to the family to invest elsewhere. 'If Lego needs [the cash] it flows back.'

As it shifts its production to low-cost countries, LEGO is building a new factory in Hungary and expanding one in the Czech Republic. It recently announced that it is to close its packing facilities at its Billund headquarters in the next two and a half years, but is investing in its moulding and engineering works there.

Questions

1 Analyse the factors that might determine demand for LEGO. [8]
2 Discuss the factors LEGO might consider before choosing a new market to target. [16]

Test your learning

Short answer questions

1 What is meant by globalisation? [2]
2 Analyse **one** way in which globalisation provides an opportunity for a business. [3]
3 Analyse **one** way globalisation can provide a threat for a business. [3]
4 State **two** reasons for increased globalisation. [2]
5 State **two** factors a business would consider when deciding which markets to enter. [2]
6 State **two** ways a business might enter a foreign market. [2]
7 Analyse **one** factor that might influence how to enter a foreign market. [3]
8 What is meant by a global strategy? [2]
9 Analyse **one** reason for adopting a global strategy. [3]
10 State **two** possible problems of entering an overseas market. [2]

Data response question

Diageo marketing overseas

Drinkers of whisky have tended to associate this drink with success. This is why the Johnnie Walker brand has used its image of a confident, successful striding man on its packaging for several years. However, people celebrate success in different ways and therefore the Diageo, the group that owns the Johnnie Walker brand, has started to adjust its marketing. In China, for example, a recent advertising campaign has featured an extreme game of golf played by two young men culminating in shots taken from a golf cart, up a tree and even beneath the chin of a crocodile. Johnnie Walker has 34 per cent of the Chinese whisky market, making it the second most popular brand behind Pernod Ricard's Chivas Regal, which has a 50 per cent share. The market is certainly worth fighting for. According to the Scotch Whisky Association, whisky exports to China have been rising rapidly. Not only are China's rapidly growing ranks of aspirational high earners eager to try upmarket international brands; the country's membership of the World Trade Organisation has also made Scotch more widely available and affordable. In recent years China has cut import tariffs on spirits from 65 per cent to 10 per cent.

Diageo introduced its strategy for expanding in China two years ago, but understanding the complexities of a different regional market is not easy.

Chinese consumers drink whisky in a more diverse range of venues than western consumers, from traditional restaurants to trendy bars and nightclubs. Tastes and spending power vary greatly among Chinese consumers, depending on where they live. And Chinese drinkers have even found a new way to drink Scotch – mixing it with iced green tea.

Diageo split the market into four consumer groups. 'The Chinese people are not monolithic,' said the managing director of Diageo China. 'The size of the market and the complex demographic composition leads to totally different consumption habits and patterns in different parts of China.'

The first, and most strategically important, consumers for Diageo are 'guanxi men' – status-driven 35–45-year-olds for whom business entertaining plays a big role.

The second are 'strong independent women' aged 35 to 45.

The third group is 'upwardly mobiles' – 25–35-year-old men and women who want to be seen at the cutting edge.

The final group, the 'choice generation', are early twentysomethings who are eager to explore and experience something new.

Diageo has also constructed a framework of seasonal promotional activity built around important dates such as Chinese New Year and National Day.

A third strand to its strategy is event sponsorship. As a sponsor of the McLaren Formula 1 team, Diageo worked with different local authorities on initiatives to promote responsible drinking, culminating in last month's Chinese Grand Prix in Shanghai.

Diageo made the most of this by launching a digital marketing campaign that resulted in 11 million Chinese viewing its ad online in the week before the event.

Questions

1 Analyse the benefits to Diageo of targeting new markets. [10]

2 Discuss the factors Diageo would consider before entering a new overseas market. [14]

3 To what extent should companies like Diageo change their marketing strategies for different markets? [16]

Essay questions

1 Discuss whether the advantages of targeting overseas markets outweigh the disadvantages. [20]

2 To what extent is greater globalisation good for business? [20]

Past paper question

Read the Forest Product Company (FPC) case study on pages 464–67 and then answer the following question.

Assess the potential impact of increasing globalisation on the marketing strategy for FPC furniture. [16]

Cambridge International AS and A Level Business Studies
9707 Paper 33 Q5 May/June 2011

27 Operations and project management

Chapter overview

In this chapter we will examine
- enterprise resource planning (ERP)
- the importance of understanding capacity
- how businesses might increase capacity utilisation
- how businesses might respond if there is a capacity shortage.

27.1 Introduction

At A2 you will build on your understanding of AS **operations management** and focus on some specific areas in detail. The key issues in operations management continue to be transforming resources in an effective and efficient process. Operations management can help a business compete in areas such as:
- the quality of what it does
- the speed with which it does it
- the costs at which it provides the goods and services
- the reliability of the products
- the flexibility of the process.

Key term

Operations management involves the planning, organising and monitoring of the transformation process turning resources into outputs.

To excel in some or all of the above operational areas will involve working closely with suppliers. The supply chain describes the different organisations involved in the transformation process from the start to the finish. When you buy a mobile phone, for example, this will be made up of hundreds of parts made from suppliers all around the world and assembled before being distributed to stores. In addition to these are the designers, the businesses transporting materials, the financial organisations helping with the funding and the marketing teams promoting the products. The production of a finished product is therefore a complex process often involving liaising and working with numerous suppliers. Throughout the process the managers will want to know what materials are available, what is being used and what is available where; this is known as enterprise resource planning (ERP) and is examined below.

In this chapter, we also examine issues relating to the maximum output a firm can a produce, which is known as capacity. A business will not want to have capacity sitting idle but at the same time won't want to have too little capacity so getting the capacity right is an important aspect of operations planning.

27.2 Enterprise resource planning (ERP)

Enterprise resource planning (ERP) involves the use of software to integrate the collection and use of information for managers throughout a business. The aim of ERP is to enable decision makers within the business to have the information they need when they need it. It also links the business to outside stakeholders such as suppliers. It should provide information in a form that is reliable, relevant and cost effective. It should enable managers to know what resources are available at any moment and this helps with planning.

ERP and businesses' efficiency

By linking together the different functions and different parts of the supply chain the business should be more efficient, more flexible and have less need to hold supplies because items can be ordered and delivered just in time. A customer may place an order and this information is immediately transferred to all the departments that need to know about it, such as finance and production. Production is now triggered to begin and this sends out orders to all the different suppliers for the right quantities of parts to arrive at the right time. This means inventory levels can be low, reducing inventory holding costs.

With better information managers should know instantly what is available, what it is possible to produce in the coming weeks; this should make the business more responsive to changes and enable better use of the resources available, so increasing capacity utilisation. This can help a business to be more efficient and to be more flexible to customer needs. It can also mean it can provide more accurate information for customers; for example, when estimating delivery times.

ERP therefore enables real time data to be available and this provides greater visibility and awareness of what is happening at each stage of the process.

Table 27.1 The impact of ERP

Factor	Impact of ERP
Inventory control	With better knowledge of demand patterns and existing inventory levels managers should know what to re-order and when, avoiding having too much inventory or running out
Costs	Better information should avoid over- or under-ordering and improve efficiency reducing costs
Pricing	Lower costs may enable lower prices Greater awareness of demand patterns may enable more dynamic pricing
Capacity utilisation	Greater awareness of how resources are being used throughout the business may enable better planning, ensuring higher capacity utilisation. For example, the business will be better placed to know whether it is able to accept an order or how it can reorganise production to make it possible to accept an order
Response to change	Better information enables a quicker and more informed response to changes; the business will know more about what is feasible given the constraints

27.3 Capacity and capacity utilisation

The **capacity** is the maximum amount a business can produce given its existing resources. The capacity of a business depends on the number and quality of its resources. What is the amount and what is the standard of equipment available? How many staff does the business have and how well trained are they? How efficient is its transformation process? Over time, the capacity can be increased with more investment, but at any one moment there will be a maximum number of orders that a business can cope with. The capacity of a bus company can be measured by how many passengers it can carry. The capacity of a restaurant is how many meals it can serve. The capacity of a school is how many students it can accept. The capacity of a plane is how many passengers it can take.

Capacity utilisation measures the existing output relative to the maximum. It can be calculated using:

$$\frac{\text{Existing output over a given time period} \times 100}{\text{Maximum possible output over a given time period}}$$
$$= \text{percentage capacity}$$

For example:

a Existing output 300 units a week, maximum output 500 units a week.

Capacity utilisation = (300/500) × 100 = 60 per cent

b Existing output 400 units a week, maximum output 500 units a week.

Capacity utilisation = (400/500) × 100 = 80 per cent

Imagine a gig where the stadium is completely sold out, with 30 000 in the audience; this means that capacity utilisation is 100 per cent, which is good for the promoter of the event. But what if you have a theatre that is half full? This means that its capacity utilisation is only 50 per cent.

Key term

Capacity measures the maximum amount of output a firm can produce at a given moment with its existing resources.

Study tip

Remember that inventory holding costs can include security, depreciation if inventories go out of date, warehousing costs and the opportunity cost of money tied up in inventory.

Maths moment

1 If capacity is 800 units and present output is 200 units what is the level of capacity utilisation?
2 If capacity utilisation is 20 per cent and capacity is 3000 units what is the present level of output?
3 If capacity utilisation is 20 per cent and present output is 4000 units what is the capacity?

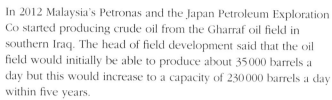

Gharraf Oil Field

In 2012 Malaysia's Petronas and the Japan Petroleum Exploration Co started producing crude oil from the Gharraf oil field in southern Iraq. The head of field development said that the oil field would initially be able to produce about 35 000 barrels a day but this would increase to a capacity of 230 000 barrels a day within five years.

The companies recently drilled four wells in Gharraf and will drill another 13 in the next six months.

Questions

1 Calculate the growth in capacity over five years. Explain how this increase might have occurred. [6]

2 Discuss the possible consequences for the business of increasing capacity. [10]

Remember that the capacity of a business will affect the sales it is trying to achieve and therefore its human resource planning and financial position. There is little point generating more demand if there is not the capacity unless the business is willing to let others produce for it and/or have queues and waiting lists.

Under-utilisation of capacity

If capacity utilisation is low, it means that the existing output is relatively low compared to what could be produced. This is inefficient because resources are not being fully utilised. The business could be producing more and, assuming the demand was there, earning more revenue and profit. The train could have more passengers, the health club could have more members, the sandwich business could be making more sandwiches. A business will, therefore, usually want a high level of capacity utilisation.

Higher levels of capacity utilisation are desirable because they spread the fixed costs of a business over more units. This helps reduce the unit cost and therefore increase profit margins. Imagine you were renting a market stall for $500 and you sold 250 items. Each item would have to earn $2 simply to cover the rental costs. If you sold 1000 items, each one would only have to earn 50 cents to cover the fixed costs: this is because as your output increases the fixed cost per unit falls. This is very significant because it means there are major cost advantages of having higher capacity utilisation. A business

with low capacity utilisation not only wastes resources but has high unit costs. This will reduce profit margins if the price stays the same. If the firm tries to increase the price to cover the higher unit costs it may find that sales fall and the situation becomes even worse.

Improving the position of the business may therefore involve increasing the capacity utilisation, either by boosting demand (which may be through marketing activities – see Chapters 25 and 26) or reducing the capacity of the business if some of it is no longer needed.

Reactions to capacity under-utilisation

Your capacity is under-utilised (i.e. capacity utilisation is low) if demand is not matching the level of output you are able to provide. For example, you have a cinema that can take 400 people but there are only 80 watching the film (this is 20 per cent capacity utilisation). You have a café with 40 tables but only four are occupied at the moment (this is 10 per cent capacity utilisation). **Capacity under-utilisation** therefore occurs when demand is too low.

In this situation the business may:

- **Do nothing** If this is seen as a temporary issue the business may accept under-utilisation for a short time (for example, when a World Cup football match is on television the number of high street shoppers falls; capacity utilisation in restaurants is usually lower during the week compared to the weekend).
- **Renew its marketing activities to boost demand** For example, changes in the promotional strategy may be made, new offers, increased efforts by the sales team or more advertising may help increase sales.
- **Reduce the level of capacity** If, over time, demand is lower than capacity the business may rationalise. **Rationalisation** means the business may reduce its capacity levels. For example, you may reduce the number of staff you have, you may sell off some of your production equipment if it is not needed or you may sell off some land if this is not required. Of course, changing capacity levels may be easier in some businesses than others. If you run a taxi or delivery business you could reduce the number of vehicles you operate fairly easily. However, if you run a cinema it is not easy to split the cinema in half to reduce the capacity. If you have a café you cannot easily sell off a quarter of it. In general, it is easier to reduce the labour input by making people redundant or asking them to go part time. Reducing the land and capital inputs can be more difficult.
- **Subcontract for other firms** If you do have excess capacity you may offer your resources to other firms and produce on their behalf. This is **subcontracting**. Some shops may rent out part of their space to other businesses, for example. A food business may offer to produce for someone else and put the other firm's brand name on the products.

Case Study

Car factory closures in Europe

The Ford Motor company was recently under pressure to close one of its factories in Europe due to high levels of excess capacity.

Figure 27.1 Workers protesting at the closure of the PSA plant at Aulnay, France

GM and PSA Peugeot had already announced layoffs and plant closures. Ford assembly plants in Southampton, England, and Genk, Belgium, may also be vulnerable. Ford is using just 63 per cent of its factory capacity in Europe.

Ford said it is developing a plan to match capacity to demand in regions that had been hit hard by the recession and where it closed a plant a decade ago and has been profitable for six of the last eight years. Car sales had been falling for nine consecutive months in Europe, as the car market there falls to its lowest level in 17 years, according to the European Automobile Manufacturers' Association.

Closing factories is a difficult and slow process in Europe due to strong labour unions and state ownership in car companies. GM has said it plans to close its plant in Bochum, Germany, at the end of 2016, the first shutdown of a German car plant since the Second World War. PSA Peugeot Citroen said it will close a French factory.

Ford last closed a major car factory in Europe ten years ago, when it shut its Fiesta assembly plant in Dagenham, England. It sold its Halewood, England, plant and two other UK factories to

India's Tata Group as part the 2008 sale of its Jaguar and Land Rover luxury lines. Ford also got rid of two major assembly plants in Europe when it sold Volvo Cars to Zhejiang Geely Holding Group Co in 2010.

Questions

1 Explain why demand may be low for cars. [6]
2 If Ford decided not to close a factory discuss the other actions it could take given its high levels of excess capacity. [10]

Capacity shortage

If demand is too high for the firm's capacity, there is a capacity shortage (e.g. there are more people wanting tickets for a gig than there are places, there are queues outside the nightclub, or there is a waiting list for a product).

In this situation a business may:

- **Do nothing** You may think that the fact that the product is in short supply relative to demand adds to its appeal. Some clubs might want to build on the image that they are difficult to get into. Morgan sports cars used a waiting list of several years but simply saw this as evidence of the appeal of their cars – they did not want to increase their output. You may also think that the excess demand is temporary and so not want to make any major changes, given that it may not last (e.g. it may be the latest fashion trend to wear a certain brand of sunglasses or T-shirt or it may just be a particularly busy day or night). In this situation people will simply have to wait. A business may start a waiting list or limit the number any one person can buy.
- **Expand capacity** If you believe demand is likely to remain high then you may increase capacity. This will require investment (for example, you may need more people, more equipment and bigger premises) but may well be worthwhile due to the extra sales you can generate.
- **Outsource** If you cannot meet all the demand yourself you may use other producers to produce for you. This increases the amount you can supply but you need to be careful that quality does not suffer and, because the other producers will want to make a profit, your own profits may be less on the units they make compared to you making them yourself. Alternatively, a business may outsource some of its non-core activities so that it can focus on the essential elements of the business. For example, in a school the governors may decide to outsource activities such as the catering, the maintenance and the security so that they can focus on the teaching and learning. This may enable managers to concentrate on what they do best and make use of the skills and experience of specialists in other areas. Caterers that supply to many schools, for example, may have economies of scale that make it cheaper to use them than to try to do it yourself. However, you obviously need to choose your partners carefully because the overall quality of what you do depends on them.

- **Increase the price** If demand is too high relative to supply, a business may increase the price to bring demand down to the 'right' level. This is what happens in many markets. If demand for a particular company's shares increases there is only a certain number available and so the holders of these can increase the price. If you have a house in an area that becomes very desirable then, given the higher levels of demand compared to supply, you can increase the price. The price can therefore act as a rationing mechanism to reduce the demand (and at the same time increase the profit margin per item).

Test your learning

Short answer questions

1 **a** What is meant by ERP?   [2]

   b Explain **one** possible benefit of ERP.   [3]

2 **a** What is meant by capacity?   [2]

   b Explain **one** factor that might influence the capacity of a business.   [3]

3 **a** What is meant by capacity utilisation?   [2]

   b If present output is 400 units and capacity is 1200 units, what is capacity utilisation?   [2]

   c If capacity utilisation is 80 per cent and output is 400 units, what is its capacity?   [2]

4 **a** What is meant by operating under capacity?   [2]

   b Explain **one** problem of operating under capacity.   [2]

5 Explain **three** ways a business might respond to excess capacity.   [6]

6 Explain **three** ways a business might respond to a capacity shortage.   [6]

7 **a** What is outsourcing?   [2]

   b Explain **one** benefit of outsourcing.   [1]

8 Explain **one** disadvantage of outsourcing.   [1]

9 If a business produces 200 units and its capacity utilisation is 70 per cent, what is its capacity?   [3]

10 Explain why higher capacity utilisation is likely to lead to lower unit costs.   [3]

Data response question

Air Mauritius

Air Mauritius recently introduced a third weekly flight to Australia with direct flights between Perth and Mauritius. The new flight represented a 50 per cent increase in seat capacity to Australia.

According to Air Mauritius this new flight confirmed its commitment to grow tourism and business between the two countries and was an attempt to increase its market share. The Australian market offers Air Mauritius great potential to grow its business and the additional capacity provides an important link for economic and tourism development. It also reflects the appeal of Mauritius as one of the world's best leisure destinations, as it is geographically positioned as an ideal place to stop on the way to Africa, the United Kingdom and Europe.

Questions

1 Explain the meaning of the following terms:

   a capacity   [3]

   b market share.   [3]

2 Explain why Air Mauritius has increased capacity.   [6]

3 Discuss the factors Air Mauritius will have considered before introducing the extra flight.   [10]

Essay questions

1 Discuss whether increasing marketing expenditure is the best response if a business is operating under capacity.   [20]

2 To what extent is outsourcing a good business strategy?   [20]

Past paper questions

1 Read the Pyramid Televisions (PT) case study on pages 454–56 and then answer the following questions.

   a Analyse possible reasons why average total costs have increased following the increase in capacity utilisation shown in Table 1.   [8]

   b Which of the two options for solving the capacity problem would you recommend to PT's Board of Directors? Support your answer by analysing data in Table 2 (including relevant calculations) and any other useful information.   [16]

Cambridge International AS and A Level Business Studies 9707 Paper 3 Q3 May/June 2008

2 Read the Forest Product Company (FPC) case study on pages 464–67 and then answer the following question.

Analyse the advantages and disadvantages for FPC of operating sawmills at nearly full capacity.   [10]

Cambridge International AS and A Level Business Studies 9707 Paper 33 Q1 May/June 2011

3 Read the Craft Designs case study on pages 459–61 and then answer the following question.

The Operations Director has proposed outsourcing all supplies of stone sculptures so that the company could start jewellery production. Discuss how Ade might try to solve what you consider to be the most important **human resource** and **operational management** problems that might result from this decision. [20]

Cambridge International AS and A Level Business Studies
9707 Paper 3 Q7 May/June 2007

28 Lean production and quality management

Chapter overview

In this chapter we examine:
- lean production
- benchmarking
- kaizen
- just-in-time (JIT) production
- quality control and assurance
- total quality management (TQM).

28.1 Lean production

Lean production aims to reduce wastage and thereby make a business more efficient. This may be crucial in an age of growing competition and there is a need to provide excellent value for money. By being more efficient a business can reduce its price and maintain its profit margins but hopefully increase sales or keep the price constant and benefit from higher profit margins.

With greater globalisation and competition from all over the world the pressure is on organisations to become more efficient. They are often facing demands for increased pay and higher input costs, but cannot easily pass these on to their customers so, to maintain profits, there is a pressing need for greater efficiencies. Managers are constantly looking for ways of reducing the cost per unit. This does not necessarily mean producing cheaply – a Ferrari car, a Chanel dress and Jimmy Choo shoes are always likely to be expensive to make. However, many managers will want to find the cheapest way of producing at a given quality level. As we saw earlier, this may be achieved by innovation. It can also be helped by trying to become leaner in the way a product is produced.

Lean production aims to reduce all forms of waste in the production process. It is an approach that was developed most fully in Japan. Waste is called muda in Japan and lean production aims to drive out all forms of muda. This includes the

waste of materials, of time, of energy and of human effort. Lean production streamlines operations so that costs are reduced and efficiency increased. To achieve this, a number of techniques have been developed (mainly in Japan) aimed at getting things right first time and reducing wastage levels.

According to Taiichi Ohno (from Toyota), the seven types of waste include:
1 Defects – these only have to be put right later on and cost money or they have to be thrown away or reworked.
2 Overproduction of goods not demanded by actual customers – if they are not needed, why produce them? They only have to be reworked or thrown away.
3 Inventories awaiting further processing or consumption – this represents idle money.
4 Unnecessary processing – why add features or extra work if it is not needed?
5 Unnecessary motion of employees – this wastes time and energy.
6 Unnecessary transport and handling of goods – again, a waste of resources.
7 Waiting for an earlier stage of the process to deliver – waiting time is idle time!

Lean production therefore aims for:
- zero delays
- zero inventories
- zero mistakes
- zero waiting
- zero accidents.

The techniques involved in lean production include:
- time-based management
- critical path analysis
- cell production
- benchmarking
- kaizen (see page 353)
- just-in-time (JIT) production (see page 354).

Lean production involves focusing on problem areas and finding the most efficient ways of doing these. Once the 'right' method has been found staff then need to be trained and shown how to do this and then follow this approach. The aim is to develop clear and reliable ways of doing things. At Toyota, for example, every activity is completely specified, then applied routinely and repetitively. This is because:

- all variation from best practice leads to poorer quality, lower productivity and higher costs
- it hinders learning and improvement because variations hide the link between them. The lean approach includes the 5 Ss:
  - Sieketsu – the aim is to standardise the approach in every area so there is a right way of doing things and this is applied consistently.
  - Seiso – employees are expected to keep their work area clean.
  - Seiton – employees are expected to organise their tools, materials and documents so they can find them easily and quickly.
  - Seiri – employees need to have key equipment only and remove unnecessary tools from their work area.
  - Shitsuke – employees are expected to follow the ways set out to complete a task.

Time-based management

With the levels of competition in most markets increasing rapidly, businesses are always looking for new ways of out-competing their rivals. Many firms have tried to use time as a competitive weapon. If an organisation is able to produce an item in a shorter period of time than its competitors, or deliver it more rapidly to customers, more sales may result. Sony keeps producing new models of its products, for example, so that by the time the competition has copied the features of the last one, it has already moved on to a new version. Domino's Pizza has competed aggressively in the fast-food market by trying to achieve pizza delivery within 30 minutes. Similarly, Dell can produce a computer to a customer's specifications within weeks. Photo developers now promise a one-hour service. Opticians can produce eye glasses in hours. Amazon can deliver within 24 hours. At Yo Sushi you can help yourself rather than wait for a waiter or waitress to come to you.

As customers become eager for 'instant' service, the ability to supply items as and when they are wanted may be crucial to a business's success. The growth of internet shopping, 24-hour telephone banking and home delivery by supermarkets all reflect a desire for quick, easy access to products. Firms must try to react by reducing the time it takes to develop products. Also, with new products being launched more frequently and with rapidly changing customer tastes, products do not tend to survive for as long as they used to in the past. More than 80 per cent of new products are likely to fail in the first few years. It may be important, therefore, to develop products very quickly to keep competitive in the market.

To speed up the development of products, businesses have adopted **simultaneous engineering** methods. These involve getting all the engineers and designers who are concerned with a project to work on it at the same time. Instead of having one person look at a product idea, develop it and then pass it on to the next person or department, time can be saved if everyone is looking at and discussing the work simultaneously. This process has become easier due to the increasing use

of information technology. This enables employees to communicate and share information more easily.

Key term

Simultaneous engineering occurs when as many activities as possible involved in developing new products are undertaken at the same time, as opposed to in sequence, to save time.

Case Study

LEGO

In 1993 after a fall in sales LEGO significantly increased the number of products it offered and invested heavily in innovation. Faced with low cost toys from China and the growing appeal of video games, LEGO decided to add LEGO-branded electronics, amusement parks, interactive video games, jewellery and education centres, and built alliances with the Harry Potter franchise and the Star Wars movies.

The company found markets with relatively little competition – free markets where it could dominate; it involved many staff and hired a diverse and creative staff; it tried to create new products that disrupted existing markets; and it listened to customer feedback. Innovation became a focus of every aspect of the company, with the goal of turning it into the world's strongest brand among families by 2005. In short, LEGO had created an innovative culture that seemingly would have been the envy of any firm. However, it almost went bankrupt. While products linked to Star Wars and Harry Potter were successful in the years films were released they were not at other times and many other products failed to take hold of the market. By 2003, the company had virtually run out of cash.

Figure 28.1 LEGOLAND Malaysia

To get the firm back on track, LEGO decided it needed to control its cutting-edge ambitions. To generate cash for its next phase, the company sold a 70 per cent stake in its successful LEGOLAND theme parks for $460 million to the Blackstone Group and closed the firm's Danish headquarters building, moving management into a nearby factory. It then outsourced the overwhelming majority of its plastic-brick production to cheaper facilities in Mexico and the Czech Republic.

The new regime at LEGO, however, did not just stop trying to innovate, according to David Robertson in his book *Brick by Brick: How Lego Reinvented its Innovation System and Conquered the Toy Industry*. Instead, it created a more organised structure for those efforts. Management gave everyone from the sales force to the headquarters staff the capability to create and suggest new avenues for growth. But their ideas were put to the test: any innovation had to prove to be consistent with the company goal of LEGO being recognised as the best company for family products.

For instance, experts generally suggest that innovation should move toward 'blue oceans', that is, markets where the product will be unique. But, as Robertson noted, 'red oceans' – meaning that blood could be in the waters from competitive sharks – exist for a reason. 'People are competing in red oceans because there is something there [worth going] after.' The company sought to compete with Lego-like toys in three dimensions and on video. It opened retail stores and created LEGO-themed board games and straight-to-DVD films.

LEGO may not regularly appear on the lists of the most innovative companies, but it is moving forward at a time when competitors such as Hasbro and Mattel are stagnating, Robertson noted. Controlled innovation has clearly worked.

Source: Adapted from 'Innovation almost bankrupted LEGO', Knowledge@ Wharton, 18 July 2012

Questions

1 Analyse two factors that might influence how much LEGO spends on innovation. [8]
2 To what extent do you think innovation guarantees business success? [16]

Time-based management also involves building a flexible production system able to respond quickly and effectively to customer demand. This requires employees and equipment that can produce 'just in time' so that production reacts to orders. If production can be made to follow demand, firms should be able to gain a time advantage over their competitors.

An important element of time-based management is scheduling activities effectively so that they are undertaken as efficiently as possible. There are various ways to do this, including using critical path (or network) analysis, which we look at in Chapter 29. This is particularly important in project-based

industries such as construction where every project may be slightly different and needs very careful coordination.

Cell production

Key term

Cell production occurs when the production process is divided into stages undertaken by teams.

Cell production is a method of organising production around teams rather than a traditional production line, and can lead to less wastage. Instead of producing items on a production line, the process is divided into a series of different stages undertaken by teams or cells. Each team is given the responsibility for a stage in the process.

An advantage of this approach is that teams are responsible for a complete unit of work. Instead of each individual working on one simple task and having no real involvement with the final product, working in cells can give employees a sense of team spirit. It can also improve quality because teams have work for which they have overall responsibility and they can clearly see the results of their efforts.

Cell production can be very motivating for employees because they feel they have more control over their own work. The team members can organise among themselves when and how items are produced. They can also share their skills and expertise.

Team members are also likely to feel much greater responsibility for their work because the next cell has the right to refuse their work if it is poor quality. Cell production involves self-checking by team members.

Hackman and Oldham (1976) developed a model of job design which highlighted the key elements of a motivating job (see Figure 28.2).

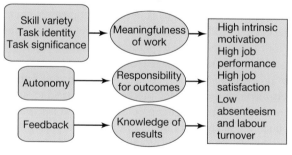

Figure 28.2 The key elements of a motivating job

This model stressed the importance of designing jobs in which individuals had:

- skill variety, i.e. they use a range of skills
- task significance, i.e. they are working on something that has some significance in terms of the overall business rather than just working on a small section and thereby not appreciating why what they do matters

- task identity, i.e. the work they do has a sense of competition (e.g. handing over a complete unit of work to the next stage of the process)
- autonomy, i.e. individuals have some independence to make decisions on how they do the work
- feedback, i.e. employees receive information on the quality of their work.

Cell production helps in most of the areas above and should therefore create more motivating work. Teams have control over what they do; together they produce a complete unit of work, they hand it over to the next cell, which will give feedback and each member of the cell may undertake a range of tasks. This should be more motivating than simply undertaking the same task again and again on a production line – in that system you probably have no idea why your part of the process matters, there is almost no skill variety or sense of task significance.

28.2 Benchmarking

Benchmarking occurs when one business measures its performance against other organisations. Firms benchmark against other organisations that are strong in particular areas. The aim of benchmarking is to learn from the best firms in the world and discover ways of improving operations. If you want to know how to manage large numbers of visitors, talk to Disney; if you want to know how to come up with great design, ask Apple; if you want to move things around reliably, talk to UPS.

Looking for the ways to improve corporate performance internally assumes that a business's staff knows the best way of doing something, or how to improve it. Analysing the actions of other organisations, especially experts in the relevant business area, means a business is more likely to find the best solution. This is particularly true if firms benchmark against the best in the world. Benchmarking may be against other firms in the same industry or even against organisations in a completely different sector. It highlights the importance of being a learning organisation and not being complacent.

Firms may use benchmarking to help them improve in areas such as:
- the reliability of their products
- their ability to send out the correct bills (also called invoices)
- their ability to deliver items on time
- the time it takes to produce a product.

Organisations undertaking benchmarking are those most eager to learn and improve and those that are unafraid to seek outside help.

Key term

Benchmarking occurs when one business decides to measure its performance against the leaders in the field.

The benchmarking process

1 The firm must plan what it wants to benchmark, which firms it wants to benchmark with, how it is going to collect the data, which resources to allocate to the project and who is responsible for the project.
2 The firm must collect data from the other firm or firms. This may be through visits to their factories or offices.
3 The firm must analyse its findings to identify how it could improve its own process.
4 The firm must adapt its findings so it can implement the new methods in its own firm given its own circumstances.

The benefits of benchmarking

By undertaking benchmarking a firm should be able to:
- develop a better understanding of customers and competitors
- have fewer complaints and more satisfied customers
- reduce waste and improve quality.

Benchmarking can be difficult because some firms will naturally be unwilling to share their information. They may want to keep their methods and processes secret and might be reluctant to provide rival businesses with ideas on how to improve. One way of avoiding this problem is to benchmark against firms in different industries.

Firms must also be careful about trying to copy another organisation's methods exactly. Every organisation has its own way of doing things, its own skills and its own circumstances. They may have to adapt the other firm's methods for their own use.

28.3 Kaizen

The belief that firms can always do better is known as 'kaizen'. Kaizen is a Japanese word meaning continuous improvement. The kaizen approach tries to get employees to improve what they do in some small way every day of every week of every year. If workers improve the quality of their work by 1 per cent every single day, the effect over just one year would be enormous. Too often, businesses seek dramatic changes instead of small, regular changes. If you want to improve your grades in your exams, it is unlikely that there is any one thing you can do that will lead to a sudden improvement in your marks. However, if you begin to change many things over time, your grade is likely to improve gradually.

The idea of continuously improving can be seen in the work of Edward Deming (see Figure 28.3 and page 357). Deming was an American who achieved great fame in Japan for his work on quality. Deming advised managers to focus on a specific problem and find the best way of doing this and set appropriate quality targets. Managers would plan what needed to be done, then do it, then check to see the results and then take action. If the targets were consistently being met, managers could then increase the level of quality they were trying to achieve and focus on how to do this. If the existing targets were not being met, managers should find out why and fix this before raising the bar.

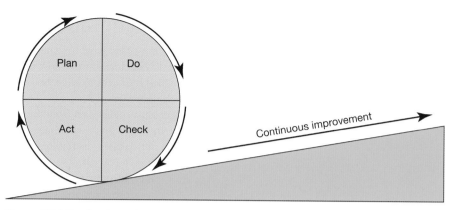

Figure 28.3 The Deming cycle

28.4 Just-in-time production

Inventories are goods that have been produced or are in the process of being produced but which have not yet been sold. As we saw at AS, just-in-time (JIT) production occurs when firms produce products to order. Instead of producing as much as they can and building up inventories, firms only produce when they know they can actually sell the items. Similarly, components and supplies are only bought in by a firm as and when they are needed. The aim of just-in-time production is to reduce a firm's inventory levels by as much as possible; in an ideal world there would be no inventories at all. Supplies would arrive and be used to produce items that are sold immediately to the final customer.

Running a just-in-time system is complex and places many demands on a business, as explained below.

- **Excellent relationships with suppliers** Businesses need to be able to rely on suppliers to deliver goods at precisely the right time. They cannot afford delays as this halts production. Also, the goods must be perfect quality; the manufacturer has no inventories to replace faulty supplies. A firm must be able to trust its suppliers completely.
- **Reliable employees** Because the business does not have many (if any) inventories at any stage of the process, the firm cannot cope with stoppages. If strikes occur, for example, the whole

production process stops. A business cannot supply customers using inventories as none exists. JIT relies upon maintaining a good relationship between employers and employees.
- **A flexible workforce** To ensure that production can respond to demand, a firm needs a flexible labour force. This means that if someone is ill, another employee must be able to cover for them, or that if demand is high in one area of the business, people can be moved to that area to help out. Firms using JIT expect employees to be ready to work anywhere, anytime. People must change to meet the demand for different products because JIT is focused entirely on matching supply to customer orders.

Introducing just-in-time production involves:
- investment in machinery which is flexible and can be changed from producing one type of item to another without much delay
- training employees so that they have several skills and can do a variety of jobs (multi-skilling)
- negotiation with employees so that their contracts are flexible and allow them to move from one job to another
- building relationships with suppliers who can produce just-in-time as well.

Problems of JIT

Although the just-in-time process has many advantages, there are several potential problems or disadvantages as well.

The system relies on suppliers providing parts and components at exactly the time they are needed. If this type of flexible and reliable supplier cannot be found, the system breaks down. JIT can also cause problems if the suppliers fail to deliver on time. The manufacturer has no buffer inventory and so cannot produce. The system also means that the firm is vulnerable to action taken by employees. Any stoppage can be extremely expensive because production is halted completely.

The earthquake in Japan in 2011 was a disaster for those directly affected by it. It also caused enormous problems for businesses operating a just-in-time process and reliant on supplies from Japan. With a delay in supplies they struggled to produce.

Switching to JIT can also lead to an increase in costs because of the extra reordering. Because parts are ordered much more frequently, the firm may lose bulk discounts and will also have more administration costs.

Case Study

Toyota

Figure 28.4 The earthquake and tsunami in Japan caused problems for companies that use JIT systems

In April 2011 the Japanese car maker, Toyota, had to temporarily halt production at its UK engine manufacturing plant on Deeside, Flintshire and five other of its factories across Europe.

The stoppage was due to a supply shortage from Japan, caused by an earthquake and tsunami.

A director of the Centre for Automotive Industry Research at Cardiff Business School, Cardiff University, said that the problem was that they relied on parts coming in from Japan.

Toyota uses a 'just-in-time system' of supply which operates without a lot of slack in the system. Once supply is stopped or interrupted it does not take much time for factories around the world to be affected.

Experts have been recommending for years that manufacturers diversify their supply base. After all, recent history is full of examples of widespread supply chain disruptions and their consequences for manufacturers reliant on too few sources – from the attacks on 11 September 2001 to Hurricane Katrina in 2005 and the cloud of volcanic ash from Iceland that shut down Europe's skies in 2010.

Questions

1 Analyse how lean production techniques might benefit Toyota. [8]

2 Discuss whether the halt in production in 2011 suggests that Toyota should stop using lean production techniques. [16]

28.5 Quality

An important aspect of operations management is making sure that the goods and services produced are of a suitable **quality**. A quality product is one that meets the specifications that the firm has set out and, in turn, meets the customers' needs. As famous management writer Peter Drucker says, 'Quality in a product or service is not what the supplier puts in. It is what the customer gets out and is willing to pay for. A product is not quality because it is hard to make and costs a lot of money, as manufacturers typically believe. This is incompetence. Customers pay only for what is of use to them and gives them value. Nothing else constitutes quality.' What is and what is not quality therefore depends on the customers' views.

Quality has been defined as 'fitness for use' by Juran (1981) and 'conformance to requirement' by Crosby (1979). A pad of paper priced at $1 or a light bulb priced at 75 cents can both be quality products, provided they do what consumers expect them to do. By comparison a $1 million house or a $400 suit may be poor quality if they do not meet consumers' expectations. The fact that these products are expensive does not mean they are necessarily of good quality. To improve the effectiveness of the business, managers must make sure that what they are producing consistently meets customers' requirements. This in turn means that to produce good products, a firm must identify exactly what customers are looking for. The firm must then specify exactly what the product has to do and make sure that these specifications are achieved every time.

To achieve quality, managers must therefore set targets based on customer needs and then make sure that the targets are being achieved. By improving the quality of their products, managers should improve customer satisfaction and lead to repeat business.

Key term

A **quality** product is one that meets customer requirements.

Quality targets

The nature of the quality targets set will depend on the type of business.

A hotel might set targets involving:
- customer satisfaction levels
- accurate billing
- speed of response, such as in reception and the restaurant.

A manufacturing business might consider:
- the proportion of products with defects

Figure 28.5 Identify needs – set quality target

- the amount of waste produced in the process
- the proportion of returned goods.

A hospital might consider:
- the time taken to see patients
- the average length of time spent by patients in hospital
- the recovery rates for different types of operation
- patient satisfaction rates.

These targets will not be fixed for ever. Once a target is achieved managers should look to make it even more challenging or find another area that needs focusing on and thereby improve the business further.

Why does quality matter?

Poor quality leads to mistakes that have to be put right or fixed. Goods may have to be thrown away. Items may be returned and have to be replaced. In a worst-case situation you may even be sued for failing to deliver the products promised. You may also lose customer goodwill and loyalty. The effects of poor quality are therefore expensive. Philip Crosby, a management writer in this area, believes that between 20 and 35 per cent of firms' revenues can be spent putting right all the consequences of poor quality. He argues that investing to prevent mistakes occurring is far cheaper than putting things right later on. Improving quality can not only improve customer satisfaction; it can also save money.

Quality control and quality assurance

The traditional approach to improving the quality of a firm's products is to put resources into inspecting the finished products to find any faults that exist and remove them. The logic behind this approach is that, if all the goods and services

with defects can be found, the customer will only receive perfect products. As a result, quality will be improved. This is known as a quality control system and it relies on the inspection of products.

In recent years, many managers have questioned whether quality control is the best approach. One problem is that quality control assumes that defects are inevitable. The task is to make sure that they are discovered before the customer receives the product. In effect, this is saying to some elements of the production team that it is acceptable for them to make mistakes, because the quality control department will find them later. This may mean that employees do not take sufficient care in their work.

The quality assurance approach puts more emphasis on preventing mistakes. If the process can be designed in a way that ensures defects do not happen (and in which employees produce correct work every time), inspection at the end of the production process is less important. This approach to quality focuses more on prevention, not just inspection. It stresses the need for employees to get it right first time.

An important part of this approach is that employees check their own work rather than rely on someone else to check it for them at the end of the process. This is known as 'self-checking'.

Under this approach, employees also have the right to reject any work of an unacceptable standard, whoever produced it. Previously, employees often accepted poor quality items as they did not feel responsible for the finished product. Faulty products were simply passed along the production line until the quality control department found the mistakes at the end. Under a quality assurance system, employees are held responsible for their own work; if they find faulty work from other employees they need to communicate with colleagues to sort it out, or report it.

Ensuring that they produce quality work is now seen as a part of everyone's job. At General Motors, for example, employees are told, 'don't accept errors, don't build errors and don't pass them on'. This is a very different view from the past, when quality was seen as something undertaken only by the quality control department.

Quality assurance requires training so that individuals can carry out their tasks effectively. It also involves choosing the right suppliers so that they deliver products without any defects: you will not check their products because you assume that they are correct; the responsibility for any problems caused later will be with the suppliers, which therefore puts pressure on them to get it right (see Figure 28.6).

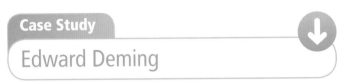

Figure 28.6 Quality assurance

Edward Deming

Edward Deming was an American quality expert who went to Japan and helped many companies there to improve their approach to quality. He was later recognised by American firms as something of a 'guru' when it came to quality.

Deming encouraged the Japanese to adopt a systematic approach to problem solving, which later became known as the Deming or Plan-Do-Check-Act (PDCA) Cycle. He highlighted that meeting and exceeding customers' requirements is the task that everyone within an organisation needs to accomplish. Furthermore, the management system has to enable everyone to be responsible for the quality of his or her output to his 'internal customers'.

Figure 28.7 The PDCA cycle

According to Deming, you must plan what needs to be done to achieve your quality targets and then implement these activities. The next stage is to study the results to see what is working and what is not. You must then take action to remedy any problems. Once these have been fixed you must plan to improve and set more demanding targets. Notice that this is an ongoing process – you are always striving to improve.

Imagine that you produce bottles of perfume and the amount in the bottles varies by + or – 0.5 per cent. Once you have made sure the variation lies within these limits, you then try to reduce the variation to + or – 0.4 per cent, and so on. Also notice that the process relies on targets and measurement; a quality process is driven by data.

Questions

1 Analyse the potential benefits to a business of Deming's quality approach. [7]

2 Discuss the problems managers might face when introducing Deming's approach. [14]

28.6 Total quality management (TQM)

Total quality management (TQM) is an approach to quality involving all the employees in the organisation. This quality assurance system appreciates that everyone within the firm contributes to the overall quality of the product or service.

TQM recognises that all employees are of equal importance, including the factory floor, the office staff, the cleaners, the maintenance staff and the delivery drivers. The way in which customers are dealt with when they ring up, the accuracy of invoices sent out and the reliability of the vans all have an impact on how customers view the firm. It is not just the people who directly make or provide the product who matter.

It is very important that all employees think about the work they do and whether it is of a suitable quality. This means that they need to think of who their customers are. These customers may be the people who actually buy the product, but include anyone for whom work is produced.

Customers are not just external (the people from outside the business who buy the product); they are also internal. Employees need to think of the requirements of all the people they produce work for and ensure they are providing exactly what is required. For example, the warehouse staff have to load materials onto the van for delivery, so the delivery drivers are the internal customers of the warehouse staff. Under the TQM approach everyone has to think about their customers' needs: what they want, what standard they want it to and when they need it by.

The TQM approach considers that employees should always aim to improve the quality of what they do. It is tempting to assume that what you are doing is good enough and, if profits are reasonable, it is easy to become complacent. Such complacency is dangerous because markets and conditions can change incredibly rapidly. To succeed, firms must be continually trying to improve what they do to ensure that they actively delight customers. Under TQM, quality is seen as a dynamic process: it is a journey, not a destination. If managers manage to improve the quality of the firm's operations, this should improve its competitiveness.

Why might employees resist a TQM approach?

Some employees may resist the introduction of a TQM approach. This could be because they see quality as the job of a separate quality control department and do not see why they should check their own work. They may think it will lead to the redundancies of colleagues in quality control if they actually manage to prevent all mistakes and so do not want to do this. They may also be reluctant to take on additional tasks. If they adopt TQM they must first be willing to reject any work that is passed to them that is not satisfactory; that may involve telling colleagues and friends to do something again, which can be difficult to do on a personal level. Also, they must check their own work before passing it on and may not see why they should do this. Some employees may also resist a TQM approach because they:

- don't see why it is necessary
- don't want to have to undertake additional training
- prefer to carry on doing things in the same old way.

Given that TQM involves a change in responsibilities and duties, managers must make sure they:

- explain why it is necessary
- provide the necessary training and support so employees feel capable and reassured
- provide appropriate rewards so employees feel they are treated fairly for taking on extra responsibilities.

Designing the product

The process of improving quality begins with a good understanding of what internal and external customers want. This involves effective market research and use of information. The better the understanding of customers' needs (including your own staff, your operations department) the more likely it is that a firm will produce something that meets their needs precisely.

The aim is to design a product to meet customers' requirements and a means of producing the product that enables the business to make an appropriate amount of profit. The design stage is absolutely critical to the success of a product and to achieving good quality. Effective planning before production begins means that the firm will produce something that customers want and that it is produced in an efficient way. The way the process is laid out, the equipment used, the level of technology involved and the way in which it is organised all have a major impact on the final quality of the goods or services.

Most companies would benefit from investing more at the design stage. If the initial design of the product and process is wrong, it is very expensive to put things right later. Unfortunately, in the rush to put products on the market, firms are willing to accept products and processes that are only adequate, rather than excellent. This is all part of a very common approach that is often more expensive in the long term. According to the UK Department of Trade and Industry, 'Many senior managers (in the UK) still consider the design function a necessary evil, a costly and non-productive unit which often delays the introduction of a new product.'

Improving quality

Quality is an important element of a firm's success. Not surprisingly then, managers should always be looking to improve the quality of their goods and services. If managers want the business to improve its quality they must make it clear that it is a priority and develop appropriate systems to make sure that employees are always trying to improve quality. Bringing about better quality involves:

- defining clearly the needs of your internal and external customers in order to set appropriate quality targets
- introducing a total quality management approach and ensuring that aiming for zero defects and getting it right first time is seen as an important element of everyone's job
- ensuring that the resources are available to enable quality targets to be achieved (e.g. sufficient training so staff can check their own work) – this may cost money at first but will save money in the long term
- working closely with suppliers to ensure they can meet your needs quickly and reliably
- ensuring that there is an ongoing programme of target setting and measuring – once targets are consistently achieved more demanding targets can then be set
- ensuring that your reward systems recognise those who achieve better quality.

Philip Crosby's Four Absolutes

Philip Crosby's name is best known for his writings on the concepts of 'Do It Right First Time'. He considers traditional quality control, the idea of acceptable quality limits (i.e. accepting a certain level of defects as acceptable) to represent failure rather than an assurance of success. In his view, firms must aim for 'zero defects' rather than 'an acceptable level of defects'. Of course, having a 'zero defects' approach will not prevent people from making mistakes, but it will encourage everyone to improve continuously.

The ultimate goal is to train all the staff and give them the tools for quality improvement and to help them to prevent mistakes occurring.

Crosby's Four Absolutes of Quality Management are:

1 Quality is defined as conformance to requirements, not as 'goodness' or 'elegance' – i.e. quality is defined by the customers, not by you!

2 The system for causing quality is prevention, not appraisal – i.e. don't fix it later – get it right first time.

3 The performance standard must be zero defects, not 'that's close enough' – i.e. don't accept mistakes.

4 The measurement of quality is the price of non-conformance – i.e. quality saves you money because it saves you all the costs of fixing the mistakes and having to rework items.

Study tip

Students often assume that improving quality increases costs. Crosby suggests it can actually save money.

Test your learning

Short answer questions

1 a What is meant by lean production? [2]
   b Explain **one** benefit of lean production. [3]

2 a What is meant by kaizen? [2]
   b Explain **one** benefit of kaizen to a business. [3]

3 a What is benchmarking? [2]
   b Explain **one** advantage of benchmarking. [1]

4 a What is meant by quality? [2]
   b Explain **one** cost of improving quality. [3]

5 a What is meant by quality control? [2]
   b Explain **one** method of quality control. [2]

6 a What is meant by quality assurance? [2]
   b Explain **one** benefit of a quality assurance. [3]

7 a What is total quality management (TQM)? [2]
   b Explain **one** reason why staff may resist TQM. [3]

8 a What is just-in-time production? [2]
   b Explain **one** reason for adopting a just-in-time approach. [2]

9 Explain the link between training and quality. [3]

10 Explain how spending more to improve quality might save costs in the long term. [3]

Data response question

Donkey recall

Chinese branches of Walmart have had to recall batches of donkey meat after they were found to contain fox meat.

The US company apologised and said it would reimburse shoppers in China who bought the 'Five Spice' donkey product when it discovered that tests showed it contained the DNA of other animals.

The problem was highlighted when a customer found the so-called donkey meat smelled and tasted unusual. The Shandong Food and Drug Administration later announced that it contained fox meat.

Walmart said that it was deeply sorry and that it showed the need to invest further in supplier management. Commentators said this could damage the Walmart brand.

Donkey meat is popular in China, though makes up a tiny proportion of all meat products consumed. Fox meat, on the other hand, is cheap because of its distinctive smell and the fact that eating it could pose serious health risks.

-Wal-mart Stores Inc., which owns the largest supermarket chain in the world and has more than 400 Walmart stores across China, has been hit with a number of scandals in the Far East in recent years.

In 2011, the Chinese government fined Walmart, along with Carrefour, a combined 9.5 million yuan ($1.5 million) for fixing product prices. In the same year the US retailer was fined in China for selling duck meat past its expiry date.

Questions

1 Analyse how Walmart's quality problem might have occurred. [10]

2 Discuss the benefits of achieving high quality for Walmart. [14]

3 To what extent do you think the poor quality of the donkey meat is likely to damage the Walmart brand long term? [16]

Essay questions

1 To what extent do you think lean production guarantees the success of a business? [20]

2 To what extent is improving quality expensive? [20]

Past paper question

Read the Sam's Fashions case study on pages 462–63 and then answer the following question.

Evaluate whether Manuel's lean production proposals are likely to increase operational efficiency without reducing customer service. [15]

Cambridge International AS and A Level Business Studies
9707 Paper 33 Q4 May/June 2010

29 Project management

Chapter overview

In this chapter we examine:
- the need for projects and project management
- network diagrams
- Critical Path Analysis (CPA).

29.1 Projects

The business environment is continually changing. This creates new opportunities and threats. To anticipate change or to react to it managers will set up project teams. These may be established to:
- develop a new product
- research a new market opportunity
- work on a new process.

Once the task is complete, the project team will be disbanded and another one created as and when required. The membership of a project team will usually depend on your ability to contribute to the task. People may be brought from different areas of the business to work on specific projects.

A project usually involves individuals collaborating in a team to achieve a particular aim. They are temporary and work within a given time and other resource constraints. Managing a project therefore involves managing a team of people to complete a task on time, to a given standard and within given budget constraints. It involves:
- good communication skills to communicate to people what is being done and what has to be done by when
- good people skills to pick the right team and to keep the team working well together
- good planning skills to establish what can be done by when and by whom
- good management skills to review progress and keep the project moving forward.

These skills are especially important given that the project may be in unfamiliar areas and/or where there is a great deal of pressure to get the task completed because it can be vital to the future of the business (e.g. a new product). They are important to ensure an innovative idea becomes a reality.

Why do projects fail?

Projects may fail because:
- not enough time is spent on the planning because of pressure or a desire to get on with the work
- the difficulties and the time and cost involved are underestimated because often these projects have not been done before so there is a lack of experience
- sometimes people want them to succeed so almost ignore the potential problems or are too confident they can overcome them
- of factors outside your control such as changes in the economy or problems with suppliers.

Case Study

Chevron

The large US oil company Chevron has recently announced it will go ahead with a $5.6 billion development project of an Angolan offshore oil field. This will be the company's second largest investment in African crude to date after its Agbami field in Nigeria.

The MafumeiraSul project will eventually pump 110 000 barrels of crude oil per day from five new platforms.

The company says this demonstrates its commitment to further developing opportunities in Angola where Chevron is a market leader.

Angola possesses Africa's third largest oil reserves.

Questions

1 Explain the factors that might delay this project. [6]
2 Discuss the factors that managers of Chevron would have considered before going ahead with this project. [10]

29.2 Critical path or network analysis

To achieve productive efficiency managers will want to plan projects as effectively as possible to ensure that time and resources are not wasted. They do not want to have people and machines sitting idle unnecessarily or materials delivered well before they are required. To help them in the planning process managers may use network analysis, also called critical path analysis (CPA).

Network analysis is a method of organising the different activities involved in a particular process in order to find the most efficient means of completing the task. The aim is to complete the project in as short a time as possible. To do this a firm will determine the exact order in which activities have to be undertaken and identify those which can be undertaken simultaneously to save time. Network analysis can be used in any type of project that involves several activities – anything from opening a new store to planning a new advertising campaign to organising the relocation of the firm. The technique was developed for DuPont in 1957 to speed up the building of a new plant.

In order to undertake network analysis managers must:
- identify all the different tasks involved in the process
- estimate the expected length of time each task will take
- determine the order in which tasks must be completed. For example, in some cases particular tasks cannot be completed until another one has taken place first (these are known as 'dependent' activities). In other cases activities can be undertaken simultaneously (these are known as 'parallel' activities because they can be undertaken at the same time as each other – 'in parallel').

Network charts

The next step is to construct a network chart. This is a diagrammatic representation of all the activities involved in the project, the order in which they must be undertaken and the times each one will take.

When drawing a network diagram the following features are used:
- a circle (called a 'node') represents the start and end of an activity
- a straight line represents the activity itself.

A line showing an activity is labelled in the following way: above the line the name of the activity is given; below the line the length of time the activity is expected to take is shown – this is known as the expected duration of the activity. In Figure 29.1, activity B is expected to last ten days; activity A is expected to last four days; activity B can only be started when activity A is completed (that is why it only begins once A is complete).

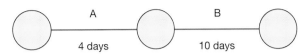

Figure 29.1

In Figure 29.2 activities C and D can only be started after activity B has been completed. Activity E can only start when C and D are finished.

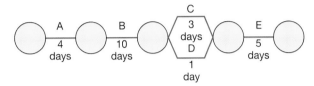

Figure 29.2

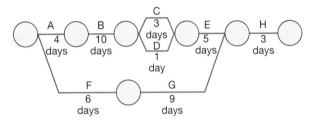

Figure 29.3

In Figure 29.3 we have added in some more activities. You can see that:
- activity F can start immediately
- G can start once F is completed
- H can start once E and G are completed.

All this information can be shown in Table 29.1.

Table 29.1

Activity	Preceded by	Duration (days)
A	–	4
B	A	10
C	B	3
D	B	1
E	C and D	5
F	–	6
G	F	9
H	E and G	3

We now have a whole network diagram. Remember the following rules when constructing a chart:
- The lines showing different activities must never cross.
- The lines showing activities should always begin and end at the mid-point of the nodes.
- The diagram must begin and end with one node.
- When drawing the activities and nodes, do not put the end node on any activity until you are sure what comes next and whether anything else must also be completed before the following activity takes place.

Adding earliest start times and latest finish times

The next stage in producing a network chart is to show various information that can be calculated from the duration of each activity. This information is shown inside the node and to do this we now draw nodes in the following way:

- The left-hand side shows the number of the node; this is used simply for reference and is done by numbering the nodes left to right.
- The right-hand side of the node is used to show two other pieces of information known as the 'earliest start time' (EST) of the next activity and the 'latest finish time' (LFT) of the activity before.

Earliest start time

The earliest start time (EST) is exactly what it says: it is the earliest time a particular activity can begin. This piece of information is shown in the top right of the node at the beginning of an activity.

As you can see in Figure 29.4, the earliest times have now been added. To calculate these figures you take the earliest start time of the activity before and add on the duration of that activity.

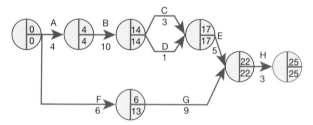

Figure 29.4

The earliest time A can start is day 0 (this is the first activity in the project); this activity takes four days so the earliest time that B can start is day 4. B takes ten days so the earliest C and D can start is day 14.

E can only start when C and D are both finished. C takes longer than D so the project must wait for this activity to be completed before moving on; the earliest that E can start is therefore day 17.

If you have a choice of numbers to add on to calculate the earliest start time, choose the bigger number; the projects cannot continue until all previous dependent activities are finished, so you must wait for the longest one to be completed. Before H can start, for example, it must wait for both E and G to be completed, which means it cannot start until day 22.

By identifying the earliest start times a firm can see when materials are likely to be needed. This means that components and supplies can be ordered to arrive just in time to be used rather than arriving too early and sitting around taking up space and costing money, or arriving late and delaying the whole project. Materials and resources for activity E, for example, do not need to be ready until day 17.

Calculating the earliest start time is therefore an important part of developing a lean approach to a project and ensuring people and materials are coordinated and ready at exactly the right moment.

Latest finish time

The bottom-right space of a node is used to show the latest finish time (LFT) of an activity. Again this shows exactly what it says – the latest an activity can be finished without holding up the whole project.

Activity H must finish on day 25 – the day the whole project can be completed; since H takes three days it means the activities before must be finished by day 22 if the project is to be completed on time. Activity E must therefore be completed at the latest by day 22. Since E takes five days this means the activities before (C and D) must be finished by day 17. Given that C takes three days (which is the longer activity out of C and D), if this stage is to be completed by day 17 the stage before must be finished by day 14.

To work out the latest finish times, therefore, you work right to left deducting the duration of a particular activity from its latest finish time to get the latest finish time of the one before. If there are two or more activities involved (such as C and D), choose the longer duration to deduct.

Rules when calculating ESTs and LFTs

- To calculate the earliest start time of an activity, work left to right and add on the duration of the next activity to the previous earliest start time; if there is a choice, choose the biggest number to add on.
- To calculate the latest finish time of an activity, work right to left and deduct its duration from the previous latest finish time; if there is a choice of numbers, choose the largest number to deduct.

Float time

Using the earliest start times and the latest finish times it is possible to calculate the float time of an activity. There are two types of float time.

- **Free float** measures how much an activity can overrun without delaying the next activity.
- **Total float** measures how much an activity can overrun without delaying the whole project.

To calculate free float you use the equation:

Free float = Earliest start time of the next activity – the earliest start time of this activity – the duration

To calculate total float use the equation:

Total float time = Latest finish time – duration – earliest start time

For example, if activity D has to be finished by day 17, can start on day 14 and lasts one day then the total float is 17−1−14 = 2 days. This activity has two days' slack – it could overrun by two days and the project would still finish on time. By comparison, if activity B has to be finished by day 14, can start on day 4 and lasts ten days, its float is 14−10−4 = 0. There is no float – it must be completed on time or the whole project will be delayed. B is therefore known as a 'critical' activity because it has no total float. By identifying all of the critical activities, the firm can see which activities must be finished on time; this is known as the **critical path**.

The critical path for the project in Table 29.2 is ABCEH because these activities have no total float time. If they are delayed at all the whole project will be late and will not be finished in 25 days.

Table 29.2

Activity	Preceded by	Duration (days)
A	–	4
B	A	10
C	B	3
D	B	1
E	C and D	5
F	–	6
G	F	9
H	E and G	3

By identifying the activities on the critical path, managers can see exactly which activities are the priority in terms of making sure they stay on time; the critical path also shows the shortest time in which a project can be completed.

Key terms

Total float time is the length of time an activity can overrun without delaying the completion of the whole project.

Free float time is the length of time an activity can overrun without delaying the start of the next activity.

The critical path refers to activities that have no float time; if they overrun at all the whole project is delayed.

The activities on the critical path will show the minimum project duration (the shortest period of time necessary to complete the project).

Dummy activities

Sometimes when constructing network diagrams the relationships get so complex that to help you draw them you need a dummy activity. This is an activity that has no time or costs involved; you include it in the diagram to help show the relationships between 'real' activities – it is simply a device you help draw the diagram.

For example:

Table 29.3

Activity	Preceded by	Duration normal time
A	(None)	3 weeks
B	(None)	4
C	(None)	5
D	A	8
E	A, B	3
F	C	5

A, B, and C have no predecessor. They all start from the first node (node 1). A can go from node 1 to node 2. B can go from node 1 to node 3. C also starts at node 1. D can only occur after activity A, so D starts at node 2.

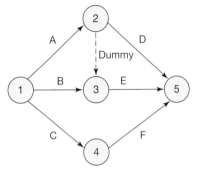

Figure 29.5 Network chart with dummy activity

Now for activity E. The difficulty here is where E should start. E can only begin after A and B. A ends at node 2 and B ends at node 3. But E poses a problem. If we joined A and B up going into node 2 so that E could start from here this would work for E but would be wrong for D; this is because it would suggest D needed both A and B to finish before it could start, which is not correct – it only needs A. The solution is to add a dummy activity that runs from node 2 to node 3, as shown in Figure 29.5. Then start E at node 3. This shows that E needs A and B whereas D only needs A, which is what we want.

Critical path analysis as a management tool

Network diagrams and critical path analysis are useful management tools in project management:

- When undertaking a critical path analysis, managers must consider exactly what activities are involved in a project. This is a useful exercise because it helps to make sure that nothing is forgotten. It also means that managers are likely to consult all the different departments and functions involved and this can help to improve everyone's understanding of the issues and get them involved in getting the project completed.
- Managers can calculate the earliest time by which the project should be completed. This can be important information for customers (e.g. the firm can announce a release date) and is

important to help plan the launch arrangements. It can also help the managers decide whether or not a deadline can be met.

- Managers can identify the 'critical' activities that must be completed in time to get the whole project finished as quickly as possible. This means that they can focus on these specific activities and make sure they do not overrun. At the same time the amount of float time on non-critical activities can be calculated. While managers cannot ignore these activities entirely it may not matter so much if they overrun (provided they do not use up all their float time); it may even be possible to transfer labour and other resources from non-critical activities to critical ones to ensure the latter are completed promptly.
- Managers may be able to produce items or develop products more quickly than the competition, providing the business with a possible competitive advantage. By seeking to reduce the time taken for a project, network analysis is an important element of time-based management.
- Managers can implement just-in-time ordering. Network analysis shows the earliest start times for each activity. Using this information, the firm can order materials and supplies to arrive exactly when they are needed and not before. This saves storage costs and also the opportunity cost of having money tied up in inventories. This can improve the firm's liquidity and free up cash which can be used elsewhere in the organisation.
- Managers can use network analysis as a control mechanism to review progress and assess whether the project is on target. If there have been delays, the effects of the earliest start times and latest finish times can be reworked to see the effect on the completion of the project.

Although some of the estimates of the likely durations may prove to be wrong, and although external factors may cause delays, this does not mean that critical path analysis is unnecessary. On the contrary, by having a network diagram the effects of any delays can be calculated relatively easily in terms of the impact on the final completion date. Critical path analysis enables managers to understand the significance and likely dangers of any delay. Projects may still overrun, but managers should be able to predict if this is going to happen as soon as a problem emerges (rather than being taken by surprise) and if possible take action to get the project back on track.

Case Study

Gautam Buddha airport

The projected duration for the completion of developments at the Gautam Buddha airport in the Himalayas has recently had to be extended to 2016 due to insufficient funds. A study in 2007–08 had estimated a total budget of $38.15 million for the airport construction project, but the estimated cost exceeded the budget after completing the final design and construction survey. The Nepalese government is now looking for additional funds of around $42 million.

To help manage the budget it was decided to start constructing the airport in two phases – Phase I and Phase II.

The plan is to construct a runway 3000 metres long instead of 2600 metres so that Boeing 777–200, Airbus A330–300, and similar aircraft can be operated. The project also includes a new terminal building instead of renovating the old one.

Questions

1 Explain two ways in which network analysis might have helped in the planning of this airport. [6]
2 Discuss whether problems such as the lack of finance make network analysis a waste of time [10]

Maths moment

Table 29.4

Activity	Preceded by	Duration
A	–	3
B	A	5
C	–	2
D	B	10
E	C, D	4
F	–	1
G	F	12
H	E	3
I	E, G	5
J	H, I	3

1 Construct the network diagram given the data in Table 29.4.
2 What is the critical path?
3 Calculate the total float and free float for each of the activities in the network.

Limitations of critical path analysis

Although critical path analysis can help business decision-making, it can have a number of drawbacks and limitations.

- It relies on the estimates for the expected duration. If these prove to be inaccurate, the calculations for earliest start times and latest finish times, and so the critical path analysis, may be wrongly identified. The estimates may be incorrect because some managers may exaggerate how long an activity takes to make it easier for them to complete within the agreed time. On the other hand, some managers may be too optimistic, particularly if these activities have not been carried out before. A more complex version of critical path analysis, called programme evaluation and review technique (PERT), includes a range of estimates for the durations of different activities; PERT produces a number of network diagrams based on optimistic, pessimistic and most likely durations of activities to take account of the fact that estimates cannot be completely relied on.

- If JIT is used for the delivery of materials, the ability to complete the project on time will depend on the reliability of suppliers. If they are late this will prevent the next activity starting on time.
- Critical path analysis simply shows the quickest way to complete a project; it does not guarantee that this is the right project to be undertaking in the first place. It may be that the firm's resources could be used more effectively elsewhere.
- All projects must be managed properly if they are to be completed on time. Drawing up a network diagram is only the starting point. Managers must agree on who is responsible for each stage of the project. They must be given the resources and budget to complete in the time agreed. There must be an effective review system to make sure the project is on schedule and to agree what action to take if it is not. A network diagram can provide a valuable focal point for the management system, but it is up to the managers to make sure that everything is implemented correctly and that each activity is completed on schedule.

Study tip

Some students argue that because the estimates of the durations of activities can be wrong or because changes can happen to delay activities this means that network diagrams are useless. In fact, it is because things can go wrong that these diagrams are so important – because you have planned out what is expected to happen this means that if something goes wrong it is possible to quickly calculate the effect of this in the project and take appropriate action.

Case Study

National Programme for IT

An ambitious multibillion pound programme to create a computerised patient record system across the entire UK NHS was scrapped in 2012. The £12.7 billion ($21.8 billion) National Programme for IT was ended after years of delays, technical difficulties, contractual disputes and rising costs.

The government decided it was better to discontinue the programme rather than put even more money into it.

An announcement has been expected for months after the National Audit Office cast serious doubt on the wisdom of ploughing further money into the scheme.

The problem, say analysts, is that the project was too ambitious and the technology kept changing. The result was that a lot of money was wasted that could have been spent on nurses and improving patient care.

The project has not delivered as targets on dates, functionality, usage and levels of benefit have been delayed and reduced. Providers of NHS care such as hospitals and GP surgeries will now be told to strike IT deals locally and regionally to get the best programes they can afford.

Questions

1 Explain why this project was scrapped. [6]
2 Discuss the possible reasons why this project might have gone wrong. [10]

Other issues in critical path analysis

Before a project is started managers must agree on a definition of success. They must set out exactly what they want to achieve otherwise subordinates may cut corners to get the project done on time. The result may be that the project is completed quickly but that the quality is poor.

Managers must also agree on what resources and spending they are willing to commit to the project. Obviously the quickest way of completing a project will depend on what facilities and resources are available and how much the firm is willing to invest into getting it completed. With more people, more money and more machines the project could probably be speeded up. Whether particular activities can be conducted simultaneously will often depend on whether the firm has or is willing to invest in the necessary resources.

Managers will also be interested in the utilisation of resources throughout the project. It may be that certain activities could be undertaken simultaneously, but that as a result some weeks would require very high levels of personnel whereas in other weeks very few people would be needed. If it adopted such an approach a firm may have to bring in extra staff for the busy week and pay its existing staff to do little in the other weeks. Rather than have such fluctuations in staffing levels managers may want to shift activities around; this may mean that the project takes a bit longer but it may nevertheless be more desirable if it means that its full-time staff are fully employed each week.

Test your learning

Short answer questions

1 What is a project? [1]

2 What does a node show? [1]

3 a What is a network diagram? [2]

   b Explain **one** benefit of constructing a network diagram. [2]

4 State **one** possible problem of constructing a network diagram. [2]

5 What is meant by the earliest start time? [1]

6 What is meant by a dummy activity? [1]

7 What is meant by free float? How is it calculated? [2]

8 What is meant by total float? How is it calculated? [2]

9 What is the critical path on a network diagram? [1]

10 What is the effect of a critical activity overrunning? Why? [2]

Data response question

Boeing Dreamliner

In 2011 Boeing's Dreamliner finally had its first commercial voyage, three years later than planned. An All Nippon Airlines (ANA) flight carried its first passengers from Tokyo to Hong Kong. The Dreamliner had originally been scheduled for delivery in 2008, but Boeing has suffered a string of setbacks throughout the project.

Problems with the Dreamliner have put its launch behind schedule, the latest being an onboard fire during test flights.

Boeing says the twin-aisle, mid-size plane features the industry's largest windows, with higher cabin humidity and cleaner air – all of which combine to allow passengers to arrive at their destinations more refreshed. Also, because of the materials used in construction – carbon fibre rather than aluminium – as well as new engines and aerodynamics, the Dreamliner is about 20 per cent more fuel efficient than other similar-sized models. This is important for the airlines that are concerned about the price of jet fuel.

Boeing plans to make ten of the Dreamliner planes a month from 2013. But the long delay has hurt its business. China Eastern Airlines recently cancelled orders for 24 Dreamliners, rather than wait for production to pick up. Boeing has more than 800 orders on its books for the 787 Dreamliner, and the average list price is $201.7 million.

Questions

1 Analyse the benefits of the Dreamliner to the airlines. [10]

2 Discuss the problems of managing a major new project such as the development of the Dreamliner. [14]

3 Discuss the possible consequences for Boeing of the delay in producing the Dreamliner. [16]

Essay questions

1 To what extent does using network diagrams ensure the success of a project? [20]

2 To what extent is effective project management the key business success these days? [20]

Past paper questions

Read the Forest Product Company case study on pages 464–67 and then answer the following questions.

a Refer to Appendix A.

   i Identify the earliest start time (EST) and latest finish time (LFT) at node 5. [2]

   ii State the length of the critical path. [1]

   iii Calculate the total float on Activity J. [3]

b To what extent will the use of critical path analysis ensure a successful completion of the new sawmill? [8]

Cambridge International AS and A Level Business Studies
9707 Paper 33 Q3 May/June 2011

30 Costing methods

Chapter overview

In this chapter we examine:
- cost and profit centres
- full and contribution costing methods
- solutions to costing problems.

The material in this chapter builds on that which we covered in Chapter 17 (Costs and break-even). You may wish to re-read that chapter before proceeding further.

Key terms

Average costs are the total cost of production divided by the number of units produced.

Direct costs can be related to the production of a particular product and vary directly with the level of output.

Indirect costs are overheads that cannot be allocated to the production of a particular product and which relate to the business as a whole.

Unit costs are the average cost of producing a single unit of output.

30.1 Issues in costing

Costs are expenses that a business has to pay to engage in its trading activities. In Chapter 17 we saw that having accurate information on costs is essential to allow managers to make a range of decisions including what prices to charge, whether a project will be profitable, and whether or not to supply a customer at a specific price.

In making such decisions managers do not simply have to know the overall level of costs but may require further details about the costs the business is likely to face. It is particularly important that they know the following.

- **Direct costs** The wage costs involved in producing as well as the materials or components that may be needed. These are the direct labour and direct materials costs respectively.
- **Indirect costs or overheads** Most of these costs relate to the business as a whole, although a small proportion of overheads may be direct and relate to a single part of a business's operations. Most businesses can face a wide range of indirect costs or overheads:
  - rent and property taxes
  - marketing and distribution costs
  - interest on loans taken out by the business
  - managers' salaries.
- **Unit costs** are the average cost of producing a single unit of output. Unit costs are calculated by dividing total production costs for a period of time by the quantity of products produced over that period. For example, if a television manufacturer produces 12 500 televisions per month and incurs direct and indirect costs of $5 million, its unit cost will be $5 000 000/12 500 = $400. Unit costs are sometimes called **average costs**.

Cost and profit centres

Key terms

A **cost centre** is a distinct part (perhaps a division or department) of a business for which costs can be calculated.

A **profit centre** is similar to a cost centre, being a part of a business for which revenues as well as costs (and thus profits) can be determined.

In many ways **cost centres** and **profit centres** are similar. They both relate to aspects of a business's operation for which it is possible to calculate important figures. In spite of this, there is a distinct difference.

For a cost centre it is only possible to calculate the associated costs. Thus, the accounts department or the department providing IT services to a business could be cost centres. For these areas it is straightforward to calculate costs such as wages and salaries, heating and lighting. However, it is impossible to calculate the revenues earned by areas of the business such as the accounts department as they do not charge separately for their services.

Profit centres can calculate costs and revenues. From this it is possible to determine the profit generated by this aspect of the business's operation. For example, the coffee chain Starbucks owns more than 17 000 outlets in over 50 countries around the world. The company operates each of its stores as a profit centre.

There are a number of ways in which a business can create cost or profit centres within its organisation.

1 Some large businesses might operate a number of factories, offices or branches. In these circumstances profit centres can be developed on a geographical basis. High street banks, such as HSBC, expect branches (or groups of branches) to achieve agreed levels of profits.

2 In manufacturing it is possible to operate smaller cost or profit centres relating to a particular product or even a single production line.

3 A relatively simple approach is to use departments or divisions as cost or profit centres. Hospitals use wards and individual departments such as X-ray to develop cost and profit centres, for example. Many airlines operate separate routes (for example, flights from Hong Kong to Shanghai) as profit centres.

4 Profit and cost centres can also relate to individual products or brands.

Why do businesses operate cost and profit centres?

There are two broad reasons why businesses decide to operate cost and profit centres.

Financial reasons

Managers can gain more detailed information from running a number of separate cost and profit centres, rather than merging all the figures into a single set of financial statements. Having separate cost centres allows managers to compare the costs incurred by various parts of the business. This enables managers to identify those less cost-efficient parts of the business. Senior managers can then attempt to reduce costs in this area, perhaps through more training of staff, creating a more profitable business. Cost centres can also play a part in setting prices – once the cost is known it is possible to set a price to make sure that the brand, product or division earns a profit.

Profit and cost centres allow businesses to take appropriate decisions at a local level. Thus, a large business may be able to set prices at a local level and to charge what the market will bear. This should lead to the business generating higher profits. Businesses may also enjoy more success in controlling costs if people at a local level are responsible for them. Employees who actually spend a firm's money can be very effective in limiting costs if given the responsibility.

Organisational reasons

The financial data provided by cost and profit centres gives managers more in-depth information about the operation of their business. Through the use of this information managers might be able to organise the business more effectively, leading to higher profits.

For example, many businesses are made up of a number of separate elements. Starbucks has more than 17 000 outlets and the data it has collected from these assists the company in deciding the best locations for new outlets. It also enables the company to identify and close unprofitable branches: it has closed more than 300 in the USA alone since 2008.

Companies can also use information from cost or profit centres in other ways. Some part of employees' pay may be linked to the success of the division, department or branch in keeping costs down, or in achieving profit targets. Companies may also use this information in setting targets for all employees, possibly as part of their appraisal system.

The drawbacks of the use of cost and profit centres

Creating a number of profit or cost centres within a business can develop rivalry between the areas. This type of competition can be a positive factor, although it can be destructive if taken too far. For example, possible customer contacts may not be passed on to rival profit centres if it might improve their financial performance.

In some circumstances it is very difficult to divide up costs to create a cost or profit centre. Thus, a manufacturing firm might find it difficult to divide up costs such as rent and rates between the three products that it produces. The case study below illustrates this point and provides an introduction to a discussion of how businesses manage their costs.

Case Study

Guillard Engineering

Guillard Engineering produces components for gas and oil companies operating rigs off the coast of East Kalimantan in Indonesia. Its factory in Balikpapan manufactures three important components: the automatic valve, the pressure sensor and the sea-bed monitor.

The managers of the business operate profit centres for each of the three products, but find it difficult to decide how to divide up the factory's rent and property taxes between the three products. The cost of rent and property taxes each year is $300 000 and this cost has to be split in some way between the three products. It is easy to identify costs such as wages, raw materials and fuel for each of the three products, but rent and property taxes remain a problem.

The Managing Director, Emmanuel Guillard, has suggested three possible approaches.

- Simply split the costs into three – that is allocate costs of $100 000 to each of the three products (and profit centres).
- Divide up the cost of rent and property taxes according to the number of employees working on each of the products.
- Divide up the cost of rent and property taxes according to the value of sales of each of the products.

The Managing Director gave an example of the amount each profit centre will be charged for rent and rates if they were divided up according to the number of employees. The number of employees is as follows:

- the automatic valve – 15 employees
- the pressure sensor – 30 employees
- the sea-bed monitor – 15 employees.

The total number of employees is 60. Thus the automatic valve profit centre should carry (15/60 × $300 000) $75 000 of the cost of rent and property taxes. The pressure sensor profit centre would be charged (30/60 × $300 000) $150 000. Finally, the amount charged to the sea-bed monitor profit centre would be (15/60 × $300 000) $75 000.

Emmanuel Guillard commented that this revealed a weakness in their use of profit centres. The profit earned by each of the three centres will vary according to the way in which the business's rent and rates were divided up between the three areas.

Questions

1 Using the data in the case study analyse two ways in which Emmanuel could divide up (or allocate) the rent and property taxes. [8]
2 Do you think that Guillard Engineering should continue to use profit centres? Justify your decision. [16]

30.2 Full costing

To calculate the total cost of producing a single unit it is necessary to include all costs, both direct and indirect. As we saw in the Guillard Engineering case study above, this can be a tricky process if it is to provide accurate costing figures. The problem centres on allocating indirect costs or overheads in a way that represents the true costs of producing a product or operating a division within a business.

Case Study

Full costing at Rajasthan Electronics

Rajasthan Electronics Ltd manufactures consumer electronics which are sold in Pakistan and other countries in Asia. The company's production is divided into three product groups: televisions, microwave cookers and digital radios.

The costs associated with the company's production over the last financial year are shown in Table 30.1.

Table 30.1

	Televisions $m	Microwave cookers $m	Digital radios $m	Total $m
Revenue from sales	286	145	225	656
Direct materials costs	107	77	78	262
Direct labour costs	97	45	87	229
Total direct costs	204	122	165	491
Allocated overheads	52	27	41	120
Total costs	256	149	206	611
Profit	30	(4)	19	45

The company's managers have used a policy of full costing to calculate its costs and profits on its three products which are made in the same factory in Faisalabad. The company's overheads were $120 million for the year. Rajasthan Electronics' managers decided to allocate the company's overheads on the basis of the percentage of revenue earned by each division. The calculations (with some rounding) carried out by the finance department are shown below:

- Allocated overheads to televisions: $120 m × 286/656 = $52 million
- Allocated overheads to microwaves: $120 m × 145/656 = $27 million
- Allocated overheads to digital radios: $120 m × 225/656 = $41 million

Total overheads = $120 million

The managers' decision to allocate overheads in this way resulted in two of its divisions earning profits while the third, the microwave division, recorded a small loss. Not all of the company's managers agreed with this approach to allocating overheads and the managers of the microwave division were angry at suggestions that production of microwaves should be stopped as they were apparently making a loss rather than a profit.

Questions

1 Analyse other possible ways that Rajasthan Electronics Ltd might have allocated its overheads. [8]
2 Do you think Rajasthan Electronics Ltd should stop producing microwave cookers? Justify your decision. [16]

Allocating costs

Full costing allocates all the costs of production (both direct and indirect or overheads) for the whole business. Therefore these costs are absorbed into each cost unit. This is also known as absorption casting.

Thus, if a business makes two or more products, or operates multiple divisions or brands, full costing entails allocating (or 'absorbing') indirect costs as accurately as possible to the different parts of the business's operations. If a business only produced two products it could allocate its overheads taking into account the type of overhead.

- Indirect costs or overheads such as rent, property taxes and fuel could be allocated or apportioned according to relative floor space taken up by the production of the two products. So, if product A takes up 60 per cent of the floor space then 60 per cent of these indirect costs should be apportioned to product A.
- Depreciation of assets such as vehicles could be apportioned according to the relative value of assets used in the production of the two products.
- Overheads wage costs associated with management and administrative staff could be allocated according to the number of people directly employed in the production of each product.

This may produce a more accurate division of the relevant overheads, though it is unlikely to be entirely accurate. Nevertheless, as many businesses produce more than a single product, especially large-scale businesses, this approach to costing is widely used. It is also accepted by many governments as the accepted method to use in preparing financial statements. This trend is also increasing as markets become more global in nature and businesses have to extend their product ranges to meet the diverse needs of customers across the world. Nevertheless, when a business produces a range of products (as in the case of Rajasthan Electronics Ltd) it requires managers to make difficult decisions to allocate overheads.

Further events at Rajasthan Electronics

The managers of the microwave division are concerned about proposals to end production of their cookers. In response they have recalculated the company's profits for the past financial year using full costing, but using a different basis for allocating overheads.

The company's operations managers have recently reported that the production of televisions uses 46 per cent of the factory's floor space, that digital radios uses 39 per cent and microwave cooker production takes place in 15 per cent of the available factory space. This was used as a basis to recalculate the profits from the three product ranges.

Their revised calculations (again with some rounding) are shown below:

- Allocated overheads to televisions: $120 m × 0.46 = $55 million
- Allocated overheads to microwaves: $120 m × 0.15 = $18 million
- Allocated overheads to digital radios: $120 m × 0.39 = $47 million

Total overheads = $120 million

This allowed the managers to present a revised set of profit figures as shown in Table 30.2.

Questions

1 Analyse the reasons why a large business might use full costing. [8]
2 Discuss whether this is a more accurate way of calculating the company's profits for its three product ranges than the approach based on the percentages of revenues earned by the divisions. [16]

Maths moment

Calculate the following using the data in the Rajasthan Electronics case study.

1 The percentage of total costs that are represented by direct labour costs.
2 The change in the company's profits if it managed to reduce its direct materials costs by 10 per cent.

In the case of Rajasthan Electronics Ltd the use of full costing makes it very difficult to judge with any certainty the precise financial position of the company's three product ranges. There is a danger that the company's senior managers may judge that the microwave division is unprofitable and decide to discontinue production of this product. This could prove to be a poor decision for two reasons.

Table 30.2

	Televisions $m	Microwaves $m	Digital radios $m	Total $m
Revenue from sales	286	145	225	656
Direct materials costs	107	77	78	262
Direct labour costs	97	45	87	229
Total direct costs	204	122	165	491
Allocated overheads	55	18	47	120
Total costs	259	140	212	611
Profit	27	5	13	45

1 The microwave division may be profitable.
2 If production of microwaves is discontinued the business's overheads are unlikely to change and will have to be paid by the remaining two divisions, which will damage the profitability of the company.

Case Study

A possible scenario at Rajasthan Electronics

As part of their case to persuade the company's senior managers to continue production of microwave cookers, the managers of the microwave division have calculated the company's profitability without microwaves and assuming that overheads do not change. Some of their figures are shown in Table 30.3.

Table 30.3

	Televisions $m	Digital radios $m	Total $m
Revenue from sales	286	225	
Direct materials costs	107	78	185
Direct labour costs	97	87	184
Total direct costs	204	165	369
Allocated overheads	67	53	120
Total costs	271		
Profit			

Questions

1 Complete Table 30.3 by calculating the missing figures. [5]
2 Do you think the decision to discontinue the production of microwave cookers would be a good one on the basis of these figures? Justify your view. [16]

There are, of course, advantages and disadvantages to using full costing. These are summarised in Table 30.4.

Table 30.4 The advantages and disadvantages of the use of full costing

Advantages	Disadvantages
• The business will have taken all of its costs into account before making pricing decisions. • Full costing is the approach that the International Financial Reporting Standards (IFRS) requires for the preparation of financial statements. • Managers have to give thought as to the most effective method of allocating overheads which may result in an accurate approach.	• It is difficult to allocate overheads accurately – the allocation is often based on proportions of direct costs. • It can result in bad decisions. Businesses may discontinue production of apparently unprofitable divisions, departments or brands. • If sales are below what is expected, allocated overheads per unit of production could be higher than forecast meaning that a price that was expected to be profitable may not be.

30.3 Contribution costing

Key terms

Profits are the amount by which revenue exceeds total costs, although there are several different measures of profit.

Contribution can be defined as the difference between sales revenue and direct costs of production.

Contribution costing calculates the cost of a product solely on the basis of direct costs, thus avoiding the need to allocate overheads.

Marginal cost is the extra cost resulting from producing one additional unit of output.

Calculating contribution and profits

The concept of **contribution** is an important one and is used in calculating break-even output. It involves the calculation of direct costs (likely to be variable costs) but not indirect costs or overheads (likely to be fixed costs).

Thus contribution can be calculated by use of the formula below:

Sales – Direct costs = Contribution

Contribution has two potential uses: firstly, it is used to pay overheads incurred by a business. Any contribution remaining after this transaction is **profit** for the business.

Contribution – Overheads = Profit

Secondly, contribution is important in calculating break-even output and is a central element of the formula that is used.

It is possible to consider contribution in two broad ways – either in relation to a single unit of output or in relation to the entire output of a particular product or business.

When contribution is calculated for the sale of a single product, we refer to it as contribution per unit. It is calculated by using the formula:

Contribution per unit = Selling price of one unit
of output – direct costs of
producing that unit

The direct cost of producing an additional unit is its **marginal cost** as we saw in Chapter 17.

For example, a brewery produces its beer with direct costs of $2.00 a bottle (the marginal cost) and sells it for $3.75 a bottle. The contribution earned from the sale of each bottle (or unit) will be $1.75.

Study tip

This way of considering contribution is particularly useful when calculating break-even. It is the basis of a simple and quick calculation, which is valuable when answering exam questions.

More on contribution costing

Contribution costing is sometimes referred to as marginal costing. **Contribution costing** excludes overheads as a central part of the calculation and only allocates direct costs.

The principle of contribution costing is valuable in a business that has a number of products, or several factories or divisions. A product or division that earns sufficient revenue to cover its overheads is likely to be viewed favourably by the managers of the business. If this is the case then the product will generate a positive contribution and assist in paying overheads or providing profit.

We can apply the contribution costing approach to the production and sale of a single unit or output or to the entire output of a product or products over some time period. If a business would incur an additional cost of $100 in producing a single extra unit of output (this is its marginal cost) but would expect to sell that product for $125, then it would make a positive contribution of $25 on that unit of output.

Alternatively we can consider contribution costing for the entire production of a particular product or products as shown in Table 30.5.

Table 30.5 Sales revenue, direct cost and contribution for a business producing three products

	Product A $	Product B $	Product C $
Revenue from sales	175 000	342 750	55 250
Direct labour costs	87 150	169 700	14 525
Direct materials costs	32 000	88 560	12 770
Other direct costs	25 450	67 425	13 050
Total direct costs	144 600	325 685	40 345
Contribution	30 400	17 065	14 905

The example in Table 30.5 shows that Product A contributes $30 400 towards paying overheads, Product B $17 065 and Product C $14 905. In total this is $62 370. If we assume that the overheads (or indirect costs) of the company for this period of time are $39 500 we can calculate the profits that the company has made.

Total contribution: $62 370
Overheads: $39 500
Profit: $22 870

If a product makes a positive contribution, as is the case in Table 30.5, then it is worth the business continuing to produce it. There may even be an argument for continuing to produce it if it makes a negative contribution, as we shall see later.

30.4 Contribution costing and decision-making

One of the key advantages of using contribution costing is that it can help managers to make some important decisions.

Special order decisions

Businesses sometimes have to make decisions on whether to accept orders that are not on their normal terms. Thus a firm might receive a large order for its products at a price significantly lower than it usually receives. Alternatively, a business might receive an order which offers a price above the usual, but which requires special features or a very early delivery date, meaning the supplier is likely to incur additional costs in fulfilling the order.

Firms faced with the dilemma of whether to accept this type of order are encountering special order decisions. In these circumstances the concept of contribution can be applied to assist the business in reaching a decision on whether or not to accept the order.

Prices lower than normal

It is not unusual for a firm to receive an order for a large quantity of its products at a price below that normally charged. Consider the case study below.

Margaret Roberts Woollens Ltd

Figure 30.1 One unit on which contribution costing could be applied

Margaret Roberts Ltd manufactures sweaters and other woollen garments for local shops at a standard price of $40. The sweaters are very popular with tourists and sell for high prices, particularly during the summer season. The cost of wool (direct materials) and the wages paid to knitters (direct labour) means that the average direct cost of producing a single woollen garment is $30. To the surprise of the managing director of the firm a large order is received from a national clothes retailer. The retailer requires 5000 sweaters and other garments, but is only willing to pay Margaret Roberts Ltd $32 per item. Should Margaret Roberts Ltd accept the order?

Contribution is the key to making this decision. The firm would earn a positive contribution on each sale. Each woollen item sold would incur variables costs of $30, but would earn revenue of $32. Thus each sale would create $2 of contribution. Therefore, meeting the order would earn the business an additional $10 000 in contribution. This *might* mean profits would rise (or losses would fall) by $10 000.

Questions

1 Analyse the reasons why accepting this order may not increase the level of profits earned by Margaret Roberts Ltd. [8]

2 Evaluate the non-financial factors the managers at Margaret Roberts Ltd might consider before deciding whether or not to accept this order. [16]

However, a number of factors need to be taken into account when taking special order decisions such as this.

- Will additional fixed costs result from accepting the order? In the circumstances above Margaret Roberts Ltd may have to hire additional factory space, increasing overheads, meaning that additional contribution is required to meet these costs before extra profits are earned. Thus if the firm has to pay an extra $10 000 in rent then profits will be unchanged as a result of accepting the order. Therefore having sufficient spare capacity is an important pre-requisite of accepting such an order.
- Might the order lead to higher variable costs? Accepting a large order might mean that workers are paid overtime, pushing up direct costs. Workers at Margaret Roberts Ltd might be paid higher hourly rates, meaning that the variable cost of producing a single item rises to $35. In these circumstances the order would not be worth accepting.
- Before accepting a special order decision (at a price below the norm) a business needs to ensure that the customer will not simply resell the product to other firms at the usual selling price, thereby making a quick profit at the expense of the manufacturer.
- A business may accept a lower price than normal, even if it doesn't produce a positive contribution, if it believes that it will result in more sales at higher prices in the future.

Study tip

When responding to questions on special order decisions (or costing decisions generally) it is important to consider non-financial factors as well as financial ones. Read the case study or stimulus material carefully to ensure you pick up on any non-financial factors that may have been included as clues.

Prices higher than normal

It may appear a stroke of good fortune for a business to receive an order at a price above that usually levied. However, if the order requires products to have a specification higher than normal or to be delivered at short notice it is likely that the supplier will face higher costs. This may make the order unprofitable.

Once again contribution is the key to the decision. If the selling price exceeds the direct costs and no additional overheads are incurred, the order would be worthwhile and would result in increased profits. Thus if Margaret Roberts Ltd had an order for a new style of sweater which needed more expensive wool than normal and had to be complete within six weeks, the firm would need to:

- calculate the extra direct costs associated with the order – overtime pay for workers and more expensive materials, for example
- consider whether it had sufficient spare capacity to meet the order – avoiding additional overheads
- decide whether accepting the order would generate extra contribution and profits.

Qualitative factors

Qualitative factors are often important in such decisions. Accepting an order such as that received by Margaret Roberts Woollens Ltd may offer long-term benefits. The customer may return with further orders and it may help to increase brand awareness in new markets. It may help the business concerned to achieve its corporate aims, especially if these are growth or increasing market share.

On the other hand, the consideration of qualitative factors may result in a decision not to supply a special order. It may be regarded as too risky. For example, managers may believe that allowing their products to be sold in large quantities at lower prices could damage its brand image. It may, for example, make the product appear less exclusive and make it difficult to charge higher prices in other markets. Sales and profit margins may fall as a consequence.

Table 30.6 Contribution and decision-making: strengths and weaknesses

Strengths	Weaknesses
• Assists managers in multi-product firms in making decisions by giving an overview of the entire business • Avoids the need for the arbitrary division of overheads • Can provide a flexible basis for pricing decisions	• Pricing decisions based on contribution do not take market conditions into account • Some costs are difficult to classify as direct or overheads • In the longer-term overheads can change, invalidating earlier decisions based on contribution

Decisions on whether to continue production

Table 30.7 An example of contribution costing

Product	A	B	C
Revenue ($000s)	242	158	485
Direct costs ($000s)	175	98	488
Contribution ($000s)	67	60	(3)

In the example shown in Table 30.7 products A and B generate a positive contribution that is available to pay overheads and provide profits. Product C incurs direct costs that are higher than the revenue earned and will not therefore help to pay

overheads. It may be appropriate to abandon this product, but a final decision will depend upon a number of factors, including the following:

- whether demand for the product may increase in the future, or if higher prices can be charged
- if the firm can increase its output of other products to use any spare capacity it may have if it ceases producing one product
- whether overheads will fall as a consequence of the decision
- the impact of the decision on the business – for example, the effects on industrial relations and productivity resulting from redundancies.

But would the business in Table 30.7 make a profit? The answer to this depends upon the level of overheads incurred by the firm. The total contribution earned by these three products is ($67 000 + $60 000 – $3000) $124 000. In these circumstances if overheads are less than $124 000, the firm will make a profit. If they exceed $124 000, a loss will result.

However, this approach to costing is based upon the business's ability to categorise its costs as direct and overheads. In many cases this is straightforward, but on occasions it may be difficult to decide, making it more difficult to use this approach to costing.

Case Study

The Marlborough Pottery

Figure 30.2 Pots – an unprofitable line?

This company makes a range of products that are sold in gift shops throughout New Zealand. The business has a reputation for high quality products and traditionally has sold to a market segment comprising older consumers, mainly female. Overall sales have declined slowly in recent years.

The company has three product lines: mugs and cups, plates and pots. The managers of the company have been concerned for some time that their business is not sufficiently profitable and is vulnerable to competition from larger firms.

In particular the management team has been dissatisfied with the profits generated by the sale of pots (Table 30.8).

The production manager has argued that the line should be discontinued if the company is to improve its profitability. He argues that if the company's overheads are divided equally between the three product lines, it is obvious that pots are not a profitable item.

Table 30.8

Product	Mugs and cups $000s	Plates £000s	Pots $000s	Total $000s
Sales revenue	575	450	227	1252
Less direct costs	352	326	189	867
Less overheads	101	101	101	303
PROFIT	122	23	(63)	82

Other managers hold different views. The finance manager offers a different presentation of the data on costs and revenues in Table 30.9. She argues that Marlborough Pottery would still face the same overheads and that to sell more mugs, cups or plates would require a price cut.

Table 30.9

Product	Mugs and cups $000s	Plates $000s	Pots $000s	Total $000s
Sales revenue	575	450	227	1252
Less direct costs	352	326	189	867
Contribution	223	124	38	385
Less overheads	171	102	30	303
PROFIT	52	22	8	82

It can be seen from the table that all the products make a positive contribution. In other words their revenues or earnings exceed the direct costs of production (labour, fuel, raw materials. etc.).

A decision to shut down the production of pots would reduce profits unless the production of other products could be increased. The financial consequences of this decision are illustrated in Table 30.10.

Table 30.10

Product	Mugs and cups $000s	Plates $000s	Total $000s
Sales revenue	575	450	1025
Less direct costs	352	326	678
Contribution	223	124	347
Less overheads	192	111	303
PROFIT			

Cutting what appears to be a relatively unprofitable line may not be worthwhile unless overheads will be reduced (for example, through the sale of a factory) or the production and sale of other products increased. The concept of contribution has been helpful in calculating the profits of the business and also in making decisions based upon financial data.

Questions

1 Use the data in the case study tables to calculate the effects on the company's profits resulting from a decision to discontinue the production of vases. [8]
2 Discuss the value of the use of contribution costing in these circumstances. [16]

Test your learning

Short answer questions

1 a Distinguish between direct costs and overheads. [3]
  b State the formula used to calculate unit costs. [2]

2 Using examples, explain the difference between a profit centre and a cost centre. [5]

3 a State **two** ways in which a large business might create cost or profit centres. [2]
  b Explain **one** financial reason why a coffee shop chain such as Starbucks might operate profit centres. [3]

4 a Define the term full costing. [2]
  b State **three** ways in which a large manufacturing business might allocate its overheads between the different products that it supplies. [3]

5 Explain why it might be difficult for the manufacturer in question 4b to allocate its overheads accurately. [5]

6 a State **two** reasons why a business might decide to use full costing. [2]
  b Explain why the use of full costing can result in poor quality decisions by managers. [3]

7 a Distinguish between profit and contribution. [3]
  b How would a business calculate the marginal cost of a single unit of output? [2]

8 Explain why contribution costing avoids the need to allocate overheads. [5]

9 Explain why a business might decide to accept an order for its products at a price of $300 per unit when its normal selling price is $400 per unit. [5]

10 a Explain **one** weakness of contribution costing. [3]

b State **two** reasons why managers might decide to continue production of a product even if its contribution is negative. [2]

Data response question

Thurgau Watches Ltd

Thurgau Watches Ltd is a manufacturer of luxury watches based in north-east Switzerland. It has three brands: the Arbon, the St Gallen and its famous Zurich watches. The company has suffered a decline in profits in recent years and is considering two possible approaches: entering new geographical markets, especially in Asia, and/or launching new products.

The company's newly appointed finance director has experienced difficulties dividing up the company's overheads and wants to use contribution costing. The company is based on a single site and most overhead costs relate to all of its production.

Table 1 Sales revenue, direct costs and overheads for Thurgau Watches Ltd for the last financial year

	Arbon watch $	St Gallen watch $	Zurich watch $
Revenue from sales	**1400000**	**3400000**	**2750 000**
Direct labour costs	456000	670000	427000
Direct materials costs	202500	1080000	721250
Other direct costs	335500	535000	605750
Total direct costs	994000	2285000	1754000
Allocated overheads	420000	1020000	825000
Profits		95 000	171 000

Sales of the Arbon watch are slowly increasing after a poor trading period, but some managers believe that it should be abandoned and the company should try to develop a new watch brand.

Last week Thurgau Watches received an order for 500 Arbon watches per year over the next three years at $2000 per watch

from a major retailer in China. This brand sells for an average of $2500 normally. The finance director estimates that the additional direct costs per year resulting from an acceptance of this order will be $975000. She is unsure whether or not to accept the order.

Questions

1 Analyse the benefits to Thurgau Watches Ltd of switching to the use of contribution costing. [10]

2 a Calculate the profit or loss earned by the Arbon watch last year. [2]

   b Calculate the total profit earned by Thurgau Watches last year. [2]

   c Assess the case for ceasing production of the Arbon watch. [10]

3 Should Thurgau Watches Ltd accept the order from China? Justify your decision. [16]

Essay questions

1 It is very common for businesses to use full costing. Does this mean that its advantages always outweigh its disadvantages? Justify your view. [20]

2 Discuss the extent to which contribution costing is the most relevant costing method for all businesses today. [20]

Past paper question

Read the Radar Cosmetics case study on pages 456–58 and then answer the following question.

Do you agree with the Chief Executive that the company should stop producing the 'Aquaskin Junior' cream? Use the quantitative data in Table 1, relevant calculations and the qualitative information available to justify your answer. [16]

Cambridge International AS and A Level Business Studies 9707 Paper 31 Q2 October/November 2010

31 Budgets

Chapter overview

In this chapter we examine:
- the purpose of budgets and the benefits and drawbacks of their use
- the meaning, calculation and interpretation of variances.

Key terms

A **budget** is a financial plan.

A **cost centre** is a distinct part (perhaps a division or department) of a business for which costs can be calculated.

A **profit centre** is similar to a cost centre, being a part of a business for which revenues as well as costs (and thus profits) can be determined.

31.1 Preparing and using budgets

What are budgets?

Budgets are financial plans. Firms plan their earnings and expenditures using budgets. Budgets are usually drawn up on a monthly basis, over the period of a financial year.

There are a number of types of budgets.

- **Sales revenue or income budgets** These set out the business's expected sales revenue from selling its products. Important information here includes the expected level of sales and the likely selling price of the product. A start-up business may have relatively low revenue budgets during its first few months of trading. It is likely that the sales revenue budgets will be increased as the business becomes better known. In contrast, an established business may have a large and loyal customer base and substantial inflows of revenue from a range of different products or brands, for different regions or from a number of subsidiary companies.

- **Production or expenditure budgets** Businesses need to plan their expenditure on labour, raw materials, fuel and other items which are essential for the process of production. Research is necessary to prepare accurate expenditure budgets. For example, an independent forecast revealed that wages in countries in Asia are expected to rise by between 2.3 per cent and 12 per cent – this would be important data for Asian firms with large workforces. The production budget will also contain forecasts for expenditure on overheads and a cash budget as well.

- **Budgeted income statements and statements of financial position** By combining sales revenue and expenditure budgets it is possible to calculate expected profits or forecast losses and therefore to draw up a budgeted income statement for the forecast trading period. At the same time managers can forecast a budgeted statement of financial position for the business.

Budgets as a measure of performance

For many businesses the figures in the profit budget will have an important influence on decision-making within the business.

If forecast profits are low or declining, the business's managers may have to take decisions to improve the financial performance of the business. This may entail changing prices and reducing costs in the short term. In the longer term management teams may consider entering new markets and developing new products as a means of improving financial performance.

However, it may be that the poor figures only relate to a single part of the business. The provision of detailed budgets on expected sales can reveal much about the forecast performance of individual **profit centres** within a large business. This information can help managers to make decisions on which areas of the business are likely to perform well and those that may not. Using this information, managers can make decisions on how to allocate financial, human and other resources most effectively.

Study tip

Remember that budgets are forecast data and may be incorrect. You should read any case study material carefully to see if there is any evidence about its likely accuracy and use this to help to develop your answers.

Similarly, information on expenditure budgets allows senior managers to examine those areas of a business that manage costs effectively. The most successful areas (possibly cost or profit centres) can become models for other parts of the business.

Case Study

Hotels in Singapore

Singapore, along with Hong Kong, has the highest rate of hotel occupancy in the world. The tourist boards in the two cities announced that in 2013 more than 85 per cent of their hotel rooms were occupied at any given time. This occupancy rate is higher than in some of the world's most popular tourist destinations such as London.

However, hotels in Singapore are forecasting that their high occupancy rates are unlikely to remain at such high levels over future years. There are two major causes of this expected decline in room occupancy rates. Firstly, a number of new hotels are due to open in the city: the number of four- and five-star hotel rooms in Singapore is expected to increase by 17.4 per cent by 2014. This is likely to reduce room rates as well as the profits earned by the hotels. Secondly, businesses are cutting their travel and accommodation budgets and fewer business people are staying in the city's hotels. Future spending on travel and accommodation, especially by Western businesses, will depend on the performance of the global economy.

City Developments Ltd (CDL) is a property company and operates four- and five-star hotels in Singapore. It 2012 it reported that its hotels were performing less strongly in financial terms. The average amount earned from its rooms was RM522 ($210) in autumn 2012. This was a decline of 3.7 per cent from the rate achieved in the summer.

Questions

1 Explain why the changes forecast in the case study might have a significant impact on the sales revenue budgets of the hotel division of CDL. [8]
2 Discuss why it might be difficult for hotel companies in Singapore to forecast future sales revenues accurately. [16]

There is the risk, of course, that the information in budgets may not prove to be accurate. For example, sales revenue budgets may be incorrect if there is an unexpected slump in sales due to,

say, a change in consumers' tastes and fashions or the entry of a new competitor into a specific market.

Why businesses set budgets

There are a number of reasons why a business will plan future costs and revenues using budgets.

- To assist businesses in controlling their finances by planning their expenditure over a future period, usually a year. It is not unusual for businesses to have budgets of many millions, or even billions, of dollars. In such circumstances it is impossible for a single person, or even a group of people, to effectively monitor these budgets to ensure costs are controlled and planned revenues earned. A system of budgets allows a large number of people within the organisation to take a share of responsibility for managing finances.
- Budgets are an effective way of ensuring that a business does not spend more than it should. As long as every employee ensures that they do not spend in excess of their budget, costs should not get out of control. Equally, if those involved in sales meet their targets then the business should earn its planned level of profit. This should help the business achieve its objectives.
- Businesses use budgets to assess the viability of new projects such as launching a new product or relocating to a new region or country. In this case the research process involved in preparing the necessary budgets is helpful and the final budget figures are likely to have a major influence on a final decision by senior managers.
- In many businesses the budgeting process can be a way in which employees are motivated. Giving relatively junior managers responsibility for setting and monitoring budgets can provide motivation (for example, by fulfilling Maslow's self-esteem needs) and may lead to an improvement in performance. Achieving the financial targets set within a budget may also improve the motivation and performance of individuals or teams.
- Monitoring budgets is a vital part of managing a business successfully. Managers can use a technique known as variance analysis (which we consider later in this chapter) to examine the difference between the budget figures they forecast and the actual figures that were recorded. This enables managers to take a range of decisions to help the business to operate smoothly and efficiently. For example, managers may spot overspending at an early stage and correct it before too much damage is done to the business's finances.

Delegated budgets

Recently, firms have given control of budgets to individuals and teams at all levels within the business. This has been accompanied by a reduction in the number of managers and an attempt to give workers more control over their working lives. Allowing them to take some decisions relating to finance through delegated budgets is an important part of this. The intentions behind these changes are:

- to reduce the number of managers, cutting wage costs
- to motivate employees by giving them more diverse and responsible jobs
- to help encourage employees at all levels to play a part in decision-making and problem-solving.

Many companies have made use of delegated budgets in an attempt to improve their performance. Their use has also been extended to organisations in the public sector, for example hospitals, schools and colleges.

The advantages and disadvantages of budgets

As with most techniques of financial control, there are advantages and disadvantages to the use of budgets.

The advantages of budgets

- Production or expenditure budgets allow managers to ensure that a business does not overspend. Senior managers receive their own budgets and can allocate these between the various parts of the department or area for which they are responsible. Figure 31.1 illustrates this process. As long as each individual budget holder makes sure that they do not spend more than the agreed figure, the business's overall expenditure should remain under control. Modern technology makes the control and monitoring of such budgets easier.

- Budgets allow senior managers to direct extra funds into important areas of the business. Thus, if a business is concerned that its product range is not selling well, it may increase its budgets in the areas of market research as well as research and development or advertising.
- Budgets can be used to motivate employees. Employees can gain satisfaction from being given responsibility for a budget. They may also gain satisfaction from keeping within a budget. As a result their level of motivation and their performance may improve, benefiting the firm as a whole. In Chapter 7 we considered motivation in more detail.
- Sales revenue budgets can also be used as targets for employees, possibly as part of the appraisal process. Employees may be motivated to improve their performance by the existence of targets in the forms of sales revenue budgets. By drawing together these sales revenue budgets the firm can attempt to achieve its overall objectives in terms of sales revenue or market share.

The disadvantages of budgets

- If a business intends that a significant proportion of its employees should manage budgets (known as delegating budgets) then training will be required. Some people will not welcome the extra responsibility or feel confident of their ability to control finances. The cost of the training could be substantial, depending on the skills of the workforce. Furthermore, there could be teething problems as employees adjust to the new roles and responsibilities.

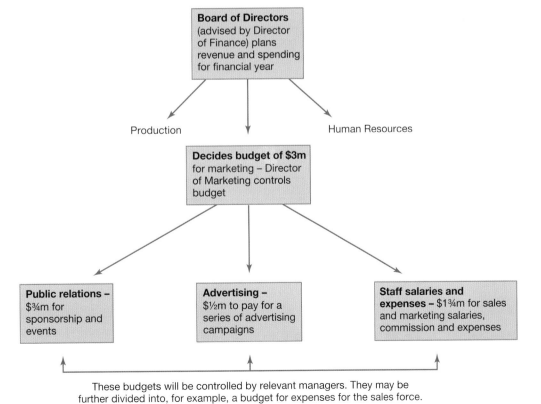

Figure 31.1 An example of using budgets within a company

Allocating budgets fairly and in the best interests of the business is difficult. Some managers may be skilled at negotiating large budgets for the areas for which they are responsible. This might be at the expense of more worthy areas. Thus, for example, a manager responsible for the sales force in existing markets may receive a large budget allocation, while insufficient funds are given to developing new markets.

Budgets normally relate to the current financial year only and are short term in nature. Thus managers might take decisions in order to keep within the current budget which is not in the longer-term interest of the business. For example, a decision to reduce the size of a workforce for budgetary reasons might result in competitors gaining more of the market over the next few years.

Case Study

Online shopping in Pakistan

Daraz, an online fashion store in Pakistan, has just released an infographic (Figure 31.2) promoting its progress so far. Since its launch in July 2012, Daraz.pk has amassed 360 brands on its site, and 14 000 clothing and accessory items – for both men and women – are now being sold there.

The really surprising figure is that over 50 per cent of Daraz's orders come from outside the major cities in Pakistan. Given that Pakistan has an internet penetration rate of only around 15 per cent, it is surprising that so many orders come from outside of better-connected urban areas. However, Daraz has delivered to over 170 cities in Pakistan, meaning there's still plenty of scope for growth.

Daraz.pk gets 500 000 unique visits per month. This compares fairly well against the 15 million visits to its sister site Zalora, which operates in ten countries across South East Asia, Australia and New Zealand.

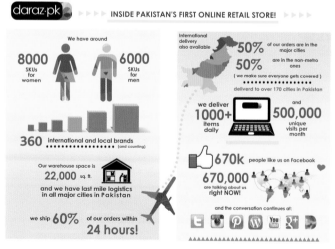

Figure 31.2 A page from the website of Daraz

Source: Adapted from Tech in Asia, 15 January 2014
http://www.techinasia.com

Daraz is delivering over 1000 items daily, though there's no indication of how much people are spending or how many orders those represent.

Questions

1 Explain why budgeting would be important to Daraz at this stage in the business's development. [8]
2 Do you believe that Daraz can draw up accurate budgets? Justify your view. [16]

The process of creating budgets

Before firms can start to write their budgets for the coming year, they need to carry out some research. This may involve:

- analysing the market to predict likely trends in sales and prices to help plan sales revenue
- analysing likely actions and reactions of competitors in the market
- researching costs for labour, fuel and raw materials by contacting suppliers and seeing if they can negotiate price reductions for prompt payment or ordering in bulk
- considering government estimates for wage rises and inflation and incorporating these into future sales revenue and expenditure budgets.

Once a business has collected the necessary data, it is normal to draw up expected revenues from selling products – the sales revenue budget. This is the first budget because, once a firm knows its expected sales, it can plan its production.

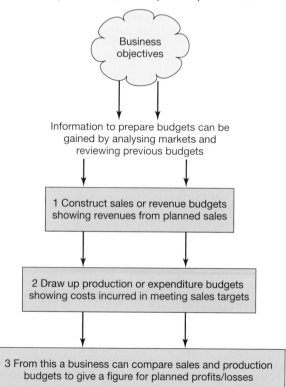

Figure 31.3 The budget setting process

Planning production will entail considering:
- the different types of goods and services that need to be produced and the quantity of goods and services that will be required
- the quantities (and cost) of materials that will be required to meet production plans – this could include components and fuel as well as raw materials
- the labour input that will be necessary for production to take place
- the overheads, sales and administration expenses that will be incurred by the planned level of production.

Taking these decisions enables the business to forecast the expenditure or costs associated with producing a sufficient quantity to match planned sales. It is vital in the setting of expenditure budgets that expendtiure on production allows a sufficient quantity and variety of products to be supplied that will match the forecasted sales. It is impossible for a business to increase its sales without producing more of its goods or services to supply to customers.

Once production budgets and sales budgets are completed, it is possible to compare revenues and expenditure. This allows managers to prepare three further budgets which provide a vital overview of the business's financial position over the future trading period. These are:
- a cash budget showing the expected sources of cash inflows and planned cash expenditures
- a budgeted income statement setting out the business's expected profits or losses
- a budgeted statement of financial position for some future date stating its forecast assets and liabilities.

Case Study

Setting a first budget

Figure 31.4 A selection of handmade soaps

Vixen Soap Ltd is due to start trading in two months' time. The company's owners, Paul and Hayley Hills, are planning to manufacture a range of handmade soaps including those made from olive oil, lavender, camomile and champagne as well as organic soaps. The intention is to sell these products using the internet and a modern and effective website has been developed to promote the new company and its products as well as to provide a method of selling the soaps.

Table 31.1 Vixen Soap Ltd's budget

Vixen Soap Ltd – Budgets			
	January $	February $	March $
Sales of scented/flavoured soaps	7450	12560	17500
Sales of organic soaps	2765	3400	4125
Total sales	**10215**	**15960**	**21625**

Purchases of raw materials	19500	14010	15550
Packaging	1215	1105	1350
Wages and salaries	3000	2850	2995
Marketing and administration	2450	2400	2450
Other costs	975	1100	1075
Total costs	**27140**	**21465**	**23420**
Profit/Loss	(16925)	(5505)	(1795)

Paul and Hayley have prepared a detailed business plan including sales, expenditure and profit budgets for the first year of trading. They conducted extensive primary and secondary market research which suggested that the company's unique range of high quality products will prove popular and sales are expected to rise steadily. However, initial costs are expected to be high as the company builds up an inventory of products ready for sale.

Paul and Hayley began the process of setting budgets by estimating the company's sales using the market research data. By combining the likely volume of sales with the expected prices, the sales revenue budget was developed. For example, Hayley had forecast that in January the company would sell 5000 bars of scented and flavoured soap at $1.49 each, giving a sales revenue of $7450.

Once the level of forecast sales was decided, it was possible for the company to calculate its expected costs of production. As with many new businesses, production costs are initially high. The company has to build up inventories of its full range of soaps to enable it to supply customers promptly. At the same time production costs have to reflect forecast sales. Thus variable costs of production are forecast to rise in February and March as sales increase.

The company's sales revenue, expenditure and profit budgets for its first three months of trading are shown in Table 31.1.

Questions

1 Explain the benefits that Paul and Hayley Hills might receive as a result of setting budgets. [8]

2 Discuss the extent to which their budgets are likely to prove to be inaccurate. [16]

Difficulties in setting budgets

Setting a budget is not always an easy exercise – all businesses encounter problems in setting accurate budgets.

- **It may be difficult to forecast sales accurately** Managers may find it difficult to estimate their sales when setting the sales revenue budget. For a new business this is a particular problem as there are no trading records on which to base forecasts. It is always easier to set a budget if a previous year's figures can be amended – for example, increasing sales by 5 per cent if the market is growing. Businesses frequently rely on market research to provide guidance in forecasting sales. If this research is inaccurate or incomplete, sales forecasts will probably prove incorrect. Changes in tastes and fashions can occur rapidly, especially in music, leisure and clothing industries, making accurate forecasts more difficult to achieve. Similarly, the pace of change in high technology industries, such as personal computers, makes the process of planning sales very tricky.

- **The danger of unexpected changes** Forecasting events for the next year is fraught with difficulty. The average wage rate in China is expected to rise by 10 per cent during 2014. If changes such as this are not forecast and incorporated into budgets it may result in expenditure above budget figures, reducing their accuracy and effectiveness as a control mechanism.

- **Decisions by governments and other public bodies** These can make it difficult to set accurate budgets. In January 2014 the Reserve Bank of India increased its interest rates from 7.75 per cent to 8 per cent in a surprise move to control inflation. This is likely to have decreased the sales of many businesses, especially those selling consumer durables and expensive products such as cars and housing which are often purchased using loans. Costs can also rise due, for example, to an increase in taxes that may not have been forecast.

- **Using managers' time effectively** Setting budgets can be a time-consuming task, especially for inexperienced managers. There is a risk that the manager may spend too long setting budgets and not devote sufficient time to other tasks. On the other hand, rushing the setting process may result in inaccurate budgets. This could prove counter-productive if sales revenue targets are unachievable and demotivate employees. Another risk is that expenditure budgets may fail to control costs, effectively damaging the financial performance of the enterprise.

Study tip

When writing answers to questions on planning finance it is important to consider the links that exist with other aspects of the process of starting a business. One such link is between sales revenue budgets and marketing. Market research may play an important part in forecasting sales and hence sales revenue. Equally, sales revenue is likely to be affected by the actions of competitors and the success of the new business's promotion.

Sources of information for budgets

The would-be entrepreneur faces a particular problem in compiling budgets – they have no previous trading records on which to base sales and expenditure figures. In contrast, if a business has traded for several years much of the budgeting process can be based upon the outcomes of previous financial years. This enables managers, for example, to predict trends in sales and seasonal effects with a greater chance of accuracy.

So, what sources of information apart from market research are available to draw up the first budgets for a new business?

- **Similar businesses** It is possible that owners of similar small businesses will be prepared to offer advice and guidance as long as the new business does not pose a direct threat to them. Thus a small business from a different geographical area might be prepared to discuss likely sales figures and associated costs safe in the knowledge that the new business will not prove to be a competitor. For example, someone considering opening a small hotel business in one area of the country may find owners in other regions willing to offer support.

- **Professional organisations** Many types of businesses operate in markets where there are professional organisations that are able to offer advice on setting up in this line of business. This advice may extend to helping to forecast sales and associated costs.

- **Bank and government organisations** Most high street banks and many government organisations can provide help with many aspects of drawing up budgets. Besides offering technical support on the process to be used these organisations may have knowledge of local market conditions.

Zero budgeting

Key term

Zero budgets exist when budgets are automatically set at zero and budget holders have to argue their case to receive any funds.

Gathering information can be time consuming even if budgets are based heavily on the previous year's figures. An alternative approach used by a number of firms is **zero budgeting**. Using this system each expenditure budget is set at zero at the start of the budget setting process. Managers responsible for the areas covered by the budget (HR managers, for example) have to bid for budget and to justify the money they request.

Using zero budgets can help firms in a number of ways.

- It avoids budgets creeping up each year as one year's budget is based on the figures from the previous year plus a little to allow for inflation. In this way it can assist a firm to control costs.
- It helps firms adjust their spending as the relative importance of areas within the firm changes. For example, the purchase of an automated switchboard might mean that the budget for this area can be reduced. This money can be used effectively elsewhere in the business.

However, the process has a number of drawbacks too.

- Zero budgeting is effective for setting production (or expenditure) budgets, but has little relevance to sales budgets. To set a zero budget for sales revenue would be ridiculous.
- Budgets might be allocated according to the negotiating skills of managers rather than the genuine needs of their areas or departments.

31.2 Variance analysis

Monitoring budgets

Setting budgets is only the first stage in the budgetary process. Once a business has planned its sales revenue and expenditure, it is essential to monitor the accuracy of these financial plans by comparing the budget figures with the actual figures resulting from the business's trading.

Budgets can also provide a wealth of information to help managers take decisions on how to improve the performance of the business.

- **Analysing budgeted and actual expenditure** This provides information on how successful the business is at controlling its costs. As a business grows it is possible to judge the ability of different parts to manage its expenditure against given targets. If one area of a business is regularly overspending its budgets, managers may take action to reduce expenditure and, by so doing, increase profitability. Relevant actions might include addressing issues such as poor motivation, quality problems or not using capacity fully. Of course if a business, or part of a business, fails to meet expenditure budgets regularly, it may be because the budgets are too low to be achievable.
- **Analysing sales revenue** A business that fails to meet its sales revenue budgets for one or more of its products may need to consider why this is occurring. Prices may be too high when compared with those of competitors, the business may not

be advertising sufficiently or not targeting the correct market segments, or the quality and/or design of the product may be inadequate. Good managers will use the information from analysing budgets to make decisions to improve the business's sales performance.

- **Analysing profits budgets** Profits below budget are likely to be a cause of concern for most businesses. These can be caused by excess expenditure or by revenue falling short of expectations or a combination of these factors. This scenario may prompt managers to examine means of cutting expenditure as well as boosting sales revenue.

Adverse and favourable variances

Key term

Variance analysis is the process of investigating any differences between forecast data and actual figures.

The process for monitoring budgets is known as **variance analysis**. A variance occurs when an actual figure for sales revenue, expenditure or profits differs from the budgeted figure. Actual sales revenue and cost figures can be higher or lower than planned; similarly, actual sales revenue or expenditure figures may be higher or lower than budgets. Variances are categorised as adverse or favourable. These two categories of variance are shown in Table 31.2.

Table 31.2 The two categories of variance

Favourable variances	Adverse variances
A favourable variance exists when the difference between the actual and budgeted figures will result in the business enjoying higher profits than shown in the budget.	An adverse variance occurs when the difference between the figures in the budget and the actual figures will lead to the firm's profits being lower than planned.
Examples of favourable variances include: - actual wages less than budgeted wages - budgeted sales revenue lower than actual sales revenue - expenditure on fuel is less than the budgeted figure.	Examples of adverse variances include: - sales revenue below the budgeted figure - actual raw material costs exceeding the figure planned in the budget - overheads turn out to be higher than in the budget.
Possible causes of favourable variances: - wages rises lower than expected - economic boom leads to higher than expected sales - rising value of currency makes imported raw materials cheaper.	Possible causes of adverse variances: - competitors introduce new products, winning extra sales - government increases business taxes by unexpected amount - fuel prices increase as price of oil rises.

The process of calculating a variance is simple, as shown by Table 31.3. It simply involves a comparison between the budgeted figure and the actual figure. In Table 31.3 the business had forecast that its sales revenue would be $840000. However, the actual figure was $790000. In this case the variance (or difference) is $50000. It is an adverse variance because it will result in the business's profits being lower than forecast or its loss larger than forecast. In contrast the business's fuel costs are only $70000 which is $5000 less than the budgeted figure. In this case this is a favourable variance because this will result in the business's profits being larger than forecast (or a smaller loss than budgeted).

Table 31.3 Calculating variances

Revenue/cost	Budget figure ($)	Actual figure ($)	Variance
Sales revenue	840000	790000	$50000 – adverse
Fuel costs	75000	70000	$5000 – favourable
Raw material costs	245000	265000	$20000 – adverse
Labour costs	115000	112000	$3000 – favourable

Carrying out regular variance analysis can give a business advance notice that its financial plans are inaccurate. Variance analysis can be carried out each month and will show before the end of the financial year that the firm's finances are not as planned. This allows the business to take action to reduce expenditure or increase revenue at an early stage. Figure 31.5 summarises the range of actions that businesses may take in response to adverse variances.

Firms may also need to respond to favourable variances. Production costs which are lower than planned may be regarded as beneficial. But sales revenue that is greater than anticipated might be caused by the firm selling more products than planned. In these circumstances, the business might not have sufficient supplies to meet future customer requirements. This could result in the loss of long-established customers and should be avoided.

There are internal connections in budgets which are important to understand. For example, if a business experiences a rise in output and sales revenue above expectations it will affect expenditure. If a product becomes unexpectedly popular and sales rise, the business may have to purchase more raw materials and hire additional labour. This is likely to result in adverse expenditure variances. Similarly, sales below those set out in the budget may lead to favourable variances for costs as expenditure falls as less is produced. We consider this further in the section on flexible budgets below.

Other factors leading to adverse and favourable variances

It may be that variances are not the result of unexpected developments and changes in the markets in which businesses operate. Poor forecasting techniques can also result in unexpected revenues and expenditures, and therefore variances.

Managers may make insufficient use of market research to forecast sales revenue. This can lead to adverse or favourable revenue variances. It may also result in inaccurate budgets for expenditure as the managers will not have forecast correctly the amount of labour and other resources that the business needs to satisfy customers' needs. Inaccurate budgets are also the result of inexperience on the part of managers and variances will be more common when a business is new to a market and has no financial records on which to base forecasts.

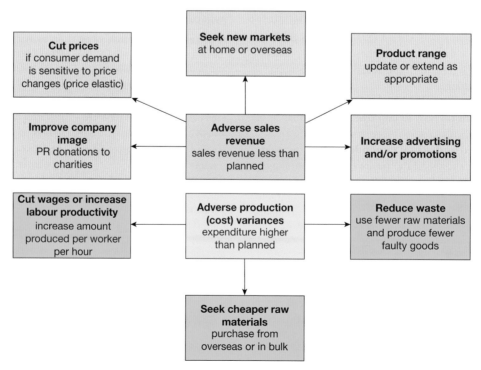

Figure 31.5 Responding to adverse variances

Study tip

Questions asking you to analyse variances are common in Business exams. It is important for you to identify those areas in which *major* differences between planned and actual expenditure or revenue have occurred. This will help to give a focus to your answer. It is also very likely that you will be asked to suggest possible causes (or cures) for the variances. Avoid simply describing the data you are given. Few, if any, marks will be awarded for this.

Case Study

Budgeting for a new factory

Figure 31.6 The GM Baojun

American car manufacturer General Motors (GM), along with its Chinese partners, has opened a second car factory to make its discount brand Baojun. The plant in the southern China city of Liuzhou is Baojun's second, producing cars with a minimum price of 40 000 yuan ($6400).

GM and its partners budgeted 8 billion yuan ($1.3 billion) to build the new factory, which will be capable of manufacturing a maximum output of 400 000 vehicles annually. The first car produced in the new factory was a Baojun 630. This model is priced at 63 000 yuan ($10 100) while the company's smaller Le Chi sells at 40 000 yuan ($6400).

The opening of this latest factory comes soon after Nissan's announcement that it intends to launch five models of the basic car Venucia in China by 2015.

The cheaper end of China's car manufacturing market is intensely competitive with joint ventures between multinational manufacturers and Chinese producers putting pressure on local manufacturers such as Chery. With Chinese incomes forecast to rise at over 7 per cent, the number of people buying cars should increase.

Questions

1 Explain two possible factors that might result in the new factory recording adverse variances. [8]
2 Do you think that the 'intensely competitive' nature of the Chinese car market is the most important reason for GM drawing up budgets for the new factory? Justify your view. [16]

Flexible budgeting

Key terms

A **flexible budget** is a budget that is designed to change along with the sales volume or production levels.
A **budget holder** is responsible for the use and management of a particular budget.

Flexible budgets or flex budgets avoid some of the problems that are associated with the use of variance analysis within normal budgets. A common problem with the use of variance analysis as we saw earlier is that some of the variances may be due to external factors such as a signifcant fall in sales due to an economy moving unexpectedly into recession. In such circumstances it can be difficult to identify how much of a variance is due to external factors and how much to poor management within the business. The use of flexible budgeting removes at least some of the effects of the external factors, allowing managers to analyse underlying issues.

Maths moment

Use the information in Table 31.4 to calculate the following.

1 The actual sales revenue required under the 'normal budget' to result in a favourable variance of $79 000.
2 If the flexed budget for sales revenue was $700 000, calculate the flexed budgets for labour and materials.

In the example in Table 31.4 the managers would be able to see that, although costs fell as a result of the large drop in sales, they didn't fall as much as may have been expected given the substantial reduction in output. Once the budget has been flexed it is simple to see that all categories of costs recorded adverse variances and that they overspent in the context of the falling level of production. Contrast this with the original budget: the favourable variances for direct costs may have suggested that the **budget holders** managed these costs effectively.

Table 31.4 An example of a flexible budget

Normal budgets ($000s)				Flexible budgets ($000s)			
	Budget	**Actual**	**Variance**	**Budget**	**Flexed budget**	**Actual**	**Variance**
Sales revenue	750	600	150 A	750	600	600	0
Overheads	200	204	4 A	200	200	204	4 A
Labour	180	162	18 F	180	145	162	17 A
Materials	220	201	19 F	220	174	201	27 A
Other costs	60	53	7 F	60	48	53	5 A
Total costs	660	620	40 F	660	567	620	53 A
PROFIT	90	(20)	110 A	90	33	(20)	53 A

Test your learning

Short answer questions

1 a Distinguish between a sales revenue and an expenditure budget. [3]

   b State **two** elements of a production budget. [2]

2 a Explain **one** way in which setting budgets for sales revenue may help a business's senior managers to take some important decisions. [3]

   b State **two** reasons why a business's sales revenue budget may prove to be inaccurate. [2]

3 Explain why a large retailer with many shops in several countries may choose to use delegated budgets. [5]

4 a State **two** reasons why setting budgets may lead to an improvement in the motivation of employees. [2]

   b Budgets are short term in nature. Explain **one** reason why this might be a problem for a business. [3]

5 a Why might it be difficult for a business to forecast its sales accurately? [3]

   b Explain how a change in the economy may make a business's budgets inaccurate. [2]

6 Explain why the first stage in setting budgets for a company is to draw up sales revenue budgets. [5]

7 a Define the term zero budgets. [2]

   b Explain **one** reason why a business might decide to use a zero budgeting system. [3]

8 a Define the term variance analysis. [2]

   b Explain **one** reason why it is important for managers to monitor budgets once they have been set. [3]

9 Using examples, distinguish between adverse and favourable variances. [5]

10 a Explain **one** factor that may lead to a business having adverse variances on its profits. [3]

    b Define the term flexible budget. [2]

Data response question

Another New Café

Nadal Ltd's cafés sell budget-priced beer, wine, coffee and tea as well as tapas and light meals. The company has succeeded despite, or maybe because of, the weak economic position of Spain. The company's brand name is associated with low prices and value for money. The company plans to expand using finance raised mainly through loans.

Last year Nadal Ltd opened its 59th café in Ronda, southern Spain. This is its first café in this part of Spain and the company has only conducted secondary market research. The new manager in Ronda has no experience of cafés or financial planning but is experienced in retail and in managing people. Despite this sales have risen steadily, if slowly, and customer feedback is positive.

Table 1 Nadal Ltd, Ronda Café. Budget figures for first three months of trading

Item	Budget ($)	Actual ($)
Sales revenue	11 500	10 990
Indirect costs	4 250	4 300
Direct costs	6 890	6 900
Profits	360	(210)

Questions

1 Analyse the problems that Nadal Ltd faced in setting its budgets for the new café. [8]

2 a Calculate the profit variance for the first three months of trading for the Ronda café. [6]

   b Assess the extent to which the advantages of drawing up budgets outweigh the disadvantages to Nadal Ltd. [10]

3 Should Nadal Ltd be pleased with the performance of its café in Ronda? Justify your decision. [16]

Essay questions

1 Discuss the extent to which it is true to say that setting budgets is of more value to managers than monitoring them. [20]

2 To what extent do you think that it would be beneficial for all managers in a business to have responsibility for budgeting? [20]

Past paper question

Read the Atlantic Steel Company case study on pages 449–51 and then answer the following questions.

a Using data in Appendix A, calculate the variances for the Newtown steel works. [6]

b Explain possible reasons for any **two** of these variances. [6]

Cambridge International AS and A Level Business Studies 9707 Paper 32 Q2a October/November 2011

32 Published accounts

Chapter overview

In this chapter we examine:
- the contents, construction and amendment of income statements and statements of financial position
- intangible assets and statements of financial position
- the role and impact of depreciation
- the methods and difficulties of valuing inventory.

Key terms

An **income statement** is an accounting statement showing a firm's sales revenue over a trading period and all the relevant costs generated to earn that revenue.

A **loss** is a situation where a business's expenditure exceeds its revenue over a specific trading period.

Profit can be defined in a number of ways, but is essentially the surplus of revenues over costs.

We looked at the contents and structures of income statements and statements of financial position in Chapter 18. This chapter considers factors that can result in amendments to these financial statements and the consequent changes that will take place. The amendments may be necessary to adjust a forecast or budgeted financial statement to show actual data. We looked at budgets in detail in the previous chapter.

32.1 Income statements

An **income statement** records a business's sales revenue and the costs that it incurred in earning that revenue. It also includes the interest that the business earned and paid, the amount of taxation paid on profits and, in the case of companies, the amount of dividends paid to shareholders.

The structure of income statements

We saw in Chapter 18 that an income statement is made up of four main sections:
1 Firstly, 'gross profit' is calculated from the difference between the revenue and the cost of the goods that have been sold.
2 From this, operating profit can be calculated by deducting the main types of expenses such as administration and selling costs.
3 The third section records profit before taxation is calculated, which is arrived at by the inclusion of interest received by the business and interest paid by it.
4 The final stage of the income statement is to calculate profit after taxation by deducting the amount of tax payable for the year.

It is possible to take this structure a stage further by explaining how the profit for the year is used. A business has two broad options on how to utilise its profits.
1 To distribute profits to its shareholders by paying them dividends (assuming it is a company).
2 To retain profits within the business for future investment.

Factors that can cause amendments in income statements

Changes in selling prices

If a business raises or reduces it price, it is almost certain that its sales revenue will alter as a consequence. A key determinant of the effect on sales revenue following a price change is price elasticity of demand. A business may be more inclined to raise its prices if it believes demand is price inelastic. In this situation sales of a product are not particularly sensitive to price and thus a price rise may increase revenue.

Changes in the volume of products sold

If a product becomes more or less popular the amount that is sold is likely to alter and so will the business's sales revenue. This may well be as a response to a price change although other factors such as changing fashions or the entry of new products onto a market may also change the quantity of products that a business sells.

Alternatively, the business may increase sales as a consequence of entering a new market or launching a new product.

Study tip

If the quantity of products sold by a business is adjusted then it is likely to have a knock-on effect on the business's costs. It is highly likely that the business's direct costs will alter and some overheads may also change, such as distribution costs. You must ensure that, when answering questions on this topic, you alter costs when necessary.

Changes in direct and indirect costs

A rise in direct or indirect costs is likely to reduce the profit recorded on a business's income statement, or to increase its losses.

An example of amending an income statement

West Kericho Estate is a well-established tea plantation in Kenya. It has recently prepared a draft of its income statement for the year, which is shown in Table 32.1 as the original figures.

However, the original figures were found to contain a number of errors.
- The company actually sold 12 500 kg of tea.
- The selling price of its tea averaged at $280 per kg over the year.
- Its administrative and other expenses were actually $901 500.
- The interest rates charged on the company's loans rose, increasing its interest charges by 20 per cent.
- The company's directors decided to increase the dividends it paid to $175 475.

These changes are shown in the right hand column of Table 32.1. There are a number of key points to note about these amendments.

Table 32.1 West Kericho Estate's original and amended income statements

	Original figures $	Amended figures $
Revenue (12 400 kg @ $275 per kg)	3 410 000	3 500 000
Cost of sales (12 400 kg @ $160 per kg)	(1 984 000)	(2 000 000)
Gross profit	**1 426 000**	**1 500 000**
Administrative and other expenses	(878 000)	(901 500)
Operating profit	**548 000**	**598 500**
Finance income (interest received)	12 000	12 000
Finance costs (interest paid)	(36 000)	(43 200)
Profit before tax	**524 000**	**567 300**
Taxation (Corporation tax @ 25%)	131 000	141 825
Profit for the year	**393 000**	**425 475**
Dividends paid	136 000	175 475
Retained profits	257 000	250 000

- The new revenue figure is calculated by multiplying the company's output of tea (in kg) by the average price per kg.
- If output changes, then the cost of sales will alter too because the quantity produced changes. Here, output rose from 12 400 kg of tea to 12 500 kg. Even though the unit cost of production was unchanged at $160 per kg, the overall cost of sales rises as output has increased.
- Gross profit changes if either revenue or cost of sales alters.
- Finance costs increased by 20 per cent, which has an effect on the profit before tax figure.
- Finally, dividends were increased leaving a slightly smaller figure for retained profits.

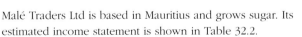

Case Study

Malé Traders Ltd

Malé Traders Ltd is based in Mauritius and grows sugar. Its estimated income statement is shown in Table 32.2.

Malé Traders Ltd has updated the information used for its income statement. The cost of its goods sold has been changed to $300 per tonne; its administrative expenses were $956 425 and it received $51 200 as interest on its bank accounts. The tax rate for profits was altered to 22 per cent. Finally, its dividends paid were unchanged.

Table 32.2 Malé Traders Ltd estimated income statement

	Original figures $
Revenue (10 425 tonnes @ $470 per tonne)	4 899 750
Cost of sales (10 425 tonnes @ $290 per tonne)	(3 023 250)
Gross profit	**1 876 500**
Administrative and other expenses	(975 450)
Operating profit	**901 050**
Finance income (interest received)	45 675
Finance costs (interest paid)	(102 300)
Profit before tax	**844 425**
Taxation (Corporation tax @ 20%)	168 885
Profit for the year	**675 540**
Dividends paid	380 000
Retained profits	295 540

Question

1 Calculate whether or not the company retained more or less profits than shown in its original forecast. [8]

32.2 Statements of financial position

Constructing statements of financial position

In Chapter 18 we saw that a **statement of financial position** has two principal elements. It records assets, which are the way in which a business uses its funds, and liabilities, which are the sources of funds used by the business.

Table 32.3 shows a statement of financial position for Western Australia Mines Ltd. This illustrates the key features of a statement of financial position: non-current and current assets, current and non-current liabilities and share capital and reserves.

The structure of a statement of financial position

The statement of financial position in Table 32.3 is separated into the various elements that make it up. When constructing a statement of financial position from given data it is necessary to separate items into assets and liabilities and to decide whether they are short-term assets or liabilities (normally received or paid within a year) or long-term. These will be recorded as non-current assets or liabilities as appropriate. Finally, funds owed to the owners of a business (shareholders in the case of a company) are listed under total equity.

Table 32.3 Some important components of a company's statement of financial position

Western Australia Mines Ltd 2012 $m		
Intangible non-current assets	417.8	(Non-current assets)
Tangible non-current assets	5 284.6	
Inventories	585.3	
Receivables and cash	720.5	(Current assets)
Other current assets	335.9	
Total assets	**7 344.1**	
Current liabilities	(1 017.0)	(Current liabilities)
Non-current liabilities	(2 038.2)	(Non-current liabilities)
Total liabilities	**(3 055.2)**	
Net assets	**4 288.9**	
Share capital	2 582.9	
Reserves & retained earnings	1 706.0	
Total equity	**4 288.9**	(Total equity – funds owed to shareholders)

Case Study

Queensland Pools Ltd

The finance director is in the process of drawing up a summary statement of financial position for the company. The following information exists for the assets and liabilities of Queensland Pools Ltd on 31 December. All figures are $000s.

- Share capital – 2000
- Current liabilities – 700
- Inventories – 800
- Other fixed assets – 1800
- Receivables – 400

- Reserves and retained earnings – 700
- Non-current liabilities – 1300
- Cash – 500
- Property – 1200

Question

1 Use Table 32.3 as a guide to draw up the statement of financial position for Queensland Pools Ltd using the data above. [8]

Amending statements of financial position

When amendments are made to a statement of financial position there are often 'knock-on' effects because of the system of double entry that is used to draw up a statement of financial position. This double entry system is used because, as we saw in Chapter 18, a statement of financial position must always balance between assets and liabilities. Therefore, if a change is made to either assets or liabilities, there has to be a compensating change to ensure that the balance is maintained.

There is a range of actions a business might take which would affect its statement of financial position. We will look at some examples of these.

- **The purchase of non-current assets** If a business purchases non-current assets such as property or vehicles then the initial effect will be to increase the value of its non-current assets on the statement of financial position. The compensating amendment could take a number of forms:
  - The business's cash balance may fall by the same figure, leaving the figure for total assets unchanged.
  - The business may arrange a long-term loan to pay for the new assets, causing a rise in liabilities to match the increased value of assets.
  - Similarly, additional shares may be sold causing an increase in total equity which represents a liability to the company.
- **The business repays a long-term loan** This action will initially reduce the company's liabilities on its statement of financial position. The compensating amendment could be one of the following.
  - The business sells additional shares to raise the funds to repay the loan. Thus, the two changes to the company's liabilities will cancel one another out on the statement of financial position.
  - The business sells an asset to generate the finance to repay the loan. This would lower the company's assets by the same amount as its liabilities are reduced.
- **The business reduces the value of some non-current assets on its statement of financial position** This is a common action taken by a business and is termed depreciation (we will look at this in more detail later in this chapter). In this case the balancing amendment is likely to be a reduction in the figure for reserves and retained earnings (and therefore total equity) of the same amount.

A wide range of other transactions will affect the statement of financial position such as the sale of inventories, or the use of an overdraft. The compensating amendments here may be a rise in the amount of cash held in the company's bank account and a rise in current assets such as inventories which may have been purchased using the overdraft facility.

Case Study

Belem Manufacturing Ltd

Table 32.4

Belem Manufacturing Ltd Statement of financial position as at 30 November	
Non-current assets	$m
Intangible assets	310
Tangible assets	6 667
Total non-current assets	6 977
Inventories	1 500
Receivables	1 075
Cash	1 000
Total current assets	3 575
Current liabilities	(4 720)
Net current assets	(1 145)
Total assets less current liabilities	5 832
Non-current liabilities	(1 041)
Net assets	**4 791**
Share capital	1 860
Reserves & retained earnings	2 931
Total equity	**4 791**

The company's managers need to incorporate a number of changes into the figures shown above. These are:

- The company has taken out an additional loan of $10 million and has purchased vehicles with this capital.
- Some of the company's customers (receivables) paid early – this amounted to $100 million.
- The company's property has increased in value by $150 million due to general rises in property prices.

The managers recognise that each of these changes will need a compensating change to ensure that the statement of financial position still balances.

Questions

1 Draw up a revised statement of financial position based on these changes and ensure that it still balances. [8]
2 Discuss the extent to which these changes have strengthened the company's financial position. [16]

32.3 Further issues on statements of financial position

Intangible assets

There is another classification of assets which is important.

- **Tangible assets** These are assets that have a physical existence and have been traditionally included on a statement of financial position. Tangible assets include land, property and vehicles.
- **Intangible assets** These assets do not take a physical form and are shown separately on the statement of financial position. Examples include:
  - patents and other rights. For example, the UK's mobile telephone companies have paid the government substantial sums for licences to operate mobile phones. These licences represent a valuable intangible asset for companies such as Vodafone.
  - brands. These can be included on a statement of financial position if they were purchased or can be separately valued. However, many brands can fluctuate in value as they may have a relatively short life.

International accounting regulations state that intangible assets can only be recorded on a business's statement of financial position if they can be separately identified and money was spent upon their purchase. An asset is separately identifiable if the business concerned is able to sell it or licence other companies to use it. For example, it would be appropriate for UK mobile telephone companies to present their licences as intangible assets as these can be separately identified and could be sold if necessary.

Brands and other intangible assets can be very valuable. Brands can account for a large proportion of a company's market value: 70 per cent for Disney, 76 per cent for Nike, and 98 per cent for Microsoft. Brands are also a means through which companies can generate cash and allow them to enter new markets and to charge premium prices.

However, it is very difficult to place an accurate value on intangible assets. Intangible assets are frequently not recorded on statements of financial position under international accounting rules because of this difficulty, except if they have been acquired as a result of a takeover or a merger. This can mean that some companies that have valuable brand names may be worth more than their statement of financial position may suggest.

It is normal for a business to **amortise** the cost of an intangible asset over each year of its life (this is especially true of patents which have a finite life) or to review its value regularly and to show impairment as and when necessary. Impairment is called for when the value of an asset on a business's statement of financial position exceeds its actual value to the business. In this case the value of the asset should be reduced and this process is called impairment.

Goodwill

Goodwill is the value of an established customer base and a good reputation to a business. It exists when a business is sold for a value greater than that which is recorded on its statement of financial position.

Goodwill is often an important factor when one business is bought by another as part of a takeover deal. Goodwill often means that a business is worth more as a going concern than the value of its assets would suggest.

Case Study

Hong Kong Stock Exchange plans takeover

Hong Kong Exchanges & Clearing Ltd, which owns and operates the Hong Kong Stock Exchange, is the world's second largest stock exchange company by value. It is planning further growth by proposing a takeover of the London Metal Exchange. The proposed deal will require the sale of $1 billion in new shares to fund its plans.

Shares of Hong Kong Exchanges & Clearing Ltd have declined by 14 per cent since its offer for the LME was revealed. Business analysts have suggested that the amount of goodwill included in the bid might be overvalued and this has made the Hong Kong Stock Exchange less attractive to shareholders.

Questions

1 Explain the effects this deal may have on Hong Kong Exchanges & Clearing Ltd's statement of financial position if it goes through. [8]
2 Discuss the possible reasons why many of the company's stakeholders may not approve of this deal. [16]

Companies that have goodwill on their statements of financial position are required to review the value of the goodwill annually and, if its value has been impaired, take the amount of the impairment as a cost on the income statement. If the value of goodwill is not impaired it can be shown in statements of financial position indefinitely.

Depreciation

Key term

Depreciation is the reduction in the value of a non-current asset over a period of time.

A business may spend its capital in two broad ways as illustrated in Table 32.5. Both types of expenditure are essential for a business's success, but only capital expenditure has any relevance to the process of **depreciation**.

Table 32.5 Capital and revenue expenditure

	Revenue expenditure	Capital expenditure
Explanation	This is spending on assets that are used up in a relatively short period of time.	This is spending on non-current assets that will be used by the business for a prolonged period of time.
Examples	Spending on fuel, components and raw materials.	Expenditure to purchase property, vehicles and production equipment.
Effects on financial statements	This type of expenditure is recorded on the income statement under headings such as 'cost of sales' and 'administrative expenses'. It will only affect the accounts in the financial year in which the expenditure occurs.	The value of non-current assets purchased through capital expenditure is shown on the statement of financial position. The reduction in value of these assets over time is listed on the income statement. This type of expenditure affects the statement of financial position and income statement for a number of years.
Possible effects on profits	Revenue expenditure is essential to production, but if not controlled, can have an immediate and damaging effect on a business's profits.	This type of spending has no immediate effect on profits. However, capital expenditure is essential if a firm is to generate long-term profits.

Depreciation is the reduction in the value of a non-current asset over a period of time. Thus, a brewery may purchase

equipment for the brewing of beer and reduce its value as shown in Table 32.6.

Table 32.6 The principle of depreciation

The Singapore Beer Company Ltd		
Year	Value of asset on statement of financial position at end of year $	Amount depreciated annually $
2011	60 000	20 000
2012	40 000	20 000
2013	20 000	20 000
2014	0	20 000

Table 32.6 illustrates the effects of depreciation on the statement of financial position and the income statement of the Singapore Beer Company. The initial cost of the brewing equipment in 2011 was $80 000. The company expects that this equipment will last for four years and have no resale value. The effect on the accounts is shown in the table. The value of the asset falls by $20 000 each year, reflecting its decline in value. The amount of the decline in value (that is depreciation) is shown as an expense on the Singapore Beer Company's income statement.

Maths moment

Recalculate the asset value and amount of annual depreciation in Table 32.6 assuming that annual depreciation is 20 per cent of the initial cost of the equipment.

Firms have to depreciate their fixed assets for a number of reasons.

1 To ensure the business is valued accurately. In the case of the Singapore Beer Company it would have been incorrect to show the value of the brewing equipment as $80 000 throughout its life. Its resale value would decline for a number of reasons:
- The equipment would lose value as a result of wear and tear.
- The production of more modern equipment would mean that the value of this 'older' style equipment declined.
- Poor or inadequate maintenance of the equipment may mean expensive repairs are necessary, further reducing the brewing equipment's value.

Thus, reducing the value of an asset in line with the factors above ensures that the value of the business recorded on the statement of financial position is a relatively accurate indication of the true worth of the business.

2 Depreciation also allows firms to calculate the true cost of production during any financial year. The Singapore Beer Company would have overstated its costs in 2011 if it had allocated the entire cost of its new brewing equipment to that

particular financial year. By depreciating the equipment by $20 000 each year for four years, one quarter of the cost of the equipment is recorded each year on the Singapore Beer Company's income statement. This helps to gain an accurate view of the profitability (or otherwise) of the business over the lifetime of the equipment.

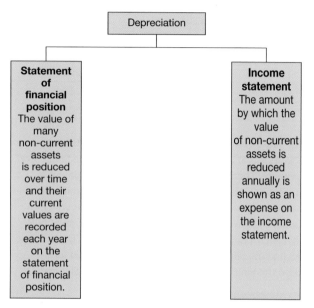

Figure 32.1 Depreciation – a link between the statement of financial position and the income statement (the valuation of inventories provides a second link)

Depreciation: a non-cash expense

Depreciation is an expense or a cost to a firm that is recorded on the income statement. However, depreciation is unusual in that it is a non-cash expense. Depreciation does not require a business to make any payment. It is recognition of the cost of providing a particular expense normally made at the time the asset was purchased. Depreciation is *not* a method of providing the cash necessary to replace the asset at the end of its useful life.

Calculating depreciation: the straight-line method

This is a simple method of depreciation that reduces the value of a non-current asset by the same amount each year until the asset is of no further use and is sold or scrapped. This method of depreciation can be calculated through the use of the formula below.

$$\text{Annual straight-line depreciation} = \frac{\text{Cost of machine} - \text{residual value}}{\text{Working life in years}}$$

The residual value of a non-current asset is the amount received when the asset is no longer required and is sold.

Case Study

Depreciation at the nightclub

Alan Cork, managing director of *Frenzy*, a nightclub in Otago, New Zealand, has just authorised the purchase of a new sound system. The new system cost $18 000 and Alan estimates that in a rapidly changing world he will need to replace it at the end of three years. The company supplying the sound system has advised Alan that the resale value after three years would be $3000.

$$\text{Annual straight-line depreciation} = \frac{18 000 - 3000}{3 \text{ years}}$$

$$= \frac{15 000}{3}$$

$$= \$5000$$

Thus the value of the new sound system on the statement of financial position of South Island Leisure Ltd (the company that owns the nightclub) would be reduced by $5000 annually. At the same time the amount of depreciation entered as a cost on the income statement would also be $5000. Thus this method of depreciation spreads the $15 000 cost of the sound system evenly over the three years of its working life.

Questions

1 Explain why this company should depreciate its assets. [8]
2 Discuss how this process would affect South Island Leisure Ltd's statement of financial position. [16]

Assessing straight-line depreciation

Straight-line depreciation offers a number of advantages to the managers and other stakeholders of a business.

- It is very simple to calculate and equally easy to understand. The value of a non-current asset can be seen to steadily decline in the business's statement of financial position.
- It does spread the cost of an asset over its working life, which is important if a business is to have an accurate view of its financial performance.

However, this approach to depreciation has a fundamental shortcoming. Its simplicity is its principal weakness. Few assets lose their value steadily over a period of time. It is much more common for an asset to lose value more heavily in the early years of its life. Thus the straight-line method may overvalue a non-current asset in the early years of its life. This is particularly true of vehicles and other technology products.

Why is depreciation important?

Depreciation is an important matter to businesses for a number of reasons.

- Depreciation provides an accurate value of a business's assets throughout their lives. This allows for a 'true and fair' assessment of the overall worth of the business at any time. Having an accurate figure for the overall value of the business is important for stakeholders such as investors and creditors.
- The amount of annual depreciation affects the overall value and profits of a business as shown in Table 32.7.

Table 32.7 The effects of depreciation

	Too much depreciation	**Too little depreciation**
Effects on statement of financial position	Non-current assets valued at less than their true worth; thus the true value of business is understated.	Non-current assets on the statement of financial position will be overvalued giving a false impression of the company's worth.
Effects on income statement	Depreciation expenses overestimated on income statement, reducing level of profits.	Low rates of depreciation will reduce the expenses incurred by a business. This will result in business's profits being higher than they would otherwise be.
Wider effects	Business may look unattractive to prospective investors. Tax liability on profits may be reduced, but tax authorities might investigate! Business may record surplus when asset finally sold.	This may make the company more attractive to investors but will also increase its tax liability.

Inventory valuation

Inventories can also be called stock. In recent years businesses across the globe have tried to minimise inventories recognising that they can be costly to store and manage and that they have the potential to tie up large amounts of cash.

It is important that a business values its inventories accurately on its statement of financial position to provide stakeholders with a figure which allows them to judge the value of the business with some degree of certainty.

Study tip

Although there are a number of methods of valuing inventory, you only need to know the net realisable value (NRV) method.

The net realisable value method of valuing inventories

There are a number of methods of valuing inventories, but we shall concentrate on a single one – the **net realisable value method** (NRV). This approach values inventories at their likely selling price after allowing a reasonable amount for the costs associated with either the eventual sale or the disposal of the asset. It is a commonly used method of valuing inventories so as to ensure that they are not over- or under-valued on a business's statement of financial position.

There are a number of stages in calculating the value of inventories using the NRV method.

1 Firstly, calculate the total value of all inventories held by the business. This is simply the amount the company could sell its assets for on the open market. As an example, take a business that manufactures cans and bottles for use in the food industry. On the day its statement of financial position is drawn up, it might have the following inventories:

- 2 000 000 cans as inventory that are sold for $0.30 each to other businesses
- 500 000 small bottles each with a selling price of $0.40
- 600 000 large bottles which can be sold for $0.60 per bottle.

The total value of the inventory is ([2 000 000 × $0.30] + [500 000 × $0.40] + [600 000 × $0.60]) = $600 000 + $200 000 + $360 000 = $1 160 000.

Maths moment

What would be the total value of the inventory above if all bottles were valued at $0.50, assuming no other changes occur?

2 The costs incurred in selling each asset the company possesses must be deducted. This would include the cost of advertising the goods for sale and expenses involved in distributing these products. Continuing our example we could assume the cost of advertising and distributing the cans and bottles is $85 000.

3 The final stage of calculating NRV entails deducting the costs associated with selling the products from the revenue raised from their sale. Thus NRV = $1 160 000 − $85 000 = $1 075 000.

The net realisable value method (NRV) is widely used to value inventories in businesses throughout the world. The International Financial Reporting Standards (IFRS) accounting rules require businesses to value inventory using the NRV method unless the cost of buying the inventories was lower. In other words IFRS rules state that inventories should be valued at cost or NRV, whichever gives the lower figure. Hence inventory that is difficult to sell may have a very low value in the statement of financial position.

Inventories, the statement of financial position and the income statement

Income statements and statements of financial position are interconnected. Earlier we saw that this relationship exists because decisions on depreciation affect the value of assets as well as the amount of expenses included in the income statement. The method used to value inventory determines a business's costs of sales and therefore its profit. The formula used in the income statement is as follows:

$$\text{Cost of sales} = \text{(opening inventory)} + \text{(inventory purchases)} - \text{(closing inventory)}$$

The value of closing inventory (i.e. at the end of the trading period) depends on how inventory is valued on the statement of financial position. The lower the value of closing inventory, the higher the costs of sales, which results in lower profit. Conversely, a higher closing inventory valuation results in lower cost of sales and higher profits. The closing inventory figure will be included in the business's statement of financial position under current assets.

The problems of valuing inventories

It can be difficult to value inventories accurately for a number of reasons.

- Some inventory may lose value because it is perishable. For example, foods may lose value as they approach the end of their saleable life – this may make the valuation of inventory a more complex task as inventory of different ages may have different values.
- Inventory may be a fashion product and therefore of less (or more) value as tastes and fashions change.

- When valuing certain inventories it can be difficult to put a market price as part of the use of the net realisable value (NRV) method. For example, a business selling antique furniture may experience problems in determining an accurate figure for some items of furniture, especially those that are unusual. With other products, such as works of art, it may be that valuations differ between different people.
- Valuations can be affected by a range of external factors. For example, a business's valuation of its inventories of oil could vary considerably as the global oil price alters. In 2013 alone, global oil prices varied between a maximum of $117 per barrel and a minimum of $97 per barrel.

Case Study
The Aura Minerals Corporation

The Aura Minerals Corporation is a mining company. It operates a number of mines in the Americas. Its mines include the San Andres Gold Mine in Honduras, the Sao Francisco and Sao Vicente gold mines in Brazil, the copper-gold-silver Aranzazu Project in Mexico, and the feasibility-stage copper-gold-iron ore Serrote Project in Brazil.

The company announced its trading figures for the third quarter of 2013 stating that its revenue fell by 9 per cent compared with the same trading period during 2012. The company mined 43 059 ounces (1220 Kg) of gold during the third quarter of 2013. The price per ounce (28.3 grams) realised by the company for gold fell from $1683 to $1643 over the same time period. The company valued its inventories using the net realisable value method.

Questions

1 Explain why inventory valuation is a particularly important issue for manufacturing businesses. [8]
2 Discuss why the use of the net realisable value method of inventory valuation might be a good choice for Aura Minerals. [16]

Test your learning

Short answer questions

1 a Define the term income statement. [2]
  b Explain the effects on an income statement of a rise in the average selling price of a business's products. [3]

2 Explain the likely consequences for a business's gross profits of:
  i a rise in its cost of sales and
  ii a rise in its expenses. [5]

3 a Explain why cost of sales is likely to alter along with the level of output of a business. [3]
  b Define the term non-current asset. [2]

4 Why is the statement of financial position an important document for a business's stakeholders? [5]

5 a Define the term goodwill. [2]
  b Distinguish, with the aid of example, between revenue expenditure and capital expenditure. [3]

6 a Define the term depreciation. [2]

b A non-current asset that was purchased for $880 000 is expected to have a residual value of $120 000 after eight years when it will be sold. Using the straight-line method of depreciation, calculate the annual depreciation figure for this asset. [3]

7 Explain why the straight-line method of depreciation may result in a non-current asset having an incorrect value on a business's statement of financial position. [5]

8 a Explain the term amortisation. [2]

b Explain **one** reason why businesses depreciate most non-current assets. [3]

9 a How does depreciation link the statement of financial position and the income statement? [3]

b Define the term inventory. [2]

10 a What is meant by the net realisable value method of valuing inventories? [2]

b Explain what effect reducing the value of inventory on a statement of financial position might have on a business's profits. [3]

Data response question

Saddlers – a growing supermarket business

Saddlers is a large supermarket business, established more than 100 years ago. The public company has 1750 stores and a fleet of 124 lorries which it uses to deliver products from its warehouses to its stores. It has started to deliver to individual customers and is purchasing vans to carry this out. The company pays $27 500 for each van and depreciates them over six years.

Saddlers is respected for its extensive range of very fresh fruit and vegetables. Saddlers purchases and stores huge amounts of oil products to heat its buildings and fuel its lorries. The company also sells non-perishable foods and has recently expanded into clothing and electrical products.

The company's stakeholders have to take a range of decisions in relation to the business. They make use of its statement of financial position and income statement to allow informed judgements on issues such as whether to supply the business, invest in its shares, lend it money or to work for the business.

Questions

1 Analyse the reasons why it is important for Saddlers to depreciate its assets. [10]

2 a Calculate the annual straight-line depreciation for the company's vans assuming they have a residual value of $9500. [4]

b Assess the extent to which Saddlers might face problems in valuing its inventory. [10]

3 Is Saddlers' statement of financial position more important to its stakeholders than its income statement? Justify your decision. [16]

Essay questions

1 To what extent does the use of the straight-line method of depreciation guarantee that a company includes accurate figures in its income statement? [20]

2 Discuss the extent to which it is possible for a business to 'improve' the figures within its financial statements. [20]

Past paper questions

1 Read the Eastern Motors (EM) case study on pages 468–70 and answer the following questions.

a Using data from Appendix A, calculate the following ratios for EM in 2008:

i Gross profit margin [3]

ii Net profit margin [3]

b Analyse **two** possible reasons for EM's falling gross profit margin [6]

c Evaluate any **two** ways in which EM might increase net profit margin [8]

Cambridge International AS and A Level Business Studies
9707 Paper 3 Q4 May/June 2009

2 Read the Curry Cuisine case study on pages 471–72 and then answer the following questions.

a Draw up a forecasted income statement (profit and loss account) for 2008 using the information in Appendix A and the management consultant's estimates (lines 59–64). [8]

b Briefly assess **two** ways in which the gross profit margin could be raised for the take-away products (calculations not needed). [8]

Cambridge International AS and A Level Business Studies
9707 Paper 3 Q3 October/November 2007

33 Analysing published accounts

Chapter overview

In this chapter we examine:
- the calculation and interpretation of profitability ratios, financial efficiency ratios, the gearing ratio and shareholder ratios
- strategies that businesses may use to improve ratio results
- limitations of accounting ratios.

Key terms

An **income statement** is an accounting statement showing a firm's sales revenue over a trading period and all the relevant costs generated to earn that revenue.

A **statement of financial position** is a financial statement recording the assets (possessions) and liabilities (debts) of a business on a particular day at the end of an accounting period. This was previously called a balance sheet.

Ratio analysis is a technique for analysing a business's financial performance by comparing one piece of accounting information with another.

We introduced **statements of financial position** and **income statements** in Chapter 18 and further investigated them in the previous chapter. This chapter examines the use of a range of ratios to analyse published accounts and to help to make informed judgements of the financial performance of businesses.

There are a number of groups that are interested in the financial information provided by businesses and especially by public limited companies. Collectively these groups can be referred to as stakeholders and they may take an interest in the published accounts of a business for a variety of reasons. For example, suppliers may want to judge the financial position of a business to evaluate whether they should offer the firm credit. Similarly, individuals contemplating buying shares in the business may try to assess the business's potential to make profits in the future. Figure 33.1 summarises stakeholder groups and their interest in a company's financial performance.

33.1 What is a financial ratio?

Ratio analysis allows stakeholders to evaluate a business's performance through the investigation of key financial statements such as the statement of financial position and the income statement. The major feature of ratio analysis is that it compares

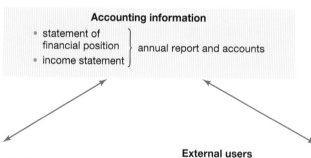

Figure 33.1 Stakeholders and financial information

two pieces of financial information. By comparing two pieces of data in this way it is possible to make more informed judgements about a business's performance. We introduced a number of financial ratios in Chapter 18. It may be worth re-reading section 18.2 before proceeding further.

Types of ratio

There are a number of ways of classifying financial ratios (see Table 33.1). One approach is to identify five main categories of ratio.

1 **Liquidity ratios**, also known as solvency ratios, measure the ability of the business to settle its debts in the short term. We looked at the acid test and the current ratio in Chapter 18.

2 **Efficiency ratios** measure the effectiveness with which an enterprise uses the resources available to it. These are also termed internal control ratios.

3 **Profitability ratios** assess the amount of gross or net profit made by the business in relation to the business's turnover or the assets or capital available to it. We explored the gross and profit margins in Chapter 18 and will encounter a further profitability ratio in this chapter. This is the return on capital employed or ROCE.

4 **Gearing** examines the relationship between internal sources and external sources of finance. It is therefore concerned with the long-term financial position of the company.

5 **Investor or shareholders' ratios** measure the returns received by the owners of the company, allowing comparison with alternative investments. For obvious reasons they are also called investment ratios.

Sources of information for ratio analysis

The most obvious sources are the published accounts of the business or businesses concerned. In particular, ratio analysis requires access to a business's statement of financial position

and income statement. However, although this might be essential information, it is not all that is required to conduct an in-depth ratio analysis of a business. Other possible sources of information include the following.

- **The financial performance of the business over recent years** Having an understanding of the trends of ratios over time can assist in making judgements. Thus a profitability ratio might appear fairly low, but if it represents a continuation of a steadily rising trend then the figure may be more acceptable to stakeholders.

- **Norms or benchmarks for the industry** The results of ratio calculations should be judged against what is normal for the industry. Thus an investor might calculate that a company's debtor day ratio is 35 days (the number of days, on average, that customers take to settle their bills). This might be acceptable for a manufacturing business, but not for a fast-food business.

- **Data on the economic environment** A decline in profit ratios might appear to reflect an unsuccessful business. However, this might be more acceptable in the context of a severe economic recession whereby sales and prices have declined.

> **Study tip**
>
> Do take care to express the results of your ratio calculations in the appropriate format. The section below offers you guidance.

Expressing ratios

Ratios are normally expressed in one of four forms:

1 as days – e.g. a business's receivables may be 43 days

2 as a percentage – ROCE expresses operating profit as a percentage of capital employed by the business

3 as a multiple – inventories (stock) are turned over (or sold) five times a year

4 as a ratio – for example the acid test ratio might have a result of 0.9:1.

Table 33.1 Types of financial ratios

Type of ratio	Liquidity ratios	Efficiency ratios	Profitability ratios	Gearing	Shareholders' ratios
Ratios used	Current ratio Acid test (or quick) ratio	Inventory turnover ratio Payable days Receivable days	Profit margin Gross profit margin Return on capital employed (ROCE)	Gearing – loans: capital employed	Dividend per share Dividend yield Price–earnings ratio
Purpose of ratios	To assess the ability of the business to pay its immediate debts	To provide evidence on how well the managers have controlled the business	To provide a fundamental measure of the success of the business	To assess the extent to which the business is based on borrowed money	To give investors information on the returns on their investment
Interested stakeholders	Creditors Suppliers Managers	Shareholders Managers Employees Competitors	Shareholders Creditors Managers Competitors Employees	Shareholders Managers Creditors	Shareholders Managers

33.2 The return on capital employed ratio (ROCE)

This is an important ratio comparing the operating profit earned with the amount of capital employed by the business. The capital employed by the business is measured by its total (or shareholders') equity plus its non-current liabilities.

The importance of this ratio is reflected in the fact that it is also termed 'the primary efficiency ratio'. The result of this ratio, which is expressed as a percentage, allows an assessment to be made of the overall financial performance of the business. A fundamental comparison can be made between the prevailing rate of interest and the ROCE generated by a business.

Return on capital employed =

$$\frac{\text{operating profit} \times 100}{\text{total equity plus non-current liabilities (capital employed)}}$$

Study tip

ROCE is one of three key ratios used to assess the financial performance of businesses. The other two are the acid test ratio and gearing. Using these three ratios enables a company's short- and long-term liquidity positions to be examined as well as a fundamental measure of its profitability. Do think about the ways in which a business may increase its ROCE figure if it is considered to be too low. This may have implications for all the functional areas of the business to increase profits and/or to reduce the amount of capital employed in the business.

Using this ratio

- A typical ROCE may be expected to be in the range of 20–30 per cent though it varies between industries and businesses. It is particularly important to compare the results from calculating this ratio with the business's ROCE in previous years and also those achieved by competitors.
- A business may improve its ROCE by increasing its operating profit without raising further capital or by reducing the amount of capital employed, perhaps by repaying some non-current liabilities.

The returns here vary enormously. The most eye-catching figure is that of Malaysia Airlines (see Table 33.2). The company's financial position has been severely affected by the rising cost of fuel and operating some uneconomic routes. At the end of 2011 the company appointed a new board of directors and this has helped as the company's ROCE for 2011 was –3.1 per cent.

Maths moment

Use the information in Table 33.2 to calculate the following.

1 Assuming no other changes, what level of operating profit would Independent Media Corporation have needed to make in 2013 to record a ROCE figure of 24 per cent?
2 Given Phoenix Beverage's 2013 profit figure, what amount of total equity plus current liabilities would be necessary to result in a ROCE figure of 15 per cent?

33.3 Efficiency ratios

This group of ratios measures the effectiveness with which management controls the internal operation of the business. They consider the following aspects of the management of an enterprise:

- how well inventories are managed
- the time that the business takes to settle its own bills
- the efficiency of creditor control, i.e. how long before customers settle their accounts.

There are a large number of ratios that fall under this heading, but we shall concentrate on just three.

Table 33.2 ROCE data for a selection of companies

Company name	Country	Type of business	Date of accounts/ Currency	Operating profit (loss)	Total equity + non-current liabilities	ROCE (%)
Infosys Limited	India	Technology	31 March 2013 Rupees million	127 990	382 320	33.5
Independent Media Corporation	Pakistan	Media	31 December 2012 Euros millions	59.7	276.3	21.6
Phoenix Beverages	Mauritius	Beers and wine	30 June 2013 Rupees 000s	95 837	2 965 266	3.2
Malaysia Airlines	Malaysia	Airline	31 December 2011 Ringgits 000s	(361 036)	11 794 472	– 3.1

Inventory turnover ratio

This ratio measures a company's success in converting inventories into sales. The ratio compares the value of inventories with sales achieved valued at cost. This permits an effective comparison with inventories, which can also be valued at cost. If the company makes a profit on each sale, then the faster it sells its inventories, the greater the profits it earns. This ratio is only of relevance to manufacturing businesses, as firms providing services do not hold significant quantities of inventories.

$$\text{Inventory turnover ratio} = \frac{\text{cost of goods sold}}{\text{average inventories held}}$$

In this form the results of calculating this ratio are expressed as a number of times a year. Century and Paper Board Mills Ltd is a Pakistani company based in Karachi and Lahore which manufactures a range of paper products. On 30 June 2013 the company held inventories valued at 2882 million Pakistani rupees (PKR). During the company's financial year which ended on that day the company had achieved sales (at cost) of PKR 11 690 million. The company's inventories turnover ratio was therefore 4.06 times.

The inventory turnover formula can be reorganised to express the number of days taken on average to sell the business's inventories.

$$\text{Inventory turnover ratio} = \frac{\text{inventories} \times 365}{\text{cost of sales}}$$

Our Century and Paper Board Mills Ltd calculation would then become PKR 2882 million × 365 divided by PKR 11 690 million giving an answer of 89.99 days. Thus, if Century and Paper Board Mills Ltd sells its complete inventories every 90 days, it will sell its inventories just over four times during a year.

Study tip

Other aspects of a business's activities can have significant impacts on the results of ratio calculations. For example, if a business uses a JIT system of inventory control it is likely to have a much higher level of inventory turnover.

Using this ratio

- The standard figure for this ratio varies hugely according to the type of business. A market trader selling fruit and vegetables might expect to sell his entire inventories every two or three days – about 100 times a year. At the other extreme an antiques shop might only sell its inventories every six months – or twice a year.
- A low figure for inventory turnover could be due to obsolete inventories. A high figure can indicate an efficient business, although selling out of inventories regularly results in customer dissatisfaction.
- Improving the inventory or stock turnover ratio requires a business to hold lower levels of inventories or to achieve higher sales without increasing levels of inventories.

Receivables (Debtors') days

This ratio is also referred to as receivables (or debtors') collection period. It calculates the time typically taken by a business to collect the money that it is owed. This is an important ratio, as granting customers lengthy periods of credit may result in a business experiencing liquidity problems. If a company has substantial cash sales these should be excluded from the calculation.

$$\text{Receivables days} = \frac{\text{receivables} \times 365}{\text{revenue}}$$

Using this ratio

- There is no standard figure for this ratio. In general a shorter figure is preferred as the business in question receives the inflow of cash more quickly. However, it can be an important part of a business's marketing strategy to offer customers a period of trade credit of perhaps 30 or 60 days.
- A rise in this ratio may be due to a number of causes. A period of expansion may mean that a business has to offer improved credit terms to attract new customers or a 'buy now pay later' offer may have been introduced.

This ratio may be improved by reducing the credit period on offer to customers or by insisting on cash payment. A more focused approach is to conduct an aged debtors' analysis. This technique ranks a business's debtors according to the period of credit taken. This allows managers to concentrate on persuading the slowest payers to settle their accounts.

Case Study

Late payment legislation

The Late Payment of Commercial Debts (Interest) Act 1998 and Late Payment of Commercial Debts Regulations 2002 give businesses in the UK the statutory right to claim interest on late payments from other businesses. The law was originally introduced in November 1998 but was amended by European Union directive in 2002.

The law allows all businesses, including public sector organisations, to claim interest from any other business or organisation if payment is late. A late payment is defined as where the agreed credit period given by the supplier to the purchaser has expired. If no credit period has been specified by the supplier the Act specifies a default period of 30 days after which interest will accumulate.

Questions

1 Explain why customers making late payments can cause problems for a small business. [8]

2 Discuss why a small business might be reluctant to claim interest from a large customer which buys a high proportion of its output and which regularly delays payment. [16]

Payables (Creditors') days

This ratio is also referred to as payables (or Creditors') collection period. It calculates the time typically taken by a business to pay the money it owes to its suppliers and other creditors. This is an important ratio, as delaying payment for as long as possible can help a business to avoid liquidity problems.

$$\text{Payables days} = \frac{\text{payables} \times 365}{\text{cost of sales}}$$

Using this ratio

- Businesses can improve their liquidity position by delaying payment, but this may result in poor relationships with suppliers who may suffer liquidity problems as a result of the delay in payment.
- Businesses may be charged interest on delayed payments which can add to costs and weaken a business's liquidity position.
- By comparing payables days and receivables days a business can assess its liquidity position. If the figure for payable days is lower then it is more likely that the business will experience liquidity problems as, on average, it is paying suppliers and other creditors more quickly than it is receiving payment from its customers.

Study tip

Payables days is not a ratio that you would normally be asked to calculate alone but it is important to use it alongside receivables days as a comparison between the two as it gives a useful insight into how the business is managing its finances efficiently.

Case Study

More on Century and Paper Board Mills Ltd

Some key data from the 2013 Annual Report for Century and Paper Board Mills Ltd is shown in Table 33.3.

Table 33.3

	2013 (PKR million)	2012 (PKR million)
Revenue	14236	12923
Cost of goods sold	11690	10823
Receivables	1185	1190
Payables	999	928

Source: Adapted from Century and Paper Board Mills Ltd Annual Report, 2012

In 2012 the company's payables and receivables ratios were as follows.

$$\text{Receivables days} = \frac{\text{receivables} \times 365}{\text{revenue}}$$

$$= \frac{\text{PKR 1190 m} \times 365}{\text{PKR 12923 million}}$$

$$= 33.61 \text{ days}$$

$$\text{Payables days} = \frac{\text{payables} \times 365}{\text{cost of sales}}$$

$$= \frac{\text{PKR 928 million} \times 365}{\text{PKR 10 823 million}}$$

$$= 31.30 \text{ days}$$

Comparing the results of these two ratio calculations it is apparent that Century and Paper Board Mills Ltd takes about two days less on average to pay its suppliers compared with the average time taken by its customers to settle their accounts.

Questions

1 Calculate the company's receivables days and payables days in 2013. [8]
2 Discuss whether Century and Paper Board Mills Ltd is managing its payables and receivables well. [16]

33.4 Gearing

Gearing measures the long-term liquidity of a business. Under some classifications of financial ratios gearing is included as a liquidity ratio. There are a number of methods of measuring gearing; we shall consider the simplest form of the ratio. This ratio analyses how firms have raised their long-term capital. The result of this calculation is expressed as a percentage.

There are two main forms of long-term finance available to businesses.

1 **Non-current liabilities** This includes preference shares and debentures (all have fixed interest payments). This is long-term borrowing and may be called loan capital.
2 **Total equity (also termed shareholder equity)** This arises from selling shares and increases in the value of the business.

The capital employed by a business is simply the total of these two. So this gearing ratio measures the percentage of a firm's capital that is borrowed.

$$\text{Gearing} = \frac{\text{non-current liabilities} \times 100}{\text{total equity} + \text{non-current liabilities}}$$

This measure of a business's performance is important because by raising too high a proportion of capital through fixed interest capital firms become vulnerable to increases in interest rates. Shareholders are also unlikely to be attracted to a business with a high gearing ratio as their returns might be lower because of the high level of interest payments to which the enterprise is already committed.

- A highly geared business has more than 50 per cent of its capital in the form of loans.
- A low geared business has less long-term borrowing and a gearing figure below 50 per cent.

Much attention tends to be given to businesses that have high gearing and are vulnerable to increases in interest rates. However, this may be considered acceptable in a business that is growing quickly and generating high profits. Furthermore, a low-geared business may be considered too cautious and not expanding as quickly as possible.

Using this ratio

- The key yardstick is whether a business's long-term borrowing is more than 50 per cent of capital employed.
- Companies with secure cash flows may raise more loan capital because they are confident of being able to meet interest payments. Equally, a business with well-known brands may be able to borrow heavily against the value of these brands to increase long-term borrowing.
- Firms can improve their gearing by repaying long-term loans or by issuing more ordinary shares.

The Duet Group in Table 33.4 is very heavily geared as it is significantly in excess of the 50 per cent standard maximum figure. The other two companies are less highly geared, although Pertamina has little potential to borrow more without being regarded as highly geared.

Maths moment

Use the information in Table 33.4 to calculate the following.

1 Assume that Pertamina's non-current liabilities in 2013 were US$13 500 m. What would have been the effect on the company's gearing ratio?
2 What figure for non-current liabilities would have been necessary in 2013 for the Duet Group to have a gearing ratio of 50 per cent?

33.5 Investors' ratios

These are also called shareholders' ratios or investment ratios. The results of this group of ratios are of particular interest to the shareholders of a company or to anyone considering purchasing shares in a particular company.

Shareholders can receive a return on their purchase of shares in two ways:

1 through dividends paid from the company's profits over the financial year
2 as a result of a rise in the price of the shares – called a capital gain.

Dividends offer a short-term return on an investment and may be of interest to shareholders seeking a quick return. However, other shareholders may seek a long-term return on their investment. They may be prepared to forgo high levels of dividends in the short term to allow profits to be invested. They hope that the business will grow, increasing the price of shares and providing a capital gain for shareholders.

There are a number of ratios that may be used by shareholders. However, we shall concentrate on ratios that compare the dividends received against the capital investment made by shareholders when purchasing shares.

Table 33.4 Gearing ratios of some leading international companies

Company	Country and industry	Date of statement of financial position/ Currency	Non-current liabilities	Total equity + non-current liabilities	Gearing (%)
Duet Group	Australia Energy supply	30 June 2012 Aus$ millions	6418	7940	80.83%
Pertamina	Indonesia Oil and gas mining	31 December 2013 US$ millions	11616	26809	43.33%
Lenovo Group Ltd	Hong Kong Computer manufacture	30 September 2012 US$ millions	601	2591	23.20%

Henry Sy

Figure 33.2 Henry Sy

Henry Sy was born in China in December 1924. He was a student at Chiang Kai Shek College and Far Eastern University.

He emigrated to the Philippines and started his commercial career by opening a small shop in Quiapo, Manila, selling shoes. He developed this business by opening two more shoe shops and then, recognising the benefits of selling a wide range of products, introduced other products into his shops, such as electrical goods. By 1972 he had created a chain of department stores: a pioneering store at Makati City followed by four other stores including one in Iloilo City which was the first outside of Metro Manila.

Not satisfied with his retail empire Henry opened some of the Philippines first shopping malls, making it easier for Filipinos to spend money! He currently owns 43 shopping malls across the Philippines and China. He has been voted Management Man of the Year by Makati Business Club and has received an Honorary Doctorate in Business Management by De La Salle University. He is thought to be the richest person in the Philippines with an estimated worth of $9.1 billion.

So why has Henry Sy been such a successful entrepreneur? In part this is because he was able to recognise an opportunity and a thorough understanding of retailing. The Philippines economy was recovering slowly from the Second World War in the 1950s. Incomes were rising and consumers were looking to spend money in shops. Fifty years later he purchased the Equitable PCI Bank and merged it successfully with another to form one of the Philippines' largest financial organisations. Henry is decisive and a natural decision-maker. This has been a valuable personal quality when combined with his ability to spot an opportunity.

Dividend per share

This is an important shareholders' ratio. It is simply the total dividend declared by a company divided by the number of shares the business has issued.

$$\text{Dividend per share} = \frac{\text{total annual dividends}}{\text{number of issued shares}}$$

Results of this ratio are expressed as a number of cents or pence per share, depending on the currency used.

In 2013 Marks and Spencer, one of the UK's best-known retailers, announced dividends totalling £293.37 million. The dividend per share for the company was calculated as follows:

Marks and Spencer's dividend per share (DPS)

= £293.77 million ÷ 1725.69 million shares

= 17.0 pence per share

It is normal for dividends to be paid in two parts: an interim dividend halfway through the financial year and a final dividend at the end of the year.

Using this ratio

- A higher figure is generally preferable to a lower one as this provides the shareholder with a larger return on his or her investment. However, some shareholders are looking for long-term investments and may prefer to have a lower DPS now in the hope of greater returns in the future and a rising share price.
- It is wise to compare the dividend per share with that offered by alternative companies. However, it is also important to bear in mind how much has to be invested to buy each share. A low dividend per share may be perfectly acceptable if the company has a low share price.
- A business can improve this figure by announcing higher dividends (and therefore reducing the amount of profit retained within the business). This may prove attractive to some shareholders, but may not be in the long-term interests of the business, particularly if profits are not rising.

Dividend yield

This ratio is really a development of the previous ratio and provides shareholders with more information. The dividend yield compares the dividend received on a single share with the current market price of that share. This provides shareholders with a better guide to a business's performance as it compares the return with the amount that would need to be invested to purchase a share. The result of calculating this ratio is given as a percentage.

$$\text{Dividend yield} = \frac{\text{dividend per share} \times 100}{\text{market price of share}}$$

Imagine a shareholder was considering investing in Marks and Spencer and noted that the share price on one particular day was 475 pence (or £4.75), and that the dividend per share for the company was 17.0 pence. He or she could calculate the dividend yield as follows.

$$\text{Dividend yield} = \frac{17.0 \times 100}{475} = 3.58\%$$

Using this ratio

- A higher return will be regarded as preferable by shareholders seeking a quick return. Longer-term investors might settle for a lower figure, allowing the firm to reinvest profits and offering the possibility of higher profits and dividends in the future.
- Results for this ratio can vary dramatically according to fluctuations in the company's share price.
- This ratio can be improved by increasing the proportion of profits distributed to shareholders in the form of dividends.

Case Study

Polymetal International announces dividends

Polymetal International plc is a mining company that specialises in precious metals with its headquarters in Russia, although its shares are sold on the London Stock Exchange. The company owns gold and silver mines in Russia and Kazakhstan. Production output in 2011 consisted of 55 per cent gold, 41 per cent silver and 4 per cent copper.

In October 2012, Polymetal International plc announced a dividend per share of £0.31 or 31 pence per share. At the time the company had 382 million issued shares and the total dividend payment was £118.42 million. At the time the company's share price on the London Stock Exchange was quoted at 1155 pence.

Figure 33.3 Polymetal International plc trades in precious metals

The company has introduced a new dividend policy paying regular dividends which will represent 30 per cent of the company's profits after tax and interest.

Commenting on the Board's decision, Vitaly Nesis, CEO of Polymetal, said: 'The implementation of our new dividend policy reflects the importance we place on delivering meaningful cash returns to our shareholders and sustainable value creation.'

Source: Adapted in part from BSR Russia

Questions

1 Explain how you think that the company's shareholders will respond to this announcement. [8]
2 Discuss the factors that might shape the shareholders' reaction. [16]

Dividend cover ratio

The dividend cover ratio shows how easily a business can pay its dividend from its profits. A high dividend cover means that the business can easily afford to pay the dividend and a low value means that the business might have difficulty paying a dividend.

$$\text{Dividend cover} = \frac{\text{profit after tax and interest}}{\text{total annual dividends}}$$

This ratio should be considered in the context of the stability of a company's profits after tax and interest payments. These profits are also referred to as earnings. A low level of dividend cover might be acceptable in a company with steady profits, but the same level of dividend cover in a company with volatile profits would indicate that future dividend payments may be at risk.

Using this ratio

- Generally speaking, a ratio of 2 or higher is considered safe – in the sense that the company can well afford the dividend – but anything below 1.5 is risky.
- If the ratio is under 1, the company is using its retained earnings from a previous year to pay this year's dividend. This is not a situation that can continue for a long time period.
- This ratio could be improved by reducing dividend payments, although shareholders and potential shareholders will not be impressed by such a move. In the longer term, increasing profitability will achieve the same aim in a way that is more acceptable to most stakeholders.

Price–earnings ratio (P/E ratio)

This ratio compares the current market price of a company's shares to its earnings per share. The P/E ratio is also called the 'price multiple'. The P/E ratio is sometimes referred to as a 'multiple' ratio, because it shows how much investors are willing to pay per dollar of earnings. If a company P/E ratio was 16, this would show that an investor is willing to pay $16 for $1 of earnings per share. An average P/E ratio is approximately 14 to 15.

To calculate the P/E ratio, it is first necessary to calculate a company's earnings per share (EPS). The EPS is the amount of the company's profits that belong to a single share. The EPS is calculated using the formula below:

$$\text{Earnings per share (EPS)} = \frac{\text{profit after tax and interest}}{\text{total number of issued shares}}$$

Once the earnings per share has been calculated then it is possible to use this information to complete the calculation of the P/E ratio.

$$\text{Price–earnings ratio} = \frac{\text{current share price}}{\text{earnings per share}}$$

Using this ratio

- In most circumstances, a higher P/E indicates that investors are anticipating higher growth in earnings in the future than in companies with a lower P/E ratio.
- Comparing the P/E ratio of a chosen company to other companies in the same industry is a valuable exercise.
- It can also be beneficial to analyse it against companies from other industries or against the company's previous P/E ratios. However, different industries can have very different growth prospects, making valid comparisons more difficult.
- One potential problem with the P/E measure arises because the denominator of the equation is earnings per share which, in turn, is based on its profit before tax. This figure can be manipulated, meaning that the P/E ratio is only as good as the data on which it is based.

Entre Rios Fruit Producers S.A.

This company is located near Concordia in Argentina. The company reported the figures shown in Table 33.5 in its Annual Report in 2012 and 2013.

Table 33.5

	2013	2012
Total annual dividends	$450 000	$425 000
Number of issued shares	1 875 000	1 850 000
Market price of share (31 December)	$4.86	$5.24
Profit after tax and interest	$787 000	$680 000

Questions

1 Use relevant ratios to compare Entre Rios Fruit Producers' financial performance in 2012 and 2013. [8]
2 To what extent do you think that Entre Rios Fruit Producers was more attractive to potential shareholders in 2012 than in 2013? [16]

33.6 The value and limitations of ratio analysis

Ratio analysis provides stakeholders with an insight into the performance of a business. However, to offer the maximum amount of information, the details gained from ratio analysis need to be compared with other data, such as that outlined below.

- **The results for the same business over previous years** This allows stakeholders to appreciate the trend of the data. Thus a low but steadily increasing figure for ROCE might be reassuring to investors.
- **The results of ratio analysis for other firms in the same industry** We have seen that results expected from various ratios vary according to the type of firm under investigation. Thus, the inventory turnover ratio will be much higher for a retailer selling perishable products than for a manufacturer. By comparing like-with-like a more informed judgement may be made.
- **The results of ratios from firms in other industries** Stakeholders can compare the ratios of a particular business with those from a wide range of firms. This might allow, for example, a comparison between two firms experiencing rapid growth. The Centre for Inter-Firm Comparisons offers anonymous data on the financial ratios of many UK firms.

Case Study

Intel

Intel is an American multinational company that manufactures semiconductor chips. It is the world's largest chipmaker, and has been the market leader since 1992. In 2011 the company earned revenue amounting to US$54 000 million and profits of US$12 900 million. It has more than 100 000 employees worldwide.

Intel holds a 17 per cent share of the global semiconductor market. While personal computer sales are slowing, they remain important, and Intel is expected to maintain its dominant market position.

Some analysts studying Intel think that it will perform less well in the future. They anticipate average earnings per share growth at around 12 per cent up to 2017, roughly half the company's figure from 2007 to 2012. Intel's forecast price to earnings (P/E) ratio is approximately 10, having recently declined. The company's shares are now priced at a level that should make the company attractive to many potential shareholders.

Investors may also be attracted by the company's dividend yield figure of 4.6 per cent. The dividend represents about 45 per cent of the company's earnings.

Questions

1 Explain the reasons why an investor might decide to buy shares in Intel. [8]
2 Evaluate the other information that would be useful to an investor considering investing in Intel. [16]

A significant weakness of ratio analysis is that it only considers the financial aspects of a business's performance. While this is undeniably important other elements of a business should be taken into account when evaluating performance.

- **The market in which the business is trading** A business that is operating in a highly competitive market might experience relatively low profits, reducing the results of ratios such as the return on capital employed (ROCE).
- **The position of the firm within the market** A market leader might be expected to provide better returns than a small firm struggling to establish itself. However, the small, struggling firm may be investing heavily in developing new products and establishing a brand identity. The struggling firm may generate large profits in the future.
- **The quality of the workforce and management team** These are important factors in assessing a business, but not ones that will be revealed directly through ratio analysis. Indeed, a business that invests heavily in its human resources may appear to be performing relatively poorly through the use of ratio analysis.
- **The economic environment** In general businesses might be expected to perform better during periods of prosperity and to produce better results from ratio analysis. During the period of poor economic performance for many major economies which started in 2008 it is reasonable to expect the financial performance of many (but not all) businesses to decline.

Test your learning

Short answer questions

1 **a** Define the term ratio analysis. [2]
  b Distinguish between efficiency ratios and profitability ratios. [3]

2 **a** What does the gearing ratio measure? [2]
  b Outline **two** sources of information that might be important when conducting ratio analysis. [3]

3 **a** State the formula used to calculate the inventory turnover ratio. [2]
  b Explain **one** reason why a company may have a low figure for inventory turnover. [3]

4 Explain why the return on capital employed (ROCE) is such an important ratio for stakeholders. [5]

5 **a** State the formula used to calculate the receivables days ratio. [2]

  b Why is it useful to use the payables days and receivables days ratios together when assessing a company's financial performance? [3]

6 Pelennor Products is a rapidly growing business providing IT services. The company's receivables (debtors') days ratio has increased from 33.2 days to 41.7 days over the past year. Explain the possible implications of this for the business. [5]

7 **a** A company has non-current liabilities totalling $456 000 and the figure for total equity is $780 500. Calculate its gearing ratio. [2]
  b Why might a business be concerned if its gearing figure was 75.6 per cent? [3]

8 Why might the dividend yield ratio provide a good measure of a company's performance for a potential shareholder? [5]

9 **a** Why might a dividend cover ratio of 1.2 be regarded as worrying by a company's shareholders? [3]

b State the formula used to calculate the price–earnings (P/E) ratio. [2]

10 a State **two** comparisons that a manager could make using the results of ratio analysis to help interpret the results. [2]

b Describe **one** aspect of a business's performance that is not covered by ratio analysis. [3]

Data response question

Lahore Construction Ltd (LC Ltd)

Over the last ten years it is estimated that the construction industry in Pakistan has contributed 2.5 per cent of the country's GDP. However, there are now fears that the industry is stagnating. LC Ltd builds houses, roads and bridges. It has suffered from declining sales recently as its house building activity has slowed and interest rates are expected to rise in the near future. However, the government is confident of attracting foreign investment into the industry.

The company's most recent accounts produced some interesting ratios as shown in Table 1.

Table 1

Ratio	Last year	The year before last
Acid test ratio	0.82:1	1.12:1
Gearing	51%	64%
ROCE	15.2%	14.1%
Total annual dividend ($m)	15.7	18.4
Number of issues shares (m)	180.39	176.82
Average share price ($)	2.42	2.20
Earnings per share (EPS) ($)	0.17	0.14

The company has faced some criticisms from its shareholders. It has repaid some of its loans, reducing its non-current liabilities. It is negotiating a $12 million contract with the Pakistan government to build new roads near to Jacobabad.

Questions

1 Analyse the benefits to LC Ltd's stakeholders of the company reducing its gearing ratio. [10]

2 a Calculate LC Ltd's dividend per share (DPS) for the two years. [4]

b Assess the extent to which LC Ltd's shareholders would be satisfied with its recent performance. [10]

3 Is it possible to judge LC Ltd's future performance from its published accounts? Justify your decision. [16]

Essay questions

1 To what extent is the ROCE a more valuable ratio for shareholders than the 'investor' ratios such as the price–earnings ratio? [20]

2 Discuss the extent to which a potential shareholder should rely on the results of ratio analysis when considering a large investment into a recently established and rapidly growing company. [20]

Past paper questions

1 Read the Atlantic Steel Company case study on pages 449–51 and then answer the following questions.

a Using data in Appendix B, analyse the financial efficiency of the business by calculating **two** appropriate ratios. [6]

b Evaluate any **two** ways in which the business might improve its financial efficiency. [8]

Cambridge International AS and A Level Business Studies 9707 Paper 32 Q3 October/November 2011

2 Read the Curry Cuisine case study on pages 471–72 and then answer the following question.

To what extent do you agree with Ling that the business would have problems raising the capital needed for the "ready made meals" project either from internal sources or from a loan? The use of relevant accounting ratios (based on the data in Appendix B) to support your judgement will be rewarded. [14]

Cambridge International AS and A Level Business Studies 9707 Paper 3 Q4 October/November 2007

34 Investment appraisal

Chapter overview

In this chapter we examine:

- the concept of investment appraisal and issues surrounding the forecasting of cash flows
- the basic methods of investment appraisal: payback and average rate of return
- discounted cash flow methods of calculating investment appraisal: net present value and internal rate of return
- assessing risks
- qualitative factors in investment appraisal.

Key terms

Cash flow is the movement of cash into and out of a business over a period of time.

Return on capital employed (ROCE) is the net profits of a business expressed as a percentage of the value of the capital employed in the business.

Risk is the chance of a misfortune occurring, possibly resulting in financial loss.

34.1 Introduction

This chapter looks at the techniques that businesses can use to make major investment decisions. It considers the reasons why businesses undertake programmes of investment and will look at financial and non-financial methods of assessing the worth of alternative investment projects.

Investment is an important term within business studies and often entails managers taking major decisions. Investment can mean a decision to purchase part or all of another business, perhaps as a result of a takeover bid. However, it is perhaps more common to use the term in relation to the purchase of a non-current asset or some other major expenditure.

What is common is that all such actions involve a degree of **risk**. This must be judged against the likely return. The final decision will depend upon managers' assessment of these two factors.

Businesses take decisions regarding investment in a variety of circumstances.

- **When contemplating introducing new products** A business may assess the likely costs and returns from investing in one or more new products.
- **Expansion** This may entail evaluating whether or not to invest in new non-current assets as part of a planned programme of growth. Tottenham Hotspur Football Club in London is planning to invest an estimated $400 million in developing a new stadium, built in part on its existing ground at White Hart Lane. The Club hopes to increase its sales revenue by attracting larger crowds into the new stadium which will have a capacity of 60 000 spectators.
- **Spending** Businesses may also use techniques of investment appraisal before spending on promotional campaigns, developing new brands or products or retraining the workforce.
- **Investing in new technology** This may be undertaken to reduce costs and improve productivity, or to meet with legal requirements or the expectations of consumers. For example, one of the world's largest mining companies, Rio Tinto, is to start using driverless trucks in its iron ore mines in Western Australia.

In each circumstance, however, the business must adopt an appropriate appraisal technique to decide whether the returns received from an investment are sufficient to justify the initial capital expenditure.

Risk and investment appraisal

Risk is an important factor within investment decision-making. Risk can be defined as uncertainty that is quantifiable or that can be measured. There are two major types of risk.

- Systematic risk relates to the environment in which a project will operate. Thus this type of risk could include a loss of sales and cash inflow due to, say, an adverse movement in the exchange rate.

- Specific risk is associated with a particular project. For example, launching a product that is entirely new and of which the firm has little experience.

Techniques of **investment appraisal** can incorporate an allowance for risk perhaps by reducing cash inflows or increasing costs. More sophisticated techniques use the theory of probability to attempt to arrive at more accurate predictions.

Risk should be distinguished from uncertainty. Uncertainty is not measurable and cannot be included in numerical techniques of investment appraisal. An investment project that appears to have a high degree of uncertainty attached to it may not be undertaken because the firm in question may be unable to assess its likely costs and benefits.

> **Key term**
>
> **Investment appraisal** is a series of techniques designed to assist businesses in judging the desirability of investing in particular projects.

Difficulties in forecasting costs and revenues

Forecasting future costs and revenues can be a very difficult and at times expensive exercise to undertake. Forecasts about future revenues could prove to be inaccurate for a number of reasons.

- Competitors may introduce new products or reduce their prices, reducing forecast sales and revenues.
- Tastes and fashions may change, resulting in an unexpected slump in demand. The popularity of flying (as a result of low-cost airlines) has led to large falls in demand for ferries and has led shipping companies to overestimate their sales.
- The economy may move into recession or slump (or alternatively into an upswing) resulting in sales figures radically different from those forecast.

Costs can be equally tricky to forecast. Unexpected periods of inflation, or rising import prices, might result in inaccurate forecasts of expenditures. This can lead to a significant reduction in actual profits when compared with forecasts.

Companies that operate in a stable economic environment are much more easily able to forecast into the future as they have confidence that their predictions on the rate of inflation, likely rate of interest, level of unemployment and hence demand are as accurate as they can make them. A stable economic environment should lead to more accurate forecasts of both costs and revenues associated with investment projects.

Investment appraisal and other business functions

It is easy to regard investment appraisal as simply a technique to be used when a business is contemplating purchasing non-current assets. However, investment appraisal can be used in relation to a number of a business's activities across each of its functional areas, all of which involve significant investment expenditure. These might include:

- investing in a major new advertising campaign
- expanding into new markets, perhaps overseas
- attempting to adjust management styles and corporate cultures, possibly entailing reorganisation and retraining
- adopting new techniques of production including JIT and kaizen
- researching and developing new products.

Investment appraisal is an important element of most aspects of business activity. It can help to quantify proposed actions by managers and provide important information to assist managers to take good quality decisions.

> **Case Study**
>
> ## Nintendo slashes sales forecasts

Figure 34.1 Nintendo has reduced its forecast sales

Nintendo has slashed the number of Wii U and 3DS consoles it expects to sell by the end of the 2013–14 financial year, which has had a knock-on effect on its financial forecasts.

In a statement, company president Satoru Iwata explained that Nintendo now expects to sell 2.8 million Wii U consoles by the end of March 2014, down from original estimates of 9 million, while 3DS projections have also been revised downwards from 18 million console sales to 13.5 million.

The knock-on effect of this is that the previous profit forecast has been revised from profit to loss. Nintendo was forecasting net profits of ¥55 billion, but is now expecting a net loss of ¥25 billion yen.

Sales in the US and European markets were significantly lower than the original forecasts. Iwata explained that despite hardware bundles and price cuts for the Wii U in western markets, sales still fell short 'by a large margin'.

The decision to downgrade sales projections for the Wii U isn't hugely surprising. Though it was projecting massive sales of 9 million consoles in October 2013 it later transpired that the company had sold fewer than 500 000 Wii Us in six months, suggesting its original forecasts were very optimistic.

Source: Adapted from IGN Topics, 17 January 2014 http://uk.ign.com

Questions

1 Explain why it is important for Nintendo to forecast its sales accurately. [8]
2 Discuss why, despite having huge resources to conduct primary market research, Nintendo appears unable to forecast its sales accurately. [16]

34.2 Financial techniques for making investment decisions

A number of techniques are available to managers to assist them in taking decisions on whether to go ahead with investments, or to help in making a judgement between two or more possible investment opportunities. This section will look at three of the most important of these techniques: payback, the average rate of return and discounted cash flow.

These financial techniques are valuable but do depend upon a number of assumptions:

- that all costs and revenues can be forecast easily and accurately for some years into the future
- that key variables (e.g. interest rates) will not change unexpectedly
- that the business in question is seeking maximum profits.

There are two major considerations for managers when deciding whether or not to invest in a non-current asset or another business:

1 the total profits earned by the investment over the foreseeable future
2 how quickly the investment will recover its cost. This occurs when the earnings from the investment exceed the cost of the investment.

The process of assessing these factors is called investment appraisal and refers to the process of assessing one or more potential investments.

Payback

Payback is a simple technique that measures the time period required for the earnings from an investment to recoup its original cost. Quite simply, it finds out the number of years it takes to recover the cost of an investment from its earnings. In spite of the obvious simplicity of the payback technique, it remains the most common method of investment appraisal used by businesses, especially small ones.

Table 34.1 A simple example of payback

Year	Cash outflow ($)	Cash inflow ($)
1	500 000	100 000
2		200 000
3		200 000
4		150 000

In Table 34.1 the calculation is simple: payback is achieved at the end of year 3, when the initial investment of $500 000 is recovered from earnings – $100 000 in year 1 plus $200 000 in each of years 2 and 3.

Calculations can be a little more complex, however, as shown in Table 34.2.

Table 34.2 A more complex example of payback

Year	Cash outflow ($)	Cash inflow ($)
1	500 000	100 000
2		100 000
3		200 000
4		300 000

In this case payback is achieved during the fourth year. The formula used to calculate the point during the year at which payback is achieved is as follows:

$$\text{Number of full years} + \left(\frac{\text{amount of investment not recovered}}{\text{revenue generated in next year}} \right)$$

In the second example the investment has recovered $400 000 after three years. Therefore $100 000 remains to be recovered in year 4 before payback point is reached. During year 4 the investment will generate $300 000. Thus:

$$\text{Payback} = 3 \text{ years} + \frac{100\,000}{300\,000} = 3\frac{1}{3} \text{ years, or three years and four months}$$

Figure 34.2 illustrates the concept of payback in the form of a graph.

Payback has the advantage of being quick and simple and this probably explains its popularity, especially with small businesses. However, it does have disadvantages. It ignores the level of profits that may be ultimately generated by the investment. For profit maximising businesses this may represent an important omission. Furthermore, payback ignores the timing of any receipts. The following example highlights this weakness.

Two investment projects, A and B, each require an investment of $1 million. Their expected earnings are shown in Table 34.3.

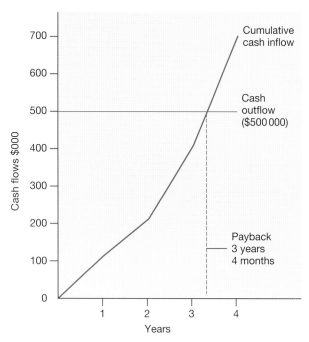

Figure 34.2 Payback on a graph

Table 34.3 Comparing investment returns

Year	Project A cash inflow ($)	Project B cash inflow ($)
1	500 000	100 000
2	300 000	100 000
3	100 000	300 000
4	100 000	500 000

Both investment projects achieve payback at the end of year 4. However, A is obviously more attractive because it yields greater returns in the early years. Payback does not take into account the timing of any income received.

Maths moment

Calculate the percentage of revenue from the four years of each of the two projects in Table 34.2 that is received in the first two years. What is the significance of this difference?

Study tip

Do not spend too long on investment appraisal calculations and do not carry out the same calculation repeatedly. Make sure you show your workings when answering questions.

Average rate of return

The average rate of return (or ARR) is a more complex and meaningful method of investment appraisal. This technique calculates the percentage rate of return on each possible investment. The resulting percentage figure allows a simple comparison with other investment opportunities, including investing in banks and building societies. It is important to

remember, however, that a commercial investment (such as purchasing CAD/CAM equipment for a production line) involves a degree of risk. The returns may not be as forecast. Therefore it is important that such an investment earns significantly more than the rate of interest available in the local bank. If the percentage return on purchasing the CAD/CAM equipment was identical to that on a high-interest account in a bank, the latter would represent the better investment, as it carries little risk.

The formula for calculating ARR is:

$$\frac{\text{average profit}}{\text{asset's initial cost}} \times 100\%$$

$$\text{average profit} = \frac{\text{total net profit before tax over the asset's lifetime}}{\text{useful life of the asset}}$$

Case Study

Miller Reprographics

Purchasing new IT equipment for Miller Reprographics is estimated to cost $120 000 and a return of $220 000 over five years is anticipated.

The total profit for the company from investing in IT over five years = $220 000 − $120 000 = $100 000.

On an annual basis this is $100 000 / 5 = $20 000

Average rate of return = $\dfrac{\$20\,000}{\$120\,000} \times 100\% = 16.67\%$

Miller Reprographics may consider this to be an attractive investment.

Questions

1 Explain why Miller Reprographics might prefer to use the average rate of return (ARR) rather than payback to judge this investment. [8]
2 Discuss the factors that Miller Reprographics might consider when deciding whether or not this really is an attractive investment. [16]

Maths moment

Use the data in the Miller Reprographics case study to answer the following question.

Calculate the total profit the company would have had to have earned to generate an ARR of 35 per cent.

The average rate of return is considered to be more useful than payback because it considers the level of profits earned from an investment rather than simply the time taken to recover costs. It also offers easier comparison with returns on other investments, notably financial investments in banks and building societies. However, this technique also fails to differentiate between investments that generate high returns in the early years and those that offer greater rewards later on.

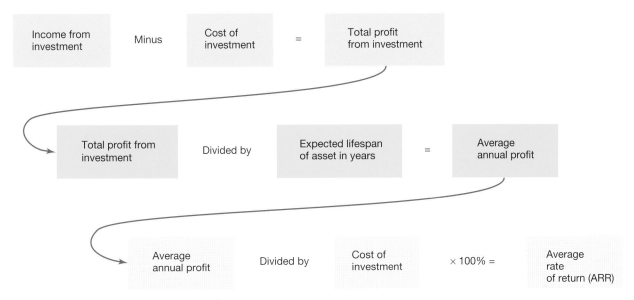

Figure 34.3 How to calculate average rate of return

Discounted cash flow

The technique of discounted cash flow takes into account what is termed the 'time value' of money. The time value of money is based on the principle that money at the present time is worth more than money at some point in the future. Thus, according to this principle, $1000 today is of greater value than $1000 in one or two years' time. There are two major reasons why this time value principle exists.

1 **Risk** – having $1000 now is a certainty; receiving the same amount at some point in the future may not occur. The full $1000 payment may not be made; indeed no payment at all may be made. An investment project may fail to provide the expected returns because of a competitor's actions, because of a change in tastes and fashions or as a consequence of technological change.

2 **Opportunity cost** is the best forgone alternative. Even if no risk existed, the time value of money would still exist. This is because the money could be placed into an interest-bearing account generating a return. Thus, if we assume that a rate of 5 per cent is available on an interest-bearing account, $1000 in one year's time is worth the same as $953 today. The reason for this is that by investing $953 at an interest rate of 5 per cent, we would have $1000 after one year.

This time–value principle means that the longer the delay before money is received, the lower its value in present-day terms. This is called present value. Table 34.4 shows two investments requiring identical outlays. Both projects also receive the same cash inflow over a four-year period and would generate the same average rate of return (10 per cent). However, the majority of the cash inflow for project A occurs in year 1, while in project B this is delayed until year 3. The time–value principle would suggest that project A is preferable to project B. To show the effect of the time principle we need

to calculate the present value of cash inflows and outflows through the use of discounting.

Table 34.4 Two similar investment projects with different time patterns for cash inflows

Year	Investment project A $000s	Investment project B $000s
0 (now)	(500)	(500)
1	400	100
2	100	100
3	100	100
4	100	400

Discounting

Discounting is the process of adjusting the value of money received at some future date to its present value, i.e. its worth today. Discounting is, in effect, the reverse of adding interest. Discounting tables are available to illustrate the effect of converting future streams of income to their present values. The rate of interest plays a central role in discounting, in the same way as it does in predicting the future value of savings. Table 34.5 shows the discounting figures and the value in present-day terms of $1000 over a period of five years into the future. If the business anticipates relatively high interest rates over the period of the investment then future earnings are discounted heavily to provide present values for the investment. Lower rates result in discounting having a lesser effect in converting future earnings into present values.

Key term

Discounting is reducing the value of future earnings to reflect the opportunity cost of an investment.

Table 34.5 The process of discounting

Year	Discounting factor used to convert to present value assuming 10% rate of interest	Present value of $1000 at a discount rate of 10% ($)	Discounting factor used to convert to present value assuming 5% rate of interest	Present value of $1000 at a discount rate of 5% ($)
0 (now)	1	1000	1	1000
1	0.909	909	0.952	952
2	0.826	826	0.907	907
3	0.751	751	0.864	864
4	0.683	683	0.822	822

The basic calculation is that the appropriate discounting factor is multiplied by the amount of money to be received in the future to convert it to its present value. Thus, at a rate of interest of 10 per cent, the present value of $1000 in two years' time is $826 ($1000 × 0.826). The present value of $1000 received in fours years' time is $683. This figure is lower because the time interval is greater and the effect of the time–value principle more pronounced.

From this example we can see that the rate of interest has a significant effect on the present value of future earnings. With a higher rate of interest, there is a greater rate of discount. Thus, the present value of $1000 in three years' time is $751 if the rate of interest is assumed to be 10 per cent. However, if the rate of interest is estimated to be 5 per cent the present value is greater: $864.

The choice of interest rate to be used as the basis for discounting is an important decision by a business undertaking investment appraisal. The discounting rate selected normally reflects the interest rates that are expected for the duration of the project. However, as we shall see later, another approach (called the internal rate of return or IRR) is to choose the rate the firm would like to earn on the project and to use this as the basis of the calculation.

Net present value

Discounting expected future cash flows is the basis of calculating net **present value**. This method of investment appraisal forecasts expected outflows and inflows of cash and discounts the inflows and outflows. To calculate net present value we need to know:
● the initial cost of the investment
● the chosen rate of discount
● any expected inflows and outflows of cash
● the duration of the investment project
● any remaining or residual value of the project at the end of the investment (if the investment is to purchase production equipment this may have scrap value once it is obsolete, for example).

The outflows of cash are subtracted from the discounted inflows to provide a net figure: the net present value. This figure is important for two reasons.
1 If the net present value figure is negative, the investment is not worth undertaking. This is because the present value of the stream of earnings is less than the cost of the investment. A more profitable approach would be to invest the capital in an interest-bearing account earning at least the rate of interest that was used for discounting.
2 When an enterprise is considering a number of possible investment projects it can use the present value figure to rank them. The project generating the highest net present value figure is the most worthwhile in financial terms. In these circumstances a business may select the project – or projects – with the highest net present values.

Here is an example of calculating net present value. *Sailing Monthly* is one of New Zealand's most popular sailing magazines. The owners of the magazine, Bure Publishing, are investigating the production of an online edition especially designed for tablet computers. The company has conducted negotiations with two software houses regarding the development of a website for its new product, e-sailing. The two software houses offered very different ideas: one (proposal A) suggested a basic product allowing Bure Publishing to offer access to the magazine at a bargain price; the other (proposal B) proposed a more sophisticated product, to a higher technical standard, offering the opportunity for premium pricing.

The cash flows associated with these proposals over a five-year period are set out in Table 34.6. These show the cost of developing the website and the expected revenues, less operating costs for the site each year. Bure Publishing estimates that a 10 per cent discount rate would reflect likely market rates of interest.

Bure Publishing would opt for proposal A on the basis of this financial information, as the net present value for proposal A (the cheaper option) is higher than that for proposal B. The net cash flow for proposal A is also positive as cash inflows exceed outflows. Therefore the investment is viable. However, non-financial information may affect this investment decision.

The internal rate of return (IRR)

This is another way in which discounting and the concept of present value can be used in the process of investment

Table 34.6 Comparing Bure Publishing's investment projects using discounted cash flow

Year	Proposal A			Proposal B		
	Annual cash flows ($)	Discounting factors at 10%	Present value ($)	Annual cash flows ($)	Discounting factors at 10%	Present value ($)
0	(212 000)	1	(212 000)	(451 000)	1	(451 000)
1	46 000	0.909	41 814	89 400	0.909	81 265
2	57 500	0.826	47 495	115 000	0.826	94 990
3	63 250	0.751	47 501	122 500	0.751	91 998
4	69 000	0.683	47 127	144 275	0.683	98 540
5	71 000	0.621	44 091	140 000	0.621	86 940
Net present value			16 028	**Net present value**		2733

appraisal. The internal rate of return does not choose a particular discounting rate. Instead a series of calculations are carried out using computers until a rate of discount is discovered which results in the net present value of the project equalling zero. That is the cash outflows and inflows when discounted at this particular rate exactly equal one another.

This rate of discount can be compared with:

● a target rate of return for which the business aims, or
● the expected rate of interest.

If the internal rate of return is higher the project should be considered viable. Although this appears to require complex calculations, computers can work out the IRR for any investment project almost instantaneously.

Study tip

You will not be asked to calculate the internal rate of return when answering questions although you do have to understand what it is and what the percentage figures using this method mean.

A comparison of investment appraisal methods

The method of investment appraisal chosen will depend upon the type of firm, the market in which it is trading and its corporate objectives. A small firm may be more likely to use payback because managers may be unfamiliar with more complex methods of investment appraisal. Small businesses also often focus on survival, and an important aspect of any investment will be how long it takes to cover the cost of the investment from additional revenues. Payback is therefore valuable for firms who wish to minimise risk.

Larger firms that have access to more sophisticated financial techniques may use the average rate of return or discounted cash flow methods. These methods highlight the overall profitability of investment projects and may be more appropriate for businesses where profit maximisation is important.

Table 34.7 A comparison of techniques of investment appraisal

Method of investment appraisal	Advantages	Disadvantages
Payback	Easy to calculate Simple to understand Relevant to firms with limited funds who want a quick return	Ignores timing of payments before payback Excludes income received after payback Does not calculate profit
Average rate of return	Measures the profit achieved on projects Allows easy comparison with returns on financial investments (bank accounts, for example)	Ignores the timing of the payments Calculates average profits – they may fluctuate wildly during the project
Discounted cash flow	Makes an allowance for the opportunity cost of investing Takes into account cash inflows and outflows for the duration of the investment	Choosing the discount rate is difficult – especially for long-term projects A complex method to calculate and easily misunderstood

Investment criteria

Once the investment appraisal process has produced an answer, this needs to be compared with something in order to make a decision. There are a number of criteria that a business may use to make an investment decision.

1 **The rate of interest** Average rate of return and net present value (NPV) methods produce figures that can be compared with the rate of interest. Any interest rate chosen for this process will be based on the interest rate set by the Bank of England or other relevant central bank. In essence, the managers of the business will seek a return that will be greater than the current and forecast interest rates if the average rate of return is used or, if they are using NPV, the interest rate that is current should produce a positive net present value.

Using the interest rate as a criterion is not straightforward. Many investment projects are long term and expenditure and returns may take place over many years. It is highly unlikely that interest rates will remain unchanged for this period of time. Therefore managers have to decide on a rate or range of rates to use in their calculations.

2 **The level of profit** We saw in Chapter 33 on interpreting company accounts that a series of ratios can be used to assess the profitability of a business. One of these (return on capital employed or ROCE) provides a figure that measures profits generated against the value of resources available to the business. It is not unusual for a business to set itself targets in terms of ROCE. Managers may insist that any new investment project should generate returns that will at least match (and hopefully exceed) the business's overall target for ROCE.

3 **Alternative investments** It would be unusual for a business to consider only a single investment project. Most managers contemplating a major investment will have other options. These could be very different investments or simple variants on the first proposal. The business may simply select the project or projects that perform the best, subject to some minimum criteria in terms of profits or percentage returns. In such circumstances opportunity cost is an important concept for managers to bear in mind.

Study tip

Investment criteria can be useful to you when responding to questions on investment appraisal. When judging whether or not a business should go ahead with a particular investment, it is important to think what criteria the business would expect the investment to meet. The case study may directly state these or they may be implied. In either case, by relating your answer to the criterion or criteria you have a basis for making a judgement that you are able to justify.

Case Study

Chinese billionaire launches takeover bid

Landbridge, owned and led by Chinese billionaire, Ye Cheng, announced in March 2014 that it is bidding to take over an Australian gas producer WestSide. Shares in WestSide rose by 13 per cent on the day the takeover bid was made public. WestSide has significant unused reserves and exploration interests in Queensland.

Landbridge, of China's Shandong Province, has offered A$0.36 per share, according to an announcement by WestSide. The bid is subject to a number of approvals, WestSide said.

Ye is chairman of the Shandong Landbridge Group. The company's businesses include logistics, petrochemicals, timber

trading and real estate. Landbridge is also an investor in Rizhao Bank, located in Shandong, which has 43 branches and 1200 employees.

Source: Adapted from Forbes.com, 10 March 2014
http://www.forbes.com

Questions

1 Explain the benefits of using the net present value approach to help to decide the financial case for major decisions such as this takeover. [8]
2 Evaluate the difficulties that Landbridge may have faced in forecasting the financial costs and returns of the takeover investment. [16]

34.3 Assessing the risks and uncertainties of investment decisions

It is not a simple matter to assess the degree of risk involved in an investment decision. Risk is the chance of something adverse or bad happening. In the context of investment decisions there are two broad possibilities: costs may be higher than forecast or sales lower than expected.

Forecasting future sales can be a very difficult, and often expensive, exercise. Market research can be used, but it is costly and not always reliable. The difficulties in forecasting sales arise from a number of factors.

- **Timescales** It is much harder to forecast sales accurately many years into the future. Over a longer timescale it is more likely that tastes and fashions may change or that new competitors or new products may enter the market.
- **New markets** If an investment project is based on a business entering a new market (either in geographical or product terms) then the business has less experience and no financial records to use as a guide in forecasting sales. In December 2012 the global retailer Tesco announced that it was pulling out of the USA having failed to break in to one of the world's toughest retail markets. Operating costs proved to be high and sales figures did not reach expectations. Apparently even one of Britain's largest companies does not find it easy to forecast its sales accurately.
- **Competitors' reactions** Deciding on a particular programme of investment may bring a business into competition with rivals in new ways. Entering a new market (as in the case of Tesco above), producing new products or developing new methods of production may all provoke a response from competitors. This may take the form of increased advertising, cutting prices

or bringing out new products. Each of these actions will impact on the sales associated with the investment project. However, not knowing the type or extent of reaction in advance makes it very difficult to estimate its effect on future sales.

Equally, costs may rise above the forecast level, reducing the returns from the investment, as we saw earlier with Tesco's unsuccessful expansion into the USA. In March 2014 the price of oil rose to more than $110 per barrel, reducing the profit margins of many companies including airlines such as Virgin Atlantic. In May 2013 oil was priced at $96 a barrel. The volatility of prices for such a fundamentally important product highlights the difficulties that firms face when attempting to forecast future costs of production.

Managers may seek to identify and manage the risk in an investment decision by taking a range of actions, including the following.

- **Purchasing raw materials on forward markets** This means that the firm concerned negotiates a price at the present time for a product to be delivered at some agreed date in the future. For example, many airlines have agreed future prices for the delivery of aviation fuel and therefore know for certain this element of their future costs. Although it removes the risk of a sudden increase in costs, it may be judged a mistake if prices fall between agreeing the deal and the delivery of the product.

- **Building in allowances for fluctuations in sales revenue and costs** Prudent managers may opt to forecast a range of sales figures and costs of production which are based on their market research, but which allow for the market to change in some way that may be either adverse or favourable. Building in this flexibility in forecasting, and thinking about how wide the ranges for sales revenue and costs should be, will help managers to judge the degree of risk as well as the value of an investment project.

- **Ensuring the business has sufficient financial assets available** If a business is trading in a volatile or rapidly changing market it would be sensible to make certain the business has sufficient resources to deal with any adverse circumstances. Tesco plans to increase its sales in China by $17 billion by 2017. The company is likely to have sufficient finance to support its ambitious plans even if sales do prove to be below forecasts for an extended period of time.

Figure 34.4 A SouthWest Airlines plane

costs) and for many years has operated a very successful strategy of hedging against oil price rises.

What is hedging? Hedging is a financial strategy that lets airlines or other investors protect themselves against rising prices for commodities such as oil by locking in a price for fuel. It has been described as everything from gambling to buying insurance.

In 2008, Southwest Airlines paid $1.98 per gallon for fuel. American Airlines paid $2.73, and United paid $2.83 per gallon in the same period. For many years hedging its expenditure on fuel has saved Southwest billions of dollars. It has sometimes meant the difference between profit and loss. However, the company's fuel strategy can also go wrong. In the autumn of 2011 the company announced a surprising third quarter loss due to wrong decisions on fuel hedging when the oil price unexpectedly fell from a peak of $125 a barrel earlier in the year.

Source: Adapted from Associated Press Report, 30 June 2008 and FT.com, 20 October 2011

Questions

1 Explain why Southwest Airlines might experience problems in forecasting its costs as part of a major programme of investment. [8]
2 Do you think that the advantages of Southwest Airlines fuel hedging strategy outweigh the disadvantages? Justify your view. [16]

Case Study

Southwest Airlines' hedging strategy

Southwest Airlines is an American low-cost airline based in Dallas, Texas. It is the largest airline in the United States by number of passengers carried domestically per year (as of 31 December 2007). In 2011 Southwest operated approximately 3400 flights each day. The company buys enormous quantities of aviation fuel (it amounts to about 30 per cent of the airline's total

Is it worth using techniques of investment appraisal?

The results of investment appraisal calculations are only as good as the data on which they are based. Firms experience difficulty in accurately forecasting the cost of many major projects. It is even more difficult to estimate the likely revenues from investment projects, particularly long-term ones. It is perhaps possible to make an allowance to represent risk, for example, the possibility of a competitor taking actions that result in sales being lower than forecast. However, uncertainty – which cannot be measured – may make any investment appraisal worthless.

In assessing the value of numerical techniques of investment appraisal, some thought has to be given to the alternative. Without the use of payback and the like, managers would operate on the basis of hunches and guesswork. Some managers may have a good instinct for these matters, whereas others may not. As markets become more complex and global, the need for some technique to appraise investments becomes greater. It is more difficult for an individual or a group to have an accurate overview of a large international market comprising many competitors and millions of diverse individuals. Detailed market research to forecast possible revenues and the use of appropriate techniques of investment appraisal may become even more important in the future.

34.4 Qualitative influences on investment appraisal

The financial aspects of any proposed investment will clearly have an important influence upon whether a business goes ahead with the plan. However, a number of other issues may affect the decision.

- **Corporate image** A firm may reject a potentially profitable investment project, or choose a less profitable alternative, because to do otherwise might reflect badly on the business. Having a positive corporate image is important in terms of long-term sales and profits and may be considered more important than gaining short-term advantage from profitable investments. In the UK the NatWest Bank has invested heavily in internet banking and had planned to close many high street branches as part of this investment programme. However, the bad publicity given to branch closures by all banks led the NatWest to reverse the closure decision. The firm's investment in internet banking may prove less profitable as a consequence.
- **Corporate objectives** Most businesses will only undertake an investment if they consider that it will assist in the achievement of corporate objectives. For example, Rolls-Royce Engineering, a company that publicly states its aim to produce high-quality products, may invest heavily in training for its staff and in research and development. This will assist in the manufacture of world-class aero engines and vehicles.
- **Environmental and ethical issues** These can be important influences on investment decisions. Some firms have a genuine commitment to trading ethically and to inflicting minimal damage on the environment. This is a core part of the business philosophy of some firms. As a consequence they would not exploit cheap foreign labour or use non-sustainable resources. Other firms may have a less deep commitment to ethical and

environmental trading but may avoid some investments for fear of damaging publicity.
- **Industrial relations** Some potentially profitable investments may be turned down because they would result in a substantial loss of jobs. Taking decisions that lead to large-scale redundancies can be costly in terms of decreased morale, redundancy payments and harm to the business's corporate image.

Study tip

It is essential to think about quantitative and qualitative factors when making decisions on investment projects. Most case studies will include some qualitative issues for you to weigh up, and a good quality answer will take these into account as well as any quantitative information.

Case Study

Cargill plans $750 million expansion in Indonesia

Global food and agriculture company Cargill has set aside US$750 million to finance its business expansion in Indonesia, particularly in the food processing industry. Bram Klaeijsen, President of Cargill Asia Pacific Holdings, said the funds would be spent from the beginning of 2014 for the following four or five years.

'We're planning to build a food [processing] complex. We will make sweeteners, oil and fats and animal food. So it's all food related and maybe some customers will come to use our products to produce goods for other customers,' Klaeijsen said.

The food processing complex will be established in the Serang area of Banten. Klaeijsen also said Cargill would try to distribute products manufactured by the new facilities to the domestic market.

'We will sell as much as we can [in] the domestic [market], but when you build a facility, you build for a certain size and to fill up, you may have to export some,' Klaeijsen said.

Cargill, based in the US state of Minnesota, started its business in Indonesia in 1974 by establishing a feed mill in Bogor, West Java. Following expansive moves, the company's products now include animal nutrition, cocoa, grain, oil seeds, palm oil and sugar.

According to Klaeijsen, Cargill now has eight animal feed plants in Indonesia.

Cargill invested in a $100 million cocoa processing facility project in Gresik, East Java in 2013. The plant, which is designed to have the capacity to process 70 000 tons of cocoa beans a year, is expected to be finished in the middle of 2014.

Source: Adapted from *The Jakarta Post*, 8 November 2013 (Raras Cahyafitri) http://www.thejakartapost.com

Questions

1 Explain why Cargill would have used investment appraisal techniques as part of its decision to invest in Indonesia. [8]

2 Do you think that qualitative or quantitative factors would have influenced Cargill more strongly in reaching the decision to invest $750 million? Justify your view. [16]

Test your learning

Short answer questions

1 **a** Define the term investment. [2]

b Explain **one** reason why forecasts of sales revenues arising from an investment may be inaccurate. [3]

2 **a** What is meant by the term risk? [2]

b Describe **one** reason why a major retailer may make a major investment. [3]

3 Thames Radio is contemplating investing in new broadcasting equipment. The cost of the investment is forecast to be £150 000. The expected additional revenue from being able to broadcast to a larger area is £40 000 per annum. What is the payback period of this investment? [5]

4 **a** Explain **one** disadvantage of using payback in the circumstances in question 3. [3]

b State the formula required to calculate average rate of return. [2]

5 Bangar Leisure is considering the purchase of a new boat for cruises in Brunei Bay. The *Royal Queen* is available at a cost of $900 000 and would cost $100 000 each year to operate. Over its ten-year life the cruiser would generate $280 000 in revenue each year. Calculate the average rate of return on this investment. [5]

6 **a** What is meant by the present value of a stream of earnings from an investment? [3]

b What is meant by the term discounting? [2]

7 Harare Printers is appraising the costs of and benefits from a new piece of machinery. The equipment costs $300 000 and has a working life of four years. The company expects to generate revenue of $120 000 each year if it purchases the machine. Calculate the net present value of this project assuming an interest rate of 10 per cent. [5]

8 **a** Explain **one** criterion that a company may use to make a decision on whether or not to go ahead with an investment programme. [3]

b State **two** reasons why it can be difficult to forecast sales. [2]

9 Explain **two** actions a business may take to manage the degree of risk involved in an investment decision. [5]

10 **a** Describe the internal rate of return method of investment. [2]

b State **three** qualitative factors a business may take into account when making an investment decision. [3]

Data response question

A risky investment?

Tangalle is one of Sri Lanka's most popular tourist destinations: its beaches are especially popular with those from overseas. This may explain a rumour that the Intercontinental Hotel Group (the world's largest hotel business) is to open a large hotel just outside the town. High potential sales is one factor influencing Leisure Group Ltd's investigation into building a new hotel in the town – its first one in the country. It will help to achieve its corporate objective of growth. Leisure Group Ltd is profitable – it most recent ROCE figure was 17 per cent.

Although Sri Lanka is increasingly popular with holidaymakers, its uncertain political situation has deterred some international travellers from visiting Tangalle. Leisure Group Ltd is ethical and committed to good employment conditions and high wages for all its employees. The company plans to build its large modern building in an unspoilt bay; this will result in the destruction of many trees and other plants.

Leisure Group Ltd's costs are shown in Table 1 and are based on the use of a construction company based in UAE.

Table 1

Year	Investment cost ($)	Profit ($)
Now (Year 0)	2 500 000	0
1	–	52 000
2	–	110 000
3	–	150 000
4	–	200 000

Questions

1 Analyse the reasons why Leisure Group Ltd's proposed investment could be considered risky. [10]

2 a Calculate the average rate of return on the proposed hotel for its first four years of trading. [6]

   b Evaluate the major qualitative issues relating to the proposed hotel. [8]

3 Should Leisure Group Ltd build the hotel? Justify your decision. [16]

Essay questions

1 To what extent does the difficulty in forecasting costs and revenues mean that investment appraisal techniques are of little value to managers planning a major investment? [20]

2 Many businesses operate in global markets. Discuss whether this means that qualitative factors should play the most important role in all investment decisions. [20]

Past paper questions

1 Read the Chan Beauty Company case study on pages 452–54 and then answer the following questions.

a Calculate for Option 2 the:

   i Average Rate of Return (ARR) [4]

   ii Net Present Value (NPV) using the 10% discount factors in Table 1. [4]

b Which of the two options would you advise June to choose? Fully support your answer by referring to your results from **a** and other information. [16]

Cambridge International AS and A Level Business Studies
9707 Paper 32 Q4 October/November 2009

2 Read the Radar Cosmetics case study on pages 456–58 and then answer the following questions.

a Calculate for the country R location:

   i Average rate of return (ARR) [3]

   ii Payback period [3]

   iii Net Present Value (NPV) at 10% discount rate. [4]

b Using your results from part **(a)**, data in Table 2 and other information, recommend the country in which Radar should locate its new factory. [14]

Cambridge International AS and A Level Business Studies
9707 Paper 31 Q4 October/November 2010

35 Strategic management

Chapter overview

In this chapter we examine:
- the meaning of strategic management
- SWOT analysis
- PEST or external environment analysis
- business vision/mission statement and objectives
- the Boston Matrix
- Five Forces analysis
- core competencies.

Figure 35.1 Strategic management

> **Key term**
>
> A **strategy** is a long-term plan to achieve an objective.

35.1 Corporate strategy, tactics and strategic management

A corporate **strategy** is the long-term plan of a business that is developed to help it achieve its corporate objectives. For example, to achieve growth a business may decide to target emerging economies such as Brazil and China as its strategy. This strategy needs to be put into effect, which involves a series of shorter-term actions known as tactics. For example, the business would need to decide when to enter these two markets, which products to offer and whether to enter an alliance with a local business. The strategy has to be right in the first place for the business to achieve its objectives – if Brazil and China are the wrong countries to target then it does not matter how good the tactics are, the business will still do badly – but the tactics also have to be right to make sure the strategy works as planned.

Strategic management is the process of developing and implementing a strategy. It involves analysing the existing situation and the strategic options available to the business, developing the long-term plan, putting the strategy into action and then reviewing to see if it needs changing.

The need for strategic management

A business needs to be constantly reviewing what it is doing because of changes inside and outside of the business. New products, new staff, new competitors, new laws, for example, mean a business has to review whether its existing plan is still appropriate. With the growth of online business does it need to have high street stores any more? With the opening up of more markets overseas should it set up in Russia? With more skilled staff should it broaden the range of services it offers? Strategic management therefore means the business needs to review and analyse its position before planning what to do next. It should ensure the business strategy is appropriate for the conditions of the moment and prepare itself effectively for the future.

Strategy and organisational structure

The strategy of a business will be closely linked to the organisational structure it adopts. This was highlighted by Alfred Chandler's famous study of four US conglomerates that dominated their industries – these were DuPont, General Motors, Standard Oil and Sears Roebuck. Chandler highlighted that these businesses managed their growth by adopting an M form of organisational structure (Figure 35.2). This means that they used a multidivisional approach in which the different countries and divisions were relatively independent but were overseen by a headquarters that coordinated them and developed the corporate strategy.

Figure 35.2 M form

Chandler defined strategy as the determination of long-term goals and objectives, the adoption of courses of action and associated allocation of resources required to achieve goals; he defined structure as the design of the organisation through which the strategy is administered. He argued that changes in an organisation's strategy led to new administrative problems which, in turn, required a new or refashioned structure for the successful implementation of the new strategy.

For example, many businesses have a functional structure when they are relatively small with few product lines (Figure 35.3a). As the business grows and introduces more products it often adopts a product approach (Figure 35.3b). This enables the managers of each division to focus on their particular products. As a business expands further and starts to operate geographically it often adopts a regional structure to focus on the specific requirements of that market (Figure 35.3c).

Alfred Chandler summarised arguing that *structure follows strategy* and so the structure must adapt as the strategy changes.

Qantas

The Australian airline Qantas recently reported its first annual loss since it was privatised in 1995, as a result of high fuel costs and growing losses at its international operations.

The firm made a net loss of 244 million Australian dollars (about US $230 million) for the year up until 30 June. Qantas also had to cancel orders for 35 Boeing Dreamliner jets worth $8.5 billion due to 'lower growth requirements'.

Growth was expected to continue to be slow due to the uncertain global economic environment. The biggest impact

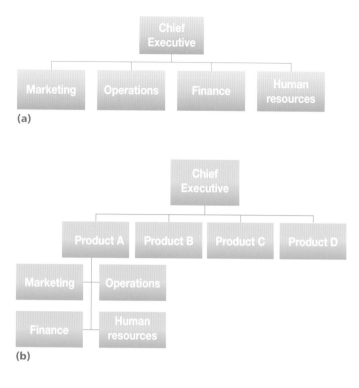

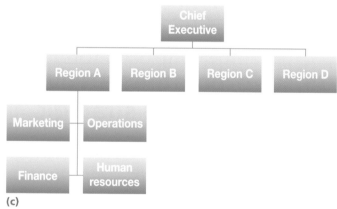

Figure 35.3 Types of structure: (a) functional, (b) product, (c) regional

on Qantas' earnings came from the growing losses at its international operations. Not only has Qantas lost passengers due to the economic crisis; it has also lost passengers to competitors. The company has tried to improve things by cancelling services on loss-making routes and trying to streamline its maintenance operations. This is likely to result in 2800 job cuts, helping to reduce costs further. Despite these job cuts, high labour costs remain a concern for Qantas.

Questions

1 Analyse two factors that might influence the strategy of a business. [8]
2 Discuss the problems a business may face by adopting a strategy of reducing its costs. [16]

How business strategy determines competitive advantage in an increasingly competitive world

The strategy of a business will determine the markets in which it competes, what goods and services it offers and how it wants to position itself relative to competitors. Will it focus just on Europe? Will it concentrate just on hair care products? Will it aim to be a premium brand or a discount business?

The success of a strategy depends on whether it fits with the strengths of the business, i.e. can it do what it sets out to do effectively and efficiently? And whether it fits the external environment – a major push for growth at a time of recession may be difficult, for example, whereas a move into products for the elderly may work if the population is ageing.

Effective strategic management understands the internal and external environment and from this develops a strategy that a business has the ability to achieve and that provides it with an advantage over rivals. Every business will be seeking to find a strategy (such as cost cutting or differentiating) that will provide it with a competitive advantage over its rivals.

The first stage in strategic management is to analyse the existing situation to identify the strategic choices available. This can be done using a SWOT analysis.

Study tip

Never underestimate the importance of getting the right strategy. If you are trying to develop your publishing business while everyone else goes online you may be doomed. If you invest in heavy petrol-consuming cars while the world becomes more concerned about the environment you will struggle. Getting the strategy right is the key to success which means you need to understand the strengths of the business and its external environment when analysing a case study.

35.2 Strategic analysis

SWOT analysis

A SWOT analysis considers the internal and external environments of a business.

S and W stand for strengths and weaknesses. These are internal features of a business at the present time.

For example, strengths may include:
- a high level of cash funds
- a strong brand name
- a good distribution network
- highly skilled staff.

Weaknesses may include:
- high borrowing
- a lack of new products being developed.

O and T stand for opportunities and threats and refer to external events that might happen in the future. Threats are events that might damage the business and opportunities might benefit the business.

Opportunities might include:
- entering new markets overseas
- an alliance with a competitor to develop new technology
- going online.

Threats might include:
- legislation that would increase wage costs
- new competitors entering the market
- takeover by a competitor.

Managers will try to identify the relevant strengths, weaknesses, opportunities and threats. They will then rank them in order of their significance – what is the biggest and most damaging threat, for example?

The process of undertaking a SWOT analysis involves discussion and in itself is useful to get managers sharing ideas and perspectives. SWOT analysis is the basis for strategic planning.

Developing of the outcome of a SWOT analysis into strategic objectives

Once a SWOT analysis has been undertaken managers should have a clearer view of what the business is good at, what its weaknesses are, what it could be doing and what it must protect itself against.

From this they can develop a strategy or series of strategies which may seek to:
- build on their strengths to exploit their opportunities; for example, use the brand to launch more products
- reduce or remove their weaknesses; for example, reducing borrowing
- protect themselves against the threats; for example, take over a competitor threatening to take more market share.

A SWOT analysis is not a one-off exercise. Given that the internal and external environment is constantly changing it should be continually reviewed and strategies adjusted accordingly. For example, a strategy of growth may be appropriate in a booming economy but in a recession it may be necessary to focus on survival.

PEST analysis

PEST analysis is a way of analysing the external macro-environment of business. It examines political, economic, social and technological factors. It can also be known as PESTEL analysis, referring to political, economic, social, technological, environmental and legal factors. Managers attempt to identify the relevant factors in their environment and again rank them according to their relative importance for the business.

- Political factors include legal issues, trade agreements and changes in government policy.
- Economic factors include the interest rate, inflation, economic growth and exchange rates.
- Social factors include demographic factors and social trends.
- Technological factors involve changes in technology.

The results of a PEST analysis will vary from business to business. For some the economic growth of a country will be vitally important; for others what the government is doing may be more significant. Furthermore, if a business operates in many different countries or has different business divisions it may need to undertake a number of PEST analyses. These need to be reviewed regularly as the external environment changes.

Study tip

The key to PEST and SWOT analysis is to prioritise the key issues in the external and internal environments. Managers can list their business strengths and weaknesses and the opportunities and threats in the environment but the key is identifying which are the most important ones and therefore being able to know where to concentrate their thinking.

The role of business vision/ mission statements and objectives in strategic analysis

Whatever strategies are developed these must fit with the overall mission or vision of the business. If the mission is to be 'the world's greatest airline' then a strategy that takes the business into soft drinks would not fit; if the mission is to be 'the leading global pharmaceutical company' then a strategy that involves retrenchment to focus on just the domestic market would not be acceptable. The mission sets out the overall guidelines within which strategies must fit. It sets the scope of the business's activities, for example, in terms of where it wants to compete, which product markets it wants to be involved in and the relative focus on different stakeholder groups.

Case Study

Strategic elements of Tata Power for 2012–13

Vision

To be the most admired and responsible Integrated Power Company with international footprint, delivering sustainable value to all stakeholders.

Mission

We will become the most admired and responsible Power Company delivering sustainable value by:

- operating our assets at benchmark levels
- executing projects safely, with predictable benchmark quality, cost and time
- growing the Tata Power businesses, be it across the value chain or across geographies, and also in allied or new businesses
- driving Organisational Transformation that will make us have the conviction and capabilities to deliver on our strategic intent
- achieving our sustainability intent of 'Leadership with Care', by having leading and best practices on Care for the Environment, Care for the Community, Care for the Customers and Shareholders, and Care for the People.

Values

Our values are SACRED to us:

- **Safety** Safety is a core value over which no business objective can have a higher priority.
- **Agility** Speed, Responsiveness and being Proactive, achieved through **Collaboration** and Empowering Employees
- **Care** Care for Stakeholders – our Environment, Customers & Shareholders – both existing and potential, our Community and our People (our employees and partners).
- **Respect** Treat all stakeholders with respect and dignity.
- **Ethics** Achieve the most admired standards of Ethics, through Integrity and mutual Trust.
- **Diligence** Do everything (set direction, deploy actions, analyse, review, plan and mitigate risks, etc.) with a thoroughness that delivers quality and Excellence – in all areas, and especially in Operations, Execution and Growth.

Source: Tatapower.com website

Questions

1 Analyse the possible reasons why Tata has the vision statement that it has. [8]
2 To what extent does producing a statement of mission and values help Tata succeed? Justify your answer. [16]

The role of Boston Matrix analysis

As part of the data gathered for a SWOT analysis a business may use the Boston Matrix, which we covered at AS (see pages 111–12). The Boston Matrix highlights the position of different products in their markets and the growth of the market as a whole. Undertaking this analysis enables a business to take a view of what the strategy should be next.

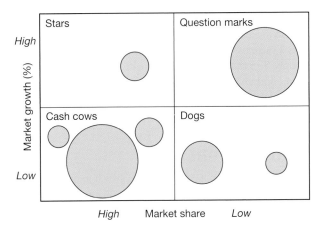

Figure 35.4 The Boston Matrix

For example:
- Dogs (low growth, low market share) – should the business sell off these products or stop producing them? Or if it invests heavily is there a chance of reviving them successfully?
- Cash cows (high market share but low market growth) – can the business milk these (i.e. take as much cash as it can from these) to finance investments elsewhere?
- Question marks (or problem children) (low market share but fast market growth) – should the business invest in these to build them up?
- Stars (high market share and growth) – should the business invest to protect these?

The business will also take an overview of its portfolio – is it too reliant on cash cows, for example? – in which case it may need investment into new products for the future. Has it got too many question marks, in which case this is quite high risk in the short term.

For very large firms the Boston Matrix is used not just for products but for the whole business. If a company owns many other companies then it may analyse the relative strength of these using the matrix and decide which ones to sell, invest in and milk.

Porter's Five Forces analysis

Businesses will also want to analyse the markets in which they operate. A common tool used for this is Porter's Five Forces analysis (see also pages 262–63). This examines five different forces which determine the likely profitability of an industry. The immediate business environment that contains these forces is known as the **micro or competitive environment**. It includes groups that the business is likely to interact with regularly; these groups exert a force on the business.

These forces are:
- rivalry
- supplier power
- buyer power
- entry threat
- substitute threat.

An understanding of the existing forces will determine the profits that can be generated but also highlight how a business might want to change its strategy to make the forces more favourable.

These forces are examined below.

Rivalry

This refers to the number of firms in the market and their relative size. If there are many firms of a similar size then the potential profits of the market have to be shared between them, reducing the likely profits of any one business. However, if the market is dominated by, say, two firms, their profits are likely to be relatively high.

Entry threat

The way a business behaves will not only be affected by the existing number of competitors in the market. It will also depend on how likely it is that other firms will enter the market in the future.

This in turn depends on the existence of **barriers to entry**. Barriers to entry are factors that make it difficult to enter a market. For example:
- **Entry costs** Heavy investment may be required to set up the business because of specialist equipment or facilities needed. You can imagine that setting up a chemical plant or car manufacturer could require quite large sums of money. This will automatically make it difficult for some entrepreneurs to enter the market. By comparison, setting up an online business might be relatively cheap.
- **Brand loyalty** If the established firms have a high level of brand loyalty then it will be more difficult for others to enter the market because of the problems gaining sufficient market share to break even. Loyalty to Nike sportswear and Twinings tea make entry into these markets quite tough.
- **Legal restrictions** If the existing provider has a patent this means you cannot imitate the invention without permission (and usually paying a licensing fee).

High barriers to entry mean that the firms already in the market are 'safe' from competition, at least for a while. This means that the competitive pressure is reduced and this may affect the quality of the service. On the other hand, if entering a market is very simple then it is highly competitive, forcing better service. For example, setting up a sandwich shop is not particularly expensive or difficult and so there is enormous pressure in terms of the prices charged and quality of food and service provided. There are always shops closing and opening and new forms of food emerging because of the very high level of competition. This is good for customers but not so good for the entrepreneurs who have to remain very responsive to market requirements to survive.

If there are very few barriers to entry this is likely to reduce the profits being earned by the established businesses in an industry. If high profits are being made by existing firms, more businesses will enter and the profits will have to be shared out among more organisations. If, however, there are high barriers to entry then existing firms can make high profits without others entering to take them away.

Buyer/supplier power

The competitive environment in a market also depends on the power of buyers and suppliers. All businesses are part of a supply chain and are reliant on other businesses or individuals that they buy from or sell to. If you are reliant on a few key suppliers then they are likely to be able to charge you more and the level of service they have to provide may not be that high because you need them so much. They are likely to be able to increase their profits at your expense – you pay them more so your profits fall and theirs increase.

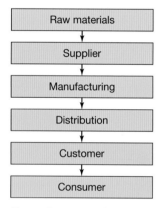

Raw materials → Supplier → Manufacturing → Distribution → Customer → Consumer

Figure 35.5 A supply chain

The power of suppliers depends on:
- the number of them and how similar their products are; if it is easy for you to switch suppliers then their power is less
- their size and the extent to which they depend on you. If the suppliers are small and rely on you then you have power over them. If you represent only a small percentage of their business then they have more power because they are more likely to reject your requests if they don't like them.

Similarly, buyer power affects what happens in a market. If buyers have a lot of power they may be able to push the price down and insist that the product is amended to meet their requirements. If buyers are powerful you are likely to receive a lower price, reducing your profits.

A buyer will have power if:
- there are relatively few buyers, so that the business relies on them heavily. For example, if a company makes very specialised technical equipment there will be a limited set of customers, so the business will need to retain those customers. On the other hand, the loss of one customer at a nightclub may not be that significant.

- they have many potential alternative suppliers so they can switch away from a business relatively easily if they need to. This puts a business in a weaker bargaining position. If you are the only firm that can produce a particularly complex piece of equipment then you have a lot of bargaining power: if you are one of many possible suppliers of paperclips you are not in such a strong position.

Substitute threat

This refers to the ease with which a buyer can switch to an alternative type of product that performs the same function. If you are charging high prices for aluminium cans, could buyers switch easily to plastic bottles? If the price of air flights is high can buyers switch to sea ferry and trains to get to their destinations? The greater the substitute threat the more buyers can move away, and therefore the less existing firms will be able to charge and the lower their profits.

Table 35.1 Five forces summary

Five forces	Effect
Barriers to entry	High barriers protect existing firms and enable higher profits
Substitute threat	Low substitute threat means customers cannot easily switch away, enabling higher profits
Buyer power	Low buyer power means established firms can charge more and earn higher profits
Supplier power	Low supplier power enables established firms to push down the price of supplies, increasing profits
Rivalry	Low rivalry means there is little competition and this enables higher profits

Case Study

Aerospace and defence industry

The global aerospace and defence industry, perhaps more than any other industry, involves huge numbers of parts to produce the finished product. A fighter jet engine, for example, has thousands of complex individual parts which means there are thousands and thousands of specialists parts suppliers.

Each and every one of them is contributing to the manufacture of planes or missiles or engines that are sold for multibillions of dollars.

The aeroplane makers like Airbus and Boeing, the engine makers such as GE and Rolls-Royce, and the defence firms including Raytheon and Northrop Grumman, are huge powerful organisations. Each of them has trading relationships with a vast number of so-called tier two and tier three suppliers, who in turn rely both on the big players and on each other.

The industry often experiences mergers and takeovers. For example, in the commercial aviation market, most deals tend to involve a tier two supplier, such as a company making the landing gear for an aeroplane, buying a tier three supplier, for example, one that makes smaller components such as nuts and bolts, or springs and levers. The deals tend to be larger than $200 million, but smaller than $500 million. They are often paid for in cash. In addition to having the right skills, suppliers must also be sufficiently large and capable to respond to the big players' requirements. Having suffered delays to major programmes, such as the Airbus A380 and the Boeing 737, as a result of difficulties in dealing with suppliers, both are eager to deal with fewer suppliers of everything from seats and curtains, to in-flight entertainment equipment and avionics.

Questions

1 Analyse who you think holds the power in the aerospace and defence industries. [8]
2 Evaluate the possible effect of this power balance on the profits being earned in the industry. [16]

Actions to change the competitive environment

Businesses try to make the competitive environment more favourable. This means that to increase their own chances of success they would want:

- a high barrier to entry so that other businesses will not enter the market: this would remove a competitive threat
- few competitors and substitutes so that customers could not easily find alternatives
- low supplier power so that they have power over suppliers. This might mean that they can demand a low price and do not have to pay quickly for the items (and so can hold on to the money and earn interest in the bank for longer)
- low buyer power, so that buyers are dependent on their products. This should make demand more price inelastic and so they may be able to charge more for their products.

Businesses will want to change the five forces to make the industry more favourable. For example, they might:

- join together in an industry association to have more buying power over suppliers
- buy competitors' companies to reduce the degree of competition in the market
- develop USPs to reduce the ability of customers to find substitutes.

Study tip

You need to be able to decide on the relative strength of the five forces in a given industry and the impact of this on the profitability of businesses. You should also consider how businesses might react to influence the forces and make them more favourable. Make sure you are clear about the difference between the substitute threat and rivalry; these are often confused. A business producing the same type of product is a rival. A business producing something that consumers might switch to is a substitute.

Core competencies analysis

Working with C.K. Prahalad, Gary Hamel developed the concept of core competencies in relation to strategic management in 1990. 'Core competencies are the collective learning in the organisation, especially how to coordinate diverse production skills and integrate multiple streams of technologies', i.e. they are the things that an organisation does extremely well and therefore its strategy should be based on this.

Hamel and Prahalad argued that if an organisation is not good at something it should consider outsourcing it to others that have competencies in these areas, i.e. business should concentrate on what they are good at.

Hamel saw strategic planning not as a series of logical steps but as moments of dramatic change. He said that 'Strategic innovation will be the main source of competitive advantage in the future.' He believed great strategies come from challenging the existing situation. He quoted Anita Roddick, the founder of Body Shop: 'I watch where the cosmetics industry is going and then walk in the opposite direction.'

'Management was designed to solve a very specific problem – how to do things with perfect replicability, at ever-increasing scale and steadily increasing efficiency. Now there's a new set of challenges on the horizon. How do you build organisations that are as nimble as change itself?'

In his book *The Future of Management* Hamel says: 'Management is out of date. Like the combustion engine, it's a technology that has largely stopped evolving, and that's not good … My goal in writing this book was not to predict the future of management, but to help you invent it.' Businesses need to think about their purpose, seek out ideas from the fringes, and in particular embrace the democratising power of the internet. They need to think of their competencies and build their strategies based on this.

Case Study

RIM

The recent resignation of RIM's co-chief executives Mike Lazaridis and Jim Balsillie came at a time when shareholders demanded a significant change in senior management. This came after falling sales, problems with the service and badly received new products. The new boss who was promoted from within announced drastic changes to the business which he claimed was suffering from 'growing pains'. He said that BlackBerry would return to focusing on what it does best: business communications for business people. This focused approach in the early days made BlackBerry one of the world's fastest growing companies. A mixture of accessible interface and trusted security made it the handset of choice for business.

However, trying to return to this strategy may be tricky given that the distinction between a business and consumer user has now blurred. For example, increasingly employees are demanding their own type of device at work such as the iPhone. RIM hopes to win back customers with developments such as BlackBerry Mobile Fusion.

Figure 35.6 The BlackBerry Mobile Fusion

Also helping the business is the strength of the BlackBerry Messenger, popular with teenagers in the Western world looking to save money on texts, and equally as popular in developing countries as a cheap means of staying in touch. However, competition from the likes of Nokia and Android-powered handsets in these markets is likely to make success difficult.

Questions

1 Explain two factors that may have caused the problems of RIM. [6]
2 Discuss whether you think RIM is doomed to failure. [10]

Test your learning

Short answer questions

1 What is meant by a corporate strategy? [2]
2 a What is meant by strategic management? [2]
   b Explain **one** possible benefit of strategic management. [?]
3 a What is meant by S and W in SWOT analysis? [2]
   b Give an example of each. [2]
4 a What is meant by O and T in SWOT analysis? [2]
   b Give an example of each. [2]
5 Explain how SWOT analysis links to strategic management. [5]
6 a What is PEST analysis? [2]
   b Give one example of P, E, S and T. [4]
7 Explain the four types of products in the Boston Matrix. [8]
8 Explain the five forces in Porter's model. [10]
9 Explain what is meant by core competencies. [2]
10 a What is a vision or mission statement? [2]
    b Explain one possible benefit to a business of having a mission statement. [3]

Data response question

Lexmark

Lexmark, the US printer maker, recently announced it would change its strategy and stop making inkjet printers and cut about 1700 jobs as part of a restructuring. The company said it was exploring the sale of its inkjet-related technology, and planned to close its manufacturing plant in the Philippines by 2015. Lexmark had been phasing out inkjet printers to focus on laser printers.

The company chairman and chief executive officer has said that it is now investing in higher value software and imaging solutions. Its revenue from its inkjet hardware business dropped 66 per cent in the first half of last year, forcing the company to cut its full-year forecast.

Most printer makers are struggling with falling sales as printing, considered one of the most dispensable parts of a company's budget, is always the first target of cost cutting.

The company expects to make annual savings of $95 million once the restructuring is complete.

Lexmark, which had about 13 300 employees worldwide at the end of last year, said it will continue to provide service, support and aftermarket supplies for its inkjet printers.

Questions

1 Analyse two possible reasons why Lexmark changed its strategy. [10]

2 Discuss the possible difficulties Lexmark may face changing its strategy. [14]

3 To what extent is cost cutting the best strategy for a business in Lexmark's position to adopt? [16]

Essay questions

1 To what extent does buyer power determine the profits made by businesses in an industry? [20]

2 Discuss the importance of strategic management for the success of a business. [20]

Past paper questions

1 Read the Craft Designs case study on pages 459–61 and then answer the following questions.

   a Evaluate the likely impact on the business of the forecast economic conditions in Appendix A. [14]

   b Discuss the relative importance of the factors, **apart from** external economic conditions, that are most likely to affect the future success of Craft Designs. [20]

Cambridge International AS and A Level Business Studies
9707 Paper 3 Q6 May/June 2007

2 Read the Forest Product Company (FPC) case study on pages 464–67 and then answer the following question.

Evaluate the importance of both SWOT and PEST analysis to FPC's directors as they analyse the two strategic options. [20]

Cambridge International AS and A Level Business Studies
9707 Paper 33 Q6 May/June 2011

3 Read the Eastern Motors (EM) case study on pages 468–70 and then answer the following question.

'Increasing opportunities for multinational investment by car manufacturers will create more threats than opportunities for EM.' (lines 35–36) To what extent do you agree with this statement? [20]

Cambridge International AS and A Level Business Studies
9707 Paper 3 Q7 May/June 2009

36 Strategic choice

Chapter overview

In this chapter we examine:
- Ansoff's Matrix
- Porter's low cost and differentiation strategies
- Force Field Analysis
- decision tree analysis.

36.1 The Ansoff Matrix

The Ansoff Matrix was developed by Igor Ansoff (1918–2002). It examines strategies in terms of the products offered and the markets a business competes in. It highlights four possible strategies open to businesses.

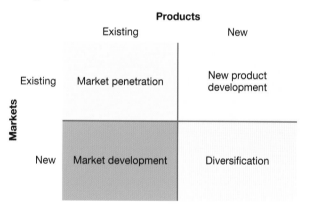

Figure 36.1 The Ansoff Matrix

Market penetration

This strategy occurs when a firm tries to sell more of its existing products to its existing customers. To achieve more sales the firm may adjust elements of its marketing mix. For example, it may increase its spending on advertising or cut its prices. This is a relatively low-risk strategy because managers are familiar with the products and markets. It may be possible to implement actions to boost sales in existing markets in the short term.

New product development

This strategy focuses on developing new products and offering these to existing clients. Firms operating in the soap, shampoo and laundry detergent markets, for example, are continually developing new brands for their customers. This strategy is risky in the sense that many new products often fail. Only one in ten new products launched survives the first two years so all the investment in developing the product can be lost.

On the other hand, managers should have a relatively good understanding of the market and their customers' buying processes, and so they may feel confident (often wrongly) that their offering will be successful despite the high failure rate of others.

Market development

This strategy occurs when a firm offers its existing products to a new market. For example, it may try to sell its products overseas or it may try to target new segments of its existing market. Many sportswear companies have successfully marketed their products as fashion items, for example. Chewing-gum companies have offered their product as an aid to giving up smoking, as something which helps prevent tooth decay and as a breath freshener; the product, therefore, has been offered to many new segments. This strategy involves quite a high level of risk because managers will not know the market well and will have to work hard to understand the segments within the market and the buying process.

Diversification

This strategy involves offering new products to new markets. For example, a chocolate company may decide to diversify into the soft drinks market. This is a high-risk strategy because the firm may have only a very limited understanding of the production and marketing requirements of the new sector. If it is successful, however, it actually reduces the firm's risk because it is operating in two different markets. If sales decline in one market, demand may be sustained or even increase in another one.

Diversification is risky in the sense that managers are operating in an unfamiliar zone. Imagine that your senior managers at school decided to move the organisation into clothes retailing as well. Of course, it is possible they could run a business like this very well, but it would be completely different from running a school and they are likely to have real problems adjusting to the different circumstances. On the other hand, by operating in different markets managers are spreading the risks of demand falling; if demand falls in one market, sales in the other market may continue to sustain the business. Market penetration, by comparison, is safe in that managers are operating within their comfort zones; your school managers are still running the school but trying to make it bigger. The managers know about education, they know the suppliers they want to work with, the competitor schools and market conditions. The danger is that the business is dependent on one market alone, which can make it vulnerable.

Study tip

Choosing where to compete (markets), what to compete with (products) and how to compete (positioning) are the key strategic decisions. Once these decisions are made the tactical decisions (i.e. the marketing mix) are more straightforward – if you know what to offer, whom to offer it to and what you are trying to achieve, the mix should follow logically. You start with the strategy and the mix follows from this.

Remember that when answering a question on strategy you don't usually have to go through all the different options; for example, you may need to select which strategy works best for the business and possibly compare with one another.

Case Study

Mars corporate fact sheet

Figure 36.2 A selection of Mars chocolate

Mars, Incorporated is a family owned company, with six industry leading business units: Chocolate, Petcare, Food, Drinks, Symbioscience and, most recently, Wrigley Gum and Sugar (after it joined with Wrigley). Headquartered in McLean, Virginia,

Mars, Incorporated operates in more than 79 countries. It is a recognised leader in confections with a wide range of product offerings including gum, mints, hard and chewy candies, lollipops and chocolate. Mars has approximately 65 000 associates worldwide and $28 billion in annual revenue.

The combination of Mars and Wrigley brings together two strong, international businesses and creates one of the world's leading confectionery companies. The portfolio spans a variety of categories such as confectionery items, main meals, side dishes, beverages, snack foods, frozen snacks, organic foods, pet foods, and now also includes Wrigley's vast portfolio of gum brands and sugar items.

Fast facts

- One of the world's largest family owned companies.
- Has more than 317 sites worldwide, including 150 manufacturing facilities.
- Products are sold in more than 180 countries.
- Mars was founded in 1911, when Frank C. Mars started making and selling butter cream candies in Tacoma, Washington, USA.
- Wrigley was founded in 1891, when William Wrigley Jr arrived in Chicago with $32 in his pocket and the ambition to start a business of his own.
- Mars' first blockbuster product was Milky Way®, invented by Frank and his son Forrest in 1923.
- In 1893, the Wrigley Company introduced Juicy Fruit® and Wrigley's Spearmint® gums, with Doublemint® making its debut in 1914.
- Mars established the Waltham Centre for Pet Nutrition in 1965 in the UK.

Mars brands

Chocolate M&M's® 3 Musketeers® Combos® Dove® Galaxy® Twix® Snickers® Mars® Milky Way® Kudos® Maltesers® Celebrations®

Petcare Pedigree® Whiskas® Cesar® My Dog® Sheba® Royal Canin® Kitekat® Frolic® Chappi® Winergy® Trill® Waltham® Aquarian® Banfield®

Food Uncle Ben's® Dolmio® Suzi Wan® Masterfoods® Seeds of Change® Ebly®

Drinks Flavia® Klix®

Mars Symbioscience focuses on innovative solutions that change the way we care for ourselves and the natural world, e.g. Mars Plantcare-Seramis®, Mars Sustainable Solutions

Wrigley gum and sugar Starburst® Skittles® Lucas® Tunes® Lockets® Kenman® Skwinkles® Rondo® Juicy Fruit® Orbit® Altoids® Life Savers ® Eclipse® Extra® Hubba Bubba® Doublemint® Spearmint® Pim Pom® Sugus®

Questions

1 Analyse two possible benefits of Mars being a family company. [6]
2 To what extent do you think Mars' strategy of operating in several different regional and product markets is a good one. [10]

36.2 Low cost vs differentiation

Another way of analysing marketing strategies was developed by Michael Porter in 1985. Porter distinguished between a low-cost and a differentiated strategy. A low-cost strategy focuses on providing similar benefits to competitors, but doing so at a lower price. This is the strategy adopted by companies such as Ryanair and IKEA. Managers of such organisations consistently look for ways of reducing costs to make their businesses leaner. They strip away costs to enable low prices. At IKEA, for example, you select your own furniture purchases, take them off the shelves on your own and take them to the tills. You then take them to your car – once again without help. You then assemble the furniture yourself at home. All of this means the labour costs of the business are reduced significantly. The stores themselves are out of town (reducing rents) and fairly basic in terms of design and layout (reducing decoration and maintenance costs). This low cost strategy by IKEA links directly to its mission 'to create a better everyday life for the many people. Our business idea supports this vision by offering a wide range of well-designed, functional home furnishing products at prices so low that as many people as possible will be able to afford them.'

To be successful with a low-cost strategy a firm must be able to deliver its products more cheaply than the competition. This may be achieved through economies of scale, special relations with suppliers or by removing some elements of the marketing mix. For example, a firm may try to make distribution more direct and so be able to avoid the middleman's profit margins; alternatively it may provide fewer additional services – some supermarkets, for example, compete on price by keeping overheads low and offering a more basic service and a more limited range of goods in the store itself.

Case Study

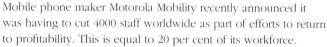

Motorola Mobility

Mobile phone maker Motorola Mobility recently announced it was having to cut 4000 staff worldwide as part of efforts to return to profitability. This is equal to 20 per cent of its workforce.

The company was bought by Google last year; it has since announced that it plans to close or merge about one-third of its 90 facilities which include offices and factories. It also announced a shift in emphasis away from low-cost non-smartphones to 'more innovative and profitable devices'.

Two-thirds of the jobs will go outside of the US, Google said. It expects the cost of severance packages to be $275 million.

Motorola, which once dominated the mobile phone market, has fallen behind its competitors, including Apple and Samsung.

Google bought Motorola Mobility last year in a $12.5 billion deal, giving it access to more than 17 000 technology patents.

It is expected that Google will bring out some innovative devices focusing on high-end smartphones, rather than low-end feature phones.

The recent success of Samsung, which has been receiving plaudits for its Nexus smartphones and tablets which use Google's Android operating system, is a model that the business could follow.

Questions

1 Analyse two difficulties that may be involved in making large scale redundancies. [8]
2 Discuss the factors that might determine whether Google was right to buy Motorola. [16]

The alternative approach is to differentiate your offering, for example by offering more benefits than your competitors. Provided the benefits are ones that customers want (e.g. a better product range, a strong brand or high levels of customer service) this should enable you to charge a higher price. For example, Bang & Olufsen produces top of the range music systems for which it charges high prices because of the quality and design; Jo Malone produces expensive but distinctive fragrances. If a business is pursuing a differentiation strategy, the distribution of product or service is often exclusive; the firm is likely to want to keep a tight control over distribution to maintain an exclusive image. The products are often innovative and the firm may invest heavily in research and development. The promotional strategy is likely to emphasise the difference between this product and rivals' products.

Inevitably firms that do differentiate their offerings successfully may be imitated over time. Just look at the way in which Coca-Cola, Dyson and Pringles have been copied. At this point the firm will only be able to justify a higher price if it can continue to stress its role as the market leader or position itself effectively as the 'first of its kind' or the best. Dyson, for example, ran an advertising campaign emphasising that, 'if you want a Dyson you have to buy a Dyson', to highlight its uniqueness; Coca-Cola often stresses that it is the 'original'.

The worst of all worlds, according to Porter, is to get 'stuck in the middle', for example, offering a product with similar benefits to competitors at a higher price – this is a no win situation.

These ideas of low costs compared to differentiation can be more fully explored using the value matrix. This looks at the benefits a business offers relative to its competitors and the price it charges.

If a business offers more benefits than its competitors it may be able to charge the same or less (if this is possible financially) or even more and still be competitive. Mont Blanc pens are very expensive but still regarded as good value because of the prestige of the brand. Bose music equipment has a high price but people are willing to pay for the design and sound quality.

If a business matches the competition in terms of the benefits offered it will have to charge the same or less to be more competitive. In the latter case the challenge is to find a way of being able to offer lower prices. This is often an issue for operations.

If a business offers fewer benefits than the competition it must charge a lot less to be competitive. Again the challenge is to find ways of doing this that cannot easily be imitated by competitors.

Study tip

Remember that while choosing the right strategy is critical, the business must also be able to deliver it. If you choose a low-cost strategy, can the business actually get its costs down? Does it have a more efficient way of providing the service than others? Does it have better relations with suppliers? Is it avoiding some costs by missing out some stages (e.g. direct selling)? You cannot sustain low prices unless you somehow have lower costs so make sure this is feasible for the business. Similarly, if you offer a differentiated product, how is it differentiated? What value have you actually created? Is this sustainable or can it be imitated easily?

36.3 Force Field Analysis

Using Force Field Analysis to make strategic choices

When making a strategic choice there will be forces pushing for change. These could be falling profits, a new management team or a falling share price. At the same time there will be resistance to change such as unwillingness by employees to change or financial constraints.

This idea of forces for change and restraining forces was put forward by Lewin in his Force Field Analysis model.

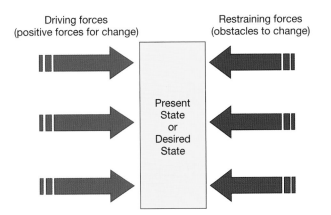

Figure 36.3 Lewin's Force Field Analysis model

At any moment the forces for and against strategic change will be balanced, which is why the business is pursuing its existing strategy.

For strategic change to occur there must be an increase in the forces pushing for change (perhaps if there is a takeover and the new owners insist on it) or a decrease in forces preventing change (for example, a training programme gives staff the necessary skills).

Managers must identify the forces for and against change and try to increase the forces for and decrease the forces against if they want change to occur.

Imagine a situation in which managers want to introduce new technology. To bring about change managers must try to increase the pressure for it. For example, they might stress to employees:

- the dangers of holding on to old technology (e.g. loss of competitiveness and the possible loss of jobs)
- the benefits of new technology (in terms of boosting competitiveness)
- the threats from competitors who are already using this technology.

Alternatively, managers might focus on reducing the resistance to change and perhaps:

- educate employees on the benefits of the change
- offer incentives to those willing to change
- threaten or intimidate those who resist
- guarantee jobs to reduce this insecurity
- offer training to those who need to re-skill.

36.4 Decision trees

In order to make the right decisions, managers may use different approaches to help them organise their information and think through the various problems. These include decision-tree analysis. Decision-tree analysis tries to estimate the possible outcomes of different courses of action and work out the likelihood of these occurring. A decision tree is a mathematical model which can be used by managers to help them make the right decision. By combining possible outcomes with the probability of them happening, managers can compare the likely financial consequences of different decisions.

The value of the technique will, of course, depend on managers' ability to accurately estimate the options and their likelihood, but it does stress the key issues of risk and rewards.

Using the decision tree model

A decision tree sets out the options to managers. Given the problem facing them, managers will identify possible courses of action. In Figure 36.4 the square highlights that a decision has to be made. The lines coming out from this are the different options; in this case there are three, including doing nothing.

Managers then have to estimate the different outcomes from each course of action; this is shown on the lines coming from the circle. A circle identifies the possible outcomes.

For each of these possible outcomes:

- The result is measured in financial terms so they can be compared.

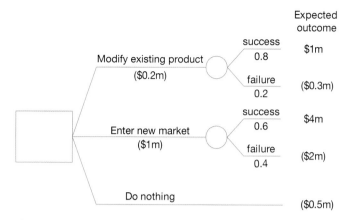

Figure 36.4 A decision tree

- The probability of each outcome is estimated. The probabilities of all the outcomes must add up to 1 (or 100 per cent); this means there is a 100 per cent chance that something will happen.

In Figure 36.4 three options are identified:

a Modify the existing product. This is expected to cost $0.2 million. The likelihood of success is 0.8, so the managers are 80 per cent confident of success perhaps because it is modifying a product they know well. The result of success would be $1 million. The probability of failure is 0.2 (20 per cent) (note: only two outcomes are given and one of these must happen so the probability of success or failure must add up to 1).

b Enter a new market. This is more expensive. The cost is estimated to be $1 million. The probability of success is estimated at 0.6 and is expected to generate returns of $4 million. The probability of failure is estimated at 0.4 and this is expected to lead to losses of $2 million.

c Do nothing. This is expected to lead to losses of $0.5 million.

Faced with a choice between these options a manager will consider the likely outcomes, the probability of these outcomes and the initial investment.

Using the data on the outcome the manager can calculate what is known as the Expected Monetary Value (EMV) of each decision. This is the average return expected from a decision, taking account of the different financial outcomes and their probability. It shows what you would expect to gain (or lose) on average if you made this decision many times. The EMV is calculated by multiplying the probability of each outcome by its financial value and adding these together; it is a weighted average of the outcomes.

For example:

a Modifying the product. There is a 0.8 chance of $1 million, i.e. this is fairly likely, but there is a 0.2 chance of losing $0.3 million. If this decision was taken many times the Expected Monetary Value (EMV) would be:

$$(0.8 \times \$1m) + (0.2 \times -\$0.3m) = \$0.8m - \$0.06m = \$0.794m$$

b Entering a new market. There is a 0.6 chance of gaining $4 million and a 0.4 chance of losing $2 million, so:

$$EMV = (0.6 \times \$4m) + (0.4 \times \$2m) = \$2.4m - \$0.8m = \$1.6m$$

If this decision were repeated many times then 60 per cent of the time you would gain $4 million and 40 per cent of the time you would lose $2 million; on average the reward would be $1.6 million.

Using the Expected Monetary Value the managers can compare this with the initial costs and estimate the likely overall return.

a Modifying the product. The expected gain is $0.794 million. Given an initial cost of $0.2 million this leads to an expected net gain of $0.594 million.

b Entering the new market. The expected gain is $1.6 million. Given an initial cost of $1 million this leads to a new gain of $0.6 million.

c Doing nothing. This is expected to lead to a loss of $0.5 million.

Based on this analysis the manager would select the option of entering a new market because it has the highest expected net gains.

In reality the number of possible outcomes might be more complicated but the same principles apply:

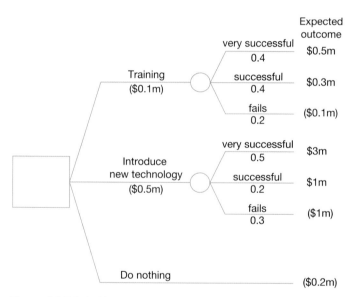

Figure 36.5 A decision tree

Calculations

a Training

$$EMV = (0.4 \times \$0.5m) + (0.4 \times \$0.3m) + (0.2 \times -\$0.1m)$$
$$= \$0.2m + \$0.12m - \$0.02m = \$0.3m$$

Net gain = EMV − initial cost = $0.3m − $0.1m = $0.2m

b New technology

$$EMV = (0.5 \times \$3m) m + (0.2 \times \$1m) + (0.3 \times -\$1m)$$
$$= \$1.5m + \$0.2m - \$0.3m = \$1.4m$$

Net gain = $1.4m − $0.5m = $0.9m

c Do nothing: Expected loss = $0.2 million.

Based on this the managers would choose new technology because it has the highest net gain of $0.9 million.

EMV

Complete the decision tree in figure 36.6, calculate the Expected Monetary Values and decide which option should be chosen.

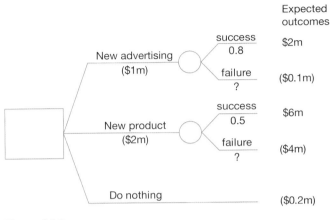

Figure 36.6

If the probability of winning $10 000 is 40 per cent and the probability of winning $20 000 is 60 per cent what is the Expected Monetary Value of this decision? What if the probability of winning $10 000 was 25 per cent and probability of winning $20 000 was 75 per cent?

Remember that managers can take action to try to increase the probability of success and reduce the probability of failure. In the case of a new product launch greater investment in market research or greater expenditure on promotion may help, for example.

The usefulness of decision trees

Decision trees are very useful because:

- They make managers think about the different options – this discussion can create new solutions which may not have been thought of if they had not gone through this process.

- It makes them consider the possible outcomes, both good and bad – this may make them realise some of the difficulties or attractions they might not have done without thinking it through in this structured way.
- It makes them quantify the possible outcomes – they have to discuss and research to find out how likely an outcome is and what it would lead to financially. This again can be very revealing.
- It means that they make a decision based on logic rather than emotions – if needs be this can be demonstrated to others to explain why a decision was made and help gain support.

However, businesses need to treat decision trees with some caution because:

- The value of a decision tree will depend on the options included – if managers fail to think of a good solution the decision made will be relatively poor.
- The values for the probabilities are estimates and therefore may not be accurate – particularly if the decision has not been made before. Also managers may suffer bias and over-estimate the possibility of success if they like the idea of the project.
- The outcomes are assessed in financial terms but some outcomes may not be easy to value – for example, the potential impact on a brand image of a poor product or the social impact of a decision.
- The trees do not take account of what might or might not fit with the ethics of the business – a decision may be profitable but unacceptable to the business. For example, it may be profitable to launch a new brand of cigarette in a country but a company may not want to associate with this type of product.
- The EMV is calculated as a weighted average – it shows what would happen on average if the decision was made many times. However, decision trees are most likely to be used for big strategic decisions that will only happen once; in this case the EMV is of limited value because you will actually receive only one of the outcomes not an average of them. The implications of this are shown below.

Remember to check where the data has come from and how likely it is the decision makers will have been able to estimate the probability and the financial value of outcomes effectively. Some outcomes will be difficult to estimate in financial terms.

Test your learning

Short answer questions

1 Explain what is meant by market penetration in the Ansoff Matrix with an example. [4]

2 Explain what is meant by market development in the Ansoff Matrix with an example. [4]

3 Explain what is meant by new product development in the Ansoff Matrix with an example. [4]

4 Explain what is meant by diversification in the Ansoff Matrix with an example. [4]

5 What is meant by risk and why does it matter when making a strategic choice? [4]

6 **a** Explain what is meant by Force Field Analysis. [2]

   b Explain how the forces for change may increase or the forces against change reduce. [5]

7 What does a decision tree show? [2]

8 Explain **two** benefits of producing decision trees. [4]

9 What is meant by the Expected Monetary Value in decision tree analysis? [2]

10 Explain two possible problems of using decision trees. [4]

Data response question

JB Hi-Fi

JB Hi-Fi was established in Melbourne, Australia by John Barbuto in 1974. It was sold to Richard Bouris and David Rodd in 1983 who grew the business before selling it on to outside investors. It was floated on the Australian Stock Exchange in October 2003.

Initially the company specialised in Hi-Fi equipment. As the demand for vinyl records declined in 1991 JB Hi-Fi cleared out their entire stock of records and sold only CDs. The chain now has stores all around Australia and some in Auckland, New Zealand's largest city, and other parts of New Zealand.

JB stores specialises in imported CDs, mainly from the United Kingdom and the United States. It has also moved away from predominantly selling music CDs, and has become a major

retailer for plasma televisions, audio/visual, digital camera photography, portable audio, in-car entertainment, computer/video games and DVD & Blu-ray movies. It also sells other accessories, such as CB radios, surveillance camera systems, musical instruments such as guitars, electronic keyboards and guitars, and DJ equipment such as CD mixers and microphones. Its profits have continued to rise when many other music retailers have struggled.

Questions

1 Analyse the factors that might determine demand for JB shares. [10]

2 Discuss the advantages and disadvantages to JB Hi-Fi of offering other products apart from CDs. [14]

3 Do you think JB Hi-Fi would be wise to diversify now into a completely new market such as clothing? Justify your decision. [16]

Essay questions

1 To what extent do you think decision trees are useful for managers? [20]

2 To what extent do you think diversification is the best strategy for a business to follow? [20]

Past paper questions

1 Read the Sam's Fashion case study on pages 462–63 and then answer the following questions.

   a Draw a decision tree based on the data provided in Appendix B. [4]

   b Calculate the expected monetary values of both Option A and Option B. [4]

   c Which option would you recommend Manuel to choose? Use information in the case and your results from part **b** to support your recommendation. [10]

   Cambridge International AS and A Level Business Studies
   9707 Paper 33 Q5 May/June 2010

37 Strategic implementation

37.1 Business plans

To implement a strategy a business will have a business plan. A business plan sets the objectives and strategy to be pursued. It then sets out in detail the actions that need to be taken to make the strategy work.

A plan sets out:
- the different tasks that need to be completed
- when each one has to be completed by
- who is responsible for each task
- what the budget is for each task
- what are the criteria for success for each task.

The value of a business plan

To produce a plan managers must think carefully about what has to be done. This in itself is useful as it helps to share ideas and information and can help identify any potential problems. The plan is then a way of coordinating all the different activities required to make the strategy successful.

At any moment the progress of the plan can be checked and if necessary action can be taken. Even if things start to go wrong having a plan is valuable because managers can assess where they are compared to where they should be and then decide what to do. Without a plan they may not recognise things have gone wrong until far too late.

The nature of the plan will vary for a start-up business compared to an established business (for example, because the

start-up will have limited experience compared to a business that has been going for some time); similarly, it will vary from a small business compared to a big business in that the latter's plan is likely to be more complex and involve more money, more products and more markets. However, for all of these businesses planning can help prevent mistakes by identifying difficulties early, coordinating actions across departments and helping take action quickly to get back on track. Even so plans must always be reviewed because external and internal conditions will change and therefore the plan may need to be flexible to keep relevant and competitive.

Study tip

Remember that having a plan is only part of the challenge of managers. To make it work it has to be implemented effectively.

37.2 Corporate culture

The strategy of a business will be influenced by its culture; this will affect whether it is a risk taker, whether it seeks short-term rewards or is willing to plan long term, whether it cares about its stakeholders and even whether it seeks to go beyond its existing borders. In this section we discuss the meaning and importance of culture.

Key term

Corporate culture refers to the values, attitudes and beliefs of a business's employees; it refers to 'how we do things around here'.

What is corporate culture?

The culture of a business (**corporate culture**), can be described as the values, attitudes and beliefs of the people working for it. It describes 'the way we do things around here' (Ouchi 1981). Hofstede (1991) describes it as 'the collective programming of the mind', which perhaps highlights how individuals' own values may change as they become accustomed to the established ways of doing things when they join a business.

In reality, there is no one culture in a business – different departments, different levels within the business, different groups of employees may all have their own way of doing things; nevertheless there may be some key areas where people generally agree and this can therefore help to define 'the overall culture' of a business.

In the same way as people can differ and their attitudes can vary enormously, so the culture of businesses can be tremendously different. For example, organisations may be:

- **Entrepreneurial** In these organisations you are highly valued if you try something, even if it does not necessarily work. The fact you had an idea and tried to make it work is regarded as worthwhile and commendable. This type of organisation may value people who 'think outside the box', try new approaches and show initiative.
- **Bureaucratic** This type of business may want people who stick to the rules and who do not make decisions for themselves. In some organisations you may not want people to start making up their own rules. At the tax office, for example, you would want all the tax forms processed in the same way. The risks of letting people use their initiative could be too high in some organisations or some parts of organisations; for example, you may want nursing staff to concentrate on administering the treatment doctors have prescribed and not diagnosing people themselves or making decisions on the medication for themselves.
- **Customer focused** Some organisations clearly value their customers (most would, we hope, but in reality not all do!). This means getting it right for the customer, who is regarded as important – staff are expected to put themselves out to make sure the customers' expectations are met. Employees are not expected to find reasons why things cannot be done. While a customer-focused approach seems sensible and certainly advisable in competitive markets, some businesses have been much more inward looking and have focused on what they could do and what they wanted to do rather than what customers wanted. British Airways had a terrible reputation in the 1970s because it placed too much emphasis on flying planes and not enough on the customer experience. Money was being invested in engines, landing gear and pilots' uniforms but not into improving the in-flight entertainment or the cleanliness of the planes. A big push to refocus on customer needs led to a change in approach (which culminated in the rebranding of the business as the 'world's favourite airline'), training all staff to place the customer first. More recently, McDonald's has been accused of being too inward looking and not appreciating the change in the market demand towards wanting healthier food. Similarly, the major American car manufacturers, such as General Motors and Ford, spent too long producing big, oil guzzling cars and did not appreciate that customers wanted more fuel efficient, smaller vehicles that were being provided by producers such as Toyota.

- **Conservative (or not!)** In these businesses there is a tendency to avoid risks. Relatively safe decisions are taken and before any new ideas are accepted there is extensive, possibly overly extensive, research. At the other extreme are high-risk organisations where decisions are made without enough thought about the resources and the dangers involved. In 2008 the global banking system underwent major shocks due in part to high-risk lending – bank managers had taken undue risks in their attempts to increase their lending and this had damaged them in the long term when borrowers could not repay.
- **Short term, long term** Some businesses are very focused on the short term (perhaps because of pressure from investors for dividends); this means they may be reluctant to invest in new product development or training. Others look more towards the long term (e.g. they might plan 15 years ahead for the next revolution in the internet).

Case Study

Johnson & Johnson

The mission statement of Johnson & Johnson highlights the importance of the customer to the business. This set of beliefs has been proved on many occasions when employees have worked hard to make sure that customer service is outstanding and that customers are treated properly.

Our Credo

We believe our first responsibility is to the doctors, nurses and patients, to mothers and fathers and all others who use our products and services. In meeting their needs everything we do must be of high quality. We must constantly strive to reduce our costs in order to maintain reasonable prices. Customers' orders must be serviced promptly and accurately. Our suppliers and distributors must have an opportunity to make a fair profit.

We are responsible to our employees, the men and women who work with us throughout the world. Everyone must be considered as an individual. We must respect their dignity and recognise their merit. They must have a sense of security in their jobs. Compensation must be fair and adequate, and working conditions clean, orderly and safe. We must be mindful of ways to help our employees fulfil their family responsibilities. Employees must feel free to make suggestions and complaints. There must be equal opportunity for employment, development and advancement for those qualified. We must provide competent management, and their actions must be just and ethical. We are responsible to the communities in which we live and work, and to the world community as well. We must be good citizens – support good works and charities and bear our fair share of taxes. We must encourage civic improvements and better health and education. We must maintain in good order the property we are privileged to use, protecting the environment and natural resources.

Our final responsibility is to our stockholders. Business must make a sound profit. We must experiment with new ideas. Research must be carried on, innovative programmes developed and mistakes paid for. New equipment must be purchased, new facilities provided and new products launched. Reserves must be created to provide for adverse times. When we operate according to these principles, the stockholders should realise a fair return.

Source: Johnson & Johnson, www.jnj.com

Questions

1 Analyse the possible benefits of outstanding customer service to Johnson & Johnson. [8]
2 Discuss the impact Our Credo might have on the performance of Johnson & Johnson. [16]

Types of culture

There are many ways of analysing the culture of a business although, given that every business will be unique, all these can do is describe in broad strokes some of the key features of an approach. One model is that of Charles Handy (1993) which outlines four types of culture.

These are:
- **Power culture** This type of culture is most common in relatively small, owner-run businesses. There is one dominant person (or a few key people) who makes all the major decisions and all employees refer to them if they want to know what to do. The 'boss' is in charge of all the operations of the business and its success depends very much on them. This can be very positive because it can lead to decisive leadership, quick decision-making and a consistent approach. However, if the business starts to grow the person or people at the centre may become overloaded and unable to cope with the number of decisions that need to be made. This can bring decision-making to a halt as employees wait to get a response. It also encourages employees to become reliant on the boss and not learn how to make decisions for themselves.
- **Role culture** This is very common in businesses as they grow and tend to adopt a more formal structure and culture. The importance of someone begins to be defined by their position in the hierarchy and their job title. This type of culture relies quite heavily on rules and procedures. To do well you need to follow the systems that are in place and do what is expected of you, rather than using your initiative to define your own job boundaries. Communication is via established channels of communication rather than being, say, informal conversation. This leads to very predictable outcomes in terms of performance. Senior managers know what is going to happen because employees do what they have been told to do. This has the value of certainty. However, the danger is that

the organisation is inflexible to change and is not prepared for unexpected challenges.
- **Task culture** This is relatively common in businesses such as design agencies or management consultancies, where the value of an individual to a project depends on their expertise rather than any formal title. In this approach teams are formed for particular projects and individuals brought into these as and when they can contribute. Your value depends on what you can add to the team rather than your age or how long you have been working there. This approach can bring together expert teams to help solve different problems; however, coordinating this approach can be difficult.
- **Person culture** This is not very common but occurs in an organisation or part of an organisation where there are groups of well-qualified individuals who respect each others' skills and knowledge. This may occur in a university or a doctors' practice, for example. Each individual is fairly self-reliant and can make decisions for themselves. They collaborate with each other and share their expertise and skills when needed but operate independently. This works well if the business can function with relatively independent units, but the danger is that the approach lacks consistency and may overlap (e.g. university lecturers designing their own courses independent of each other and the student finding that elements of these courses overlap). Unfortunately, sometimes the individuals will resist if a more centralised approach is needed, because they are used to their independence.

National culture

In 1966 Geert Hofstede undertook what has become some of the most famous research on national cultural differences. Around 116 000 employees at all levels of the multinational company IBM across 50 countries were involved. The result was a massive amount of data on employees within the same organisation but in different countries. This took Hofstede 15 years to analyse. He concluded that there were five major dimensions that can describe a national culture:
- **Power distance** is the extent to which there is a difference between who has the power within a business (e.g. a difference between the boss and the subordinate). A low power distance means that power is distributed fairly equally; a high power distance means there are big differences in power – for example, there are many levels of hierarchy in organisations.
- **Uncertainty avoidance** is the extent to which employees need to know exactly what they are supposed to do and how success is measured. A high uncertainty avoidance means employees want clear guidelines on what to do; a low uncertainty avoidance means employees are willing to be given general guidelines but do not need a high level of detail on what to do and when.
- **Individualism vs collectivism** measures the extent to which employees feel they are supposed to be part of a team, part of the business 'family', or whether they want to work and look after themselves.

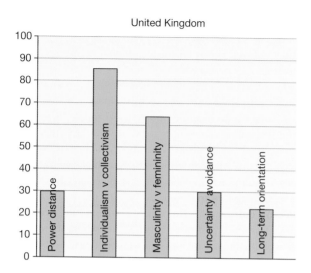

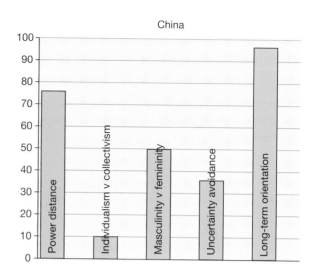

Figure 37.1 National cultures: the UK and China

- **Masculinity vs femininity** measures the extent to which employees feel they need to be dominant and assertive (masculine) or whether they feel that concern for others is more important (feminine).
- **Long-term orientation** measures the extent to which individuals planned ahead. Is the long term 5 years or 20 years?

There can be significant differences between societies in terms of how they score on these scales, and managers need to be aware of these differences when having meetings, making decisions and working with overseas partners. The differences that exist can be because of their history, society, traditions and politics. Look below at Hofstede's findings on the UK and China, for example. These are shown graphically in Figure 37.1.

The UK is strong on individualism – people recognise and reward individual performance rather than team players; the UK is low on long-term orientation, tending to be short-term planners. China, by comparison, tends to plan for the long term but places less emphasis on the individual. In China the hierarchy is accepted much more than in the UK. You can imagine how these differences could cause problems in business. Chinese managers might be interested in projects that generate a return in the long term; UK managers might not. In the UK junior managers might be asked for their opinion even if it contradicts the senior managers; in China they might not.

Of course, these findings do not represent every individual and every business in a given country (in fact, with globalisation and greater diversity among staff it becomes difficult to talk of a British or Chinese company), and these features will change over time. Nevertheless, they highlight that there can be significant differences in cultures between regions and this needs to be remembered when doing business with foreign partners. An understanding of Hofstede's cultural dimensions can help managers to understand the way business is done in different countries.

Case Study

Culture clash

Mike Lynch is the founder of the company Autonomy which was based on research he had done on search techniques in Cambridge in the 1990s. Its search software allows companies to gain more from the institutional knowledge that is in the company's email messages, PowerPoint presentations, and elsewhere on the corporate network. Autonomy was recently bought for $10 billion by Hewlett-Packard. Not long after, the chief executive of HP sacked Lynch.

Some say the problem was that there was a culture clash between Autonomy and HP. Autonomy was more entrepreneurial while HP was a much bigger corporation with more systems and procedures. Soon after the takeover as many as a quarter of the staff at Autonomy left the business because they did not like the 'HP way'.

Questions

1 Analyse the ways in which the culture of the two businesses might have differed. [8]
2 Do you think that it matters to HP that there was a culture clash with Autonomy? [16]

Case Study

W.L. Gore

Whenever business experts make lists of the best American companies to work for, or whenever consultants give speeches on the best-managed American companies, W.L. Gore is high on the list. It has a rate of employee turnover that is about a third the industry average. It has been profitable for 35 consecutive years and has growth rates and an innovative, high-profit product line that is the envy of the industry. Gore has managed to create a small company ethos so infectious and sticky that it has survived the firm's growth into a billion-dollar company with thousands of employees. And how did it do that? By (among other things) adhering to the Rule of 150.

Bill Gore, the founder of Gore Associates, a privately held, multimillion-dollar firm, understood from the start that smaller is often better and designed his organisation according to the Rule of 150 – each facility is limited to 150 associates. The size limitation enables this organisation to grow; yet it continues to behave like a small entrepreneurial start-up. This has not only proven to be a profitable strategy, but also it has created a culture of highly committed employees. Gladwell, in his book *Tipping Point* (2002), comments:

'This organizational strategy is not unique to Gore and Associates. Semco, a Sao Paulo, Brazil-based manufacturer of industrial machinery, has a similar size strategy and, like Gore and Associates, Semco has experienced remarkable success (Semler, 1993). Semco has, in fact, grown 24 per cent annually for the past ten years – without an organizational chart or headquarters facility. Ricardo Semler, chairman of the board, reflecting on the decision to forego a traditional corporate structure, comments that traditional organizational hierarchies are "a source of control, discrimination, and power mongering". The fact that Semco operates in a South American culture with patriarchal national values that are quite different from this company's participative organizational values, makes this a particularly noteworthy example of the paradoxical nature of successful organizations.'

Questions

1 Analyse the possible reason why W.L. Gore may be such an excellent company to work for. [8]
2 Discuss the ways in which the decisions made regarding the structures of their businesses might affect or reflect the cultures of W.L. Gore and Semco. [16]

Study tip

Remember that culture cannot be changed quickly and that the 'right' culture for an organisation may depend on the type of business it is and the environment it operates in. Remember also that the culture of a business can vary between different departments or divisions.

The importance of corporate culture

The culture of a business or a part of a business matters because it determines how employees will behave in any given situation.

This can work in an organisation's favour. Companies such as Google have a culture that recognises and rewards creative talent and technological skills. Bright computer programmers will go far in this organisation regardless of their age and, to some extent, regardless of their formal qualifications; if they can do it and prove they can do it they will probably be promoted. This encourages ideas and new thinking which helps keep Google ahead of its rivals. A culture of accuracy and attention to detail, by comparison, may ensure your firm of accountants does not make any mistakes.

On the other hand, a culture can limit a firm's success. In some retail organisations the customer seems an unwelcome visitor! Customers are not truly valued and employees do not make the effort to provide good customer service. This will lose business over time.

In other organisations, the unwillingness to take risks may mean market opportunities are missed. In Marks and Spencer ten years ago the culture was one of unquestioning agreement with the chief executive's decisions; this meant that when the wrong products were ordered and the wrong approach to displays was chosen no one dared to question. The culture did not encourage a questioning approach which meant that even though staff may have seen the iceberg ahead they did not shout out the dangers because they simply followed the course the captain set for them.

The importance of culture in terms of the success (or failure) of a strategy should not be underestimated. Is the business full of ideas, encouraging initiative, stressing the value of working hard and working effectively? Are new projects met with open arms? Do individuals take care to get it right and show commitment to a project? All these issues depend on the culture of a business. It determines what people do, how they work together, how much effort they make, what they strive for and basically determines how the business 'ticks'. Whatever strategies you bring in, whatever ideas you have, the culture of the business will influence whether they are implemented, how they are implemented and the level of commitment to them by employees.

Case Study

The Five Principles of Mars

Quality

The consumer is our boss, quality is our work and value for money is our goal.

Our company is dedicated to the highest quality in all the work we do. Quality is the uncompromising standard for our actions, and it flows from our passion and our pride in being part of the Mars community. Quality work, which results from our personal efforts, is the first ingredient of quality brands and the source of our reputation for high standards.

Responsibility

As individuals, we demand total responsibility from ourselves; as associates, we support the responsibilities of others.

Mutuality

A mutual benefit is a shared benefit; a shared benefit will endure.

We believe that the standard by which our business relationships should be measured is the degree to which mutual benefits are created. These benefits can take many different forms, and need not be strictly financial in nature. Likewise, while we must try to achieve the most competitive terms, the actions of Mars should never be at the expense, economic or otherwise, of others with whom we work.

Efficiency

We use resources to the full, waste nothing and do only what we can do best.

How is it possible to maintain our principles, offering superior value for money and sharing our success? Our strength lies in our efficiency, the ability to organize all our assets – physical, financial and human – for maximum productivity. In this way, our products and services are made and delivered with the highest quality, at the least possible cost, with the lowest consumption of resources; similarly, we seek to manage all our business operations with the most efficient processes for decision-making.

Freedom

We need freedom to shape our future; we need profit to remain free.

Mars is one of the world's largest privately owned corporations. This private ownership is a deliberate choice. Many other companies began as Mars did, but as they grew larger and required new sources of funds, they sold stocks or incurred restrictive debt to fuel their business. To extend their growth, they exchanged a portion of their freedom. We believe growth and prosperity can be achieved another way.

Source: The Five Principles of Mars, www.mars.com

Questions

1 Analyse the factors that might influence the culture of Mars. [8]
2 Discuss the ways in which the culture of Mars might affect the behaviour of employees and its business performance. [16]

37.3 Developing a change culture

Changing culture can be important but difficult. Businesses will want to have a culture that is open to change and be willing to embrace a new strategy and implement it fully.

According to Kotter and Schlesinger (1979) the main reasons why people resist change are:

- self-interest – they do not want the effort of change or are better off as they are (e.g. their status or importance might be less after the change)
- misunderstanding and lack of trust – they do not understand why change is necessary and/or are suspicious about why the change is happening
- they prefer the status quo – they would rather keep things as they are because they feel comfortable with it
- they do not think the new idea will work – they think there are flaws in this and therefore it would be wrong to pursue it.

To change the culture of an organisation you need to change what people value and what they believe is important. This can happen but often takes time. Imagine you were someone who does not like sport, who sees no point in taking part in it if you do not like it and who likes the freedom your sixth form gives you to choose whether to participate. If the school headteacher suddenly decides that your views on the importance of sports at school is wrong and that from now on it will be compulsory you would probably argue about this. It is possible that over time you could be convinced that compulsory sport at school would help your academic performance or help you feel better in yourself, but simply being told that this is true would not necessarily work. You would want to see some evidence or try it out for a while to see for yourself, or be talked through the arguments for and against until you were convinced and agreed with the arguments being made. Unfortunately, businesses do not always have time to go through this process with every member of staff. Sometimes culture needs to be changed faster than a process of education and discussion allows; sometimes leaders may think it is better to push on and let people see the benefits rather than spend the time trying to convince them in advance.

To achieve change quickly managers may:

- offer incentives for those who agree to the changes and start adopting them (higher marks for those who participate in sport); this is a 'carrot' approach
- punish those who do not adopt the changes (lower marks for those who do not participate in sport); this is the 'stick' approach.

Neither the carrot nor the stick approach will in itself change people's attitudes. They are simply changing behaviour. They do not change what you believe, simply what you do. This means people will not be very committed to the changes. However, in the long term if the changes are proved to be beneficial people may change their attitudes as well.

Other approaches include:

- educating people about the benefits of change
- reassuring people about the change, to reduce fears
- providing resources to enable people to prepare and train for change
- focusing on key people to get their support; once they are won over others will follow.

37.4 Leading and managing change

Given that change is going to occur both internally and externally, managers must consider the best way(s) of managing it.

Resistance to change may come in many forms, such as:

- a lack of effort to learn the necessary new skills or a general lack of cooperation
- a demand for more pay
- a refusal to use the new systems
- a demand for extended discussion to slow down the process of change.

Figure 37.2 highlights the different states that employees might be in when managers are introducing change. This model by Zeira and Avedisian highlights that the openness and readiness for change will depend on how dissatisfied employees are with the present situation and the extent to which they think they will suffer from change. The more dissatisfied they are and the less they think they will personally suffer as a result of it, the more open they will be to change.

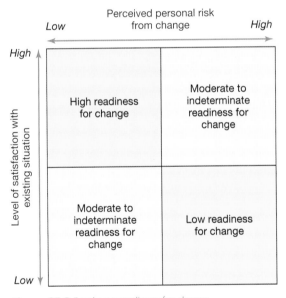

Figure 37.2 Employee readiness for change

Change may not happen because there is resistance to it. Also, it may be that the business lacks the resources to bring it about.

We may know we need to update our database systems, improve our websites or refurbish our stores but lack the resources to do so. Often the very time when change is needed (when a business is doing badly) is when a business is short of resources to bring it about.

The lack of resources may involve a lack of:

- money, for example, a business may not have the cash or access to credit to invest
- skills, for example, a business may not have the talents, experience and abilities within its organisation to manage a change or bring about change effectively. This may be due to the recruitment policy, a lack of training and/or a new situation arising which requires new skills it does not have
- time – you should never underestimate time as a resource.

There may be many changes managers want to bring about but they may be so busy firefighting (see Mintzberg's analysis of what managers do on pages 41–43) that they cannot implement all the changes they would like to.

Another problem that can occur is that managers simply do not recognise that change is needed. They may be too inward looking and not appreciate that their market has changed. A manager like this is a reactive rather than a proactive manager.

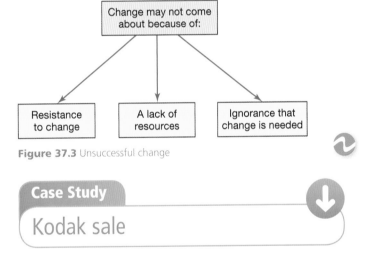

Figure 37.3 Unsuccessful change

Case Study

Kodak sale

In 2012 Kodak announced it may sell off its still-camera film and photo paper divisions.

This meant an end to Kodak making films for still cameras, photo papers, souvenir photo products at theme parks, scanners and picture print-out kiosks at stores. It left the business focused on printers, cinema film stock and chemicals.

Kodak had already stopped making digital cameras as part of efforts to reduce its losses. The company had struggled to compete with increasingly sophisticated cameras on mobile phones.

It has also been trying to raise funds by selling off more than 1100 digital imaging patents.

Apple and Google had been reported to have made rival bids for the patents. Sources suggest the offer price for the portfolio would be about $500 million – well below the $2.6 billion estimate that Kodak had suggested it could be worth.

Questions

1 Analyse the reasons why Kodak may have sold off its film and paper divisions. [8]
2 Discuss the ways in which culture can affect the success of a business strategy. [16]

Why can change go wrong?

Kotter (1990) studied more than 100 companies going through change and identified the following most common errors made by managers trying to bring about change:

1 Too much complacency – it is common to think problems can be dealt with later. Managers need to create a sense of urgency when introducing change.
2 Failing to build a substantial coalition – this means that forces opposing change often undermine the changes that managers are trying to bring in. Managers need to build a coalition to gain support and help push the change through.
3 Underestimating the need for a clear vision – without a clear vision of where you are headed you may end up with a series of initiatives that are rather disconnected.
4 Permitting roadblocks against the vision; allowing things to get in the way and delay change – managers need to empower people to clear obstacles.
5 Not planning or achieving short-term wins – it is important to sustain momentum. Managers need to secure short-term wins to show they can succeed.
6 Declaring victory too soon – managers need to keep moving.
7 Not anchoring changes in corporate culture – managers need to anchor change and make sure it is part of the culture (for example, by rewarding those who have helped bring it about).

Kotter stressed the importance of using the sequence in the order shown above to bring about effective change.

37.5 Developing a strategy to manage change

Managers will need to consider the right strategy to manage change in any given situation. This will depend on factors such as:
- the potential level of resistance
- the extent to which the reason for change is understood
- the resources and time available.

In some cases the focus may be on informing staff. In other cases persuading them of the need for change or the benefits of change is more significant. On some occasions the strategy may need to concentrate on forcing it through.

Huawei

Huawei is a leading global ICT solutions provider. Through our dedication to customer-centric innovation and strong partnerships, we have established end-to-end capabilities and strengths across the carrier networks, enterprise, consumer, and cloud computing fields. We are committed to creating maximum value for telecom carriers, enterprises and consumers by providing competitive ICT solutions and services. Our products and solutions have been deployed in over 140 countries, serving more than one-third of the world's population.

Huawei's vision is to enrich life through communication. By leveraging our experience and expertise in the ICT sector, we help bridge the digital divide by providing opportunities to enjoy broadband services, regardless of geographic location. Contributing to the sustainable development of society, the economy, and the environment, Huawei creates green solutions that enable customers to reduce power consumption, carbon emissions, and resource costs.

Focus on Strategy, Simplify Management, Increase Efficiency
We have weathered another turbulent year: the downward spiral in the global economy, an investigation into cyber security allegations by a particular committee of the US Congress, political upheavals in the Middle East and Northern Africa, as well as natural disasters including floods and earthquakes. I would like to express my most sincere gratitude to our customers, suppliers, and partners across the world. My thanks also go out to our staff members for your dedicated work and to your loved ones for their support. Without your support, Huawei wouldn't have outperformed the market in 2012.

… Statistics show that the data created in 2012 alone is equal to all the data created in human history before 2012 and this trend will continue. Rapid transmission of data to every corner of the world is an inevitability, which will create incredible demands. … Seizing opportunities, focusing on strategy, and simplifying management are the core measures that we will take to achieve effective growth in the next five years.

As a professional ICT solutions provider, we are committed to achieving 'high bandwidth, multiple services, and zero wait time'. After two decades of development, we are now able to gather all the required human resources and materials to strengthen our investment in the major pipes, including information access, convergence, transmission, switching, and storage. Our historical mission and strategic opportunity is to achieve breakthroughs in key technologies and align our offerings with market demands. Our strategic objective in 2013 is to establish our leading positions in Mobile Broadband (MBB), Fixed Broadband (FBB), and backbone network solutions. Our value does not simply lie in our capability to help customers lower their procurement costs. More importantly, it lies in our capability to increase their competitiveness and profitability. Our goal is to become our customers' trusted partner.

We should devote our limited energy to specific business objectives, and avoid the impulse to expand business blindly. Managers who expand business blindly must be held accountable … Responsibility and performance are the most important basis for selecting and assessing managers at Huawei. In 2013, we must continue to simplify our internal management: We must delegate more authority to field offices, shift the focus of our HQ organizations to service, support, and supervision, streamline HQ organizations, and simplify processes. Moreover, we must focus less on expense settlement intended for performance appraisals, optimize value assessment and distribution mechanisms, and motivate our staff members to apply full effort to create value.

Source: Guo Ping, Huawei Rotating and Acting CEO, 31 December 2012, www.huawei.com

Questions

1 Analyse the ways in which Huawei wants to develop how it manages its people. [8]

2 Discuss the external factors that influence Huawei's strategy. [8]

Techniques to implement and manage change successfully

Change is most likely to be successful if:

- those affected by the change were involved in bringing it about (rather than having it imposed on them)
- those involved in the change feel they have an opportunity to air their views
- the benefits of the change are made clear to those involved
- individuals feel able to cope with the change; they feel they have the resources and skills to deal with it
- the people involved agree with the reasons for the change.

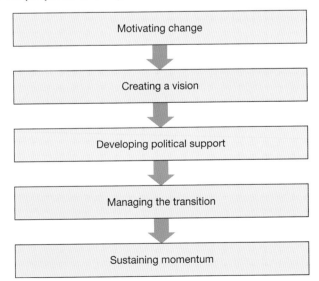

Figure 37.4 Successful change

37.6 Contingency planning

Businesses operate in uncertain and risky environments. Managers are always making decisions about the future and inevitably are not sure of exactly what the future will be like. This makes planning even more important; planning for a situation that is expected but also reviewing the plan regularly to assess where the business is compared with where it expected to be, and to decide what to do next to get back on track if necessary. One type of planning is known as **contingency planning**. This occurs when a firm prepares for unlikely events, such as:

- a fire
- the bankruptcy or insolvency of a major customer
- the closure of an important supplier
- a major computer virus attacking the database
- an epidemic causing illness among staff.

Contingency plans might include:

- using two suppliers for the same part or component in case there are problems with one of them; this can safeguard supply
- paying a fee to be able to use computer facilities or office space elsewhere in case of flooding, earthquake or a terrorist attack
- training employees in several tasks so they can take over from others if there are major absences, illnesses or strikes
- ensuring new products are in development so that if there is a problem with existing products they can be replaced.

However, you cannot afford to have a contingency plan for every event (such as alien invasion or being hit by a meteorite). Managers must therefore decide exactly which events are worth preparing for and how many resources to put into contingency planning. Should the firm have back-up plans in case there are problems with suppliers? Should it have a plan for what to do if there is a safety problem with one of its products? What about planning for a situation where a competitor makes a takeover bid? Decisions must be based on the likely risk and damage of any event.

A contingency plan should provide a sense of direction and enable each element of the business to see how it should contribute. It should help managers set their priorities and allocate their resources.

The greater the likelihood of an event and the greater the potential damage if it does occur, the more likely a firm is to plan for it. Food manufacturers, for example, are likely to plan for a situation where their products are contaminated and they have to recall them. An airline will plan for a crash. An oil transportation business will prepare for a spillage.

> **Key term**
>
> **Contingency planning** involves preparing for unexpected events.

Lehman Brothers

After the terrorist attacks on 11 September 2001 Lehman Brothers, an investment bank which had offices just across the road from the World Trade Center, was able to restart its business in New York almost immediately. This was thanks to careful advance planning which meant its computer systems allowed many of its staff to work from home, and others to set up in hotel rooms as a temporary measure. As a result, it came through the period after 11 September better than some of its competitors that suffered much less physical damage and disruption. (Despite such contingency planning Lehman Brothers later collapsed in the financial crisis of 2008, showing that no business is ever completely safe.)

Questions

1 Analyse the contingencies a bank might plan for.   [8]
2 To what extent is planning for terrorist attacks a good use of resources?   [20]

The need for contingency planning highlights the dynamic nature of business and the need to be prepared for the unexpected. Obviously a firm cannot prepare for every emergency but it is worth highlighting the biggest risks and preparing for these. Firms must continually examine their own operations and their environment to check that they are prepared for possible changes in the future; in this way managers will be proactive (anticipating and preparing for change) rather than reactive (having to react to crises as they develop).

Of course this does not mean that companies that have contingency plans are safe from disaster; unfortunately managers often do not or cannot foresee what events will occur. In 2008, for example, there was a major global financial crisis that few had predicted. This led to a problem gaining credit and lower customer spending which damaged many businesses, very few of which would have had any form of plan for this scenario.

Case Study

Disaster planning

In 2008 more than 5 million Southern Californians signed up to simultaneously drop to the floor on a given day and huddle face down under tables and desks for two minutes of imagined seismic turmoil in the biggest US earthquake drill ever.

The Great Southern California ShakeOut drill was organised by scientists and emergency officials as part of a campaign to prepare the region's 22 million inhabitants for a catastrophic quake that experts say is inevitable and long overdue.

Figure 37.5 Pupils at a school taking part in the Great Southern California ShakeOut drill

The exercise is based on the premise of a magnitude 7.8 quake striking the San Andreas Fault, similar in strength to a devastating quake that had hit China earlier in the year.

At precisely 10a.m. on a given day people in classrooms, offices and homes throughout the region had to 'drop, cover and hold on' for two minutes, the duration of the hypothetical quake. They were guided by a public service message distributed to businesses and schools and played over the airwaves by radio and TV stations.

Questions

1 Analyse the possible impact of an earthquake on businesses in the area.   [8]
2 To what extent would disaster planning be useful for all businesses?   [16]

The impact of a crisis

When a disaster does occur, such as a fault in the product or a fire at the factory, this can cause panic. It is hoped that the firm will have a contingency plan which it can put into action, but even so this is likely to be a stressful time. It is easy to rush into a decision at times like these because of the pressure to do something and be seen to be doing something – this can lead to rushed and inappropriate decision-making. On the other hand, if you delay too long the crisis may get worse. As well as sorting out the crisis itself, the firm may have to handle the press as well. When managing a crisis it is important to:
- identify the 'facts' as soon as possible. What is the scale of the problem? How many people are likely to be affected?
- establish good communication systems. Managers must make sure that everyone is 'on line' and reacting in the same way. If, for example, different managers are giving the press different information following a scare about the safety of the product,

this will create the impression they are not in control and the public may lose faith.

- have the authority and resources to make decisions quickly, rather than having to consult endless committees.

Scenario planning

This is another technique to help managers plan ahead. In this approach managers try to imagine three or four possible scenarios that might develop in the future in their industry. Scenario planning does not assume the future will be like the past, but asks managers and experts to think of what the world might look like in the future. This could be very different from the past (as we have seen with the rapid collapse of financial markets in 2007 and 2008 across the world). This technique has been used widely by Shell, where managers work with experts to create possible visions of what the world might look like in the future. For example, one scenario might include a stable political position in the Middle East, high levels of oil production and a low oil price. Another might focus on high levels of intervention by the government to reduce car usage, leading to high taxes and low levels of demand. Managers then work on how these scenarios might affect the business and the implications for their strategy. Schwartz describes scenarios as: 'Stories that can help us recognise and adapt to changing aspects of our present environment. They form a method for articulating the different pathways that might exist for you tomorrow, and finding your appropriate movements down each of those possible paths.'

Test your learning

Short answer questions

1 a What is a business plan? [2]

   b Explain **one** element of a business plan. [3]

2 Explain **one** benefit of producing a business plan. [3]

3 Explain **one** problem of producing a business plan. [3]

4 What is meant by corporate culture? [2]

5 What is a power culture? [2]

6 What is a task culture? [2]

7 What is meant by an innovative culture? [2]

8 Explain the link between culture and strategic management. [5]

9 a What is meant by contingency planning? [2]

   b Explain **one** benefit of contingency planning. [3]

10 What is meant by crisis management? [2]

Data response question

About Lenovo

The Lenovo brand was created in 2004 but the company behind it– Legend Holdings– has been around since 1984. Originally formed in Hong Kong, Legend grew to become the largest personal computer manufacturer in China. In 2004 it changed its name to Lenovo and in 2005 it acquired the Personal Computing division of IBM.

Lenovo is now worth over $20 billion and employs more than 26 000 employees in over 60 countries, selling to customers in over 160 countries. The company is building on its base in China to expand globally. In particular it is growing in markets in the West, having previously focused on the East. It is planning five or ten years ahead and investing heavily for the future.

The approach of the company is to achieve balance. It sales are balanced between different products and markets. It focuses on short-term issues while also planning for the long term. It has a market share of over 30 per cent in China and was also developing new markets. In managing the business they balance leadership with listening to others. As a result the company is the fastest growing PC business in the world and is number one in China and Japan and number one in the world for large business and public sector customers. Other achievements include:

- enormous success with its ThinkPad notebook
- the launch of a smartphone in China
- the launch of a new family of tablets targeting consumer and commercial markets.

The Lenovo business is built on product innovation, a highly efficient global supply chain and a well implemented strategy. The company develops, produces and markets reliable, high quality, secure and easy-to-use technology products and services for customers who want technology that does more.

It has a long-term goal of becoming the leading personal technology company in the world. It aims to achieve this by leading in three areas:

- product innovation and quality in personal computers
- leading the industry with a range of products such as devices, services, applications and content that seamlessly connect to people and the web
- becoming recognised as the one of the best, most trusted and respected companies to work for and do business with.

The values of the company are an integral part of its success. They define how its people work and what the business represents. Its values include:

- serving customers
- trust and integrity

- teamwork across cultures
- innovation and entrepreneurial spirit.

To achieve the innovation it values the company has 46 world class laboratories including research centres in Yokohama, Japan; Beijing, Shanghai and Shenzhen in China and Morrisville in the USA. Its innovation strategy focuses on:

- the majority of development ideas being ones that can be brought to market within 24 months
- some investment in longer term research, targeting 'game changing' developments.

The company employs more than 3000 engineers, researchers and scientists. The company has a track record on over 2000 patents and more than 100 major design awards. Acquisitions and collaborations with others in the industry enable Lenovo to stay ahead of market trends and provide a strong portfolio of products. Through innovation the company believes it can meet customer needs and also become more environmentally friendly, meeting climate and energy concerns.

Source: Adapted from www.lenovo.com

Questions

1 Analyse the benefits of investing in innovation.   [10]

2 To what extent do you think the culture of a business such as Lenovo is vital to its success?   [14]

3 To what extent does Lenovo's strategy seem a good one?   [16]

Essay questions

1 To what extent do you think it is easy to change the culture of a struggling business?   [20]

2 How important do you think culture is in determining the success of a business?   [20]

Past paper question

Read the Sam's Fashion case study on pages 462–63 and then answer the following question.

Manuel is proposing significant organisational changes. Discuss how managers such as Manuel can minimise workforce resistance during a period of change.   [20]

Cambridge International AS and A Level Business Studies 9707 Paper 33 Q7 May/June 2010

All the questions below are taken from Cambridge International's past A level Business Studies unit three examination papers. The questions represent only part of the whole paper. In each chapter we have recommended that you answer at least one part of these questions. However, you should attempt as many complete sets of questions as possible once you have studied the necessary chapters.

A Level Paper 3

Atlantic Steel Company (ASC)

The current situation
ASC is a public limited company which produces steel. It was privatised in November 2005 after 35 years of state ownership and control. Since privatisation, the profit-focused objectives of the shareholders and the directors they elected have led to many changes within the business. Table 1 summarises some of these changes following privatisation.

Table 1 ASC data comparing 2005 with 2010   *5*

	2005 (before privatisation)	2010 (after privatisation)
Annual labour productivity	600 tonnes per worker	940 tonnes per worker
Number of steel works	20	14
Total staff employed	44 000	32 000
% of staff belonging to a Trade Union	78	48
Average ASC wage as % of industry average wage	89	105
% of total output exported	23	45
Average price of ASC steel as % of average industry price	82	98

10

15

The company accountant is forecasting profit before tax (net profit) for the 2011 financial year of $35m. In 2005 ASC lost $45m despite substantial Government subsidies.

Long-term plan and corporate objectives
One of the first actions made by the new directors was to establish a five year plan for ASC. This contained the long-term objectives of the business and details of the main strategic decisions needed to achieve them.   *20*

Long-term corporate objectives are:

- Achieve 2.5% global market share in steel by 2011

- Become one of the five most efficient steel producers in the world.

Strategic decisions include: *25*

- Close least efficient steel works

- Acquire, through takeovers, smaller competitors with good productivity records.

Fluctuating global demand for steel

Steel is used in many industries such as construction, car manufacturing and shipbuilding. There are seasonal changes in demand for steel in some countries due to poor weather conditions affecting output in major industries. The ASC marketing department uses the moving average method and other techniques to forecast these seasonal demand changes. These forecasts are used by both the human resources and the operations management departments.

Cyclical demand changes are more difficult to predict. Global demand for steel increased steadily during the 10 years to 2008. In that year demand rose by 11% to 1.22 billion tonnes. However, the global recession cut demand for steel by 15% in 2009 and demand fell again in 2010. ASC, like all of the world's steel makers, has been greatly affected by this cyclical demand.

The Chief Executive Officer reported to directors at a Board meeting in 2010 that: 'Our long-term strategic plan may have to be radically changed as a result of this recession. This will have great effects on the objectives and strategies used by all departments of the business.'

The directors of ASC took very rapid action as soon as it became clear that the fall in demand for steel would be serious and prolonged:

- Two steel works were closed, reducing the overheads of the business

- Some staff in steel works kept open were either offered redundancy or re-employment on flexible employment contracts

- Steel stocks were increased to prevent output being reduced at some works

- Investment in fully automated computer controlled equipment was increased to make ASC's steel more competitive.

Further closures seem inevitable

Even if global steel demand increases, the directors of ASC are determined to continue closing low productivity works that have spare capacity. The directors are going to decide which of two works to close at the next Board meeting. They think that closing one of these works, both of which are located in the same country, will increase demand for the output of the other. The Operations Director has produced the data contained in Table 2.

Table 2 Comparative data for two steel works

	Steel works A	Steel works B
Contribution towards ASC's profit in 2010	($5m)	($7m)
Average age of equipment	15 years	11 years
Number of workers employed	5 500	7 000
Unemployment rate in the region	12%	18%
Output of carbon pollution in 2010	55 000 tonnes	43 000 tonnes
Distance from major customer	55 kilometres	120 kilometres
Size of Government grant offered to keep plant open	$5m total grant to be paid in 2012	$1.4m per year for 6 years

Global recession – it's not all bad

The global economic downturn led to the closure of several major steel works owned by ASC's competitors. This reduced competition in some countries. ASC was able to take over a small maker of specialist steel, forced into liquidation, at a price the directors believed was below net asset value. Substantial increases in unemployment in many countries have made recruitment for most businesses much easier than when the world economy was booming.

Variance analysis reveals problems

The Finance Director is undertaking variance analysis for most of ASC's steel works. By investigating the major adverse variances, he believes that the recession is not the only factor causing them. The data for the Newtown steel works is contained in Appendix A.

Financial efficiency

75

Despite the decisions taken by the company, the period of falling steel demand has worsened the cash flow position of the business. The changes in the financial efficiency of the business in 2011 can be assessed by ratios calculated from the data given in Appendix B. These can then be compared with the results for 2010 in Appendix C.

Appendix A Budget and actual data for Newtown steel works, 2011

80

	Budget for year ending 31 October 2011	Actual data for year ending 31 October 2011
Revenue	$306m	$272m
Material costs	$125m	$118m
Labour costs	$113m	$106m
Allocated overhead costs	$40m	$41m
Profit	$28m	$7m

85

Appendix B Accounting data for ASC, $m

	As at 30 September 2011
Trade receivables (debtors)	300
Inventories (stocks)	195
Trade payables (creditors)	250
Annual revenue (sales turnover) (for year ending)	2500
Cost of sales (cost of goods sold) (for year ending)	1750

90

Appendix C Financial efficiency ratios, 2010

95

	As at 30 September 2010
Inventory (stock) turnover	15
Days sales in trade receivables (debtor days)	33

Section A

Answer **all** questions in this section.

1 Analyse the opportunities and threats of a global recession for ASC. [10]

2 a i Using the data in Appendix A, calculate the variances for the Newtown steel works. [6]

    ii Explain possible reasons for any **two** of these variances. [6]

  b Discuss the impact of ASC's privatisation on the company's stakeholders, using the data in Table 1, and other relevant information. [16]

3 a Using data in Appendix B, analyse the financial efficiency of the business by calculating **two** appropriate ratios. [6]

  b Evaluate any **two** ways in which the business might improve its financial efficiency. [8]

4 The ASC marketing department uses a number of sales forecasting techniques including the moving average method. Evaluate the usefulness of sales forecasting to ASC. [12]

Cambridge International AS and A Level Business Studies 9707 Paper 32 Q1, 2, 3 & 4 October/November 2011

Chan Beauty Company (CBC)

June Chan's beauty business

June had always been ambitious and self motivated but she never imagined her business empire would be so successful. After completing a hairdressing course at college she used all of her savings and a bank loan to start her own business, CBC, providing hairdressing for women. June worked 13 hours a day and took no holiday for a year and within 12 months she was able to repay the bank loan. She had even saved up enough to put a deposit on another hairdressing shop that was for sale. After three years, June was the main shareholder in a private limited company operating three hairdressing shops in different towns and two 'fitness and beauty' centres that offered keep fit classes as well as beauty treatments. She now looked around for new challenges.

Ethical beauty products

One idea that June wanted to develop was to create a range of ethical beauty products for both men and women. She made small batches of creams, soaps and shampoos and they were very successful in one of the hairdressing shops in the town of Urbis. Average customer incomes were high in this town and customers seemed prepared to pay high prices for socially responsible products. June wanted to manufacture these products on a much larger scale. The products would not be tested on animals and would contain only natural ingredients such as cocoa butter and nut oils. These would be purchased from small, local suppliers who would receive prices above the market average to encourage long term sustainable development.

Meeting Jon Kiplagat was a big step in June's life. He was a rich businessman who had used much of his wealth to support charities. He offered to help finance a factory to produce June's ethical beauty products in exchange for a 45% stake in CBC.

He explained that he was not interested in managing the factory, short term profits were not a priority and June would have complete control.

Within 4 months:

- Premises had been found and fitted with large scale batch production equipment

- The first products had been made

- Some large retail customers had been signed up on short term contracts.

Poor communication

The products proved to be popular but not very profitable because of production and supply problems. June had no experience of managing a factory. She left the running of it to a senior supervisor but problems soon became apparent. Suppliers complained of receiving confusing orders. Retail customers could not get enough stock of the most popular ranges, but their telephone calls for more deliveries went unanswered. Different departments of the factory appeared not to be communicating with each other. The factory workforce had agreed to work flexibly, switching from one task to another. Workers were paid a good salary but they did not like the formal instructions pinned to the notice-board each morning giving details of the daily jobs with no thought given to their preferred work groups. Initial production problems had often gone unsolved as the staff had not been consulted about the most likely causes.

The business now

CBC is made up of the three original hairdressing shops, the factory and eight fitness and beauty centres. June's leadership style as Managing Director is not autocratic as she is keen to see managers develop. She concentrates on developing new ideas for company expansion as she finds this much more exciting than day-to-day routine details. At present, June is considering two strategies for the growth of the company.

Option 1: Market development – selling ethical beauty products in other countries. This would involve exporting the beauty products to Country X. June is keen on this idea – she wants to run an international business empire! The Marketing Director warned, however, that: 'Consumer tastes may be very different and does it have the same youthful population profile as our own country? We would also need to consider the impact that the appreciation of our currency's exchange rate would have.' June had estimated some investment appraisal results for this strategy – see Appendix A.

Option 2: Diversification – selling a range of clothing. June believes that consumers are starting to reject cheap clothes made in factories with low wage workers who are often still children. 'If we sold a range of clothing to complement our beauty products we could use the term "ethically produced clothes" as a useful marketing weapon,' the Marketing Director said to June. 'I am sure that we would not need to do much market research as we know our hair and beauty customers so well anyway. I have done some quick calculations of potential future cash flows from this strategy.' He presented the following net cash flow forecasts to June for Option 2:

Year 0 (capital cost)	Year 1	Year 2	Year 3	Year 4
($6m)	$2m	$3m	$6m	$4m

Cityville hairdressing shop – should we close this?

At a recent CBC Board of Directors meeting, June was disappointed to see the financial performance of the original hairdressing shops. She admitted to herself that she had ignored this side of the company in recent years and now the Finance Director showed her the data in Appendix B. 'It seems obvious to me that we should shut down Cityville hairdressers,' June said. 'This will increase the overall profitability of the company and free up funds for investment in my new ideas.' 'But,' replied the Finance Director, 'it would be a financial mistake to shut this Cityville shop now and do not forget that three of the employees there have been working for you for several years.'

Future issues

June's satisfaction over the success of her business was shattered by the news of Jon Kiplagat's death. He had left shares in all of his business interests to his son, Jim. Jim puts profit as his main objective. He is very keen to get involved in helping to manage the company. June wondered how to keep control of the company especially as it might be necessary to sell more shares privately to raise finance for the new growth strategy. At around the same time, the Business News carried two significant reports. One was about the slower rate of economic growth and the other gave details of new foreign competitors in the beauty product market.

Appendix A Estimated investment appraisal data for Option 1: Market Development

Average Rate of Return over 4 years	26.7%
Net Present Value @ 10% discount rate	$4.25m
Payback period	2 years
Initial capital costs	$4m

Appendix B Data for the three hairdressing shops. Year ending 31/10/09

	Newtown	Cityville	Urbis
Number of customers	6500	4800	9500
Average price per customer	$12	$8	$16
Total variable costs	$25000	$12000	$28000
Fixed costs of shop	$10000	$9000	$16000
Allocated share of Head Office overheads	$22000	$28000	$30000
Labour turnover	10%	33%	8%
% of customers who complained	1%	8%	3%
Change in unemployment rate over last 12 months in each town	+2%	−3%	−1%

Table 1 10% discount factors

Year 0	Year 1	Year 2	Year 3	Year 4
1	0.91	0.83	0.75	0.68

Section A

Answer **all** questions in this section.

1 a Analyse **two** possible reasons for the communication problems in the factory. [8]

b Evaluate **two** ways in which communication might be improved in the factory. [10]

2 Using the data in Appendix B, calculate the impact on the company's annual profit of closing the Cityville hairdressing shop. [8]

3 a Calculate for Option 2 the:

i Average Rate of Return (ARR). [4]

ii Net Present Value (NPV) using the 10% discount factors in Table 1. [4]

b Which of the two options would you advise June to choose? Fully support your answer by referring to your results from **4a** and other information. [16]

4 Assume Option 1, the market development option, is chosen. Discuss the important features of a marketing plan for a successful launch in your country of the ethical beauty products. [16]

Cambridge International AS and A Level Business Studies 9707 Paper 32 Q1, 2, 4 & 5 October/November 2009

Pyramid Televisions (PT)

PT is based in Country Y and manufactures televisions (TVs). The business undertakes all Processes in TV production including research and development, manufacture of components and final assembly. This is unusual in the industry, but the directors believe it ensures excellent product quality. Business is booming for PT. Demand from the home market and export markets is at an all time high. Exports have been boosted by a recent depreciation of Country Y's currency exchange rate. Demand from home market consumers has risen due to low interest rates. The government in Country Y has recently stated its policy of low interest rates is helping to reduce unemployment. Some economists doubt whether this policy can continue. The rate of inflation has just risen for the fifth month in a row.

Capacity issues

PT operates three factories in different locations. Each one specialises in TVs of different sizes and styles. All factories have reached their maximum production capacity with the recent employment of a third shift of workers, working at night for which they are paid a bonus. Average fixed costs have fallen as capacity utilisation reached its maximum. However, the overall efficiency of production has declined. This is shown in Table 1:

Table 1 Average costs of production in existing factories

Rate of capacity utilisation in the business (%)	Average fixed costs per TV ($)	Average variable costs per TV ($)	Average total costs per TV ($)
70	20	55	75
80	18	50	68
90	16	54	70
100	14	60	74

Machinery in two of the factories is unreliable due to continuous working and lack of time for maintenance. Purchased in 2003, the machinery is old by TV industry standards. Technology is changing so rapidly that factory machines need updating every two years. The Operations Director has two alternative proposals for solving the problems of full capacity and declining efficiency. She outlined them at the last Board of Directors' meeting:

'**Option 1:** We could build a large new factory. This could be in a region of high unemployment where government grants are available. Also, planning laws are less strict so it would not matter if the factory was next to a housing estate. This new factory would double the business's production capacity. The three old factories would be closed.

Option 2: This is cheaper. It involves updating the oldest machinery with new, much quicker, robot-controlled equipment to assemble TVs. Production capacity will increase. These machines take up a lot of space. To increase capacity further I propose buying in components from a low cost foreign supplier rather than making the components ourselves.'

Financial issues

The Operations Director continued: 'I have forecast some of the financial data for these two options. It is clear that both options will offer a lower break-even level of production than at present.' She presented the data in Table 2 to her fellow directors.

Table 2 Financial forecasts for the two options

	Option 1	Option 2
Capital cost	$25m	$12m
Annual fixed costs	$21m	$12m (total for 3 factories)
Average variable cost per TV	$30	$40
Average TV selling price (to retailers)	$60	$60
Expected annual maximum capacity	1.5 million	1.2 million (total for 3 factories)

Current production capacity and level of sales is 750 000 units per year. The finance for either option would be borrowed. Although PT is profitable, retained profits are quite low. The directors have recently adopted a policy of paying high dividends to shareholders. 'By calculating some ratios from this year's accounts we should be able to convince the bank to lend the finance we will need,' said the Finance Director confidently.

Marketing issues

The Chief Executive is concerned that a high proportion of the company's TVs are being sold through discount shops. 'They offer low prices but awful customer service. There is no consumer advice given, they are often in out-of-town locations and they offer no after-sales service. I want PT to control the marketing mix of its own products. We could add value to the product. By offering consumers an excellent retail experience we could charge higher prices. Quality of service could become a unique selling point for us. I want PT to take over the "TV4U" chain of shops. This will cost about $10m. It offers us a great chance to become a fully vertically integrated TV business.' Some of the other directors were less keen. They raised questions about the cost of the shops and whether they had the management skills to operate shops as well as factories. 'With either Option 1 or 2 costing so much, could PT afford this takeover?' asked the Finance Director.

Research and development (R and D) issues

PT's R and D department has created inventions in the last two years but none have proved to be successful. In contrast, its major competitor has introduced a number of new ideas, such as very high definition screens. These product innovations have helped to make demand for the competitor's TVs less price elastic than PT's products.

The R and D Director had his own ideas why his department had failed to produce successful innovations. 'The rigid structure of the business, with its many levels of hierarchy, does not work for us. The R and D department needs regular and frequent contact with all other departments to make sure we invent products that consumers might want and that we can produce cost-

30

35

40

45

50

55

60

65

70

effectively. My department is too isolated. I recommend that the whole company switches to a matrix, team based structure.'

Industrial relations issues

The full capacity working had led to workers demanding higher pay or a share of company profits. Many workers belong to the Trade Union of Manufacturing Workers (TUMW) but this is not recognised by PT for negotiations. A union representative is demanding that unless PT managers negotiate with the union to resolve the dispute about pay levels the union members would go on strike. This would be bad news for PT as retailers might stock up with competitors' products. PT's management recognise that this dispute needs to be resolved quickly.

Appendix A Market research data for PT and its major competitor

	PT TVs	Major competitor's TVs
Increase in sales last year when average consumer incomes in Country Y increased by 5%	5%	10%
Increase in sales resulting from 10% increase in promotional spending by both companies	4%	8%

Section A

Answer **all** questions in this section.

1 a Discuss how PT's management might resolve the pay dispute with the workers. [10]

   b Assess the advantages and disadvantages to the Research and Development department of changing the organisational structure of the business. [10]

2 Analyse possible reasons why average total costs have increased following the increase in capacity utilisation shown in Table 1. [8]

3 Which of the two options for solving the capacity problem would you recommend to PT's Board of Directors? Support your answer by analysing data in Table 2 (including relevant calculations) and any other useful information. [16]

4 a Using the data in Appendix A calculate, for both PT and its major competitor, the:

   i Income elasticity of demand

   ii Promotion elasticity of demand. [8]

   b Discuss possible changes to PT's future marketing strategy based on these results and other information in the case. [14]

Cambridge International AS and A Level Business Studies 9707 Paper 3 Q1, 2, 3 & 4 May/June 2008

Radar Cosmetics

Good news for Radar Cosmetics

'Sales of branded cosmetics in Asia hit all time high!' announced the Daily Echo headline last month. This is excellent news for Radar. The company manufactures cosmetics, shampoos and creams. Women, and increasingly men too, buy these products to look more beautiful! The increase in sales of cosmetics and similar products has been due to rising disposable incomes amongst the 18–35 year old, middle income market segment in country P. This is the main market for Radar products, accounting for 80% of the company's total sales.

Research and Development success

For years Radar had struggled with a poor brand image and lack of product focus. The business used to make products for supermarkets which sold them under the supermarkets' 'own name'

labels. This changed when Radar's small research and development team of scientists developed a
new range of skin creams. Radar's scientists made two claims about these creams:

- They definitely reduced the signs of ageing in 75% of users.
- Three separate products have been developed – creams A, B and C – to suit different ethnic
  skin types.

The directors of Radar made a strategic decision. The company stopped making skin creams for
other companies and launched its own range of three expensive up-market creams. The brand
'Aquaskin' was created. A large marketing budget paid for advertisements on TV and in fashion
magazines which created much consumer interest. The advertisements stated its unique selling
point as: 'Aquaskin is an entirely natural product, is not tested on animals and is guaranteed to make
you look younger'. Clever publicity was arranged with the support of an Olympic swimming gold
medallist. She was paid by Radar to suggest that 'Aquaskin keeps my skin fresh each day even after
6 hours training in the pool'. Sales of Aquaskin products were 50% above the company's target in
the first two years despite prices being 20% above those of most competitors' products.

Extending the product range

Encouraged by this success, Radar introduced other products under the same brand name.
'Aquaskin Junior' was aimed at young people. The Marketing Director had said at a directors
meeting: 'Young people can be tricked into buying these products, even at high prices, by telling
them that famous models and sports stars use them. 10–17 year olds are more worried about
their appearance than they used to be. This junior range is certain to sell well. There is no need to
research this market segment. The Aquaskin name is so well known that the junior range will sell
itself without much promotion'. The Finance Director presented the following data to the Board one
year after the 'Aquaskin Junior' launch.

Table 1 2010 cost and sales data

	Aquaskin Junior	Aquaskin Cream A	Aquaskin Cream B	Aquaskin Cream C
Labour costs per 100 units	$40	$60	$30	$80
Material costs per 100 units	$200	$300	$100	$600
Allocated fixed factory and Head Office costs	$190 000	$250 000	$450 000	$350 000
Selling price per 100 units to retailers	$400	$500	$250	$900
Sales (boxes of 100 units)	1000	12 000	20 000	6000

On seeing these figures, the Chief Executive quickly suggested that: 'These are bad results for the
Aquaskin Junior range. I believe that we should stop making this product immediately. This would
increase our annual profit by $30 000.'

New factory location could reduce costs

Radar has always manufactured its products in country P. However, wage rates and land prices
are at least 50% higher than in countries R and S. The directors plan to establish a new factory
abroad to manufacture products under the 'Aquaskin' brand. This would lead to the closure of one
of the two existing factories in country P. The Operations Director had produced a report about two
possible factory sites – one in country R and one in country S. Here is some of his report.

- The employment laws in country R are the same as in country P.
- Country R is in a large free trade area with many other countries and is a well known tourist
  destination.
- The opportunities for joint ventures and accepting sub-contracted work are likely to be higher in
  country S due to the huge cosmetics industry already based there. This would offer opportunities
  for economies of scale.

10

15

20

25

30

35

40

45

50

55

- The initial investment in country R for the factory capacity required would be at least $3.5m, based on a five year lease of the property.

- The expected cash inflows from the country R location over this time period are forecast to be:

	Year 1	Year 2	Year 3	Year 4	Year 5
Expected cash inflows $m	2.5	2.5	3.0	4.0	6.0

60

- Cash outgoings are expected to be 50% of cash inflows in any one year.

- Data on the location in country S are contained in Table 2.

Table 2 Financial forecasts for factory location in country S

Average rate of return (ARR) (first 5 years)	40%
Payback	3 years
Net present value over 5 years (at 10% discount rate)	$3.6m
Capital cost including property lease for 5 years	$8 million

65

The Operations Director concluded: 'However, these figures are only part of the issue. We need to consider so many qualitative factors too. The relative appeal of these two locations to some of our senior managers will be one factor.'

70

Temporary and flexible labour contracts

Having a new factory in a low cost location would mean the inevitable closure of one of the two existing plants. The Human Resources Director suggested that moving the factory to either country R or S would give Radar the chance to save even more on labour costs by using temporary and flexible labour contracts. 'We can vary the number of workers and the hours they work according to seasonal demand. If they don't meet our quality standards we can replace them quickly.'

75

Another news story

The directors of Radar have just been called to an emergency meeting. Today's Daily Echo reported: 'Former Radar employee claims that Aquaskin **IS** tested on animals! Many consumers now claim it hasn't made them look any younger!'

80

Radar's directors have many important decisions to make over the next few days – and how to deal with this bad publicity is one of them.

Appendix A Forecasted data on country P and other countries Radar sells in

	Country P	Other countries
Annual GDP growth rate 2010–2015	2.0%	3.5%
Annual total population growth rate 2010–2015	1%	1.8%
Annual population growth: 10–17 year olds 2010–2015	4%	2%
Inflation 2011	4.5%	2.5%
Change in interest rate in 2011	+2%	+1.5%

85

90

Appendix B 10% discount factors

Year	1	2	3	4	5
Discount factor	0.91	0.83	0.75	0.68	0.62

Section A

Answer **all** questions in this section.

1 Analyse the benefits to Radar of further investment in research and development (R and D). [10]

2 Do you agree with the Chief Executive that the company should stop producing the 'Aquaskin Junior' cream? Use the quantitative data in Table 1, relevant calculations and the qualitative information available to justify your answer. [16]

3 Evaluate the benefit to Radar of preparing a detailed marketing plan before launching a new product such as the 'Aquaskin Junior' cream. [16]

4 a Calculate for the country R location:

   i Average rate of return (ARR) [3]

   ii Payback period [3]

   iii Net present value (NPV) at 10% discount rate. [4]

   b Using your results from part **a**, data in Table 2 and other information, recommend the country in which Radar should locate its new factory. [14]

Cambridge International AS and A Level Business Studies 9707 Paper 31 Q1, 2, 3 & 4 October/November 2010

Craft Designs

Recent rapid growth

The growth of Ade's business had surprised everyone, especially Ade. Since starting the private limited company twelve years ago it has become the market leader in the tourist gift market in his country. The company produces stone sculptures, wooden carvings and printed textiles. 90% of sales are to tourists, either through Ade's own shops or other retail outlets. There is no doubt that the rapid expansion of the business has been helped greatly by the 300% increase in foreign tourists visiting the country over the last 10 years. *5*

Ade has always been an independent person. His first job in the local soft drinks business had frustrated him despite offering a regular income and secure working conditions. He disliked working for a large organisation in which he had no real responsibility or chance of promotion. When the drinks firm was taken over he, with several other workers, was made redundant. Several of his *10*
colleagues immediately started looking for new jobs but Ade used the first two weeks after his redundancy to think seriously about his future.

He believed he was a natural salesman since winning the Young Enterprise Award at school for his own 'mini company' selling home made sweets. Ade's winning smile and quick sense of humour helped him to break all sales records! He wanted to use his skills to his own advantage. He had a *15*
small amount of savings and he decided to use these to set up his own market stall, selling printed textiles that his sister and her friends were already making for a large retail store in town.

Now, twelve years later, he has several small workshops producing quality sculptures, wooden carvings and printed textiles. Ade still purchases about half of the finished goods needed from independent producers. This outsourcing of supplies gives the business great flexibility without *20*
having to build further workshops. One of the main problems with outsourcing from other producers is the need for additional quality control checks. About half of all products are sold through the company's retail shops, located in all of the major tourist areas. The rest are sold, on credit, to other gift shops.

The growth of the business has brought both its rewards and problems. At the most recent Board of Directors meeting the following issues had been discussed.

25

Product portfolio

Although growing in overall size, the tourist market is changing. Fewer family groups visited the country last year. These visitors had tended to buy large gifts for their homes. However, recently there has been a huge increase in the number of young travellers. These younger tourists seemed to fall into two distinct groups. The first group are dominated by high income earners who visit the country to stay at luxury lodges and hotels. The other main group is made up of tourists who take part in 'environmentally aware' or 'eco-tourism' holidays, visiting the country's beautiful nature reserves. This group is often worried about the exploitation of scarce resources. Market research evidence also seems to suggest a move away from large-scale traditional craft gifts towards jewellery made from precious metals and gem stones. Ade realised the company had to adapt to keep up with these changing tastes.

30

35

He was keen to move into the jewellery market, but realised the specialist nature of the product and the segmentation of the market. Workshop space was not currently available to expand into jewellery production but the Operations Director put forward a rather surprising proposal at the meeting.

40

'Look at this financial data (Table 1). The workshop production of stone sculptures is unprofitable. This situation results from higher raw material costs – stone supplies are now running out in our country – and lower than expected price rises for the finished goods. If we stopped producing these stone products, this would free up workshop space for jewellery production. We could then totally outsource production of stone products to manufacturers in other countries with greater reserves of the natural stone. Our staff will need retraining to make jewellery or, if they cannot learn the new skills required, they will have to be replaced by new workers.'

45

The directors studied the following table produced by the Operations Director but they were not all convinced by his arguments.

Table 1 Financial data for the three products manufactured by Craft Designs

50

For year ending 31/5/07	Stone sculptures ($000)	Wooden gifts ($000)	Printed textiles ($000)
Sales revenue (from products made in own workshops)	4 000	3 000	6 000
Direct material costs	2 000	500	1 500
Labour costs	1 000	1 000	2 000
Allocated factory overheads	500	300	300
Allocated administration overheads	750	600	600
Profit / (Loss)	(250)	600	1 600

55

Economic conditions

The growth of the company had occurred during a period when the macro-economic conditions in the country had been favourable. Recently, some economists have been suggesting that significant changes might be needed in Government economic policy to keep the economy growing steadily. Ade showed the Government economic forecasts in Appendix A to the other directors. He said: 'Our company will undoubtedly be affected if these forecasts turn out to be true'.

60

65

Control of working capital

The Finance Director produced the financial data contained in Appendix B. She commented that: 'We have not managed to control our finances as well as planned. Rapid sales growth has not improved our working capital position. If I were to calculate the debtors days and stock turnover ratios, the results would reinforce the need to take action to improve our financial efficiency. Unfortunately, all possible actions involve some drawbacks to the business.'

70

Appendix A Government Economic Forecasts

	End of 2007	End of 2008	End of 2009
Inflation (annual %)	10	20	18
Unemployment as % of working population	7	8	9
Exchange rate index (2006=100) *	100	95	90
Interest rates (%)	8	14	12

* The exchange rate index measures the average value of a country's currency. A higher value would indicate a currency appreciation.

Appendix B Extract from Craft Designs published accounts for year ending 31/5/07

Sales Revenue	$28m
Gross profit	$12m
Debtors	$7m
Stocks including work in progress	$4m
Short term creditors	$12m
Cash	$1m

Section A
Answer **all** questions in this section.

1 Evaluate the likely impact on the business of the forecast economic conditions in Appendix A. [14]

2 a Using the two ratios suggested by the Finance Director, analyse and comment on the financial efficiency of Craft Designs. [10]

  b Outline **two** drawbacks to the ratio analysis that you have conducted. [4]

  c Discuss **two** ways in which the Finance Director could improve the financial efficiency of the company. [8]

Section B
Answer **one** question from this section.

3 Discuss the relative importance of the factors, **apart from** external economic conditions, that are most likely to affect the future success of Craft Designs. [20]

4 The Operations Director has proposed outsourcing all supplies of stone sculptures so that the company could start jewellery production. Discuss how Ade might try to solve what you consider to be the most important **human resource** and **operational management** problems that might result from this decision. [20]

Adapted from Cambridge International AS and A Level Business Studies 9707 Paper 3 Q3, 4, 6 & 7 May/June 2007

Sam's Fashions (SF)

Time for action

'Sales volumes are up yet our profit margins and net profits are down. We must take action to increase profits or the shareholders could vote us off the Board'. The warning of the Chief Executive of Sam's Fashions, Manuel, was clear. At the last Annual General Meeting of this public limited company, many shareholders had been disappointed about the falling profits. They were worried about the proposal to reduce dividends and the impact this could have on the share price of the company. The decision to cut retail prices last year by 5% on average had helped sales volume in the short term – but with the result of reducing profit margins.

5

Manuel, the son of SF's founder, and the other directors knew that important strategic decisions needed to be taken. The business was experiencing difficult trading conditions as a result of a lengthy global recession and increased competition. In the past, the growth of SF's business had been based on the strategy of the founder Sam Little. His vision had been to 'manufacture and sell quality clothing at premium prices to high income professional women'. The high quality of the clothes was supported by the luxurious furniture and fittings in the shops and the well trained and experienced sales staff.

10

Strategies for recovery

15

Manuel put forward two marketing strategies at a recent Board of Directors meeting. These are called Options A and B.

Option A: E-commerce and telephone sales

- Close most of the shops which have very high overheads, and sell through e-commerce (Internet) and telephone ordering.

20

- These methods, directed at the same market segments as currently targeted, should increase sales and market share.

- Access to high income female consumers in other countries will increase. Lower overhead costs could allow slightly reduced prices to be charged without cutting the net profit margin.

- Staff for these e-commerce operations and telephone sales could be based abroad in very low wage countries. 'We must cut our major cost – labour. Making our shop workers redundant will save costs in the long term, and using the cheapest labour we can find abroad should keep shareholders happy,' explained Manuel.

25

Human resources issues for Option A

If Option A is chosen there will be completely different staffing requirements. Most shop staff will no longer be required. How many e-commerce and telephone staff will the company need? Surely the number of operators will need to vary during the year, with festivals likely to lead to much higher demand? The training of software engineers and computer operators will be very important to give a reliable service. Manuel is keen to move the whole e-commerce and telephone sales operation abroad, but the Marketing Director wondered about the possible impact on customer service that this might have.

30

35

Option B: Mass Marketing

- Use existing shops to enter the mass market with fewer styles and lower prices.

- New clothing designs will appeal to cost conscious adults.

- For the first time SF will design, produce and stock clothes for children and men as well as women.

40

- These clothes will be targeted at families who are on a tight budget due to the recession but who still want fashionable clothes.

- 'We could use our established brand name in advertising to sell to the mass market. We might be able to persuade consumers that our products are of the same high quality, even though we would actually be using much cheaper materials. The most important factor affecting the success of this strategy would be a high marketing budget though' explained Manuel.

Operational management issues for Option B

Option B will need the operations management department to change production and stock control methods. SF's three factories will need to change not just clothing styles but the speed of manufacture and the quality of clothes. Instead of making relatively few high quality items of each style, many thousands of identical items of a few styles will need to be made. Manuel told the Operations Director to consider lean production ideas to keep costs low. 'We need to turn new fashions and styles into clothes in the shops as quickly as possible. Stocks must be minimised but there should be good choice in the shops too. We need to minimise waste at all levels of production. Workers need to be made more responsible for quality. I suggest you look again at using the cheapest dyes and colourings for our materials even though they may pollute the local water supplies', suggested Manuel when explaining his ideas to the Operations Director.

Organisational changes

Manuel is also keen to cut costs at Head Office. The business has five levels of hierarchy and narrow spans of control. This structure reflected Sam's attitude towards leading people – control was more important than trust. Manuel, who took over from Sam just before the company converted to public limited status last year, wants change. He believes that managers and workers could be given more authority and encouraged to take some responsibility for making decisions. He wants to delayer the structure – perhaps by taking out two levels of management. Staff will need to retrain in two-way communication methods, establish effective teamwork and become multi-skilled. Manuel believes that there will be some redundancies and other workers will need to re-apply for newly created posts. His aim is to make the Head Office organisation 'leaner' and more cost effective.

Appendix A Financial data on Sam's Fashions Financial Year ending 31st May

	2009	2010
Total dividends	$70m (paid)	$60.2m (proposed)
Dividend per share	$0.50 (paid)	$0.43 (proposed)
SF's share price at end of year	$5.00	$3.50
Net profit	$200m	$150m
Capital employed	$1000m	$990m
Retained profits	$45m	$15m

Appendix B Forecasted probabilities and economic pay-offs (over 5 year period) from the marketing strategies

	Probabilities of success/failure	Forecasted economic pay-off
Option A Capital cost $5m	0.70 probability of success 0.30 probability of failure	$12m gain $2m loss
Option B Capital cost $3m	0.50 probability of success 0.50 probability of failure	$10m gain $1m loss

Section A

Answer **all** questions in this section.

1 Assuming Option A is chosen, evaluate the importance of effective planning and management of human resources to the success of this option. [16]

2 Evaluate whether Manuel's lean production proposals are likely to increase operational efficiency without reducing customer service. [15]

3 a Draw a decision tree based on the data provided in Appendix B. [4]

 b Calculate the expected monetary values of both Option A and Option B. [4]

 c Which option would you recommend Manuel to choose? Use information in the case and your results from part **b** to support your recommendation. [10]

Section B

4 Manuel is proposing significant organisational changes. Discuss how managers such as Manuel can minimise workforce resistance during a period of change. [20]

Adapted from Cambridge International AS and A Level Business Studies 9707 Paper 33 Q2, 4, 5 & 7 May/June 2010

Forest Product Company (FPC)

FPC is a public limited company. The business owns forests in several low-income developing countries. The main operations of FPC are:

- Wood-cutting: cutting down mature hardwood trees and selling the wood cut from them

- Furniture making: making wooden furniture.

Wood-cutting

The wood-cutting division of the business earns 80% of FPC's total revenue. Many thousands of trees are cut each year. These are transported by trucks and ships to large sawmills, where the trees are split and cut into wood of all sizes. 85% of total output is sold to businesses in 35 different countries. It is used for furniture, house construction and boat building.

Furniture-making

15% of all FPC wood is supplied to the company's furniture-making division which operates two factories. These produce traditional styles of furniture. The furniture is sold through independent 'low price' retailers in several countries. Sales volume of these products has fallen in the last two years. Consumers are showing increased interest in modern imported furniture made from a variety of materials, not just wood. Imports have become cheaper due to lower tariffs. FPC does not promote its own furniture ranges – it depends on the retailers to do this.

Environmental problem

FPC's mission statement is: 'Managing the world's forests carefully for a sustainable future – for all of us'. FPC's commitment to this statement is being challenged by pressure groups opposed to the expansion of FPC's operations in the Lotus forest. The company bought this huge forest as part of its takeover of Far East Forest Company in 2010. It is now clear that FPC's directors had been attracted by the low price for this takeover and they had not undertaken sufficient in-depth research into the operations of the Far East Forest Company. The Lotus forest is located within an area of outstanding natural beauty which has just been given National Park status. This means that existing agreements with the Government to cut trees will not be renewed when they end in 3 years' time. FPC has decided to beat this deadline by accelerating its tree-cutting programme and constructing a new access road through several small villages.

Pressure groups are now campaigning for consumers to stop buying FPC products.

The Chief Executive Officer of FPC has stated that: 'The trees in this forest are very old and large. Increased tree cutting from the Lotus forest will have a much more significant impact on sales turnover than costs over the next year. I forecast that company sales from wood will rise by 15% and that our company's gross profit margin will rise to 72%. Overhead costs, including depreciation on new equipment, should only increase by 5%'. *30*

Organisational structure

The hierarchical structure of the Operations Department of FPC is shown in Appendix B. The new Chief Executive Officer, appointed last year, considers that this is not a suitable structure. She thinks it does not give staff the opportunity for personal development and is inappropriate for the company, especially if it continues to expand into other countries and, possibly, other product markets. *35*

Full capacity at sawmills

Table 1 indicates that the company is operating its sawmills at nearly full capacity. This helps to make FPC one of the lowest cost suppliers of wood in a competitive market. However, the safety record is poor at several sawmills and essential maintenance on heavy electric saws and trucks used to move wood is often hurriedly done. *40*

Table 1 Annual output and capacity at FPC's sawmills

	Total annual capacity (000s tonnes)	Actual annual output (000s tonnes)
2008	45	42
2009	46	44.5
2010	48	47

45

To increase capacity and allow the sawmills to deal with the expected increase in the number of trees cut down in the Lotus forest, a new sawmill is planned. The Operations Director said: 'If we can get this operating within 4 months we will avoid having to sell whole trees that have not been sawn. Critical path analysis should guarantee that this time limit is met'. The Operations Director has prepared the network analysis shown in Appendix A. *50*

Strategic options

The directors of FPC aim to satisfy shareholders' demands for higher dividends by increasing FPC's profits. They are discussing two options for the company. *55*

Option 1: Expansion of furniture making by a merger with, or takeover of, a large Asian furniture manufacturer

At a recent Board meeting the Marketing Director said: 'This form of growth could allow us to integrate with an under-performing furniture manufacturer at relatively low capital cost. It would increase our furniture-making capacity and offer economies of scale, allowing FPC to compete with cheaper imports. Depending on the exchange rates, we could even consider selling to retailers in European and American markets. I am sure that the same marketing strategy that we use now would appeal to consumers in those markets'. *60*

Option 2: Exploitation of other primary products

65

The Finance Director suggested at the same meeting that: 'We are largely a supplier of primary products. Why not use our experience and business contacts to exploit other primary products? Much of our land that was once covered with trees contains important minerals and metals. If we developed large opencast mines we could extract these commodities and diversify our product range'. *70*

The Chief Executive Officer disagreed: 'We have always allowed villagers back on to their land once all the trees have been cut. We do not have the experience or the capital equipment needed for mining. The changes needed to our staff training, workforce plan and operations would be very substantial. We should focus on trees and wood-cutting – this is much less risky.'

Appendix A Network analysis for the new sawmill

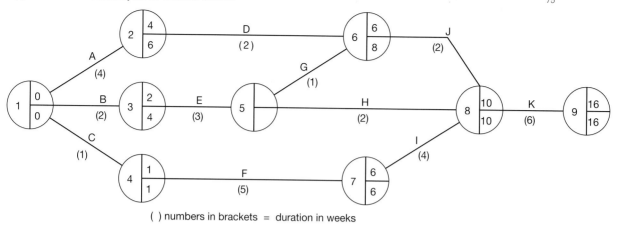

( ) numbers in brackets = duration in weeks

Appendix B Organisational chart for the Operations Department in FPC

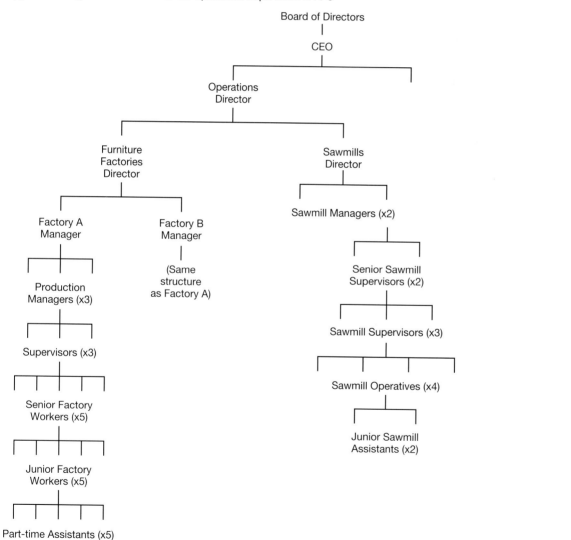

Appendix C Income Statement (Profit & Loss Account) for FPC, Year ending 31 May 2011 ($m)

Revenue (sales)	50 (80% from sawmills; 20% from furniture sales)
Cost of sales (cost of goods sold)	15
Gross profit	35
Overhead costs	28
Profit before tax (net profit)	7

80

Section A

Answer **all** questions in this section.

1 Analyse the advantages and disadvantages for FPC of operating sawmills at nearly full capacity. [10]

2 a Refer to Appendix A.

    i Identify the earliest start time (EST) and latest finish time (LFT) at node 5. [2]

    ii State the length of the critical path. [1]

    iii Calculate the total float on Activity J. [3]

  b To what extent will the use of critical path analysis ensure a successful completion of the new sawmill? [8]

3 Assess the potential impact of increasing globalisation on the marketing strategy for FPC furniture. [16]

Section B

4 Evaluate the importance of both SWOT and PEST analysis to FPC's directors as they analyse the two strategic options. [20]

Adapted from Cambridge International AS and A Level Business Studies 9707 Paper 33 Q1, 3, 5 & 6 May/June 2011

CAR MANUFACTURER AT A CROSSROADS

Introduction

Eastern Motors (EM) is a public limited company that manufactures cars in eight factories. It makes and sells cars with brand names that are well known worldwide. The company's main products are family cars that are sold to mass markets at competitive prices.

Marketing of EM cars

EM's cars are sold in 35 countries. The company does not operate its own retail outlets. It sells all of its cars through independent agents. There are several benefits of this. EM does not have to obtain detailed market knowledge of each country its products are sold in. It leaves this to each country's agent. Selling cars to consumers is the responsibility of these agents and they also bear the significant cost of stock holding cars.

EM is planning to start selling its cars in Country Z for the first time. The Marketing Director plans to open an EM owned car retailing business in Country Z. 'For the first time we will have complete control over the marketing strategies for our cars' she told her sales team.

Environmental pressures

The challenge of climate change is having an impact on governments and consumers all over the world. Some governments are increasing taxes on the most polluting and powerful cars. Pressure groups in some countries are encouraging buyers to move away from buying big cars towards purchasing smaller cars using fuels other than petrol – such as hybrid cars. This attempt to change consumer buying habits is being supported by some famous film actors selling their big and environmentally damaging cars and buying hybrid cars instead which are powered by petrol and electricity.

Main competitors

Asiatic Cars and Western Vehicles are EM's main rivals. These companies used to only sell cars in similar market segments to EM, but they now also produce larger and more powerful models and fast sports cars. These types of cars sell for prices, on average, 25% higher than EM's cars. Both companies use more extensive above and below the line promotion than EM. In addition, Asiatic Cars and Western Vehicles have recently started to obtain raw materials, steel and other supplies from low labour cost countries and this has reduced their costs of production.

Eastern Motors' profit margins on the decline

Although EM's total profits have remained steady in recent years, profit margins have fallen. Data to support this is shown in Appendix A – together with an inter-firm comparison with its two main rivals. EM directors are very worried about these declining profit margins. They believe that they result from increased competition and over-capacity in the world car industry. The recent rapid growth of multinational car manufacturers and free international trade has forced car prices down. EM's Marketing Director reported at a recent international car exhibition that 'Increased opportunities for investment by multinational car companies will create more threats than opportunities for EM'.

All EM directors are agreed that the trend in falling profit margins must be reversed. If the trend continues, total profits will eventually fall. This will mean that any future expansion will be likely to need external finance to pay for it.

Human resources problem

Appendix B refers to employee performance data in the eight EM factories. The Northcape factory was only opened two years ago in a low income country with few legal controls over employee welfare. In an attempt to cut costs, EM introduced a different management and motivational strategy within the Northcape factory compared with all its other factories. The Human Resources director has been trying to find out why the employees in this factory seem to perform less effectively than in the other EM factories. 'If we can increase productivity and reduce wastage and absenteeism in the Northcape factory then this will make us more competitive.'

Strategies for the future

'No business can stand still for long' announced the Chief Executive at a recent board meeting. 'The mass market for cars is changing. Consumers want much more variety and car models that suit their incomes and life styles. We should start making luxury cars and sports cars. Look at the data I have produced.' (See Appendix C.) 'It shows our sales performance compared to our main rivals. I also have data on Research and Development spending. It is my belief that if we increased spending on technological research into new types of engines and car designs we would be certain to increase our sales and profits very quickly. Research and Development spending always creates innovative products and increases profits.'

50

55

Appendix A Data for Eastern Motors 2008 $m

Sales revenue	Gross profit	Net profit
16350	3600	1520

Inter-firm comparison between EM and two rival car manufacturers

60

	Eastern motors		Asiatic Cars		Western Vehicles	
	Gross profit margin %	Net profit margin %	Gross profit margin %	Net profit margin %	Gross profit margin %	Net profit margin %
2006	35	16	37	20	42	23
2007	32	12	34	20	40	22
2008	–	–	30	15	36	20

65

Appendix B EM Employee and output data 2008

	Northcape Factory	Other EM factories
Number of workers employed	5500	5000 (average)
Number of workers leaving during the year	1000	750 (average)
Proportion of workers who left during year (labour turnover)	See question 2(a)	15%
Total output of cars	385000	450000 (average)
Output of cars per worker (labour productivity)	See question 2(a)	90
Wastage rate as % of total output	7	5 (average)
Annual days lost through absenteeism	27500	15000 (average)
Team working	No	Yes
Pay system	Piece rate	Salary
Quality circles used	No	Yes
Full-time, permanent contracts	15% of workers	90% of workers

70

75

80

Appendix C Sales and market data and spending on Research and Development

- In 2008, world demand for family cars increased by 5%.

- World demand for luxury and sports cars increased by 9%.

- Annual world economic growth is forecast to fall from 6% to 3% for the period 2009–2012.

	EM	Asiatic Cars	Western Vehicles
2008 Sales growth (number of cars)	8%	16%	11%
2008 Sales growth (value of sales)	2%	15%	8%
Number of different car models sold	8	16	12
Research and Development spending 2008	$0.5bn	$2bn	$4bn

85

90

Section A

Answer **all** questions in this section.

1 Assume Eastern Motors has a factory in your country. Analyse the impact of any **two** legal controls on this factory's operations. [8]

2 a Using data from Appendix B, calculate for the Northcape factory in 2008:

   i The proportion of workers who left [2]

   ii Output of cars per worker. [2]

  b 'If we can increase productivity and reduce wastage and absenteeism in the Northcape factory then this will make us more competitive.' (lines 46–47)

  Recommend an appropriate Human Resources strategy to achieve this objective. Support your recommendation. [16]

3 a Using data from Appendix A, calculate the following ratios for EM in 2008:

   i Gross profit margin [3]

   ii Net profit margin. [3]

  b Analyse **two** possible reasons for EM's falling gross profit margin. [6]

  c Evaluate any **two** ways in which EM might increase its net profit margin. [8]

Section B

4 'Increasing opportunities for multinational investment by car manufacturers will create more threats than opportunities for EM.' (lines 35–36) To what extent do you agree with this statement? [20]

Adapted from Cambridge International AS and A Level Business Studies 9707 Paper 3 Q1, 2, 4 & 7 May/June 2009

Curry Cuisine

Setting the scene

From an early age Ling was determined to become a chef owning her own restaurant. After completing a college catering course she was lucky enough to gain a junior chef's position in the smartest restaurant in town, the Asian Experience. She had to work long hours and put up with some dreadful working conditions. Despite being an expensive restaurant, the kitchen was small and always very hot and crowded. Chefs had to work under great pressure but they were paid a good hourly wage rate. Ling worked hard but this did not prevent her from being bullied and shouted at by the Head Chef. He seemed to believe that shouting instructions was the only way to ensure staff worked hard. Ling felt that she was being discriminated against. Chas, another young worker, was unhappy with the working conditions but both he and Ling tried to ignore the problems as they wanted to progress their careers.

5

10

The business start-up

Ling and Chas struck up a friendship and decided to use their experience to set up a restaurant together. After three years they had had enough of being shouted at! They were offered premises in the centre of town. They did not want to lose this site so they hurriedly signed a ten year lease. They decided that the restaurant would specialise in curries and other Asian dishes – they called it Curry Cuisine. They could not afford any market research but they often cooked this type of meal for their friends and it was always very popular.

15

The joint owners set up the business as a partnership. They each invested $10 000 of their own savings and the rest of the capital needed, $80 000, was financed by a variable interest rate bank loan.

20

They had to employ a trained restaurant manager as their own experience had been gained in kitchens. The building needed more work doing to it than they had predicted. However, the choice of location turned out to be crucial to the success of the business. They realised that a newly completed large office development was leading to many new customers. The key selling point of the restaurant was that every customer had food that was freshly prepared, even if there was a wait before it was served. This involved very labour intensive job production.

25

Expansion – then problems occur

The success of this first restaurant surprised Chas and Ling as they spent little on promotion. "Word of mouth" from satisfied customers proved to be the most effective way of encouraging new trade. It soon became clear that the existing premises were too small and a new location was found. The building was three times larger than their first restaurant with a huge kitchen. Ling recruited many more staff. She was careful to follow all of the legal requirements in the selection of staff. She wanted skilled workers who could work in a team with the minimum of management supervision. Ling wanted to encourage initiative and responsibility as she thought this would bring the best out of the workers. All staff were offered a chance to be in a profit-sharing scheme.

30

35

Chas took charge of fitting out the kitchen with new equipment. This included huge new fuel efficient cookers that allowed very accurate temperature settings. Strict health and safety laws had recently been passed. Chas was determined that the new restaurant would exceed all minimum standards. This would encourage good workers to look for jobs there and would give customers confidence too. Initially, the restaurant was popular but sales soon started to fall. Other restaurant businesses offering freshly prepared food had opened in the same area. This increased competition. Ling had to make some staff redundant which she did after a careful appraisal of every worker including an interview with each one.

40

The decline in the number of customers meant that there was now excess capacity in the kitchen. Cash was flowing out of the business to pay overheads and interest and Chas and Ling realised that quick action was needed to save the business.

45

The "ready made meals" proposal

Chas was sure that the way forward was to diversify into a different market segment. Returning from a holiday in Europe he had been amazed at the number of restaurants offering packaged "ready made meals" sold as "take-aways" as well as still running a normal restaurant service. The most successful ones sold these packaged "ready made meals" at very competitive prices. "We could adapt the unused space in the kitchen and, by building an extension, set up batch production for the most popular dishes. Computer controlled equipment could mix and cook the dishes and package them ready to be taken away. A delivery service would expand the market further. We could create a web site that would allow customers' orders to be placed "online". By keeping the same brand name for these meals we would not need to spend anything on promotion." 50 55

Ling was excited by the proposal but needed convincing. She asked a management consultant to prepare a report on the likely impact of the project on the business.

The management consultant's report was optimistic. Compared to the latest data available (see Appendix A) the sales of the business could double within one year, but the overall company gross profit margin would fall to 30%. Overhead expenses would rise by 40%. A further loan of $60 000 with an annual interest of 10% would be needed if the capital required could not be gained from internal sources. The report did suggest that planning permission for the kitchen extension might be difficult to gain as the dirt and fumes from this would affect local residents. 60

Chas was keen to go ahead immediately with the project. Ling, however, advised caution. She was not sure the business could raise the capital needed for the high technology equipment from internal sources or bank loans. Also, did they have enough information to market this new type of product successfully? What objectives were the partners trying to achieve? What type of customer would use the take-away service? What prices should be charged? Were there any local competitors? Would the use of batch production have a negative impact on the image of the business? Ling wanted to discuss these and other issues with Chas but he could not see any problems – only future profits! 65 70

Appendix A Profit and Loss Account for year ending 31/10/07

	$000
Sales Revenue	90
Costs of goods sold	54
Gross Profit	36
Overhead costs	15
Interest	8
Net profit	13

75

Appendix B Other accounting data for year ending 31/10/07

80

	$000
Fixed assets	130
Current assets	75
Of which: Stocks	20
Current liabilities	85
Long term borrowing	50
Capital employed	120

85

Section A

Answer **all** questions in this section.

1 a Analyse **two** possible problems that might result from the approach to managing staff used within the Asian Experience kitchen. [6]

   b Evaluate the appropriateness of Ling's approach to managing staff within the Curry Cuisine restaurant. [14]

2 a Draw up a forecasted Profit and Loss Account for 2008, using the data in Appendix A and the management consultant's estimates. (lines 59-64) [8]

   b Briefly assess **two** ways in which the gross profit margin could be raised for the take-away products (calculations not needed). [8]

3 To what extent do you agree with Ling that the business would have problems raising the capital needed for the "ready made meals" project either from internal sources or from a loan? The use of relevant accounting ratios (based on the data in Appendix B) to support your judgement will be rewarded. [14]

Section B

4 Assume that Chas and Ling decide to go ahead with the "ready made meals" proposal. Evaluate the arguments for and against developing a marketing plan for this project. [20]

Adapted from Cambridge International AS and A Level Business Studies 9707 Paper 3 Q2, 3, 4 & 7 October/November 2007

Index

above the line promotion 124

absenteeism 52, 279

absorption (full) costs 181

ACAS (Advisory, Conciliation and Arbitration Service) 84

accountability 35, 303–4

accounting 192–204, 388–96
    case studies 194, 196, 197, 198, 201, 203, 204, 389–91, 392, 394, 396
    financial ratios 197–201
    financial statements: limitations/uses 202–4
    financial statements: stakeholders 201–2
    income statements 156, 192–5, 377, 381, 388–90, 394, 396
    statements of financial position 156, 195–7, 377, 381, 390–6

accounts analysis 398–407
    efficiency ratios 399, 400–2
    financial ratios 197–201, 398–407
    gearing 399, 402–3
    investors' ratios 399, 403–6
    ratio analysis, value/limitations of 406–7
    return on capital employed ratio (ROCE) 400

acid test (quick) ratio 198–9

acquisitions (takeovers) 221, 316

Acts of Parliament 282

advertising 120–1, 123, 257, 311

Advertising Standards Authority (ASA) 257

Advisory, Conciliation and Arbitration Service (ACAS) 84

amortisation 392

annualised hours contracts 276, 277

Ansoff Matrix 322, 430–1

appraisal systems 82, 146, 318

appreciation 239, 240

arbitration 84, 292

ARR (average rate of return) 412–13

assessment centres 74

assets 153, 154–5, 195, 391, 392
    sale and leaseback 157–8, 164, 173, 174, 175, 199

authority 39, 49, 295, 306

autocratic leadership 46

autonomous work groups 66, 284–5

average costs 182, 367

average rate of return (ARR) 412–13

backward vertical integration 222

bad debts 171

balance of payments 227, 228

bank loans 158, 159

barriers to entry 262, 425

batch production 139

behavioural segmentation 95

behavioural theories of leadership 45–8

below the line promotion 124

benchmarking 353

binding arbitration 292

bonuses 62

booms 230–1, 232, 233

Boston Matrix 111–12, 424–5

brand awareness 89

branding 122, 123
    employer branding 280, 285, 290

brand loyalty 262, 425

break-even 177
    analysis 185–90
    case studies 186, 188
    charts 186–8
    contribution and 185

break-even analysis 185–90
    changing variables and 189–90
    uses/limitations 190

break-even charts 186–8

BRIC (Brazil, Russia, India, China) nations 5, 338, 339

Brin, Sergey 306

budgeted income statements 377, 381

budgeted statements of financial position 377, 381

budget holders 385

budgets 30, 124, 377–86
    case studies 378, 380, 381–2, 385
    preparing/using 377–83
    variance analysis 184, 378, 383–6

buffer inventories 148, 150

bureaucratic approach 438

business activity 1–7, 252–70
    case studies 2–3, 5, 7, 252–3, 254, 257, 260–1, 265, 266–7, 269–70
    competitors/suppliers and 252, 261–3
    demographic changes and 252, 267–70
    environmental factors and 252, 268–9
    legal influences 252
    legislation and 254–7
    government intervention 253–4
    social influences 252, 263–70
    success/failure 6–7
    technology and 252, 258–61

business angels 159

business culture 48

business cycle 228, 230–3

business expansion 154

business finance 153–65
    capital, need for 153–4
    capital expenditure 156, 393
    case studies 153, 155, 156–7, 158, 159, 160–1, 162, 163, 165
    revenue expenditure 156, 393
    sources of finance 156–65
    sources of finance: choice of 162–5
    working capital 154–5, 158, 197

business growth 221–5

business letters 313

business objectives 1, 27–31
    case studies 27, 28, 31
    and decision-making 29–31

business plans 437
business revenues 177–8
business size 23–6
    case studies 24, 25
business strategy
    business cycle and 233
    and economic environment 228–9
    and exchange rates 241
business structure 14–22, 216–25
    business growth 221–5
    case studies 15, 19, 20–1, 217, 219, 222, 224–5
    economic sectors 14–15
    governments and 220–1
    international trading links 218–20
    legal structures 15–22, 162–3
    local/national/international businesses 216–18
buyer/supplier power 262, 426
by-products 2
CAD (Computer Aided Design) 137, 259
CAM (Computer Aided Manufacturing) 137, 259, 260
capacity 110, 137, 345–8
capacity shortage 347–8
capacity under-utilisation 345–7
capacity utilisation 110, 345
capital 2, 132, 153–5, 195
    venture capital 159, 164, 165
    working capital 154–5, 158, 197
capital expenditure 156, 393
capital intensive processes 132
CAPP (Computer Aided Process Planning) 259
cartels 249
cash budgets 381
cash cow products 111–12
cash flow 167–75
    case studies 168, 169, 171, 173–4
    discounted cash flow 413–15
    and product life cycle 110
cash flow forecasts
    improving 172–5
    in practice 169–72
    reasons for 167–9
cell production 352–3
centralisation 299, 306–7
chains of command 298
change 442–5
channels of distribution (place) 106, 124–7
charts
    break-even charts 186–8
    inventory (stock) control charts 149
    network charts 361–3
    organisational charts 295, 297, 298, 300, 301, 302
CIVETS (Cambodia, Indonesia, Vietnam, Egypt, Turkey, South Africa) nations 338
collective bargaining 255, 256, 275, 290, 291
collective labour law 254, 255–6
commission 62
common law 282
communication 310–18
    barriers to 316–17
    case studies 310–11, 314, 315, 318
    effective communication 317–18
    electronic communication 313–14, 315
    improvements in 285, 317–18
    leadership styles and 46, 49, 316
    managers and 41, 49
    methods of 312–16
    organisational structure and 297, 298, 300
    problems 146
    reasons/need for 311–12
    record keeping 316
    speed of 315
    technology and 259, 316, 317
    theory of 310–11
    trade unions and 290
communication channels 312
community
    community cooperatives 18
    and social responsibilities 264, 265
companies 17–18
competition 261–2
competitive (micro) business environment 426, 427
competitive pricing 115
competitive threshold 6
competitors 224, 261–3, 252
Computer Aided Design (CAD) 137, 259
Computer Aided Manufacturing (CAM) 137, 259, 260
Computer Aided Process Planning (CAPP) 259
conciliation 84, 292
confidence levels 331
conglomerate integration 223
conservative approach 438
consultants 276
Consumer Credit Act 1974 257
consumer markets 92, 94
Consumer Price Index (CPI) 234
consumer products 96, 97
Consumer Protection from Unfair Trading Regulations 2007 257
consumer protection legislation 256–7
content theories of motivation 54–60
contingency planning 445–7
contractionary fiscal policy 246
contractors 276
contracts of employment 75, 76–7, 276, 277
contribution 182, 183–4, 185, 371–2
contribution costing 371–5
contribution per unit 185
contribution pricing 183
control 164
convenience goods 96, 125
cooperatives 18–19
core competencies analysis 427
core workers 276–7
corporate culture 437–42
corporate image 418
corporate objectives 281, 418
corporate social reports (CSRs) 263, 265–6
corporate social responsibility (CSR) 28
corporation tax 193
correlation 328, 329
cost centres 181, 367–8, 377, 378
costing methods 367–75
    case studies 368–70, 371, 373, 374–5
    contribution costing 371–5
    decision making 372–5

full costing 369–71
  issues in 367–9
cost-plus pricing 182–3
cost-push inflation 234–5
costs 177–85, 193, 345
  case studies 178, 179, 181–2, 184
  cost information: revenue and 177–82
  cost information: uses of 182–5
  forecasting 410
  see also costing methods; opportunity
      costs
counter-cyclical policies 231–3, 234
CPI (Consumer Price Index) 234
created value 135
creditors 164, 195
  and social responsibilities 264
creditors' (payables) days 402
critical path (network) analysis 361–5
  limitations of 364–5
  as management tool 363–4
cross-price elasticity of demand 321
crowdfunding 160, 161, 162, 253
CSR (corporate social responsibility) 28
CSRs (corporate social reports) 263, 265–6
current assets 154–5, 195
current liabilities 154–5, 195
current ratio 198
customer-focused approach 438
customer (market) orientation 92
customers
  and integration 223
  and marketing mix 106–7
  and social responsibilities 264
cyclical unemployment 236, 237, 238
data gathering 331–2
Davidson, Hugh 88
debentures 159
debt factoring 172–3, 174
debtors' (receivables) days 401, 402
debts 171
decentralisation 299, 306–7
decisional management 42
decision-making 44, 317
  business objectives and 29–31
  contribution costing and 372–5
decision trees 433–5
Deed of Partnership 17
deindustrialisation 219
delayering 303, 305
delegated budgets 378–9
delegation 47, 299
  accountability and 303–4
  and motivation 304
  and trust 306
Delphi technique 330
demand, *see* supply and demand
demand-pull inflation 234
de-mergers 223
Deming, Edward 353, 357
Deming (PDCA) cycle 354, 357
democratic leadership 46–7
demographic changes 252, 267–70

demographic segmentation 95
depreciation 239, 240, 393–5
design 358
desk (secondary) market research 100, 330
differentiation strategy 432
direct costs 180, 193, 367
direct mail 122, 123
directors 43–4
direct taxes 244, 246–7
disciplinary procedures 77, 78–9
discounted cash flow 413–15
discounting 173, 413–15
discrimination 282
diseconomies of scale 144, 146–7, 223
dismissals 77, 80
  unfair dismissals 255–6, 283
disseminators 42
distributed profits 194
distribution channels 124–5, 127
distribution outlets 124, 125–7
disturbance handlers 42
diversification 430–1
diversity 84
dividend cover ratio 405–6
dividend per share (DPS) 404
dividends 18, 403
dividend yield 405
division of labour 55
dog products 111–12
DPS (dividend per share) 404
dummy activities 363
economic environment 227–50
  business cycle 228, 254
  business strategy and 228–9
  economic growth 227–8, 229–30
  exchange rates 228, 239–42
  government objectives 227–9
  government policies 231–3, 244–8
  income/wealth redistribution 228, 242–3
  inflation 227, 228, 234–6
  market failure 249, 274
  unemployment 227, 228, 236–9
economic growth 227–8, 229–30
economic sectors 14–15
economies of scale 144–5, 147, 222
effective communication 317–18
effectiveness/efficiency 133–5
efficiency ratios 399, 400–2
elasticity of demand 116–20, 320–2
electronic communication 313–14, 315
emails 313, 315
emotional intelligence (EQ) 49–50
employee cooperatives 18
employee participation 66–7
employee performance 276–80
employee performance reports 41
employees
  and financial statements 202
  and integration 223
  and social responsibilities 264, 265
employee shareholders 66
employee welfare 81–4

employer branding 280, 285
    trade unions and 290
Employment Act 1980 255
Employment Equality (Age) Regulations 2006 255
employment legislation 254–5, 256, 282–4
Employment Relations Act 1999 255
employment tribunals 77
empowerment 65, 304
EMV (Expected Monetary Value) 434, 435
enterprise 1–13
    business activity 1–7
    case studies 2–3, 5, 7, 8, 9, 10–12
    entrepreneurs 7–11
    social enterprise 11–13
enterprise resource planning (ERP) 344–5
entrepreneurial approach 438
entrepreneurs 7–11, 42
    government help 10–11
    qualities needed 9–10
entry costs 262, 425
environmental issues 12, 252, 268–9
EQ (emotional intelligence) 49–50
Equalities Act 2010 255
equality 84
equity (share) capital 153, 154, 159–60
ERP (enterprise resource planning) 344–5
ethical behaviour 30–1
European Union law 282
exchange rates 228, 239–42
    business strategy and 241
    changes in 240, 242
expansion: investment appraisal and 409
expansionary fiscal policy 246
expectancy theory (Vroom) 60
Expected Monetary Value (EMV) 434, 435
expenditure (production) budgets 377, 381
extension strategies 108–9
external diseconomies of scale 147
external economies of scale 147
external growth 25, 221–5
externalities 220
external recruitment 72–3
extrapolation 328–9
family businesses 24–6
feedback 311
field (primary) market research 100, 330
figureheads 42
finance 156–65
    external sources of 158–60, 162
    internal sources of 157–8, 162
    short-/long-term sources of 157
financial accounting 204
financial ratios 197–201, 398–407
financial reports 41
financial statements 201–4
fiscal policy 244, 246–8
fixed costs 178, 180
flexibility 138, 164
flexible budgets 385–6
flexible workforces 276–7, 354
float time 362–3
flow production 139

focus groups 103
Force Field Analysis 433
forecasting
    cash flow 167–75
    costs 410
    revenue 410
    sales 331–2
formal communication 313
forward vertical integration 222
Four Absolutes of Quality Management 359
franchises 19–21, 322
free float time 362–3
frictional unemployment 236, 237
Friedman, Milton 35
fringe benefits 66
full costing 369–71
full (absorption) costs 181
functional structures 300–2
gearing 399, 402–3
generation Y 61
geographic segmentation 95
Gini coefficient 242
globalisation 338–9
global strategies 341
global warming 268
Goleman, Daniel 49
goods 2: *see also individual goods*
goodwill 392–3
government expenditure 247–8
government grants 161, 164
government intervention 231–3, 234, 236, 238, 243,
        249–50, 253–4
    counter-cyclical policies 231–3, 234
    economic policies 244–8
    response to market failure 249
governments
    and business structure 220–1
    and economic environment 227–9, 231–3, 244–8
    and entrepreneurs 10–11
    and integration 224
gross profit 192
gross profit margin 200
Hawthorne effect 56–7
health and safety
    as measure of employee performance 279
    trade unions and 290
health and safety legislation 256, 283
hedging 417
Herzberg, Frederick 54, 57, 58–60, 62, 64, 67, 304
hierarchical structures 300
hierarchy of needs (Maslow) 57, 58, 59–60, 62
high-risk approach 438
hire purchase 174
HM Revenue and Customs (HMRC) 202
horizontal communication 312, 313
horizontal integration 222
horizontal loading 64–5
HRM, *see* human resource
        management
HR outsourcing 275
human needs 53–4
Human Relations School 49, 56–7

Index

human resource management (HRM) 69–85, 272–93
  case studies 70, 71, 74, 77, 79, 80–1, 82–3, 84–5, 273, 275, 277, 278, 279, 283–4, 287, 289, 291, 292
  definition of 69–71
  disciplinary procedures/redundancy/dismissal 77–80
  employee performance: improving 279–80
  employee performance: measures of 276–9
  employee welfare/morale 81–5
  employment documents 75–7
  flexible workforces 276–7
  hard/soft strategies 272–6
  labour legislation 282–4
  management by objectives 281
  management–workforce cooperation 284–5
  negotiation 290–2
  no strike deals 293
  recruitment and selection 72–5
  trade unions, role of 288–90
  training 80–1, 279–80
  workforce planning 286–8
human resource (workforce) planning 286–8
hygiene (maintenance) factors 59, 62
impairment 392
imported inflation 235
income (sales revenue) budgets 377, 378, 379, 380, 383
income elasticity of demand 321–2
income redistribution 228, 242–3
income statements 156, 192–5, 377, 381, 388–90, 394, 396
income tax 193
incorporation 17
indirect costs (overheads) 180, 181–2, 193, 367, 370
indirect taxes 244, 246–7
individual bargaining 290, 292
individual labour law 254, 255
industrial democracy 284
industrial disputes 292
industrial (producer) goods 125
industrial products 97
inflation 227, 228, 234–6
informal communication 313
informational management 42
infrastructure 247–8
innovation 138
installations 97
intangible assets 392
integration 222–4
intellectual capital 2, 132
interest rates 163, 228, 232–3, 235
  changes in 244–5
  as investment criterion 415–16
internal diseconomies of scale 146
internal economies of scale 144–5
internal growth 25
internal rate of return (IRR) 414–15
internal recruitment 72
international businesses 216–17
international markets 92, 339–42
  case studies 339–40, 341–2
international trade 218–20
internet: and marketing mix 127–8
interpersonal management 42
interviews 74, 313

intranets 314
inventories 148–51, 195, 345
  valuation of 395–6
inventory management 148–51
  case studies 150, 151
inventory out 149
inventory turnover ratio 401
investment 134, 220, 247–8
  criteria 415–16
investment appraisal 409–19
  assessing risks/uncertainties 409–10, 413, 416–18
  case studies 410–11, 412, 416, 417, 418–19
  financial techniques for making investment decisions 411–16
  qualitative influences on 418–19
investors' (shareholders') ratios 399, 403–6
invoice discounting 173
IRR (internal rate of return) 414–15
JIT (just-in-time) production 150–1, 317, 354–5, 364, 365
job advertisements 75–6
job descriptions 75, 76
job enlargement 64–5
job enrichment 64
job production 139
job re-design 64–5
job rotation 65
Jobs, Steve 47, 326
joint ventures 21, 224, 225
just-in-time (JIT) production 150–1, 317, 354–5, 364, 365
kaizen (continuous improvement) 353–4
knowledge management 305
labour 2, 132
labour costs 185
labour intensive processes 132
labour legislation 282–4
labour markets 248
labour productivity 52, 272, 277–8
labour supply 287
labour turnover 52, 70, 71, 274, 278–9
laissez-faire leadership 48
laissez-faire policy 253
land 1–2, 132
leaders 42
leadership 39, 43–9
  leadership styles 45–9, 273, 316
lead time 148
lean production 150–1, 350–5
  case studies 351–2, 355
  see also JIT (just-in-time) production
leasing 172, 174
legal structures
  and business structure 15–22, 162–3
  changes in 21–2
legislation
  business activity and 254–7
  collective labour law 254, 255–6
  common law 282
  employment laws 254–6, 282–4
  European Union law 282
  health and safety laws 256, 283
level of economic activity 227
levels of hierarchy 298
  and spans of control 305

liabilities 154–5, 195, 403
liaison 42
limited liability 17
line managers 307–8
liquidity 195
liquidity ratios 198–9, 399
loan capital 153, 154
loans 158, 159, 175
local businesses 216
localised strategies 341
location 140–4
long-term approach 438
long-term borrowing 197, 391
losses 192, 388
low-cost strategy 432
McClelland, David 60–1
McGregor, Douglas 48–9
macro business environment 426
maintenance (hygiene) factors 59, 62
management 39–50
    case studies 40, 42, 44, 45, 47
    cooperation with workforce 284–5
    emotional intelligence 49–50
    functions of 40–3
    knowledge management 305
    leadership 39, 43–9
    and managers 39–43
    time-based 351–2
management accounting 204
management by objectives (MBO) 281
management teams 65
managers 44
    and communication 41, 49
    and financial statements 202
    and management 39–43
    and stakeholders 36
marginal costs 180, 182, 371, 372
margin of safety 189
market analysis 325–33
market development 430
market failure 249, 274
market growth 93
marketing 87–97, 320–36
    case studies 88, 89, 91, 93–4, 96, 322–5, 326–7, 329–31, 332–5
    coordinated marketing mix 333–6
    definition of 88
    elasticity of demand 320–2
    and environmental issues 269
    market analysis 325–33
    market features 92–4
    niche/mass marketing 94
    planning 320
    producer/consumer markets 94
    product development 322–5
    role of 87–9
    segmentation methods 95–7
    supply and demand 89–91
    technology and 258
marketing expenditure budget 124
marketing mix 105–29
    4Cs 106
    7Ps 105–6

case studies 106, 109, 112, 113, 114, 115, 118–19, 121, 122, 123, 126–9
    channels of distribution (place) 106, 124–7
    coordinated marketing mix 333–6
    customers and 106–7
    effectiveness of 128–9
    internet and 127–8
    price elasticity of demand 116–20
    pricing 105, 112–16
    product 106, 107, 127
    product life cycle 107–12
    promotion 66, 106, 120–4, 127
marketing objectives 88–9, 333, 334
marketing plans 320
marketing strategies 89, 333, 334–6
market (customer) orientation 92
market penetration 430
market research 99–104, 330–1
    case studies 100–2
    cost effectiveness 103–4
    definition of 99–100
    primary/secondary 100–2, 330
    quantitative/qualitative 103
    results 103
    sampling 102–3
market segmentation 95–7
market share 88–9, 92, 93, 222, 325
market size 92, 325
market structure 261–2
market structures 129
Maslow, Abraham 49, 54, 57, 58, 59–60, 62, 67, 304
mass customisation 139
mass marketing 94
mass production 139
materials 97
matrix structures 302
Max-Neef, Artur Manfred 53
Mayo, Elton 49, 54, 56–7, 67
MBO (management by objectives) 281
meetings 313, 314
memoranda 313
merchandising 122, 123
mergers 221, 316
merit goods 14
micro (competitive) business environment 426, 427
microfinance 160
migration 238
minimum project duration 363
minimum wage 255, 282–3
MINT (Malaysia, Indonesia, Nigeria, Turkey) nations 338
Mintzberg, Henry 41–3
mission statements 28, 146, 281
MNCs (multinational corporations) 216–18
monetary policy 244–6
monitors 42
monopolies 129, 220, 249
Morita, Akio 323–4, 326
mortgages 159
motivation 52–67, 134, 146, 280, 285
    case studies 52–3, 54, 56, 57, 59, 61, 64, 66–7
    cell production and 352–3
    content theories 54–60

definition of 52–3

delegation and 304

financial 62–4

HR strategies and 272, 274

human needs 53–4

managers and 41

non-financial 64–7

process theories 60–1

motivators 59

moving averages 328

multinational corporations (MNCs) 216–18

national businesses 216

national culture 439–40

nationalisation 14, 220–1

national markets 92

National Minimum Wage Act 1998 255

natural monopolies 220

need theory (McClelland) 60–1

negotiation 290–2

negotiators 42

Neo-Human Relations School 49, 57–60

net present value (NPV) 414–15

net profit 192–3

net realisable value (NRV) method 395–6

network (critical path) analysis 361–5

network charts 361–3

niche marketing 94

niches 24

non-binding arbitration 292

non-current assets 153, 174, 195, 391

non-current liabilities 195, 403

no strike deals 293

NPV (net present value) 414–15

NRV (net realisable value) method 395–6

objectives 114, 146

management by 281

off-the-job training 81

oligopoly markets 129, 325

on-the-job training 81

operating profit 193

operation processes 138–40

operations 131–5

capital/labour intensive processes 132

case studies 132, 134–5

creating value 135

effectiveness/efficiency 133–5

operations management 131–2, 344–8

capacity/capacity utilisation 345–8

case studies 346, 347

enterprise resource planning 344–5

targets 138

operations planning 137–47

case studies 139–41, 142–3, 145

flexibility and innovation 138

influencing factors 137

location 140–4

operations methods 138–40

scale of production 144–7

opportunities 327

opportunity costs 4–5, 163, 164, 180

and investment appraisal 413

organisational charts 295, 297, 298, 300, 301, 302

organisational structures 295–308

case studies 296, 299, 301, 303, 305, 307

formal/informal 298–9

key factors in 303–8

and strategy 421–2

types of 300–3

output 133–4

outsourcing 275, 347

overdrafts 158, 164, 173

overheads (indirect costs) 180, 181–2, 193, 367, 370

overtrading 171

partnerships 17, 161, 162, 163

part-time working 276

patents 324, 425

payables (creditors') days 402

payback 411–12, 415

pay systems 280

performance-related pay 62, 63, 280

piece rate pay 48, 49, 55, 62, 280

team pay 280

PDCA (Deming) cycle 354, 357

pendulum arbitration 292

penetration pricing 115

P/E (price–earnings) ratio 406

performance

budgets as measure of 377–8

employee performance 276–80

performance-related pay (PRP) 62, 63, 280

peripheral workers 276–7

perks 66

personal selling 121, 123

person culture 439

personnel management 69

person specifications 75, 76

PERT (programme evaluation and review technique) 364–5

PEST (political, economic, social, technological) analysis 5, 423–4

piece-rate pay 48, 49, 55, 62, 280

planning

contingency planning 445–7

enterprise resource planning 344–5

human resource (workforce) planning 286–8

operations planning 137–47

scenario planning 447

pollution 2, 268

Porter, Michael 262–3, 432

Porter's Five Forces analysis 262–3, 425–6

positive externalities 220

power culture 439

PPA (product portfolio analysis) 111

PR (public relations) 121, 123

presentations 313

present value 414–15

pressure groups 263

price discrimination 119–20

price–earnings (P/E) ratio 406

price elasticity of demand 116–20

price inelastic demand 118

price skimming 115

pricing 105, 112–16, 127, 345

cost-plus pricing 182–3

pricing strategies 115–16

primary (field) market research 100, 330

primary sector 2, 14

private limited companies 18, 163

private sector 14–15, 220: see also privatisation

privatisation 14, 220, 221, 248, 253

process innovation 138

process theories of motivation 60–1

producer (industrial) goods 125

producer markets 92, 94

product 106, 107, 127

product development 322–5, 430

product differentiation 107

production

    batch production 139

    cell production 352–3

    and environmental issues 269

    flow production 139

    just-in-time production 150–1, 317, 354–5, 364, 365

    lean production 150–1, 350–5

    scale of 144–7

    technology and 259

production (expenditure) budgets 377, 381

production teams 65

productivity 133–5, 227, 228

product life cycle 107–12

product orientation 92

product portfolio analysis (PPA) 111

profitability ratios 200–1, 399

profit centres 367–8, 377–8

profit margin 200

profits 23, 167–8, 192, 371, 372, 388

    distributed profits 194

    gross profits 192, 200

    net profits 192–3

    operating profits 193

    retained profits 154, 157, 164, 194

profit sharing 63

profit targets 184–5

programme evaluation and review technique (PERT) 364–5

project management 360–5

    case studies 360, 364, 365

    critical path (network) analysis 361–5

    projects 360

promotion 66, 106, 120–4, 127

promotional elasticity of demand 321

promotional mix 120–4

PRP (performance-related pay) 62, 63, 280

psychographic segmentation 95

psychometric tests 74

public limited companies 18, 162, 163

public relations (PR) 121, 123

public sector 14–15, 220

purchasing: and environmental issues 269

QE (quantitative easing) 246

quality 355–9

    case studies 357

    improving 358

    total quality management (TQM) 357–9

quality assurance 356–7

quality circles 65, 66, 284, 285

quality control 356

quality targets 355–6

quantitative easing (QE) 246

quantitative/qualitative market research 103

question mark products 111–12

quick (acid test) ratio 198–9

quota samples 102–3

random samples 102

ratio analysis 197

    stakeholders and 398–9

    value/limitations 406–7

rationalisation 346, 347

ratios

    acid test (quick) ratio 198–9

    current ratio 198

    dividend cover ratio 405–6

    efficiency ratios 399, 400–2

    financial ratios 197–201, 398–407

    inventory turnover ratio 402

    liquidity ratios 198–9, 399

    price–earnings ratio 406

    profitability ratios 200–1, 399

R&D (research and development) 322–4

receivables (debtors') days 401, 402

recessions 229, 231, 232

record keeping: communications 316

recoveries (upswings) 230, 232

recruitment and selection 72–5

redundancies 77, 79–80

redundancy pay 79–80

regional markets 92

regional trading blocs 219

relative poverty 228

relocation 143

reorder level 148

reorder quantity 148

reports 313

research and development (R&D) 322–4

reserves 195, 196

resource allocators 42

responsibility 295, 306: see also accountability; social responsibility

retail cooperatives 18

retained profits 154, 157, 164, 194

return on capital employed ratio (ROCE) 400, 407, 416

revenue 177–82

    forecasting 410

revenue expenditure 156, 393

rights issues 163

risks

    and investment appraisal 409–10, 413, 416–18

    and rewards 7–8

rivalry 425

ROCE (return on capital employed ratio) 400, 407, 416

role culture 439

salaries 62

sale and leaseback 157–8, 164, 173, 174, 175, 199

Sale of Goods Act 1979 257

sales forecasts 331–2

sales patterns 325

sales promotions 121, 123

sales revenue (income) budgets 377, 378, 379, 380, 38

sales targets 88

sampling 102–3

scale of production 144–7

scenario planning 447

Index

Scientific School of Management 48–9, 54, 55–6

secondary (desk) market research 100, 330

secondary sector 14

Selective Finance for Investment (SFI) 161

semi-variable costs 179

service sector 2

share (equity) capital 153, 154, 159–60

shareholder concept 35

shareholder (total) equity 195–6, 403

shareholders 17, 18, 66, 161, 163

    employee shareholders 66

    and financial statements 202

    and integration 223

    and social responsibilities 264

shareholders' (investors') ratios 399, 403–6

share issues 163, 164

shopping goods 96, 113, 124

short-term approach 438

short-term loans 174

simultaneous engineering 351

skill shortages 238–9

slumps 229, 231, 232

small businesses 23–5

social accounting 265

social enterprise 11–13

social performance reports 41

social responsibility 35, 263–5, 270

    corporate social responsibility 28

sole traders 15–16, 162, 163

spans of control 298–9

    and levels of hierarchy 305

specialisation 145

specialist products 96

special order decisions 183–4, 372–4

specific risk 410

spending: investment appraisal and 409

spoken communication 313

spokespersons 42

sponsorship 121

staff managers 307–8

stakeholder concept 35

stakeholders 33–7, 197

    case studies 34, 36, 37

    importance/influence of stakeholders 34–7

    and integration 223–4

    and ratio analysis 398–9

    and social responsibilities 263, 264

    stakeholder groups 33–4

star products 111–12

start-up capital 153, 154

statements of financial position 156, 195–7, 377, 381, 390–6

    amendments to 391

status 66

stock (inventory) control 149, 150–1

strategic alliances 224, 225

strategic analysis 423–8

    Boston Matrix 111–12, 424–5

    PEST analysis 5, 423–4

    Porter's Five Forces 262–3, 425–6

    SWOT analysis 335, 423

strategic choice 430–5

    Ansoff Matrix 322, 430–1

    case studies 431, 432, 435

    decision trees 433–5

    Force Field Analysis 433

    low cost vs differentiation 432–3

strategic implementation 437–47

    business plans 437

    case studies 438–9, 440–2, 443–5, 446

    change culture 442

    contingency planning 445–7

    corporate culture 437–42

    leading/managing change 443–4

    managing change 444–5

strategic management 421–8

    case studies 422, 424, 426–8

    organisational structures and 421–2

    strategic analysis 5, 111–12, 262–3, 335, 423–8

strategy 28–9

stratified samples 102

structural unemployment 236–7, 238

subcontracting 138, 346, 347

substitutes 326, 426

supervisors 44

suppliers 252, 261–3

    and financial statements 202

    and social responsibilities 264, 265

supplies 97

supply and demand 89–91

supply chains 426

supply-side policies 244, 248

SWOT (strengths, weaknesses, opportunities, threats) analysis 335, 423

Sy, Henry 404

systematic risk 409

tactics 29

takeovers (acquisitions) 221, 316

tangible assets 392

Tannenbaum and Schmidt continuum 46

target audience 315

task culture 439

taxes 243

    corporation tax 193

    direct taxes 244, 246–7

    income tax 193

    indirect taxes 244

    tax avoidance 217

    see also fiscal policy

Taylor, Frederick Winslow 48–9, 54, 55, 62

team pay 280

teamworking 57, 65, 134

technical economies of scale 145

technology

    and business activity 252, 258–61

    and communication 259, 316, 317

    investment appraisal and 409

    and marketing 258

    and production processes 259

technology grants 161

telephone communication 313, 315

temporary workers 276

tertiary sector 14

text messages 314, 315

Theory X/Theory Y (McGregor) 48–9

threats 327
time-based management 351–2
time-based pay 62
total costs 179–80, 182
total (shareholder) equity 195–6, 403
total float time 362–3
total quality management (TQM) 357–9
total revenue 118
trade credit 164, 171, 172
Trade Descriptions Act 1968 257
trade payables 172, 174, 175
trade receivables 172, 174, 175
Trade Union Act 1984 255
Trade Union Reform and Employment Rights Act 1993 255
trade unions 256, 275
    legislation 255, 284
    no strike deals 293
    role in HRM 288–93
training 65–6, 80–1, 133, 279–80, 318
trait theory of leadership 45
transfer payments 247
transformation process 1–4
    inputs 1–2
    outputs 2–4
trends 325
Triple Bottom Line 12–13
trust 304, 306
two-factor theory (Herzberg) 57, 58–60, 62
two-way communication 312, 313
unemployment 227, 228, 236–9
unfair dismissal 255–6, 283
union recognition 288
unique selling point (USP) 107
unit costs 367
unlimited liability 16, 17
unsecured borrowing 245

upswings (recoveries) 230, 232
value of sales 325
variable costs 179, 180, 186–7
variable pay 63
variance analysis 184, 378, 383–6
venture capital 154, 159, 164, 165
vertical communication 312, 313
vertical integration 222–3
vertical loading 64
video conferencing 314, 315
viral marketing 123
visual communication 314
volume of sales 325
Vroom, Victor 60
wage rises 234–5
wages 62
wealth redistribution 228, 242–3
weather elasticity of demand 321
websites 314
welfare
    employee welfare 81–4
    welfare benefits 243
window dressing 199, 203
worker representatives 44
workforce
    cooperation with management 284–5
    flexible workforces 276–7, 354
workforce performance 285
workforce (human resource) planning 70, 286–8
working capital 154–5, 158, 197
Working Time Regulations 1998 255
works councils 66, 284, 285
World Trade Organisation 338
written communication 313
zero budgets 382–3
zero-hours contracts 277

Acknowledgements

For Poppy, Imogen, Archie and Alastair with love (Malcolm Surridge)

With thanks to Seth, Romily, Clemency and Ali (Andrew Gillespie)

Many thanks to Nina and Will for their support during the writing of this book (Malcolm Surridge & Andrew Gillespie)

The Publishers would like to thank the following for permission to reproduce copyright material:

Photo credits:

p.2 © Simon Reddy / Alamy; **p.9** © Awfully Chocolate; **p.15** *l* © rgbspace – Fotolia, *r* © Kadmy – Fotolia; **p.19** *t* © Ben & Jerry's Homemade, Inc., *b* © Domino's Pizza UK & IRL Limited; **p.20** © T.M.O.Buildings / Alamy; **p.24** © timothyfrance/Demotix/Corbis; **p.28** © Goh Seng Chong/Bloomberg News via Getty Images; **p.35** © Bachrach/Getty Images; **p.41** © Aaron Amat – Fotolia; **p.47** *t* © Michael Buckner/Getty Images; **p.47** *b* © Keystone USA-ZUMA/Rex Features; **p.59** © Special Collections Dept., J. Willard Marriott Library, University of Utah; **p.80** © Center Parcs; **p.82** *all* © Google; **p.83** *all* © Google; **p.91** © WestEnd61/Rex Features; **p.96** © BIC Group; **p.101** © Trevor Snapp/Bloomberg via Getty Images; **p.109** © Prashanth Vishwanathan/Bloomberg via Getty Images; **p.121** © Ian Waldie/Bloomberg via Getty Images; **p.122** © ARND WIEGMANN/Reuters/Corbis; **p.126** © Ed Lallo/Bloomberg via Getty Images; **p.134** *l* © redav – Fotolia; **p.134** *r* © Mary Evans Picture Library / Alamy; **p.139** © Hyundai Motor UK Ltd; **p.141** © Keystone USA-ZUMA/Rex Features; **p.156** © imageBROKER / Alamy; **p.161** © CARE International UK (www.lendwithcare.org); **p.162** © 2009 Martin Jardine Photography, Courtesy of The Brooklyn Warehouse; **p.204** © ZUMA Press, Inc. / Alamy; **p.219** © KonArt – Fotolia; **p.222** Photo courtesy of ExxonMobil; **p.233** © Asim Hafeez/Bloomberg via Getty Images; **p.259** © GM Corp.; **p.280** © PATRICE COPPEE/AFP/Getty Images; **p.287** © SeongJoon Cho/Bloomberg via Getty Images; **p.306** © Justin Sullivan/Getty Images; **p.310** © Erik Hildebrandt, Courtesy of Cathay Pacific; **p.323** © INTERFOTO / Alamy; **p.324** © Balint Porneczi/Bloomberg via Getty Images; **p.327** *a* © Imagestate Media (John Foxx), **b** © commerceandculturestock/Moment/Getty Images, **c** © alexandre zveiger – Fotolia, **d** © ginosphotos/iStock/Thinkstock, **e** © Picturenet/Blend Images/Thinkstock; **p.331** © Todd Gipstein/Corbis; **p.335** © Art Directors & TRIP / Alamy; **p.339** © Mike Ehrmann/Getty Images; **p.340** © MANPREET ROMANA/AFP/Getty Images; **p.341** LEGO and the LEGO logo are trademarks of the LEGO Group © 2013 The LEGO Group; © 2013 Lucasfilm Ltd. LLC & TM. All rights reserved.; **p.347** © THOMAS SAMSON/AFP/Getty Images; **p.351** © epa european pressphoto agency b.v. / Alamy; **p.355** © Tomohiro Ohsumi/Bloomberg via Getty Images; **p.373** © cedrov – Fotolia; **p.374** © Zoja – Fotolia; **p.381** © volff – Fotolia; **p.385** © Imaginechina/Corbis; **p.404** © AP/Press Association Images; **p.405** © Polymetal International plc; **p.410** © epa european pressphoto agency b.v. / Alamy; **p.417** © Nicholas Burningham / Alamy; **p.428** © 2014 BlackBerry; **p.431** © Realimage / Alamy; **p.446** © David McNew/Getty Images.

t = top, *b* = bottom, *l* = left, *r* = right

Acknowledgements:

p.3 Case study- transformation processes, adapted from Open University material from *http://openlearn.open.ac.uk*; **p.5** Figure 1.4 Brazil about to overtake US as world's sixth biggest economy graph, from International Monetary Fund; **pp.10-11** Ease of doing business ranking, from The World Bank (2012); **p.15** Cuba case study text, from *www.ukti.gov.uk/export/countries/americas/caribbean/cuba/overseasbusinessrisk.html*, Foreign & Commonwealth Office, © Crown copyright; **p.19** Figure 2.2 Cooperatives around the world, from The International Cooperative Alliance; **pp.20-21** Toni&Guy case study, adapted from *The Independent* (15 October, 2006), *www.independent.co.uk*, reproduced by permission of ESI Media; **p.21** Franchise case study, from *www.dailybread.co.in/franchise*; **p.27** Tesco growth case study from *www.tesco.com*; **p.28** Intel case study, adapted from *www.intel.com*; **p.31** Ethics at Texas Instruments case study, from *http://www.ti.com/corp/docs/csr/corpgov/ethics/*; **p.34** Gold Fields Ghana engages stakeholders case study, from Joy Online, *http://business.myjoyonline.com/pages/news/201302/101803.php*; **p.36** Hitachi case study, adapted from *Contributing to a Sustainable Society as a Good Corporate Citizen*, from *http://www.hitachi.com/csr/csr_images/csr2012e_007-008.pdf*; **p.47** Richard Branson assesses Apple's Steve Jobs case study, adapted from *the Daily Telegraph* (6 October 2011), from *http://www.telegraph.co.uk/technology/steve-jobs/8811232/Virgins-Richard-Branson-Apple-boss-Steve-Jobs-was-the-entrepreneur-I-most-admired.html*; **p.49** Goleman's four competencies of emotional intelligence, adapted from Transgrowth, *http://www.transgrowth.com/transgrowth_website/emotional_intelligence.php*; **p.50** Figure 6.5 The importance and benefits of emotional intelligence, redrawn from *Emotional Intelligence 2.0*, *www.talentsmart.com*, reproduced by permission of Travis Bradberry, President, Talent Smart; **p.54** Working at Google case study, from *www.Google.co.uk*; **p.72** Figure 8.2 The process of recruitment and selection diagram, from *Resourcing and Talent Planning Survey (2012)*, Chartered Institute of Personnel and Development (CIPD); **p.73** Figure 8.3 The most effective methods of attracting applicants from potential employees in the UK in 2013, from *Resourcing and Talent Planning Survey,*

Acknowledgements

2013, CIPD; **p.74** Case Study: Recruitment is competitive in the Gulf States, adapted from *Gulf News*, 4 February 2014, *http://gulfnews. com/business/general/corporate-websites-yield-more-job-recruits-1.1286337*; **p.76** Figure 8.5 A job advertisement for the United Nations, from *The Economist*, 15 September 2012; **p.78** Figure 8.6; Disciplinary procedures, from *'Discipline and Grievances at work'*, ACAS; **p.80** Case Study: Centre Parcs, from *www.centreparcs.co.uk*; **p.82** Working at Google case study, adapted from *http://www. google.co.uk/about/corporate/company/culture.html*; **p.83** Table 8.3 Weekly working hours in a selection of OECD countries, 2000 and 2012, from *http://oecdilibrary.org/employment/average-annual-working-time_20752342-table8*; **pp.84-85** Equality and diversity at the University of Cambridge, adapted from the website of the University of Cambridge, © 2013 University of Cambridge, The Old Schools, Trinity Lane CB2 1TN; **p.89** BAT in Russia case study, from British American Tobacco Russia; **p.96** BIC case study, from *www. bicworld.com/en/products/details/417/cristal-for-her*, reproduced by permission of BIC UK & Ireland Limited; **p.101** Table 10.2 Market share of comics in Asia, market research by Hakuhodo, Japan, from *http://www.bbc.co.uk/news/business-14526451*; **pp.101-102** Africa case study, from *http://www.mckinsey.com/global_locations/africa/south_africa/en/rise_of_the_african_consumer*; **p.106** Case Study: Doing Business in Africa; from *www.accenture.com*; **p.109** Segway case study, adapted from *www.segway.com*; **p.114** Figure 11.9 Competitors in the UK soft drinks market, Mintel Group (2010); **p.115** Vertu ti case study, from *www.vertu.com*; **p.118** Table 11.3 Summary table: price elasticity and revenue, from Bohi (1981); Cheng, and Capps Jr (1988); Gwartney, and Stroup (1997); Houthakker, and Taylor (1970); US Department of Agriculture; **p.121** Richard Branson case study, adapted from *www.news.bbc.co.uk/go/pr/fr/-/1/ hi/business/5368602.stm*; **p.122** Table 11.5 Best global brands, from Brand Finance plc., *http://brandirectory.com/league_tables/table/ global-500-2012*; **pp.128-129** Barbie case study, adapted from *http://en.wikipedia.org/wiki/Barbie_dolls*; **p.134** Finance against warehouse receipts case study, adapted from *www.standardchartered.com*; **pp.135-136** The Singapore Economy data response question, from Singapore Ministry of Manpower, *http://www.mom.gov.sg/skills-training-and-development/productivity/Pages/what-is-productivity.aspx*; **p.141** Dov Charney case study, adapted from *www.americalapparel.net*; **p.147** Pantaloon Retail Ltd data response question, adapted from *http://articles.marketwatch.com*; **p.150** Car dealerships in China case study, from *www.chinadaily.com.cn*; **pp.160-161** Lend with care case study, from CARE International UK, *http://www.lendwithcare.org/entrpreneurs/index/7486*, reproduced by permission of CARE International UK; **p.178** Palm oil prices, adapted from *The Star Online* (Malaysia), *http://www. thestar.com.my/Business/Business-News/2014/03/06/Dry-spell-to-affect-CPO-Prices-could-hit-RM3000-per-tonne/*; **p.194** Table 18.1 Rolls Royce summarised income statement, from Rolls Royce Holdings plc., *Annual Report, 2013, http://www.rolls-royce.com/Images/ RR_Full%20Report_tcm92-55530.pdf*; **p.196** Figure 18.4 Statement of financial position, adapted from Burberry plc., *Annual Report, 2013, http://www.burberryplc.com/documents/full_annual_report/burberry_areport_2012-13.pdf*; **p.197** Table 18.2 Statement of financial position, Rolls Royce Holdings plc., *Annual Report, 2013, http://www.rolls-royce.com/Images/RR_Full%20Report_tcm92-55530.pdf*; **p.198** Lucy Hornby, Case study: Chinese steel manufactures face liquidity problems, adapted from BD Live, *http://www. bdlive.co.za/world/asia/2014/02/27/liquidity-problems-bit-in-chinas-steel-sector* (27 February, 2014); **p.204** Table 18.6 Case study: Tesco's American enterprise struggles, from *Annual Report 2013, http://files.thegroup.net/library/tesco/annualreport2013/pdfs/tesco_ annual_rep[ort_2013.pdf*; **p.219** Figure 19.1: Growth in GDP and trade, from HSBC Bank,October 2013, *https://globalconnections. hsbc.com/united-kingdon/en/tools-data/trade-forecasts/global*; **p.220** Figure 19.3 Growth in exports, from HSBC Bank, October 2013, *https: globalconnections.hsbc.com/united-kingdon/en/tools-data/tradeforecasts/global*; **p.229** Figure 20.3 Economic growth in the UK, from Office for National Statistics (ONS); **p.230** Angela Monaghar, 'UK economy grew unexpectedly fast in 2013', adapted from *The Guardian*, 28 January 2014, *http://www.theguardian.com/business/2014/jan/28/uk-economy-2013-fastest-growth-fourth-quarter-gdp*, copyright Guardian News & Media Ltd 2014, reproduced by permission of the publisher; **p.233** Case Study: Pakistan's Cental Bank Forecasts 4% Economic Growth, adapted from *Dawn* (15 January 2014), *http://www.dawn.com/news/1080523/pakistans-central-bank-forecasrs-upbeat-4pc-growth*; **p.234** Figure 20.7 UK inflation rate 2004-14, from Trading Economics/ONS; **p.235** Figure 20.8 Inflation in China 2004-14, from Trading Economics/National Bureau of Statistics in China; **p.235** Figure 20.9 Inflation in Russia 2004-14, from Trading Economics/Federal State Statistics Service; **p.237** Figure 20.10 UK unemployment 2005-14, from Trading Economics/ONS; **p.238** Figure 20.12 World Map showing the countries that have had net outflows and inflows of migrants.World migration patterns, originally published by Liu Institute for Global Issues, UBC, from *http://essay-eb.blogspot.co.uk/2012/07/the-urge-to-migrate-began-in-wild-berry.html*; **p.241** Figure 20.14 US Dollar Argentine Peso Exchange Rate, from *www.bloomberg.com*; **p.242** Figure 20.15 Map showing The distribution of income in countries throughout the world, from *http://www.globalpolicy.org/images/pdfs/Gini_Coefficient_ Map.pdf*, CIA – *The World Factbook*, 2009; **p.243** Taxes, benefits and the effects on household incomes in 2011, from ONS, *http:// www.ons.gov.uk/ons/rel/household-income/the-effects-of-taxes-and-benefits-on-household-income/2010-11/etb-stats-bulletin-1011.html*; **p.245** Case Study: Credit Card worries in Singapore, adapted from *The Real Singapore*, 2 October 2013, *http://therealsingapore.com/ content/more-people-singapore-finding-it-hard-pay-credit-card-debt*; **p.248** Case Study: Japan's economy shows signs of recovery, adapted from the *New York Times*, 11 July 2013, *www.nytimes.com/2013/07/12/business/global/japans-economy-on-road-to-recovery-central-bank-says.html?_r=o*; **p.257** Case Study Queensland unveils new fast food laws, adapted from ABC News, *http://www.abc.net. au/news/2011-12-04/qld-new-fast-food-laws/3711496*; **p.260** Case Study Google's culture, from *http://www.google.com/corporate/ culture.html*; **p.267** Table 21.2 One-person households by age in the UK, 2003–26, from News Distribution Service, *http://nds.coi.gov. uk/content/detail.asp?NewsAreaID=2&ReleaseID=191108*; **p.265** Case Study Richard Anderson, Unilever says sustainability key to new business model, adapted from BBC News Business, *http://www.bbc.co.uk/news/business-11755672* (15 November, 2010); **p.266** Case study: Apple is the world's most admired company, adapted from *Time*, 27 February 2014, *http://time.com/10351/fortune-worlds-most-admired-company-2014/*; **p.267** Figure 21.6 The age structure of the UK's population 2003–41, graph from Government Actuaries Department; **p.268** Figure 21.7 Global emissions of carbon dioxide 1990-2008, from The United States Environmental Protection Agency, *http://www.epa.gov/climatechange/science/indicators/ghg/global-ghg-emissions.html*; **p.268** Figure 21.8 Evidence of rising average global temperatures 1880–2010, from Earth Policy Institute, *http://www.earth-policy.org/indicators/C51/global_temperature_2010*; **p.273** Case study: Appointing an HR Manager, adapted from Sancus Associates website, *http://www.sancusassociates.com/vacancies/2014/02/10/hr-manager-international-automotive-company-shanghai-36465946*, reproduced by permission of Phaidon International; **p.275** Case study: Outsourcing and HR, adapted from HRM Asia, 3 October 2013, *http://www.hrmasia.com/resources/outsourcing/hr-outsourcing-talking-point/179976/*; **p.276** Comparative data on percentages of employees working part time and on temporary contracts in 2002 and 2012, from OECD, *http://Stats.oecd.org/Index.aspx?DataSetCode=TEMP_1*; **p.277** Simon Neville, 'McDonald's tie nine out of 10 workers to zero-hour contracts', adapted from *The Guardian*, 5 August 2013, *http:www.theguardian.com/business/2013/aug/05/mcdonalds-workers-zero-hour-contracts*, copyright Guardian News & Media Ltd 2013, reproduced by permission of the publisher; **p.278** Figure 22.2 Reasons for leaving employment in a sample of jobs in the UK, 2012, from CIPD *Annual Survey Report, 2012*, *http://www.cipd.co.uk/binaries/5874%20RTP%20SR%20(WEB).pdf*; **p.279** More feedback from CIPD case study, from CIPD *Annual Survey Report, 2012*, *http://www.cipd.co.uk/binaries/5874%20RTP%20SR%20(WEB).pdf*; **p.280** Table 22.3 M. Thompson, Team pay versus individual pay from *eam-working and Pay (1995)*, Institute for Employment Studies, *http://www.employment-studies.co.uk/summary/summary.php?id=281*; **pp.283-284** Case Study Workplace accidents in Zimbabwe, adapted from *New Zimbabwe*, 19 August 2013, *http://www.newzimbabwe.com/business-12094 NSSA+38+killed+in+workplace+accidents/business.aspx*; **p.296** Table 23.1 Case study: The structure of HSBC, from *http://www.hsbc.com/1/2/about/group-structure*; **p.297** Figure 23.2 The simplified organisational structure for the HSBC, from *http://www.hsbc.com/1/2/about/group-structure*; **p.305** Case Study Google, from *http://www.google.co.uk/intl/en/about/company/facts/culture/*; **p.307** Case Study Opodo, adapted from Opodo and Eye for Travel websites, *Opodo website http://opodo.com/about/about.html* and *Eye for Travel http://www.eyefortravel.com/node/13603*; **p.314** Figure 24.5 Jerome Briner, Oral and visual information, as cited by Paul Martin Lester in *Syntactic Theory of Visual Communication* (California State Unniversity at Fullerton, 1994-1996), reproduced by permission of Paul Lester; **p.318** Case Study: APN News and Media, adapted from APN News and Media website; **pp.322-323** Case Study The leading investors in R&D in Europe, from European Commission, *http://ec.europa.eu/enterprise/newsroom/cf/itemdetail.cfm?item_id=6312*; **pp.323-324** Case Study Akio Morita, adapted from *Economist.com*, 7 November 2008; **p.325** Case Study R&D Spendin, OECD; pp.326-327: Case study Africa, from *http://www.accenture.com/SiteCollectionDocuments/Local_South_Africa/PDF/Accenture-The-Dynamic-African-Consumer-Market-Exploring-Growth-Opportunities-in-Sub-Saharan-Africa.pdf*; **pp.334-335** Case Study Unileve, from *www.unilever.com*; **pp.338-339** Case Study NFL, from *Looking beyond the obvious*, Ernst & Young, 2013, *http://media.nzherald.co.nz/webcontent/document/pdf/20134/Globalisation%202013.pdf*; **pp.339-340** Case Study: Tesco withdraws from Japanese market, adapted from *www.ft.com http://www.ft.com/cms/s/0/7cd29322-d39a-11e0-bc6b-00144feab49a.html#axzz2LolqUZow*; **pp.351-352** Case Study Lego, from The Wharton School, *http://knowledge.wharton.upenn.edu/article.cfm?articleid=3050*; **p.380** Online shopping in Pakistan, adapted from *Tech in Asia*, 15 January 2014, *http://www.techinasia.com/rocket-internet-pakistan-estore-daraz-gets-1000-orders-per-day/*; **p.402** Table 33.3 More on Century and Paper Board Mills Ltd case study, adapted from Century and Paper Board Mills Ltd, *Annual Report, 2012*, *http://www.centurypaper.com.pk/admin/upload/Century%20Report%202012.pdf*; **p.405** Polymetal International announces dividends case study, adapted in part from BSR Russia, *http://www.bsr-russia.com/en/mining/item/2513-special-dividend-of-us$-050-per-share-approved-by-the-polymetal-international-plc-board.html*; **pp.410-411** Case Study: Nintendo slashes sales forecasts, adapted from *IGN Topics*, 17 January 2014, *http://uk.ign.com/articles/2014/01/17/nintendo-cuts-wii-u-sales-forecast-from-9-million-to-28-million*; **p.416** Case Study: Chinese billionaire launches takeover bid, adapted from *Forbes.com* (10 March 2014), *www.forbes.com/sites/russellflaneery/2014/03/10/australias-westside-shares-rise-13-after-takeover-bif-by-chinese-billionaires-firm*; **p.417** Case Study Southwest Airlines' hedging strategy, adapted from *Associated Press Report*, 30 June 2008, *http://www.msnbc.msn.com/id/25419436/* and *FT.com*, October 20th, 2011, *http://www.ft.com/cms/s/0/4df11e88-fb28-11e0-8756-00144feab49a.html#axzz1ckCHXAvF*; **p.418** Case Study: Cargill plans $750 million expansion in Indonesia, adapted from *The Jakarta Post*, 8 Nov 2013, *http://www.thejakartapost.com/news/2013/11/08/cargill-plans-750-million-expansion-indonesia.html*, reproduced by permission of The Jakarta Post, Editorial Dept.; **p.424** Strategic Elements of Tata Power for 2012-13 case study, from Tata Power, *http://www.tatapower.com/aboutus/vision-mission-values.aspx*; **pp.438-439** Case Study Johnson & Johnson, from *www.jnj.com*; **pp.441-442**: Case Study The Five Principles of Mars, from *Mars, www.mars.com*. All Rights Reserved. October; **pp.444-445** Case Study Huawei, from Guo Ping, Huawei Rotating and Acting CEO, 31 December 2012,*www.huawei.com*; **p.447** Data response question case study: About Lenovo, from *www.lenovo.com, http://www.lenovo.com/lenovo/us/en/our_company.html*.

Permission for re-use of all (c) Crown copyright information is granted under the terms of the Open Government Licence (OGL).

Every effort has been made to trace and contact copyright holders, and the publishers apologise for any omissions or error which they will be pleased to rectify at the earliest opportunity.